Laboratory Phonology 7

Phonology and Phonetics
4-1

Editor
Aditi Lahiri

Mouton de Gruyter
Berlin · New York

Laboratory Phonology 7

edited by
Carlos Gussenhoven
Natasha Warner

Mouton de Gruyter
Berlin · New York   2002

Mouton de Gruyter (formerly Mouton, The Hague)
is a Division of Walter de Gruyter GmbH & Co. KG, Berlin.

∞ Printed on acid-free paper which falls within the guidelines
of the ANSI to ensure permanence and durability.

Die Deutsche Bibliothek − *Cataloging-in-Publication Data*

Laboratory phonology / ed. by Carlos Gussenhoven ; Natasha Warner.
− Berlin ; New York : Mouton de Gruyter, 7. − (2002)
(Phonology and phonetics ; 4,1)
ISBN 3-11-017086-8
ISBN 3-11-017087-6

© Copyright 2002 by Walter de Gruyter GmbH & Co. KG, D-10785 Berlin.
All rights reserved, including those of translation into foreign languages. No part of this
book may be reproduced in any form or by any means, electronic or mechanical, including
photocopy, recording, or any information storage and retrieval system, without permission
in writing from the publisher.
Printing & Binding: Hubert & Co., Göttingen
Cover design: Christopher Schneider, Berlin.
Printed in Germany.

Table of Contents

List of authors ... ix

Acknowledgements ... xi

Introduction ... xiii
   Carlos Gussenhoven & Natasha Warner

Part 1: Phonological Processing and Encoding ... 1

The role of the lemma in form variation ... 3
   Daniel Jurafsky, Alan Bell & Cynthia Girand

Phonological encoding of single words: In search of the lost syllable ... 35
   Niels O. Schiller, Albert Costa & Angels Colomé

Temporal distribution of interrogativity markers in Dutch: A perceptual study ... 61
   Vincent J. van Heuven & Judith Haan

Phonological Encoding in speech production: Comments on Jurafsky et al., Schiller et al., and van Heuven & Haan ... 87
   Willem P. J. Levelt

Word-specific phonetics ... 101
   Janet B. Pierrehumbert

Phoneme frequency in spoken word reconstruction ... 141
   Danny R. Moates, Z. S. Bond & Verna Stockmal

Temporal neutralization in Japanese ... 171
   Haruo Kubozono

A typological study of stress 'deafness' 203
  Sharon Peperkamp & Emmanuel Dupoux

Confluent talker- and listener-oriented forces in clear 237
speech production
  Ann R. Bradlow

Phonological Processing: Comments on Pierrehumbert, 275
Moates et al., Kubozono, Peperkamp & Dupoux,
and Bradlow
  Anne Cutler

Part 2: In the laboratory and in the field: relating 297
phonetics and phonology

Explosives, implosives and nonexplosives: The phonological 299
function of air pressure differences in stops
  G. N. Clements & Sylvester Osu

Assimilatory processes and aerodynamic factors 351
  Maria-Josep Solé

Tonal association and target alignment in European 387
Portuguese nuclear falls
  Sónia Frota

Gestural overlap and recoverability: Articulatory evidence 419
from Georgian
  Ioana Chitoran, Louis Goldstein & Dani Byrd

The Phonetics-Phonology Interface: Comments on 449
Clements & Osu, Solé, Frota, and Chitoran et al.
  Bruce Hayes

The search for primitives in phonology and the explanation 455
of sound patterns: The contribution of fieldwork studies
  Didier Demolin

Acoustic correlates of rhythm class   515
  Esther Grabe & Ee Ling Low

From pitch accent to stress accent in Basque   547
  José I. Hualde, Gorka Elordieta, Iñaki Gaminde
  & Rajka Smiljanić

Lexically contrastive stress accent and lexical tone in Ma'ya   585
  Bert Remijsen

Field work and phonological theory: Comments on   615
Demolin, Grabe & Low, Hualde et al., and Remijsen
  W. Leo Wetzels

Underspecified recognition   637
  Aditi Lahiri & Henning Reetz

Speech recognition: Comments on Lahiri & Reetz   677
  Dafydd Gibbon

Subject Index   687

Author Index   693

Language Index   717

List of authors

Alan Bell	University of Colorado, Boulder, Colorado, USA
Z. S. Bond	Ohio University, Athens, Ohio, USA
Ann R. Bradlow	Northwestern University, Evanston, Illinois, USA
Dani Byrd	Haskins Laboratories, New Haven, Connecticut, USA and University of Southern California, San Diego, California, USA
Ioanna Chitoran	Dartmouth College, Hanover, New Hampshire, USA
G. N. Clements	CNRS, Paris, France
Angels Colomé	Universitat de Barcelona, Spain
Albert Costa	Harvard University, Massachusetts, USA
Anne Cutler	Max Planck Institute for Psycholinguistics, Nijmegen, The Netherlands
Didier Demolin	Université Libre de Bruxelles, Belgium
Emmanuel Dupoux	Laboratoire de Sciences Cognitives et Pycholinguistiques (EHESS/CNRS), Paris, France
Gorka Elordieta	University of the Basque Country, Vitoria-Gasteiz, Spain
Sónia Frota	Universidade de Lisboa, Portugal
Iñaki Gaminde	University of the Basque Country, Vitoria-Gasteiz, Spain
Dafydd Gibbon	Universität Bielefeld, Germany
Cynthia Girand	University of Colorado, Boulder, Colorado, USA
Louis Goldstein	Yale University and Haskins Laboratories, New Haven, Connecticut, USA
Esther Grabe	University of Cambridge, United Kingdom
Carlos Gussenhoven	University of Nijmegen, The Netherlands
Judith Haan	University of Nijmegen, The Netherlands
Bruce Hayes	University of California at Los Angeles, USA
Vincent J. van Heuven	Universiteit Leiden, The Netherlands
José Ignacio Hualde	University of Illinois at Urbana-Champaign, USA
Daniel Jurafsky	University of Colorado, Boulder, Colorado, USA
Haruo Kubozono	Kobe University, Japan
Aditi Lahiri	Universität Konstanz, Germany
Willem P. J. Levelt	Max Planck Institute for Psycholinguistics, Nijmegen, The Netherlands
Ee Ling Low	Nanyang Technological University, Singapore
Danny R. Moates	Ohio University, Athens, Ohio, USA
Sylvester Osu	LLACAN-CNRS, Villejuif, France
Sharon Peperkamp	Laboratoire de Sciences Cognitives et Pycholinguistiques (EHESS/CNRS), Paris and Université de Paris VIII, Saint Denis, France

List of authors

Janet B. Pierrehumbert	Northwestern University, Evanston, Illinois, USA
Henning Reetz	Universität Konstanz, Germany
Bert Remijsen	Universiteit Leiden, The Netherlands
Niels O. Schiller	Universiteit Maastricht, The Netherlands and Max Planck Institute for Psycholinguistics, Nijmegen, The Netherlands
Rajka Smiljanić	University of Illinois at Urbana-Champaign, USA
Maria-Josep Solé	Universitat Autònoma de Barcelona, Spain
Verna Stockmal	Ohio University, Athens, Ohio, USA
W. Leo Wetzels	Vrije Universteit, Amsterdam, The Netherlands
Natasha Warner	Max Planck Institute for Psycholinguistics, Nijmegen, The Netherlands and University of Arizona, Tucson, Arizona, USA

Acknowledgements

The Seventh Conference on Laboratory Phonology could not have been held the way it was without the financial support of the Royal Dutch Academy of Sciences, the Netherlands Organization for Scientific Research, the University of Nijmegen, the Arts Faculty of the University of Nijmegen and the Max Planck Institute for Psycholinguistics. Neither would it have been possible without the commitment of our stalwart co-organizer Toni Rietveld, our efficient conference assistants Petra van Alphen, Aoju Chen, Nicole Cooper and Andrea Weber, our quietly competent webmaster Keith Alcock, or our reassuringly professional administrative assistant Marlene Jonas. We are greatly indebted to them all. We would also like to thank the many reviewers of the abstracts, the speakers, and the contributors to the 45 poster presentations. Thanks also go to Pieter Nieuwint for enlivening the conference dinner with a LabPhon song which he composed specially for the occasion.

We owe the smooth progress in the production of these proceedings to the advice of the standing Laboratory Phonology Committee, in particular the former series editors Mary Beckman and John Kingston, who unofficially continued their good services during the transition to the new publisher, as well as to all the authors and reviewers. We are grateful to Jeroen van de Weijer for preparing the indices and to Ursula Kleinhenz and Annelies Aurich of Mouton de Gruyter for the efficient and friendly way in which they oversaw the production process.

Introduction

Carlos Gussenhoven and Natasha Warner

The Seventh Conference in Laboratory Phonology was co-hosted by the University of Nijmegen and the Max Planck Institute for Psycholinguistics from 28 June to 1 July 2000, and was the first conference in the series to be held outside an English-speaking country. The organisational format which had made the first six conferences so successful was followed in Nijmegen, too. Thematically, the conference's location is reflected in the two parts into which this volume has been divided. Part 1 deals with phonological issues from a psycholinguistic perspective, while Part 2 deals with the relation between phonetics and phonology in a way that was envisaged by the organizers of the first conference, Mary Beckman and John Kingston, at a time when the combined study of phonological representations and the phonetic record was not yet self-evident. As a whole, the volume comprises the written versions of 17 oral presentations and five commentaries, one of which, that by Dafydd Gibbon, represents a contribution that was invited after the conference. The number of commentaries reflects the original sub-thematic structure of the conference, which was divided into fives sections. Two of these, Phonological Encoding and Phonological Processing, represented the psycholinguistic half, while three, Field work and phonological theory, Speech technology and phonological theory, and the Phonology-Phonetics interface, reflected other local interests.

The series of Laboratory Phonology conferences has played a crucial role in healing the 'cultural fissure' between phoneticians and phonologists which still existed in 1987 when the first conference was organised (Kingston & Beckman, 1990). Today, it is not only the previous volumes of *Papers in Laboratory Phonology* that testify to the fruitful re-union of two fields of enquiry which had slowly been drifting apart since the advent of the structuralist phonology of the Prague School. Numerous monographs and journal articles show that, as an approach to the issue of the nature of speech communication, laboratory phonology comes as naturally to the field as do experimental, empirical approaches in other sciences.

These days, the question might be asked whether there is now a cultural fissure to be healed between laboratory phonologists and psycholinguists. It would hard to argue that there is no categorical division, if the answer depends on how researchers see themselves and in which journals they publish their research results, but the more interesting question is whether the research issues are really different. The aim of phonology is to characterize the phonological well-formedness of linguistic expressions, while that of psycholinguistics is to chart the processes that lead speakers to produce and hearers to perceive linguistic expressions. Despite this difference in aim, many phonological questions seem inherently psycholinguistic, while conversely, psycholinguists often address phonological issues in refreshingly new and more researchable ways.

The question how the pronunciation of words is represented has led to phonological theories that assume relatively sparse underlying representations and more detailed surface representations, augmented in Lexical Phonology with one or more intermediate representations, the latter position now being controversial. In what is still the mainstream view, a distinction is moreover drawn between these 'declarative' representations and 'procedural' implementation. As an example of a merging of psycholinguistic and phonological research, psycholinguistic findings showing that detailed phonetic information about ambient pronunciations is stored and reproduced by speakers are expanded on and incorporated into a model of speech production by Janet Pierrehumbert, someone who is widely regarded as an eminent representative of the laboratory phonology tradition, but who with equal grace and dispatch applies herself to the investigation of psycholinguistic issues. Implicitly, the phonological model is biased towards production, and conceptually it is thus perhaps more easily mappable onto Pim Levelt's model of phonological encoding than onto models of speech perception that figure in Anne Cutler's commentary. In general, psycholinguistic models could account for behaviour that would be totally at odds with the predictions of phonological models. Experimental phonetic data, with a strong computational component, allow a test of the issue, and Jurafsky et al. find mostly in favour of the traditional linguistic interpretation of categories. Schiller et al.'s lack of evidence for the syllable in production tasks suggests that perception and production strategies need not involve phonological elements in equal measure. Indeed, one thing that readily emerges from the pages of this volume is that the distinction between production and perception is relevant to the phonological model.

Inevitably, the results of some psycholinguistic investigations seem to impinge more immediately on phonologists' concerns than others. For example, Peperkamp et al.'s finding that speakers of Polish, with its predictable but bi-locational stress, behave as if stress is represented in their words, unlike speakers of Hungarian or French, whose stress is equally predictable but additionally occurs in a fixed location, is closely related to issues of concern to phonology. On the other hand, the vowel mutability effect investigated by Moates et al. is more strictly psycholinguistic in nature, addressing a difference in processing of vowels and consonants which has no immediate impact on phonological thinking. There are also contributions that would appear to address both scientific communities in like measure, such as Grabe & Low's on the gradient nature of rhythm class, van Heuven & Haan's on listeners' use of phonetic information that is available well before the occurrence of the phonological element, the final F0 rise, that encodes the relevant information in the grammar, and Lahiri & Reetz's on the viability of a word recognition algorithm based on phonologically underspecified lemmas, as well as Dafydd Gibbon's reaction to the latter paper.

More 'traditional' Laboratory Phonology concerns are also likely to be relevant to the concerns of psycholinguists. The extent to which speakers and listeners are collusive looms large in the contributions by Bradlow and Kubozono. By showing that clear speech retains the coarticulations of fast speech, Bradlow shows that speaking is a sympathetic activity, in which the speaker's own interests are weighed against those of the listener. Kubozono's contribution demonstrates the language-specific nature of the way a speech community may respond to the natural limitations of the speech process, as shown by the way hearers and speakers effectively abandon the exploitation of inefficient cues like word-final vowel quantity.

However, it is clearly not the case that the two fields of inquiry have pooled all their research questions. Neither do we wish to imply that it would be a good idea to do so, since the vastness of the scientific challenge posed by the speech process will inevitably require the development of different kinds of expertise. Research questions that fall more precisely within the expertise of phonologists include the nature of the factors that play a role in shaping phonetic behaviour and phonological grammars, an issue that is nicely laid out in Demolin's contribution, while Clements and Osu's closely argued introduction of [± obstruent] demonstrates that what is traditionally the core task in phonology, the identification of distinctive features, has not yet been completed — and indeed requires careful phonetic research. The close connection between phonetics and phonology is further underscored by Solé's demonstration that the anticipation of the articulation of Catalan trills will selectively frustrate the articulatory postures required for preceding fricatives, thus accounting for the details of fricative-to-[r] assimilations. Equally, Chitoran et al.'s account of the class of 'harmonic' stop clusters of Georgian, whose status as single complex segments is explained by the preservation of the acoustic identity of the first closure in front-to-back sequences, brings gestural phonetics into the delineation of a phonological category. Hayes extends their line of reasoning to explain the absence of 'harmonic' labial-coronal stop clusters, thus identifying a hitherto unattested operation of an ingressive velaric airstream mechanism in language (cf. Catford, 1977: 73).

Prosodic structure has been a recurring theme at Laboratory Phonology conferences, which is in part explained by the unreliability of introspective data in this area. Frota's measurements of the alignment of pitch events allow her to speculate on the appropriate phonological representation of bitonal pitch accents in European Portuguese, while Remijsen's comprehensive phonetic investigation of Ma'ya stress and tone supports an elegant alternative to an earlier more elaborate analysis. This allows him to contribute to the typological debate, already conducted in these very pages by Wetzels, in part on the basis of his data and those of Hualde et al. The latter show how a Tokyo-type pitch accent system in northern Basque gradually gives way to a stress system of the type found in Spanish in more southern varieties, which may lead one to wonder if such a development is necessarily dependent on the availability of a dominant stress language in the neighbourhood.

The dissemination of the results of Labphon7 has involved the transition to a new publisher and new series editors. To mark the coming of age of the Labphon conference proceedings, we have decided to drop the prefix *Papers in* from the title. They will appear as a subseries in Aditi Lahiri's Phonetics and Phonology Series, a niche which is appropriate both to the thematic continuity of the proceedings and their relatively infrequent appearance. We are proud to be given this chance to contribute to a successful continuation of the Laboratory Phonology enterprise.

References

Catford, J. C.
    1977   *Fundamental Problems in Phonetics*. Edinburgh: Edinburgh University Press.
Kingston, J. & Beckman, M. E. (editors)
    1990   *Papers in Laboratory Phonology I: Between the Grammar and Physics of Speech*. Cambridge: Cambridge University Press.

Part I
Phonological Processing and Encoding

The role of the lemma in form variation

Daniel Jurafsky, Alan Bell and Cynthia Girand

Abstract

We investigate the role that lemmas and wordforms (lexemes) play in form variation in lexical production, using a corpus-based methodology which is sensitive to lexical frequency effects. Average durations and reduction frequencies seem to show differences between the surface forms corresponding to different lemmas for the words *of*, *that*, and *to*. But after controlling for such factors as rate of speech, segmental context, neighbouring disfluencies, and, crucially, predictability from neighbouring words, almost all of these differences disappear. The remaining differences do not require phonetic encoding to be directly sensitive to lemma differences even for homophones. Nor do the results suggest a role for lemma frequency in lexical production, despite its key role in lexical comprehension. Instead, a 'multiple lexeme' model of lexical representation, in which different lemmas are differentially linked in the lexicon to different wordforms can account for lemma-based form differences. Our results further suggest that the lexical specifications of these wordforms include more fine-grained phonetic detail than has been previously suggested.

1. Introduction

A key problem in building a complete model of the lexicon is understanding the complex relationship between semantically and syntactically defined lexical entries ('lemmas' in the terminology of Levelt (1989), and phonological forms ('wordforms' or 'lexemes'). One reason for the complexity is that the relationship is not one-to-one. For example, in homophones like *still*, a single wordform /stɪl/ is linked with many different lemmas, including verbs ('to quiet'), nouns ('equipment for distilling' or 'silence'), adverbs ('yet' or 'nevertheless'), and adjectives ('silent', 'not moving'). The complementary situation of a single lemma linked with multiple wordforms includes well-known instances of allomorphy such as the realization of the English indefinite article as *a* or *an*, or the definite article *the* as [ðə] or [ði].

In addition to such lexically based form variation, recent corpus-based studies have shown extensive form variation in the pronunciations of what may be single lemmas (Jurafsky et al., 1998; Bell et al., 1999). For example, the phonetically transcribed Switchboard corpus (Greenberg et al., 1996) contains 33 pronunciations for the word *the*. Besides the two allomorphs [ðə] and [ði], most of the other surface realizations are due to segmental and prosodic context and to production factors like speaking rate. But in some cases, where multiple lemmas are mutually associated to a phonological form, it may be that the lemma difference plays a role in the surface realization. The impressionistic summary of Roach (1983), while noting the extensive contextual variation for most English function words, describes lemma-based variation for different functions of *that*, *some*, *there*, and *must*. Such a difference has been repeatedly noted between the pronoun *that* (*That was pretty heart-rending for her*) and the complementizer *that* (*I can't say that I'm an expert on the region*) (Jones, 1947; Jespersen, 1933; Berkenfield, 2000).

In this paper we examine the role of the lemma in explaining these kinds of variation, focusing on four very frequent function words: *to*, *that*, *of*, and *you*. The variation in these four function words provides a suitable locus for this study for several reasons. First of all, they have distinguishable functions that are plausibly instantiated as different lemmas. Second, the functions are plausibly assumed to share phonological forms or lexemes. Third, they exhibit extensive surface variation. Fourth, they are very frequent, permitting enough observations to distinguish the various sources of the variation. For example, the word *to* is very frequent (occurring 68,352 times out of about three million words in Switchboard, thus consisting of about 2% of the word tokens), is commonly assumed to have a single lexeme/wordform /tu/, has (at least) two lemmas — an infinitive marker (*we had to do it*) and a preposition (*I would have gone to the store*), and has a lot of surface variation (appearing as [tu], [tə], [tɨ], [tʌ], etc.).

We also chose to investigate function words, rather than content words, because function words are much less likely to receive sentence accent, which interacts strongly with reduction, and which we could not control adequately in our corpus. Note that the term *function word* is here no more than a convenient descriptive label; our study will not allow us to make any claims about, for example, differential processing of function and content words, or the exact nature of the set of function words.

When two or more lemmas systematically vary in their surface realizations there are three main classes of explanations for the variation:

1. **Contextual:** The variation is due to contextual and production factors acting on a single phonological form, as sketched in Figure 1.

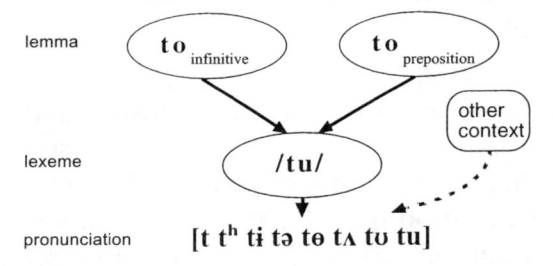

Figure 1: The contextual model: two lemmas share a wordform but there is no effect of these different lemmas on wordform variation. Variation is accounted for solely by effects of context not mediated through the lemma or through the wordform.

2. **Multiple lexeme:** The variation is due to multiple phonological forms, possibly differentially linked to the lemmas (Figure 2).

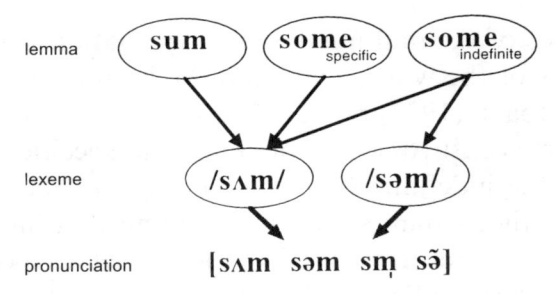

Figure 2: The multiple lexeme model. Different lemmas are linked in overlapping ways to different wordforms.

3. **Lemma-based:** The variation is due to differences in the lemmas (e.g. frequency) sharing a single phonological form (Figure 3).

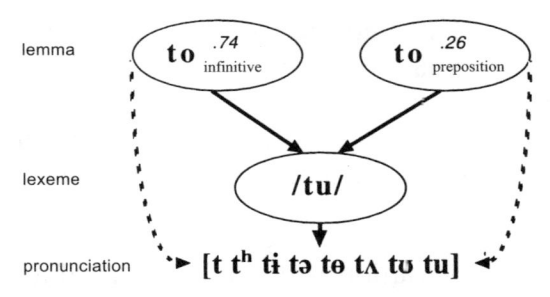

Figure 3: The lemma-based model: Two lemmas share a wordform and some of the wordform variation is accounted for by the effects of lemma differences (such as frequency) on lexical access and/or other production processes. The lemmas *too* and *two* are omitted.

These explanations are of course not exclusive, and many combinations and variants are possible for any given case.

The contextual explanation, sketched in Figure 1, suggests that pronunciation variation is not represented in any way in the lexicon. Rather, whatever variation in wordform we see depends only on contextual factors such as prosodic, segmental or syntactic context, production factors like rate of speech, or sociolinguistic factors. This explanation of variation appears to be the cause of most kinds of variation, if impressionistic summaries like Roach's or the relative rarity of diachronic homonym splits like that of New York and Philadelphia *can* are any guide (Ferguson, 1975; Labov, 1989).

An example of the multiple lexeme explanation is given by the various senses of the word *some* (and the homonym *sum*), shown in Figure 2. Roach (1983) points out that there are pronunciation differences between two senses of *some*, the specific *some animal broke it* and the indefinite *have some more tea*. These differences are most directly accounted for by assuming that indefinite *some* is linked to two wordforms /səm/ and /sʌm/, while specific *some* is linked only to /sʌm/. (*Sum* is also of course linked only to /sʌm/.) Figure 2 sketches this kind of lemma effect.

Similarly, although the split between the New York and Philadelphia English noun *can* (*can of beans*; /keːən/) and auxiliary *can* (*can I*; /kæn/) may have had its original source in a prosodically conditioned longer noun *can* (perhaps also abetted by its lower lexical frequency), it likely passed through a stage where the two lemmas differentially selected multiple wordforms.

The lemma-based explanation, sketched in Figure 3, assumes that the variation in surface form is somehow caused directly by a property of the different lemmas, such as their frequencies. For example, if the lemmas differ in frequency, this difference might account for some of the surface variation, even though they share a single phonological form. One way that this might happen is for less frequent lemmas, being accessed more slowly, to sometimes slow up one or more of the steps in the phonetic encoding process. We will call this the lemma frequency hypothesis.

The lemma frequency hypothesis is not compatible with current phonological theory or most models of speech production, which generally assume that multiple lemmas have no direct effect on surface variation (Levelt et al., 1999). Furthermore, previous research such as Jescheniak & Levelt (1994) has argued convincingly that the wordform and not the lemma is the major locus of frequency effects in the lexicon, at least so far as they affect lexical access speed in production. Still, we feel it is worth examining the lemma frequency effect. One main reason is that there is robust evidence for a lemma frequency effect in comprehension. For example, Hogaboam & Perfetti (1975), Simpson (1981), Simpson & Burgess (1985), and many more recent studies have found that the rate of rise in activation for a particular lemma in comprehension is a function of the lemma's relative frequency. Since there are many differences between lexical comprehension and production, it is crucial to understand exactly which kinds of frequency effects are not symmetric in this way.

A second reason to investigate the lemma frequency effect is that an initial, raw measurement of word durations does seem to give preliminary evidence of a frequency effect. For example, as we will show below, in our corpus the more frequent infinitive lemma for *to* is much shorter on average (with an average raw length of 110 ms) than the less frequent preposition lemma for *to* (with an average raw length of 140 ms). Berkenfield (2000) found similar relations between frequency and shorter duration for the word *that* in a different speech corpus.

Lemma frequency is also a convenient avatar for general lemma effects because in addition to predicting that the lemma will affect the reduction of the wordform, it makes a more specific prediction about the direction of the reduction: more frequent lemmas will have shorter wordforms.

2. Methodology

This paper is based on a new corpus-based methodology to explore the interaction of frequency, lemma, and wordform. Our method is to show how various frequency factors affect the duration, reduction, or lenition of words in a corpus. That is, rather than using carefully controlled materials in production studies in laboratory settings, we use a very large database of natural speech and use multiple regression to control for factors that influence the duration or reduction of words. Our study is based on the Switchboard corpus of 2430 telephone conversations between strangers, collected in the early 1990s (Godfrey et al., 1992).

We coded each instance of the four words *to*, *that*, *of*, and *you* for their different syntacto-semantic lemmas. For example, we investigated four different *that*s (complementizer, pronoun, determiner, and relative pronoun) and two different *to*s (preposition, infinitive marker). Lists and examples of each sense are given below. The different lemmas of a word may differ in frequency. The infinitive *to*, for example, is about three times as frequent as the preposition *to*.

The phonological variable we used to study these parts of speech was the reduction or lenition of the word's pronunciation in conversational speech. Based on our previous work (Jurafsky et al., 1998; Bell et al., 1999) we coded three measures of reduction for *that*, *to*, *of*, and *you*: duration in milliseconds, reduced vowel, and deletion of final consonants.

In earlier work (Jurafsky et al., 2001), we have shown that this methodology is quite sensitive to word frequency. In natural speech, frequent words are shorter in duration, have a greater proportion of reduced vowels, and are more likely to have deleted coda consonants than rarer words. This effect holds even after controlling for the many factors that we and others have shown influence reduction in function words, including the speaker's rate of speech (in syllables per second), whether the speaker was having planning problems (as indicated by neighboring disfluencies), the position of the function word in the utterance, the segmental context, the contextual predictability of the function word, and sociolinguistic factors such as age and sex.

In the experiments described in this paper, then, we controlled all our data for these factors and then tested whether the more frequent lemma (e.g., the infinitive *to*) was shorter than the less frequent lemma (e.g., the preposition *to*). Since we did see such a difference in raw durations (for example infinitive *to* is in fact shorter on average than preposition *to*) we expected to see this difference after controlling for other factors.

2.1 The Switchboard dataset

Our dataset of the four function words was drawn from the Switchboard corpus of telephone conversations between strangers, collected in the early 1990s (Godfrey et al., 1992). The corpus contains 2430 conversations averaging six minutes each, totaling 240 hours of speech and about three million words spoken by over 500 speakers. The corpus was collected at Texas Instruments, mostly by soliciting paid volunteers who were connected to other volunteers via a robot telephone operator. Conversations were then transcribed by court reporters into a word-by-word text.

Approximately four hours of speech from these conversations were phonetically hand-transcribed by students at UC Berkeley (Greenberg et al., 1996) as follows. The speech files were automatically segmented into pseudo-utterances at turn boundaries or at silences of 500 ms or more, and a rough automatic phonetic transcription was generated. The transcribers were given these utterances along with the text and rough phonetic transcriptions. They then corrected the phonetic transcription, using an augmented version of the ARPAbet, and marked syllable boundaries, from which durations of each syllable were computed.

This phonetically transcribed corpus contains roughly 38,000 transcribed words (tokens). Our total dataset is drawn from the set of all instances of *of, that, you*, and *to*, after screening for transcription errors. Each of our analyses of reduction are based on the tokens remaining after excluding various non-comparable items, as explained below in section 2.3.

Each observation was coded for two or three factors reflecting reduction:

vowel reduction: We coded the vowel of each function word as *full* or *reduced*. The full vowels included basic citation or clarification pronunciations, e.g. [ði] for *the*, as well as other non-reduced vowels. The reduced vowels that occurred in the function words were [ə] and [ɨ].[1] Table 1 shows full and reduced-vowel pronunciations of the four words.

duration: the duration of the word in milliseconds.

coda obstruent deletion: for *that* and *of*, whether the word-final obstruent was deleted.

Table 1: Common pronunciations of the four function words by vowel type.

	Full	Reduced
of	[ʌv], [ʌ], [ʌvv] [ɪ], [i], [ɑ]	[ə], [əv], [əf]
to	[tu], [ɾu], [tʊ], [tɪ], [tʌ]	[tə], [tɨ], [ə]
that	[ðæ], [ðæt], [æ], [ðɛ], [ðɛt], [ðɛɾ]	[ðɨt], [ðɨ], [ðɨɾ]
you	[yu], [u], [yɪ], [ɪ], [i]	[yɨ], [y], [ɨ]

2.2 The regression analysis

We used multiple regression to evaluate the effects of our predictability factors on reduction. A regression analysis is a statistical model that predicts a *response variable* (in this case, the word duration, the frequency of vowel reduction, or the frequency of coda deletion) based on contributions from a number of other *explanatory factors* (Agresti, 1996). Thus when we report that an effect was significant, it is meant to be understood that it is a significant parameter in a model that also includes the other significant variables. In other words, after accounting for the effects of the other explanatory variables, adding the explanatory variable in question produced a significantly better account of the variation in the response variable. For duration, which is a continuous variable, we used ordinary linear regression to model the log duration of the word. For vowel quality and coda deletion, which are categorical variables, we used logistic regression.

All of the analyses assume that the items of the sample are independent. This is not strictly true, since some of the function words come from the same pseudo-utterances (and more generally, from the same conversations). We do not expect that this would influence the results much, but it does mean that the significance levels we report are somewhat overstated, and hence they should be interpreted with caution.

2.3 Control factors

The reduction processes are each influenced by multiple structural and performance factors that must be controlled to assess the contribution of lexical category to reduction. We briefly review these factors here and our method of controlling for them. First, we excluded tokens of *of*, *you*, *to*, and *that* based on the following three factors:

– **special forms:** We excluded cliticized words (e.g., *you've*, *that's*, etc.), Such forms made up about nine percent of the total occurrences of the four function words; tokens of *that's* accounted for almost 80 percent of the excluded items. Also excluded were about 100 items whose extreme or aberrant parameter values indicated a high likelihood of coding error.

– **prosodic position:** We removed words which began or ended the pseudo-utterances of our dataset, because of the incomparability of the predictability measures for such items and their high correlation with special prosodic contexts. Such words made up about 14 percent of the items. Recall that these conversational fragments were bounded either by turns or long pauses. Thus, all turn-initial and turn-final items were excluded. Many items that were initial or final in an intonational phrase would also have been excluded, leaving only such items that fell within the pseudo-utterances. Based on two subsamples of the data coded for prosodic units, we estimate that perhaps 10 percent of the remaining data consists of items that were initial or final in the intonational phrase.

– **planning problems:** Previous work has shown that when words are followed or preceded by disfluencies indicating planning problems (pauses, filled pauses *uh* and *um*, or repetitions), their pronunciations are less reduced (Fox Tree & Clark, 1997; Jurafsky et al., 1998; Bell et al., 1999; Shriberg, 1999). Partly for this reason and partly because the interpretation of the predictability variables in such contexts was unclear, these items, about 18 percent of the remaining data, were excluded.

We then controlled other variables known or suspected to affect reduction by entering them first in the regression model. Thus the full base model for an analysis was a regression on the following set of control factors:

– **rate of speech:** Speech researchers have long noted the association between faster speech, informal styles, and more reduced forms. For a recent quantitative account of rate effects in Switchboard, see Fosler-Lussier & Morgan, 1999. We measured rate of speech at a given function word by taking the number of syllables per second in the smallest pause-bounded region containing the word. Our regression models all included log rate; log squared rate, found to be a significant factor in our work with larger samples, was included in models where it was an appreciable factor.

– **segmental context:** A general fact about reduction processes is that the form of a word is influenced by the segmental context – for example, consonant deletion is favored when a segment is preceded by or followed by a consonant. We controlled for the class (consonant or vowel) of the following segment. For vowel reduction, we also controlled for whether the target syllable was open or closed (e.g., *it* vs. *to*), since we know from studies in larger samples that this variable interacts closely with segmental context (the latter factor was ignored in some regressions where its effect was negligible).

- **Reduction of following vowel:** The prosodic pattern of the utterance plays a crucial role in reduction. Since our current dataset does not mark stress or accent, the only prosodic control was whether the vowel in the syllable following the target word was reduced or full. (This partially controls for stress since the reduction of the following vowel should correlate with its stress level, and hence the stress level of the target word.)
- **Probability of word given neighboring words:** In earlier work (Jurafsky et al., 2001), we showed that the conditional probability of a word given the previous and following words played an important role in its reduction. We therefore included four probabilistic control factors: the conditional probability of the target word given the previous word, the joint probability of the target word with the previous word, the conditional probability of the target word given the following word, and the joint probability of the target word given the following word. The next section summarizes the definitions of these probabilities and the effects we found in this earlier work.

We also included terms for some of the interactions between these variables where their effect was appreciable.

Several factors that have been reported to influence reduction were not controlled in this study. First, our definition of words was quite simplified; we assume that anything bounded by spaces in the text transcriptions was a word. Thus *most of*, for example, was taken to be two words.

Other factors not controlled included the segmental environment of the preceding word, finer details of the the segmental environment of the following word, and social variables, i.e. register, age, sex, and social class. We expect that the remaining segmental factors would have relatively little effect on duration or on the role of the predictability measures, but we have not examined this possibility. When we controlled for some social variables in earlier work (Bell et al., 1999), the effects on reduction were relatively small and the robust effects of the predictability measures were little diminished. The effects of prosodic structure, stress, and accent are only partially and indirectly controlled by the variable of reduction in the following vowel and the exclusion of beginnings and ends of pseudo-utterances. Work in progress in which we controlled for an approximation to position in the intonational phrase showed that while initial and final tokens in this domain were significantly longer, controlling for these items had little effect on the predictability measures. The effect of pitch accent is discussed below in section 3.4.

2.4 Effects of probability of word given neighboring words

Jurafsky et al. (2001) proposed the *Probabilistic Reduction Hypothesis*: Word forms are reduced when they have a higher probability. In that paper we showed specifically that target words which have a higher probability given neighboring words are shorter. We use two measures (the *joint probability* and the *conditional probability*) of the predictability of a word given the previous and given the following word. The *joint probability* of two words $P(w_{i-1}w_i)$ may be thought of as the prior probability of the two words taken together, and is estimated by just looking at the relative frequency of the two words together in a corpus:

$$(1) \qquad P(w_{i-1}w_i) = \frac{C(w_{i-1}w_i)}{N}$$

The *conditional probability of a word given the previous word* is also sometimes called the *transitional probability* (Bush, 1999; Saffran et al., 1996). The conditional probability of a particular target word w_i given a previous word w_{i-1} is estimated from a sufficiently large corpus, by counting the number of times the two words occur together $C(w_{i-1}w_i)$, and dividing by $C(w_{i-1})$, the number of times that the first word occurs:

$$(2) \qquad P(w_i|w_{i-1}) = \frac{C(w_{i-1}w_i)}{C(w_{i-1})}$$

The difference between the conditional and joint probability is that the conditional probability controls for the frequency of the conditioning word. For example, pairs of words can have a high joint probability merely because the individual words are of high frequency (e.g., *of the*). The conditional probability would be high only if the second word was particularly likely to follow the first. Most measures of word cohesion, such as conditional probability and mutual information, are based on such metrics which control for the frequencies of one or both of the words (Manning & Schütze, 1999).

In addition to considering the preceding word, we measured the effect of the following word by the two corresponding probabilities. The *joint probability of a word with the next word* $P(w_i w_{i+1})$ is estimated by the relative frequency of the two words together:

(3) $$P(w_i w_{i+1}) = \frac{C(w_i w_{i+1})}{N}$$

Similarly, the *conditional probability of the target word given the next word* $P(w_i | w_{i+1})$ is the probability of the target word w_i given the next word w_{i+1}. This may be viewed as the predictability of a word given the word the speaker is about to say, and is estimated as follows:

(4) $$P(w_i | w_{i+1}) = \frac{C(w_i w_{i+1})}{C(w_{i+1})}$$

Jurafsky et al. (2001) showed that all of these measures played a role in reduction; words which were highly probable by any of these measures were shorter, more likely to have a reduced vowel, and more likely to have a deleted consonant.

Since our 38,000 word corpus was far too small to estimate word probabilities, we used the entire 2.4 million word Switchboard corpus (from which our corpus was drawn) instead. See Jurafsky et al. (1998) for details about the backoff and discounting methods that we used to smooth the estimates of very low frequency items. We then took the log of these probabilities for use in our regression analyses.

2.5 Earlier results on sensitivity of our methodology to lexical frequency

The hypothesis that more frequent forms are more likely to be reduced in lexical production has been widely proposed (Schuchardt, 1885; Jespersen, 1922; Zipf, 1929; Martinet, 1960; Oldfield & Wingfield, 1965; Fidelholz, 1975; Hooper, 1976; Phillips, 1984; Jescheniak & Levelt, 1994; Bybee, 2000; Rhodes, 1992, 1996).

In Jurafsky et al. (2001), we used our corpus-based methodology to examine the role of various probabilistic measures, including lexical frequency, on reduction. We examined 2042 tokens of words ending in the phoneme /t/ or /d/, again from the 38,000 word phonetically-transcribed Switchboard database. We examined two dependent measures: the duration of the word in milliseconds (only for monosyllabic words) and deletion of the final /t/ or /d/. We found a strong effect of relative frequency on both kinds of reduction ($p < .0001$). For duration, high frequency words (at the 95th percentile of frequency) were 18% shorter than low frequency words (at the 5th percentile) and high frequency words (at the 95th percentile) were 2.0 times more likely to have deleted final /t/ or /d/ than the lowest frequency words (at the 5th percentile).

These results suggest that our corpus-based methodology is indeed sensitive to lexical frequency. But our previous results did not distinguish between lemma frequency and wordform frequency. Testing the differential role of the two requires labeling each wordform observation for its associated lemma. This coding process is described in the next section.

2.6 Coding for lexical category

We coded the four function words *that*, *to*, *of*, and *you* for their syntactic categories. In each case we coded fine-grained categories which were then collapsed into broader categories for our analyses. Tables 3–5 show examples of the different lexical categories we coded for the four words.

Table 2: Lexical category coding for *to*.

Count	%	Syntactic Category	Example from Switchboard
543	74%	**infinitive marker**	is that a tough system **to** be in?
195	26%	**preposition/particle**	she is a great comfort **to** me
738	100%	**Total**	

For *that*, there are four traditional part-of-speech or syntactic category differences: determiner, pronoun, complementizer, and relativizer. Some previous studies of form variation have treated complementizers and relativizers together (Jespersen, 1933), while others have distinguished all four (Berkenfield, 2000). We chose to look at all four. We did not, however, study subtypes of these categories such as the differences between subject and object pronouns, or between subject and object relatives, mainly since neither the literature nor our intuitions gave us any reason to expect a duration or reduction difference between subject and object pronouns. But in order to make it clear what the categories encompass, we give more details of subtypes of these categories in Table 3.

Table 3: Lexical category coding for *that*.

Count	%	Syntactic Category	Example from Switchboard
294	37%	**pronoun**	
		subject	**that** didn't help at all
		non-subject	and we keep thinking about **that**
183	23%	**complement**	
		verbal complement	like uh one company had proposed to me **that** i could come back to work after having the baby um
		verbal extraposition	and uh it's always occurred to me **that**
		nominal complement	I just finished fuming at the fact **that** we pay an eight and a half percent sales tax ...
170	21%	**rel. pronoun**	
		subject relative	found a bunch of memos **that** were uh supposedly from...
		non-subj. relative	you get on a topic **that** you know you enjoy...
102	13%	**determiner**	...and fines and things of **that** nature
42	5%	**other**	idioms (*that is*), intensifiers, etc.
791	100%	**Total**	

For *of*, the different lemmas are strongly related to the different syntactic constructions they can occur in, for example as the complement of a verb or preposition (e.g., *thought of, outside of*) or as a partitive (e.g., *some of, all of*) (Table 4).

18 Daniel Jurafsky, Alan Bell and Cynthia Girand

Table 4: Lexical category coding for *of*.

Count	%	Syntactic Category	Example from Switchboard
230	40%	**partitive**	e.g., one **of** them, type **of** job, all **of**, some **of**
100	18%	**complement**	e.g., thought **of**, outside **of**, in front **of**
95	17%	**genitive/other post-nominal**	e.g., friend **of** mine, matter **of** concern, things **of** that nature
146	26%	**assorted idioms**	e.g., kind **of**, lot **of**, sort **of**, matter **of** fact
561	100%	**Total**	

For *you*, we distinguished four potential lemmas. We considered the *you* of the phrase *you know*, the referential pronoun *you*, and a non-referential or generic pronoun *you* (*yeah then you have to get up the next day and move it on*). We also distinguished auxiliary-inverted and non-inverted instances of the referential *you* (Table 5).

Table 5: Lexical category coding for *of*.

Count	%	Syntactic Category	Example from Switchboard
359	47%	**you know**	it was **you** know in the seventies
212	27%	**generic**	yeah then **you** have to get up the next day and move it on
172	22%	**referential**	
83	11%	aux-inverted	well do **you** drink soda and such?
89	12%	not aux-inverted	and **you** only get one of them
743	100%	**Total**	

3. Results

We ran separate regressions for each of the four words.

3.1 Effect of the lemma on variation in *to*

As Table 2 shows, the frequency of the infinitive lemma was 2.8 times greater than the frequency of the preposition lemma. If lemma frequency plays a role in lexical production, as the lemma frequency hypothesis suggests, we would expect the infinitives to be shorter than the prepositions after controlling for other variables in our regression. In addition, we would expect the infinitives to have a greater percentage of reduced vowels than the prepositions. If we look at the values of tokens of the two lemmas in the corpus after excluding items but not controlling for any other factors, this is indeed the case, as we see in Table 6.

Table 6: Lemma counts, proportions, raw durations, and raw percentage of reduced vowels for infinitival and prepositional *to*. Lemma counts and proportions are based on the total sample. Durations and reduced vowel percentages are based on the sample after excluding non-comparable items.

Lemma	Count	Proportion of Occurrences (percent)	Average Duration (ms)	Percent Vowel Reduction
Infinitive	543	74	109	78
Preposition	195	27	138	56

The differences in all three variables are highly significant ($p < .0001$), and are in the direction predicted by the lemma frequency hypothesis. We used a binomial test for the lemma frequency difference ($z_c = 7.2$). To examine the differences in duration and in vowel reduction of the two categories, we made a planned comparison between the infinitive and the preposition categories in linear regressions for duration, and in logistic regressions for vowel reduction. These comparisons yielded values of $F(1,567) = 28.4$ for duration, and $\chi^2(1) = 21.9$ for vowel reduction.

These differences, however, are not controlled for factors known to influence reduction. We thus added control variables for rate of speech and for following segmental context to the regression models. There remained a difference in duration ($F(1,564) = 12.1$, $p = .0005$), and in vowel reduction ($\chi^2(1) = 5.7$, $p < .05$) between infinitival and prepositional *to*. The infinitives were shorter in duration and had a greater probability of having a reduced vowel.

Still not controlled in these comparisons are the effects of local predictability. We therefore included four local predictability variables into our base model for the regression:

1. Joint probability of target and previous word
2. Joint probability of target and following word
3. Conditional probability of target given following word
4. Conditional probability of target given previous word

After adding these variables, no effect of the lemma categories on either duration or vowel reduction remained ($F < 1$, $\chi^2 = 1.1$). That is, there was no difference between the duration or vowel quality of infinitive *to* and preposition *to*. This was a surprising result, as the difference in raw durations was so large.

3.2 The roles of predictability and lemma category

The fact that no effect of lexical category remains after controlling for predictability implies that there must be some connection between lemma category and predictability. And indeed there is. The average conditional probability of prepositional *to* given the following word is 0.032, whereas the average conditional probability of infinitival *to* is 0.190. That is, infinitival *to* is more predictable. We might further inquire, however, about the symmetry of the relationship. Are lexical category and predictability here merely correlated, so that either is an equally good predictor of reduction?

Or is predictability a separate factor, whether we categorize the data by lemma or not? This latter model is what was suggested by our earlier work in which we found a robust effect of predictability on reduction throughout a very wide range of word classes, word frequencies, and word contexts.

We tested whether predictability is a separate factor by examining the effect of predictability after controlling for lemma. As we expected, the predictability variables remain highly significant. This means that predictability completely accounts for any predictive power that the lemma variable offers, and offers further explanatory power, e.g. it accounts for the reduction of tokens within each of the two lemma categories. This suggests that predictability and not lemma is the factor accounting for the difference between surface pronunciations of *to*.

In other words, the lemma categories only appeared to account for the reduction and duration difference for *to* because it happens that the more reduced infinitival *to*s are also more predictable.

3.3 Lexical categories of *of*

Recall that the lexical categories for *of* included complements (*thought of*), partitives (*one of them*), genitives/postnominals (*friend of mine*), and high-frequency idioms *kind of, sort of*). Their frequencies, average durations, and average coda deletion are summarized in Table 7. The lemmas did not differ in frequency of vowel reduction.[2]

Table 7: Lemma counts, proportions, raw durations, and raw percentage of deleted codas for *of*. Lemma counts and proportions are based on the total sample. Durations and reduced vowel percentages are based on the sample after excluding non-comparable items.

Lemma	Count	Proportion of Occurrences (percent)	Average Duration (ms)	Percent Coda Deletion
Partitive	230	54	82	55
Complement	100	24	94	39
Genitive/Postnominal	95	22	103	38

The frequency of partitives is obviously much greater than that of complements and genitive/postnominals, whose frequencies do not differ significantly.

To examine the differences in the durations and coda deletion of the categories, we made planned comparisons between the frequent partitive and the other two categories, and then between the latter two categories, using contrast variables in linear regressions for duration, and in logistic regressions for coda deletion. Partitives differ from complements/genitives both for raw duration ($F(1,474) = 16.6, p = .0001$) and raw proportion of coda deletion ($\chi^2(1) = 13.7, p < .0005$). The differences between complements and genitives are not significant. Note that the lemma frequency hypothesis predicts that partitives should be shorter and more reduced than complements and shorter and more reduced than genitives, which is the case.

When we control for rate and contextual factors (without predictability), both duration ($F(1,471) = 14.9, p = .0001$) and coda deletion ($\chi^2(1) = 11.2, p < .001$) remain significant. Finally, controlling also for predictability, we still found effects of lemma on coda deletion, but not on duration ($F < 1$). Partitives were marginally more likely to have deleted codas than the combination of complements and genitives ($\chi^2(1) = 5.1, p < .05$).[3]

These results suggest that surface pronunciations of the (more frequent) partitive lemma for *of* are more reduced than surface pronunciations of the (less frequent) complement or genitive lemmas. While the predictability variables completely eliminated any lemma effect for *to*, this was not the case for *of*.

3.4 Lexical categories of *that*

The frequencies, average durations, average reductions, and average coda deletion of the four major lexical categories of *that* are summarized in Table 8.

Table 8: Lemma counts, proportions, raw durations, and raw percentage of reduced vowels and deleted codas for *that*. Lemma counts and proportions are based on the total sample. Durations and deleted coda and reduced vowel percentages are based on the sample after excluding non-comparable items.

Lemma	Count	Proportion of Occurrences (percent)	Average Duration (ms)	Percent Vowel Reduction	Percent Coda Deletion
Pronoun	294	37	186	2	56
Relative	170	21	132	18	50
Complementizer	183	23	154	22	43
Determiner	102	13	142	0	75

From Table 8 we observe that the pronoun *that* is the most frequent of the four lemmas of *that* that we consider, and the determiner or demonstrative *that* is the least frequent, with relative marker *that* and complementizer *that* falling in between. All the frequency differences between the categories are significant except for that between complements and relative markers (z_c from 4.1 to 9.6, $p < .0001$). Berkenfield (2000) investigated the durations of these same four lemmas for 305 observations of *that* in a corpus of conversational speech taken from the television program *The Newshour with Jim Lehrer*. She found a similar ranking of the raw durations, although not quite the same. In her data, as in ours, pronouns were longest. But in her data determiners were the next longest, followed by complementizers, with relative clause markers the shortest. That is, in her data, determiners and relative clause markers are switched in their order from our Switchboard data. Berkenfield (2000) also found that while the pronoun lemma for *that* was the most frequent in Switchboard, it was the complementizer lemma that was by far the most frequent in written corpora like the Brown corpus (Francis & Kučera, 1982), and news programs like the Lehrer Newshour. Thus it is not clear what the correct prediction would be of the lemma frequency hypothesis.

All corpora agree, however, that the determiner lemma is the least frequent. It is also less likely to have a reduced vowel than complementizers or relative markers. This difference cannot be attributed to rate, contextual factors, or predictability; it remains highly significant after controlling for these factors ($\chi^2(1) = 23.5$, $p < .0001$). The duration and likelihood of coda deletion of determiners, however, do not differ significantly from complementizers or relative markers.

Pronouns appear to be much like determiners in that they, too, are less likely to have reduced vowels than the complementizers and relative markers. But unlike determiners, they are longer than the other lemmas (including determiners) after accounting for the control factors ($F(1,421) = 20.7$, $p < .0001$). They do not differ in likelihood of coda deletion.

Complementizers are less reduced than relative markers: they are longer ($F(1,419) = 9.2$, $p < .005$) and marginally less likely to have deleted codas ($\chi^2(1) = 5.1$, $p < .05$); but they do not differ in likelihood of vowel reduction.

It may be that the occurrence of accent is an important factor in these results. While we do not have enough data coded for accent to control for this factor, a small portion of the Switchboard corpus has been coded for accent under the direction of Stefanie Shattuck-Hufnagel and Mari Ostendorf. They generously made an alpha-release of their accent-coded corpus available to us, and we examined the overlap between their corpus and ours, a small subset consisting of 10 percent or less of our entire dataset. There were 180 tokens of our four function words in this sample, if we include the disfluent contexts. Of these, 16 were accented. Only *that*s received accent at all frequently, 10 out of the 36 tokens coded; *Of*s were accented once out of 45 tokens; *to*s, once out of 53; *you*s, 4 times out of 46. This is encouraging in that it affords some confidence that the results for *of* and *to* are unlikely to be much influenced by accent.

Of the 36 tokens of *that* coded for pitch accent, only the determiners (4 accented of 11) and the pronouns (6 of 14) received accent; not surprisingly, all accent-coded occurrences of complementizers and relative markers were unaccented. However, it appeared that the disfluent contexts favored accent somewhat. In fluent contexts, only two of eight determiners and two of nine pronouns were accented. Although, for example, the average duration of the accented pronominal *that*s was longer than the duration of the unaccented ones (256 ms versus 142 ms), the sample is simply too small to demonstrate significant differences of duration either for the accent or lemma categories.

Until the influence of accent can be further determined, any conclusions about pronunciation differences linked to *that* lemmas must remain guarded. The lesser reduction found for determiners is surely affected to some extent by the presence of accented items, and is in any case suspicious without any accompanying difference in duration. At least for pronouns there are strong effects both for reduction and duration, but until the factor of accent can be controlled, we can only conjecture that a noncontextual effect may exist. The relatively weak difference in duration between complementizers and relative markers remains, however, since accent is unlikely to account for any difference between them.

3.5 Lexical categories of *you*

Unlike the other three words, the two main lemmas we investigated for *you* (the referential and the generic/nonreferential) did not differ significantly in raw duration or reduction. None of the differences in duration or vowel reduction between generic and referential lemmas shown in Table 9 are significant.

Table 9: Lemma counts, proportions, raw durations, and raw percentage of reduced vowels for *you*. Lemma counts and proportions are based on the total sample. Durations and reduced vowel percentages are based on the sample after excluding non-comparable items.

Lemma	Count	Proportion of Occurrences (percent)	Average Duration (ms)	Percent Vowel Reduction
You know	359	47	105	49
Generic, non-referential	211	27	109	26
Referential	172	22	118	22

After controlling for the base model including predictability, the items were still the same; referential and non-referential observations of *you* did not differ in surface pronunciation.

4. Conclusions

We investigated the role that lemmas play in wordform variation, using a corpus-based methodology which is sensitive to lexical frequency effects. Raw duration and reduction measures seem to show differences between the surface forms corresponding to different lemmas for the words *of*, *that*, and *to*. But after controlling for such factors as rate of speech, segmental context, neighboring disfluencies, and, crucially, predictability from neighboring words, almost all of these differences disappeared.

For the word *to*, for example, we found no separate effect whatsoever of the lemma for wordform variation. That is, we could account for most or all of the variation in surface form of *to*, solely based on the control factors described above. The most important such control factor was the predictability of the word given the neighboring words. When this factor was included in our regression, it accounted for all of the differences between the different surface realizations of *to*.

While we found no evidence for a lemma effect for *to*, we did find a small lemma effect for *of*, even after controlling for predictability. The partitive *of* (*one **of** them*) is more likely to have a deleted coda than the genitive *of* (*friend **of** mine*) and the complement *of* (*to think **of***). Since the partitive is also more frequent, the direction of the difference is consistent with the hypothesis that the more frequent lemma will show more reduction. However, we found no effect of lemma on the duration or vowel reduction for *of*.

Our results on *that* are inconclusive. First, after controlling for predictability and other factors, the pronoun *that* (*thinking about **that***) is longer and more likely to have a full vowel than the relative (*a topic **that** you enjoy*) or complementizer *that* (*proposed to me **that** I could*). Second, the determiner *that* (*things of **that** nature*) was more likely to have a full vowel than the complementizer or relative *that*. Both these differences, though, are clearly related to prosody; the pronoun *that* and the determiner *that* are both much more likely to receive accent than the complementizer or relative marker.

The third result with *that* is less likely to be influenced by accent. The relativizer sense of *that* is shorter and has more coda deletion than the slightly less frequent complementizer sense of *that*. This difference is unlikely to be caused by lemma frequency, since the relative frequencies of the complementizer and relativizer lemmas were not significantly different.

Finally, we found no effects of lemma on the word *you*.

In summary, although we were able to account for most of the differences between surface forms of different lemmas via these contextual factors, four differences remained significant even after controlling for these factors. As we suggested above, two of these, the less reduced forms of the determiner and pronominal lemmas for *that*, may turn out to actually be effects of pitch accent.

Thus two differences remained. First, the frequent partitive sense of *of* was more likely to have a deleted coda than the less frequent genitive or complement senses. Second, the relativizer sense of *that* is shorter and has more coda deletion than the equally frequent complementizer sense of *that*.

The fact that these two differences remained despite our control for context suggests that the contextual model of lexeme variation may not be sufficient to explain pronunciation variation. The contextual model predicts that all variation in surface pronunciation should be accounted for by context or by production factors, and that neither the lemma nor the lexeme should have a role. This model is not sufficient to explain the variation we see in *of* and *that*.

But the differences in *of* and *that* are also not compatible with the lemma frequency model of form variation. The relativizer and complement lemmas for *that* have the same frequency, but still differ in duration and coda deletion percentage. Even the result for *of*, where the more frequent partitive had more coda deletion than the rarer genitive and complementizers, is not strong evidence for the lemma frequency model. This is because if the reduction of *of* is caused by frequency, we would also expect reduction differences between other lemmas whose frequency difference is as great as the difference in *of*. The frequency ratio between the partitive and complement/genitive lemmas for *of* is 2.4 to 1. But the frequency ratio between the infinitive and preposition lemmas for *to* is about the same (2.8 to 1), but *to* shows no lemma-based effect on reduction.

Even if in time numerous instances of association of frequent lemmas with reduced non-contextual pronunciations were found, it does not follow that production models should incorporate the lemma frequency hypothesis. The association would more plausibly be accounted for by diachronic preferences rather than synchronic structures. A homonym split could begin with a differentiation of pronunciations that was at first purely contextual, with reduced forms occurring in more frequent, more predictable, and possibly less prosodically prominent constructions or contexts. If the contextual differences became lexicalized, this would lead to some of the distinctions in reduction becoming encoded in the lexicon, and would leave an association of more reduction with the more frequent lemmas.

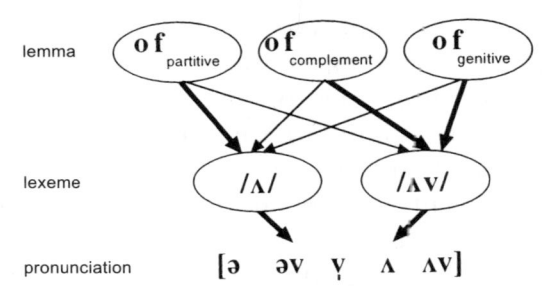

28 Daniel Jurafsky, Alan Bell and Cynthia Girand

Figure 4: A possible multiple lexeme model of *of*, showing more coda deletion in partitive *of*, and less coda deletion in genitive and complement *of*.

Our conclusion that the lemma frequency hypothesis does not hold for speech production is nicely consonant with the result of Jescheniak & Levelt (1994). But it does point out an intriguing difference between lexical access in comprehension, where lemma frequency effects are robust and have been reported cross-linguistically (Li & Yip, 1996; Ahrens, 1998), and lexical access in production (with, it seems, no lemma frequency effect). Lemma frequency, then, is a feature that seems to play different roles in language comprehension and production, a fact that should clearly be further studied.

Even if there is not sufficient support for the lemma frequency hypothesis, it is still necessary to consider whether there are cases which require the lemma-based model involving other factors than frequency. Diachronically, we assume such differences would arise by lexicalization of contextual differences. The issue is whether the differences are incorporated in the lexeme or in the lemma, i.e. whether the multiple lexeme model or the lemma-based model applies.

Recall that the multiple lexeme model suggested that different lemmas are differentially linked in the lexicon to different wordforms. Perhaps, for example, as shown in Figure 4, all lemmas for *of* are linked to the wordforms [ʌv] and [ʌ], but the genitive or complement *of* is linked more preferentially to the wordform [ʌv], while the partitive *of* is linked more preferentially to [ʌ]. Similarly, the relativizer sense of *that* could be preferentially linked to [ðæ], while the complementizer sense of *that* could be preferentially linked to [ðæt].

The multiple lexeme model might be able to handle such results. But recall that the relativizer sense of *that* is also *shorter* than the complementizer sense of *that*, even after controlling for the greater incidence of coda reduction. That is, the difference between these two forms is not just purely representable as a segmental difference. This suggests that the specifications of wordforms include more phonetic detail than just phonological categories. We found a related result in our earlier work (Jurafsky et al., 2001), where we showed that reduced forms of very predictable words are shorter even after controlling for segmental changes (vowel reduction or coda deletion).

One recent approach to phonological representation and production does offer a possible solution to these data. Pierrehumbert (2001) and others have recently proposed exemplar-based models of phone and word production. In exemplar-based models, each category is stored in memory as a cloud of exemplars of that category. Thus in Pierrehumbert's model, for example, phones and words are both stored as clouds of exemplars. Production of a phone or word takes place by randomly activating and then producing a particular exemplar. Pierrehumbert (2001) then proposes that the production process is not quite random; in leniting contexts it has a very slight bias in its selection process toward shorter forms. This models the general historic tendency of words to lenite. Pierrehumbert's model also predicts the effects of wordform frequency on reduction. A more frequent wordform will produce more exemplars, each of which is very slightly biased toward reduction. Over time, the exemplar cloud of a very frequent word will tend to consist of somewhat more reduced exemplars.

Such an exemplar-based model can explain the non-segmental nature of the differences we show in the production of *that*. Two lemmas, say the complementizer and relativizer *that*, may begin with a direct mapping to a single wordform. Over time, the lemmas may begin to be differentially mapped to different wordforms. These wordforms may have a clear segmental difference, as shown in Figure 2 and Figure 4, or the two wordforms may be segmentally identical. Either way, these different wordforms would themselves consist of clouds of exemplars. The exemplars for the more frequent wordform would in general be more reduced than the exemplars for the other; some of these reductions might be segmental, but many might simply consist of slightly shorter durations for the individual phones in the word. Such an exemplar-based model might also model our word predictability effects by including some exemplar clouds for two-word or three-word phrases. While this exemplar-based explanation is clearly only a vague and preliminary attempt at a model, it is an exciting possibility which deserves further study.

Such examples suggest that it will always be possible to explain any non-contextual variation with a multiple lexeme model, provided that it is sufficiently elaborated. If so, there would be no need to resort to lemma-based models. The result of our study of lemma variation, therefore, is that there are cases which appear to require more complex representations at the lexeme level than have been commonly assumed. Ultimately, of course, we require independent evidence, from controlled experiments or other sources, for models like that sketched in Figure 4, or for models to account for variation at a finer level of detail than traditional phonological categories.

We are currently working on adding further prosodically-coded data to the accent-coded portion of Switchboard coded by Stefanie Shattuck-Hufnagel and Mari Ostendorf, so as to be able to reanalyze the pronoun and determiner senses of *that* after controlling for accent.

In addition to these conclusions about the process of lexical production, we would like to end with a methodological insight. We hope to have shown that a corpus-based methodology such as ours can augment traditional controlled psycholinguistic experiments to help provide insight into psychological processes like lexical production. Corpus-based methods have the advantage of ecological validity. The difficulty with corpus-based methods, of course, is that every possible confounding factor must be explicitly controlled in the statistical models. This requires time-consuming coding of data and extensive computational manipulations to make the data usable. Creating a very large hand-coded corpus is difficult, as we saw with our inability to completely control for pitch accent for the word *that*. But when such control is possible, a corpus provides natural data whose frequencies and properties may be much closer to the natural task of language production than experimental materials can be. Obviously, it is important not to rely on any single method in studying human language; corpus-based study of lexical production is merely one tool in the psycholinguistic arsenal, but one whose time, we feel, has come.

Acknowledgements

This project was partially supported by the National Science Foundation via NSF IIS-9733067 and IIS-9978025. Many thanks to Michelle Gregory, William D. Raymond, Eric Fosler-Lussier, Joan Bybee, and Janet Pierrehumbert for fruitful discussions. We are also grateful to Stefanie Shattuck-Hufnagel and Mari Ostendorf, who generously took the time and effort to release to us a preliminary version of their prosodically coded portion of Switchboard. Finally, we owe a particular debt of gratitude to Stefanie Shattuck-Hufnagel and to the editors of this volume, all of whom gave extraordinarily helpful comments and spotted many errors and inconsistencies which greatly improved our paper. Of course all remaining errors are our own.

Notes

1 In general we relied on Berkeley transcriptions for our coding, although we did do some data cleanup, including eliminating some observations we judged likely to be in error; see Jurafsky et al. (1998) for details.
2 The two frequent idioms *kind of* and *sort of*, which constituted 12% of the tokens, are not compared here, since they may well be acting as a lexicalized category on their own, rather than playing the part of partitives or genitives. However, the duration of *of* in these idioms is shorter (74 ms) and they have more frequent deletion of the coda (64%).
3 In all of these comparisons, we included the frequent and probably lexicalized *lot of* in the partitive category. These tokens made up 20% of the total sample of partitives. Analyses on the smaller restricted set of partitives excluding *lot of* showed little difference from those reported here.

References

Agresti, A.
    1996   *An Introduction to Categrical Data Analysis.* New York: John Wiley & Sons.

Ahrens, K. V.
    1998   Lexical ambiguity resolution: Languages, tasks, and timing. In Hillert, D. (ed.), *Syntax and Semantics, Vol* **31**: *Sentence Processing: A Crosslinguistic Perspective.* San Diego: Academic Press.

Bell, A., Jurafsky, D., Fosler-Lussier, E., Girand, C. & Gildea, D.
    1999   Forms of English function words – Effects of disfluencies, turn position, age and sex, and predictability. In *Proceedings of the 14th International Congress of Phonetic Sciences*, **99**, 395–398.

Berkenfield, C.
    2000   The role of syntactic constructions and frequency in the realization of English *that*. Master's thesis, University of New Mexico, Albuquerque, NM.

Bush, N.
    1999   The predictive value of transitional probability for word-boundary palatalization in English. Master's thesis, University of New Mexico, Albuquerque, NM.

Bybee, J. L.
    2000   The phonology of the lexicon: evidence from lexical diffusion. In Barlow, M., & Kemmer, S. (eds.), *Usage-based Models of Language*, (pp. 65–85). Stanford: CSLI.

Ferguson, C. A.
    1975   "Short a" in Philadelphia English. In E. Smith, (ed.), *Studies in Linguistics in Honor of George L. Trager*, (pp. 259–274). The Hague: Mouton.

Fidelholz, J.
    1975   Word frequency and vowel reduction in English. In *Papers from the 11th Regional Meeting Chicago Linguistic Society*, **75**, (pp. 200–213). Chicago: University of Chicago.

Fosler-Lussier, E. & Morgan, N.
    1999   Effects of speaking rate and word frequency on conversational pronunciations. *Speech Communication*, **29**, 137–158.

Fox Tree, J. E. & Clark, H. H.
    1997   Pronouncing "the" as "thee" to signal problems in speaking. *Cognition*, **62**, 151–167.

Francis, W. N. & Kučera, H.
    1982   *Frequency Analysis of English Usage.* Boston: Houghton Mifflin.

Godfrey, J., Holliman, E. & McDaniel, J.
    1992   SWITCHBOARD: Telephone speech corpus for research and development. In *Proceedings of the 1992 IEEE International Conference on Acoustics, Speech, and Signal Processing*, **92**, 517–520. IEEE.

Greenberg, S. Ellis, D. & Hollenback, J.
    1996   Insights into spoken language gleaned from phonetic transcription of the Switchboard corpus. *Proceeding of the 1996 International Conference on Spoken Language Processing*, **96**, 24–27.

Hogaboam, T. W. & Perfetti, C. A.
1975 Lexical ambiguity and sentence comprehension. *Journal of Verbal Learning and Verbal Behavior*, **14**, 265–274.
Hooper, J. B.
1976 Word frequency in lexical diffusion and the source of morphophonological change. In Christie, W. (ed.), *Current Progress in Historical Linguistics*, (pp. 96–105). Amsterdam: North Holland.
Jescheniak, J. D. & Levelt, W. J. M.
1994 Word frequency effects in speech production: Retrieval of syntactic information and of phonological form. *Journal of Experimental Psychology: Learning, Memory and Cognition*, **20**, 824–843.
Jespersen, O.
1922 *Language*. New York: Henry Holt.
Jespersen, O.
1933 *Essentials of English Grammar*. New York: Henry Holt.
Jones, D.
1947 *An English Pronouncing Dictionary*. New York: E. P. Dutton.
Jurafsky, D., Bell, A., Fosler-Lussier, E., Girand, C. & Raymond, W. D.
1998 Reduction of English function words in Switchboard. In *Proceedings of the 1998 International Conference on Spoken Language Processing*, **89**, 3111–3114.
Jurafsky, D., Bell, A., Gregory, M. & Raymond, W. D.
2001 Probabilistic relations between words: Evidence from reduction in lexical production. In J. Bybee & P. Hopper (eds.), *Frequency and the emergence of linguistic structure,* (pp. 229–254). Amsterdam: Benjamins.
Labov, W.
1989 The exact description of the speech community: Short a in Philadelphia. In R. Fasold & D. Schiffrin (eds.), *Language Change and Variation*, (pp. 1–57). Washington, D. C: Georgetown University Press.
Levelt, W. J. M., Roelofs, A. & Meyer, A. S.
1999 A theory of lexical access in speech production. *Behavioral and Brain Science*, **22** Vol. **1**, 1–75.
Levelt, W. J. M.
1983 *Speaking: From Intention to Articulation*. Cambridge, MA: MIT Press.
Li, P. & Yip, M. C.
1996 Lexical ambiguity and context effects in spoken word recognition: Evidence from Chinese. In *Proceedings of the 18th Conference of the Cognitive Science Society*, **96**, 228–232.
Manning, C. D. & Schütze, H.
1999 *Foundations of Statistical Natural Language Processing*. Cambridge, MA: MIT Press.
Martinet, A. (Ed.)
1960 *Elements of General Linguistics*. Chicago: University of Chicago Press.

Oldfield, R. C. & Wingfield, A.
  1965   Response latencies in naming objects. *Quarterly Journal of Experimental Psychology*, **17**, 273–281.
Phillips, B. S.
  1984   Word frequency and the actuation of sound change. *Language*, **60** Vol **2**, 320–342.
Pierrehumbert, J. B.
  2001   Exemplar dynamics: Word frequency, lenition and contrast. In J. Bybee & P. Hopper (eds.), *Frequency and the Emergence of Linguistic Structure*, (pp. 137–157). Amsterdam. Benjamins.
Rhodes, R. A.
  1992   Flapping in American English. In W. U. Dressler, M. Prinzhorn & J. Rennison (eds.), *Proceedings of the 7th International Phonology Meeting*, (pp. 217–232). Rosenberg and Sellier, Turin.
Rhodes, R. A.
  1996   English reduced vowels and the nature of natural processes. In B. Hurch & R. A. Rhodes (eds.), *Natural Phonology: The State of the Art*, (pp. 239–259). The Hague: Mouton de Gruyter.
Roach, P.
  1983   *English Phonetics and Phonology*. Cambridge: Cambridge University Press.
Saffran, J. R., Aslin, R. N. & Newport, E. L.
  1996   Statistical cues in language acquisition: Word segmentation by infants. *Proceedings of the 18th Conference of the Cognitive Science Society*, **96**, 376–380.
Schuchardt, H.
  1885   *Über die Lautgesetze: Gegen die Junggrammatiker*. Robert Oppenheim, Berlin. Excerpted with English translation in T. Vennemann and T. H. Wilbur, (eds.), *Schuchardt, the Neogrammarians, and the Transformational Theory of Phonological Change*, Athenaum Verlag, Frankfurt, 1972.
Shriberg, E.
  1999   Phonetic consequences of speech disfluency. *Proceedings of the 14th International Congress of Phonetic Sciences*, **99**, 619–622.
Simpson, G. B.
  1981   Meaning dominance and semantic context in the processing of lexical ambiguity. *Journal of Verbal Learning and Verbal Behavior*, **20**, 120–136.
Simpson, G. B. & Burgess, C.
  1985   Activation and selection processes in the recognition of ambiguous words. *Journal of Experimental Psychology: Human Perception and Performance*, **11**, 28–39.
Zipf, G. K.
  1929   Relative frequency as a determinant of phonetic change. *Harvard Studies in Classical Philology*, **15**, 1–95.

Phonological encoding of single words: In search of the lost syllable

Niels O. Schiller, Albert Costa and Angels Colomé

Abstract

Syllables seem to be very salient units in speech perception and production. Yet, experimental evidence for the role of a syllabic unit in production is scarce. In this paper, we first review the support for the existence of syllabic units in speech production. Especially relevant in this area are results that were obtained with the masked priming paradigm. We show that using this paradigm with comparable methodologies has led to contradictory results in the past. This may have to do with the fact that mostly Germanic languages were tested. Here, we will mention data from English demonstrating that the visibility of the prime (masked or unmasked) and the time between prime and target presentation (i.e., stimulus onset asynchrony or SOA) are not crucial for obtaining the syllable priming effect. However, we will also present data from Spanish, i.e. a Romance language, showing that the failure to replicate the syllable priming effect is not restricted to Dutch and English. Finally, we present two experiments from French, the second of which seems to show a weak syllabic effect. Taken together, these results do not support the view that the syllable plays an independent role in phonological encoding.

1. The origin of the syllable priming hypothesis

The syllable plays an important role in modern approaches to phonology (see Blevins, 1995 for a recent overview). Some phenomena such as syllable-initial aspiration of plosives in English or syllable-final devoicing of obstruents in Dutch or German can easily be described with reference to the syllable as a unit (see Kenstowicz, 1994). However, syllables may be useful not only as phonological but also as psycholinguistic units. In language acquisition, for example, syllables are important units in the process of acquiring the phonological system of a language (Gerken, 1994; Liberman, Shankweiler, Fischer & Carter, 1974; Wijnen, Krikhaar & Den Os,

1994; for an overview see Macken, 1995). Recently, Levelt, Schiller & Levelt (2000) described the process of acquiring syllable structure in Dutch using *Optimality Theory* (OT). It was shown that Dutch children between one and three years of age followed a pattern of syllable structure acquisition that increased in complexity and could be captured by an OT grammar.

Also, for the adult speaker/listener syllables may play an important role. For instance, in a seminal paper, Mehler, Dommergues, Frauenfelder & Segui (1981) observed that when participants were asked to monitor words for certain sequences of sounds, they were faster to do so when the target sequence (e.g., /pal/) corresponded to the first syllable of a carrier word (e.g., *pal.mier*) than when it did not match the first syllable (e.g., *pa.lace*; dots are used to indicate syllable boundaries throughout this paper). CV targets were responded to faster in carrier words that started with a CV syllable (hereafter *CV words*) than in carrier words starting with a CVC syllable (hereafter *CVC words*), and CVC targets yielded faster reaction times (RTs) for CVC words than for CV words, even though the entire CVC phoneme string is present in both types of units. This *syllable match effect* was interpreted as evidence for the existence of the syllable as a prelexical speech segmentation unit.

This effect has been replicated in many other Romance languages but not in Germanic languages (see Cutler, 1997 for a summary). In English, for instance, stress is important for the perception of words (a stress-rhythm language; Cutler & Norris, 1988), while moras play a crucial role for the perception of Japanese (a mora-rhythm language; Otake, Hatano, Cutler & Mehler, 1993). In speech production, evidence for syllabic units is more scarce than in speech perception (see Schiller, 1998 for a review). However, in two recent papers, Ferrand and co-workers claimed to have found syllable priming effects in French (Ferrand, Segui & Grainger, 1996) and English (Ferrand, Segui & Humphreys, 1997) speech production. These authors presented a visually masked letter string before a target word or picture that had to be named (see Figure 1). The letter string was orthographically and/or phonologically related to the target but participants were generally not able to recognize it. Masking the primes has the advantage of minimizing the possibility of task-specific strategic effects. In one condition, the prime corresponded to the first syllable of the target name. In the other condition, it was one segment longer or shorter than the target's first syllable. Ferrand et al. (1996, 1997) found that when the prime matched the first syllable of the target (e.g., *ca* – CA.ROTTE *'carrot'* or *car* – CAR.TABLE *'school bag'*), naming latencies were significantly shorter than when the prime did not match the first syllable (e.g., *ca* – CAR.TABLE or *car* – CA.ROTTE).

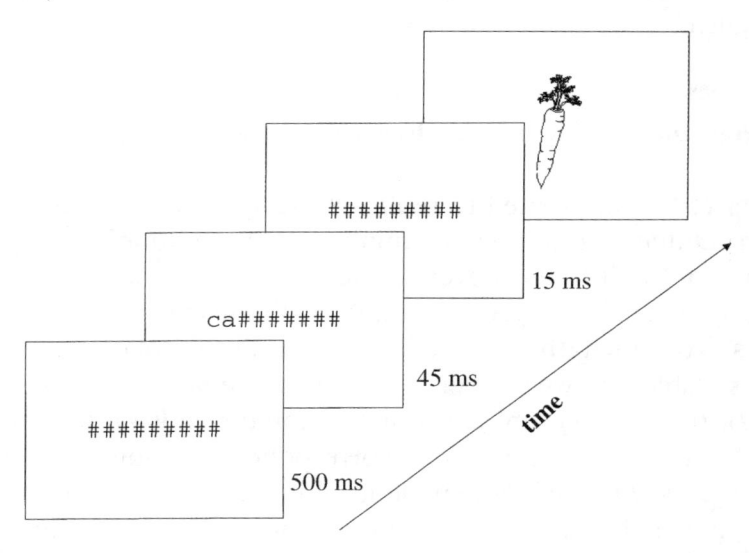

Figure 1: Illustration of one experimental trial in the experiment: Each trial comprises four different screens. First, the forward pattern mask is presented for 500 ms. Then, the prime is in view for a brief period of time, e.g., 45 ms. The prime is immediately followed by the backward pattern mask for 15 ms. Finally, the target is presented.

This *syllable priming effect* was accounted for in terms of the (pre)-activation of syllabically structured phonological output units.[1] "Sublexical orthographic units that are activated upon prime presentation will send activation directly to the syllabic output units thus facilitating the pronunciation of any target stimulus that shares the same syllable units" (Ferrand et al., 1996, p. 714). However, this explanation presents some problems, at least for English. Given the irregular grapheme-to-phoneme correspondence in English, it is not clear how orthographic syllables are able to (pre)activate the appropriate phonological syllables for speech output in English. To give an example, how does the speech production system "know" that the visual prime *de* corresponds to the phonemic sequence /dɪ/ when *de.tect* is the target or to the phonemic sequence /deɪ/ when *de.but* is the target? Both words are bisyllabic and have final stress. The model Ferrand et al. (1996, 1997; see also Ferrand & Grainger, 1994), presented to account for their syllabic effect, does not solve the problem of spelling inconsistency in English.

2. Does the syllable priming hypothesis also hold for Dutch?

Schiller (1998) attempted to replicate the syllable priming effect in Dutch. Dutch is a Germanic language that is phonologically very similar to English. However, Dutch is characterized by a very transparent spelling system. Dutch distinguishes short and long vowels. Vowel length is marked in Dutch in the following way: In open syllables, vowels receive a long pronunciation (e.g., *de.ler* /delər/). In closed syllables, pronunciation depends on the spelling: Double marking of the vowels corresponds to a long pronunciation (e.g., *deel.tje* /deltjə/), single marking means short pronunciation – and slightly more open articulation of the vowel (e.g., *del.ta* /dɛlta/). On the basis of the transparent spelling in Dutch, syllabic priming effects are to be expected: *de* /de/ should prime the CV word *de.ler* /delər/ but not the CVC word *del.ta* /dɛlta/, and for the prime *del* /dɛl/ the reverse should be true. However, this is not what Schiller (1998) obtained. He never found a syllable priming effect across a series of five experiments. Instead, he consistently obtained *segmental overlap effects* – the longer the overlap in segments between prime and target, the shorter the naming latencies. Syllabic overlap did not play a separate role (e.g., the letter string *del* primed both the CV word *de.ler* ('divisor') and the CVC word *del.ta* ('delta') significantly more than the letter string *de*). This effect could not be due to residual visual overlap between the masked letter prime and the target because the effect was not only obtained with words but also with pictures. In Experiment 5 of that study, Schiller (1998) showed that for six-letter words identity priming yielded shorter RTs than having only the first five letters of the word. This in turn was more efficient than having the first four letters of the word, etc. Having only the onset of a word still yielded significant priming effects as compared to a control condition in which no linguistic information about the target word was contained. Schiller (1998) accounted for this effect by the (pre-) activation of phonological segments facilitating their retrieval when the target has to be encoded phonologically for production. He suggested that the visually masked primes first activate orthographic units, but these do not send activation directly to articulatory output units. Instead, they activate sublexical phonological units, which correspond to segments.

There are at least two unpublished dissertations that also looked at masked syllable priming. Evinck (1997) used the same methodology and materials as Ferrand et al. (1996) but could not replicate their syllable priming effect in French. Boelhouwer (1998) aimed at obtaining a syllable priming effect in Dutch, but equally without success. These two additional failures to replicate further demonstrate the weakness of the syllable priming effect.

3. The syllable priming effect is in fact a segmental priming effect – Further evidence from English

To further investigate the segmental priming effect, more experiments were carried out in English. As we mentioned earlier, Ferrand et al. (1997) reported a syllable priming effect for English, although this effect was unambiguously obtained in only one of the five experiments in that study. However, it was never obtained in a series of seven new experiments (Schiller, 1999, 2000). Instead, using the same methodology as in the Ferrand et al. (1997) study, the segmental overlap effect (Schiller, 1998) was replicated in English several times using different materials and tasks (word and picture naming). To account for the priming effect in a language like English where the grapheme-to-phoneme mapping variability is very high, a *multiple activation account* was invoked. Orthographic segments activate a whole set of possible phonological correspondences. The amount of activation may possibly be weighted by the frequency with which a particular grapheme is pronounced as a particular phoneme. The more segments from the target are activated, the larger the priming effect. On this account, the letters 'pi' prime *pilot* (/paɪlət/) and *pillow* (/pɪləʊ/) to the same extent and the letters 'pil' prime the same targets significantly more.

All the studies referred to above used slightly negative stimulus onset asynchronies (SOAs) and subliminal primes to investigate the syllable priming effect, that is, the target picture or word appeared on the screen a small number of milliseconds after the prime was presented on the screen. SOA and visibility of the prime are crucial, at least in masked priming. Therefore, it may be that slight variations of these two factors have large effects on the outcome of the experiment. We tried to investigate these potential effects systematically. First, we investigated the influence of presenting the prime at different moments in time relative to the presentation of the target picture or word. That is, we varied the SOA over a range from negative to positive SOAs. Second, we manipulated the visibility of the prime from masked (subliminal visibility) to unmasked (full visibility). In the following, we describe two experiments that were carried out in English.

In the first experiment, we tested the effect of CV, CVC, and control primes on naming of CV and CVC picture targets (for details about the procedure and design, see Schiller & Costa, submitted). Masked primes were presented at three SOAs relative to picture onset (−200 ms, 0 ms, +200 ms) (see Figure 2). At SOA −200 ms, the prime appears on the screen 200 ms before the target. The reverse condition holds at SOA +200 ms, i.e., first the target appears on the screen, 200 ms later the prime. At SOA 0ms, the prime is presented superimposed on the target, i.e., they are presented simultaneously, but the prime is replaced after some milliseconds by the backward mask. The predictions were clear: the syllable priming hypothesis predicts that CV targets should be named faster when presented with CV primes as compared to CVC or control primes (Ferrand et al., 1997). CVC targets should only

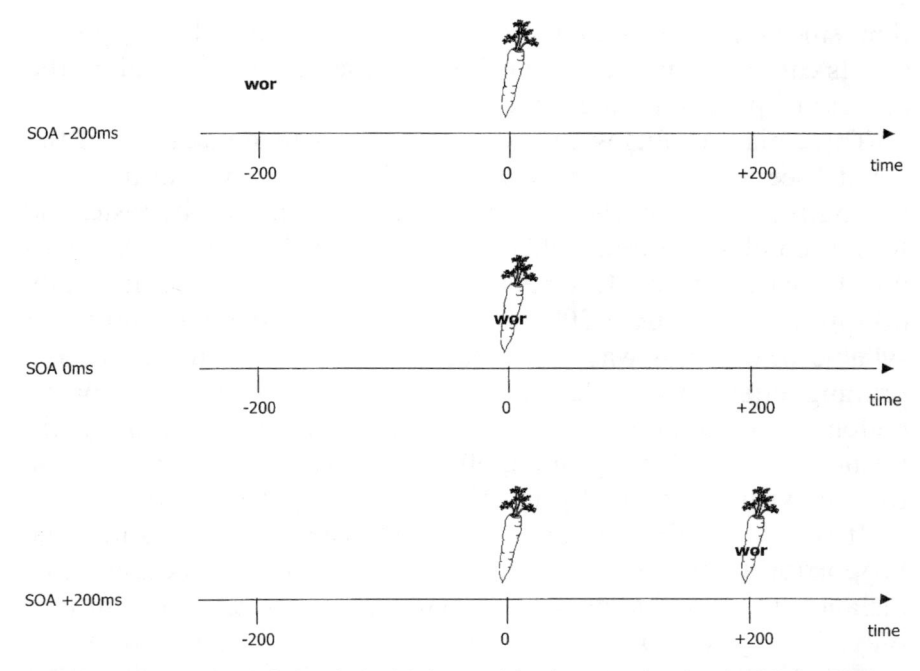

Figure 2: Illustration of the three SOAs used in the experiment: At SOA –200 ms (upper panel), the prime precedes the presentation of the target picture by 200 ms. At SOA 0 ms (middle panel), the prime is presented superimposed on the target. Finally, at SOA +200 ms (lower panel), the prime appears superimposed on the target after the target alone had been in view for 200 ms.

show priming when preceded by CVC primes but not when preceded by CV or neutral primes. The segmental overlap hypothesis (Schiller, 1998, 1999, 2000), however, predicts that CVC primes should be more effective than CV primes independent of the target structure. Both of these predictions are valid at least for short negative SOAs (such as –200 ms) and SOA 0 ms. At later, positive SOAs (such as +200 ms) the prime is no longer presented before the target. According to Levelt's model of phonological encoding (Levelt & Wheeldon, 1994; Levelt, Roelofs & Meyer, 1999), syllables are not stored in the lexicon but are computed at later stages of phonological encoding as the result of a syllabification process. Therefore, this theory might predict a syllable structure effect at SOA +200 ms even though it does not for earlier prime presentation, since one may assume under this theory that syllabic priming effects can only emerge if the prime is presented late enough in the process of producing the target.

Three main results were observed (for a detailed analysis of the results, see Schiller & Costa, submitted). First, there was an effect of length of prime in the RTs: The longer the prime, the faster the RTs. Second, the priming effect was modulated by the SOA. Priming decreased from SOA –200 ms to SOA 0 ms, until it finally disappeared at SOA +200 ms. Third, and most importantly, no syllabic interaction was observed; that is, the magnitude of the priming effect was independent of whether or not the prime matched the structure of the first syllable of the target. Why did we not find a syllabic priming effect? A possible answer could be that the visually masked primes were not fully processed.

It is possible that under constrained visual conditions in some proportion of the trials the primes were not fully processed. For instance, the prime *pi* may be partially processed to an extent that only the segment *p* could produce an effect. If this is true, the expected syllabic effect of the prime *pi* could not arise, since that prime would not be processed as an entire syllable. The same is true for CVC primes such as *pic*. In this case, it may be that the prime was encoded as *pi*, and therefore this prime might be facilitating the retrieval of the syllable *pi* in a CV word, such as *pi.lot*, but not the expected retrieval of the syllable *pic* in CVC words, such as *pic.nic*. If this was the reason for the lack of syllabic effects in that experiment, increasing the probability of full processing of the prime should also increase the probability of obtaining a syllabic effect.

In the second experiment, we made the primes clearly visible instead of masked. For SOAs of −200 ms and 0 ms, the results of the second experiment replicate the observations of the first one. For SOA +200 ms, a reliable priming effect (without segmental overlap effect) was obtained in the second, but not in the first experiment.

The outcome of these two experiments suggests that, first, the lack of syllabic effects cannot be attributed to partial processing of the primes since even with clearly visible primes the syllabic effect was not found. Second, we have shown that a syllabic effect did not arise even when we tried to tap into different stages of phonological encoding by varying the SOA. Third, when primes and target shared some segments, a priming effect was found, the magnitude of which depended exclusively on the length of the prime (at least at SOA −200 ms and SOA 0 ms). These results are in line with the results obtained by Schiller (1998, 1999, 2000) where an increase of the number of shared segments resulted in an increase of the magnitude of the priming effects.

4. Is the syllable priming effect a phenomenon of syllable-timed languages?

An interim summary of the data would state then that in Dutch and English, segments but not syllables can be primed using the masked priming paradigm. However, the question of whether the syllable priming effect in French (Ferrand et al., 1996) remained valid was still open, and also whether or not it holds for other Romance languages. Romance languages are claimed to have a prosodic structure that relies on syllables as primary rhythmic units to a larger extent than Germanic languages such as Dutch or English, which are generally claimed to have a stress-based rhythm (Abercrombie, 1967; Pike, 1946). Therefore, it could be the case that there is a correlation between the primary prosodic unit of a language and the presence of a syllable priming effect as there is in perception (Cutler, 1997).

The precise nature of such a correlation in models of phonological encoding (e.g., Dell, 1986, 1988; Levelt et al., 1999), however, is not clear. Levelt's model, for instance, assumes that the metrical frame is built or retrieved (depending on the language and the status of the word) at the same time that the segments are retrieved. Segments are then serially assigned to the metrical frame on the basis of syllabification rules. This general architecture holds for *all* languages, whether syllable-timed or stress-timed. Thus, there is no principled difference in phonological encoding of syllable-timed languages that would make the syllable priming effect expected in French in this model. It could be that when syllables play a role in the rhythmic organization of a language, they can be primed, whereas syllables cannot be primed if they are not very salient units in a particular language because they do not contribute to the rhythm.

Spanish is another syllable-timed language. Therefore, data from Spanish may be interesting with respect to the syllable priming effect. If the syllable priming effect is a property of syllable-timed languages, the effect should emerge in Spanish. Colomé and Costa carried out two word-naming experiments with masked syllable primes to investigate the syllable priming effect in Spanish. The results of these experiments are reported below.

4.1 Experiment 1: Word Naming in Spanish with 28 ms prime

4.1.1 Method

Participants. Eighteen undergraduate students at Barcelona University took part in the third experiment. All of them came from Spanish monolingual families. They received extra course credit for their participation.

Materials. Two sets of 36 words were employed (see Appendix A). In both sets, half of the stimuli were bisyllabic and half were trisyllabic words. In Set A, words were grouped in pairs that shared the first three segments (e.g., *mono* 'monkey' – *monja* 'nun'). In one of the groups, the first three segments corresponded to the initial syllable (e.g., *mon.ja*). In the other group, they consisted of the first syllable and the onset of the second one (e.g., *mo.no*). In Set B, stimuli could not be paired, but there was the same number of CV and CVC initial syllables both within the bisyllabic and the trisyllabic words. All stimuli were presented in white and centred on a black screen.

Procedure. Participants were tested individually in a soundproof booth, using a very similar procedure to the one employed by Ferrand et al. (1996, 1997). They were invited to fixate the hash marks that would appear at the beginning of each trial and to name the word that would replace them as soon as possible and without making errors. Each trial had the following structure. First, a forward mask consisting of hash marks was displayed for approximately 500 ms. It was immediately followed by the prime in lower case, which remained on the screen for 28 ms. Afterwards, a backward mask appeared for 14 ms. Then, the target word was presented, in capital letters to reduce the visual overlap between prime and target. The prime-target SOA was therefore −42 ms. The target remained in view until the participant responded or for a maximum of 2000 ms. Finally, there was a blank screen for 1000 ms before next trial started. Reaction times (RTs) were measured from target onset. The EXPE program (Pallier, Dupoux & Jeannin, 1997) was used to display the stimuli and record the RTs. Participants were never informed about the existence of the primes. Before the experimental session started, they received a training block where all the targets appeared preceded by the neutral prime.

Design. All words were presented three times, once with each type of prime. Primes could be either the first two (CV) or the first three (CVC) letters of the target. In addition, there was a neutral prime consisting of the characters %&$. All primes were followed by a number of hash marks to equate the length in letters of prime and target word. Three blocks of stimuli with pauses between them were created with the following restrictions: a) no more than four consecutive stimuli of the same set; b) maximally two primes of the same condition in a row. We also checked that the two words in a pair of Set A did not appear consecutively.

4.1.2 Results and Discussion

RTs less than 300 ms or greater than 1600 ms were excluded from the analysis. These trials, together with ones where participants stuttered or produced a non-linguistic sound before the response and where the computer failed to record the response, constituted only 1.3% of the trials, so no error analysis was conducted.

Mean naming latencies are summarized in Table 1. We used these data to run two ANOVAs with three factors: Set (A or B), Prime Type (CV or CVC) and Target Structure (CV or CVC). F values are reported separately for participants (F_1) and items (F_2).

The main effect of Set was significant only by participants ($F_1(1,17) = 6.89$, $p < .05$; $F_2(1,68) = 1.08$, n.s.). None of the interactions of this variable, either with Prime Type ($F_1(1,17) = 3.16$, n.s.; $F_2(1,68) = 2.47$, n.s.) or Target Structure (both Fs < 1), nor the three-way interaction between Set, Prime Type and Target Structure ($F_1(1,17) = 1.17$, n.s.; $F_2 < 1$) reached significance, so we decided to pool both sets in the following comparisons. Neither the main effect of Target Structure nor its interaction with Prime Type were significant (all Fs < 1). Finally, the main effect of Prime Type was only significant by participants ($F_1(1,17) = 9.06$, $p < .01$; $F_2(1,68) = 1.18$, n.s.). Both CV and CVC primes differed significantly from the neutral condition ($t_1(17) = 8.77$, $p < .01$; $t_2(71) = 4.50$, $p < .01$ and $t_1(17) = 8.63$, $p < .01$; $t_2(71) = 5.53$, $p < .01$, respectively).

Table 1: Mean naming latencies for Experiment 1 in ms (with % errors).

Set	Prime Type	Target Structure CV	CVC
A	CV	457 (0.0)	457 (1.6)
	CVC	454 (1.6)	461 (1.2)
	Neutral	464 (1.4)	471 (1.9)
	Δ (CV−CVC)	3	−4
B	CV	464 (0.7)	466 (1.4)
	CVC	459 (0.9)	458 (1.4)
	Neutral	474 (1.4)	474 (1.2)
	Δ (CV−CVC)	5	8

4.2 Experiment 2: Word Naming in Spanish with 42 ms prime

Experiment 1 did not show any sign of a syllable priming effect. Instead, Prime Type showed a tendency towards a segmental overlap effect: CVC primes were on average more efficient than CV primes. However, this effect was only significant by participants but not by items.

One reason why this effect did not reach significance might be that the prime exposure duration was too short. Schiller (1998,

1999, 2000) used slightly longer prime exposure durations than in Experiment 1. Presenting the prime too briefly may render it ineffective. Therefore, we decided to run another experiment in Spanish with a slightly longer prime exposure duration.

4.2.1 Method

Participants. Twenty-four undergraduate students from the same population described in the previous experiment participated in Experiment 2.

Materials, Procedure, and Design. Everything remained the same as in Experiment 1 except for the exposure time of the prime, which was extended to 42 ms (i.e., one screen refresh cycle more than in the previous experiment). Thus, the SOA between prime and target was −56 ms in Experiment 2.

4.2.2 Results and Discussion

Naming latencies shorter than 300 ms and longer than 1600 ms were excluded. Altogether, only 1.7% of the total data were considered errors, so we did not run an error analysis. As for the RTs, Table 2 shows the mean naming latencies for each of the conditions. An ANOVA was conducted again with three main factors: Set (A or B), Prime Type (CV or CVC) and Target Structure (CV or CVC).

The main effect of Set was significant only by participants – but not by items – ($F_1(1,23) = 6.75$, $p < .05$; $F_2(1,68) = 2.17$, n.s.) and neither the interactions with Target Structure (both Fs < 1) or Prime Type ($F_1(1,23) = 2.80$, n.s.; $F_2(1,68) < 1$) nor the three-way interaction between Set, Target Structure and Prime Type reached significance (both Fs < 1), so we decided to run a joint analysis of the material from both Sets.

The difference between the two Target Structures was significant only by participants ($F_1(1,23) = 6.53$, $p < .05$; $F_2(1,68) < 1$). The interaction of Target Structure and Prime Type was not significant (both Fs < 1), so, again, there was no syllable priming effect.

The main effect of Prime Type, however, was significant ($F_1(1,23) = 11.82$, $p < .01$; $F_2(1,68) = 5.11$, $p < .05$), indicating that the longer the prime was, the easier it was to name the target, irrespective of syllabic structure. That is, a segmental priming effect was obtained. Furthermore, we conducted two planned comparisons to check whether both CV and CVC primes differed significantly from the neutral condition; t values were significant by participants and items ($t_1(17) = 7.81$, $p < .01$; $t_2(71) = 7.55$, $p < .01$ and $t_1(17) = 8.99$, $p < .01$; $t_2(71) = 9.23$, $p < .01$, respectively).

Table 2: Mean naming latencies for Experiment 2 in ms (with % errors).

Set	Prime Type	Target Structure CV	CVC
A	CV	490 (1.2)	495 (2.8)
	CVC	488 (2.1)	492 (2.1)
	Neutral	509 (1.6)	511 (2.3)
	Δ (CV−CVC)	2	3
B	CV	499 (0.9)	505 (1.6)
	CVC	493 (1.6)	494 (1.2)
	Neutral	518 (1.4)	511 (1.9)
	Δ (CV−CVC)	6	11

The outcome of this experiment did not show any sign of a syllable priming effect. Instead, segmental priming effects were obtained. The Spanish results from two experiments speak clearly against the syllable priming hypothesis. That is, although Spanish is generally considered to rely on syllables as rhythmic units, no syllabic priming effects were obtained. Instead, the overall pattern across both experiments more closely resembles the segmental priming effect: The longer the prime, the shorter the RTs. However, it could be the case that Spanish is not the best example of a syllable-timed language. Sebastián-Gallés, Dupoux, Segui & Mehler (1992), for instance, could replicate the perceptual syllable monitoring effect from French (Mehler et al., 1981) with Spanish materials only when participants performed an additional memory task, whereas

Bradley, Sánchez-Casas & García-Albea (1993) replicated the original French perceptual result for Spanish without this additional procedure. This may be taken as an indication that Spanish is not as syllable-timed as French. Note that we understand the phonological distinction of syllable vs. stress-timed as a continuum rather than a categorical classification.

Furthermore, the Spanish experiments have one drawback, namely that only word naming but no picture naming experiments were reported. Generally speaking, qualitative differences have never been found between word and picture naming in masked priming (Ferrand et al., 1996; Schiller, 1998, 1999, 2000). Only quantitative differences have been obtained, namely that form priming effects in picture naming are usually larger than in word naming, as seen in the current experiments. Nevertheless, it may be the case that the word-naming task is carried out without accessing the lexicon, e.g., via non-lexical grapheme-to-phoneme conversion (GPC) rules. Such a strategy is especially likely in an orthographically transparent language like Spanish. The failure to replicate the syllable priming effect in Spanish may be a consequence of such a strategy, if syllabic units are only involved in phonological encoding when access to the word form lexicon is involved, but not when targets are produced purely on the basis of GPC rules. Therefore, two picture naming experiments were carried out; however, not in Spanish but in French. French is a prototypical syllable-timed language. If the syllable priming effect holds for what are considered to be syllable-timed languages, we should observe it in French. Furthermore, since we employed a picture-naming task, the target cannot be produced on the basis of GPC rules. If the syllable priming effect is contingent on accessing the lexicon, we should observe it. The results of the French experiments are reported below.

4.3 Experiment 3: Picture naming in French with 34 ms prime

French is the prototype of a syllable-timed language. Bonin, Peereman and Schiller carried out a series of picture naming experiments in French using visually masked primes that either matched or mismatched the first syllable of the target's name. The methodology of these experiments closely followed the original Ferrand et al. (1996) experiments.

4.3.1 Method

Participants. Twenty-six students of the University Blaise Pascal from Clermont-Ferrand (France) participated in the third experiment. All were native speakers of French and had normal or corrected-to-normal vision. Participants received course credits for taking part in the experiment.

Materials. The materials consisted of 48 bi- and trisyllabic French words corresponding to pictorial objects (see Appendix B). All items were grouped into pairs beginning with the same three segments but differing in syllable structure (CV or CVC). The items were matched for number of letters, number of syllables, and frequency of occurrence. The objects were presented as simple line drawings. Materials partially overlapped with the materials used by Ferrand et al. (1996). However, Ferrand et al. (1996) used only ten pairs.

Procedure. The procedure was similar to the one described for the previous experiments. The presentation of the trials was controlled by PsyScope. Pictures were used as targets. Prime exposure duration was 34 ms (i.e., two screen refresh cycles of the monitor used in the Clermont-Ferrand laboratory).

Design. The design was similar to the one described in Experiment 1 except that no control prime condition was included.

4.3.2 Results and Discussion

The results are summarized in Table 3. There were no significant effects in the errors. RT analysis revealed that the main effect of Prime Type (CV or CVC) was only marginally significant by participants ($F_1(1,25) = 3.74$, $p < .06$) and not significant by items ($F_2(1,46) = 1.99$, n.s.). The main effect of Target Structure (CV or

CVC) was not significant (both Fs < 1), and the interaction of Prime Type and Target Structure was not significant either. That is, there was no syllable priming effect.

Table 3: Mean naming latencies for Experiment 3 in ms (with % errors).

	Target Structure	
Prime Type	CV	CVC
CV	864 (8.2)	852 (8.7)
CVC	871 (7.7)	875 (6.6)
Δ (CV−CVC)	−7	−23

The results of this experiment are somewhat inconclusive, since neither syllabic effects nor segmental overlap effects were observed. However, RTs are considerably longer (> 860 ms) than in the original Ferrand et al. (1996) study (approximately 730 ms). This may simply be a consequence of the fact that different and more pictures were used in this study than in the Ferrand et al. (1996) study. However, participants might have generated an internal deadline and not responded before that deadline, which would result in a ceiling effect and rather long RTs. As a result, any differences between the priming conditions may have been lost. Furthermore, we should consider the possibility that the primes were not effective using such a short prime exposure duration. In the first Spanish experiment (see above) as well as in the studies by Evinck (1997) and Boelhouwer (1998) very brief prime exposure durations (28 ms) were used also, but no effects were found. Therefore, a second experiment was carried out using a slightly longer prime exposure duration. Furthermore, it was stressed in the instructions that speed was important for the responses.

4.4 Experiment 4: Picture naming in French with 51 ms primes

4.4.1 Method

Participants. Twenty-eight students from the same pool as described in the previous experiment took part in Experiment 4.

Materials, Procedure, and Design. The same procedure, materials and design were used as in the previous experiment except that the prime exposure duration was extended to 51 ms and participants were asked to respond as fast as they could.

4.4.2 Results and Discussion

The results of Experiment 4 are summarized in Table 4. The error analysis did not reveal any significant results. In the RT analysis, neither the main effects of Target Structure nor of Prime Type were significant (all Fs < 1). However, it can be seen from Table 4 that CV primes were more effective for CV targets than for CVC targets and that for CVC primes the situation was reversed. This looks like a syllable priming effect, although the interaction between Prime Type and Target Structure is only significant by items ($F_1(1,27) = 3.64$, p = .067; $F_2(1,46) = 4.25$, p = .044). One reason why the syllable priming effect is weaker here than in the original study by Ferrand et al. (1996) may be the difference in magnitude of the effects: There is a big difference between the effects obtained here (9 and 16 ms) and in the Ferrand et al. (1996) study (35 and 49 ms). This is surprising if one considers that the prime exposure duration was longer here (51 ms) than in the Ferrand et al. (1996) study (29 ms). When we used a similar prime exposure duration (34 ms; Experiment 3), we obtained inconclusive results (see above). However, Experiment 4 showed that under certain circumstances it may be possible to obtain a syllabic effect in French speech production using masked priming.

Table 4: Mean naming latencies for Experiment 4 in ms (with % errors).

	Target Structure	
Prime Type	CV	CVC
CV	737 (6.1)	745 (4.9)
CVC	746 (5.5)	729 (6.1)
Δ (CV−CVC)	−9	16

General Discussion

The present results have several theoretical implications. Our data suggest that one cannot use the syllable priming effects obtained with this paradigm to support the idea that syllabic units are encoded during phonological encoding. Recall that the syllable priming effect observed by Ferrand et al. (1996, 1997) was the most compelling evidence for the existence of syllabic units in phonological encoding. The English results referred to in this study support the segmental overlap effect, the Spanish results (Experiments 1 and 2) also support the segmental overlap effect, and the French results (Experiments 3 and 4) provide some weak evidence for the syllable priming hypothesis. None of the four experiments reported in this paper resulted in a clear syllable priming effect, but one of them resulted in a clear, i.e. statistically significant, segmental overlap effect. Shall we then reject the assumption that syllables are represented during speech production? There are at least four reasons to believe that such a conclusion would be premature.

First, there are some results (Costa & Sebastián-Gallés, 1998; Ferrand & Segui, 1998; Sevald, Dell & Cole, 1995) suggesting that syllables are at play during phonological encoding as abstract structures into which the phonological segments are inserted during a process of segment-to-frame association (see Levelt & Wheeldon, 1994; but see also Roelofs & Meyer, 1998).

Second, it is possible that the (masked) priming paradigm is not a good paradigm to investigate syllabic priming effects in phonological encoding. Ferrand et al. (1996, 1997) are the only authors who have obtained a syllable priming effect so far, and even an exact replication of the latter study failed (Schiller, 2000). It is unclear, though, what the problem with this paradigm is. One may argue that the effects observed with this paradigm have nothing to do with phonological encoding. However, the paradigm is sensitive to phonological primes in general, as demonstrated by the fact that the length of the primes affected the magnitude of the priming. Therefore, we have to conclude that if a syllable priming effect exists at all, it is extremely unstable.

Third, although linguistic and psycholinguistic descriptions do not necessarily completely overlap, linguistic theory is clearly simplified by postulating syllabic units (e.g. Kenstowicz, 1994, p. 250). There are linguistic processes that make reference to the syllable, such as syllable final devoicing (e.g. in Dutch or German) and syllable initial aspiration of plosives (e.g. in English), and these processes imply that syllabic units exist.

Fourth, it is possible that the relevant phonological units involved in speech production depend on language-specific properties of the language being spoken. This cross-linguistic hypothesis finds some support in the results presented in this paper. The fact that the syllabic effect arises only for a clear so-called syllable-timed language (i.e. French) may suggest that the syllable is a relevant representational unit in some languages but not in others.

However, it may also be argued that syllables are not used as phonological planning units in phonological encoding, but are rather just a consequence of the open-close articulatory modulation associated with the production of vowels (opening movements) and consonants (closing movements) (MacNeilage, 1998). Therefore, syllables may just be an epiphenomenal consequence of the necessity of generating a maximally pronounceable and perceivable stream of sounds, i.e., an alternation of vowels and consonants, as suggested by Ohala (1998).

Further research is needed to determine under which conditions syllables play a role during phonological encoding. The evidence collected with the masked priming paradigm in favor of the syllable as a functional unit in phonological encoding of English should be carefully reconsidered. However, we provided some evidence that under appropriate masking conditions the syllable may play a role in French speech production.

Acknowledgements

The work reported in this paper was supported by a fellowship of the Royal Dutch Academy of Arts and Sciences to Niels O. Schiller, a grant NS22201 from NIH and a Fullbright Fellowship from the Spanish government to Albert Costa, and a PhD fellowship (FI/FIAP97) from the Comissionat per a Universitats i Recerca de la Generalitat de Catalunya to Angels Colomé, and by Spanish MEC research grant PB97−977 and Catalan Government research grant GR00083. Furthermore, the authors wish to thank Patrick Bonin, Ronald Peereman, and

Nuria Sebastián-Gallés for helpful discussion of the data, and an anonymous reviewer for comments on the manuscript, Pam Miller for proofreading the paper, and Anouk Cuijpers for help with editing the manuscript.

Notes

1 An input account was excluded on the basis of lexical decision experiments that did not show any facilitation (i.e., a syllable priming effect) under the same priming conditions.

References

Abercrombie, D.
    1967   *Elements of General Phonetics.* Edinburgh: Edinburgh University Press.

Blevins, J.
    1995   The syllable in phonological theory. In J. A. Goldsmith (ed.), *The Handbook of Phonological Theory*, (pp. 206–244). Cambridge, MA: Blackwell.

Boelhouwer, B.
    1998   *From letter strings to phonemes: The role of orthographic context in phonological recoding.* PhD dissertation, Nijmegen University.

Bradley, D. C., Sánchez-Casas, R. M. & García-Albea, J. E.
    1993   The status of the syllable in the perception of Spanish and English. *Language and Cognitive Processes*, **8**, 197–233.

Costa, A. & Sebastián-Gallés, N.
    1998   Abstract phonological structure in language production: Evidence from Spanish. *Journal of Experimental Psychology: Learning, Memory, and Cognition.* **24**, 886–903.

Cutler, A.
    1997   The syllable's role in the segmentation of stress languages. *Language and Cognitive Processes.* **12**, 839–845.

Cutler, A. & Norris, D. G.
    1988   The role of strong syllables in segmentation for lexical access. *Journal of Experimental Psychology: Human Perception and Performance*, **14**, 113–121.

Dell, G. S.
    1986   A spreading-activation theory of retrieval in sentence production. *Psychological Review*, **93**, 283–321.

Dell, G. S.
1988 The retrieval of phonological forms in production: Tests of predictions from a connectionist model. *Journal of Memory and Language*, **27**, 124–142.

Evinck, S.
1997 *Production de la parole en français: Investigation des unités impliquées dans l'encodage phonologique des mots* [Speech production in French: Investigation of the units implied during the phonological encoding of words]. PhD dissertation, Bruxelles University.

Ferrand, L. & Grainger, J.
1994 Effects of orthography are independent of phonology in masked form priming. *The Quarterly Journal of Experimental Psychology*, **47A**, 431–441.

Ferrand, L. & Segui, J.
1998 The syllable's role in speech production: Are syllables chunks, schemas, or both? *Psychonomic Bulletin & Review*, **5**, 253–258.

Ferrand, L. Segui, J. & Grainger, J.
1996 Masked priming of word and picture naming: The role of syllabic units. *Journal of Memory and Language*, **35**, 708–723.

Ferrand, L., Segui, J. & Humphreys, G. W.
1997 The syllable's role in word naming. *Memory & Cognition*, **35**, 458–470.

Gerken, L. A.
1994 Young children's representations of prosodic phonology: Evidence from English-speakers' weak syllable productions. *Journal of Memory and Language*, **33**, 19–38.

Kenstowicz, M.
1994 *Phonology in generative grammar*. Cambridge, MA: Blackwell.

Levelt, W. J. M. Roelofs, A. & Meyer, A. S.
1999 A theory of lexical access in speech production. *Behavioral and Brain Sciences*, **22**, 1–75.

Levelt, C. C., Schiller, N. O. & Levelt, W. J. M.
2000 The acquisition of syllable types. *Language Acquisition*, **8**, 237–264.

Levelt, W. J. M. & Wheeldon, L.
1994 Do speakers have access to a mental syllabary? *Cognition*, **50**, 239–269.

Liberman, I. Y., Shankweiler, D., Fischer, F. W. & Carter, B.
1974 Explicit syllable and phoneme segmentation in the young child. *Journal of Experimental Child Psychology*, **18**, 201–212.

Macken, M. A.
1995 Phonological acquisition. In J. A. Goldsmith (ed.), *The Handbook of Phonological Theory*, (pp. 671–696). Cambridge, MA: Blackwell.

MacNeilage, P. F.
1998 The frame/content theory of evolution of speech production. *Behavioral and Brain Sciences*, **21**, 499–546.

Mehler, J., Dommergues, J. Y., Frauenfelder, U. & Segui, J.
   1981   The syllable's role in speech segmentation. *Journal of Verbal Learning and Verbal Behavior*, **20**, 298–305.

Ohala, J. J.
   1998   Content first, frame later. *Brain and Behavioral Sciences*, **21**, 525–526.

Otake, T., Hatano, G., Cutler, A. & Mehler, J.
   1993   Mora or syllable? Speech segmentation in Japanese. *Journal of Memory and Language*, **32**, 358–378.

Pallier, C., Dupoux, E. & Jeannin, X.
   1997   EXPE: An expandable programming language for on-line psychological experiments. *Behavior Research Methods, Instruments, & Computers*, **29**, 322–327.

Pike, K. L.
   1946   *The Intonation of American English.* Ann Arbor: University of Michigan Press.

Roelofs, A. & Meyer, A. S.
   1998   Metrical structure in planning the production of spoken words. *Journal of Experimental Psychology: Learning, Memory, and Cognition*, **24**, 922–939.

Schiller, N. O.
   1998   The effect of visually masked syllable primes on the naming latencies of words and pictures. *Journal of Memory and Language*, **39**, 484–507.

Schiller, N. O.
   1999   Masked syllable priming of English nouns. *Brain and Language*, **68**, 300–305.

Schiller, N. O.
   2000   Single word production in English: The role of subsyllabic units during phonological encoding. *Journal of Experimental Psychology: Learning, Memory, and Cognition*, **26**, 512–528.

Schiller, N. O. & Costa, A.
   submitted   The role of the syllable in phonological encoding: Evidence from masked priming. *Journal of Memory and Language*.

Sebastián-Gallés, N., Dupoux, E., Segui, J. & Mehler, J.
   1992   Contrasting syllabic effects in Catalan and Spanish. *Journal of Memory and Language*, **31**, 18–32.

Sevald, C. A., Dell, G. S. & Cole, J. S.
   1995   Syllable structure in speech production: Are syllables chunks or schemas? *Journal of Memory and Language*, **34**, 807–820.

Wijnen, F., Krikhaar, E. & Den Os, E.
   1994   The (non)realization of unstressed elements in children's utterances: Evidence for a rhythmic constraint. *Journal of Child Language*, **21**, 59–83.

Appendix A (Spanish materials)

SET A:

Target Structure

CV	CVC
1. bo.lo (skittle)	bol.sa (bag)
2. ca.sa (house)	cas.co (helmet)
3. pi.no (pine tree)	pin.za (clothes peg)
4. ma.no (hand)	man.cha (stain)
5. ba.la (buttlet)	bal.sa (raft)
6. co.no (cone)	con.cha (shell)
7. pa.la (spade)	pal.co (box)
8. ro.sa (rose)	ros.ca (thread)
9. mo.no (monkey)	mon.ja (nun)
10. sa.le.ro (salt cellar)	sal.chi.cha (sausage)
11. ca.la.mar (squid)	cal.ce.tín (sock)
12. pa.no.cha (corncob)	pan.te.ra (panther)
13. mo.ne.da (coin)	mon.ta.ña (mountain)
14. ba.na.na (banana)	ban.de.ra (flag)
15. ca.me.llo (camel)	cam.pa.na (bell)
16. pa.lo.ma (pigeon)	pal.me.ra (palm)
17. ve.ne.no (poison)	ven.ta.na (window)
18. ma.no.pla (mitten)	man.za.na (apple)

SET B:

Target Structure

CV	CVC
1. ca.ma (bed)	fal.da (skirt)
2. va.so (glass)	dis.co (record)
3. ve.la (candle)	mos.ca (fly)
4. co.la (queue)	tan.que (tank)
5. me.sa (table)	bom.ba (bomb)
6. ra.mo (bouquet)	ban.co (bench)
7. pe.sa (weight)	rom.bo (rhombus)
8. ra.na (frog)	ces.ta (basket)
9. cu.na (cradle)	cal.vo (bald)
10. co.ne.jo (rabbit)	pas.ti.lla (pill)
11. gu.sa.no (worm)	lám.pa.ra (lamp)
12. pe.lo.ta (ball)	cas.ti.llo (castle)

13. co.me.ta (kite)
14. te.ne.dor (fork)
15. ca.mi.sa (shirt)
16. ma.le.ta (suitcase)
17. cá.ma.ra (camera)
18. pe.lu.ca (wig)

pes.ta.ña (eyelash)
pis.ci.na (swimming pool)
can.gu.ro (kangaroo)
ban.de.ja (tray)
pis.to.la (pistol)
ves.ti.do (dress)

Appendix B (French materials)

(Targets are listed in French orthography except where phonemic transcription is necessary to show syllable structure.)

SET A:

Target Structure

CV
so.leil (sun)
ca.rotte (carrot)
se.rinque (syringe)
ce.rise (cherry)
fi.let (net)
ga.rage (garage)
ma.ri.o.nette (puppet)
pa.lace (palace)
ca.ca.huette (peanut)
ca.puche (capuchin)
vo.lant (steering wheel)
ca.ra.bine (carbine)
ca.ra.vanne (caravan)
ca.sier (canterbury)
ma.rin (sailor)
ba.leine (whale)
pi.scine (swimming pool) /pi.sin/
bi.son (bison)
ca.rafe (carafe)
ma.ra.cas (maracas)
ca.ril.lon (carillon)
ha.ri.cot (bean)
ba.ril (keg)
ca.lu.met (calumet)

CVC
sol.dat (soldier)
car.touche (cartridge)
ser.pent (snake)
cer.veau (brain)
fil.tre (filter)
gar.çon (boy)
mar.gue.rite (daisy)
pal.mier (palm tree)
cac.tus (cac.tus)
cap.sule (seal)
vol.can (volcano)
car.table (satchel)
car.net (note book)
cas.tor (beaver)
mar.mite (pot)
bal.con (balcony)
pis.to.let (pistol)
bis.cuit (cracker) /bis.kwi/
car.pette (rug)
mar.cas.sin (young wild boar)
car.quois (quiver)
har.pon (harpoon)
bar.be.le (barbed wire)
cal.mar (squid)

Temporal distribution of interrogativity markers in Dutch: A perceptual study

Vincent J. van Heuven and Judith Haan

Abstract

A set of 128 different intonation patterns were synthesized on a single Dutch sentence with (potential) pitch accents on the subject (sentence-initial position) and on the object (sentence-medial position). The sizes of the accents were 0, 4, 8 and 12 semitones (st) in all 16 logical combinations. The accents were superposed on four different baseline slopes (-3, -1.5, 0 and $+1.5$ st/s), and utterances could or could not end in a terminal rise H% (0,8 st). The 128 versions were presented to two groups of 20 native Dutch listeners. One group heard the 128 complete utterances and identified each version as either a statement or a question. The second group performed a gating task: they first heard (16) different versions that were truncated after the subject accent (gate 1), then (the same 16) with the truncation point delayed to the onset of the object accent (gate 2), next the (64) different versions with the truncation point at the end of the object accent (gate 3), and finally the (64) versions with the truncation point at the onset of the (potential) terminal rise (gate 4). On hearing each gated stimulus listeners guessed whether they had heard the beginning of a statement or of a question. The results of both experiments were analysed in order to reveal the temporal development of cues that signal statement versus declarative question in Dutch. Sentence type is clearly signalled well before the terminal rise is heard. In terms of the experimental variables, the overall f_0 trend (slope of baseline) is the most important early cue, followed by the size of the object accent. All early cues were overruled by the information in the terminal boundary. However, the percept of statement vs. question suffered significantly when early cues were contradictory to the absence versus presence of a terminal rise. The results bear on the issue whether the signalling of sentence type can still be modelled by a sequential, linear tone model or whether some global tone shape feature needs to be involved.

1. Introduction

The smooth exchange of information requires the exploitation of several distinct sentence types or speech acts. Among the most important of these are the expression of statement (presenting facts or beliefs) and the asking of questions (prompting the listener to take a turn and supply some information that is explicitly targeted by the speaker). The signalling of statement versus question seems universal (Sadock & Zwicky, 1985: 195). In the large majority of the world's languages, the contrast is expressed by lexico-syntactic devices, as well as by intonational means. The statement type is generally considered the unmarked choice, requiring no special sign. Question is the marked sentence type, signalled lexically by a question word (a wh-word or question particle) or by dedicated syntactic means such as inversion of subject and finite verb. Whilst the lexico-syntactic question devices may vary considerably across languages, the apparent universal lies in the prosodic interrogativity marking: is has been claimed that questions are universally differentiated from statements by a higher beginning, a higher end and, more generally, by a higher overall pitch level throughout the utterance (Hermann, 1942; Lindsey, 1985). That is, apart from the canonical final rises, questions have been shown to display (some combination of) higher onset, raised register, raised peaks, and less downward or even upward overall trend. Obviously, such early cues have the advantage of drawing a listener's attention to the interrogative character of the utterance before it is finished, facilitating the subsequent response.

Although 'some high-pitched element' would appear to be a (near) universal characteristic of question intonation, languages may differ considerably in their choice of phonological tone configurations and phonetic implementation of the interrogative sentence type (Gussenhoven & Chen, 2000). Haan, van Heuven, Pacilly & van Bezooijen (1997) presented systematic analyses of the Dutch sentence melodies of statements and of three types of questions derived from these statements, i.e., wh-questions, yes/no-questions, and declarative questions (the latter differing from the corresponding statement in intonation only). The results revealed clearly different intonation profiles for each of these four sentence types. Moreover, although the three question types typically ended in a H% high boundary tone (the spoken equivalent of the question mark), all the sentence types were differentiated from the statement version at some earlier point in the time course of the utterance. Figure 1 shows averaged stylised pitch patterns for the statement and declarative question versions of the utterance *marina wil haar mandoline verkopen(?)* 'Marina wants her mandolin sell(?)', i.e. 'Marina wants to sell her mandolin(?)', spoken twice by five males and five females in three different positions in a short paragraph.[1]

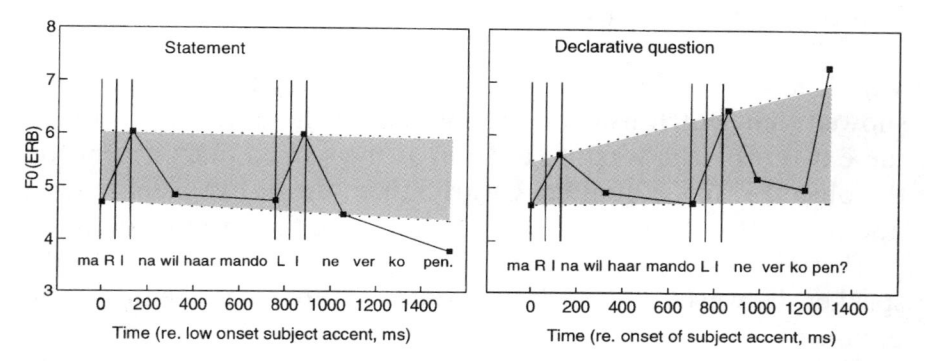

Figure 1: Stylised pitch contours (F_0 in ERB) for statements and declarative questions averaged over five male and five female speakers. Each data point nominally represents 100 measurements. Vertical lines represent the onset and nucleus segments of accented syllables. Low declination lines were drawn connecting the low onset pivot point to the last relevant low pivot. Note that the L% target extends clearly below the low declination line. The high declination lines connect the accent peaks on subject and object.

A number of differences are visible between the statement and question versions:

- The question ends with a high boundary tone H%; the statement with the low boundary tone L%.
- The two accents in the statement are of roughly equal size; the accents are unequal in the question version:
  - The first pitch accent (i.e. on the subject) is smaller in the question than in the statement.
  - The second (final) pitch accent (i.e. on the object) is larger in the question than in the statement.
- The statement shows downtrend in the (imaginary) line connecting the low-pitched turning points in the contour, whilst a slight uptrend is shown in the question version.[2] This effect was noted earlier in a comparison of statements and echo questions in Danish (Thorsen, 1980).

— The accent peak on the object is reached slightly (ca. 40 ms) later (relative to either syllable or vowel onset) in the question version than in the statement. A rightward shift of the final accent peak in questions was reported for other languages as well, e.g. by Gósy & Terken (1994) for Hungarian, and by Makarova (1999) for Russian.[3]

Van Heuven & Haan (2000), using a gating task (see below), showed that Dutch listeners reliably detect the difference between these two prosodic versions as soon as the second pitch accent (on the object) is made audible. Clearly, then, the native listener need not await the end of the sentence (containing the terminal question marker H%) in order to know the sentence type intended by the speaker. However, it is unclear at this juncture what cue or combination of cues enables the listener to achieve this. Is it the large size of the object accent, or is it the difference between the small-sized subject accent and the large object accent? Or is the relevant cue not in the scaling of the accents but in the slope of the pitch trend in the low pivot points (i.e. presence versus absence of downtrend in the baseline)? Or are there still other cues in the signal that we did not measure?

This type of problem cannot be solved by analysing natural speech, since the various cues always co-occur. We need a way to disentangle them, and vary each cue orthogonally to the others. The only way to achieve this is to set up a listening experiment in which the necessary variations in pitch pattern are artificially generated. Fortunately, we have at our disposal signal processing techniques (such as PSOLA, cf. Moulines & Verhelst, 1995) that allow us to create intonation patterns of our own choosing, and superpose these onto a pre-recorded human utterance, generally with little audible loss of sound quality or naturalness.

We created an orthogonal multidimensional stimulus space by introducing controlled variations along four dimensions (for details cf. § 2.1):

1. Size of subject accent: varying from absent to extremely large.
2. Size of object accent: same range of variation as that of subject.

3. Slope of the baseline connecting low turning points of accents, from gentle downtrend to slight uptrend.
4. Presence versus absence of terminal rise H%.

Naturally, we expect the largest, even overriding, effect of H%: if the terminal rise is present, the overall percept will be that of a question, but the result may be less than convincing if the earlier prosody of the sentence does not set up the expectation of an interrogative, e.g. through clear downtrend or pitch accents of equal size. Specifically, we have reason to believe that the perception of interrogativity interacts with the way pitch accents are realised. Statements typically have pitch accents on two constituents, i.e. on the topic and on the comment. However, when a speaker asks a question, there would appear to be a tendency to avoid accenting both topic and comment, presumably because there is a stronger need to mark the comment more clearly as new, and mark the topic as having continued relevance, not requiring a further attention marker. Consequently, when listeners hear (or expect to hear) a relatively high, single accent peak, they will be biased into assuming that the speaker intends a question.

Alternatively, our listeners' responses may be relatively independent of the specifics of the pitch contour and rather be governed by the overall shape of the sentence melody. Assuming, for instance, that listeners in most languages, including Dutch, will perceive interrogativity whenever the utterance has a concentration of high pitch towards the end of the utterance, similar results will be found for any combination of higher and later accent peaks, and a high terminal boundary tone. Under this view, the large object accent in the question version in figure 1 would be primarily motivated by the speaker's wish to elevate the average pitch towards the end of the utterance, rather than by considerations of focus.

We ran two experiments. In the first experiment the subjects heard only parts of sentences, which were truncated at one of several carefully chosen points in time. This so-called gating technique has enjoyed increasing popularity in experimental research aiming to trace the ability of listeners to set up expectations of upcoming events, and to determine the nature of the acoustic properties in early portions of the speech utterance that enables the listener to generate such projections (Grosjean, 1983). In our case, we applied this technique to see how well listeners differentiate between statement and declarative question at each of these points in the temporal development of the intonation pattern.

In the second experiment, the full set of variations was offered once more, to a fresh group of listeners, in order to determine the effects of the above four types of pitch variation when the utterance is not presented repeatedly in chunks of increasing length, but uninterruptedly as in normal speech situations.

2. Method

2.1 Stimulus material

The material for both experiments was constructed from a single question utterance *maRIna wil haar mandoLIne verkopen?* [ma'rina ʋɪl har mɑndo'linə vərkoːpə] (cf. p. 1), spoken by a female speaker of Standard Dutch with H*L pitch accents (indicated by small caps in the orthographic representation above) on the subject and object of the sentence, and with a high boundary tone (H%). The recording was transferred from DAT to computer memory and downsampled to 16 kHz (16 bits amplitude resolution). Pitch extraction was performed by the autocorrelation method implemented in the Praat (Boersma & Weenink, 1996) speech processing package. The pitch curve was interactively stylised with 9 pivot points interconnected with straight lines in a log-frequency (semitone) by linear time representation (see also figure 1), such that no audible difference existed between the original and the stylised pitch curves. By manipulating only the frequency values but leaving the time coordinates unaltered, 128 different pitch patterns were then generated according to the following schema:

1. *Size of subject accent.* The excursion size on the stressed syllable of the subject *maRIna* was varied in 4 steps: 0, 4, 8 and 12 semitones (st) above the baseline.

2. *Size of object accent*. The excursion on the object (*mandoLIne*) was also varied in four steps (same four steps as subject accent).
3. *Trend*. The slope of the baseline connecting the minima in the stylised pitch contour was varied in four steps: -3, -1.5, 0 and $+1.5$ semitones per second (st/s). Here, the sentence-initial pitch pivot point was kept constant (as did our speakers), yielding a natural sounding range of overall trend varying from rather steeply dropping, through level pitch, to slightly rising.
4. *Boundary tone*. An H% boundary rise of 8 st was either present or absent.

The set of stimuli is schematically represented in figure 2.

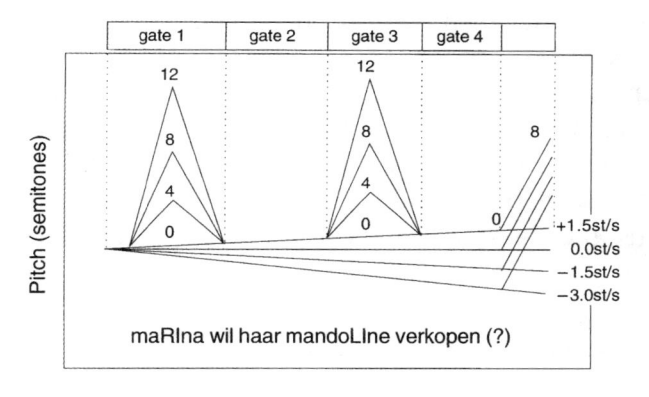

Figure 2: Schematic representation of stimulus materials used in experiments 1 and 2. The 4 × 4 combinations of rise-fall accents were superposed on each of the 4 baselines.

For experiment 1, the stimuli were organised into sets of 16 to 64 variations, depending on the truncation condition (or 'gate').

Gate 1. The truncation point was set at the end of the subject accent. This yielded 16 different stimuli: 4 subject accent sizes × 4 baseline slopes. These 16 stimuli were generated in random order, preceded by 4 practice items, yielding a set of 20 trials.

Gate 2. The truncation point was moved to the onset of the rise belonging to the second accent; the same 16 combinations of subject accent and baseline slope were used, in a different random order. This yielded the second set of 20 trials (including 4 practice trials).

Gate 3. The truncation point was set at the offset of the object accent; variation of subject accent, object accent and baseline yielded 64 combinations, in random order. The third set was preceded by 1 practice trial.

Gate 4. The truncation point was shifted to the onset of the terminal rise; this yielded the same 64 combinations (in a different random order) as in gate 3 (plus 1 practice trial) but followed by a longer stretch of baseline.

The total of 170 stimuli (including practice trials) were played back in blocks of 10 trials, with 3-second intervals between trials (offset to onset) and a 5-second interval plus a beep between blocks. In the order of presentation shorter gates always preceded longer gates.

For experiment 2, the entire set of 128 complete utterances (4 subject accents × 4 object accents × 4 baseline slopes × 2 boundary tones) were played back in random order, preceded by two practice items, in blocks of 10 trials, with 5-second intervals between trials and 7-second intervals + beep between blocks.

2.2 Subjects and procedure

Two groups of 20 native Dutch listeners participated in the experiment. Both groups comprised volunteers, students and researchers at the Department of Linguistics and Phonetics at Leiden University. Group 1 listened to the 170 truncated (gated) stimuli played to them through high-quality loudspeakers (Quad ESL-63) in a quiet, medium-sized seminar room. Subjects were instructed (in writing) to indicate for each trial on their answer sheets whether they thought they heard the beginning of a statement or of a (declarative) question, with binary forced choice. Experiment 1 lasted about 30 minutes.

The subjects in experiment 2 (group 2) performed a dual task. On hearing each stimulus they were to indicate on their answer sheets (i) whether they judged the stimulus to be a statement or a question, with binary forced choice, and (ii) how clearly they thought the stimulus represented a prototypical exemplar of a statement or question, depending on their response to (i).[4] Experiment 2 lasted about 20 minutes.

3. Results

3.1 Experiment 1: gated sentence fragments

Overall effect of gate length. We will first present the results for experiment 1 (gating). In order to obtain an overview of the most important results of this experiment, figure 3 shows percent question responses (and by implication percent statement responses, i.e., the complement to 100 percent) as a function of gate (truncation points 1 through 4) broken down further by slope of the baseline (but accumulated across all sizes of subject and object accents).

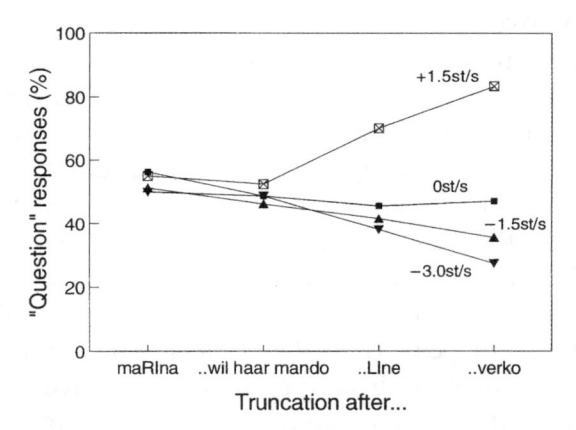

Figure 3: Percent 'question' responses as a function of truncation point, broken down by baseline slope.

During the first two gates the listeners do not differentiate statement from question; responses are random during these early gates. However, some differentiation is observed at the third truncation point, where the object accent is first made audible. Here the rising baseline clearly triggers more question responses than the level and falling baseline conditions. The same pattern of results, but more clearly differentiated, is obtained at gate 4, when the stimulus is truncated just before the onset of the final rise.

The data were submitted to a repeated measures analysis of variance (RM-ANOVA) with slope of baseline and gate number as fixed, within-subject factors. All p-values reported are Huynh-Feldt corrected. The effects of gate, $F(3,57) = 1.4$ (ins.), and of slope, $F(3,57) = 17.7$ ($p < .001$) are not relevant to the present issue. Importantly, however, the interaction between slope and gate reaches significance, $F(9,171) = 7.9$ ($p < .001$), which indicates that the differentiation between statement and question increases for longer gates. Specifically, there is no effect of slope during gates 1, $F(3,57) < 1$, and 2, $F(3,57) < 1$, but significant effects of slope of increasing magnitude are found for gates 3, $F(3,57) = 27.9$ ($p < .001$) and 4, $F(3,57) = 38.7$ ($p < .001$).

These data show that the slope of the baseline used to generate our stimuli provides an important perceptual cue for the sentence type (statement versus question) before the end of the sentence is reached. Moreover, since the data were pooled across excursion sizes of subject and object accent, the cue provided by the baseline would appear to be independent of other interrogativity cues. These observations should not be interpreted as meaning that listeners project the sentence type on the perceptual cue afforded by the baseline as such. It may be the case, for instance, that listeners only attend to the relative pitch difference between the accent peaks in the stimuli. A more detailed analysis of the results may then reveal that more 'question' responses are given if the object has a higher accent peak than the subject. This condition will be met more often in stimulus types with a positive slope for the baseline. Let us therefore examine the results in more detail, for increasing gate lengths and for different sizes of subject and object accents.

Effects at gate 1. Figure 4 presents percent question responses at gate 1 (when just the portion of the sentence is heard up to and including the subject accent), broken down by size of the accent and by baseline slope. The results reveal no effect of baseline slope at this early point in the utterance, as is to be expected given the absence of any overall effect of baseline slope before truncation point 3 is reached. Moreover, there is no systematic effect of the excursion size of the subject accent either, with just one exception. Only when the subject accent is extremely large (12 st, which is twice the normal size of a Dutch pitch accent, cf. 't Hart, Collier & Cohen, 1990) do we find a clear propensity on the part of our listeners to project an interrogative utterance. The overall effect of subject accent, $F(3,57) = 8.5$ ($p < .001$) is significant but only because the 12-st accent differs significantly from the other excursion sizes, which do not differ from each other (Bonferroni posthoc tests, $p < .05$). This finding is compatible with our suggestion that a single (and therefore contrastive) accent may bias the listener into believing that the utterance will develop into a question. Alternatively, the large accent elevated the mean pitch of the stretch of speech heard up to the truncation point. Since questions are (universally) cued by high pitch somewhere in the utterance, the unusually high mean pitch in the audible onset portion of the utterance may be responsible for the strength of the interrogative projection.

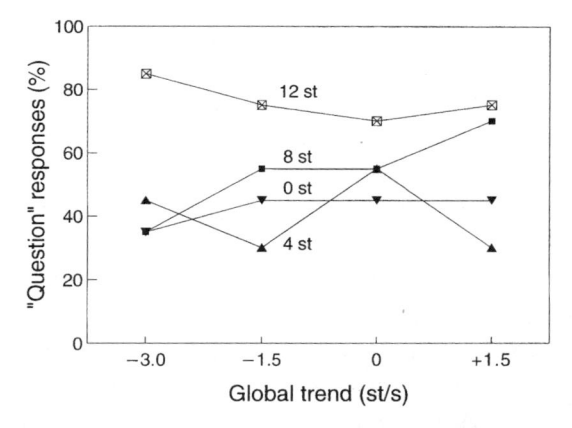

Figure 4: Percent question responses as a function of size of subject accent and global pitch trend, at truncation point 1.

Effects at gate 2. Figure 5 is organised in the same way as figure 4 but now the truncation point is delayed to the onset of the object accent. At gate 2 no information is given to the listener about the size (or even the existence) of the object accent.

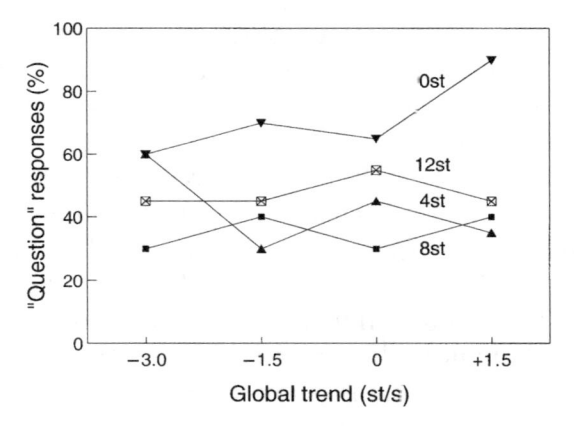

Figure 5: As figure 4, at truncation point 2.

Again, there is no systematic overall effect of baseline slope (which will not be manifest until gate 3, see figure 3). This time, however, the stimuli with a 0-st (i.e. no) accent on the subject are most strongly associated with interrogativity (supporting the expectation derived from the acoustic profile of the declarative question type in figure 1. The effect of subject accent is significant, $F(3,57) = 3.5$ (p = .024), but only because the 0-st accent differs from the other three conditions, which do not differ from each other. Note that baseline slope has a considerable effect (60% question responses for downtrend to 90% questions for uptrend, with intermediate scores for flatter slopes) if there is no accent on the subject. No effect of baseline slope is seen when there is an accent on the subject (whether small or large). It seems, therefore, that the information in the baseline can be picked up by the listener at a relatively early point in time, but only if its course is uninterrupted by (accent-lending) pitch obtrusions. This observation ties in with the result of Gussenhoven, Repp, Rietveld, Rump & Terken (1997) that only the declination portion before the (first) accent but not the post-accentual stretch of baseline provides the reference for the perceptual scaling of accentual prominence.

The stimuli with larger than 0-st subject accents are never associated with questions; at best, the 12-st subject accents are indifferent between statement and question, and the smaller subject accents are associated with statement; there is no effect of baseline slope in these stimuli. It is unclear to us why the addition of just a stretch of baseline after the subject accent caused the 12-st accents – which were strongly associated with interrogativity in gate 1 – to drop to indifferent between question and statement. This effect is commensurate neither with the contrastive accent hypothesis nor with the alternative elevated mean pitch explanation entertained above.

The next two figures present the effects of baseline slope and size of object accent on percent question responses, with the data accumulated across subject accents. Figure 6 presents the data at truncation point 3 (object accent audible); figure 7 shows the data at gate 4, including both the object accent and the stretch of baseline up to the point in time where the final rise would begin.

Effects at gate 3. Figure 6 shows that the size of the object accent has a powerful effect on the projection of interrogativity, $F(3,57) = 17.1$ (p < .001) by an RM-ANOVA with slope of baseline and size of object accent as fixed, within-subject factors. The interrogativity percept is strongest for the 12-st object accent, and gets progressively weaker (in fact crossing over to statement for the smaller object accents of 8 and 4 st). Bonferroni posthoc tests for contrast show that all accent sizes differ from each other, except 4 versus 8 st. This effect is in line with the expectation that

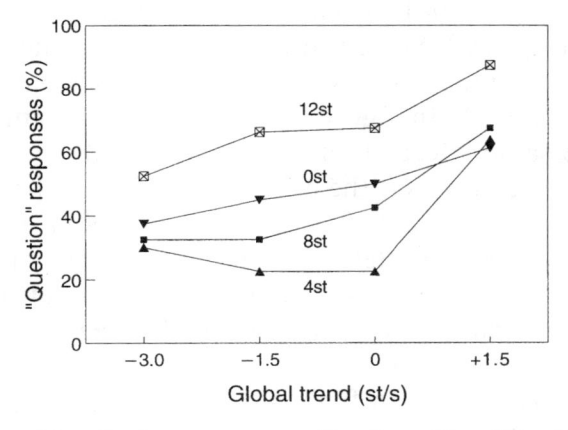

Figure 6: Percent 'question' responses as a function of baseline slope and size of object accent, at truncation point 3.

74 Vincent J. van Heuven and Judith Haan

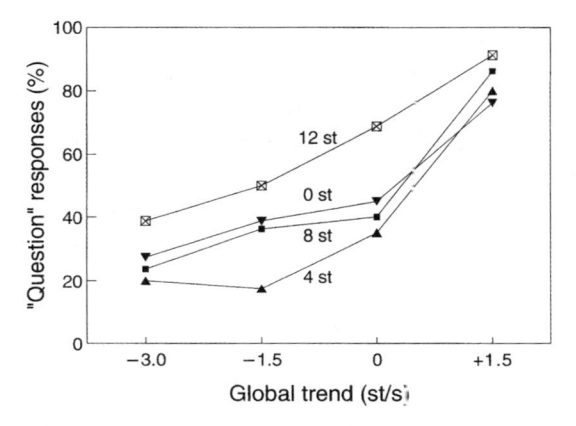

Figure 7: As figure 6, at truncation point 4.

would be derived from the acoustic profile of the declarative question type in figure 1, where the object accent was clearly larger than the subject accent. However, when there is no accent on the object at all (0 st), interrogativity perception is in between that found with 12 and 8 st. Possibly, when there is no accent on the object (0 st), any accent on the subject, but especially the larger types, may be interpreted as contrastive, and be associated with interrogativity. Possibly then, hearing a single accent, whether on the object or on the subject, biases the listener towards the question interpretation. Finally, there is an effect due to baseline slope, $F(3,57) = 27.9$ (p < .001), which is to be expected given the earlier discussion of figure 3. Specifically, the rising baseline slope differs from the other three slopes, which do not differ from each other.

Effects at gate 4. In figure 7, at truncation point 4, we find basically the same effect of size of object accent, $F(3,57) = 12.9$ (p < .001); here, however, the effect of baseline slope has become stronger than at gate 3, $F(57) = 38.7$ (p < .001). In fact, some 80% questions are projected regardless of size of object accent if the general pitch trend is upwards. All differences between baseline slopes are significant, except the contrast between flat (0 st/s) and slightly falling (-1.5 st/s).

Subject versus object. In figures 8 and 9 the effect of excursion size of the object accent is pitted against that of the subject accent. The results were very similar for truncation points 3 and 4, so that

Interrogativity markers in Dutch 75

we have accumulated the data across these two gates. However, given that baseline slope has a strong effect as of gate 3 (see figure 3), we present the results separately for global uptrend (figure 8) and for the flat and falling trends combined (figure 9).

When the baseline slope is upwards (figure 8), question perception is always above 60%, showing, once more, the strength of the baseline parameter. Generally, we observe no systematic overall effect of size of subject accent, $F(3,57) = 2.1$ (ins.). The size of the

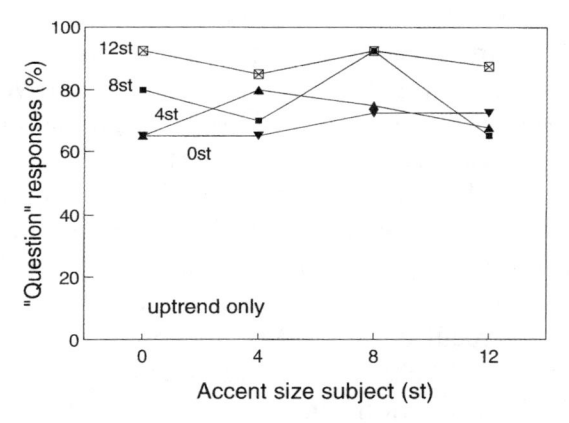

Figure 8: Percent 'question' responses broken down by size of object accent (across) and of subject accent (separate lines), at truncation points 3 and 4 combined. The baseline slope is upwards.

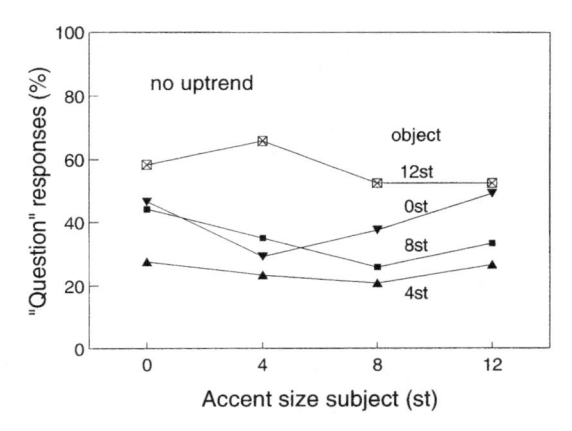

Figure 9: As figure 8, but baseline slope is either flat or falling.

object accent, however, matters, $F(3,37) = 5.7$ (p = .002): when there is no object accent, between 65 and 75% question responses are obtained, depending on the subject accent (slightly more question responses for 8 and 12-st subject accents); when the object accent is 12 st, about 90% question responses are obtained irrespective of subject size, and values of around 80% are found with object accents of 4 and 8 st, without any systematic interaction with subject accent size. Statistically, only the 12-st object accents differ significantly from the other three sizes, which do not differ among each other. Of course, larger object accents − on average − boost both mean and maximum pitch towards the final portion of the utterance, which would be in line the alternative account of the preponderance of question responses for larger object accents in terms of the overall shape hypothesis (p. 4).

When the global pitch trend is either flat or falling (figure 9), percent question responses is generally below 50 (i.e., statement rather than question). Only when the object accent is large (12 st) do we obtain more than 50% question projections, more strongly so if the subject accent is small (4 st) or absent (0 st). For smaller object accents the likelihood of statement responses increases steadily, with the exception, again, of 0-st object accents. When there is no accent on the object, a large subject accent tends to increase the chances of a question response (50% maximally, and excluding the accent-less utterances). Once more, this finding suggests that a single-accent sentence is conducive to projecting interrogativity. The effect of object accent size is significant, $F(3,57) = 18.1$ (p < .001); all accent sizes differ from each other, except the 0 vs. 4-st pair. Finally, and predictably from the results we presented above, there is no overall effect of subject accent, $F(3,57) = 2.0$ (ins.).

3.2 Experiment 2: complete utterances

Let us now turn to the results of experiment 2, where a fresh group of listeners decided whether they heard a question or a statement when the entire utterance was presented. Crucially, half of the complete utterances contained a terminal pitch rise, the prototypical interrogativity marker. We want to know whether hearing the final pitch rise, or its absence, obliterates all earlier projections of the sentence type as entertained by the listener during the earlier time-course of the utterance, or whether the final evaluation weighs the earlier cues along with the terminal boundary cue. The relevant results are presented in figure 10, where percent question responses is plotted as a function of global pitch trend, broken down by utterances ending in the terminal rise H% and those that do not.

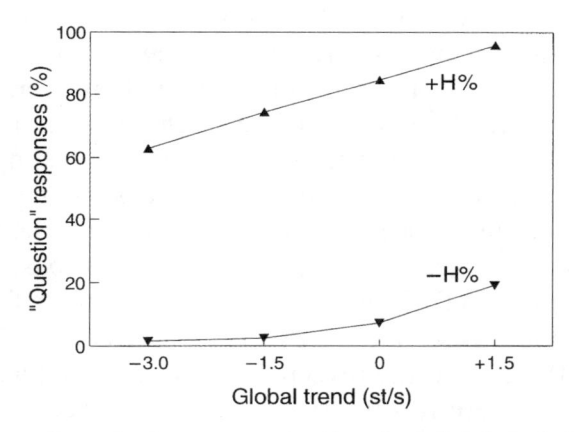

Figure 10: Percent 'question' responses as a function of global pitch trend, broken down by presence versus absence of H% (complete sentences).

The terminal pitch rise exerts an almost categorical effect. If H% is present, there is always a majority of question responses; whenever H% is absent, the perceived sentence type is statement, $F(1,19) = 235.3$ (p < .001). However, there is a quite noticeable effect of the slope of the baseline, $F(3,57) = 28.4$ (p < .001). First, utterances without a terminal rise are less unanimously perceived as statements when the baseline is flat or upwards. Second, and more importantly, stimuli bounded by H% obtain (near) perfect question scores only if the baseline slope is upwards. Each time the baseline slope is decreased by a quantum of 1.5 st/s, the number of perceived questions drops by approximately 10%, leaving a mere 60% question responses for +H% utterances with the steepest downslope of baseline (-3 st/s).

Finally, we will briefly discuss some effects and interactions of the excursion size of subject and object accents. For sentences without the terminal rise, we do not obtain any effects of either subject or object accent when the baseline is flat or falling: all the stimuli are perceived as clear statements here. However, when the baseline slope is upwards, the size of the object accent matters: there are some 40% question responses when the object accent is large (12 st), but percentages drop for 8-st (20%) and 4-st (5%) object accents. Here, of course, baseline slope and size of the object accent conspire to elevate the (mean) pitch towards the end of the sentence, even if there is no high boundary tone, so that these observations do not necessarily support the idea that contrastive accent is associated with question responses. However, when there is no object accent (0 st), a (therefore single) accent on the subject generates roughly 25% question responses, suggesting that contrastive accentuation weakens the statement percept.

For complete utterances ending in a terminal rise, we find no further effects of subject and object accents if the baseline slope is upward (ceiling effect). When the baseline is flat or falling, there is plenty of room for secondary effects of subject and object accent size. As was the case in the presentation of the sentence fragments in experiment 1, here too the size of the object accent has an important effect: the smaller the object accent, the less convincing the question percept. Again, the size of the subject accent has no overall effect, but does matter when the object is unaccented.

4. Conclusions

Summing up the effects observed in the gating experiment, we draw the following conclusions at the observational level:

- Statements are differentiated from questions before the end of the sentence; differentiation is found by the time the accent on the object is heard.
- The slope of the baseline used to construct our stimuli is one important parameter that distinguishes statement (falling slope) from question (rising slope).

- Utterances that have, or are expected to have, a single (large) accent are more readily interpreted as questions than utterances with two (smaller) accents.
- A (large) accent on the object is more compatible with interrogativity than a (large) accent on the subject.

Clearly, these effects allow Dutch listeners to generate expectations as to the speech act (making a statement, or asking a question) on-line as the utterance develops in time. Normally, the on-line expectations are confirmed by the presence or absence of the sentence-final rise. In our experiment 2, however, the stimulus manipulations were such that the presence or absence of the terminal rise could clash with the listener's expectation based on the earlier prosody of the utterance. In the case of such a clash, the effect of H% is strongly attenuated, impairing the communication of interrogativity to the listener.

These conclusions suggest that the marking of interrogativity in text-to-speech systems (reading machines) can be considerably improved by implementing the various cues that we discovered in our research. Not only will the final product sound more convincing, but also, and possibly more importantly, the listener is given the means to project the speech act as it develops in time.

5. General discussion

Our experiment employed a set of 128 intonationally different versions of one meaningful Dutch sentence. The set was created through systematic variation of four parameters, i.e., size of subject accent, size of object accent, slope of baseline, and presence vs. absence of H%. It is important to point out that we claim no theoretical status for these parameters; they were adopted as convenient descriptive devices to allow us to compactly characterize the perceptually relevant aspects of our speakers' statement and question utterances, and to construct a four-dimensional stimulus space that adequately sampled the range of variation found in the natural utterances. In particular, we do not claim that the slope of the baseline is an entity that is voluntarily manipulated by the human speaker in order to signal the contrast between statement and (declarative) question.

In the preceding sections we have developed two possible mechanisms that the speaker may use to signal the contrast between statement and (declarative) question, which we will refer to as the compositional approach versus the integral approach. The integral approach involves a general strategy on the part of the speaker, not just in Dutch, but probably in the majority of the world's languages, to encode questions by generating a sentence melody with a globally rising shape. From this point of view it would make sense if the speaker were to reduce the peaks of accents in the early portions of the utterance, whilst increasing the peaks of the final accents. The globally rising shape of the melody would be brought out even more clearly by superposing the small subject accent and large object accent on a rising baseline. The global rising shape would then culminate in the terminal high boundary tone. This effectively describes the overall intonational shape of the declarative question. The overall shape of statements, by contrast, would lack all these ingredients. This view, however, would require that the speaker employs a dedicated mechanism for encoding sentence types, that generates planned overall rising versus falling melodic patterns for questions and statements, respectively.

We contrast this view with what might be called a minimalist view on the encoding of sentence type that involves no special, dedicated global shapes. In this compositional view, the global rising shape of question melody would fall out as a by-product of two independently motivated tonal devices: (i) ending the question in a high boundary tone, and (ii) contrastive accentuation of the comment in question sentences, such that size of the object accent is increased while the size of other accents in the sentence is decreased. We will briefly discuss these two devices.

High boundary tone. In the first place, it is clear that our listeners overwhelmingly relied on the presence of a final rise on the last syllable. Speakers, also, use this rise as their foremost intonational device. Investigation of our corpus of 600 Dutch questions (cf. p. 1) showed that this rise occurred in more than 95% of the yes-no questions and declarative questions; even in wh-questions the percentage was as high as 63%, despite frequent claims that this question type typically lacks final rises. As the final rise has traditionally been regarded as the hallmark of question intonation, this finding does not come as a surprise.

A potentially more interesting question is whether in actual speech production there is a (causal) relationship between the presence of a final rise and the slope of the baseline of the utterance. In the earlier production study, when wh-questions featured final rises, baseline slopes tended to be shallower than in wh-questions ending in low pitch. Consequently, it seems plausible that the final rise, as planned by the speaker, has the effect of gradually raising the pitch minima in earlier parts of the question. As the results of experiment 2 showed, a (gently) rising baseline is an important additional (and early) perceptual cue to the interrogative character of the utterance. Still, we would argue that the upward slope of the baseline that we found in our production study, falls out as a by-product of an attempt on the part of the speaker to economize on articulatory effort: given that questions typically involve a large final accent followed by a high boundary tone, the speaker elevates his pitch minima towards the end of the utterance. So, in our view, what the speaker aims for is not an upward slope of baseline, but ease of articulation in the production of high pitch targets towards the end of the utterance.

Contrastive focus. Second, interrogativity was also found to be signalled by a relatively salient accent, in particular on the object. This confirmed our earlier impression (inspired by the inequality of consecutive accent peaks in the production data) that questioning involves contrastivity. Increasing the (relative) salience of an accent peak is an intonational device for encoding contrastive focus (e.g. Eady, Cooper, Klouda, Müller & Lotts, 1986; Bartels & Kingston, 1994; Rump & Collier, 1996). This increased salience conveys that the reason for bringing the item in focus is to establish it as the correct item from an (implicit) set of alternatives (cf. Chafe, 1976).

Our suggestion that the raising of accent peaks in questions likewise reflects contrastivity is built on assumptions that would seem uncontroversial. First, utterances are to be divided into the universal pragmatic constituents topic (representing what the utterance is 'about') and comment (representing what is being said with respect to that topic). Asking a question implies that the questioner has reasons to suppose that, with respect to a particular topic, some comment can be made. Accordingly, a provisional comment is profferred by the speaker with a view to checking its correctness. Second, pragmatic constituents to which a speaker chooses to call a listener's attention, are brought in intonational focus. However, speakers may have different reasons for highlighting a constituent, viz. (i) to (re)introduce it to the current discourse (i.e., the topic is focused), (ii) to add new information (i.e., the comment is focused), and (iii) to indicate that it is the correct item from some subset (i.e., the comment is contrastively focused). That is, given the various discoursal functions of focus different focus types have to be distinguished.

In our view, questions typically differ from statements in the distribution of focus type. Considering that the comment constituents in questions do not seek to add new information but merely check correctness, questions allow only the contrastive focus type (iii), whose prosodic correlate is a raised accent peak. Thus, in yes-no/declarative questions the speaker checks whether his comment is the correct member of an implicit set of other potentially appropriate comments respecting this particular topic. In wh-questions the comment corresponds to the wh-phrase, which explicitly indicates a limited range of possibilities only one of which is correct (for more details, see Haan, 2002). Independent evidence for this approach is afforded by clefting questions; in cleft structures, the highlighted element is claimed to have the full implication of contrastive focus (e.g. Quirk, Greenbaum, Leech & Svartvik, 1987). For example, an adequate paraphrase of the declarative question *Marina wil haar mandoline verkopen?* would be: 'Is it selling her mandolin that Marina wants to do?', reflecting contrastive focus on the comment.

The experiment described in this paper was not constructed to allow us to choose between the integral versus the compositional view on question intonation. Nevertheless, there is some circumstantial evidence in the data that would support the compositional view. It was shown repeatedly that a single large (8 or 12 st) accent on the subject (i.e., not followed by an accent on the object) yields fewer statement judgments than smaller subject accents or subject accents followed by larger than 0-st object accents. Note that such contrastive subject accents – which occur early in the utterance – cause the global melodic shape to be falling, which should yield more statement judgments. Apparently, then, any contrastive (i.e., single) accent – whether on the subject or on the object – seems to be (weakly) associated with interrogativity.

Finally, we should realise that the integral and the compositional accounts of the observations are not mutually exclusive. It may be argued that the integral mechanism reflects a (near) universal tendency based, for instance, on the iconic use of high pitch whereby high and rising pitch (characteristic of young and/or small creatures) is used to express subservience and dependence (as required when asking a question) and low pitch (characteristic of strong and large creatures) corresponds with dominance (Ohala, 1984).

Acknowledgements

This research was funded in part by the Netherlands Organisation for Scientific Research (NWO) under grant 200–50–073 (principal investigators: Renée van Bezooijen and Vincent van Heuven). The experiments were run by Rembrandt Hissink, Myrthe Lems and Els Nachtegaal as part of a research seminar in Experimental Phonetics at Universiteit Leiden supervised by the authors. We thank Bob Ladd for discussion and improvements.

Notes

1 The means underlying the f_0 pivot points in Figure 1 were based on a selection of the production data such that data points that could not be realistically modelled in terms of a rise-fall accent configuration were excluded. For instance, missing data were entered for the third and fourth pivot points when the two rise-fall accents were linked into a flat hat contour, and for the sixth and seventh pivot points when the object accent was directly linked to H% without an intervening fall. Missing values were then replaced by the mean f_0 and relative timing values for the speaker concerned.

2   The baselines in Figure 1 were drawn conservatively. The alternative would have been to draw linear regression lines through the six (in statements) or seven (in questions) non-terminal pivot points. The regression line for statements would have the same (downward) slope as in figure 1, but it would be considerably more steeply rising in the case of the declarative questions.
3   Moreover, Gussenhoven & Chen (2000) have shown that the rightward peak shift, even when it is not accompanied by a larger excursion size, provides a cue to the perception of interrogativity for native listeners of Dutch, Chinese and Hungarian, when judging stimuli in an unfamiliar language. However, the effect of peak shift was clearly smaller than that of excursion size (or peak height); even a 120-ms peak shift could not create a convincing cross-over from statement to question (43% question responses for 0-ms, monotonically increasing to 57% question responses for 120-ms peak shifts).
4   The correlation between percent perceived questions and quality of question prosody proved almost perfect. Therefore, we will only present results in terms of percent perceived questions.

References

Bartels, C. & Kingston, J.
    1994   Salient Pitch Cues in the Perception of Contrastive Focus. In P. Bosch and J. van der Sandt (eds.), *Focus and Natural Language Processing*, IBM Working Papers of the Institute for Logic and Linguistics, 1–10.

Boersma, P. & Weenink, D.
    1996   Praat: a System for Doing Phonetics by Computer. *Report of the Institute of Phonetic Sciences, University of Amsterdam*, **132**.

Chafe, W.
    1976   Givenness, Contrastiveness, Definiteness, Subjects and Topics. In: C. Li (ed.), *Subject and Topic*. New York: Academic Press, 25–56.

Eady, S. J., Cooper, W. E., Klouda, G. V., Müller, P. R. & Lotts, D. W.
    1986   Acoustical Characteristics of Sentential Focus: Narrow vs. Broad and Single vs. Dual Focus Environments. *Language and Speech*, **29**, 233–251.

Gósy, M. & Terken, J.
    1994   Question Marking in Hungarian: Timing and Height of Pitch Peaks. *Journal of Phonetics*, **22**, 269–281.

Grosjean, F.
    1983   How Long is the Sentence? Prediction and Prosody in the On-line Processing of Language. *Linguistics*, **21**, 501–509.

Gussenhoven, C. & Chen, A.
2000   Universal and Language-specific Effects in the Perception of Question Intonation. *Proceedings of the Sixth International Conference on Spoken Language Processing*, Beijing, **2**, 91–94
Gussenhoven, C., Repp, B. H., Rietveld, A., Rump, H. H. & Terken, J.
1997   The Perceptual Prominence of Fundamental Frequency Peaks. *Journal of the Acoustical Society of America*, **102**, 3009–3022.
Haan, J.
2002   *Speaking of Questions. An Exploration of Dutch Question Intonation.* LOT Dissertation Series, Nr **52**, Netherlands Graduate School of Linguistics, Utrecht.
Haan, J., van Heuven, V. J., Pacilly, J. J. A. & van Bezooijen, R.
1997   On the Anatomy of Dutch Question Intonation. In H. de Hoop and J. Coerts (eds.), *Linguistics in the Netherlands 1997*. John Benjamins, Amsterdam, 99–110.
Hart, J. 't, Collier,R. & Cohen, A.
1990   *A Perceptual Study of Intonation.* Cambridge: Cambridge University Press.
Hermann, E.
1942   *Probleme der Frage*. Nachrichten Akademie von Wissenschaft. Göttingen.
Heuven, V. J. van & Haan, J.
2000   Phonetic Correlates of Statement versus Question Intonation in Dutch. In A. Botinis (ed.), *Intonation: Analysis, Modelling and Technology* (pp 199–143). Amsterdam: Kluwer.
Lindsey, G. A.
1985   Intonation and Interrogation: Tonal Structure and the Expression of a Pragmatic Function in English and Other Languages. PhD dissertation, University of California, Los Angeles.
Makarova, V.
1999   Pitch Peak Alignment in Russian Declaratives, Interrogatives and Exclamations. *Proceedings of the 16th International Congress of Phonetics Sciences*, San Francisco, 1173–1176.
Moulines, E. & Verhelst, W.
1995   Time-domain and Frequency-domain Techniques for Prosodic Modification of Speech. In W. B. Kleijn and K. K. Paliwal (eds.), *Speech Coding and Synthesis* (pp 519–555). Amsterdam: Elsevier Science.
Ohala, J. J.
1984   An Ethological Perspective on Common Cross-language Utilization of F0 in Voice. *Phonetica*, **41**, 1–16.
Quirk, R., Greenbaum, S., Leech, G. & Svartvik, J.
1987   *A Grammar of Contemporary English.* Harlow (Essex, UK): Longman.
Rump, H. H. & Collier, R.
1996   Focus Conditions and the Prominence of Pitch-Accented Syllables. *Language and Speech*, **39**, 1–17.

Sadock, J. & Zwicky, A.
    1985   Speech Act Distinctions in Syntax. In T. Shopen (ed.), *Language Typology and Syntactic Description*, Vol 1., (pp 155–196). Cambridge: Cambridge University Press.

Thorsen, N.
    1980   A Study of the Perception of Sentence Intonation – Evidence from Danish. *Journal of the Acoustical Society of America*, **67**, 1014–1030.

Phonological encoding in speech production: Comments on Jurafsky et al., Schiller et al., and van Heuven & Haan

Willem J. M. Levelt

1. Introduction

What is phonological encoding? An introductory answer to this question may be helpful for a discussion of the preceding three papers. The term 'phonological encoding' has multiple uses, as Pat Keating signalled during the meeting from which this book stems in her introductory presentation: it can denote the encoding *by* phonology or the encoding *of* phonology. In the reading literature, for instance, the standard use of the term is this: 'Phonological encoding is writing a letter or word based on its sounds'[1] i.e., the encoding of phonology *by* orthographic units. This is not the topic of the present section. The other use of the term, encoding *of* phonology was introduced in my book *Speaking* (1989). After a discussion of grammatical encoding, phonological encoding was introduced as follows:

"Second, there is *phonological encoding*. Its function is to retrieve or build a phonetic or articulatory plan for each lemma and for the utterance as a whole. The major source of information to be accessed by the Phonological Encoder is *lexical form*, the lexicon's information about an item's internal composition. Apart from the lemma information, an item in the lexicon contains information about its morphology and its phonology [...] Several phonological procedures will modify, or further specify, the form information that is retrieved. [...] The result of phonological encoding is a *phonetic* or *articulatory plan*. It is not yet overt speech; it is an internal representation of how the planned utterance should be articulated — a program for articulation." (p. 12)

Introducing this use of the term to denote the speaker's phonological preparation of the utterance by no means amounted to an introduction of the study of this process. Clearly, the study of phonological encoding has its roots in speech error analysis, going back as far as Meringer & Mayer's (1895) careful analysis of form errors in spontaneous speech. They distinguished between meaning-based substitutions (such as *Ihre* for *meine*) and form-based substitutions (such as *Studien* for *Stunden*), which suggested the existence of two levels of processing in speech production, one of which concerns form encoding. This notion was elaborated in much detail by Garrett (1975). He discovered that word exchanges (such as *he left it and forgot it behind*) can be between phrases or clauses, but preserves grammatical category and grammatical function. By contrast, sound exchanges (such as *rack pat* for *pack rat*) mostly happen between juxtaposed or close-by words, which can differ in grammatical category and function. Apparently two levels of processing are involved in utterance generation, which Garrett called the 'functional' and 'positional' levels. The latter involves morphological processes such as affixation and all further phonological (though not phonetic) processing. Except for details of phonetic preparation this level of processing coincides with 'phonological encoding' as outlined above.

A landmark development in modelling the process of phonological encoding was Shattuck-Hufnagel's (1979) Scan-Copier Model, with its slots-and-filler mechanism of word form encoding in utterance context. The review of phonological encoding in Levelt (1989) is largely inspired by this modelling effort. The Scan-Copier Model was based on both a detailed corpus analysis of phonological speech errors and on the results of systematic error-inducing experiments, an important methodological innovation, which brings us to laboratory phonology.

In retrospect, the laboratory study of phonological encoding was quite late to develop. Whereas the experimental study of speech perception was a long established field by 1975, the laboratory study of speech production was either articulatory phonetics, the study of the vocal tract's production of speech sounds, or reading-based study of prosody. There existed a tacit but quite general disbelief that one would ever be able to gain experimental output control over a speaker's natural utterance production, including phonological encoding.

This has drastically changed. A range of experimental paradigms have been invented over the past quarter century that do provide for that type of output control. Among them are the above-mentioned error-induction paradigms, introduced by Baars et al. (1975). But more importantly, there are the chronometric naming paradigms stemming from an old tradition in studies of reading and picture naming (cf. Levelt, 1999 for a review). That tradition first touched issues of phonological encoding when Lupker (1982) discovered that the latency of naming a picture was reduced when simultaneously with the picture a visual distractor word was presented that rhymed with the target picture name (as compared to a situation where a non-related distractor word was presented). This 'orthographic' facilitation is really phonological facilitation. It is also obtained when the distractor word is presented auditorily. Any segmental phonological correspondence between distractor and target can induce facilitation (Schriefers et al., 1990; Meyer & Schriefers, 1991). The contribution of Schiller et al. in the present section uses orthographic picture/word interference to study, cross-linguistically, whether syllable priming exists in phonological encoding.

Together with picture/word interference, a range of other chronometric paradigms were developed to study phonological encoding (see Levelt, 1999 for review), among them the 'implicit priming paradigm' (Meyer, 1990). If subjects are induced to produce a block of words that are word-initially phonologically identical (such as *loner, local, lotus* − 'homogeneous' block), word onset latencies are shorter than when the same words are produced in 'heterogeneous' blocks (e.g. the word *loner* among *beacon* and *major*). The shared word onset in a homogeneous block is an 'implicit' phonological prime. The method has been profitably used to study various issues of phonological encoding, among them: Is phonological encoding an incremental procedure? The clear answer is 'yes'. Only word initial primes are effective. Sharing word final phonology (as in *deed, feed, seed*) is entirely ineffective. This doesn't contradict the just mentioned rhyme priming effects in picture/word interference. These arise at an earlier level of the encoding process. In phonological encoding, a first step is to 'spell out' the target word's phonological code, largely its segmental composition; it is most unlikely that the stored code has syllable structure, because syllable structure can be highly context dependent (Levelt, 1992). Typically a word's segments are simultaneously activated; the spell-out can be primed through any segment in the code. During a next stage the code is used to compute the phonological word proper. This is an incremental process of syllabification. The domain of syllabification can be smaller (compounds) or larger (clitics) than the input lexical word. And syllabification is incremental. It starts word-initially, synthesizing one syllable after another. This process is the one accessed by the implicit priming paradigm. The paradigm has also been used to show that the elements of incremental encoding are segments, not features. Implicit priming is back to zero when the word initial segments in a block differ by just one feature, as in *noga, modem* (Roelofs, 1999). In a modified form the paradigm has further been used to study metrical aspects of word encoding. The evidence, reviewed in Levelt et al. (1999), supports the notion that, at least for Dutch, a phonological word's stress pattern is computed 'on-line'. It is probably the case that only irregularly stressed words carry metrical information in their stored phonological codes.

The two ordered operations of retrieving the stored phonological codes and using them in incremental prosodification (syllabification, metrical encoding, as well as higher levels of prosodification) are followed by phonetic encoding. As incremental prosodification proceeds, the resulting syllabic and larger prosodic structures should acquire phonetic shape. How do speakers incrementally prepare the articulatory gestures for the subsequent syllables in their prosodic contexts? One hypothesis, originally proposed by Crompton (1982) and further developed in Levelt (1989) and Levelt & Wheeldon (1994), is that frequently used syllabic gestures are stored as abstract motor schemas, somewhere in premotor/Broca cortex. This hypothetical repository has been called the 'mental syllabary'. And indeed, as Schiller has shown (see Levelt et al., 1999), English and Dutch speakers do more than 80% of their talking with no more than 500 different syllables. My rough estimation is that, on average, we have used each of these syllables almost 100.000 times at reaching adulthood, i.e., some 13 times every single day[2].

Many of these syllables are themselves high-frequency words and there is no reason why even multisyllabic high-frequency words (such as *about* or *really*) wouldn't be similarly stored in this speech motor repository. Levelt et al. (1999) suggest a mechanism by which these high-frequency target syllables are incrementally selected, as phonological syllabification proceeds. This cannot be the full story, of course. Speakers are also able to phonetically encode low-frequency and even new syllables. In addition, phonetic encoding involves the further coarticulatory integration of successive articulatory syllables.

The three papers discussed here address different aspects of phonological encoding. Jurafsky et al. focus on the issue of modularity in phonological encoding: do homophonous words behave similarly in phonetic encoding, as the above theory predicts, or is their phonetics co-determined by their specific lexical frequency? As mentioned, Schiller et al. consider whether accessing the phonological code already involves accessing syllable structure. Van Heuven et al., finally, address higher levels of phonological encoding and decoding, relating to intonational accentuation in statements versus questions. I will now consider these contributions in turn.

2. Commentary

The empirical basis of the staged model of phonological encoding, summarized above, is formed by chronometric laboratory data, mostly response latencies in word and phrase production experiments. In their article, Jurafsky et al. managed to test aspects of that theory against the wider empirical domain of naturalistic speech data. If homophones, such as the pronoun *that* and the complementizer *that*, share their phonological code but not their lemma, as Levelt et al. (1999) claim to be the case, could one still observes articulatory differences between them in natural connected speech? Strictly speaking, the theory, and in particular Roelofs's (1997) computational model WEAVER++, predict only that there will be no difference in latency. Latency differences, however, are exactly what is hard to observe in naturalistic data; one has no natural anchor point for word onset latency. Jurafsky et al. checked instead how the word is realized, its duration, its vowel quality, its coda. It conforms to the nature of the theory to predict that homophones are phonetically realized in the same way (but see below for a qualification). In particular, the frequency of the lemma should be irrelevant. If not, one has a so-called 'lemma effect'. Of course, one should correct for confounding factors, such as position of the word in the utterance, etc. My reading of Jurafsky et al.'s data is that, after applying a range of careful controls, there are by and large no lemma effects left. This certainly reflects the spirit of our theory. Still, there are some effects. In particular, there is less coda reduction in partitive *of* than in genitive and complement *of*. Also, determiner *that* never showed vowel reduction as the other *that* lemmas do, and pronominal *that* tends to be longer than the other *that*s. Is there a left-over confounding factor involved? My only hunch is that these differences may relate to the prosodic structure of the word's immediate environment. The data base did not allow for the marking of stress and accent, but it could certainly have been the case in this corpus that the determiner *that* is more often accented, in particular contrastively, than for instance the relative *that*. This needs further testing.

The analysis raises a further theoretical issue worth considering. How does onset latency (the strict empirical domain of the theory in Levelt et al., 1999) relate to articulatory realization, in particular word duration? Is the realization of the articulatory gesture, in particular its duration, affected by the flow of activation at higher levels of processing? How modular is articulation? Kello et al. (2000) argue against full modularity. In their experiments they used a Stroop task, in which the subject names the colour of a printed word. If the word happens to be the name of a different colour (e.g. the word GREEN printed in red), colour naming latency is substantially slower than when the word is the name of the colour (e.g. the word RED printed in red) or a neutral word (e.g. the word CHAIR printed in red). This is called 'Stroop interference'. In Kello et al.'s experimental results this difference in latencies had no counterpart in the articulatory durations of the colour word response ('red'). So far, articulation seemed to be modular with respect to higher level interference. However, when the authors applied a response deadline, requiring a speeded response, they found some evidence for prolonged articulatory duration under Stroop interference. Kello et al. concluded that a modular system can change its architecture to a cascading one, dependent on the specific task demands. I will call this 'restricted modularity'. However, they obtained this effect in only one of their experiments, precisely the one in which 25% of the data had to be removed for various reasons.

Damian (submitted) took up this topic in two carefully controlled experiments. The first one was a picture/word interference task. Here he obtained the usual phonological facilitation effect when the name of the auditory distractor word was phonologically related to the name of the target picture. This facilitation in naming latencies did not 'spill over' to articulatory durations, just as there was no spill over in Kello et al.'s original Stroop experiment. However, even when Damian applied a deadline, which speeded up the responses, again not the slightest effect of phonological relatedness showed up in the response durations. In a second experiment Damian affected response latencies by way of a semantic manipulation. A block of pictures to be named was either homogeneous in semantic category (e.g., all vehicles, or all vegetables) or heterogeneous (a mix of vehicle, vegetable, etc.). Semantic homogeneity leads to substantial interference, i.e., longer response latencies (Kroll & Stewart, 1994; Damian et al., 2001). In agreement with the original Kello et al. data and with the previous picture/word interference data, there was no concomitant effect on articulatory durations. But neither was such an effect obtained when Damian applied a deadline, which led to generally shorter naming latencies. In other words, in carefully controlled experiments, no 'spilling over' or cascading under time pressure could be demonstrated. Thus, so far there is no good evidence against the modularity of articulation. This, however, may have theoretical repercussions for analyses such as those reported by Jurafsky et al. Assume that a lemma effect does exist. It should show up in response latencies. But if articulation is indeed modular, the lemma effect will not affect articulatory duration. Worse, if Kello et al. were to be right after all, there will not be a spill-over at normal, non-speeded articulation rates. Under both theoretical cases, therefore, a null effect in Jurafsky et al.'s data does not guarantee the absence of a lemma effect. Still, if an even more detailed analysis of these duration data showed a lemma effect, then both theoretical positions (full and restricted modularity) would be in trouble.

Let me now turn to Schiller et al.'s contribution on syllable priming. Syllable priming has never been a happy topic. In a most careful dissertation, Baumann (1995) showed that, whatever one does experimentally, it is impossible to obtain a syllabic priming effect by way of auditorily presented syllable primes. Of course, one always finds auditory priming, but it is irrelevant whether the prime corresponds exactly to a syllable of the target word. The only thing that matters is the number of phonological segments shared between prime and target. We call this the *segmental priming effect*: the more shared segments, the more effective the prime is. This work was done on Dutch and German and one shouldn't exclude the possibility that specific syllabic priming (beyond segmental priming) would be possible for other languages, for instance syllable timed languages. In their paper Schiller et al. provide convincing evidence against syllable priming in Dutch, English, Spanish, and with a slight hedge, also in French, even though Spanish and French are clearly syllable-timed.

It is theoretically important to observe that the non-existence of syllable priming is in fact predicted by the WEAVER++ model of phonological encoding (Roelofs 1997, see also Levelt et al., 1999). As mentioned in the introduction, auditory and orthographic priming affect the level of phonological code retrieval. The code is, however, not a syllabified structure. A syllable prime has no special status in code retrieval. Could it affect syllabification? In the theory each auditory or orthographic input segment can prime all related gestural scores in the syllabary. But again, the syllabic status of the prime is irrelevant. If the first syllable of a target word is of the type CVC, then a corresponding CV prime will prime it partially, a corresponding CVC prime will prime it fully, and a corresponding CVCC prime will prime it fully and the next syllable partially. The total amount of priming, therefore, is simply a function of the number of segments, not of syllable structure. In short, WEAVER++ predicts prime length effects, but no syllable effects.

It is essentially for the same reason that WEAVER++ predicts a number-of-segments effect in phonological word encoding, but no number-of-syllables effect. This was recently challenged by Santiago et al. (2000) on the basis of MacKay's Node Structure Theory (NST). They claimed to have obtained a number-of-syllables effect but no (independent) length effect. However, the authors had not fully controlled for word length in their experiments. A reanalysis by Roelofs (2002) shows that there is only a length effect in the reported data, no independent number-of-syllables effect.

However, the total absence of syllable priming and syllable structure effects in latency measurements of phonological encoding does not mean at all that syllables are not essential planning units in speech production. Syllables are among the earliest acquired and most frequently produced motor programs in our repertoire. They are, in fact, so heavily overused, that it would be impossible *not* to store them. Of course, one can construct new ones, but that is an exceedingly rare event. In our theory, phonetic, articulatory syllables are major, ultimate targets of form encoding. It should be added that these gestural scores may well have internal hierarchical structure not unlike the syllabic structures proposed in NST. Motor priming experiments by Sevald, Dell & Cole (1995) show that such phonetic syllabic structure is independent of phonemic content.

The paper by van Heuven and Haan, finally, moves us beyond phonological word encoding. It addresses an important issue in higher, supra-word level phonological encoding. From the point of view of encoding, the main data reported are the measured sentence melodies of statements versus declarative questions. In these measurements the syntax was kept constant; we are getting a pure view of intonational differences between the two sentence moods. Clearly and expectedly, the two melodies differ markedly in their boundary tones. But the more interesting finding is that they also differ in other respects. Apparently, speakers give away the mode of their utterance long before they generate the boundary tone. There is, in particular, a difference in the balance of the two pitch accents in the sentence melody. To the best of my knowledge, this phenomenon has not been reported before. The authors argue convincingly that this difference results from an amalgam of several encoding processes. It is not the case that the speaker decides to make an interrogative statement and then incrementally installs these melodic features. Rather, each feature is installed for its own reason. In particular, if the speaker wants to invite the interlocutor's confirmation that a particular referent was involved in some state of affairs, the speaker will focus that referent by means of a pitch accent. In itself, this has nothing to do with interrogation, but it does cause the characteristic imbalance of pitch accents. It should not be too complicated to elaborate this decompositional approach, and test it in the laboratory.

One advantage of this theory of intonational encoding is that it allows for a limited planning window. Speakers are often under so much time pressure that they cannot afford much 'look ahead' in their conceptual, grammatical and phonological encoding. The architecture of speech encoding must allow for piecemeal, incremental planning (Levelt, 1989). A decompositional stepwise encoding of question intonation relieves the speaker of attentionally loading long-term planning, but still, the outcome will be a natural pitch contour. I am not claiming that speakers always operate at such a minimal look ahead level. When there is no particular time pressure, or when the speaking situation is a more formal one, incremental encoding units can become larger, especially for skilled speakers.

It should not go unnoticed that the main experimental contribution of van Heuven and Haan's paper is their finding that listeners can, by and large, pick up the characteristic pre-boundary pitch cues. However, that moves us beyond phonological encoding.

The studies discussed in this section support a general view of phonological encoding as a multilevel, incremental process. The levels of encoding, from intonational to syllabic, involve dedicated and rather modular operations. Incrementality is achieved by minimizing 'look ahead' at all levels of processing.

Notes

1 Glossary 'Learning to read ... reading to learn' of the National Center to Improve the Tools of Educators.
http://ldonline.com/ld_indepth/reading/ltr-cec/ltr7-cec.html
2 Assuming 45 talking minutes a day, two words per second, 1.5 syllable word length.

References

Baars, B. J., Motley, M. T. & MacKay, D.
    1975   Output editing for lexical status from artificially elicited slips of the tongue. *Journal of Verbal Learning and Verbal Behavior*, **14**, 382–391.

Baumann, M.
    1995   *The production of syllables in connected speech.* PhD dissertation, Nijmegen University.

Crompton, A.
    1982   Syllables and segments in speech production. In A. Cutler (ed.), *Slips of the Tongue and Language Production.* The Hague: Mouton.

Damian, M. F.
    submitted   Articulatory duration in single word speech production.

Damian, M. F., Vigliocco, G. & Levelt, W. J. M.
    2001   Effects of semantic context in the naming of pictures and words. *Cognition*, **81**, B77–B86.

Garrett, M. F.
    1975   The analysis of sentence production. In G. H. Bower (ed.), *The Psychology of Learning and Motivation*, Vol **9** (pp 133–178). New York: Academic Press.

Kello, C. T., Plaut, D. C. & MacWhinney, B.
    2000   The task-dependence of staged vs. cascaded processing: An empirical and computational study of Stroop interference in speech production. *Journal of Experimental Psychology: General*, **129**, 340–361.

Kroll, J. & Stewart, E.
- 1994 Category interference in translation and picture naming: Evidence for asymmetric connections between bilingual memory representations. *Journal of Memory and Language*, **33**, 149–174.

Levelt, W. J. M.
- 1989 *Speaking. From Intention to Articulation.* Cambridge MA: MIT Press.

Levelt, W. J. M.
- 1992 Accessing words in speech production. Stages, processes, and representations. *Cognition*, **42**, 1–22.

Levelt, W. J. M.
- 1999 Models of word production. *Trends in Cognitive Sciences*, **3**, 223–232.

Levelt, W. J. M. & Wheeldon, L.
- 1994 Do speakers have access to a mental syllabary? *Cognition*, **50**, 239–269.

Levelt, W. J. M., Roelofs, A. & Meyer, A. S.
- 1999 A theory of lexical access in speech production. *Behavioral and Brain Sciences*, **22**, 1–38.

Lupker, S. J.
- 1982 The role of phonetic and orthographic similarity in picture-word interference. *Canadian Journal of Psychology*, **36**, 349–367.

Meringer, R. & Mayer, K.
- 1895 *Versprechen und Verlesen.* Stuttgart: Goschensche Verlag. (Re-issued, with introductory essay by A. Cutler and D. A. Fay (1978). Amsterdam: Benjamins.)

Meyer, A. S.
- 1990 The time course of phonological encoding in language production: The encoding of successive syllables of a word. *Journal of Memory and Language*, **29**, 524–545.

Meyer, A. S. & Schriefers, H.
- 1991 Phonological facilitation in picture-word interference experiments: Effects of stimulus onset asynchrony and types of interfering stimuli. *Journal of Experimental Psychology: Learning, Memory Cognition*, **17**, 1146–1160.

Roelofs, A.
- 1997 The WEAVER model of word-form encoding in speech production. *Cognition*, **64**, 249–284.

Roelofs, A.
- 1999 Phonological segments and features as planning units in speech production. *Language and Cognitive Processes*, **14**, 173–200.

Roelofs, A.
- 2002 Syllable structure effects turn out to be word length effects: Comments on Santiago et al. (2000). *Language and Cognitive Processes*, **17**, 1–13.

Santiago, J., MacKay, D. G., Palma, A. & Rho, C.
2000 Sequential activation processes in producing words and syllables: Evidence from picture naming. *Language and Cognitive Processes*, **15**, 1–44.

Schriefers, H., Meyer, A. S. & Levelt, W. J. M.
1990 Exploring the time course of lexical access in speech production: Picture-word interference studies. *Journal of Memory and Language*, **29**, 86–102.

Sevald, C. A., Dell, G. S. & Cole, J. S.
1995 Syllable structure in speech production: Are syllables chunks or schemas? *Journal of Memory and Language*, **34**, 807–820.

Shattuck-Hufnagel, S.
1979 Speech errors as evidence for a serial-ordering mechanism in sentence production. In W. E. Cooper & E. C. T. Walker (eds.), *Sentence Processing: Psycholinguistic Studies Presented to Merrill Garrett*, (pp. 295–342). Hillsdale, NJ: Erlbaum.

Word-specific phonetics

Janet B. Pierrehumbert

Abstract

In standard models of phonetic implementation, surface phonological representations arise as words are retrieved from the lexicon and assembled in a buffer, where the phrasal intonation and prosody are added. These (categorical and hierarchical) representations provide the input to the phonetic implementation rules, which map them into motor gestures and acoustic outcomes. The model has been highly successful in handling across-the-board effects on phonetic outcomes, including language-specific phonetic patterns of allophony and shifts in overall voice level or force of articulation. The very causes of this success render it unable to handle instances of word-specific phonetic detail, which have now come to light through large-scale experimental and sociolinguistic studies. This paper summarizes the evidence that long-term representations of words include more phonetic detail than previously imagined. It sketches a hybrid model of speech production, in which exemplar theory is used to model implicit knowledge of the probability distributions for phonological elements as well as of word-specific phonetic patterns. Production goals for specific phonological elements are biased by stronger activation of exemplars associated with the current word. Thus, experience with specific words influences the exact production goals for those words, even as the phonological decomposition plays the dominant role. The consequences of this model for the production of morphologically complex words are also explored. The model also provides a mechanism for the subphonemic paradigm uniformity effects which other authors have recently documented.

1. Introduction

A long-standing forte of the Laboratory Phonology series has been work on phonetic implementation of phonological representations. Numerous studies in this series have elucidated the patterns of variation in the realization of phonological categories in different segmental and prosodic contexts, and such studies now provide one of the main lines of evidence about the cognitive representation of sound structure.

In a consensus view of phonetic implementation, lexemes (the phonological representations of words) are abstract structures made up of categorical, contrastive elements. The phonetic implementation system relates this abstract, long-term, categorical knowledge to the time course of phonetic parameters in particular acts of speech. In fluent mature speakers, the phonetic implementation system is a modular, feed-forward system, reflecting its nature as an extremely practiced and automatic behavior. Lexemes are retrieved from the lexicon, and assembled in a phonological buffer in which phrasal prosody and intonation are also assigned. The fully formed hierarchical structures thus assembled provide the input to the phonetic implementation rules, which compute the degree and timing of articulatory gestures. The model is feedforward because no arrows go backwards, from articulatory plans to phonological encoding, or from the phonological encoding to the lexical level (apart from some post-hoc monitoring which permits people to notice and correct speech errors). It is modular because no lexeme information can influence the phonetic implementation directly, bypassing the level of phonological buffering.

Though highly successful in explaining a wide range of data, such models are now challenged by a number of studies demonstrating the existence of word-specific phonetic detail. In modular feed-forward models, the (categorical) form of the lexeme wholly determines the phonetic outcome. If two words differ at all in their phonetics, then they differ categorically, and accordingly one job of the phonology is to identify a category set which captures all systematic differences amongst words. Another feature of these models is they do not take on the job of describing systematic phonetic variation related to sociostylistic register. Though the authors of such models would no doubt acknowledge the existence of such variation, they have not undertaken to provide a formal treatment of the cognitive capabilities which permit it. These limitations in formal models of speech production are related, because some cases of word-specific phonetic detail can be traced to the typical patterns of word usage in different social contexts. Developing the next generation of speech production models which can handle such variation is an important goal, because control of subphonemic variation is an important aspect of the human language capability. Its interaction with the more categorial aspects of linguistic competence appears to be highly structured, and it promises to be a rich source of information about the architecture of language. In the theoretical stance taken here, categorical aspects of phonological competence are embedded in less categorical aspects, rather than modularized in a conventional fashion. The reader is referred to Pierrehumbert (2000) and Pierrehumbert, Beckman & Ladd (2001) for a more detailed defence of this stance.

Production models based on exemplar theory can readily capture findings of word-specific allophonic detail. In such models, each word can be associated with an empirically determined frequency distribution over phonetic outcomes. The distributions are continuously updated based on experience, and nonphonemic differences in these experiences accrue in the representations. For example, if some word is most often produced in leniting contexts, its long-term representation will show more lenition. If it is most often produced in a particular sociostylistic register, its long term representation will show the hallmarks of that register. The chief drawback of this approach is that it handles none of the data which motivated the standard modular feedforward models.

In this paper, I sketch out a hybrid model which generates word-specific allophony while still retaining the insights of the modular feedforward models. I will first review the major lines of evidence for the modular and exemplar-based models. Then I will show how each line of evidence is handled in the hybrid model.

2. Modular Feedforward Models

Modular feedforward models of phonetic implementation were developed on the basis of experimental work in psycholinguistics and phonetics. Psycholinguistic studies have concentrated on the speed and accuracy of word production in various tasks. Experiments on induction of speech errors provide one of the earliest lines of evidence that lexemes are first copied into a phonological buffer before being pronounced. In Shattuck-Hufnagel's highly influential account (Shattuck-Hufnagel, 1979) errors in the copying and checkoff procedures explain the statistical patterns of anticipation, perseveration, and transposition errors. Competing models which lack buffering have difficulties in explaining transposition errors. A set of experiments by Sternberg et al. (1978) and Sternberg et al. (1980) on the latency to begin speaking provides evidence that assembly of longer phonological plans takes longer than assembly of shorter plans — further evidence that such an assembly process is critically involved. A long series of experiments by Levelt and colleagues (see Levelt, 1989; and also the WEAVER model presented in Roelofs, 1997) used a variety of speech production tasks. A critical finding from this work is that some predictable features of word prosody are computed on-line rather than stored in long-term representations.

This general class of experimental results brings home the fact that in both speech perception and speech production, a correspondence is established between events which unfold in time (the speech signal) and the metatemporal long-term representations of words. The long-term representations are metatemporal in the sense that they are about sequences of phonological events that unfold in time. They describe such events, but they themselves are not events that occur in time. This means that there is a discrepancy in logical type between lexical representations (which are long-term — or nearly permanent — memories), and speech events (which occur in time and and which are as evanescent and irreversible as other other physical events). In the terms of psychology, lexical representations are examples of declarative memories: "I know **that** the word *evanescent* has such-and-such articulatory and acoustic events in such-and-such order." The phonetic implementation rules provide an example of procedural knowledge: "**how** to say /v/." The mere fact of this distinction provides a basic argument for a modular theory.

Detailed studies of phonetic implementation rules have concentrated on phonetic variability related to the phrasal context of a word. The original goal of these studies was to explore the psychological reality of hierarchical structures and/or to delineate the architecture for fluent and natural-sounding speech synthesis systems. Quantitative studies of f0 showed that the phonetic realization of any given tonal element can only be computed if a complete phrasal phonological structure is available (see Pierrehumbert & Beckman, 1988, and literature reviewed there). More recent work has extended these findings to the domain of segmental allophony. In addition to the well-known case of phrase-final lengthening, phrasal prosody is now known to affect aspiration and glottalization (Pierrehumbert & Talkin, 1992; Pierrehumbert, 1994; Pierrehumbert & Frisch, 1996; Dilley, Shattuck-Hufnagel & Ostendorf, 1996), as well as the force, accuracy, and duration of the other aspects of consonantal articulation (de Jong, Beckman & Edwards, 1993; de Jong, 1995; Keating et al., forthcoming).

Such studies provide a prima-facie case for a level of phonological encoding which is distinct from the lexeme level. Phrasal prosody depends on the syntactic structure and pragmatic force of a sentence, which are productively determined when words are combined. In intonation languages such as English, the tonal elements also are assigned at the phrasal level. The phonological buffer proposed by Shattuck-Hufnagel and Sternberg et al. provides a locus for the calculation of phrasal prosody and intonation. Detailed phonetic effects of phrasal phonology are then taken to arise from the way that the fully parsed contents of this buffer are executed by the motor system. The execution is known to be language-particular (since allophonic details for even the most comparable phonemes differ from one language to another); however, it is of course constrained by human capabilities for articulation and perception.

Such studies of phonetic implementation bring home the success of modular feed-forward models in explaining across-the-board effects of all types. Across-the-board effects are ones which pertain to all words which share the triggering phonological context. There are several different kinds of examples of such effects. One is allophonic rules which are peculiar to a language or dialect. For example, in American English, intervocalic word-internal /t/s in a falling stress context (as in the word *pretty*) is typically produced as a voiced flap. In many dialects of British English, the voicelessness of the /t/ is preserved in the same context even if the closure is reduced. A related fact is the outcome of Neogrammarian sound changes (which enter the language as allophonic processes and may eventually become fossilized across the entire vocabulary). For example, the Germanic affrication of Indo-European stops affected all words containing the target stops. Changes in stylistic register are also across-the board, in that they affect all words throughout a phrase. In a clear speech style, the speaker produces all words more slowly and with more articulatory effort. Raising the voice causes all words to be louder and have a higher f_0.

However, as we will see below, the assumption that such effects are across-the-board is not fully correct. The effects are across-the-board in that broad classes of words are eligible to undergo them, and they can even apply to novel words. A person who flaps the /t/ in *pretty* and *Betty* will find that an invented *Bretty* is also eligible for flapping. But detailed studies have shown that the probability and extent of reduction processes is word-dependent. Dependence on both word frequency and on morphological relatives has been documented. In the next session, I review reports of word-specific subphonemic detail.

3. Long term word-specific phonetic patterns

Reports of allophonic effects related to word frequency and/or contextual predictability go back to Zipf or earlier. They are usefully reviewed in the contribution by Jurafsky, Bell & Girard to this volume, and I will not repeat this review here. Both in experiments and in corpora of natural conversation, words which are highly expectable are produced faster and less clearly than words which are rare or surprising. What does this mean for the architecture of the cognitive model? An important issue is whether such effects are generated on-line (and if so, by what means) or whether they result from long-term storage of different phonetic patterns for different words. The primary concern of this paper is the relationship of long-term representations to production patterns, and so my primary focus will be patterns which do not plausibly result from on-line control of speech style and therefore implicate long-term memory.

Consider first the effects of contextual predictability, the main topic of Jurafsky et al. (this volume). For any given word, contextual predictability results in differential lenition rates depending on how much novel information the word contributes (above what is in any case inferrable from the thread of the conversation and the neighbouring words). Such effects can be viewed as an on-line modification of speech style. The standard modular model does not generate such effects, but it can be readily modified to do so. When a lexeme is retrieved and loaded into the phonological buffer, assume that a gradient value representing the ease of retrieval is passed to the buffer as a quantitative attribute of the Prosodic Word node. This parameter would control, or rather play a part in controlling, an overall parameter of articulatory clarity and effort. This would be a direct formal analogue of the gradient pitch range parameters which full-blown f_0 synthesis algorithms, such as Pierrehumbert & Beckman (1988), employ to generate tonal outcomes under varying conditions of intonational subordination.

A similar line of reasoning may be available for the finding by Wright (1997) that CVC words produced in citation form show a dependence of formant values on lexical neighbourhood density. Words with a high neighbourhood density have many lexical neighbours which differ in just one phoneme (according to the metric used). Words with a low neighbourhood density have few such neighbours. Wright (1997) found that the vowel space was expanded in words with high neighbourhood density. Since high neighbourhood density slows word recognition in perception experiments (an effect attributed to lexical competition), it is at least possible that neighbourhood density would also slow lexeme retrieval in production. If so, Jurafsky et al. (this volume) would predict an on-line effect on speech clarity.

The pervasiveness and automaticity of such reduction effects suggests, of course, that this description is a piece of formalism in search of an explanation. Jurafsky and colleagues are actively seeking to identify the underlying cognitive or neural factor which creates such an intimate connection between the ease of lexical retrieval and speech style.

Whatever this factor may prove to be, it predicts the existence of reduction effects related to word frequency. First, word frequency is uncontroversially related to resting activation levels, so that even out of context, frequent words are retrieved faster. Second, word frequency is correlated with contextual predictability. Since (by definition) high frequency words occur more often in running speech than low frequency words, any given high frequency word is more likely or unsurprising in the average context than a low frequency word. Furthermore, a high frequency word is more likely to occur a short time after a previous mention of the same word. Thus, on-line tracking of predictability would have the result that the aggregate statistics for high-frequency words would display higher average predictability, and hence more lenition on the average. A surface pattern of reduction related to word frequency is not enough in itself to argue for long-term storage of word-specific allophonic detail. As far as long-term storage goes, then, the most telling phenomena are ones which do not involve the connection of frequency or neighbourhood density to lenition.

One example of such a phenomenon is provided by an experiment reported in Goldinger (2000). Goldinger carried out a speech production experiment in order to elucidate the nature and role of long-term memory of specific voices. Goldinger's prior work on speech perception had indicated that long-term memory of words includes traces of the specific voices in which the words were spoken (Goldinger, 1996). In the production experiment, subjects first made a baseline recording of a set of test words by reading the words from a screen. The next day, they carried out a task in which they heard words in various voices and located the word in a visual display on a computer screen. Five days later, they returned to the lab and read the words for a second time, providing a set of test utterances for a second experiment. AXB stimuli for the second experiment were constructed from the baseline recordings, the test recordings, and the stimuli of the first experiment. The word in the X position was one which had been played to the first group of subjects for the visual search and identification task. The words in the A and B positions are baseline and test utterances by the first group of subjects (balanced for position in the presentation). Then, a new group of 300 subjects listened to the AXB stimuli and made judgments of "which utterance was a better imitation of the middle word." Overall performance was well above chance on this task, indicating that the test utterances resembled the speech stimuli of the first experiment more than the baseline stimuli did. More importantly, the word frequency and the number of repetitions of the word on Day 2 had a strong impact on the success rate in the AXB task. Low frequency words which had been heard many times were most reliably identified as imitations. This specific pattern in the data indicates that the subjects success in the AXB task could not be an artifact of some global effect, such as overall fluency on the word set. Instead, it is word-specific.

The modular feed-forward model summarized above has a certain capability for handling the finding that long-term perceptual memories of words include voice information. Clearly, words have numerous associations or connotations, which would figure in the lexical model as a set of links to the words. Nothing in the model prevents specific words from evoking specific voices or sets of voices. However, the modular feed-forward model cannot handle the finding that these voice memories for words impact phonetic details in production. In this approach, retrieval of the lexeme means that a categorical encoding of that lexeme is loaded into the phonological buffer for execution. If the voice memories do not result in a categorically distinct form of the lexeme, they can have no impact on the production of the form. With the data in Goldinger (2000) showing gradient effects of word frequency and repetition count on perceived accuracy of imitation, the strict modularity of the standard model does not appear to be viable.

Bybee (2001) reviews a considerable body of literature on leniting historical changes, including both her own work and the landmark paper Phillips (1984). An example of such a change would be reduction of full vowels to schwa, with eventual loss of the schwa and the syllable it projected. Such changes are typically more advanced in high-frequency words than in low frequency words; the effects of word frequency appear to be gradient. Another example is provided by English doubly-marked past tense verbs (such as *left*, past tense of *leave*). As shown in Bybee (2000b), the rate of /t/ reduction and/or deletion in such forms is a function of their frequency. As a static state of affairs, such a difference can, in principle, be accounted for by an on-line factor, as discussed above, However, this proposal fails to account for the fact that historical leniting changes advance on a scale of decades. They advance in two senses. Phonological sequences which are at first lenited become more and more lenited until they disappear entirely. Leniting changes which first become evident in high-frequency words typically spread to low-frequency words, in the end affecting the entire vocabulary. An example is provided by the history of French. In French, the post-tonic syllables of Latin eventually disappeared entirely, leaving an entire lexicon with word-final stress.

To model the progress of such effects requires a model in which the lexical representations of words include incrementally updated information about the phonetic distribution for each word. An across-the board effect, in the form of a consistent leniting bias on the productions, explains why all words are affected. However, high frequency words are affected more, because they are produced more often and so more memories of them in their lenited form accrue, once the lenition gets underway. Exactly such a model is developed in Pierrehumbert (2001), on which more below.

Word-specific effects in historical change are not confined to word-frequency effects. Yaeger-Dror & Kemp (1992) and Yaeger-Dror (1996) document a vowel shift in progress in Quebecois French. They found that a particular group of words failed to shift despite exhibiting the phonological sequence which was targeted in the change. These words were a group of semantic associates, representing organs of the church, the military, and the schools. Yaeger-Dror was not able to identify any phonological properties shared by these words which distinguished them from words which did undergo the shift.

A phonetic pattern with a morphosyntactic component is discussed in Hay (2000). Hay examined the production of /t/ in words such as *swiftly* and *listless*. Target word pairs in the study were phonologically matched, and differed in their degree of morphological decomposability, as predicted by Hay's model. Taking into account psycholinguistic results on morphological parsing, Hay predicts that complex words of equal frequency will be perceived as more decomposed when the base is more frequent than the word itself, and less decomposed when the base is infrequent compared to the word itself. For example, *swiftly* is highly decomposible because *swift* is readily perceived inside *swiftly*. However, *list* is not perceived inside *listless*. Hay found a significant effect of decomposibility on the /t/ allophony. (It appears to be gradient, though a larger data set would be desirable.) The more decomposible the form is, the more strongly the /t/ is pronounced. Note that this effect is in the opposite direction from an effect of base frequency per se. Given Hay's experimental design, the bases of the more decomposible words were **more** frequent than the bases of the less decomposible words. Nonetheless, they were produced with a **stronger** /t/. Thus, the pattern could not result from an on-line effect of the frequency of stem (as related to ease of access of the stem). Nor do they relate to word frequency of the complex form, since this factor was controlled in the experiment. The pattern can be generated in the model described below, in which the long-term representations of words include probability distributions over phonetic outcomes.

Mendoza-Denton (1997) and Hay, Jannedy & Mendoza-Denton (1999) hint at how word-frequency effects and lexical field effects may come together in the cognitive model. Mendoza-Denton (1997) reports the degree of raising and fronting of /ɪ/ in the speech of Latina gang girls in California. Hay et al. (1999) studied the degree of monophthongization of the diphthong /aɪ/ (a characteristic of African-American Vernacular English) in the speech of the African American TV personality Oprah Winfrey. Monophthongization of /aɪ/ might be viewed as a lenition, but raising and fronting of a lax front vowel to its tense variant is clearly not a lenition. However, in both studies, the shift is most marked in high-frequency words which serve as markers of sociolinguistic register. Fronting and raising of /ɪ/ was greatest on the word *nothing*, which acts as a discourse marker in the dialect in question. Monophthongization of /aɪ/ was strongest on the word *I*. In addition to interacting with word frequency, these words reflected the sociolinguistic situation of the speaker. For the gang girls, the shift was most advanced for core gang members. Oprah Winfrey displayed the ability to shift her speech style between a more AAVE influenced style to a more mainstream style, depending on the subject matter she was speaking about. Another striking example of gradual adaptation of sociolinguistic style is provided by Harrington, Palethorpe & Watson (2000). This study, based on decades of radio broadcasts by Her Majesty Queen Elizabeth II, showed that she has gradually shifted her pronunciation in the direction of the Southern British English which has become fashionable with younger speakers.

4. Exemplar production models

The results reviewed in the last section all point to a model in which speakers learn implicit frequency distributions over phonetic outcomes, these distributions are stored in long-term memory, and they are subject to incremental updating. The psychological literature on categorization in perception provides precedents for models of this class. The approach I will be working with here is exemplar theory.

The critical ingredients in exemplar theory are a map of the perceptual space and a set of labels over this map. A clear example of a map is provided by the lowest level of encoding in visual perception. This is a sort of mental movie screen on which the neural signals from the retina are displayed. An example of a long-term memory of a visual map would be a long-term memory of a visual environment, such as one's own bedroom. The labels would be objects in this scene, such as *bed, lamp, bookcase*.

For phonetics, the relevant physical domain is the articulatory/acoustic space, whose dimensions are the relevant dimensions of contrast in articulation and acoustics. This domain provides the perceptual map for phonetic encoding and memory. The familiar $F1-F2$ space for vowels shows part of the information encoded in this map, but the real map is of course much higher dimensional. The higher dimensional space is still a space, however, in the sense that a metric is defined along each dimension. Thanks to this metric it is possible to quantify the distance between any two stimuli in some single respect, or in all respects. The labels over the map are the inventory of phonological primitives, e.g. phonemes, features, or other phonological units.

According to exemplar theory, people have detailed long-term memories of particular percepts, and these are stored as locations on the map. These are the "exemplars" of the theory. Exemplars are categorized using the label set, and this has the result that each label is associated with a large set of remembered percepts. These implicitly define the region of the map which corresponds to that label. For example, the set of exemplars labelled with /i/ implicitly defines the region of the formant space which corresponds to that vowel; at the center of this distribution, the exemplars are numerous whereas towards the margins of the distribution, the exemplars become much sparser. A fresh stimulus is classified as follows. The perceptual encoding of the stimulus causes it to be placed at some location on the map. Given that location on the map, a statistical choice rule determines its most probable classification, given the number, location, and labelling of the previously stored exemplars in the region of the fresh stimulus. As discussed in Johnson (1997) and Pierrehumbert (2001a), this approach is highly successful in capturing the interaction of similarity and frequency in perceptual classification. It is also successful in handling prototype effects. Of course, we view the model as a logical schema rather than taking it as a literal picture of activity in the brain. Any model which stores implicit and incrementally updatable frequency distributions over a cognitive map will show similar behaviour; it is not important that all percepts are individuated as separate memories in the long term. The statistical choice rule is presumably physically implemented through activation and lateral inhibition of labels competing over a neighbourhood of the map.

The phenomena described in the last section are all patterns of speech perception. Classical exemplar theory says nothing whatsoever about production. Therefore, the model must be extended if it is to be applied. Goldinger (2000), Pierrehumbert (2001a), and Kirchner (forthcoming) all adopt a similar viewpoint on how to obtain productions from an exemplar model. The basic insight, which appears to originate with work on motor control by Rosenbaum et al. (1993), is that activating the group of exemplars in a subregion of the perceptual map can specify a production goal which corresponds to the aggregate or average properties of the members of the group. To produce an /i/, for example, we activate the exemplars in some area of the /i/ region in the vowel space. This group of /i/s serves as a goal for the current production, much as a perceived object can serve as a goal for a reaching motion.

Models of this general class predict strong effects of degree of language exposure on production. Acquiring a fully native accent in a language involves building up probability distributions for all the different phonological elements in their various contexts, a task of empirical estimation which requires hearing and encoding a very large amount of speech. A variety of consequences is predicted from low levels of exposure, for example in the phonetic patterns which result from attempting to imitate a different dialect. This imitation will succeed only if the speaker has some amount of exposure to the dialect, and it is to be expected that the most frequent and perceptually salient features of the dialect would be imitated the most accurately, since utterances exhibiting these features would serve to establish labels and phonetic distributions characteristic of the dialect. However, without very extensive experience with the dialect, errors in establishing the label set and effects of undersampling would combine to predict various kinds of over- and under- generalization in phonetic outcomes. It is also important to note that the exemplar space itself provides a strong cabability for generalization based on phonetic similarity. Other types of generalizations are also supported by the model, because the model has multiple levels of representation. For example, the characteristic stress pattern of nouns and verbs differs in English, and learning this generalization requires access to the syntactic level, at which the variables N (noun) and V (verb) are defined. Although such phenomena are not the focus of the present paper, nothing about the model prevents relations of abstract levels of description to be established with other. even more abstract, levels.

In formalizing the model, I will adopt the specifics of Pierrehumbert (2001a). In this model, production of the phonological category represented by any specific label involves making a random selection from the exemplar cloud for that label. The selection is random because of the kind of variability which is displayed in productions. If the production model always selected the single best exemplar (by any measure), then the production goal would be invariant. In fact, however, the outcomes vary with variables at nonphonological levels (such as speech rate, style, and speaking conditions). The aggregate effect of such variation as viewed from within the phonological model is random variation over the exemplar cloud; I will return below to the hidden systematicity which a more complete model should capture. The mathematical nature of random sampling does of course entail that the location selected is more likely to be in a densely populated part of the exemplar cloud than in a sparse part.

The specific equations of this model are as follows, repeated from Pierrehumbert (2001a). The exemplar list $E(L)$ consists of the list of exemplars $\{e_1^L, ..., e_n^L\}$ associated with label L. To decide which label to assign to a new utterance with phonetic characteristic x, we define a score for each label by the equation

$$(1) \qquad score\,(L, x) = \sum_{i=1...n} W(x - e_i^L)\, exp\left(-\frac{t - T_i}{\tau}\right)$$

where W is a window function, t is the current time, T_i is the time at which the ith exemplar was admitted to the list, and τ is the memory decay time. Different exemplars have different strengths in the model, because memories are assumed to decay in time. An exponential decay of the exemplar strength is used to model this effect. The window function is a square in Pierrehumbert (2001a) but other choices are possible.

In production, a target x_{target} is obtained by picking an exemplar randomly from the exemplar list of the desired label. Since the probability (or strength) of each exemplar is time-dependent, old exemplars are only rarely used as targets. The actual production target is formed by taking a group of exemplars around this random element. This is necessary for the system to behave correctly as experience increases. If just a single exemplar is chosen as the target, and if it is produced with some probabilistic degree of error (arising as random variation in the motor system), then the phonetic distribution for any given label will spread out more and more. In fact, experience tends to make distributions sharpen up, a phenomenon known as entrenchment. Using a region around x_{target} to control productions puts an anti-diffusive factor in the model, which causes productions to be biased towards the center of the distribution. Specifically, n_{trench} closest exemplars to x_{target} are selected using the memory-weighted distance

$$(2) \qquad d_i = \left| x_{target} - e_i^L \right| exp\left(-\frac{t - T_i}{\tau}\right)$$

A new target is formed by taking the memory-weighted mean of these n_{trench} values. In the limit of very large n_{trench}, the production target becomes fixed at the memory weighted mean of the exemplar list. The final x_{target} is then produced with some random error ϵ.

$$(3) \qquad x = x_{target} + \epsilon$$

In the case of a leniting bias, this equation has the form:

$$(4) \qquad x = x_{target} + \epsilon + \lambda$$

On the assumption that exemplar clouds are associated with phonological units — such as phonemes — models of this class readily handle phonologization of phonetic tendencies. The model discussed in Kirchner (forthcoming) uses spreading activation in a connectionist framework to derive specifics. Clearly, an exemplar production model has to associate exemplars with phonological units, either directly or indirectly. Otherwise, it would be impossible to pronounce novel forms, such as words learned through reading.

One might also assume that exemplar clouds are directly associated with words. Clearly, rather complex memories can be associated with particular labels; for example, I associate a mental image of the photograph on Keith Johnson's web site with the label *Keith Johnson*. Equally, I could associate a recollection of a sizable speech fragment with the word that it instantiates. To do this, it is necessary to impute a temporal dimension to the perceptual map; but this is probably necessary even for modeling phonological units, since phonological units have characteristic dynamics. On the assumption that exemplar clouds contain longer perceptual traces which are directly associated with word labels, the approach readily handles most of findings of the last section; only Hay's results on morphological decomposibility require further apparatus which will be provided below.

Specifically, in Goldinger's (2000) experiment, the exemplar distribution associated with each word would be impacted by the repetitions of the word encountered on Day 2 of the experiment. The more repetitions encountered, the more the distribution would be impacted. Furthermore, for low frequency words, the proportion of exposures which occurred in the context of the experiment would be higher than for more common words. Thus, the proportional effect of the target voices on the mental representation would be higher for low frequency words than for high frequency words, as Goldinger actually found.

Wright's (1997) findings would fall out from the fact that words with a low neighbourhood density are (all else equal) more readily recognized than words with a high neighbourhood density. If a word has no similar competitors, then even a rather slurred example of it will be recognized as a token of the word. As a result, the exemplar distribution for successfully recognized instances of low density words will include more reduced tokens than for high density words. This account leaves us with two different mechanisms for explaining Wright's data, and in fact, both could be involved.

The findings about Quebec French in Yaegor-Dror & Kemp (1992) and Yaegor-Dror (1996) would fall out if words in a particular semantic domain are dominantly used in a social group dominated by older speakers and/or in a formal speech register. In this case, the frequency distributions for words used colloquially in everyday interactions would drift while those in the exceptional semantic field would stay in place.

Pierrehumbert (2001a) assumes that exemplar clouds are associated with phonological units as exhibited in words. Consider the process of vowel reduction in the context of sonorants, one of the initial cases for which Bybee established a relationship between word frequency and degree of reduction. (See Bybee, 2001) To model this effect, it is necessary to assume that the change in progress refers to a structural description within each word, namely the vowel-sonorant combination targeted by the change. A persistent tendency to hypoarticulation of this combination is a language-specific instantiation of broad tendencies to hypoarticulate as discussed in Lindblom (1983). It induces the persistent production bias represented by the variable λ in equation (4). It is also necessary to assume that phonetic distributions for individual words are maintained. The perceptual memories of the lenited word tokens accumulate, incrementally updating the distribution for the word. Since high frequency words are produced more often than low frequency ones, the listener encounters more numerous word tokens which have been affected by the leniting change. As a result, the frequency distribution of outcomes for high frequency words is shifted further in the direction of the historical change than for low frequency words. Obviously, this treatment is not confined to lenition; any systematic bias on the allophonic outcome would incrementally impact high frequency words at a greater rate than low frequency words. In short the model is applicable to any Neogrammarian sound change, by which I mean sound changes which get started in the phonetic implementation and eventually sweep through the vocabulary. (Analogical sound changes, in which words shift their pronunciations categorically through pressure from morphological relatives are generally agreed to arise a a different level in the system).

In this treatment, the exemplar distributions associated with particular phonological units arise as the union of the relevant temporal subparts of exemplars associated with words. For example, each words containing the vowel /o/ would contribute the region which manifests the /o/ to the exemplar distribution for that phoneme. Of course the allophony of this vowel depends on the segmental context and other factors, such as word frequency. This

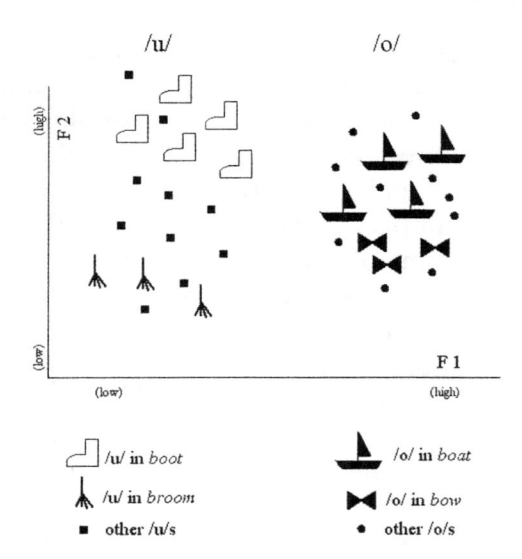

Figure 1: Hypothetical distributions of exemplars for /o/ and /u/.

situation is illustrated by Figure 1, showing exemplar locations for /o/ in *bow* and *boat*, as well as /u/ in *broom* and *boot*. The perceptual memories of in *boot* and *boat* have generally higher F2 values than most other words with the respective vowels, because the /t/ causing fronting of the round back vowels. Since some instances of the word *bow* occur in coronal contexts, some of these /o/s could be rather fronted, too.

However, some awkward and crucial issues about the relationship of word-level and phoneme-level labelling of the exemplar space are swept under the rug in Pierrehumbert (2001a). Specifically, the entire production model presupposes that the perceptual labelling of the space is simply used "in reverse" in production. When a label is activated through the speaker's lexical choice, then a region of the exemplars associated with that label is activated and guides the production. With word-level labels being associated directly with the exemplar space, it is unclear what enforces a phonological decomposition of the word in the first place. Why couldn't the exemplars of any given word provide a holistic plan for the production of that word? If this were possible, two awkward consequences would ensue. First of all, there would be no necessary reason why productions of a word would actually be subject to the persistent bias which encapsulates the historical change in progress. Recall that the allophonic principle has a structural description, and therefore entails a phonological decomposition of the word. Direct linking of words to phonetic outcomes bypasses this level of analysis entirely, and so it is unclear why the leniting bias would impact every production of the word. In fact, the general assumptions of spreading activation models (to which exemplar models are closely related) would be that frequently used activation pathways tend to be more active. High word frequency would tend to enhance the "holistic" route of word production, if such were available, thus exempting high frequency words from a historical change in progress. Obviously, this is contrary to the finding that high frequency words tend to lead Neogrammarian sound changes.

A second, and conceptually related, problem relates to the fact that Neogrammarian sound changes normally sweep through the vocabulary. Even if allophonic rules are not absolutely across the board, they are nearly across the board. Cases such as that of vowel change in Quebec French are unusual, and even in this case there are only two classes of words — the majority that undergoes the change and a semantic group that resists it. The long-term results of a system in which words activated exemplar clouds directly (without implicating a phonological decomposition) would, however, be arbitrary phonetic dispersion. Because of the cumulative nature of the perception-production loop in this model, tiny differences between words build up over time as a function of differences in their social and linguistic contexts of use. Thus, the words would disperse through the available regions of the phonetic hyperspace. The notion that words can be mapped directly to phonetic outcomes is at odds with the phonological principle, according to which human languages are characterized by the repeated use of a small number of phonological elements which are found in many different combinations to make words. Though this characterization of language is not absolutely true (as we have seen), it is approximately true and the fact that language can be approximated in this way is an important one.

In the next section, I sketch and compare two alternative models for overcoming these problems.

5. Models

The two models I will discuss share a number of features. First, in both the production system is closely tied to the perceptual system, with the same levels of representation appearing in both perception and production. As discussed, these include the lexical network itself (in which only lexeme information interests us here) and the exemplar space over which frequency distributions are built up. Secondly, in both there is an intermediate level of representation, that of phonological encoding, which has a privileged position amongst the labels over the exemplar space. It is the level at which time actually unfolds (in contrast to the lexicon and the exemplar space, which are long-term memories of linguistic events).

In production, this intermediate level corresponds directly to the level of phonological encoding and buffering found in modular feed-forward models, as discussed in section 2 above. In particular, I assume that this level represents procedural knowledge; that phonological representations of words are incrementally loaded into this buffer; that a complete phonological parse including metrical and intonational structure up to the phrasal level is assigned here. Thus, the major deviation from previous views is the radically representational concept of phonetic implementation. The contents of this buffer are not subject to phonetic implementation rules in the traditional sense. Instead, they probabilistically evoke regions of the exemplar space as production goals.

In perception, there is increasing experimental evidence for an analogous level of processing, which is termed the Fast Phonological Preprocessor (or FPP) in Pierrehumbert (2001b). This level uses language-specific but still general knowledge of the phonotactic and prosodic patterns of a language to parse the incoming speech stream. The critical function of this level is hypothesizing possible word boundaries, that is, identifying temporal locations in the speech stream at which a lexical search should be initiated. All current models of word recognition (such as Norris 1994, Vitevich & Luce 1998, Norris, McQueen & Cutler, 2000) describe word recognition in terms of words being incrementally activated as a reflex of their similarity to the speech stream. Simultaneously activated words compete through mutual inhibition, until one candidate wins over the others. There is clear evidence that staggered or partially overlapping candidates are implicitly considered during word recognition. For example, during processing of the word *festoon*, the word *tune* might be activated beginnning at the /t/. In short, multiple desynchronized word candidates are maintained in parallel as the competition plays out. However, it would be problematic to assume that fresh lexical searches are launched absolutely continuously — for example, every 5 msec, representing the temporal resolution of some digital speech processing systems. The kind of partial overlaps which have been reported arise when junctural statistics or prosody suggest that a word boundary might be present (See e.g Cutler & Norris, 1988; McQueen, 1998; Content, Dumay & Frauenfelder, 2000). The activation of *tune* in *festoon* occurs because most English words begin in a stressed syllable, and the stress is accordingly a probabilistic cue for a word boundary. The word *emu* is not necessarily activated in processing the word *honeymoon*, even though it is possible to find an acoustic subregion of this word which sounds a great deal like *emu* when played in isolation. By hypothesizing possible word boundaries, the FPP places practical bounds on the number of number of possibly staggered candidates maintained in parallel.

According to Norris et al. (2000), decontextualized phoneme decisions (as in a phoneme monitoring experiment which requires subjects to push a button for any word containing /p/) are made in a module which is distinct from the FPP and which is influenced by lexical matches (if any). This suggestion, which I take to be well-supported, liberates the FPP from the task of providing a phonemic transcription. This is a welcome result, since the FPP is a bottom-up processor and the efforts of phoneticians and speech engineers show bottom-up phonemic transcription to be extremely problematic. It is statistically fragile and it discards allophonic information which is demonstrably used in recognizing words. For example, Dahan et al. (2000) show that misleading coarticulatory information affects the time course of lexical matching as reflected in eye-tracking data. Furthermore, if subphonemic information were discarded during lexical access, then there would be no way that it could accumulate in long-term memories associated with particular words.

My conclusion, then, is that the FPP maintains extremely detailed phonetic encoding, and that its primary contribution is to add parsing information. A mental image of a grainy spectrogram decorated with a prosodic parse can provide a mnemonic for this conclusion. The results of lexical access and even post-lexical decisions can continue to add labelling to this same structure. Fragments of phonetic streams labelled in this way provide material for the labelled exemplar space.

Now, I come to two alternatives on how detailed phonetic outcomes can be associated with particular words under this model. The examples I will be using come from a pilot experiment on glottalization at a morpheme boundary, in the words *preoccupied*, *high-octane*, *overarching*, *realignment*, and *reenact* as produced in sentence contexts. Such glottalization is not contrastive in English, and it shows a considerable range of phonetic variation, from a full glottal stop to creaking voicing to a merely pressed voice quality. The target words all have somewhat idiosyncratic meanings, with the least familiar to foreign readers possibly being *high-octane* on the meaning of "forceful". Baseline data were also collected on the rate of glottalization at word boundaries for vowel initial words following a function word, in sequences such as "to Egypt" and "are available". In this experiment, stress was manipulated through design of the materials, and speech style was manipulated through direct instructions to the five subjects, who were Northwestern undergraduates enrolled in introductory linguistics courses. The summary data show a cumulative interaction of stress, morphosyntactic status, and speech style, as shown in the following table. The patterns shown were also found within the speech of individuals. The lexical issue which appears in these data is the relationship of allophony in a base form to allophony in a derived form. In the discussion, I will also return to some of the phenomena summarized above which are not exemplified in this data set.

124 Janet B. Pierrehumbert

Table 1:

	Stress-Clear	Stress-Normal	Unstress-Clear	Unstress-Normal
BaseL	100%	80%	52%	8%
Mor. Complex	75%	20%	12%	0%

The most straightforward extension of the modular feed-forward model would seek to model the probability distributions for the phonetics of individual words via links from the lexemes to units of phonological encoding. Note that all of the words in the data set have idiosyncratic meanings, and thus must be lexical entries. In order to generate the various outcomes, this model requires that glottalization be available as a category in the phonological encoding. I will transcribe it as a glottal stop, /ʔ/, despite its wide phonetic range.

Figure 2 sketches how this would generate the contrasting outcomes for the two words *high-octane* and *reenact*, each of which has glottalization at the VV hiatus some of the time. In order to illustrate the point, rates of glottalization in this figure are taken from data on these stress configurations in the clear speech condition, since no glottalization of stem-initial schwa was found in the normal speech condition.

Note that the final distribution of glottalization for *reenact* shows a less frequent and less extensive glottalization than for *high-octane*. The prosodic parse for *high-octane* shows stress on the second vowel, and the exemplar cloud associated with this position has more frequent and more forceful glottalization than for the unstressed case. In a classic modular feed-forward model, this regularity would be described by having two different phonetic implementation rules, one for the stressed condition and one for the unstressed condition. In the present model, these rules are replaced by associations between phonological fragments (including relevant prosodic structure) and probability distributions over the degree of glottal constriction.

Now, let us consider the speaker who glottalizes more in *high-octane* than in *reenter*. This outcome can be encoded, if not necessarily explained in the model, provided that the mental representa-

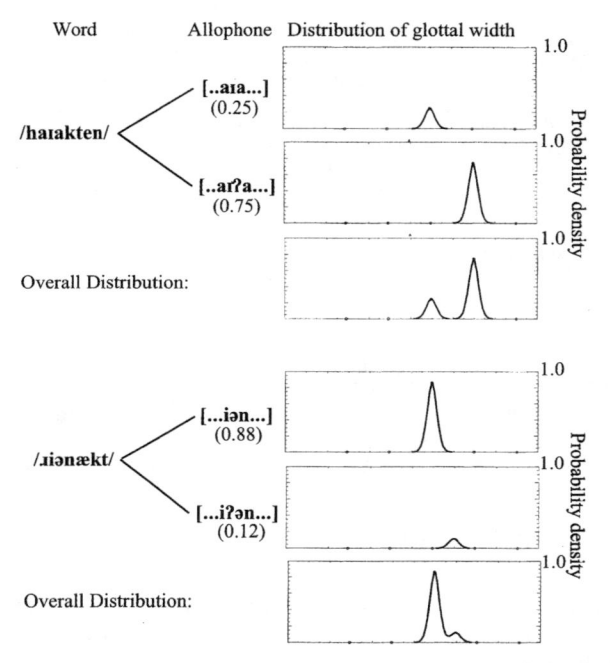

Figure 2: Contributing and total frequency distributions for degree of glottal adduction (spread ... constricted), with two rules for glottal stop insertion.

tions maintain implicit frequency counters on the pronunciations as encountered in perception. (Rates of glottalization in this figure are taken from pooled data on these words in the normal speech condition.)

By comparing the displays for *high-octane* in Figures 2 and 3, we can also see how clear speech style would be modelled under this approach. It must affect the probabilities for the rules mapping to allophonic outcomes, in order to model the fact that glottal stop insertion is most frequent in clear speech. In addition it must affect the force and speed of articulation, a factor not illustrated here.

Speaking more generally, assume that the model maintains for each word a probability distribution over some number of categorically different phonetic outcomes. For words such as *cat*, these might be an aspirated released /t/, a plain /t/, and unreleased plain /t/, a glottalized /t/, and a glottal stop, providing in effect a five-step scale along the dimension of [spread glottis] − [constricted

126   Janet B. Pierrehumbert

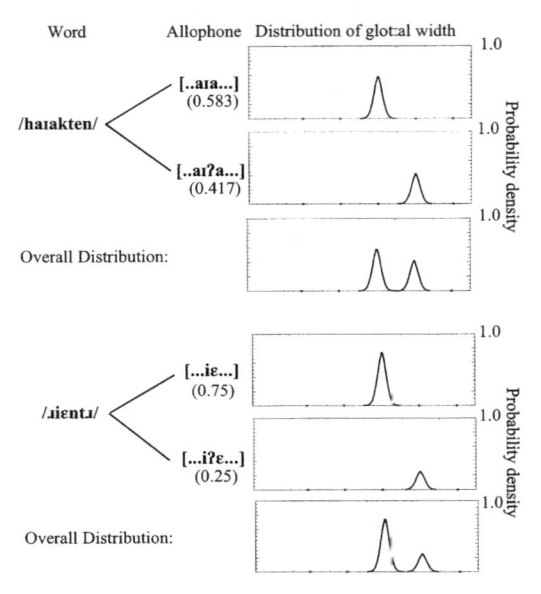

Figure 3: Contributing and total frequency distributions for degree of glottal adduction (spread ... constricted) for two words with idiosyncratically different rates of glottalization.

glottis]. Production of each outcome in turn relates to a probability distribution over the phonetic space. In this case, the total space of outcomes for each word is a weighted sum of the distributions for the variants. This can be conceptualized as a set of mountains which maintain their location but differ in their height, as in Figure 4a. However if the distributions are wide compared to the separation between them, the peaks in the result need not correspond to the peaks in the underlying distributions. This is shown in 4b, which provides a strong appearance of gradient effects over the phonetic space. In particular, a variable mixture of two distributions can cause the mean and even the mode to exhibit a gradient dependence on the proportion describing the mixture. An approach in which superficial distributions such as 4b are uniformly attributed to mixtures of underlying categories will be termed the "secret categories" approach. Since a distribution such as 4b can arise mathematically either as a wide distribution for a single label, or a mixture of the different distributions for a set of labels, further considerations must be brought to bear to evaluate this approach.

Word-specific phonetics   127

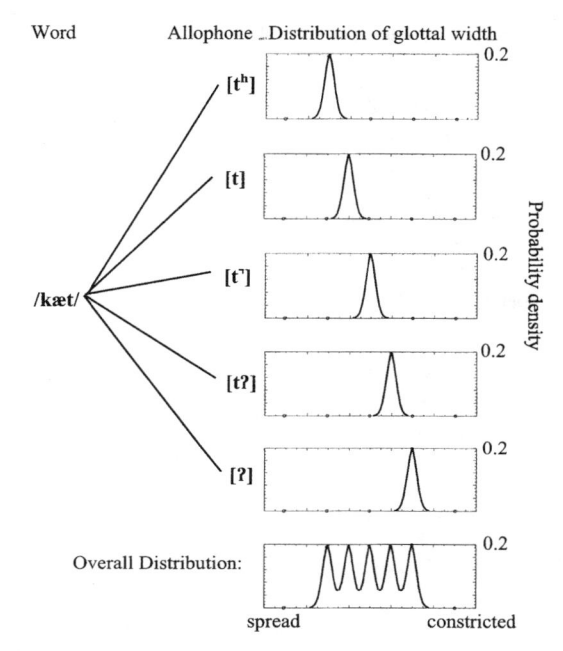

Figure 4a: Mixtures of sharp categories.

A second model, and the one I will advocate, draws on the proposals made in Johnson (1997) about speaker normalization. Johnson (1997) builds on findings that people have long term memories of the specific voices in which words were spoken to propose that the exemplar space is labelled by speaker as well as phonologically. Speaker normalization occurs through attentional weighting of the exemplars. For example, in attempting to classify an incoming stimulus as /ɛ/ or /ɪ/, the basic statistical choice rule would be sensitive to all /ɛ/s or /ɪ/s in the neighbourhood of the incoming stimulus. If I know I am listening to my 11-year old daughter, however, I can weight more highly exemplars which originated from her speech. Since her vocal tract is shorter than that of an adult, the net effect would be to shift the F2 boundary for /ɛ/ versus /ɪ/ in this perceptual classification, a typical example of successful speaker normalization. Extended to production, this would mean that activating memories of a particular speaker does not in itself cause speech to come pouring out. However, if one is

128 *Janet B. Pierrehumbert*

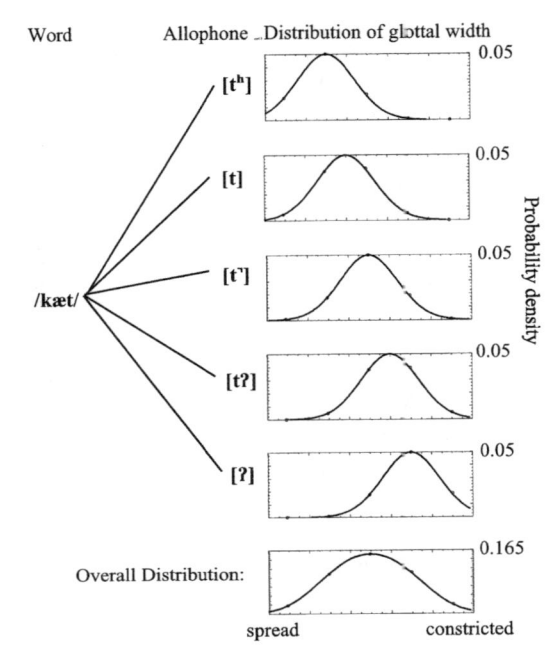

Figure 4b: Mixtures of soft categories.

speaking, then activating memories of a particular speaker can bias the productions which occur. The productions would be biased towards phonetic imitations of the speaker in question, because exemplars of that speaker's productions would be more activated and thus acquire a disproportionate role in shaping production targets.

Implementing this model is a very straightforward extension of the equations introduced above. For each exemplar e_i, define a weighting coefficient A_i^t. This is the extent of activation of exemplar e_i at time t due to its originating in the current word. The value of this coefficient depends on time because the activation is temporary. Now, recall that a weighting coefficient related to the temporal decay of the exemplars was already included in the model, namely.

$$(5) \qquad exp\left(-\frac{t - T_i}{\tau}\right)$$

The overall weighting of the exemplar can then be treated as a product of our two coefficients (for some appropriate choice of units).

(6) $\quad exp\left(-\dfrac{t - T_i}{\tau}\right) A_i^t$

This overall weighting will then be active at all three critical points in the dynamics of the model: Highly weighted exemplars will play a stronger role in classification. They will be more frequently selected as the core of a production target. And they will be more influential in the aggregate target computed from the neighbourhood of the core. An important corollary of the weighting scheme is that the influence of particular words on phonetic outcomes is secondary, with the actual phonological makeup of the words providing the primary influence. That is, individual words can be shifted or biased within the space provided by their phonological makeup, but not into regions of phonetic hyperspace which are not used generally in the language. This is correct, and goes towards explaining why many of the patterns in question have only been found recently as large scale studies become possible.

This model will tend to transfer allophony from a base form to a morphologically related complex form, without requiring an allophone to be projected as a category. For the glottalization, this works as follows, assuming that word-initial glottalization is provided by a direct mapping from the triggering context (the word-initial vowel) to dimensions of the exemplar space such as vocal fold adduction. Consider the word *realign*. Consider first the evolution of the situation for an initial condition in which *realign* has no glottal attack on the second syllable, just like *realize*. (1) When *realign* is activated, activation spreads to *align*. (2) Producing *realign* involves producing a schwa in the second syllable. Examples of the schwa which originate from this word are weighted in establishing the production plan. In the initial condition, these have no glottal attack. (3) Because of the spreading activation of *align*, exemplars originating from this word as also weighted. These exemplars have a glottal attack. (4) *realign* is therefore probabilistically produced with a glottal attack, though on average less than *align*. (5) Tokens of *realign* which have glottalization update the exemplar distributions (of other speakers), as do ones which lack glottalization.

Now consider the contrary case, in which *realign* is productively generated as a neologism from *re-* and *align*. Under this scenario, the initial condition is that in which the word *align* is actually produced, and therefore one would find exactly the same rate of glottal attacks in both words. If *realign* becomes stored in the lexicon as a unit, then its production entails activation of the exemplar space for the VV hiatus, and this exemplar space will include exemplars of unanalyzed words such as *realize*. Though tokens of *realign* (insofar as they are available) are positively weighted in establishing the production goal, they are not the sole factor. In this case, *realign* will evolve to shower fewer and weaker glottal attacks than *align*. To summarize, then, the pronunciation of nondecomposed *realign* will tend to evolve towards the phonetic pattern of *align*, to the extent to which the word *align* is perceived within *realign*. The pronunciation of transparently decomposed *realign* will evolve toward the phonetic pattern of *realize*, to the extent that the word becomes lexicalized as a whole. If the word is partially or sporadically decomposed, the phonetic pattern will end up in the middle. The underlying assumption, is that morphological decomposition is gradient. This assumption follows from current morphological processing models notably Caramazza, Laudanna & Romani (1988), Frauenfelder & Schreuder (1992), Schreuder & Baayen (1995), Wurm (1997), Baayen & Schreuder (1999), and Hay (2000). Unlike generative linguistic models, in which a given word either is or is not morphologically decomposed, the processing models suggest that examples can be found all along the scale from fully simplex to fully decomposed. The glottalization results in Table 1 are what the model would predict for semi-decomposed words — for each stress and speech style condition, the rate of glottal attacks within the complex words is less than that at a full-fledged word boundary. The model also predicts gradient allophonic results as a reflex of gradient decomposability. This is exactly the finding of the Hay (2000) experiment on /t/ allophony discussed above.

Of course, one would not wish to deny that transfer can also occur at a categorical level. Examples are provided by speech errors such as *fat* for the past tense of *fit* (under the pressure of *sit/ sat*); and the paradigm levelling which is widely attested in historical morphology. In such cases, however, one observes two qualitatively different outcomes without examples of any in between. Speech errors such as *fat* do not necessarily imply the existence of a set of intermediate cases along the vowel height dimension.

The model predicts a cumulative effect between the probability/ degree of glottalization, and any bias represented by the parameter λ. λ was introduced to describe a persistent leniting bias. However, the work by Lindblom to which it hearks back proposes a continuous scale of hypo- to hyper-articulation (Lindblom, 1984) The clear speech style in the data set obviously provides an example of hyper-articulation. The results of Table 1 are broadly in line with prediction. They give percentages of tokens which crossed a threshhold of glottalization. All of these percentages are shifted up under the clear speech condition, preserving, however, the rank ordering of the cases. More detailed consideration of these numbers raises some issues, since λ only shifts the degree of some gesture which is already planned, and does not bring it into being if it did not exist in the first place. The shift of 80 to 100 percent (for the case of a stressed word boundary), or 0 to 12 percent (for unstressed morpheme boundaries) would thus need to be interpreted as threshholding artifacts. Such numbers would follow under the assumption that a sampling of x_{target}s for the former case are all glottalized to some degree in normal speech (with 20 percent of targets showing such slight glottalization that it is below threshhold), and that the sampling x_{target}s for the latter case includes at least some number of tokens with a glottal adduction gesture, which is amenable to being strengthened. These assumptions would need to be validated with more conclusive measures, such as stereofibroscope pictures of the vocal folds. There is also a hint in the numbers that the influence of morphological relatives actually increases for the clear speech condition. If this proves to be the case, then the parameter λ is in the wrong place in the model; an effect of this type would require λ to bias the underlying sampling for the production plan, rather than shifting the production plan post-hoc.

Thus, the second model readily captures the tendency for morphologically complex forms to be influenced by the allophony of the base. It predicts that complex forms are **more** influenced by the allophony of an embedded morphological relative than by the allophony of a phonologically embedded word which is unrelated. For example, insofar as the word *mislay* is decomposed, it would be more influenced by *lay* (predicting a well-voiced /l/) than by *sleigh* (predicting a largely devoiced /l/). This prediction follows because *mislay* activates *lay*, which would then bias the set of exemplars contributing to the production goal. In contrast, *mislay* does not activate *sleigh* (in fact, it competes with it in perception). Thus *sleigh* has no particular privilege to affect the pronunciation of *mislay*, with any commonalities coming about solely from the common phonological content.

Further cases of allophonic transfers from morphological relatives are discussed in Steriade (2000) and Rialland (1986). The model predicts in particular the existence of cases in which relationship of phonetic outcomes to morphological relatedness is gradient. More large-scale experiments are needed to evaluate this prediction.

Another line of argument for the second model over the secret categories approach depends some general observations about categorization systems. When the equations presented above are applied iteratively in a simulation of the production-perception loop, two qualitatively different outcomes readily arise for cases like Figure 4b. In one outcome (representing a parameter range with a high degree of entrenchment), the distributions are gradually sharpened up until they become well separated, as in Figure 4a. The other outcome (representing a lesser degree of entrenchment), the distributions spread out. Over more and more intervals of the phonetic space, a competition arises between a more frequent label and a less frequent one. In this case, more and more tokens are assimilated to the more frequent categories until the less frequent labels are gobbled up and the distinctions in the system have collapsed. Notice that the slightest difference in frequency tends to become amplified over iteration, since the perceptual classification is de facto biased towards the higher frequency label in any neighborhood. I have not actually been able to find a parameter range for this model which shows stable overlapping distributions. Given the complex nonlinear character of this model, there is at present no mathematical proof that all cases such as 4b are unstable. However, phonetic typology strongly suggests that situations such as 4b evolve towards either a sharper category system or a category collapse. The most studied cases of overlapping phonetic distributions are the "near-mergers" discovered by Labov, Karan & Miller (1991) in speech communities with varied dialects. In these cases, the overlapping categories carry a much higher functional load than those discussed here, because they distinguish words for some speakers and also provide socioeconomic information about speakers. Nonetheless, the actual perceptual discriminability of the labels is less than a statistical phonetic analysis would support, and the labels tend to collapse. The suggestion that the secret and non-meaning-bearing categories of the phonetic implementation system show stability properties which are not found even for lexically distinctive phonological units appears to be highly problematic. The second model makes it possible to reserve the projection of categories for situations when when a phonetic contrast is plainly bimodal and/or carries a high functional load.

More generally, the secret categories model relies on something like an IPA fine transcription to achieve coverage of the phonetic gradients which are observed. This is a level I have attacked elsewhere on the grounds that it has difficulty modelling the gradient cumulative effects in phonetic implementaion which are observed in experiments on continuous speech. (See Pierrehumbert & Beckman, 1988 regarding f_0, and Pierrehumbert & Talkin, 1992, regarding aspiration and glottalization). Direct mapping of more abstract entities to quantitative parameters meets with more success. A similarly broad issue is the reliance of the secret categories model on multiple representations for the same word. As argued in Bybee (2000a), there are strong cognitive pressures to maintain only a single representation for any given word. Lastly, the second model is more parsimonious. Findings on speaker normalization and long-term memory of particular voices strongly suggests that we need attentional weighting on the exemplar space. In fact, a weighting scheme is needed to describe any kind of contextual effect which gradiently shifts category boundaries in either production or perception. Reusing this independently motivated device would appear to be preferable to proliferating categories over anything that would otherwise be viewed as a phonetic continuum.

6. Conclusion

The empirical studies which gave rise to modular feed-forward models of speech production provide strong evidence for distinguishing three levels in the cognitive system: lexemes, phonological encoding, and quantitative knowledge of phonetic outcomes. These levels are found in both perception and production. The models are successful in capturing the productiveness of speech processing and the existence of across-the-board effects.

More recent and detailed studies show that phonetic outcomes are not as across-the-board as they originally appeared. A number of cases have come to light in which allophonic details are systematically associated with words. Some of these effects (most notably those involving word accessibility in context) may arise on-line, but others are difficult to explain without assuming that individual words have associated phonetic distributions.

Exemplar-based production models provide a method for integrating these findings with prior work. Phonetic implementation rules are modelled through a correspondence between phonological labels and frequency distributions over the phonetic space. Individual words can bias the set of exemplars which serve as production goals. By assuming that words bias productions — rather than providing holistic production goals — the approach captures the fact that word-specific phonetic effects are second-order effects. The approach also makes it possible to capture cases of allophonic transfer between morphological relatives. Because of averaging in the system, it can capture gradient effects related to degree of morphological decomposibility. It establishes a connection between the likelihood of effects and their degree. Interactions at more abstract levels of representation must also be posited to handle nongradient effects.

Weighting of exemplars by individual words is not the only weighting in the system. Sociostylistic register and other contextual and attentional factors are clearly important. For this reason, the system does not predict an exhaustive match between perception and production. If speech tokens were perceived but not committed to long-term memory, they would fail to influence production. If the contexts for perception and production differed, differences in the exemplar sets activated for any given label would also ensue. Likewise, the connection of personal identity to sociostylistic register could also give rise to differences.

References

Baayen, R. H. & Schreuder, R.
   1999   War and Peace: Morphemes and Full Forms in a Noninteractive Activation Parallel Dual-Route Model. *Brain and Language*, **68**, 213−217.

Bybee, J.
   2000a   Lexicalization of sound change and alternating environments. In Broe, M. and Pierrehumbert, J. (eds.), *Papers in Laboratory Phonology V: Acquisition and the Lexicon*, (pp. 250−269). Cambridge UK: Cambridge University Press.

Bybee, J.
   2000b   The phonology of the lexicon; evidence from lexical diffusion. In Barlow, M. & Kemmer, S. (eds.), *Usage-Based Models of Language*, (pp. 65−85). Stanford: CSLI.

Bybee, J.
   2001   *Phonology and Language Use*. Cambridge UK: Cambridge University Press.

Caramazza, A., Laudanna, A. & Romani, C.
   1988   Lexical access and inflectional morphology. *Cognition*, **28**, 297−332.

Content, A., Dumay, N. & Frauenfelder, U.
   2000   The role of syllable structure in lexical segmentation: Helping listeners avoid mondegreens. In A. Cutler, J. M. McQueen & R. Zondervan, *Proceedings of SWAP (Spoken Word Access Processes)*, Nijmegen, Max Planck Institute for Psycholinguistics. 39−42.

Cutler, A. & Norris, D.
   1988   The role of strong syllables in segmentation for lexical access. *Journal of Experimental Psychology: Human Perception and Performance*, **14**, 113−121.

Dahan, D., Magnuson, J. S., Tanenhaus, M. K. & Hogan, E. M.
  2000   Tracking the time course of subcategorical mismatches on lexical access: Evidence for lexical competition. In A. Cutler, J. M. McQueen & R. Zondervan (eds.), *Proceedings of SWAP (Spoken Word Access Processes)*, Max-Planck Institute for Psycholinguistics, Nijmegen, (pp. 67–70).

de Jong, K., Beckman, M. E. & Edwards, J.
  1993   The Interplay between prosodic structure and coarticulation. *Language and Speech*, 36, 197–212.

de Jong, K. J.
  1995   The supraglottal articulation of prominence in English: Linguistic stress as localized hyperarticulation. *J. Acoust. Soc. Am.*, 97, 491–504.

Dilley, L., Shattuck-Hufnagel, S. & Ostendorf, M.
  1996   Glottalization of word-initial vowels as a function of prosodic structure. *Journal of Phonetics*, 24, 423–444.

Frauenfelder, U. H. & Schreuder, R.
  1992   Constraining Psycholinguistic Models of Morphological Processing and Representation: The Role of Productivity. In G. Mooij & J. van Marle, (eds.), *Yearbook of Morphology 1991*. Dordrecht: Kluwer Academic Publishers. 165–185.

Goldinger, S. D.
  1996   Words and voices: Episodic traces in spoken word identification and recognition memory. *Journal of Experimental Psychology: Learning, Memory, and Cognition*, 22, 1166–1183.

Goldinger, S. D.
  2000   The role of perceptual episodes in lexical processing. In A. Cutler, J. M. McQueen & R. Zondervan, *Proceedings of SWAP (Spoken Word Access Processes)*, Nijmegen, Max Planck Institute for Psycholinguistics. 155–159.

Harrington, J., Palethorpe, S. & Watson, C. I.
  2000   Does the Queen speak the Queen's English? *Nature*, 408, 927–928.

Hay, J. B.
  2000   *Causes and Consequences of Word Structure*. PhD dissertation, Northwestern University. (Downloadable from http://www.ling.canterbury.ac.nz/jen/)

Hay, J. B., Jannedy, S. & Mendoza-Denton, N.
  1999   Oprah and /ay/: Lexical Frequency, Referee Design and Style. Paper R3TEL1, *Proceedings of the 14th International Congress of Phonetic Sciences*. 1389–1392.

Johnson, K.
  1997   Speech perception without speaker normalization. In K. Johnson & J. W. Mullennix (eds.), *Talker Variability in Speech Processing*, (pp. 145–166). San Diego: Academic Press.

Keating, P., Cho, T., Fougeron, C. & C. Hsu
    forthcoming   Domain-initial articulatory strengthening in four languages. In R. Odgen, J. Local & R. Temple (eds.), *Papers in Laboratory Phonology VI*. Cambridge: Cambridge University Press.

Kirchner, R.
    forthcoming   Preliminary thoughts on "phonologisation" within an exemplar based speech processing model. *UCLA Working Papers in Linguistics* Volume 6.

Labov, W., Karan, M. & Miller, C.
    1991   Near mergers and the suspension of phonemic contrast. *Language Variation and Change*, **3**, 33–74.

Levelt, W. J. M.
    1989   *Speaking*. Cambridge MA: MIT Press.

Lindblom, B.
    1983   Economy of speech gestures. In MacNeilage, P. (ed.), *The Production of Speech*. (pp. 217–245). New York: Springer-Verlag.

McQueen, J. M.
    1998   Segmentation of Continuous Speech Using Phonotactics. *Journal of Memory and Language*, **39**, 21–46.

Mendoza-Denton, N.
    1997   *Chicana/Mexicana Identity and Linguistic Variation: An Ethnographic and Sociolinguistics Study of Gang Affiliation in an Urban High School*. Ph.D dissertation, Stanford University.

Norris, D., McQueen, J. M. & Cutler, A.
    2000   Merging information in speech recognition: Feedback is never necessary. *Behavioral and Brain Sciences*, **3**, 299–325.

Phillips, B. S.
    1984   Word Frequency and the actuation of sound change. *Language*, **60**, 320–42.

Pierrehumbert, J.
    1994   Prosodic Effects on Glottal Allophones. In O. Fujimura & M. Hirano (eds.), *Vocal Fold Physiology: voice quality control*. (pp. 39–60). San Diego: Singular Publishing Group.

Pierrehumbert, J.
    2000   The phonetic grounding of phonology. *Les Cahiers de l'ICP, Bulletin de la Communication Parlé*, **5**, 7–23.

Pierrehumbert, J.
    2001a   Exemplar dynamics: Word frequency, lenition, and contrast. In J. Bybee & P. Hopper (eds.), *Frequency Effects and the Emergence of Linguistic Structure*. (pp. 137–157). John Benjamins, Amsterdam.

Pierrehumbert, J.
    2001b   Why phonological constraints are so coarse-grained. In J. M. McQueen & A. Cutler (eds.), *SWAP* special issue, *Language and Cognitive Process*, **16**, 691–698.

Pierrehumbert, J. & Beckman, M. E.
1988   *Japanese Tone Structure.* LI Monograph, **15**. Cambridge, MA: MIT Press.
Pierrehumbert, J., Beckman, M. E. & Ladd, D. R.
2001   Conceptual Foundations of Phonology as a Laboratory Science. In Burton-Roberts, N., Carr, P. & Docherty, G. (eds.), *Phonological Knowledge*, (pp. 273–304). Oxford, UK: Oxford University Press.
Pierrehumbert, J. & S. Frisch,
1996   Synthesizing Allophonic Glottalization, J. P. H. van Santen, R. Sproat, J. Olive, & J. Hirschberg, (eds.), *Progress in Speech Synthesis*, (pp. 9–26). New York: Springer-Verlag.
Pierrehumbert, J. & D. Talkin,
1992   Lenition of /h/ and glottal stop. In G. Doherty & D. R. Ladd (eds.), *Papers in Laboratory Phonology II: Gesture, Segment, Prosody.* (pp. 90–179. Cambridge, UK: Cambridge Univ. Press.
Rialland, A.
1986   Schwa et syllabes en Français. In L. Wetzels & E. Sezer (eds), *Studies in Compensatory Lengthening.* (pp. 187–226). Dordrecht: Foris Publications.
Roelofs, A.
1997   The WEAVER model of word-form encoding in speech production. *Cognition*, **64**, 249–284.
Rosenbaum, D. A., Engelbrecht, S. E., Bushe, M. M. & Loukopoulos, L. D.
1993   A model for reaching control. *Acta Psychologica*, **82**, 237–250.
Schreuder, R. & Baayen, R. H.
1995   Modeling Morphological Processing. In I. B. Felman (ed.), *Morphological Aspects of Language Production.* (pp. 131–156). Hillsdale, NJ: Lawrence Erlbaum Associates,
Shattuck-Hufnagel, S.
1979   Speech errors as evidence for a serial order mechanism in sentence production. In W. E. Cooper & E. C. T. Walker (eds.), *Sentence Processing: Psycholinguistic Studies Presented to Merrill Garrett.* Hillsdale, NJ: Lawrence Erlbaum.
Steriade, D.
2000   Paradigm Uniformity and the phonetics-phonology interface. In M. Broe & J. Pierrehumbert (eds.), *Papers in Laboratory Phonology V: Acquisition and the Lexicon.* (pp. 313–335). Cambridge UK: Cambridge University Press.
Sternberg, S., Monsell, S., Knoll, R. L. & Wright, C. E.
1978   The latency and duration of rapid movement sequences: Comparisons of speech and typewriting. In G. E. Stelmach (ed.), *Information Processing in Motor Control and Learning.* New York: Academic Press.

Sternberg, S., Wright, C. E., Knoll, R. L. & Monsell, S.
    1980   Motor programs in rapid speech: Additional evidence. In R. A. Cole (ed.), *Perception and Production of Fluent Speech*. Hillsdale NJ: Lawrence Erlbaum Associates.
Vitevich, M. & Luce, P.
    1998   When words compete: Levels of processing in perception of spoken words. *Psychological Science*, **9**: 4, 325–329.
Wright, R.
    1997   Lexical competition and reduction in speech: A preliminary report. Research on spoken language processing: Progress report **21**. Bloomington, IN: Indiana University. (Related paper also forthcoming in Papers in Laboratory Phonology VI).
Wurm, L. H.
    1997   Auditory Processing of Prefixed English Words is Both Continuous and Decompositional. *Journal of Memory and Language*, **37**, 438–461.
Yaeger-Dror, M.
    1996   Phonetic evidence for the evolution of lexical classes: The case of a Montreal French vowel shift. In G. Guy, C. Feagin, J. Baugh & D. Schiffrin (eds.), *Towards a Social Science of Language* (pp. 263–287). Philadelphia: Benjamins.
Yaeger-Dror, M. & Kemp, W.
    1992   Lexical classes in Montreal French. *Language and Speech*, **35**, 251–293.

Phoneme frequency in spoken word reconstruction

Danny R. Moates, Z. S. Bond and Verna Stockmal

> Words were made of the strong bones of consonants with the vowels floating above like invisible spirits (cited in Pickett, 1999).

Abstract

In the word reconstruction task, participants hear a nonword and are asked to change either one vowel or one consonant to produce a word. Van Ooijen (1996) found that participants were generally better and faster at changing vowels than at changing consonants and preferred to change a vowel if given a choice. She labeled these effects "vowel mutability." Vowel mutability has been replicated in spoken Spanish, spoken Dutch, and printed English. There is at present no confirmed explanation for vowel mutability.

We investigated whether the frequency of use of target phonemes accounts for vowel mutability, comparing high and low frequency vowels and consonants in target words. The results showed a significant vowel mutability effect and a significant effect for phoneme frequency in certain conditions, but the two effects did not interact. Hence, phoneme frequency does not explain vowel mutability.

We review current hypotheses about the source of vowel mutability and models of spoken word recognition for an explanation of the phoneme frequency effect. No model suggests an explanation for phoneme frequency effects in word reconstruction; however, a strategy hypothesis may offer an explanation.

1. Introduction

When given a non-word such as /wɛdo/, listeners generally find it easier to convert it to *widow* /wɪdo/ than to *meadow* /mɛdo/. This example represents the fundamental findings of the word reconstruction task, introduced by van Ooijen (1996). Participants are given a non-word and instructed to change it to a real word by substituting just one consonant or just one vowel. Van Ooijen found that participants made fewer errors in changing a vowel than in changing a consonant and were generally faster in changing a vowel. When permitted to change either a vowel or a consonant, participants made vowel changes more quickly and accurately than consonant changes. Collectively, van Ooijen (1996) labeled these effects vowel mutability.

Van Ooijen (1996) proposed that vowel mutability results from a mechanism for dealing with uncertainty about precise vowel identity. That is, in ordinary conversation listeners are often uncertain about vowel identity because of factors such as speech rate, speaker dialect, and phonemic inventory (pp. 579–580). She concludes by pointing to the importance of an investigation of the relation between vowel mutability and the size of the vowel inventory of a language. If the size of a language's vowel inventory contributes to vowel mutability, then languages with a small, highly distinctive set of vowels should not show vowel mutability.

Marks, Moates, Bond & Vazquez (submitted) tested the effect of vowel inventory with Spanish, which has only five vowels, and found a robust vowel mutability effect. Moates & Russell (1999) found that vowel mutability is not limited to spoken language. Cutler, Sebastián-Gallés, Vilageliu & van Ooijen (2000) investigated vowel mutability in both Spanish and Dutch, a language with a vowel inventory roughly equal to its consonant inventory. They found the effect in both languages and concluded that the size of vowel inventories does not explain vowel mutability. Instead, Cutler et al. (2000) suggested that listeners' performance is determined by intrinsic differences between the information provided by vowels and that provided by consonants.

According to Landauer & Streeter (1973), there are significant differences in the distribution of phonemes in high and low frequency words. For example, /n, l, t/ occur more often in high frequency words, whereas /z, p, g/ occur more often in low frequency words. They found that these differences had perceptual consequences. High frequency words containing phonemes characteristic of high frequency words were more intelligible in noise than equally high frequency words containing phonemes characteristic of low frequency words. This finding suggests that there may also be a phoneme frequency effect occurring within the word reconstruction task. We offer here the hypothesis that the frequency of use of the phoneme being recovered influences the ease of reconstructing the target word.

We distinguish between the frequency of phoneme types and the frequency of phoneme tokens. The frequency of phoneme types is the frequency with which individual phonemes occur in the words of the language. For example /n/ occurs in more words than any other phoneme in English (Shriberg & Kent, 1982). The frequency of phoneme tokens, however, takes account of the fact that some words – and hence their phonemes – are used very often, and other words and their phonemes are used rarely. Thus, /n/ not only occurs in many words, but it also occurs in *and*, *in*, and *not*, which are among the most frequently used words in English. An estimate of phoneme token frequency is available in Mines, Hanson & Shoup (1978), who recorded everyday conversations in a sample of 26 adult speakers, transcribed approximately 10 minutes of spontaneous speech for each speaker, and tallied the frequency of use for each phoneme (token frequency) in these conversations. The data base contains 103,887 phoneme tokens. The norms show relative frequency of use for each phoneme. The schwa is the most frequent, at 7.30%, followed by /n/ at 6.72%. These norms offer an estimate of token frequencies for American English phonemes, and it is these norms that we have used to construct the materials described below.

In the present study, participants were required to reconstruct a word by changing a consonant (consonant condition), a vowel (vowel condition), or any segment (that is, although a target could be reconstructed by either a consonant or vowel change, the participants were instructed to simply change one segment (free choice)). The words to be reconstructed varied in the frequency of the phoneme to be recovered. A portion of the words for both vowel and consonant targets required reconstructing a word that contained a high frequency phoneme not found in the non-word. For example, the nonword /sedli/ had the vowel target word /sædly/ *sadly* in which the vowel /æ/ is a high frequency vowel.

Similarly, the nonword /plos/ had the consonant target word /klos/ *close* in which the consonant /k/ is a high frequency consonant. The remainder of the words for both vowel and consonant targets required reconstructing a word that contained a low frequency phoneme not found in the non-word. For example, the nonword /sedli/ had the consonant target word /sefli/ *safely* in which the /f/ consonant is a low frequency consonant, and the nonword /plos/ had the vowel target word /plʌs/ *plus* in which the /ʌ/ vowel is a low frequency vowel. In the consonant condition, participants were expected to reconstruct /sefli/ *safely* from the nonword /sedli/, and in the vowel condition they were expected to reconstruct /sædli/ *sadly* from that same nonword. In the free-choice condition, participants could reconstruct either /sædly/ or /sefli/, whichever they preferred. Within these conditions, we offered the following hypotheses.

1.1 Hypotheses

1.1.1 Forced choice

The vowel condition produces fewer errors in reconstructing words containing the high frequency vowels than in reconstructing words containing the low frequency vowels. Similarly, the consonant condition produces fewer errors in reconstructing words containing the high frequency consonants than in reconstructing words containing the low frequency consonants. This hypothesis assumes that phoneme token frequency, analogous to word frequency, influences ease of access to lexical entries.

1.1.2 Free choice

In the free-choice condition participants produce more correct words containing the high frequency phonemes than words containing the low frequency phonemes. This hypothesis also assumes that phoneme token frequency influences ease of access to lexical entries.

1.1.3 Frequency

The frequency of occurrence of target phonemes is responsible for the vowel mutability effect. Because target phonemes are matched on phoneme token frequency for both vowels and consonants, there should be no difference between vowels and consonants except for the frequency effects described in Hypotheses 1.1.1 and 1.1.2.

2. Method

2.1 Participants

Ninety-one students in introductory courses in Psychology or Hearing and Speech Sciences participated for a small amount of course credit. All participants were native speakers of American English and reported normal speech and hearing.

2.2 Materials

Fifty-four non-words were created. Each non-word could be changed into two different English words by altering either one vowel or one consonant, e.g., /hʌndəl/ could be changed to /hændəl/ *handle* by changing the vowel or to /bʌndəl/ *bundle* by changing the first consonant. The goal was for each non-word to have exactly two real word neighbors, one created by changing a vowel, the other created by changing a consonant. That goal was met for 48 of the 54 non-words.

The phonemes which had to be substituted into an item in order to make a real word were the target phonemes. Thirteen vowel target phonemes were selected to go with 13 consonant target phonemes of similar phoneme token frequency. Each of the 13 vowel target phonemes appeared in one or more of the 54 vowel target words, and each of the 13 consonant target phonemes appeared in one or more of the 54 consonant target words. It was not possible to match the token frequency of the target vowel and target consonant for a particular non-word, but across the two sets of 13 vowel target phonemes and 13 consonant target phonemes, the token frequencies were equivalent (mean for high frequency vowels = 2.74, mean for high frequency consonants = 2.64, t = 0.23, p = 0.83, df = 11; mean for low frequency vowels = 1.03, mean for low frequency consonants = 0.91, t = 0.56, p = 0.59, df = 11). These high and low frequency sets differed significantly in token frequency (mean for high frequency vowels = 2.74, mean for low frequency vowels = 1.03, t = 4.54, p <0.001, df = 11; mean for high frequency consonants = 2.64, mean for low frequency consonants = 0.91, t = 5.79, p < .001, df = 11). Frequency information for each phoneme is given in Table 1.

Several factors were controlled in selecting materials. First, the frequency of the target words was balanced between vowel words and consonant words (mean for vowels = 29.46; mean for consonants = 31.74, t = 0.24, p = 0.81, df = 106), using the actual values (from a corpus of 1,014,000 lemmas) from the Francis & Kučera (1982) corpus. Word frequencies for target words with high and low frequency consonants and vowels were also balanced (high frequency vowel word mean = 25.06, low frequency vowel word mean = 34.86, t = 0.37, p > .05, df = 55; high frequency consonant word mean = 37.58; low frequency consonant word mean = 25.50, t = 0.67, p > .05, df = 24). Second, a few of the non-words could be reconstructed as more than two possible words. The numbers of possible vowel and consonant words were balanced (mean for vowels = 1.11, mean for consonants = 1.04). Third, for half the items the phoneme replacing the vowel preceded the phoneme replacing the consonant, and in the other half the order was reversed. Fourth, in about half the items (41%) the frequency of the word created by changing a vowel was greater than the frequency of the word created by changing a consonant, and the reverse was true for the other half of the items. Fifth, in 96%

Table 1: Token frequencies (in percent) and number of tokens for vowel and consonant target phonemes

Vowel	Token Frequency	Number of Tokens	Consonant	Token Frequency	Number of Tokens
High Frequency					
i	3.69	4	d	3.33	8
ɪ	3.64	4	k	3.10	12
ɛ	3.21	5	m	2.99	1
ai	2.97	4	z	2.75	4
æ	2.25	7	b	1.90	5
o	1.85	3	p	1.79	6
e	1.57	8			
Mean	2.74			2.64	
Low Frequency					
ʌ	1.46	7	f	1.55	2
a	1.43	1	h	1.31	3
u	1.13	3	g	1.18	5
ɔ	0.77	4	θ	0.70	1
ʊ	0.76	1	dʒ	0.56	3
au	0.64	3	ʃ	0.56	2
			tʃ	0.50	2
Mean	1.03			0.91	

of the possible vowel words, the vowel change occurred before the uniqueness point of the word and similarly for 91% of the possible consonant words. Finally, the location of the phoneme to be changed was distributed in approximately the same proportions across the beginning, middle, and end positions of the non-words (first, middle, or last third of phonemes) for both vowels (.37, .48, and .15, respectively) and consonants (.44, .31, and .24, respectively). An additional nine non-words were created to serve as practice items.

All 54 non-words were tape recorded by a male native speaker of American English who produced the words in citation form. The speaker was originally from a southern state and so tended to produce relatively high versions of unstressed vowels. The speaker used the vowel /ɑ/ in words such as /kɑstlɪ/ *costly*, as is common for residents of the Midwest. To ensure that the non-words corresponded to their target words, the speaker silently spoke the two target words before speaking aloud the non-word, e.g., *cobra* /kobrə/, *zebra* /zibrə/, /kibrə/. Each non-word was spoken twice to ensure clarity for listeners. Ten seconds separated onsets of successive non-words.

Three randomizations of the 54 non-words were constructed. Each third of the list was used in one of the three conditions: vowel replacement, consonant replacement, and free choice (either vowel or consonant replacement) so that each participant was exposed to all three conditions. Within each randomization, the order of conditions was counterbalanced. Participants were assigned to each of the six possible orders of conditions for each of the three randomizations, producing a total of 18 groups. Three to 11 participants served in these 18 groups. The experiment was conducted using a within-subjects comparison for the vowel, consonant and free choice conditions. This design has been used in previous word reconstruction studies and was selected for comparability.

2.3 Procedure

The 91 participants were tested in small groups in a quiet classroom. Each heard one randomization of the 54 non-words through loudspeakers in the classroom ceiling and wrote the word that came to mind on a prepared answer sheet. Responses could be scored for correct vs. erroneous word reconstructions but not for reaction time. Participants were told that they would be hearing a series of spoken non-words that were similar to real words. They were asked to change one, and only one, of the sounds in the non-word to convert it to a real word and to write that word on their answer sheet. They were asked not to respond with foreign words, proper nouns, hyphenated words, or contractions and to give only one-word responses. These general instructions were followed by more specific instructions at the beginning of each of the three conditions. For the vowel condition, participants were asked to substitute only one vowel in the non-word in order to produce a word. For the consonant condition, participants were asked to substitute only one consonant in the non-word in order to produce a word. For the free-choice condition, participants were asked to substitute either a vowel or a consonant — whichever came to mind first — in the non-word in order to produce a word. In each condition, participants were given three examples for practice.

The target words were largely low frequency words, and some may have been unknown to some participants. To control for this source of error, following completion of the task, participants were given a randomized list of the 24 lower frequency target words plus 24 non-words and were asked to circle any items they thought were not words. Inclusion of the 24 non-words was a protection against guessing. If a real word was circled, then no error was scored on that target word for that participant.

3. Results

Overall, the error rate approached 60%. Because of this high error rate, reaction time measures might have been unreliable. Participant responses were scored for three kinds of errors: no response within the 10−second interval; mistake, a response which did not meet the criteria stated in the instructions; and an intrusion, a response which changed a consonant in the vowel condition or vice versa. The word check task showed that most participants knew all of the real words.

3.1 Vowel, consonant and free-choice conditions

Separate analyses of variance were conducted with both participants (F_1) and items (F_2) as random factors. This statistical procedure is recommended because both participants in an experiment and specific linguistic test items are selected to represent much larger populations. Means and standard deviations of errors in the vowel, consonant, and free-choice conditions are shown in Table 2.

Table 2: Means, standard deviations, and proportions of errors in the consonant, vowel, and free-choice conditions. In each condition, participants were responding to 18 items.

	Condition		
	Consonant	Vowel	Free Choice
Mean	11.58	8.48	7.34
Standard Deviation	2.30	2.72	2.48
Proportion	0.64	0.47	0.41

3.1.1 Condition by randomization

A 3 x 3 ANOVA on errors across subjects with condition (vowel, consonant, free choice) as a within-subject variable and randomization (1, 2, 3) as a between-subject variable revealed that the main effect for condition [$F_1(2,176) = 80.72$, $p < .001$] and the interaction [$F_1(4,176) = 2.70$, $p < .05$) were significant, but there was no main effect for randomization [$F_1(2,88) < 1$]. Post-tests were not performed on the interaction because they would not be interpretable. Tukey HSD post-tests on the main effect for condition showed that the mean error for consonants (11.58) was significantly greater than that for vowels (8.48) and for free choice (7.34). The mean errors for the vowel and free-choice conditions were also significantly different.

In the analysis across items, only 48 items were included because, due to a problem with the randomizations, only those 48 had appeared in all three versions of the test. The main effect for condition was significant [$F_2(1.44, 67.9) = 22.83$, $p < .001$], with Greenhouse-Geisser correction for degrees of freedom. The main effect for randomization was not significant [$F_2(1.98, 92.81) < 1$] nor was the interaction [$F_2(3.67, 172.7) = 2.015$, $p > .05$]. Tukey HSD post-tests showed that the mean error for consonants (67.21) was significantly greater than that for vowels (46.66) and for free choice (41.69). The mean errors for vowels and free choice were not significantly different.

As in all previous word reconstruction studies, participants found changing vowels in the non-words easier than changing consonants. When the participants could change either a consonant or a vowel (free-choice condition), they performed better than in the consonant change condition though not necessarily better than in the vowel change condition.

3.2 Vowel and consonant condition

3.2.1 Target segment frequency

Participants produced fewer errors for words with high frequency target segments than for words with low frequency target segments. Means and standard deviations of errors for high and low frequency vowel target words and high and low frequency consonant target words are shown in Table 3. The values given are proportions of errors in each condition.

Table 3: Means and standard deviations for proportions of errors for high and low frequency vowel target words and high and low frequency consonant target words.

	Vowels		Consonants	
	High Freq	Low Freq	High Freq	Low Freq
Mean	0.45	0.54	0.62	0.70
SD	0.18	0.22	0.16	0.19

Note. The number of target words with high frequency segments was about twice the number with low frequency segments. Proportions were constructed on the number of available targets.

Separate ANOVAS with participants and items as random factors were conducted on error rates to assess the effects of type of target (vowel, consonant) and frequency of target (high, low). The analyses showed a main effect for vowel/consonant [$F_1(1,90) = 70.41$, $p < .001$; $F_2(1,92) = 9.19$, $p < .01$] and a main effect for frequency in the subject analysis [$F_1(1,90) = 25.75$, $p < .001$] but not in the item analysis [$F_2(1,92) < 1$]. The interaction was not significant [$F_1(1,90) < 1$; $F_2(1,92) < 1$]. Consistent with hypothesis 1.1.1, there were more errors for words containing low frequency target segments than for words containing high frequency target segments, but this effect appeared only in the subject analysis. Contrary to hypothesis 1.1.3, the vowel/consonant variable was significant in both subject and item analyses. The effect size for the consonant/vowel variable, as measured by eta squared, was considerably larger ($\eta^2 = .439$ for participants; $\eta^2 = .091$ for items) than that for the frequency variable ($\eta^2 = .222$ for participants; $\eta^2 = .005$ for items).

In order to investigate whether the frequency of the target phoneme might predict error frequency, a linear regression was calculated. The predictor variables were vowel/consonant status of the target word and the frequency of its target phoneme. The regression produced an R^2 of .106 which was significant for vowel/consonant status as a predictor (t = 3.04, p < .005, df = 93) but not for phoneme frequency (t = 1.36, p > .05, df = 93). The regression outcome is consistent with the ANOVA item analysis.

3.2.2 Replacing segment frequency

Because the frequency of the target phoneme affected word reconstruction, the token frequencies of the phonemes which replaced the targets in creating non-words could also have affected the task. To test this possibility, the replacing phonemes were divided into high vs. low categories according to frequency, using a median split. Table 4 shows means and standard deviations for the proportions of errors occurring for both high and low frequency replacing phonemes in the vowel and consonant conditions.

Separate ANOVAs with subjects (F_1) and items (F_2) as random effects were performed on proportions of errors. For both, 2 × 2 ANOVAs having type of phoneme (vowel, consonant) as one variable and frequency of the replacing phoneme (high, low) as the second were carried out. The main effect for vowel/consonant was significant, [$F_1(1,90) = 84.96$, p < .001, $\eta^2 = .486$, $F_2(1,92) = 8.62$, p < .005, $\eta^2 = .086$]. Vowels produced fewer errors than did consonants. The main effect for frequency was also significant, [$F_1(1,90) = 38.76$, p < .001, $\eta^2 = .301$, $F_2(1,92) = 4.76$, p < .05,

Table 4: Means and standard deviations for proportions of errors for high and low frequency replacing vowels and consonants

	Vowel		Consonant	
	High Freq	Low Freq	High Freq	Low Freq
Mean	0.42	0.55	0.64	0.71
SD	0.20	0.20	0.18	0.18

$\eta^2 = .049$]. Items with high frequency replacing phonemes produced fewer errors. The interaction was not significant [$F_1(1,90) = 3.59$, p > .05, $F_2(1,92) = 1.20$, p > .05].

Although the replacing segment was selected in order to form possible English words rather than in any systematically controlled manner, it is worth noting that non-words formed with higher frequency replacing segments produced fewer errors than those with low frequency replacing segments.

The appearance of a phoneme token frequency effect for the replacing phonemes raised the possibility that it was the source of the phoneme token frequency effect for the target phonemes. This hypothesis is not supported. The correlation between frequencies of replacing vowels and target vowels was small and non-significant, r = .01, p > .05. Similarly, the correlation between frequencies of replacing consonants and target consonants was small and non-significant, r = −.13, p > .05.

3.3 Phoneme frequency in the free-choice condition

In the free-choice condition participants produced either a vowel word or a consonant word, whichever came to mind first. Participants were expected to reconstruct words having high frequency vowel targets more often than words having low frequency vowel targets, and words having high frequency consonant targets more often than those having low frequency consonant targets.

Because the task was a free-choice task, responses were scored for proportions correct rather than for errors. Mean correct proportions of high and low frequency vowel and consonant target words are given in Table 5. Within each randomization and within each of the three orders, the number of high and low frequency vowel and consonant targets differed. These values were the basis for calculating proportions correct.

Table 5: Means and standard deviations for proportions of correct high and low frequency vowel and consonant substitution responses in the free-choice condition

	Vowel		Consonant	
	High Freq	Low Freq	High Freq	Low Freq
Mean	0.31	0.32	0.27	0.28
SD	0.15	0.22	0.13	0.22

Separate ANOVAs with subjects (F_1) and items (F_2) as random effects were performed on proportions of correct responses. Both ANOVAs evaluated the vowel/consonant and frequency variables. The vowel/consonant effect was marginally significant in the subject analysis, [$F_1(1, 90) = 3.41$, p = .07] but not significant in the item analysis, [$F_2(1,92) = 1.38$, p > .05]. The main effect for frequency was not significant in either analysis, [$F_1(1, 90) < 1$, $F_2(1,92) < 1$] nor was the interaction, [$F_1(1, 90) < 1$, $F_2(1,92) < 1$].

Across the whole set of materials 50 participants made more vowel than consonant responses, and 29 participants made more consonant than vowel responses (with 12 ties), whereas 30 items received more vowel than consonant responses and 18 items received more consonant than vowel responses (with 0 ties). Forty-three participants made more responses to high frequency targets than to low frequency targets while 48 participants made more responses to low frequency than high frequency targets (with no ties). Among the items, only 24 had one high frequency and one low frequency target, i.e., a high frequency vowel and a low frequency consonant or vice versa. For 12 of these items, the high frequency target was selected more often than the low frequency target.

3.4 Phonological variables

3.4.1 Feature differences

As a measure of phonetic similarity, the distance in distinctive features between the target and the replacement segment, either consonant or vowel, was established using the feature system described in O'Grady, Dobrovolsky & Aronoff (1997). A one-way ANOVA on the numbers of features separating target and replacement segments showed no significant difference in the proportion of errors for each item [$F(3,34) = 1.42$, $p > .05$] for vowel features and [$F(8,39) < 1$] for consonant features. This finding is consistent with van Ooijen's (1996), who failed to find a significant relationship between feature differences and reaction time in word reconstruction.

3.4.2 Target position

As a control for position effects, the target segments were distributed approximately proportionally at the beginning, middle and end of the vowel and consonant target words. The control was effective in that the proportions of errors across positions were not different for either consonants [$F_1(2,45) < 1$; $F_2(2,45) < 1$] or for vowels [$F_1(2, 45) < 1$; $F_2(2,45) = 1.074$, $p > .05$].

3.4.3 Length of target word

Target words varied in length between 4 and 8 phonemes. Linear regression on target word length predicting error rates found no relationship between the two [$r^2 = .014$, $F(1,46) < 1$].

3.5 Error types

Although participants made more errors when they had to reconstruct words with consonant targets than words with vowel targets, the types of errors in the two conditions were quite similar. By far the most common type of error was no response; participants simply could not think of a word which could be reconstructed from the non-word. This error type was more common in the consonant response condition than in the vowel response condition. Mistakes occurred at similar rates in the two conditions, and intrusion errors were rare.

4. Discussion

Phoneme token frequency was hypothesized to account for vowel mutability. The present study provides partial evidence for a phoneme token frequency effect, but that effect does not account for vowel mutability. These matters are discussed in detail below.

4.1 Hypothesized effects

Hypothesis 1.1.1 predicted that participants would have more difficulty in reconstructing the target words containing the low token frequency phonemes than in reconstructing the target words containing the high token frequency phonemes. That hypothesis was supported in the subject analysis but not the item analysis, giving partial evidence for the influence of phoneme token frequency. The effect is analogous to the widely observed effect for word frequency, in which low frequency words are more difficult to access than high frequency words. It suggests that frequency of use is a part of representations of individual phonemes and influences identification of these phonemes. That influence appears also to extend to the identification of words in which the phonemes are embedded. Activation of individual phonemes thus influences activation of whole words, at least as exemplified in the word reconstruction task used in the present study. This effect accounted for variance ($\eta^2 = .222$) equal to about half that accounted for by the vowel/consonant variable ($\eta^2 = .439$), so it carries some weight in the processing of words.

The phoneme token frequency variable was not significant in the item analysis, suggesting that the effect is unique to the present items and may not generalize to another sample of items drawn from the same population. The sample of items used in the present study comes close to being the entire population of relevant items. The controls applied to the selection of items, especially the requirement that each non-word have only two real word neighbors, were sufficiently stringent to exhaust the relevant entries in the Francis & Kučera (1982) word list. That requirement was necessary in order to minimize competition among lexical entries and maximize the opportunity for phoneme token frequency effects to emerge. Subsequent studies may expand the number of real word neighbors for a non-word in order to explore the relation between phoneme token frequency and neighborhood density.

The phoneme token frequency effect was tested again in Hypothesis 1.1.2, which stated that, in the free-choice condition, participants would produce more correct words containing high frequency phonemes than words containing low frequency phonemes. This effect was not significant in either the subject or item analysis. The vowel/consonant effect, however, was significant. The pattern of effects across the forced-choice and free-choice conditions is a clear one. In the forced-choice condition, both the vowel/consonant effect and the phoneme token frequency effect are highly significant, though the vowel/consonant effect is stronger than the frequency effect. In the free-choice condition, the vowel/consonant comparison, which is the stronger variable, is marginally significant at best, and the frequency variable is not significant at all. The free-choice condition thus appears to be a less revealing condition in which to study these variables.

Hypothesis 1.1.3 stated that matching vowel and consonant target words on phoneme token frequency would remove the vowel mutability effect. Hypothesis 1.1.3 was clearly disconfirmed. The vowel/consonant effect was significant in both subject and item analyses in the forced-choice conditions and marginally significant in the subject analysis in the free-choice condition. Focusing on the forced-choice conditions, this effect has been observed in all studies of vowel mutability since van Ooijen's (1996) first report. It has occurred in spoken materials in English (the present study; van Ooijen, 1996), Dutch (Cutler et al., 2000), and Spanish (Cutler et al., 2000; Marks et al., submitted) as well as in printed materials in English (Moates & Russell, 1999). It is thus a highly reliable effect and is general to the auditory and visual modalities.

Focusing on the free-choice condition, the marginal significance in the preference for vowel words over consonant words in the present study reflects the instability of the effect in other studies. The preference for vowel changes was significant in both the Dutch and Spanish studies in Cutler et al. (2000) as well as in Experiment 2 for Marks et al. (submitted). It was not significant in Experiment 1 for Marks et al. (submitted) nor in the studies by van Ooijen (1996) and Moates & Russell (1999). Thus, the selection of a vowel word rather than a consonant word − given a choice − is probably a small effect relative to the very reliable effect for ease of reconstructing vowel words over consonant words.

Analyses of both the forced-choice and free-choice data showed the interaction between the vowel/consonant variable and the phoneme token frequency variable to be wholly non-significant, with $F < 1$ in all cases. Instead the vowel/consonant effect and the phoneme token frequency effect (to the degree that it appears) were statistically additive, each contributing to the observed results but not influencing the other.

Given the limited evidence for the influence of phoneme token frequency, it would be helpful to look for this effect in other tasks. Word reconstruction may not be the best task for looking at phoneme token frequency, because participants are not exposed directly to the target words where phoneme token frequency is manipulated. Gating, shadowing, and phoneme monitoring all give participants direct exposure to the targeted phonemes and would permit varying the range of phoneme token frequency more widely than was possible in the present study.

4.2 Vowel mutability

Phoneme token frequency emerges as a variable contributing to word reconstruction but not one that explains vowel mutability. Explaining vowel mutability was the goal of the present study, so how shall we explain vowel mutability? Three hypotheses bear consideration.

4.2.1 Phonology

Vowels are phonetically more similar to one another than are consonants. Vowels share the same manner of articulation, though consonants do not. Further, vowels are distinguished from consonants by features such as [vocalic] or [vocoid] which define primary class nodes in feature geometry (Roca & Johnson, 1999). The difference in ease of reconstructing vowel and consonant words may reflect these phonological differences.

If the phonological properties distinguished by features such as [vocalic] produce vowel mutability, then other features high in the feature hierarchy may also influence word reconstruction. Evidence for such an effect would support the hypothesis that phonological features affect vowel mutability. Marks, Moates, Bond & Stockmal (in press) have provided such evidence for the feature [sonorant], which distinguishes obstruents from resonants. In a word reconstruction task, non-words were created by replacing one obstruent with another obstruent (*cavalry* /kævəlri/: /bævəlri/) or with a resonant (*cavalry* /kævəlri/: /mævəlri/). A second set of non-words was created by replacing one resonant with another resonant (*nonsense* /nansəns/: /ransəns/) or with an obstruent (*nonsense* /nansəns/: /zansəns/). Participants made fewer errors in reconstructing target words in which the replacing consonant was from the same class as the target consonant (resonant, resonant; obstruent, obstruent) than in reconstructing target words in which the replacing consonant was from the opposite class (resonant, obstruent; obstruent, resonant). It was more difficult to reconstruct the target word when the listener had to cross the [sonorant] boundary, suggesting that phonological representations for lexical entries are sensitive to major class features.

4.2.2 Vowel variability

Van Ooijen (1996) suggested that listeners expect vowels to be more variable in their realizations than consonants. The phonetic context for a vowel may produce more variability in vowel phonemes than in consonant phonemes, so listeners are less sure about which vowel phoneme a given token represents. That uncertainty makes them more likely to change an initial hypothesis about a vowel when the initial hypothesis does not activate a real word. It is possible, however, that the variability of vowel tokens is related to the size of a language's vowel inventory.

4.2.3 Lexical neighbors

Cutler et al. (2000) noted that changing a consonant in a word is more likely to produce a real word neighbor than changing a vowel. They reviewed the vocabularies of English, Dutch, and Spanish and found that changing a consonant in a word is about twice as likely to produce another word (e.g., *pat* as a neighbor for *cat*) as changing a vowel (e.g., *kit* as a neighbor for *cat*). Listeners thus learn that, when normal lexical access fails, it is better to adjust vowel information, since that is more likely to yield the correct lexical candidate, than consonant information, which is more likely to result in a mistake, that is, the wrong lexical neighbor. As a result of learning these structural regularities in the lexicon, listeners develop a bias in the lexical access process that favors vowel change over consonant change.

4.3 Models of spoken word access

In lexical access, words appear to compete with other words having similar phonological form (Connine, Titone, Deelman & Blasko, 1997; McQueen, Norris & Cutler, 1994; Tabossi, Burnai & Scott, 1995) as well as with words that begin in the same way (Marslen-Wilson, 1990; Zwitserlood, 1989). Although activation of a target word may be inhibited by mismatch in just one phoneme (Marslen-Wilson & Zwitserlood, 1989), phonological similarity produces activation for words with shared phonemes (Connine et al., 1997; Goldinger, Luce, Pisoni & Marcario, 1992; Radeau, Morais & Segui, 1995; Slowiaczek & Hamburger, 1992; Slowiaczek, McQueen, Soltano & Lynch, 2000).

Phoneme token frequency was hypothesized to explain vowel mutability, but it is, instead, a novel experimental effect that does not interact with vowel mutability. Can this effect be explained by existing models of spoken word access? Four models bear considering: The Cohort Model (Marslen-Wilson, 1987; 1990; Marslen-Wilson & Welsh, 1978), TRACE (Elman & McClelland, 1986; McClelland & Elman, 1986), Shortlist (Norris, 1994), and PARSYN (Luce, Goldinger, Auer & Vitevitch, 2000).

4.3.1 Word reconstruction

All four models assume the activation of a set of word candidates, followed by competition among the candidates based on their degree of activation. Because of this assumption, all four models explain how target words in the word reconstruction task can be reconstructed. The presented non-word overlaps the target word in all but one phoneme. The overlap should be sufficient in many cases to include the target word in the set of activated word candidates. In the present study there were only two real word neighbors for each non-word, so these would have little competition for recognition if they were in the set of activated word candidates.

4.3.2 Phoneme token frequency effect

None of the four models appears to explain the phoneme token frequency effect. The Cohort and TRACE models do not represent frequency of use for individual phonemes, only for whole words and so cannot respond to varying phoneme frequency. Phoneme frequency effects, however, might be explained in some later version of the TRACE model by coding the links between phonemes and their words for frequency of use of the phonemes.

In contrast, both Shortlist and PARSYN explicitly represent frequency of use for phonemes. Shortlist has a level for the analysis of phonemes that is autonomous from the level for lexical representations. It codes both frequency of use for phonemes and the phonotactic properties of the phonological input. In the word reconstruction task, however, the phonemes in the target words are replaced by other phonemes in the non-word that is presented to listeners, so frequency values for the target phonemes are not available for the phoneme analyzer in Shortlist, rendering it unable to explain a phoneme token frequency effect. PARSYN has the same problem. In brief, none of these four models seems to explain a phoneme token frequency effect.

4.3.3 Frequency effect for replacing phonemes

If these models do not explain the phoneme token frequency effect, can they nonetheless explain the frequency effect for the replacing phonemes? The replacing phonemes were directly available to listeners and also showed significant frequency effects.

As noted above, neither the Cohort Model nor TRACE represents phoneme frequency and so offers no means for responding to variations in phoneme frequency even when the phonemes are directly available to perception. In contrast, Shortlist and PARSYN have prelexical processors that are sensitive to the frequency values of the replacing phonemes. Both models predict that low frequency replacing phonemes would send less activation to the lexical level than high frequency replacing phonemes. Because the replacing phonemes are inappropriate for identifying the target word, low frequency replacing phonemes should interfere less with recognition of the target word. Paradoxically, the results of the present study show just the reverse effect: Low frequency replacing phonemes produced more errors in word reconstruction than did high frequency replacing phonemes.

4.4 Explanation of the phoneme token frequency effect

Existing models of spoken word recognition do not explain the phoneme token frequency effect, because most models do not represent phoneme token frequency. The two models that do, Shortlist and PARSYN, require direct access to the phonemes. In the word reconstruction task, the phonemes whose frequency is being manipulated in the target words have been replaced in the nonwords with other phonemes. Thus the phoneme analyzer (in Shortlist) and the pattern level processor (in PARSYN) do not get access to the target phonemes. If existing models of spoken word recognition do not explain phoneme token frequency, how may we think about it?

All the models discussed above assume the processing of phonemes to be fast and automatic. The word reconstruction task, however, allows up to 10 seconds for a participant to process a nonword, thus permitting such processing to become strategic rather than automatic. The error rate in this task was over 50%, and even when participants did identify the target word correctly, they did not necessarily do so immediately. Knowing that some phoneme in the nonword had to be changed, participants may have substituted more familiar (frequent) phonemes first, inserting these more available sounds into the non-word in an effort to convert it to a word. This explanation for phoneme token frequency may be tested by reducing the usual 10−second presentation time to 1−2 seconds so that participants could not employ a strategy.

The same explanation may be appropriate for the frequency effect for the replacing phonemes, namely, high frequency phonemes produced fewer errors. As noted in 4.3, existing models of spoken word recognition do not explain the phoneme token frequency effect for the replacing items. Only Shortlist and PARSYN represent frequency information, and they predict greater interference from high frequency replacing phonemes compared to low frequency replacing phonemes, just the reverse of what was observed. As with the target items, the most appropriate explanation for the frequency effect may be a strategic one. Knowing that they had to change some sound in the nonword, participants may have started with the more familiar (frequent) sounds in the nonword, thus favoring the high frequency phonemes.

4.5 Autonomous vs. interactive models

Current models of spoken word access are divided on the question of whether top-down feedback is necessary from the lexical level to lower levels of processing. The interactionist model TRACE (Elman & McClelland, 1986; McClelland & Elman, 1986) posits top-down activation from lexical nodes to phoneme nodes such that lexical decisions influence phoneme identification. Supporters of autonomous models such as Shortlist (Norris, 1994) and PARSYN (Luce et al., 2000) argue that feedback from the lexical level down to the phoneme level is neither necessary nor desirable and that the phenomena that are explained by the top-down feedback in interactionist models are explained more parsimoniously in autonomous models featuring wholly bottom-up processing (see especially Norris, McQueen & Cutler, 2000; Pitt & McQueen, 1998).

If subsequent research shows phoneme token frequency to be a reliable effect in ordinary listening, it could be explained by a top-down model such as TRACE if the model were revised. The revision would require different weights on the links from phoneme nodes to word nodes, and these weights would build up as a function of the frequency of use of the links from phoneme nodes to word nodes. The explanation of the phoneme token frequency effect in such a revised model would rely essentially on bottom-up processing. By itself, that change would probably not explain the phoneme token frequency effect as it appears in the word reconstruction task because the frequency-bearing phonemes are hidden. Even with the frequency-weighted links, an explanation of the phoneme token frequency effect in the word reconstruction task would require that correctly recognized words feed excitation back down to their member phonemes, inhibiting the replacing phonemes and activating the target phonemes. These phonemes would then send activation back up to the lexical nodes, differentially according to their frequency of use, in a manner that would lead to greater recognition of words having high frequency phonemes. The target phonemes would receive no bottom-up activation, only top-down activation, and such activation would be the source of the phoneme token frequency effect.

In contrast, autonomous models such as Shortlist and PARSYN have a prelexical level of processing for analyzing such phonological properties as phoneme token frequency. Shortlist and PARSYN, in particular, explicitly represent phoneme token frequency as a component of prelexical processing. If the phoneme token frequency effect is shown to be reliable in ordinary listening settings, it will have a clear explanation in these models, and that explanation also will rely essentially on bottom-up processing.

5. Conclusion

The vowel mutability effect remains unexplained. Several potential explanations for it have been rejected, and the three possible ones described in 4.2 are largely untested. Every reported investigation of vowel mutability has confirmed the effect. An effect of such stability is a continuing challenge for investigators of spoken word recognition.

The present study offers partial evidence for a phoneme token frequency effect. In the forced-choice condition, it appeared in both the target phonemes and in the replacing phonemes. In the free-choice condition, it did not appear at all. The effect may simply be due to a strategy that is specific to the word reconstruction task. Further research should establish the validity and generality of the effect by testing it with other tasks. How reliable is it across tasks? How sensitive are listeners to phoneme token frequencies? To the degree that the effect is supported as a valid phenomenon, then questions will emerge about the mechanism responsible for it. The models of spoken word access reviewed above do not explain the effect, at least as it occurs in the word reconstruction task. That task is unusual, however, in that it hides the frequency information from listeners. The effect may be stronger in tasks such as lexical decision or shadowing which present the target words directly to the listeners. If so, then phoneme token frequency effects may offer a new venue for exploring spoken word recognition.

Acknowledgements

We thank Bruce Carlson, Patrick Munhall, and Paul Weiland for statistical advice and assistance and James McQueen for helpful comments on an earlier version of this article.

References

Connine, C. M., Titone, D., Deelman, T. & Blasko, D.
  1997   Similarity mapping in spoken word recognition. *Journal of Memory and Language*, **37**, 463–480.
Cutler, A., Sebastián-Gallés, N., Vilageliu, O. S. & van Ooijen, B.
  2000   Constraints of vowels and consonants on lexical selection: Crosslinguistic comparisons. *Memory & Cognition*, **28**, 746–755.
Elman, J. & McClelland, J.
  1986   Exploring lawful variability in the speech waveform. In S. Perkell & D. H. Klatt (eds.), *Invariance and Variability in Speech Processing*, (pp. 360–385). Hillsdale, NJ: Erlbaum.
Francis, W. N. & Kučera, H.
  1982   *Frequency Analysis of English usage: Lexicon and Grammar.* Boston: Houghton Mifflin.
Goldinger, S. D., Luce, P. A., Pisoni, D.B. & Marcario, J. K.
  1992   Form-based priming in spoken word recognition: The roles of competition and bias. *Journal of Experimental Psychology: Learning, Memory and Cognition*, **18**, 1211–1238.
Landauer, T. K. & Streeter, L. A.
  1973   Structural differences between common and rare words: Failure of equivalence assumptions for theories of word recognition. *Journal of Verbal Learning and Verbal Behavior*, **12**, 119–136.
Luce, P. A., Goldinger, S. D., Auer, E. T., Jr. & Vitevitch, M. S.
  2000   Phonetic priming, neighborhood activation, and PARSYN. *Perception & Psychophysics*, **62**, 615–625.
Marks, E. A., Moates, D. R., Bond, Z. S. & Stockmal, V.
  2002   Word reconstruction and consonant features in English and Spanish. *Linguistics*, **40**, 421–438.
Marks, E., Moates, D. R., Bond, Z. S. & Vazquez, L.
  submitted   Vowel mutability: The case of monolingual Spanish listeners and bilingual Spanish-English listeners. *Southwest Journal of Linguistics*,
Marslen-Wilson, W. D.
  1987   Functional parallelism in spoken word recognition. *Cognition*, **25**, 71–102.
Marslen-Wilson, W. D.
  1990   Activation, competition, and frequency in lexical access. In G. T. M. Altmann (ed.), *Cognitive Models of Speech Processing: Psycholinguistic and Computational Perspectives*, (pp. 148–172). Cambridge, MA: MIT Press.
Marslen-Wilson, W. D. & Welsh, A.
  1978   Processing interactions and lexical access during word recognition in continuous speech. *Cognitive Psychology*, **10**, 29–63.

Marslen-Wilson, W. D. & Zwitserlood, P.
    1989   Accessing spoken words: The importance of word onsets. *Journal of Experimental Psychology: Human Perception & Performance*, **15**, 576–585.

McClelland, J. & Elman, J.
    1986   The TRACE model of speech perception. *Cognitive Psychology*, **18**, 1–86.

McQueen, J. M., Norris, D. G. & Cutler, A.
    1994   Competition in spoken word recognition: Spotting words in other words. *Journal of Experimental Psychology: Learning, Memory & Cognition*, **20**, 621–638.

Mines, M. A., Hanson, B. F. & Shoup, J. E.
    1978   Frequency of occurrence of phonemes in conversational English. *Language and Speech*, **21**, 221–241.

Moates, D. R. & Russell, S.
    September, 1999   Word reconstruction with printed materials. Paper presented at the conference on Basic Mechanisms of Language and Language Disorders, Leipzig.

Norris, D.
    1994   Shortlist: A connectionist model of continuous speech recognition, *Cognition*, **52**, 189–234.

Norris, D., McQueen, J. M. & Cutler, A.
    2000   Merging information in speech recognition: Feedback is never necessary. *Behavioral and Brain Sciences*, **23**, 299–370.

O'Grady, W., Dobrovolsky, M. & Aronoff, M.
    1997   *Contemporary Linguistics, an Introduction*. New York: St. Martin's Press.

Ooijen, B. van
    1996   Vowel mutability and lexical selection in English: Evidence from a word reconstruction task. *Memory & Cognition*, **24**, 573–583.

Pickett, J. M.
    1999   *The Acoustics of Speech Communication*. Boston: Allyn & Bacon.

Pitt, M. A. & McQueen, J. M.
    1998   Is compensation for coarticulation mediated by the lexicon? *Journal of Memory and Language*, **39**, 347–370.

Radeau, M., Morais, J. & Segui, J.
    1995   Phonological priming between monosyllabic spoken words. *Journal of Experimental Psychology: Human Perception & Performance*, **21**, 1297–1311.

Roca, I. & Johnson, W.
    1999   *A Course in Phonology*. Oxford: Blackwell.

Shriberg, L. D. & Kent, R. D.
    1982   *Clinical Phonetics*. New York: Wiley.

Tabossi, P., Burani, C. & Scott, D.
   1995   Word identification in fluent speech. *Journal of Memory and Language*, **34**, 440–467.
Slowiaczek, L. M. & Hamburger, M.
   1992   Prelexical facilitation and lexical interference in auditory word recognition. *Journal of Experimental Psychology: Learning, Memory and Cognition*, **18**, 1239–1250.
Slowiaczek, L. M., McQueen, J. M., Soltano, E. G. & Lynch, M.
   2000   Phonological representations in prelexical speech processing: Evidence from form-based priming. *Journal of Memory and Language*, **43**, 530–560.
Zwitserlood, P.
   1989   The locus of the effects of sentential-semantic context in spoken-word processing. *Cognition*, **32**, 25–64.

Appendix

NON-WORD	VOWEL WORD	CONSONANT WORD
kərʌkt	correct	corrupt
dətæn	detain	detach
plinli	plainly	cleanly
mʊdnɪs	madness	goodness
hərɛs	harass	caress
səpraim	supreme	surprise
wɛdo	widow	meadow
karsɪt	corset	carpet
ɪnæpt	inept	enact
tʃɑstli	chastely	costly
fɛntly	faintly	gently
æfər	offer	adder
əfrɔd	afraid	abroad
flɔri	flowery	glory
hʌndəl	handle	bundle
rʌtʃli	richly	roughly
əlɛf	aloof	allege
sedli	sadly	safely
ʌbli	ably	ugly
vɛto	veto	ghetto
plos	plus	close
daʊbɔi	doughboy	cowboy
galɪʃ	ghoulish	polish
ədrɔs	address	across

ɪˈrɛpt	erupt	erect
bɪldoz	bulldoze	dildos
kʌndrɪd	kindred	hundred
prɔər	prayer	drawer
kɑrɪdʒ	courage	porridge
sprɛl	sprawl	spread
skaitʃ	sketch (scotch)	skies
ˈkɑntʌkt	contact	conduct
prɔɪl	prowl	broil
sɔrˈve	survey	sorbet
kənfɔin	confine	conjoin
dɪˈpʌkt	depict	deduct
ˈɛbsɛs	excess	abscess
brʌdɪŋ	breeding	brushing
frɛdmən	freedman	freshman
kastəl	coastal	hostile
frænt	front	grant
dɪslaidʒ	dislodge	dislike
dʒæstʃər	gesture	pasture
kibrə	cobra	zebra
plaimɪt	plummet	climate
mændfʊl	mindful	handful
ʌkwərd	awkward	upward
gedɪns	guidance	cadence
mɛdʒɪk	magic	medic
dɪsˈklom	disclaim	disclose
θrav	thrive	throb
dɔtfʊl	doubtful	thoughtful
ɛkspəndʒ	expunge	exchange
pərez	peruse	parade

Temporal neutralization in Japanese

Haruo Kubozono

Abstract

This paper argues that essentially the same type of temporal neutralization is observed in four manifestations of Japanese: phonology, phonetics, auditory perception, and visual perception, i.e. speech perception on the sole basis of visual information. It is demonstrated, first of all, that phonologically long vowels tend to shorten in word-final position in a wide range of phonological processes. It is then shown that essentially the same tendency is observed in visual perception as well, where word-final contrasts between short and long vowels become literally invisible to native speakers, but not to non-native speakers. This paper proposes several acoustic and perceptual factors that are to be held responsible for this position-dependent invisibility of temporal distinctions.

1. Introduction

The primary goal of this paper is to demonstrate and explain the temporal neutralization in (Tokyo) Japanese of word-final vowels within four central areas of speech research: phonology, phonetics, auditory perception, and visual perception (i.e. speech perception on the basis of visual information). There appear to be striking correspondences in the way these four areas exhibit neutralization in moraic structure between short and long vowels specifically in word-final contexts.

The analyses in this paper sprang from two independent sources of interest. One is bimodal perception, generally known as the 'McGurk Effect', or the idea that visual information as well as auditory information provides useful cues in the perception of speech (McGurk & McDonald, 1976). Research on bimodal perception has centered largely on segmental distinctions, e.g. [ba] vs. [ga], and little is known about the role of visual information in the perception of prosody (cf. Takano et al., 2000). This is especially true in the case of Japanese, where visual information is said to play a relatively minor role in distinguishing segmental contrasts

(Sekiyama & Tohkura, 1991; Shigeno, 1998). More crucially, it remains unclear how facts about bimodal perception generally relate to phonological structure. The lack of work in this area of speech research contrasts strongly with the increasing interest in prosody and its relation to speech perception (Cutler et al., 1983; Cutler, 1994). Research in this latter area has filled much of the gap between phonological studies and the studies of speech perception.

The other source of interest that has led to the current study is in the phonological neutralization of vowel length in Japanese. As is well known, Japanese is a typical 'mora language' (see Kubozono, 1999b, for a summary of the role of the mora). The distinction between monomoraic and bimoraic syllables in particular is of crucial importance; it exhibits considerable temporal differences, more so than appears to be the case in syllable-based languages. Contrary to this general idea, Japanese reportedly shows a tendency towards word-final shortening of long vowels (Alfonso, 1980; Sibata, 1995), which can potentially lead to the loss of this crucial distinction. However, it is unclear how general this reported tendency is in Japanese phonetics and phonology – whether it only implies sporadic instances of vowel shortening or rather represents a very general process. If the latter is the case, it is then worth asking why such a seemingly anti-rhythmic phenomenon should occur.

I will attempt to integrate into a single picture the two major fields of interest described above. In order to do this, this paper will consider, after a brief introduction to the mora system of Japanese in the next section, how temporal neutralizations occur in the four independent areas: phonology (section 3), auditory perception (section 4), visual perception (section 5) and phonetics (section 6). Section 7 presents a summary.

2. Mora and syllable in Japanese

2.1 Two Types of Syllables

Japanese contrasts monomoraic and bimoraic syllables, as illustrated in (1) and exemplified in (2) (glosses are given in (14) below).

(1) a.   σ   b.   σ
         /| /\
        / μ   / μ μ
       / | / | |
      (C) V   (C) V V
                         (C) V C

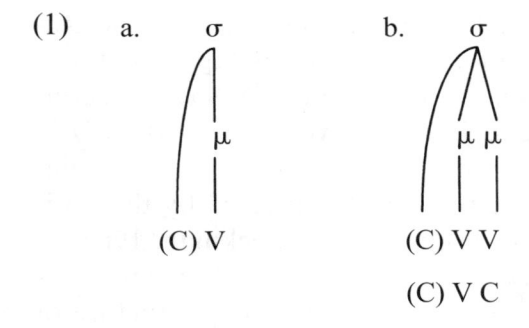

(2)   Word-medial   Word-final
   a. Moraic nasal (N)   taniN−taNniN   tani−taniN
   b. Short/long vowel   sado−saado   sado−sadoo
   c. Moraic obstruent   kako−kakko   ———
   d. Diphthong   kaga−kaiga   kaiga−kaigai

As shown in (2), there are four types of bimoraic syllables in Japanese: those including a long vowel, a diphthongal vowel sequence, or a short vowel followed by one of two coda consonants. The coda consonant can be either a 'moraic nasal' (*hatuon*), symbolized as 'N', or the first part of a geminate obstruent known as a 'moraic obstruent' (*sokuon*) and symbolized as 'Q'. These coda consonants are homorganic with the following consonant, and the moraic nasal is realized as a velar or uvular nasal in word-final position. The moraic obstruent Q can only occur word-medially. The four kinds of 'non-syllabic moras' illustrated in (2) make up bimoraic syllables together with a preceding mora that can potentially form a syllable on its own.

2.2 Arguments for the Mora

The mora in Japanese plays various roles as a basic unit of timing (Kubozono, 1999b). This function shows up very clearly in phonetics, where the mora serves as a basic unit of isochrony or speech rhythm (Port et al., 1987; Han, 1994; see Beckman, 1982 and Ramus et al., 1999 for different views of what makes Japanese mora-timed). Thus trimoraic words such as *saado* and *sadoo* are about one and a half times as long as bimoraic words such as *sado* in (2). This temporal structure is quite independent of word accent: acoustic durations of moras are not directly affected by the position of pitch accent in the word (Sugito, 1980; Beckman, 1986).

The temporal aspect of the mora is also clear in Japanese phonology. Most accent rules are sensitive to the moraic structure of the word (McCawley, 1978; Haraguchi, 1996; Poser, 1984; Kubozono, 1988), although some require information on syllable structure, too (Kubozono, 1999b; Kubozono, 2001). As another example, vowel coalescence yields long vowels in its output, thus preserving the mora length of the original words. (3a) represents a case where a diphthong in careful speech alternates with a long vowel in casual speech. (3b), by contrast, represents a historical change whereby a diphthong turned into a long vowel (see Poser, 1988, for similar evidence for compensatory lengthening in Japanese).

(3) a. da<u>i</u>.kon → d<u>ee</u>.kon 'radish'
    b. ka<u>u</u>.be → k<u>oo</u>.be 'Kobe (placename)'

One also finds strong evidence for the mora from psycholinguistic studies of speech. Thus studies on speech errors have shown that the mora serves as a basic weight unit; in substitution and transposition (metathesis) errors, for example, bimoraic syllables tend to interchange with two monomoraic syllables much more often than with a single monomoraic syllable (Kubozono, 1985, 1989). Finally, recent cross-linguistic studies on speech perception have provided abundant evidence that speakers of different languages employ different strategies of speech segmentation (i.e. segmentation of continuous speech into discrete linguistic units) and that these strategies are closely linked to the rhythmic structure of individual languages (Cutler et al., 1983; Cutler 1994). In the case of Japanese, it has been shown that the mora serves as a basic unit of speech segmentation (Cutler & Otake, 1994).

3. Temporal neutralization in phonology

We have seen that the mora plays a pivotal role as a temporal unit in various aspects of speech in Japanese. Since the distinction between bimoraic and monomoraic syllables is vital for mora timing as against syllable timing, it would be expected that these two types of syllable structures should be strictly distinguished from each other. However, careful examination of various phonological phenomena in Japanese – both diachronic and synchronic – reveals that the underlying moraic structure is subject to change in one certain context. Specifically, long vowels tend to shorten in word-final positions, becoming indistinguishable from their short counterparts. This position-dependent neutralization occurs in a wide range of phonological phenomena from vowel coalescence to some morphophonological processes.

3.1 Historical Change

Historically, long vowels, especially /oo/, have tended to shorten word-finally, particularly in bisyllabic Sino-Japanese compounds (Kubozono, in press). (4) gives typical words in which vowel shortening has occurred historically (Matsumura ed., 1995). The same morphemes affected by this historical change are still pronounced with a long vowel in compound-medial position, as shown in the parentheses.

(4) a. ai.soo → ai.so 'sociability' (soo.zoo 'imagination')
    b. nai.syoo → nai.syo 'a secret' (syoo.mee 'proof')
    c. sen.zyuu → sen.zyu 'Senju (placename)' (zyuu.syo 'address')
    d. teu.teu → tyoo.tyoo → tyoo.tyo 'butterfly'

On the other hand, it is difficult to find examples like those in (5) in which long vowels shortened in word-medial position, and this occurred only in morpheme-final position in compound words (morpheme boundaries are shown by /+/).

(5)   sayoo+na.ra → sa.yo.na.ra 'good-bye'
        tuu+ya → tu.ya 'a wake'

The words in (6) represent an ongoing phonetic change in contemporary Japanese. Alfonso (1980) notes that this kind of vowel shortening takes place only if the first syllable of bisyllabic words contains a moraic nasal or obstruent, but it also occurs after other bimoraic syllables. Forms with a short final vowel seem especially popular among young speakers. Again, long vowels tend to shorten in word-final positions, but not in word-medial positions.[1]

(6)   men.doo → men.do 'trouble'
        sen.see → sen.se 'teacher'
        o.ben.too → o.ben.to 'lunch'
        kak.koo → kak.ko 'appearance'
        nyoo.boo → nyoo.bo 'wife'
        kai.syoo → kai.syo 'resourcefulness'
        a.ri.ga.too → a.ri.ga.to 'thank you'

Note that this is not generally observed with any bimoraic syllables other than long vowels (see Kubozono, in press, for a couple of exceptions).

3.2 Vowel Shortening in Synchronic Processes

3.2.1 Vowel coalescence and shortening

Vowel coalescence, which is quite productive in contemporary Japanese, creates vowel alternations between a diphthong and a monophthong according to speech style: diphthongs in careful speech tend to become monophthongs in casual speech (Kubozono, 1999a). The resulting monophthongs are generally lengthened, preserving the original mora count (7).

(7)   a. ita-i → itee 'painful, ouch'
        b. sugo-i → sugee 'great'
        c. atu-i → atii 'hot'

In very casual (and fast) speech, however, this lengthening optionally fails to apply — or, equivalently, lengthened vowels are again shortened. Thus we have such forms as /ite/ and /suge/ for /itee/ and /sugee/. Interestingly, this shortening occurs only at the end of a prosodic word, and is invariably blocked when the word forms a larger prosodic word with a following clitic-like element such as the sentence-final particle *na*. Consequently, such forms as */ite-na/ and */suge-na/ are unacceptable while their counterparts with a long vowel, i.e. /itee-na/ and /sugee-na/, are perfectly acceptable (8).

(8)   Underlying   Casual speech   Very casual speech   Gloss
    a.   it<u>ai</u>   itee, itee-na   ite, *ite-na   'ouch!'
    b.   sug<u>oi</u>   sugee, sugee-na   suge, *suge-na   'great!'
    c.   at<u>ui</u>   atii, atii-na   ati, *ati-na   '(It's) hot'

Optional vowel shortening in word-final position is observed in the pronunciation of numbers, too. Numbers are subject to a bimoraic minimality constraint when they are enumerated (Itô, 1990). In the examples in (9), numbers of an underlying monomoraic length are pronounced with a bimoraic duration: /ni/ '2' → [ni:], /go/ '5' → [go:]. This lengthening is often optionally blocked, however, when the number stands at the end of the expression. The number 5 at the end of the words in (9a–c) is thus pronounced with either a long or short vowel. Note that this optional shortening (or blocking of lengthening) does not occur when the number comes to stand in a non-final position, as in (9d,e).

(9)   a.   7<u>2</u>1−5<u>555</u> /nana nii iti goo goo goo go(o)/ (reciting a phone number)
      b.   51<u>5</u> /goo iti go(o)/ (arbitrary number)
      c.   57<u>5</u> /goo siti go(o)/ (rhythm of *haiku* poetry)
      d.   5<u>7</u>5<u>77</u> /goo siti goo siti siti/ (rhythm of *tanka* poetry)
      e.   51<u>5</u> ziken /goo iti goo ziken/ 'May 15 Incident (Coup)'

3.2.2 Vowel shortening in clipped compounds

The peculiar behaviour of word-final long vowels is also observed in the morphological process of compound clipping (or truncation) in Japanese. This process most typically involves taking the initial two moras of each component word to produce a four-mora word, or a word consisting of two bimoraic feet (foot boundaries are denoted by [ ]) (10). This process is basically independent of syllable structure, so that any syllable combination is viable as long as four-mora outputs are produced (Itô, 1990; Kubozono, 1999b). In (10), H and L stand for heavy (bimoraic) and light (monomoraic) syllables, respectively.

(10) a. LL+LL se.ku.syu.a.ru ha.ra.su.men.to → [se.ku][ha.ra] 'sexual harassment'
 b. LL+H po.ket.to mon.su.taa → [po.ke][mon] 'Pokémon, pocket monster'
 c. H+LL han.gaa su.to.rai.ki → [han][su.to] 'hunger strike'
 d. H+H han.bun don.ta.ku → [han][don] 'a half day off (= a half + holiday)'

However, when the second component word begins with a heavy syllable containing a long vowel, the long vowel is usually shortened, producing a three-mora output.[2]

(11) a. te.re.hon kaa.do → [te.re]ka 'telephone card'
 b. ba.su.ket.to syuu.zu → [bas]syu 'basketball shoes'
 c. dan.su su paa.tii → [dan]pa 'dance party'
 d. kan.nin.gu pee.paa → [kan]pe 'crib sheet'

In contrast, long vowels are not generally shortened if they come from the first component word, as shown in (12a). They are occasionally shortened as in (12b), but in such a case the following material usually fills in the empty mora slot.[3]

(12) a. waa.do pu.ro.se.saa → [waa][pu.ro] 'word-processor'
kaa na.bi.gee.syon → [kaa][na.bi] 'car navigation'
ziin.zu pan.tu → [zii][pan] 'jeans'
b. paa.so.na.ru kon.pyuu.taa → [pa.so][kon] 'personal computer'
suu.paa kon.pyuu.taa → [su.pa][kon] 'super computer'

In sum, long vowels behave differently in word-final and word-medial syllables of truncated compound nouns. Vowel shortening typically occurs in word-final positions, just as in the other cases. This peculiar behaviour of long vowels also contrasts with the behaviour of other non-syllabic moras: moraic nasals, for instance, are hardly ever deleted, even if they appear word-finally (e.g. /po.ke.mon/ and /han.don/ in (10)). This suggests that neutralization of bimoraic and monomoraic syllables is restricted to word-final vowel length contrasts. The same position-dependent neutralization of long and short vowels is observed in the formation of *Zuzya-go*, a secret language used by Japanese jazz musicians, which was analyzed extensively by Itô et al. (1996) and Kubozono (in press).

4. Auditory perception

This section presents evidence from the auditory domain for neutralization of final vowel length. Kato (1999) and Tanaka et al. (1994) have found that native speakers of Japanese are more sensitive to temporal distortions in the initial portion of sound sequences than in a later portion, both for speech and non-speech stimuli. These results suggest that listeners gradually lose sensitivity to the temporal structure of auditory stimuli as they hear the stimuli from the beginning to the end.

Sukegawa et al. (1999) report an experiment more specific to vowel shortening. They had a native speaker of Japanese read the test sentence in (13), which contains the bisyllabic word /koo.koo/ 'high school'.

(13)   Dore-ga <u>kookoo</u>-tuki no daigaku?
'Which university has an attached high school?'

They then edited this recording with a computer program to shorten each of the two long vowels in /koo.koo/ in ten degrees. They presented these temporally distorted stimuli to four native speakers of Japanese, who were asked to judge whether each stimulus was /koo.koo/ (vs. /ko.koo/ and /koo.ko/). Three of the four subjects were less sensitive to temporal distortions in the word-final long vowel than the word-medial one. The second syllable of /koo.koo/ in (13) is not strictly word-final since the word arguably forms a compound with the morpheme /tuki/ 'attached'. However, it is interesting that Sukegawa et al.'s subjects nevertheless responded differently to the temporal distortions of the two long vowels in the word /koo.koo/.

5. Visual perception

We have seen a marked tendency towards a position-dependent neutralization of vowel length in both phonology and auditory perception. Interestingly enough, essentially the same position-dependent confusion occurs in 'visual perception' of speech, where listeners are only given visual stimuli. The series of 'perception' experiments to be described in this section were not designed to explore the McGurk Effect with Japanese listeners, i.e. to address the question of to what extent listeners rely on visual cues when they actually perceive speech. Rather, they were carried out to see what listeners could (or could not) perceive on the basis of the visual information alone when they are deprived of auditory stimuli. These experiments, therefore, do not allow us to look directly into the mechanism or strategies of speech perception. Yet, the results which we will see shortly suggest that 'visual perception' has a close bearing on phonology, phonetics and auditory perception, and is indeed constrained by the same principle of temporal neutralization governing the latter three areas of speech.

5.1 Experiment 1

5.1.1 Method

Materials
Stimuli in (14) consisted of 15 pairs of two words contrasting in the presence or absence of one of the four types of non-syllabic moras in (2) above: the moraic nasal, the moraic obstruent, the second half of a long vowel, and the second half of a diphthong. The contrast in the presence or absence of these moraic elements occurs either word-medially or word-finally, except the moraic obstruent, which can occur only word-medially. The accentuation of the pairs was controlled so that the two members of each pair have an identical accent pattern (with the exceptions of two pairs, /obasaN/−/oba'asaN/ and /o'kasaN/−/oka'asaN/).

(14)		Word-medial contrast	Word-final contrast
	Moraic Nasal	ama−aNma 'a nun', 'massage'	aNma−aNmaN 'massage', 'bean-jam bun'
		taniN−taNniN 'others', 'teacher in charge'	tani−taniN 'a valley', 'others'
	Short/long vowel	sado−saado 'Sado Island','third'	sado−sadoo 'Sado Island', 'tea ceremony'
		obasaN−obaasaN 'aunt', 'grandmother'	
		biru−biiru 'building', 'beer'	rubi−rubii 'type-setting term', 'ruby (gem)'
		okasaN−okaasaN 'Mr/Ms. Oka', 'mother'	kyoozyu−kyoozyuu 'professor', 'within today'
	Moraic obstruent	kako−kakko 'past', 'bracket'	———

	syutyoo−syuttyoo 'claim', 'business trip'	
Diphthong	kaga−ka<u>i</u>ga 'Kaga (placename)', 'painting'	kaiga−kaiga<u>i</u> 'painting', 'foreign land'

The total of 30 test words were randomized and numbered. They were read in isolation by a native female speaker of Tokyo Japanese, and were simultaneously recorded with a digital video camera. On the basis of this recording, the following three kinds of stimuli were produced: (i) visual stimuli (video playback without sound), (ii) auditory stimuli (cassette tape playback), and (iii) audio-visual stimuli (video playback with sound).

Subjects
Participants were 46 native adult speakers of Japanese who had no reported hearing problems, and twelve hearing impaired adult speakers of Japanese. The hearing unimpaired subjects lived in the Kansai area, although they were originally from various parts of Japan. The hearing-impaired subjects were all from Kansai and lived there at the time of the experiment.

Most of the hearing impaired subjects became impaired prelingually. Ten subjects are diagnosed as Grade 2 on the hearing impairment scale, which means that they can hear virtually nothing in natural conversation. The other two subjects are diagnosed as Grade 3, which means that they can only hear a person when the person speaks extremely loudly in front of them. All the hearing impaired subjects use the Japanese sign language and lip-reading in daily communication. These hearing-impaired subjects were included in the visual perception experiment in order to see how much more accurately they were able to perceive temporal differences on the basis of visual information alone.

Task
Hearing impaired subjects were presented only with the visual stimuli. Hearing unimpaired subjects participated in all three tests, taking the visual test first and then the auditory or audio-visual

test. In each type of test, each subject heard each test word once and was asked to choose between the two members of the minimal pair after the playback of each test word. The two words were printed on an answer sheet for a total of 30 responses.

5.1.2 Results and analysis

As expected, hearing unimpaired subjects showed very good performance in the auditory and audio-visual tests. None of the subjects, in fact, made any errors for any word pair in the audio-visual test. They gave almost perfect scores in the auditory test as well. They did not make any errors in distinguishing between long and short vowels, either in word-medial or word-final positions. Some errors were attested with the moraic nasal and the diphthong only when they appeared in word-final positions. However, the subjects' performance remains very high: the percentage of correct answers was 97% for the word-final moraic nasal and 94% for the word-final diphthong. Overall, hearing unimpaired subjects had little or no difficulty in distinguishing between bimoraic and monomoraic syllables in both the audio-visual and auditory tests.

However, a substantially different result was obtained for the visual test. Figures 1 and 2 show the results of this test with the two groups of subjects, respectively.

As can be seen, both groups of subjects generally achieved very good performance in the visual perception test, too. Although not as good as in the auditory or audio-visual tests, the average percentage of correct answers in this test is over 80% for each of the subject groups, much higher than the chance level of 50%. This suggests that visual information alone contains very useful cues for perceiving temporal differences such as those found in the test words.

On the other hand, Figures 1 and 2 suggest that visual information was not useful at all in distinguishing between pairs that contrasted in vowel length word-finally. To confirm this, a three-factor mixed ANOVA was carried out, with the between-subjects factor hearing group (hearing unimpaired vs. impaired) and the within-subjects factors mora type (non-syllabic moras except the ob-

184   *Haruo Kubozono*

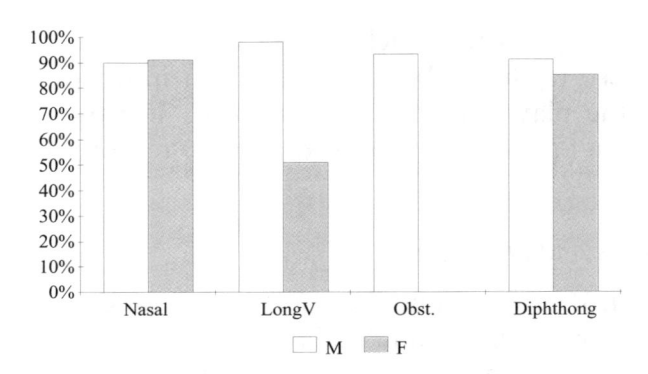

Figure 1: Performance of hearing unimpaired Japanese subjects in visual perception test: percentage of correct answers for the four types of moras in two word positions, word-medial (M) and word-final (F).

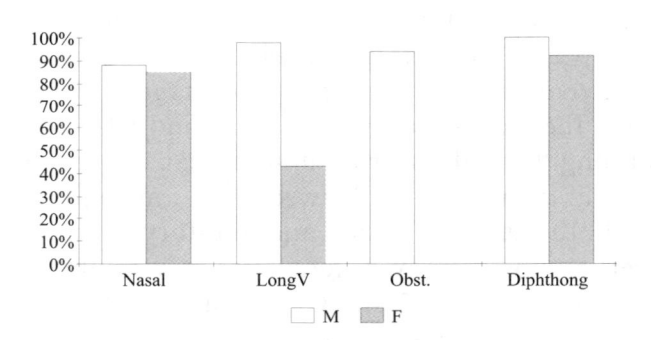

Figure 2: Same as Figure 1 for hearing impaired subjects.

struent, which was not included since it can only occur word-medially) and word position of the non-syllabic mora (medial vs. final). The measure was the percentage of correctly perceived items. Although the three-way interaction was not significant, the interaction of mora type and word position was significant ($F(2,336) = 63.61$, $p < .001$), and so were the main effects of mora type ($F(1,336) = 31.72$, $p < .001$) and word position ($F(2,336) = 89.67$, $p < .001$). No other factor or interaction of factors was significant. The simple effect of word position was significant for long/short vowels for both groups of speakers (unimpaired: $F(1,90) = 180.53$, $p < .0001$; impaired: $F(1,22) = 68.17$, $p < .0001$), but no significant positional effect was found for the nasal or the diphthong for either group of subjects. This suggests that the significant main effect of word position is mainly due to the long/short vowels.

In sum, Japanese subjects cannot 'see' the difference between long and short vowels in word-final positions, while they can in word-medial positions. This is true not only of hearing unimpaired subjects but of hearing impaired subjects as well, who are expected be more skillful in lip-reading than the unimpaired subjects.

The fact that Japanese subjects cannot correctly perceive word-final distinctions in vowel length may not be very surprising if we consider the phonetic nature of long/short vowels and the special status of the word-final position. First, as their names suggest, long and short vowels differ primarily in duration. In contrast, presence or absence of moraic nasals and diphthongs involves a segmental change as well as a change in duration. This segmental cue is absent in the contrast between long and short vowels, regardless of position. Second, it is to be expected that contrasts in vowel length can be seen much more clearly in word-medial positions than in word-final positions. The timing between the vowel and the following material gives a useful cue to the duration of the vowel itself but this 'external' timing cue is not available if the vowel appears in word-final positions, where it is not followed by any phonetic material. This prediction is tested in Experiment 2.

5.2 Experiment 2

5.2.1 Method

Methods were the same as in Experiment 1, except that test words were placed in a carrier sentence, /kare wa ... to itta/ 'He said...', which was pronounced by a male native speaker of Japanese at a natural speed. A total of 25 native hearing-unimpaired Japanese speakers, all of whom had participated in Experiment 1, served as subjects.

5.2.2 Results and analysis

The results of this experiment, shown in Figure 3, differ from those of the previous experiment (Figure 1) in several striking ways.

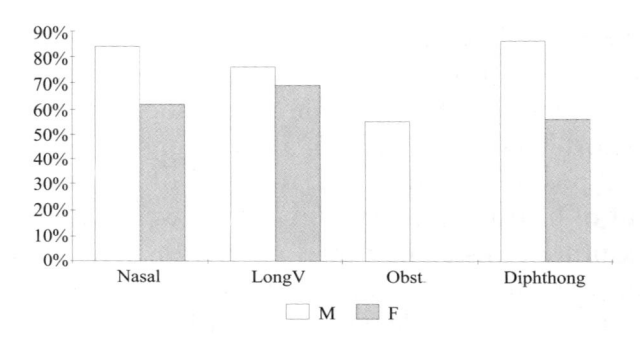

Figure 3: Same as Figure 1 for words in frame sentences.

A two-factor ANOVA (word position and mora type) reveals that the interaction between word position and mora type is not significant. However, the main effect of word position was significant, with word-final contrasts more difficult to perceive than their word-medial counterparts $(F(1,138) = 19.22$, $p < .001)$. The averages in the figure suggest that this main effect of word position is mainly due to the moraic nasal and the diphthong, although there is no significant difference among the three mora types with regard to the effect of word position. This contrasts with the result from Experiment 1, where we saw that the simple effect of word position was significant only for long/short vowels and not for other mora types.

A post-hoc comparison of the data in Figure 3 with the hearing unimpaired subjects' visual perception data from Experiment 1 was performed to investigate the effect of frame sentence vs. stimuli in isolation. This was analyzed using a three-factor ANOVA with the factors word position, mora type, and stimulus environment (frame sentence vs. isolation). This statistical test showed a significant interaction of the three factors $(F(1,276) = 12.44$, $p < .001)$. It also showed that the main effect of stimulus environment as well as the main effect of word position was significant: $F(1,276) = 22.16$, $p < .001$; $F(1,276) = 36.28$, $p < .001$. This suggests that the minimal pairs of test words were generally more difficult to distinguish visually when they are pronounced in a sentence than in isolation.

This difference seems to contradict the prediction stated at the end of Experiment 1, namely, that temporal distinctions will be easier to perceive when they are followed by some phonetic material than otherwise. However, the overall effect of stimulus environment can be attributed to an independent factor. Acoustic measurements of the test words show that heavy syllables actually had considerably shorter durations when they were pronounced in a sentence than when they were pronounced in isolation (Table 1), indicating faster speech in the sentences.

Table 1: Comparison of the acoustic durations (in ms) of vowels in the auditory stimuli in Experiments 1 and 2.

	bi_ru	bi_i_ru	sad_o	sa_a_do
Experiment 1	172	356	112	331
Experiment 2	105	191	86	203

	rub_i	rub_i_i	sad_o	sad_o_o
Experiment 1	120	256	93	267
Experiment 2	86	187	63	193

Given this unexpected background factor, one would anticipate that all the temporal distinctions in the test words in (14) should be harder to perceive in frame sentences than in isolated words. This has turned out to be true, as can be seen from the comparison of Figure 1 and Figure 3. However, there is one exception, which is the distinction between long and short vowels in final position. In fact, comparison of the averages in Figures 1 and 3 suggest that long/short vowels in final position were easier to distinguish when they were pronounced in sentences than in isolation.

Moreover, statistical analysis of the data in Figure 1 showed a significant effect of position for long/short vowels, but not for the other mora types. On the other hand, statistical analysis of the data in Figure 3 reveals a different tendency, with the moraic nasal and the diphthong apparently showing a stronger positional effect than long/short vowels. This latter positional effect can be attributed, at least in part, to a phonetic tendency whereby heavy syllables including diphthongs and the moraic nasal are generally shorter in word-final position than in word-medial position when they are pronounced in sentences (Ujihira & Kubozono, 2000). Despite this phonetic tendency, it is noteworthy that long/short vowels did not exhibit a noticeable positional effect in Figure 3. This, too, suggests that word-final contrasts in vowel length become, other things being equal, relatively less difficult to distinguish when the stimuli are presented in a sentence than in isolation.

Thus, comparison of the results of Experiment 2 with those of Experiment 1 seems to support the idea that temporal differences in vowel length are easier to perceive if the vowel is followed by some material. In other words, the material that follows the vowel provides some external timing cue to the perception of the duration of the vowel itself and, hence, to the identification of long vs. short vowels. This additional timing cue is largely absent in word-final positions if the word is pronounced in isolation.

5.3 Experiment 3

It is by now largely clear why temporal confusion in visual perception is most likely to occur in word-final positions and with contrasts in vowel length if stimuli are presented in isolation. Specifically, word-final distinctions between long and short vowels lack both a segmental and an external timing cue, whereas other types of temporal distinctions as well as word-medial contrasts in vowel length have either or both of the cues at hand. However, this does not necessarily mean that visual information contains no cue to the word-final distinction between long and short vowels when the words are pronounced in isolation. It may be that some non-temporal cues are present in the visual stimuli but somehow not used by native speakers of Japanese, i.e. that the invisibility of vowel length is specific to Japanese speakers. To solve this question, a third experiment was carried out, this time with non-native learners of Japanese as subjects.

5.3.1 Method

Methods were the same as in Experiment 1, except that subjects were nine unimpaired adults whose native languages were Thai, English, Romanian, Korean, Mandarin Chinese, or Marathi (a language spoken in India). All were fairly competent in Japanese, speaking it as their second or third language. They arrived in Japan at ages ranging from 21 to 33 and had lived there for about two years on average (ranging from six months to six years) at the time of the experiment.

5.3.2 Results and analysis

Just like native Japanese subjects, the non-native subjects were able to perceive temporal distinctions quite accurately based on auditory and audiovisual information. Their scores on these two tests were very high with the average percentage of correct answers reaching 97% (auditory test) and 98% (audio-visual test). The final diphthong was most difficult to perceive in the auditory test (88% correct), but a three-factor ANOVA with the factors media type (two media), word position and mora type showed no significant three-way interaction.

While the non-native subjects displayed basically the same patterns as the native Japanese subjects in auditory and audio-visual tests, they performed in a substantially different way in the test where only visual stimuli were presented. The results of this visual test are summarized in Figure 4.

A three-factor ANOVA (three media types, word position and mora type) showed no significant three-way interaction, but a significant two-way interaction between media type and word position ($F(2,144) = 9.74$, $p < .0001$). No other two-way interaction was significant. The main effect of media type was also significant ($F(2,144) = 15.92$, $p < .0001$), and so was the main effect of word position ($F(1,144) = 14.44$, $p < .001$). Specifically, the simple effect of word position was significant for the visual test ($F(1,48) = 13.64$, $p < .001$), but not for the auditory ($F(1,48) = 1.15$, $p > .1$) or audio-visual test ($F(1,48) = 0.06$, $p > .5$). This indicates that word-

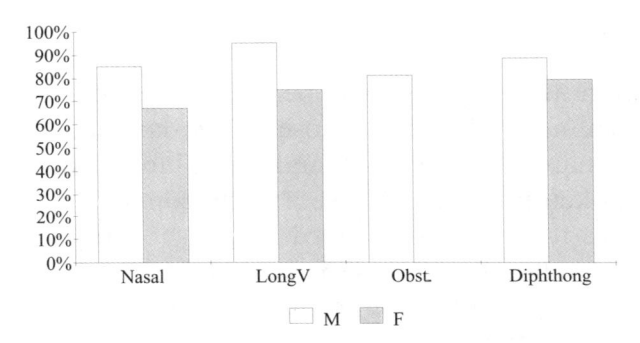

Figure 4: Same as Figure 1 for hearing unimpaired non-Japanese subjects.

final distinctions are harder to perceive than word-medial distinctions only for the visual test.

A more revealing fact about Figure 4 is that non-native subjects attained relatively high accuracy (75%) in distinguishing long/short vowels in word-final positions. This suggests that non-native hearing unimpaired subjects were able to perceive this type of temporal distinction better than the hearing unimpaired native subjects (Figure 1). To confirm that this is actually the case, a three-factor ANOVA was conducted with the factors language background (native vs. non-native hearing unimpaired), word position and mora type. This revealed a significant three-way interaction ($F(2,318) = 8.86$, $p < .001$) and also a significant two-way interaction between language group and mora type ($F(2,318) = 4.31, p < .05$) and between word position and mora type ($F(2,318) = 33.51, p < .0001$), but not between language group and word position. Moreover, two-factor ANOVAs showed a significant interaction between word position and mora type for the native subject group ($F(2,324) = 31.42$, $p < .0001$), but not for the non-native subject group ($F(2,48) = 0.14, p > .5$). This suggests that the significant positional effect that was observed for long/short vowels in Figure 1 is no longer present in the data in Figure 4.

A post hoc comparison of the non-native subjects' visual perception data and the native unimpaired subjects' visual data was performed using the three-factor ANOVA mentioned above. This comparison showed no significant difference between the two language groups ($F(1,318) = 0.001$, p > .5), but did reveal that non-native subjects' perception of word-final long/short vowels was significantly better than that of the native subjects ($F(1,53) = 9.53$, p < .01). This contrasts strongly with the fact that non-native perception is generally worse than or just as good as native perception with respect to other types of temporal distinctions, e.g. word-final contrast in the moraic nasal ($F(1,53) = 12.71$, p < .001), and word-medial long/short vowels ($F(1,53) = 0.57$, p > .1).

This suggests that visual information does contain a certain secondary cue to the distinction between long and short vowels in word-final positions. Non-native subjects used this secondary cue when 'seeing' prosody, whereas native Japanese subjects — both the hearing impaired and unimpaired — simply did not. This difference between native and non-native perception may be related to Sekiyama's two findings about bimodal perception by non-native listeners (Sekiyama, 1997a,b): (a) that Chinese speakers who live in Japan, as well as native English speakers, show a stronger McGurk effect than native Japanese listeners when listening to Japanese; and (b) that Japanese speakers show a stronger McGurk effect when listening to English than when listening to their native language.

Given the native vs. non-native difference in the visual perception experiments, the next question to ask is what the secondary visual cue is. To tackle this question I compared the performance of the three subject groups with respect to the three word-final long/short vowels, i.e. /i/, /u/ and /o/, in the visual tests. The results of this analysis are shown in Figure 5. A two-factor ANOVA was conducted with the factors subject group (three subject groups) and vowel type (three word-final vowels). This statistical test did not show a significant two-way interaction or any significant main effect of the vowel type, but the main effect of subject group was significant ($F(2,192) = 8.62$, p < .001). Specifically, non-native subjects performed better than native unimpaired subjects ($F(1,163) = 12.85$, p < .001) and native impaired subjects ($F(1,61) = 19.32$, p < .0001), but no significant difference was found between the two native groups ($F(1,172) = 1.82$, p > .1).

192 *Haruo Kubozono*

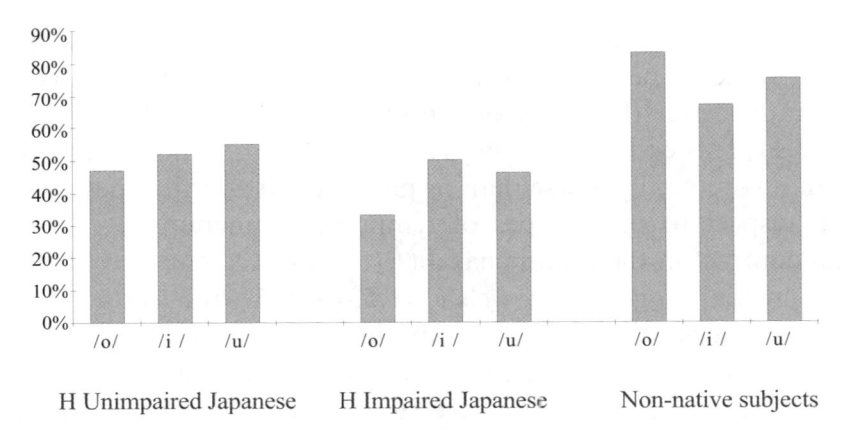

Figure 5: Word-final contrast in vowel length: percentage of correct answers in visual perception tests for three groups of subjects and three different vowels

Although not statistically significant, results in Figure 5 suggest that non-native speakers were slightly better on the /o/–/o:/ pair than on the other two vowel pairs, whereas the two native groups were not. This non-significant tendency shown by non-native subjects may be linked to the differing degrees of lip protrusion shown by different vowels in Japanese. According to Kiyoshi Honda (personal communication), long /o:/ and short /o/, but not /i:/–/i/ or /u:/–/u/, exhibit a considerable difference in the degree of lip protrusion in Japanese. Given this difference, a tentative explanation for the non-native speakers' surprisingly good perception of word-final vowels is that they relied on the differing extent of lip protrusion as well as temporal cues. This interpretation probably squares with a remark some of the non-native subjects made after the experiment that long and short vowels can be distinguished by the shape of the speaker's mouth.

It is quite possible that non-native speakers, too, relied on visual cues other than lip protrusion. However, it seems safe to conclude that native Japanese speakers rely almost exclusively on temporal cues when using visual information to perceive the vowel length contrast, whereas non-native speakers are sensitive to redundant non-temporal cues as well.

6. Acoustic measurements

Having seen that word-final contrasts between long and short vowels are prone to neutralization in both phonology and visual perception of speech, there are two interrelated questions that remain unanswered: why are word-final contrasts in vowel length invisible in Japanese phonology, and how is this phonological invisibility related to the invisibility of the same type of temporal contrast in the visual perception of speech? These questions can be answered by considering in more detail the perceptual and phonetic characteristics of long and short vowels in word-final positions.[4]

In the foregoing discussion of visual perception it was pointed out that word-final contrasts in vowel length inherently have several disadvantages as compared to other types of temporal contrasts. That is, neither a segmental nor an external timing cue is available for this particular type of temporal distinction, whereas these cues as well as an internal durational cue are available for other types of temporal distinctions. This is summarized in Table 2. (Recall that the moraic nasal and obstruent in word-medial posi-

Table 2: Types of temporal distinctions and availability of visual cues.

	Durational cue	External timing cue	Segmental cue
Moraic nasal			
taniN—taNniN	YES	YES	NO
tani—taniN	YES	NO	YES
Long/short vowel			
biru—biiru	YES	YES	NO
rubi—rubii	YES	NO	NO
Moraic obstruent			
kako—kakko	YES	YES	NO
Diphthong			
kaga—kaiga	YES	YES	YES
kaiga—kaigai	YES	NO	YES

tion are homorganic with the following consonant and do not have their own place of articulation.)

This picture applies to auditory perception in a straightforward manner. For example, presence or absence of the moraic obstruent in word-medial position is signaled not only by the durational difference of the intervocalic consonants themselves, but also by the onset of the following vowel. Likewise, distinctions between word-medial long and short vowels can be perceived on the basis of the onset of the following segment as well as the inherent durational differences between the two kinds of vowels. However, their word-final counterparts, e.g. /rubi/−/rubii/, can basically be distinguished by the inherent durational difference and nothing else. Thus, long and short vowels in vowel-final position have the fewest perceptual cues among the seven types of distinctions in Table 2. If phonological patterns are affected by what happens in auditory perception at all, it is not surprising to find that the vowel length distinction in word-final position, and not other types of temporal distinctions, tends to be neutralized in phonological phenomena.

In addition to these considerations about the perceptual characteristics of temporal contrasts, acoustic characteristics of long and short vowels in word-final position also help to account for the phonological invisibility of word-final vowel length. Kaiki & Sagisaka (1992) report that Japanese vowels are phonetically shorter in sentence-final positions than in non-final positions. They did not find any substantial effect on vowel duration word-finally, nor did they discuss the shortening effect separately for short and long vowels. However, since the stimuli used in Experiments 1 and 3 were recorded as isolated words, they are effectively sentences. If so, sentence-final shortening may well make the final long vowels in the stimuli rather similar to short vowels, reducing the usefulness of the duration cue.

In order to find out if this explanation is possible, I measured the duration of each vowel in the stimuli in Experiments 1 and 3. Specifically, I compared vowel durations in final and medial positions (Table 3) and also the duration of the vowel in the long and short member of each pair (Table 4).

Table 3: Acoustic comparison (in ms) of vowels in the two word positions

/i/	biru	172	/u/	rubi	175		rubii	183	/i:/	biiru	356
	rubi	120		biru	132		biiru	96		rubii	256

Table 4: Acoustic comparison (in ms) of long and short vowels in the two word positions

a. word-medial contrast

/i:/	biiru	356	/a:/	saado	331
/i/	biru	172	/a/	sado	112
	difference	184		difference	219

b. word-final contrast

/i:/	rubii	256	/o:/	sadoo	267
/i/	rubi	120	/o/	sado	93
	difference	136		difference	174

The results in Table 3 show that the word-final vowels, whether long or short, were shorter by about 30% on average than their word-medial counterparts. The results in Table 4 show that the durational differences between long and short vowels were smaller in word-final positions than in word-medial positions. Although the durational ratios between long/short vowels are much the same across the two word positions, i.e. the ratio of about 2:1 in the case of /i:/−/i/ and the ratio of nearly 3:1 in the case of other vowels, the absolute differences between the two word positions are considerable: a difference of about 200 ms (184−219 ms) for word-medial contrasts and a difference of about 150 ms (136− 174 ms) for word-final contrasts. If these results are found to hold for larger numbers of tokens, such a positional effect on the durations of long vs. short vowels could reduce the usefulness of the durational cue to the distinction in word-final position. The same effect will also explain, at least in part, why hearing impaired subjects performed no better than hearing unimpaired subjects in Experiment 1 (section 5.1) although the former group should be generally more skillful than the latter in using visual information for speech perception.

The data in Table 3 square with the data reported by Ujihira & Kubozono (2000), who made acoustic measurements of long vowels in word-medial and word-final positions. They found out that long vowels were significantly shorter finally than medially.

7. Conclusion

This paper has examined a linguistic context in which monomoraic and bimoraic syllables are neutralized in Tokyo Japanese. While temporal distinctions between these two types of syllables are crucial for the mora-based rhythm of Japanese, they are sometimes neutralized. However, this type of temporal neutralization is highly restricted: it only occurs in word-final positions and, moreover, only affects the contrast between long and short vowels. What is most interesting is the finding that tendencies towards this highly constrained neutralization of mora timing are observed in four independent areas of speech: phonology, auditory perception, visual perception and acoustic data. In other words, the four areas are constrained in the same way with respect to temporal neutralization.

In the perception of speech with visual information but without sound, word-final contrasts in vowel length are literally invisible to native Japanese subjects, hearing impaired and unimpaired alike. This suggests that there is a striking correspondence between phonological invisibility and visual invisibility, at least as far as temporal structure is concerned. The visual perception experiments further revealed some differences between native and non-native subjects. Most crucially, non-native speakers of Japanese are able to perceive word-final distinctions in vowel length more accurately than native speakers. A closer examination of the visual perception data suggests that native Japanese subjects rely primarily on temporal visual cues to distinguish between long and short vowels, while non-native subjects seem to make use of some non-temporal visual cues as well, such as the differing degrees of lip protrusion.

Finally, this paper considered the reasons why word-final contrasts in vowel length are prone to neutralization in Japanese in general. A set of phonetic factors was proposed to explain this position-dependent neutralization. Seen from a perceptual point of view, word-final long and short vowels potentially have fewest phonetic cues available for perceptual distinction. They lack a segmental cue, for example, which will potentially enhance the durational difference in other types of temporal contrasts, e.g. /ka/ vs. /kai/ and /ta.ni/ vs. /ta.niN/. They also lack an external timing cue, a cue to the duration of a vowel or consonant that is signaled by the temporal onset of the following phonetic material. This additional timing cue is generally available for temporal distinctions in word-medial positions, e.g. /ka.ko/ vs. /kak.ko/, /sa.do/ vs. /saa.do/, but not for word-final distinctions, e.g. /ta.ni/ vs. /ta.niN/, /sa.do/ vs. /sa.doo/. It was argued that these perceptual disadvantages lie behind the invisibility of vowel length contrasts in word-final position in both phonology and visual perception.

Word-final contrasts in vowel length are further weakened by the acoustic characteristics of long and short vowels in word-final position. Acoustic data suggest that vowels, both long and short, tend to become phonetically shorter in word-final positions. It is not clear why this position-dependent shortening occurs, but it obviously reduces the durational difference between long and short vowels in this particular position. It was proposed that it consequently reduces the usefulness of the durational cue and, together with the perceptual disadvantages mentioned above, triggers the neutralization of word-final contrasts in question both in phonology and in visual perception.

Acknowledgements

I am grateful to Keiko Ishii for her assistance in conducting the experiments and to Tadahisa Kondo, Michinao Matsui and Akira Ujihira for their assistance with the statistical analysis of the data. I benefited from discussions with many people, particularly Reiko Mazuka, Akiko Hayashi, Reiko Yamada, Hiroaki Kato, Minoru Tsuzaki and Kiyoshi Honda. I am indebted to an anonymous reviewer and Anne Cutler for their invaluable comments on an earlier version of this paper. All errors that remain are my own.

Notes

1. Long vowels sometimes tend to shorten at the end of the first component word of compound expressions: e.g. mendoo kusai → mendokusai 'trouble, smelly; troublesome', obentoo-bako → obentobako 'lunch, box; lunch box', kakkoo ii → kakkoii 'appearance, good; good-looking'.
2. Exceptions include the following: pa.to.roo.ru kaa → [pa.to][kaa] 'patrol car', kan.sai suu.paa → [kan][su.pa] 'Kansai Supermarket'. In the first example, the word-final long vowel is retained, whereas in the second example, the long vowel is shortened but the empty mora slot is filled by the subsequent mora.
3. The only exception I know to this rule is the word /te.re.ko/, which comes from /tee.pu re.koo.daa/ 'tape recorder'.
4. Another hypothesis is that vowel length is not very distinctive in word-final positions in Japanese, at least not as contrastive as vowel length in word-medial positions or as the moraic nasal in word-final positions. However, this functional possibility cannot be empirically supported. An analysis of the NTT Database (NTT, 1999) shows that long vowels appear in word-final positions almost as frequently as in word-medial positions. Moreover, the difference in frequency between word-medial and word-final long vowels is basically the same as the difference between word-medial and word-final moraic nasals. These results suggest that word-final long vowels are potentially as contrastive as their word-medial counterparts and also as word-final moraic nasals.

References

Alfonso, A.
    1980   *Japanese language patterns*, Vol. 2. Tokyo: Sophia University.
Beckman, M. E.
    1982   Segment duration and the 'mora' in Japanese. *Phonetica*, 39, 113–135.
Beckman, M. E.
    1986   *Stress and non-stress accent*. Dordrecht: Foris Publications.
Cutler, A.
    1994   Segmentation problems, rhythmic solutions. *Lingua*, 92, 81–104.
Cutler, A. & Otake, T.
    1994   Mora or phoneme? Further evidence for language-specific listening. *Journal of Memory and Language*, 33, 824–844.
Cutler, A., Mehler, J., Norris, D. G. & Segui, J.
    1983   A language-specific comprehension strategy. *Nature*, 304, 159–160.
Han, M. S.
    1994   Acoustic manifestations of mora timing in Japanese. *Journal of the Acoustical Society of America*, 96, 73–82.

Haraguchi, S.
  1996   Syllable, mora and accent. In T. Otake & A. Cutler (eds.), *Phonological Structure and Language Processing: Cross-linguistic Studies*, (pp. 45–75). Berlin: Mouton de Gruyter.
Itô, J.
  1990   Prosodic minimality in Japanese. *CLS 26–II: Papers from the Parasession on the Syllable in Phonetics and Phonology*, 213–239.
Itô, J., Kitagawa, Y. & Mester, A.
  1996   Prosodic faithfulness and correspondence: Evidence from a Japanese argot. *Journal of East Asian Linguistics*, 5, 217–94.
Kaiki, N. & Sagisaka, Y.
  1992   The control of segmental duration in speech synthesis using statistical methods. In Y. Tohkura, E. Vatikiotis-Bateson & Y. Sagisaka (eds.), *Speech Perception, Production and Linguistic Structure*, (pp. 391–402). Tokyo: Ohmsha.
Kato, H.
  1999   *Perceptual characteristics of temporal structures in speech: towards objective assessment of synthetic speech*. PhD. dissertation, Kobe University.
Kubozono, H.
  1985   Speech errors and syllable structure. *Linguistics and Philology*, 6, 220–243.
Kubozono, H.
  1988   *The organization of Japanese prosody*. PhD. dissertation, University of Edinburgh [Kurosio, 1993].
Kubozono, H.
  1989   The mora and syllable structure in Japanese: evidence from speech errors. *Language and Speech*, 32 Vol 3, 249–278. Reprinted in C. W. Kreidler (ed.), *Phonology: Critical Concepts*, Vol 3, (pp. 196–226). London: Routledge.
Kubozono, H.
  1999a   *Nihongo no onsei (The sound system of Japanese)*. Tokyo: Iwanami Shoten.
Kubozono, H.
  1999b   Mora and syllable. In N. Tsujimura (ed.), *The Handbook of Japanese Linguistics*, (pp. 31–61). Oxford: Blackwell.
Kubozono, H.
  2001   Epenthetic vowels and accent in Japanese: facts and paradoxes. J. van de Weijer & T. Nishihara (eds.), *Issues in Japanese phonology and Morphology*, (pp. 113–142). Berlin and New York: Mouton de Gruyter.
Kubozono, H.
  in press   The syllable as a unit of prosodic organization in Japanese. In C. Féry & R. van de Vijver (eds.), *The Syllable in Optimality Theory*, (pp. 129–156). Cambridge: Cambridge University Press.

Matsumura, A.
 1995 *Daizirin* (Japanese Dictionary). Tokyo: Sanseido.

McCawley, J. D.
 1978 What is a tone language? In V. Fromkin (ed.), *Tone: A Linguistic Survey*, (pp. 113−131). New York: Academic Press.

McGurk, H. & McDonald, J.
 1976 Hearing lips and seeing voices. *Nature*, **264**, 746−748.

NTT Communication Science Laboratories
 1999 *Nihongo no goi tokusei (Lexical properties of Japanese)*. Tokyo: Sanseido.

Port, R. F., Dalby, J. & O'Dell, M.
 1987 Evidence for mora timing in Japanese. *Journal of the Acoustical Society of America*, **81**, 1574−85.

Poser, W.
 1984 *The phonetics and phonology of tone and intonation in Japanese*. PhD dissertation, MIT.

Poser, W.
 1988 Glide formation and compensatory lengthening in Japanese. *Linguistic Inquiry*, **19**, 494−502.

Ramus, F., Nespor, M. & Mehler, J.
 1999 Correlates of linguistic rhythm in the speech signal. *Cognition*, **73**, 265−292.

Sekiyama, K.
 1997a Cultural and linguistic factors in audiovisual speech processing: the McGurk Effect in Chinese subjects. *Perception and Psychophysics*, **59** Vol **1**, 73−80.

Sekiyama, K.
 1997b Audiovisual speech perception and its inter-language differences. *The Japanese Journal of Psychonomic Science,* **15**, 122−127.

Sekiyama, K. & Tohkura, Y.
 1991 McGurk Effect in non-English listeners: few visual effects for Japanese subjects hearing Japanese syllables of high auditory intelligibility. *Journal of the Acoustical Society of America*, **90**, 1797−1805.

Shigeno, S.
 1998 Individual differences observed in McGurk Effect. *The Japan Journal of Logopedics and Phoniatrics*, **39** Vol **3**, 267−273.

Sibata, T.
 1995 *Nihongo wa omosiroi (Japanese is fun)*. Tokyo: Iwanami.

Sugito, M.
 1980 Akusento Intoneesyon no hikaku (Comparison of accent and intonation of Japanese and English). In T. Kunihiro (ed.) *Noti-eigo hikaku kooza (Comparative studies of Japanese and English)*, (pp. 107−183). Tokyo: Taishukan.

Sukegawa, Y., Maekawa, K. & Uehara, S.
    1999   An experimental phonetic study of Japanese vowel shortening and its implications to pronunciation training. (In Japanese) In Y. Sasaki-Alam (ed.), *Linguistics and Japanese Language Education*, (pp. 81−94). Tokyo: Kurosio Publishers.

Takano, S., Tsuzaki, M. & Kato, H.
    2000   Perceptual sensitivity to temporal distortion of visual, auditory and bimodal speech. *Journal of the Acoustical Society of Japan* (E), **21** Vol **1**, 41−43.

Tanaka, M., Tsuzaki, M. & Kato, H.
    1994   Discrimination of empty duration in the click sequence simulating a mora structure. *Journal of the Acoustical Society of Japan* (E), **15** Vol **3**, 191−192.

Ujihira, A. & Kubozono, H.
    2000   On the neutralization of vowel length in Japanese. Paper presented at the annual meeting of the Phonetic Society of Japan. September, 2000.

A typological study of stress 'deafness'

Sharon Peperkamp and Emmanuel Dupoux

Abstract

Previous research has shown that native speakers of French, as opposed to those of Spanish, exhibit stress 'deafness', i.e. have difficulties distinguishing stress contrasts. In French, stress is non-contrastive, while in Spanish, stress is used to make lexical distinctions. We examine three other languages with non-contrastive stress, Finnish, Hungarian and Polish. In two experiments with a short-term memory sequence repetition task, we find that speakers of Finnish and Hungarian are like French speakers (i.e. exhibit stress 'deafness'), but not those of Polish. We interpret these findings in the light of an acquisition framework, that states that infants decide whether or not to keep stress in their phonological representation during the first two years of life, based on information extractable from utterance edges. In particular, we argue that Polish infants, unlike French, Finnish and Hungarian ones, cannot extract the stress regularity of their language on the basis of what they have already learned. As a consequence, they keep stress in their phonological representation, and as adults, they do not have difficulties in distinguishing stress contrasts.

1. Introduction

It has long been known that speech perception is influenced by phonological properties of the listener's native language (Sapir, 1921; Polivanov, 1974). Much experimental evidence has been gathered concerning this influence, suggesting that listeners use a set of language-specific phoneme categories during speech perception. For instance, Goto (1971) has documented that Japanese listeners map American [l] and [r] onto their own, single, [ɾ] category, and, as a result, have a lot of difficulties in discriminating between them. Similarly, the contrast between the retroflex and dental stops [t] − [t̪] is very difficult for the English, but not for the Hindi speaker (Werker & Tees, 1984b). This contrast is, in fact, phonemic in Hindi, whereas neither of the stop consonants involved occurs in English; rather, English uses the alveolar stop [t].

The influence of suprasegmental properties of the native language has also been investigated. Research in this area has concentrated on the perception of tone (Kiriloff, 1969; Bluhme & Burr, 1971; Gandour, 1983; Lee & Nusbaum, 1993; Wang, Spence & Sereno, 1999), but the perception of stress was recently investigated as well. In particular, Dupoux, Pallier, Sebastián-Gallés & Mehler (1997) found that French subjects exhibit great difficulties in discriminating non-words that differ only in the location of stress. In French, stress does not carry lexical information, but predictably falls on the word's final vowel. Speakers of French, then, do not need to process stress to identify lexical items; given its fixed position, stress may instead be used as a cue to word segmentation (Rietveld, 1980).

The term 'deafness' is meant to designate the effect of listeners having difficulties in discriminating non-words that form a minimal pair in terms of certain non-native phonological contrasts, be it segmental or suprasegmental. We put the term 'deafness' between quotes, since listeners do not completely fail to perceive these contrasts (see Dupoux, Peperkamp & Sebastián-Gallés (2001) for extensive discussion on this issue). Segmental 'deafnesses' have been shown to arise early during language development. In fact, at 6 months, infants begin to lose their sensitivity for non-native vowel contrasts (Polka & Werker, 1994), while between 10 and 12 months, they lose the ability to discriminate non-native consonantal contrasts (Werker & Tees, 1984a). Suprasegmental 'deafnesses', by contrast, have not yet been attested experimentally in infants. However, it has been shown that 6- and 9-month-old infants are sensitive to suprasegmental properties of words in their native language (Jusczyk, Cutler & Redanz, 1993; Jusczyk, Friederici, Wessels, Svenkerud & Jusczyk, 1993). We therefore assume that suprasegmental 'deafnesses' similarly arise during infancy.

In this paper, we propose to extend the study of stress 'deafness' initiated by Dupoux et al. (1997). Two questions appear to be pertinent. The first one concerns the linguistic parameters that govern the presence of stress 'deafness'. Dupoux et al. (1997) suggest that the stress 'deafness' in French speakers is due to the fact that

French has non-contrastive stress. This hypothesis, however, needs to be tested with speakers of other languages with non-contrastive stress. French might indeed be a special case, in that — as is sometimes suggested — it has no word stress at all (Grammont, 1965); stress 'deafness', then, might be restricted to French only. Alternatively, as we will argue here, languages with non-contrastive stress might vary on other dimensions that are relevant for stress 'deafness'; accordingly, not all of these languages necessarily yield stress 'deafness'. The second question concerns the point during language development at which stress 'deafness' arises in infants. Dupoux & Peperkamp (2002) proposed a framework that allows us to explore these two questions simultaneously. In this framework, the perception of stress is assessed cross-linguistically in adults and inferences are drawn concerning the early acquisition of non-contrastive stress. In this paper, we will take up this framework and present experimental data concerning the perception of stress by adult speakers of several languages.

The outline of this paper is as follows. In section 2, we present the theoretical framework, state our assumptions, and outline different predictions regarding the perception of stress in four classes of languages with non-contrastive stress. We exemplify our typology with languages belonging to each one of the four classes in section 3. In section 4, we recall the results of Dupoux et al. (2001), attesting stress 'deafness' in French speakers with a new paradigm, and report on two new experiments with the same paradigm. These latter experiments assess the perception of stress by speakers of Finnish, Hungarian, and Polish. Section 5 contains our conclusions.

2. Theoretical framework

2.1 Stress 'deafness' as a window onto early language acquisition

It is largely agreed upon that words are stored in a mental lexicon. As to the phonological representation of words in this lexicon, two opposite views have been advanced in the literature. On the one hand, Klatt (1980), Marslen-Wilson & Warren (1994), and Goldinger (1998) argue for a universal acoustically or phonetically based representation of words. On the other hand, Church (1987), Frazier (1987), and Mehler, Dupoux & Segui (1990) propose that words are represented in an abstract phonological format that is tuned to the properties of the maternal language. Mehler et al. (1990) argue that from the onset of lexical acquisition, infants store words in this language-specific phonological format. They claim that having learned beforehand a language-specific phonological representation helps lexical acquisition. That is, a given word can surface in a near infinity of phonetic forms that − if the lexicon were constructed on the basis of a universal phonetic representation − would all be mapped onto separate lexical entries. By contrast, knowledge of what constitutes a lexical entry should facilitate the subsequent task of finding word meanings.

In Dupoux & Peperkamp (2002), we endorsed the hypothesis by Mehler et al. (1990) and further proposed that tuning of the phonological representation occurs during the first two years of life, before full mastery of the language. Such tuning, we argued, is based on an analysis of distributional regularities of the phonetic stream, rather than on a contrastive analysis involving minimal pairs. Given that infants have a limited knowledge of their language during the tuning of the phonological representation, they may include certain non-contrastive variation simply since they fail to observe its non-contrastiveness. In addition, we proposed that once tuned, the phonological representation of words becomes fixed and is relatively unaffected by later acquisitions in either the same or a different language (for empirical support, see Goto, 1971; Best, McRoberts & Sithole, 1988; Pallier, Bosch & Sebastián-Gallés, 1997; Dupoux et al., 1997; Dupoux, Kakehi, Hirose, Pallier & Mehler, 1999). This, then, allows us to gain insight into the nature and content of the phonological representation by conducting experiments in adults.

In the present study, we concentrate on the perception of stress, and focus on languages in which stress is signaled only by suprasegmental properties, i.e. duration, pitch, and energy. Regarding the representation of stress, the infants' problem is to decide, on the basis of a limited amount of information, whether stress is contrastive or not in their language, and, consequently, whether it should be encoded in the phonological representation or not. We dub this binary option the Stress Parameter and propose that it is set within the first two years of life. In its default setting, stress is encoded in the phonological representation. We distinguish three cases regarding the setting of the Stress Parameter during acquisition. Suppose a language with non-contrastive stress. If by the time the Stress Parameter is set infants can observe the stress regularity, they will set the Stress Parameter such that stress is not encoded. If, by contrast, they fail to deduce that stress is non-contrastive, they will redundantly keep stress in the phonological representation. Finally, for languages with contrastive stress, infants will observe no stress regularity and hence correctly keep stress in the phonological representation.

One might want to argue that infants simply attend to one-word utterances in order to deduce whether stress is contrastive. However, infant-directed speech does not necessarily contain many one-word utterances (Aslin, Woodward, LaMendola & Bever, 1996; Van de Weijer, 1999), and it is unclear how infants could distinguish between one-word and multi-word utterances (Christophe, Dupoux, Bertoncini & Mehler, 1994). Alternatively, we propose that in order to set the Stress Parameter, infants rely on cues concerning the distribution of stresses at utterance boundaries.[1] Indeed, if word stress is regular, then this regularity will be present at either the beginning or the end of utterances, depending on whether stress is assigned at the left or the right edge of the word, respectively. For instance, in French, all utterances end with a stressed syllable. Assuming that the location of main stress in the last word of the utterance does not differ from that of other words, infants can deduce that stress is always word-final and hence need not be encoded. In Spanish, by contrast, stress is largely unpredictable and falls on one of the word's last three syllables (Navarro Tomás, 1965). Hence, utterances neither begin nor end consistently with a main stressed syllable. Neither utterance edge thus presents a regular surface stress pattern, and infants therefore decide to keep stress in the phonological representation. Finally, in section 2.3 we will see cases in which infants might fail to deduce that stress is non-contrastive; this concerns languages in which the stress regularity is harder to extract from one of the utterance edges than in French. Before going in detail into the predictions of our framework, though, we will spell out various assumptions that underlie our proposal.

2.2 Background assumptions

First of all, we assume that utterance edges are easily attended to by young infants. This is an uncontroversial claim, since utterance edges are typically signaled by pauses in the discourse and/or by universal prosodic markers such as final lengthening. Experimental evidence that infants can segment speech into utterances is provided by Hirsh-Pasek, Kemler-Nelson, Jusczyk, Wright Cassidy, Druss & Kennedy (1987).

Stress can be instantiated by a variety of phonetic cues, i.e. duration, pitch, and energy (Lehiste, 1970). Our second assumption is that infants can perceive word stress categorically by the time they come to fix the Stress Parameter. This is a relatively strong assumption, since there is no one-to-one correspondence between the abstract notion of linguistic stress and the three phonetic cues. On the one hand, the relative weighting of these three cues in the realization of stress is language-specific. For instance, in languages with contrastive vowel length, duration is used to a lesser extent than pitch and energy; and in languages with lexical tone, pitch is avoided as a stress cue (Hayes, 1995). We assume that by the time they set the Stress Parameter, infants have acquired a sensitivity to the way in which word stress is realized in their language. In particular, we assume that they know whether their native language is a tone language, a pitch accent language, or a stress language, and whether or not it uses contrastive vowel length. An indication that this is a realistic assumption is that newborns rapidly become attuned to some global suprasegmental and rhythmic properties of their native language (Mehler, Jusczyk,

Lambertz, Halsted, Bertoncini & Amiel-Tison, 1988; Moon, Cooper & Fifer, 1993; Mehler, Bertoncini, Dupoux & Pallier, 1996; Nazzi, Bertoncini & Mehler, 1998; Ramus, Nespor & Mehler, 1999). On the other hand, in addition to signaling word stress, duration and pitch typically serve various grammatical functions. For instance, they are used to mark phrasal boundaries, focused constituents, and interrogatives. We assume that by the time they set the Stress Parameter, infants know the language-specific cues that signal the boundaries of prosodic constituents such as phonological utterances, intonational phrases, and phonological phrases (Nespor & Vogel, 1986). This assumption is supported by the fact that during the first year of life, infants develop a sensitivity to increasingly smaller prosodic units (Hirsh-Pasek et al., 1987; Gerken, Jusczyk & Mandel, 1994). Similarly, we assume that infants know the language-specific intonation contours that are associated with interrogatives, focused constituents, etc.

Third, we assume that the Stress Parameter is set at roughly the same age in all languages. This follows from a more general assumption that languages are equally learnable. Along the same lines, we assume that the tuning of the phonological representation is finished at a certain age, regardless of the language under consideration. This is important, since, as we will show below, languages differ considerably as to when the Stress Parameter can be set correctly in principle.

Fourth, we assume that infants acquire aspects of their maternal language in basically three steps. First, they acquire the segmental inventory between 6 and 12 months (Kuhl, Williams, Lacerda, Stevens & Lindblom, 1992; Polka & Werker, 1994; Werker & Tees, 1984a). Second, they acquire the inventory of function words between 10 and 12 months (Shady, 1996). Third, starting at around 10 months, they begin to acquire a lexicon of content words (Benedict, 1979; Hallé & Boysson-Bardies, 1994). Neither the function nor the content words are linked to a meaning at this stage. That is, they are stored in a recognition lexicon, containing word forms only. Regarding the difference between function words and content words, the former share a number of acoustic, phonological, and distributional properties that set them apart from the latter. In particular, they are mostly high frequent, unstressed, monosyllables that typically occur at phrasal edges, and have a simple syllable structure, a short duration, and a low relative amplitude. This might explain why infants can strip function words off the speech signal before they can segment content words out of the speech signal (Shi, Morgan & Allopenna, 1998). At 12 months, the content word lexicon is still very small (around 40 words), but it grows rapidly; at 16 months, for instance, it contains around 100 words (Benedict, 1979).

Our final assumption concerns the linguistic input and states that stress is phonologically transparent at utterance edges. By this we mean that the distribution of word stress is not obscured at utterance edges, in that initial or final words do not have a deviant stress pattern. In particular, contrastive stress should not be neutralized at the beginning or end of some phrasal constituent; such unattested neutralization would give rise to a regular pattern at one of the utterance edges, thus inducing infants to incorrectly conclude that stress is not contrastive (Peperkamp, 2000).[2]

2.3 Hypotheses and predictions

Our central hypothesis is that before having acquired the entire lexicon, infants use stress patterns at utterance edges to infer whether stress is contrastive or not and, hence, set the Stress Parameter. However, the stress regularity of languages with predictable (i.e. non-contrastive) stress is not always as easy to extract from one of the utterance edges as it is in French, the language introduced in section 2.1. For instance, in Hungarian, stress falls on the word-initial syllable. Due to the presence of utterance-initial unstressed function words, though, not all utterances begin with a stressed syllable. In Dupoux & Peperkamp (2002), we established a typology of languages with non-contrastive stress. This typology distinguishes four classes of languages with a phonological stress rule, corresponding to four types of information that are needed to correctly set the Stress Parameter. In languages of Class I, the stress rule can be acquired on the basis of a universal phonetic representation only; in languages of Class II, it can be acquired once language-specific phonological information has been extracted; in languages of Class III and IV, it can be acquired only after all function words and all content words, respectively, can be segmented out of the speech stream.

Given our assumption about the time course of language acquisition in section 2.2, the stress rules of languages belonging to Class I are the first that can be acquired, followed by those of languages in Class II, III, and IV, respectively. This yields the following prediction regarding the cross-linguistic pattern of attested stress 'deafness': 'deafness' in speakers of a language of Class N implies 'deafness' in speakers of all languages belonging to the same or to a lower Class. To see why, suppose a language with a purely phonological stress rule belonging to Class N, the adult speakers of which are stress 'deaf'; we take this as an indication of the absence of stress in the phonological representation of words. Hence, before the Stress Parameter gets set, infants acquiring this language have correctly inferred that stress is non-contrastive and needs not be encoded. In other words, infants have access to the type of information necessary to deduce the stress rule at hand. But then they have also access to the types of information necessary to compute stress rules of other languages belonging to the same or to a lower class. Therefore, infants acquiring any language of Class N or less can deduce that stress is not contrastive before the setting of the Stress Parameter, and, as a consequence, adult speakers of such a language should be stress 'deaf' as well.

There are thus four theoretical possibilities as far as the cross-linguistic perception of stress is concerned, depending on the moment during language development at which the Stress Parameter gets set. First, the Stress Parameter could be set at a late point in development, that is, after much of the lexicon of word forms has been acquired. This possibility corresponds to the idea that the phonological representation encodes all and only those features that are used contrastively in the lexicon (cf. Dupoux et al., 1997). We refer to this hypothesis as the Lexical Parameter Setting hypothesis. It predicts that stress 'deafness' should be attested in speakers of languages belonging to any of the four classes, since in none of these classes is stress used contrastively. Second, the

Stress Parameter could be set after the acquisition of all other phonological properties of the language as well as of the set of function words, but before the acquisition of a full word form lexicon. This predicts that only languages belonging to Class I−III should yield a 'deafness'. Third, the Stress Parameter could be set after most of the phonology of the language has been acquired, but prior to the acquisition of the function words. This predicts that 'deafness' should be restricted to languages belonging to Class I and II. Finally, the Stress Parameter could be set on the basis of phonetic information only, in which case only languages belonging to Class I should yield a 'deafness'. We globally refer to the last three hypotheses as Non-lexical Parameter Setting hypotheses. They predict the existence of languages with non-contrastive stress whose speakers nonetheless encode stress in the phonological representation.

Table 1 summarizes the predictions from the four hypotheses, where each column represents a cross-linguistic possibility ('+' stands for the presence of stress 'deafness' and '−' for its absence); the absence of stress 'deafness' in languages with predictable stress is shaded.

Table 1: Four alternative hypotheses regarding the presence (+) or absence (−) of stress 'deafness' in speakers of languages belonging to Class I−IV or having contrastive stress

Language Class	Lexical Parameter Setting (Dupoux et al. 1997)	Non-lexical Parameter Setting		
		Phonetics, phonology, and function words available	Phonetics and phonology available	Phonetics only available
Class I	+	+	+	+
Class II	+	+	+	−
Class III	+	+	−	−
Class IV	+	−	−	−
Contrastive stress	−	−	−	−

Our aim, then, is to experimentally assess the perception of stress by adult speakers of languages belonging to each one of the four classes. If we find that speakers of languages belonging to any of the four classes exhibit stress 'deafness', as represented in the first column of Table 1, then the Lexical Parameter Setting hypothesis is corroborated. By contrast, if we find one of the three remaining cross-linguistic patterns in Table 1, then the corresponding Non-lexical Parameter Setting hypothesis is corroborated. Finally, if we find a cross-linguistic pattern that is not included in Table 1, then the whole theoretical framework of Dupoux & Peperkamp (2002) has to be revised.

Before turning to the experiments, we will discuss examples of languages belonging to the four different classes of our typology, and spell out the predictions according to the various Non-lexical Parameter Setting hypotheses. (Recall that according to the Lexical Parameter Setting hypothesis, all languages in the typology should yield stress 'deafness'.)

3. Exemplification of the typology

3.1 Class I

Examples of languages belonging to Class I are French and Finnish. First, in French, stress falls on the word's final vowel (Schane 1968). Function words, which are typically unstressed elements, attract stress if they are phrase-final.[3] This is illustrated in (1).

(1) a. coupez   [kupé]   'cut$_{IMP-PL}$'
    b. coupez-les   [kupelé]   'cut$_{IMP-PL}$-them'
    c. coupez-vous-en   [kupevuzã]   'cut$_{IMP-PL}$-yourself$_{PL-DAT}$-of them'

Moreover, although eurhythmic principles induce destressing rules in French, the final and strongest stress of an utterance is never reduced (Dell, 1984). Hence, neither the occurrence of phrase-final function words nor destressing interferes with the observability of the stress rule at utterance endings. That is, all utterances in

French have stress on their final vowel.[4] Infants, then, can infer that stress is not contrastive by focussing on universal phonetic cues at utterance endings. In fact, the utterance's final vowel can be singled out on the basis of the acoustic signal only.

Second, in Finnish, stress is word-initial (Karlsson, 1999). This is illustrated in (2).

(2) a. usko [úsko] 'belief'
    b. uskollisuus [úskolːisuːs] 'fidelity; loyalty'

There are no unstressed function words that appear phrase-initially. Moreover, monosyllabic content words are not destressed when they are involved in a stress clash.[5] All utterances therefore have stress on the first vowel, and infants can extract the stress rule by focussing their attention on universal phonetic cues at utterance beginnings.

Given that the French and Finnish stress rules can be deduced without having access to any language-specific cues, French- and Finnish-acquiring infants can deduce the stress rule of their language before the Stress Parameter needs to be set. All three Non-lexical Parameter Setting hypotheses therefore predict that adult speakers of these languages exhibit stress 'deafness'.

3.2 Class II

An example of a language belonging to Class II is Fijian (Schütz, 1985; Dixon, 1988; Hayes, 1995). In this Austronesian language, word stress falls on the final syllable if it is heavy; otherwise stress is penultimate. The language has only two syllable types, (C)VV and (C)V, where the former is heavy and the latter is light. There are no phrase-final unstressed function words. Examples from Dixon's (1988) description of the Boumaa dialect are given in (3); syllable boundaries are indicated by dots.

(3) a. kám.ba   kam.bá.ta   'climb − climb it'
    b. te.ʔe.vúː   te.ʔe.vúː.na   'start − start$_{TR}$'
    c. pu.lóu   pu.lóu.na   'be covered − cover$_{TR}$'

The language permits monosyllabic words provided they are heavy. If a monosyllable is preceded by a word ending in a long vowel or a diphthong, a stress clash arises. We do not know if and how stress clash is resolved in Fijian. Clearly, if the second stress undergoes destressing, utterance-final stress clash configurations will disrupt the surface stress pattern. Abstracting away from this potential confound, however, we can formulate the following surface generalization: in utterances that end in a word with a final long vowel or a diphthong, the final syllable is stressed, while in utterances that end in a word with a final short vowel, the penultimate syllable is stressed. Once infants have acquired the distinction between heavy and light syllables, they can observe the stress regularity. Speakers of Fijian, then, are predicted to exhibit stress 'deafness' if syllable structure and the distinction between light and heavy syllables are available to infants at the time they set the Stress Parameter. Thus, among the Non-lexical Parameter Setting hypotheses, only the last one predicts that speakers of Fijian are not stress 'deaf'; according to this hypothesis, the Stress Parameter is set before the acquisition of both other phonological properties and the set of function words. The remaining hypotheses predict that speakers of Fijian are stress 'deaf'.

3.3 Class III

In languages belonging to Class III, stress is predictable and observable *modulo* the occurrence of function words. In fact, contrary to the situation in French described in section 3.1, function words are typically unstressed, regardless of their position in the utterance. Consider, for instance, the case of Hungarian. In this language, stress falls on word-initial syllables, and function words are systematically unstressed (Vago, 1980). This is illustrated in (4).

(4) a. emberek   [émberek]   'men'
    b. az emberek [azémberek]   'the men'

In Hungarian, then, utterances that begin with a function word have stress on the second syllable, while all other utterances have stress on the first syllable. Hungarian has monosyllabic content words, but stress clash resolution does not interfere with this surface stress pattern, since utterance-initial words are never destressed (Vogel, 1988).

In order for infants to discover the stress rule of Hungarian, they should strip off utterance-initial function words and look for generalizations in the remaining string. That is, after removing the initial function word(s), infants can discover that the remaining string of content words always begins with a stressed syllable. If infants have acquired the set of function words prior to setting the Stress Parameter, they should thus exhibit stress 'deafness' as adults. Among the Non-lexical Parameter Setting hypotheses, then, only the first one predicts that speakers of Hungarian are stress 'deaf'; according to this hypothesis, in fact, the set of function words is available by the time the Stress Parameter gets set. The remaining hypotheses predict that speakers of Hungarian are not stress 'deaf'.

3.4 Class IV

Languages in Class IV have a stress rule that is observable only if the boundaries of content words are available. Consider, for instance, Polish, a language in which word stress is on the penultimate syllable (Comrie, 1967; Hayes, 1995). Some examples are given in (5).

(5) a. gázet – gazéta – gazetámi   'newspaper $_{\text{GEN-PL; NOM-SG; INST-PL}}$'
    b. jézyk – jezýka – jezykámi   'language $_{\text{NOM-SG; GEN-SG; INST-PL}}$'

Polish has many monosyllabic content words. If a monosyllabic word is followed by another monosyllabic word or by a disyllabic word, a stress clash arises, which is resolved by destressing of the first word (Rubach & Booij, 1985). Destressing therefore does not interfere with the generalization concerning surface stress patterns at utterance edges, which can be formulated as follows: in utterances that end in a monosyllabic word, the final syllable is stressed, whereas in all other utterances, the penultimate syllable is stressed.[6]

In order to extract the rule regarding penultimate stress, infants should have access to content word boundaries. Stress 'deafness' in adults, then, depends upon the availability of full word segmentation by the time the Stress Parameter gets set. Hence, none of the Non-lexical Parameter Setting hypothesis predicts a stress 'deafness' in speakers of Polish. Rather, such a 'deafness' is predicted only by the Lexical Parameter Setting hypothesis.

4. Experiments assessing the perception of stress

In the remaining part of this paper, we report on experiments assessing the perception of stress by adult native speakers of French and Finnish (Class I), Hungarian (Class III), and Polish (Class IV).[7] As a control language, we use Spanish, which does not belong to any of the four classes since it has contrastive stress. We predict that native speakers of Spanish will not exhibit stress 'deafness'.

Before turning to the experiments, however, we should define what is meant exactly by studying the perception of stress cross-linguistically. Recall from section 2.2 that the acoustic correlates of stress, i.e. duration, pitch and energy, are not used to an equal extent in all languages to realize stress. In this study, we manipulate all three stress cues, in order to create a maximally perceptible contrast that contains valid stress cues in all languages under consideration. Using these very different stimuli ensures that whenever a stress contrast is not perceived in a given language, the 'deafness' effect is not due to the confusability of the stimuli. One caveat is in order, though: it is important to make sure that we do not manipulate variables that could be perceived as something other than stress in a given language. For instance, in languages with contrastive vowel length, such as Finnish and Hungarian, duration is avoided as a correlate of stress (Hayes, 1995). Therefore, when processing a foreign language with duration as a phonetic correlate of stress, speakers of languages with contrastive length might map stressed vowels onto long vowels and unstressed vowels onto short vowels. Thus, they can assimilate stress to length, and consequently, stress 'deafness' will not be observed. This is why, given that our sample of languages include Finnish and Hungarian, we take special care to insure that the durational cues of our stimuli do not yield the perception of a lexical vowel length contrast.

4.1 General method

Dupoux et al. (2001) present a novel paradigm for assessing the perception of stress, based on a short term memory task. In this paradigm, the recall performance of a stress contrast is compared with that of a control phonemic contrast, across different levels of memory load. The experiment is divided into two parts. In each part, subjects are required to learn two CVCV non-words that are a minimal pair differing only in one phonological dimension, i.e. place of articulation of the second consonant or location of stress. In each part, subjects are taught to associate the two non-words to the keys [1] and [2], respectively, of a computer keyboard. After some training with an identification task, subjects listen to longer and longer random sequences of the two non-words, which they are required to recall and transcribe as sequences of [1] and [2]. Within the sequences, the non-words are randomly instantiated by one of 6 acoustically different tokens. The length of the sequences varies from 2 to 6, and is augmented by one after 8 trials. Hence, each part of the experiment contains 40 (5 × 8) trials. The segmental contrast in the first part is phonemic in all languages under consideration and hence equally easy for all subjects; this contrast is thus used to establish baseline performance.

In order to diminish the likelihood that subjects use explicit recoding strategies, the stimuli are short and the tokens in the sequences are separated from one another by a very short interval, i.e. 80 ms. Moreover, in order to prevent subjects from using echoic memory, every sequence is followed by the word 'OK'. On average, the experiment lasts about 20 minutes. Responses that are a 100% correct transcription of the input sequence are coded as correct; all other responses are coded as incorrect, regardless of the number of tokens within the sequence that are transcribed incorrectly. Among the incorrect responses, those that are a 100% incorrect transcription — i.e. with each token of the sequence labeled incorrectly — are coded as reversals. Subjects with more reversals than correct responses in either the phoneme or the stress condition are rejected, the high percentage of reversals suggesting that they might have confused the number key associated to the first item with the one associated to the second item.

In Dupoux et al. (2001), we used the novel paradigm to test the perception of stress by speakers of French and Spanish. In a previous experiment, using a different paradigm, Dupoux et al. (1997) found that speakers of French, but not those of Spanish, exhibit stress 'deafness', i.e. they had much more difficulties with the stress contrast than with the phonemic contrast. These results were confirmed with the novel paradigm. That is, in Experiment 3 of Dupoux et al. (2001), we compared the phonemic contrast [kúpi — kúti] with the stress contrast [mípa — mipá], and found that the French subjects made significantly more errors with the latter ($F(1,11) = 71.0; p < .0001$), whereas the Spanish subjects showed a non-significant trend in the other direction ($F(1,11) = 3.7; .1 > p > .05$). The interaction between the factors language and contrast was highly significant ($F(1,22) = 70.3; p < .0001$).

4.2 Experiment 1: Finnish

In the first of the two experiments to be presented in this paper, we used the same materials and the same paradigm as Dupoux et al. (2001) to test 12 native speakers of Finnish, a language with contrastive vowel length. As in French and Spanish, all the items are composed of existing phonemes in Finnish that appear in a combination in accordance with the phonotactics of the language. Hence, apart from the location of stress, they are possible but nonexisting words.

The recordings, used previously for the French and Spanish subjects, were made by a female trained phonetician whose native language is Dutch. The mean durations of the tokens used for the phonemic and the stress contrast were 439 ms, and 513 ms, respectively. In order to introduce more phonetic variation among the tokens, we manipulated the global pitch with a waveform editor. Specifically, the pitch contours of the 6 tokens of each item were multiplied with the values 95, 97, 99, 101, 103, and 105, respectively (see Dupoux et al., 2001, for discussion). Figure 1 displays the pitch contours of the 6 tokens of each item used for the stress contrast before the global pitch modifications were realized, as well as the mean duration and intensity of their segments. As can be seen, the pitch contours of the [mípa] tokens and those of the [mipá] tokens are highly dissimilar. Indeed, all tokens of [mípa] show a drop in pitch between the first and second syllable, the magnitude of which is between 7 and 9 semitones, whereas all tokens of [mipá] show an increase in pitch between the first and second syllable of a magnitude between 4 and 5 semitones. There are also significant differences in the mean duration of segments in stressed versus unstressed syllables. This is seen most prominently in the vowels. Indeed, across the two sets of tokens, stressed vowels are on average 21 ms longer than unstressed vowels, a numerically small but significant difference given the small between-token variance ($F(1,5) = 43.2; p < .001$). Finally, stressed vowels are on average 3.7

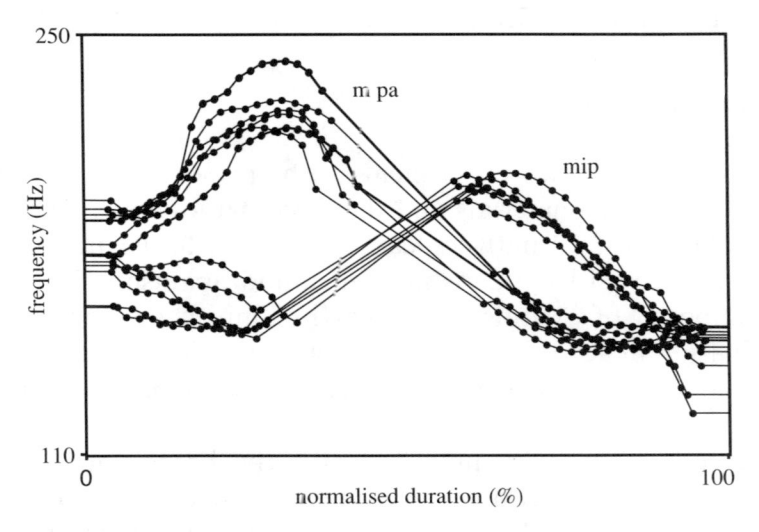

Figure 1: Acoustic measurements of 6 tokens [mípa] and 6 tokens [mipá] used in Experiment 1
a. f_0 as a function of normalised duration

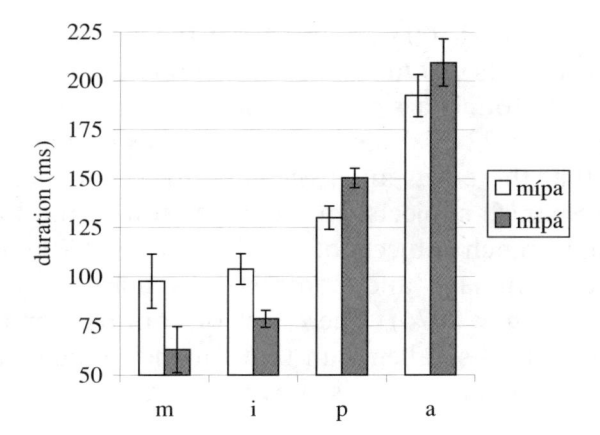

b. Duration of segments

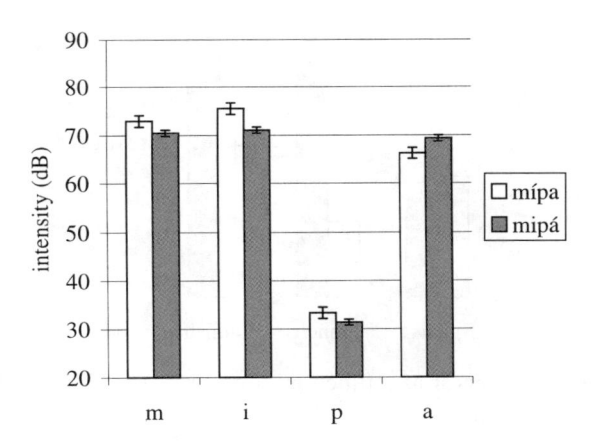

c. Intensity of segments

dB louder than unstressed vowels, again, a numerically small but significant difference ($F(1,5) = 78.2; p < .001$).[8]

In an informal pilot with a native speaker of Finnish, we found that the stressed vowels in [mípa] and [mipá] were not perceived as long vowels. We thus decided to run the experiment with the 12 Finnish subjects using the same recordings of the four non-words. The results were that analogously to the French subjects in Dupoux et al. (2001) the Finnish subjects made significantly more errors with the stress contrast than with the phonemic contrast

($F(1,11) = 15.9$; $p < .003$). Comparing the Finnish subjects with the Spanish subjects of Dupoux et al. (2001) in a post-hoc analysis of variance, we found a significant interaction between language and contrast ($F(1,22) = 19.5$; $p < .0001$). This interaction was due to the fact that there was an effect of contrast for the Finnish but not for the Spanish subjects. In a comparison of the Finnish subjects with the French subjects of Dupoux et al. (2001), the interaction between language and contrast was marginally significant ($F(1,22) = 3.6$; $p < .074$). The effect of contrast for the Finnish subjects was indeed smaller than that for the French subjects.

A summary of the results is shown in Figure 2.

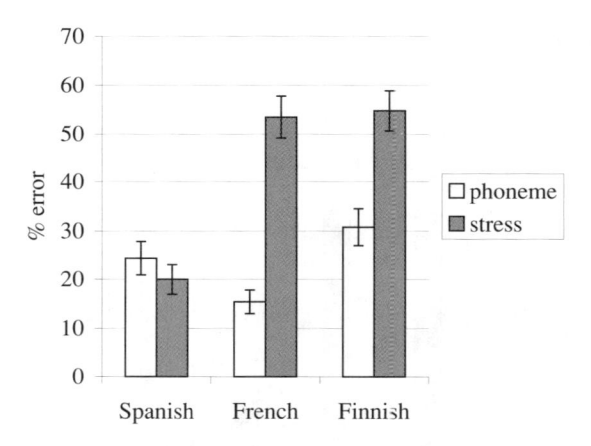

Figure 2: Percent recall error as a function of contrast for 12 Spanish, 12 French, and 12 Finnish subjects

The Finnish results replicate the results with the French subjects in Dupoux et al. (2001), thus corroborating the hypothesis that Class I languages yield stress 'deafness'. This is an interesting result in itself, since it shows that stress 'deafness' is not limited to a single language, and, moreover, that it is independent of the position of word stress in the language. Recall, in fact, that stress is word-final in French and word-initial in Finnish. If we are correct in positing that infants acquire the stress regularity of their language by focusing on utterance edges, these results are evidence that infants can focus equally well on utterance endings and on utterance beginnings.[9]

To sum up, native speakers of French and Finnish, as opposed to native speakers of Spanish, exhibit stress 'deafness'. The 'deafness' effect appears to be somewhat larger in the French than in the Finnish subjects; this difference, however, is not significant. We need to test more subjects to verify whether the interaction between language and contrast reaches significance. If this turns out to be the case, then a possible explanation might be related to the fact that in Finnish but not in French, vowel length is contrastive. That is, despite our precautions, some Finnish subjects might encode stressed vowels as long vowels, and hence rely on the lexically distinctive property of vowel length to do the task.

4.3 Experiment 2: Hungarian and Polish

In our second experiment, we tested the perception of stress by native speakers of Hungarian and Polish, languages belonging to Class III and Class IV, respectively. Given that [kúti] is a real word in Hungarian, we could not use the pair [kúpi – kúti] of the previous experiments. We therefore chose new items, which are possible but non-existing words not only in Hungarian and Polish, but also in Finnish, Fijian, and our control language Spanish, allowing us to use the new materials in future experiments.

For the phonemic contrast, we used the pair [níka – níta]. As in the previous experiment, all segments making up the items are phonemic in the languages at hand, and appear in a phonotactically legal combination. There are two reasons why the pair [níka – níta] is comparable to the pair [kúpi – kúti] used in Experiment 1 as far as perceptual difficulty is concerned. First, the consonants involved in the two contrasts, i.e. [p], [t], and [k], are all unvoiced stops; the place of articulation of the consonant present in both pairs, i.e. [t], lies between that of the consonants with which it forms a contrast, i.e. [p] and [k], respectively. Moreover, the consonantal contrasts [p – t] and [t – k] are known to be equally difficult to perceive (Miller & Nicely, 1955). Second, the consonants are embedded within comparable vocalic contexts, consisting of two different cardinal vowels each that differ on either the front/

back dimension ([kúpi − kúti]) or on the height dimension ([níka − níta]). Specifically, in both pairs, one of the consonants shares its place of articulation with the following vowel and the other one shares its place of articulation with the preceding vowel. Thus, in [kúpi − kúti], [p] and the preceding [u] are both labial, while [t] the following [i] are both coronal; and in [níka − níta], [t] and the preceding [i] are both coronal, while [k] and the following [a] are both dorsal. Therefore, there is no reason to believe that coarticulation will make one of the contrasts more difficult than the other.

As to the stress contrast, we constructed 10 minimal pairs, in order to show that the 'deafness' effect is not limited to a single non-word. These pairs are shown in (6).

(6)   [kánu − kanú]   [númi − numí]
        [míku − mikú]   [támi − tamí]
        [nátu − natú]   [támu − tamú]
        [nímu − nimú]   [tímu − timú]
        [núma − numá]   [túka − tuká]

All items were recorded 6 times by the same speaker that recorded the materials for the experiments reported in the previous section. The mean duration of the tokens for the phonemic contrast was 444 ms. The mean duration of the tokens for the stress contrasts was 425 ms. In this experiment, we wanted to reduce the importance of duration as a stress cue, in order to prevent Hungarian subjects from relying on the lexical difference between short and long vowels. The speaker therefore took special care to reduce the durational differences with respect to that in the materials used in Experiment 1. As in Experiment 1, we introduced more phonetic variation among the tokens, by multiplying the pitch contours of the 6 tokens of each item with the values 95, 97, 99, 101, 103, and 105, respectively.

We carried out several acoustical analyses of the stress tokens. Due to the large number of tokens, we restricted these analyses to only one token per item. For each of the 20 items, we randomly chose one of the 6 tokens for the analyses. Figure 3 displays the pitch contours of these tokens before the global pitch modifications were realized, as well as the mean duration and intensity of their segments.

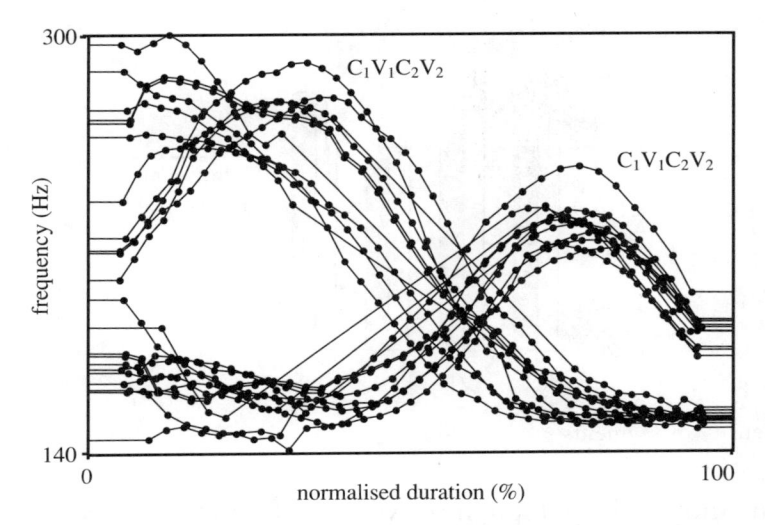

Figure 3: Acoustic measurements of 10 items $C_1V_1C_2V_2$ (one token per item) and 10 items $C_1V_1C_2V_2$ (one token per item) used in Experiment 2
a. f_0 as a function of normalised duration

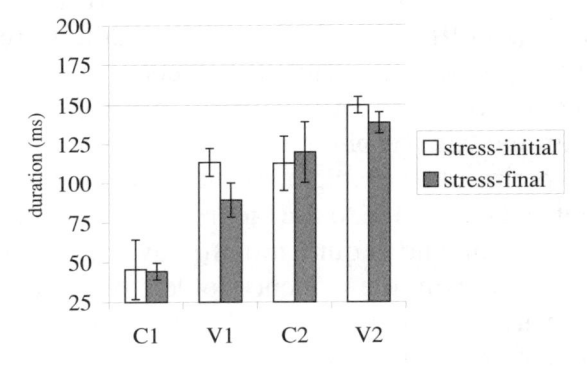

b. Duration of segments

The durational difference between stressed and unstressed vowels is 6.5 ms ($F(1,9) = 5.7$; $p < .04$), which is smaller than the corresponding difference in the stimuli in Experiment 1. Duration, then, is a less important stress cue than in the previous experiments, as desired. As to the pitch contours of the stress-initial tokens and those of the stress-final tokens, they are again highly dissimilar, and even more so than in Experiment 1. Indeed, all stress-first

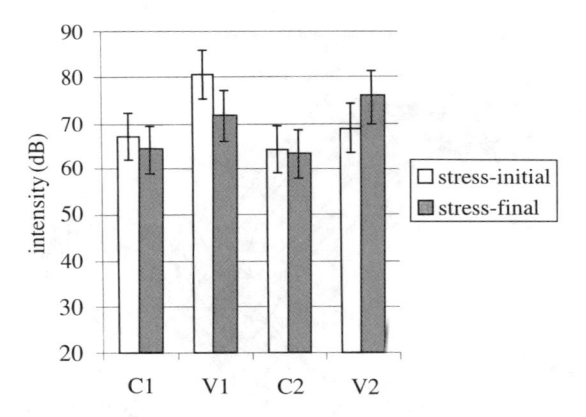

c. Intensity of segments

tokens show a drop in pitch between the first and the second syllable, the magnitude of which is between 9 and 11 semitones; all stress-second tokens show an increase in pitch between the first and the second syllable, the magnitude of which is between 6 and 8 semitones. Stressed vowels are on average 8 dB louder than unstressed vowels ($F(1,9) = 116.5$; $p < .001$), again a greater difference than in the previous experiment.[10] Hence, in this new recording, the reduction of duration as a stress cue appears to be compensated by an increase of pitch and energy as stress cues.

As to the experimental paradigm, we made one change with respect to Experiment 1. That is, due to the fact that the experiment requires a lot of concentration and is quite long (on average 20 minutes), we shortened it by taking out the sequences of length 3 and 5. Hence, we used only sequences of length 2, 4, and 6. An analysis of the results obtained in Dupoux et al. (2001) shows that using only these sequence lengths does not impair the power of the paradigm.

We tested 10 native speakers of Hungarian and 10 native speakers of Polish. Each subject was tested on the phonemic contrast and on one of the stress contrasts. One Hungarian and one Polish subject were replaced, due to too many reversals among their responses with the stress contrast and with the phonemic contrast, respectively. We found that the Hungarian subjects exhibited stress 'deafness'; that is, they made significantly more errors with the stress contrast than with the phonemic contrast ($F(1,9) = 37,4$; p

< .0001). The Polish subjects also made more errors with the stress contrast, but the effect was only marginally significant ($F(1,9) = 4.5; p < .056$). The interaction between language and contrast was also marginally significant ($F(1,18) = 3.4; p < .084$).

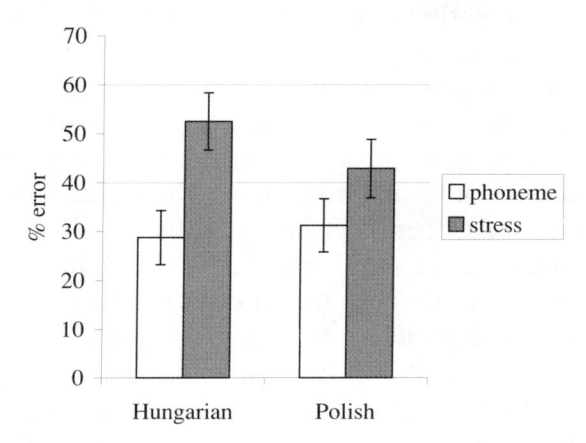

Figure 4: Percent recall error as a function of contrast for 10 Hungarian and 10 Polish subjects

These results show that Hungarian subjects are stress 'deaf'. Polish subjects, by contrast, are not stress 'deaf'; indeed, they did not make significantly more errors with the stress contrast than with the phoneme contrast. In Polish, vowel length is not contrastive but is used as a stress cue. Consequently, for some Polish subjects the materials in set 2 might have been ambiguous as far as stress is concerned, the vowel length difference between stress-initial and stress-final items not being sufficiently large. This could explain why we found a tendency towards stress 'deafness' in the Polish subjects.

Before closing this section, some additional remarks concerning Polish are in order. It is well-known that the Polish stress rule has some lexical exceptions, which are borrowings of mainly Greek and Latin origin, with either antepenultimate (7a,b) or final stress (7c).

(7) a. muzyka [múzika] 'music'
    b. uniwersytet [univérsitɛt] 'university'
    c. menu [menú] 'menu'

We assume that the existence of several lexical exceptions does not interfere with the classification of Polish as having a regular phonological stress rule. In particular, due to their small number as well as their low frequency of occurrence, infants are likely not to take lexical exceptions into account while deducing the stress regularity of their language, if they are exposed to them at all.

We take the presence of lexical exceptions as an indication that speakers of Polish cannot be stress 'deaf'. Indeed, if they were, they would not perceive lexical exceptions as being deviant and hence they would not be able to produce them with the exceptional stress pattern. Consequently, foreign loans should be completely regularized to the native stress pattern.[11] This is indeed what happens in, for instance, French, which does not have any lexical exceptions and whose speakers typically do not recall where stress falls in foreign words. Based on a large sample of languages, Peperkamp (submitted) argues that languages with non-contrastive stress present lexical exceptions if and only if they belong to Class IV, suggesting that speakers of languages belonging to Class I–III but not those of languages belonging to Class IV exhibit stress 'deafness'.

4.4 General discussion

Using a paradigm that we initially set up to study the perception of stress in French and Spanish, we presented experiments in three new languages that exemplify different levels of our linguistic typology. In order to get a clearer idea of the overall pattern of results, we need a direct comparison of the results obtained with the French, Finnish and Spanish subjects on the one hand and those obtained with the Hungarian and Polish subjects on the other hand. Before conducting such a comparison, however, an important caveat has to be raised. Indeed, in these two sets of languages, we used different sets of stimuli for both the phonemic and the stress contrast. Given our constraint on the non-word status of the items as well as the differences in the use of vowel length in the various languages, it is extremely hard to construct materials that can be used in all five languages. The materials of set 1 contained stressed vowels that were longer than those of the materials in set 2. Speakers of languages without contrastive vowel length use duration as a stress cue and are thus best tested with set 1. By contrast, speakers of languages with contrastive vowel length are best tested with set 2, since the materials in set 1 might induce them to perceive a lexical vowel length contrast. In our experiments, Finnish and Polish were tested with materials from the non-optimal set. That is, Finnish subjects, who use vowel length contrastively, were tested with set 1, while Polish speakers, who do not use vowel length contrastively, were tested with set 2. Stress 'deafness', therefore, might be underestimated in Finnish subjects and overestimated in Polish subjects.

This being said, in order to compare the different languages, we define a stress 'deafness' index for a population as the mean percentage of errors made with the stress contrast minus the mean percentage of errors made with the phonemic contrast. For each language in our sample, Table 2 displays the stress 'deafness' index, together with information concerning the class to which the language belongs, the status of vowel length in the language, and the stimuli that were used in the experiment.

Table 2: Stress 'deafness' index and information regarding class membership, status of vowel length, and stimulus set for five languages tested in Experiment 3 of Dupoux et al. (2001) and in Experiments 1 and 2 of the present paper

language	stress 'deafness' index	Class	vowel length	stimuli
French	38.1	I	non-contrastive	set 1
Finnish	24.0	I	contrastive	set 1
Hungarian	23.7	III	contrastive	set 2
Polish	11.6	IV	non-contrastive	set 2
Spanish	−4.4	control	non-contrastive	set 1

According to the stress 'deafness' index, speakers of French exhibit the strongest effect, followed by speakers of Finnish, Hungarian, and Polish, respectively. Interestingly, the gradual nature of the 'deafness' effect goes in the direction of our language typology, in that the strongest 'deafness' effect is found in a Class I language, i.e. French, and the weakest 'deafness' effect is found in a Class IV language, i.e. Polish. The intermediate languages, Finnish and Hungarian, belong to Class I and Class III, respectively. It appears, then, that the size of the 'deafness' effect correlates with the ease with which the stress regularity can be acquired by infants. Note that the numerical difference between Finnish and French might be due to the underestimation of 'deafness' in Finnish that we discussed earlier.

We also ran a series of t-tests for the 'deafness' index computed for each individual subject across the different languages. The t-tests are corrected for multiple comparisons, using a Bonferroni corrected p-value of .005. We found that French yielded a significantly higher 'deafness' score than all other languages except Finnish. Similarly, Spanish had a significantly lower score than all other languages except Polish. No other comparison reached significance. Considering French and Spanish as two anchor points, we thus find that Finnish patterns with the former and Polish patterns with the latter; Hungarian is situated in the middle and differs significantly from both anchors.

These results allow us to discard the Lexical Parameter Setting hypothesis, according to which all languages with non-contrastive stress should yield an equal amount of stress 'deafness'. This hypothesis is falsified, given that both Hungarian and Polish yield significantly less stress 'deafness' than French and that Polish does not differ significantly from Spanish. Regarding the Non-lexical Parameter Setting hypothesis, recall that it is actually a grouping of three hypotheses, that vary in the amount of non-lexical information that they state is available for the setting of the Stress Parameter. Given that we did not test speakers of a language belonging to Class II, we cannot distinguish the hypothesis according to which only phonetic information is available from that according to which additional phonological information is available. Both correctly predict that Polish (Class IV) does not differ from the control language Spanish, and that Hungarian (Class III) differs from French (Class I). However, these hypotheses cannot account for the fact that Hungarian also differs from Spanish; according to these hypotheses, in fact, speakers of Hungarian, similarly to those of Spanish, should have no problem with the perception of stress contrasts. The third Non-lexical Parameter Setting hypothesis states that in addition to phonetic and phonological information, the set of function words is available before the Stress Parameter needs to be set. Analogously to the first two, this hypothesis also correctly predicts the pattern of results regarding Polish and fails to account for Hungarian, although for a different reason. That is, under this hypothesis, the difference between Hungarian and Spanish is accounted for, while the difference between Hungarian and French is not.

Due to the intermediate status of Hungarian, our pattern of results is thus intermediate between that predicted by the last non-lexical hypothesis discussed here and that predicted by the first two. Speculatively, we would like to offer two possible explanations for this fact. First, the Stress Parameter might not be binary. It has indeed been proposed that the initial tuning of the phonological representation of words is gradual rather than discrete. For instance, Jusczyk (1993) argues that early exposure to a language results in a deformation of the acoustic space, with relevant dimensions being blown up and irrelevant dimensions being squeezed down. Second, the Stress Parameter might be binary but set according to a statistical criterion, resulting in individual variation. Consequently, in cases where the stress regularity is fairly complex to extract, as in Hungarian, only a certain proportion of infants correctly detects the presence of the regularity and hence becomes stress 'deaf'; the remaining infants would simply fail to detect the regularity and hence retain stress in the phonological representation. We then predict the presence of a bimodal distribution of individual responses, a prediction which can be put to test if a larger number of subjects is used.

5. Conclusion

The present paper is a first step towards a more comprehensive cross-linguistic examination of the perception of suprasegmental information. The results can be accounted for in terms of our acquisition framework; specifically, they support the notion that decisions regarding the format of the phonological representation of words are made before much of a lexicon of word forms is available. Several questions, though, remain open, and future research can be carried out along various directions.

First, we need to replicate our findings in the languages that we have tested so far, and test the generality of our results by independently manipulating duration and pitch of stressed vowels in the stimuli. We also need to test a language belonging to Class II to complete our survey. Furthermore, in order to show that the location of word stress *per se* does not interfere with the presence of stress 'deafness', more cross-linguistic experiments should be carried out with languages that share the location of word stress but belong to different classes of our typology. In particular, we tested two languages with initial stress (i.e. Finnish and Hungarian), but only one language with final stress (i.e. French) and only one language with penultimate stress (i.e. Polish). Given the fact that Polish is the only language in which stress does not fall at one of the word edges, we would especially like to test another language with prefinal stress but belonging to a different class.

Second, it would be interesting to show that the stress 'deafness' effect found with our task truly reflects a property of the phonological representation of words. One way to test this would be to explore with a lexically pertinent task how speakers of a language with stress 'deafness' represent words in a foreign language with contrastive stress that they have learned as a second language. We predict that such speakers fail to build two separate lexical entries for words forming a minimal stress pair.

Third, we might test more directly the hypothesis that infants can set the Stress Parameter by focusing on utterance boundaries. A first step in this direction would be to perform acoustical analysis on natural utterances in the various languages of our sample, in order to determine whether word stress can indeed be observed above and beyond sentence level suprasegmental phenomena. A second step would be to directly probe the age at which infants of languages for which we have found a 'deafness' become less sensitive to stress.

Finally, our framework can be extended to include languages in which the segmental phonology can help to distinguish between stressed and unstressed syllables. For instance, many languages have a rule that reduces certain unstressed vowels; the presence of a reduced vowel, then, is an indication of the absence of stress (Hayes 1995). Cutler (1986) and Cutler and Van Donselaar (2001) found contrastive results in English and Dutch, two languages with vowel reduction. Cutler (1986) used minimal stress pairs in English in which vowel reduction exceptionally does not apply, such as *fórbear – forebéar*. She found that speakers of English do not process stress on-line in order to identify lexical items, and argued that this is due to the fact that English has only a very small number of true minimal stress pairs (that is, pairs of words in which vowel reduction does not apply). Cutler & Van Donselaar (2001) similarly used true minimal stress pairs in Dutch, a language in which the number of such pairs is equally small. They found that speakers of Dutch, contrary to those of English, do use stress on-line in order to identify lexical items. Their interpretation of this finding relies on the observation that English and Dutch differ in the amount of vowel reduction that applies; whereas unstressed syllables in English almost invariably have a reduced vowel, Dutch has much less vowel reduction. Cutler & Van Donselaar, then, raised the hypothesis that a given contrast is not used for lexical access if and only if its information value is relatively low. That is, speakers of English, but not those of Dutch, can rely on the parasitic, segmental, cue of vowel reduction in order to identify stressed syllables. This hypothesis, though, cannot account for the present pattern of results, since in the languages with non-contrastive stress that we tested, the information value of the stress cues is zero.

To conclude, we hope to have convinced the reader that studying models of early language acquisition in a cross-linguistic perspective can open interesting and novel issues in speech perception research. These issues can be tested in adults, and, ultimately, in infants.

Acknowledgments

Research for this paper was funded by grants from the French Ministry of Education, Research, and Technology (Groupement d'Intérêt Scientifique 'Sciences de la Cognition', and Action Concertée Incitative 'Cognitique'), as well as by a grant from the Centre National de la Recherche Scientifique ('Aide à Projet Nouveau'). We are grateful to the Finnish, Hungarian, and Polish cultural institutes in Paris, who provided us with testing facilities. We would like to thank Katherine White for help in running the subjects and Inga Vendelin for practical assistance. Thanks are also due to Anne Christophe, François Dell, Jacques Mehler, Marina Nespor, Christophe Pallier, Franck Ramus, and two anonymous reviewers for comments and discussion.

Notes

1 The idea that infants can bootstrap into phonological regularities of their language by focusing on utterance edges was first explored in Bourgeois (1991).
2 By contrast, rhythmic readjustments in stress clash configurations potentially interfere with the transparency of stress at utterance edges. We test only languages in which this is not the case (cf. section 3).
3 Exceptions are *je* 'I' and *ce* 'it'. These words have schwa as their vowel, which is deleted in phrase-final position, as in *suis-je* [sɥiʒ] 'am I' and *est-ce* [ɛs] 'is it'.
4 In southern varieties of French, utterance-final words can end in an unstressed schwa. In these varieties, the acquisition of the stress regularity is more complex, in that infants first have to acquire the difference between full vowels and schwa. Consequently, these varieties belong to Class II rather than to Class I.
Note also that, alternatively, French has been characterized as having phrasal stress, with stress falling on phrase-final syllables (Grammont 1965). The question as to whether French has word stress or phrasal stress is irrelevant to our point, given that under both assumptions, all utterances end in a stressed syllable.
5 This observation is based on judgments of our own recordings of four female native speakers.
6 In the literary language, there are three enclitics that fall outside the stress domain, i.e. *by*, *śmy*, and *ście*. With these enclitics, then, antepenultimate stress is yielded. Examples are *róbiłby* 'he would', *robílismy* 'we did', and *robíliscie* 'you$_{PL}$ did'. The latter two, however, can also surface with penultimate stress, and this variant is the most frequent one (Booij & Rubach 1987). We assume that infant-directed speech does not contain sequences of host plus enclitic with antepenultimate stress.
7 Fijian, the Class II language in our sample, presents two problems. First, the official language of Fiji being English, it is hard to find native speakers who

were raised in a monolingual environment. Second, there is much dialectal variation, and it is still unclear whether this variation concerns the stress pattern.

8   The root mean square of the signal in the portion of speech corresponding to each segment was measured and converted to an intensity value in dB by a logarithmic transform (this was done with the Praat software). The dB-value for each vowel was then entered into a two-way ANOVA with stress and vowel position as main factors.

9   Aslin, Woodward, LaMendola & Bever (1996) show that when American and Turkish mothers teach their 12−month-old infants new words, they tend to put these words in utterance-final position. This suggests that infants might be more focused on utterance endings that on beginnings, whence the non-triviality of the present finding.

10 See note 8.

11 Our subjects informed us that lexical exceptions are explicitly taught as such to school children. Moreover, they are sometimes regularized, either by movement of the stress, or − in the case of antepenultimate stress − by deletion of the vowel in the penultimate syllable. This regularization, however, is not generalized.

References

Aslin, R., Woodward, J., LaMendola, N. & Bever, T.
    1996   Models of word segmentation in fluent maternal speech to infants. In J. Morgan & K. Demuth (eds.), *Signal to Syntax. Bootstrapping from Speech to Grammar in Early Acquisition*, (pp. 117−134). Mahwah, N. J.: LEA.

Benedict, H.
    1979   Early lexical development: comprehension and production. *Journal of Child Language*, **6**, 183−200.

Best, C., McRoberts, G. & Sithole, N.
    1988   Examination of perceptual reorganization for non-native speech contrasts: Zulu click discrimination by English-speaking adults and infants. *Journal of Experimental Psychology: Human Perception and Performance*, **14**, 345−360.

Bluhme, S. & Burr, R.
    1971   An audio-visual display of pitch for teaching Chinese tones. *Studies in Linguistics*, **22**, 51−57.

Booij, G. & Rubach, J.
    1987   Postcyclic versus postlexical rules in lexical phonology. *Linguistic Inquiry*, **18**, 1−44.

Bourgeois, T.
1991   Instantiative Phonology. PhD dissertation, University of Arizona.
Christophe, A., Dupoux, E., Bertoncini, J. & Mehler, J.
1994   Do infants perceive word boundaries? An empirical study of the bootstrapping of lexical acquisition. *Journal of the Acoustical Society of America*, **95**, 1570–1580.
Church, K.
1987   Phonological parsing and lexical retrieval. *Cognition*, **25**, 53–69.
Comrie, B.
1967   Irregular stress in Polish and Macedonian. *International Review of Slavic Linguistics*, **1**, 227–240.
Cutler, A.
1986   Forbear is a homophone: Lexical prosody does not constrain lexical access. *Language and Speech*, **29**, 201–220.
Cutler, A. & Van Donselaar, W.
2001   Voornaam is not a homophone: Lexical prosody and lexical access in Dutch. *Language and Speech*, **44**, 171–195.
Dell, F.
1984   L'accentuation dans les phrases en français. In F. Dell, D. Hirst & J.-R. Vergnaud (eds.), *Forme sonore du language*, (pp. 65–122). Paris: Hermann.
Dixon, R.
1988   *A Grammar of Boumaa Fijian*. Chicago: University of Chicago Press.
Dupoux, E., Kakehi, K., Hirose, Y., Pallier, C. & Mehler, J.
1999   Epenthetic vowels in Japanese: a perceptual illusion? *Journal of Experimental Psychology: Human Perception and Performance*, **25**, 1568–1578.
Dupoux, E., Pallier, C., Sebastián-Gallés, N. & Mehler, J.
1997   A destressing 'deafness' in French? *Journal of Memory and Language*, **36**, 406–421.
Dupoux, E., Peperkamp, S. & Sebastián-Gallés, N.
2001   A robust paradigm to study stress 'deafness'. *Journal of the Acoustical Society of America* **110**, 1606–1618.
Dupoux, E. & Peperkamp, S.
2002   Fossil markers of language development: phonological 'deafnesses' in adult speech processing. In J. Durand & B. Laks (eds.), *Phonetics Phonology, and Cognition*. (pp. 168–190). Oxford: Oxford University Press.
Frazier, L.
1987   Structure in auditory word recognition. *Cognition*, **25**, 157–187.
Gandour, J.
1983   Tone perception in Far Eastern languages. *Journal of Phonetics*, **11**, 149–175.

Gerken, L. A., Jusczyk, P. & Mandel, D.
1994   When prosody fails to cue syntactic structure: 9-month-olds' sensitivity to phonological versus syntactic phrases. *Cognition*, **51**, 237—265.
Goldinger, S.
1998   Echoes of echoes? An episodic theory of lexical access. *Psychological Review*, **105**, 251—279.
Goto, H.
1971   Auditory perception by normal Japanese adults of the sounds 'l' and 'r'. *Neuropsychologia*, **9**, 317—323.
Grammont, M.
1965   *Traité de phonétique*. Paris: Delagrave.
Hallé, P. & De Boysson-Bardies, B.
1994   Emergence of an early receptive lexicon: infants' recognition of words. *Infant Behavior and Development*, **17**, 119—129.
Hayes, B.
1995   *Metrical Stress Theory*. Chicago: The University of Chicago Press.
Hirsh-Pasek, K., Kemler-Nelson, D., Jusczyk, P., Wright Cassidy, K., Druss, B. & Kennedy, L.
1987   Clauses are perceptual units for young infants. *Cognition*, **26**, 269—286.
Jusczyk, P.
1993   From general to language specific capacities: The WRAPSA model of how speech perception develops. *Journal of Phonetics*, **21**, 3—28.
Jusczyk, P., Cutler, A. & Redanz, N.
1993   Preference for the predominant stress pattern of English words. *Child Development*, **64**, 675—687.
Jusczyk, P., Friederici, A., Wessels, J., Svenkerud, V. & Jusczyk, A.
1993   Infants' sensitivity to the sound pattern of native language words. *Journal of Memory and Language*, **32**, 402—420.
Karlsson, F.
1999   *Finnish: An Essential Grammar*. London: Routledge.
Kiriloff, C.
1969   On the auditory perception of tones in Mandarin. *Phonetica*, **20**, 63—67.
Klatt, D.
1980   Speech perception: A model of acoustic-phonetic analysis and lexical access. *Journal of Phonetics*, **7**, 279—312.
Kuhl, P., Williams, K., Lacerda, F., Stevens, K. & Lindblom, B.
1992   Linguistic experience alters phonetic perception in infants by six months of age. *Science*, **255**, 606—608.
Lee, L. & Nusbaum, H.
1993   Processing interactions between segmental and suprasegmental information in native speakers of English and Mandarin Chinese. *Perception and Psychophysics*, **53**, 157—165.

Lehiste, I.
1970   Suprasegmentals. Cambridge, MA: MIT Press.
Marslen-Wilson, W. & Warren, P.
1994   Levels of perceptual representation and process in lexical access: words, phonemes, and features. *Psychological Review*, **101**, 653–675.
Mehler, J., Bertoncini, J., Dupoux, E. & Pallier, C.
1996   The role of suprasegmentals in speech perception and acquisition. In T. Otake & A. Cutler (eds.), *Phonological Structure and Language Processing. Cross-linguistic Studies*, (pp. 145–169). Berlin: Mouton de Gruyter.
Mehler, J., Dupoux, E. & Segui, J.
1990   Constraining models of lexical access: The onset of word recognition. In G. Altmann (ed.), *Cognitive Models of Speech Processing: Psycholinguistic and Computational Perspectives*, (pp. 236–262). Cambridge, MA: MIT Press.
Mehler, J., Jusczyk, P., Lambertz, G., Halsted, H., Bertoncini, J. & Amiel-Tison, C.
1988   A precursor of language acquisition in young infants. *Cognition*, **29**, 144–178.
Miller, G. & Nicely, P.
1955   An analysis of perceptual confusions among some English consonants. *Journal of the Acoustical Society of America*, **27**, 338–352.
Moon, C., Cooper, R. & Fifer, W.
1993   Two-day-olds prefer their native language. *Infant Behavior and Development*, **16**, 495–500.
Navarro Tomás, T.
1965   *Manual de prononciación española*. Madrid: Consejo Superior de Investigaciones Científicas.
Nazzi, T., Bertoncini, J. & Mehler, J.
1998   Language discrimination by newborns: Towards an understanding of the role of rhythm. *Journal of Experimental Psychology: Human Perception and Performance*, **24**, 1–11.
Nespor, M. & Vogel, I.
1986   *Prosodic Phonology*. Dordrecht: Foris.
Pallier, C., Bosch, L. & Sebastián-Gallés, N.
1997   A limit on behavioral plasticity in speech perception. *Cognition*, **64**, B9–B17.
Peperkamp, S.
2000   *Two typological gaps in stress systems: arguments from early language acquisition*. Handout of a talk presented at the Fourth Utrecht Biannual Phonology Workshop, Utrecht, The Netherlands.
Peperkamp, S.
submitted   Lexical exceptions in stress systems: Arguments from early language acquisition and adult speech processing.

Polivanov, E.
1974 The subjective nature of the perceptions of language sounds. In E. Polivanov, *Selected Works. Articles on General Linguistics* (compiled by A. Leont'ev), (pp. 223−237). The Hague: Mouton.

Polka, L. & Werker, J.
1994 Developmental changes in perception of non-native vowel contrasts, *Journal of Experimental Psychology: Human Perception and Performance*, **20**, 421−435.

Ramus, F., Nespor, M. & Mehler, J.
1999 Correlates of linguistic rhythm in the speech signal. *Cognition*, **73**, 265−292.

Rietveld, A.
1980 Word boundaries in the French language. *Language and Speech*, **23**, 289−296.

Rubach, J. & Booij, G.
1985 A grid theory of stress in Polish. *Lingua*, **66**, 281−319.

Sapir, E.
1921 *Language*. New York: Harcourt Brace Jovanovich.

Shady, M.
1996 *Infants' sensitivity to function morphemes*. PhD dissertation, State University of New York at Buffalo.

Schane, S.
1968 *French Phonology and Morphology*. Cambridge, MA: MIT Press.

Schütz, A.
1985 *The Fijian Language*. Honolulu: University of Hawaii Press.

Shi, R., Morgan, J. & Allopenna, P.
1998 Phonological and acoustic bases for earliest grammatical category assignment: a cross-linguistic perspective. *Journal of Child Language*, **25**, 169−201.

Vago, R.
1980 *The Sound Pattern of Hungarian*. Washington, D.C.: Georgetown University Press.

Vogel, I.
1988 Prosodic constituents in Hungarian. In P. M. Bertinetto & M. Loporcaro (eds.), *Certamen Phonologicum. Papers from the 1987 Cortona Phonology Meeting*, (pp. 231−250). Torino: Rosenberg & Sellier.

Wang, Y., Spence, M. & Sereno, J.
1999 Training American listeners to perceive Mandarin tones. *Journal of the Acoustical Society of America*, **106**, 3649−3658.

Weijer, J. van de
1999 *Language Input for Word Discovery*. PhD dissertation, University of Nijmegen.

Werker, J. & Tees, R.
- 1984a Cross language speech perception: Evidence for perceptual reorganization during the first year of life. *Infant Behavior and Development*, **7**, 49–63.

Werker, J. & Tees, R.
- 1984b Phonemic and phonetic factors in adult cross-language speech perception. *Journal of the Acoustical Society of America*, **75**, 1866–1878.

Confluent talker- and listener-oriented forces in clear speech production

Ann R. Bradlow

Abstract

The overall goal of this study was to examine the acoustic-phonetic modifications that characterize clear speech with particular attention to features that are generally taken to reflect the talker-oriented force towards ease-of-articulation. Two specific clear speech features were investigated: the extent of CV coarticulation and vowel space expansion as a function of vowel inventory size. In particular, the purpose of this study was to investigate whether coarticulatory influences are minimized, maintained or exaggerated in clear speech, and whether clear speech hyper-articulation is limited to segments that are likely to be perceptually confused or if clear speech is produced with "global" hyper-articulation. Results showed that clear speech involves both the maintenance of coarticulation, and similar amounts of vowel space expansion for English monolinguals and Spanish-English bilinguals when producing either English or Spanish. The maintenance of coarticulation in clear speech suggests that it is under talker control and likely serves some listener-oriented purpose. Furthermore, the inventory-independent vowel space expansion suggests that talkers spare no effort in producing clear speech and instead "globally" hyperarticulate, even for segments that are unlikely to be perceptually confused with their distant neighbors. These data are interpreted within a framework that views talker- and listener-oriented forces as confluent rather than opposing.

1. Introduction

Speech communication is often characterized in terms of a constantly shifting balance between talker- and listener-oriented forces (e.g. Lindblom, 1990). Within this general theoretical framework, the talker-related principle of ease of articulation stands in opposition to the listener-related requirement for sufficient perceptual contrast. Furthermore, this balance between talker- and listener-oriented forces is viewed as variable depending on the communicative situation. If the situation places extra demands on the listener then talkers will hyper-articulate; whereas, in favorable listening conditions talkers will be free to hypo-articulate. This view of spoken language as a dynamic interaction of competing forces has become very influential in current thought on all aspects of linguistic structure. In particular, many phonological processes and typological patterns are explained as alternative resolutions to the competing constraints imposed by the talker-oriented principle of economy of effort and the listener-oriented principle of sufficient contrast (e.g. Flemming, 1995; Boersma, 1998).

A common and highly effective method for directly observing the effects of this talker-listener balance is to observe the effects on speech production of different communicative situations. Typically, listener-related demands are manipulated either explicitly through the introduction of interfering noise or implicitly through the use of various instructions to the talkers (e.g. Cutler & Butterfield, 1991; Lively, Pisoni, Summers & Bernacki, 1993; Johnson, Flemming & Wright, 1993; Moon & Lindblom, 1994). Experimenters can then observe how talkers adapt to the demands of the communicative setting in a way that reflects tacit knowledge about the task of the listener. Studies using this type of methodology have shown that when talkers believe that the listener is more likely to encounter speech perception and lexical access difficulties, they spontaneously adjust their articulatory patterns to produce speech that is "clearer" than speech produced under highly favorable listening conditions. Importantly, several previous studies have shown that clear speech does indeed result in improved intelligibility (Picheny, Durlach & Braida, 1985) and numerous specific acoustic-phonetic markers of the clear speech mode have been identified (Picheny, Durlach & Braida, 1986; Payton, Uchanski & Braida, 1994; Uchanski, Choi, Braida, Reed & Durlach, 1996). These include, amongst others, increased overall duration and vowel space expansion. As an aside, it is important to note that, although clear speech is typically slower than conversational speech, the rate adjustment is neither the only nor the primary adjustment; that is, it is possible to produce fast, clear speech (Krause & Braida, 1995). These studies of clear speech provide strong support for the idea that talkers vary their articulation along a "hyper-hypo" continuum in response to the communicative situation.

Another critical testing ground for the view of speech communication as a balance between the talker's need for ease-of-articulation and the listener's need for sufficient-contrast is the study of the nature and origin of coarticulation. Within this general conceptual framework, coarticulation is viewed as the primary means by which talkers exercise their need to reduce effort. Therefore, in accordance with this view, the examination of coarticulatory patterns under various conditions should provide insight into the mechanisms that underlie the talker-oriented tendency towards hypo-articulation. Indeed, several studies have shown that segments in prosodically strong positions appear to resist coarticulation relative to segments in prosodically weak positions (e.g. Nord, 1974; Fowler, 1981; Engstrand, 1988; Cho, 1999). Similarly, there is some evidence that citation speech shows less extensive context-dependent variability than spontaneous speech (Krull, 1989; Duez, 1992). These data seem to suggest that talkers reduce the extent of coarticulatory influences when they want to increase the salience of all or some portion of an utterance.

However, an important generalization that has emerged from the extensive literature on coarticulation is that, at least to some extent, coarticulation is under talker control. Apparently talkers deliberately introduce this source of intra-talker variability into the stream of speech. Supporting evidence comes from cross-language studies showing substantial variation in coarticulatory patterns. Interestingly, these cross-linguistic differences are only partially determined by the underlying system of phonemic contrasts (see Manuel, 1999 for a review of this issue). For example, Beddor & Krakow (1999) report that even though both English and Thai have nondistinctive vowel nasalization, they differ dramatically in the degree to which a vowel preceding a nasal consonant is nasalized. English speakers typically allow extensive anticipatory vowel nasalization in CVN(C) syllables (about 80% of the vowel duration), whereas Thai speakers typically show more limited anticipatory vowel nasalization in CVN syllables (about 45% of the vowel duration). Furthermore, in a laboratory production study, Whalen (1990) showed that coarticulatory influences were exaggerated when the identity of the upcoming segment was known in advance relative to a condition where its identity was delayed for the talker. Studies such as these (among numerous others) suggest that coarticulation may serve some communicative function, and that it is planned by the talker and advantageous for the listener.

This suggestion runs contrary to the idea that coarticulation reflects the talker-related tendency towards ease of articulation. Furthermore, this raises the possibility that coarticulation is at least partially a listener-oriented source of variability, perhaps arising from perceptual mechanisms that (in parallel to production mechanisms) are optimized to extract information that is distributed over time rather than organized into discrete units. A prediction of this possibility is that even under decidedly listener-oriented conditions, coarticulation will be maintained rather than diminished since it serves both talker- and listener-oriented needs.

With this background in mind, the overall goal of the present study was to investigate coarticulatory patterns under conditions that demand hyper-articulation, that is, in clear speech. Specifically, this study compared the extent of vowel variability in conversational and clear speaking modes for high vowels that occurred in CV syllables where C varied in place-of-articulation. Furthermore, a cross-language approach was adopted as a means for assessing the extent to which the underlying system of phonemic contrasts determines hyper-articulatory patterns. In particular, I wanted to see whether when producing clear speech, talkers of a language with an uncrowded vowel space (such as Spanish with just five monophthongs) would take the opportunity afforded by the "listener friendly" vowel space to economize on effort by expanding the vowel space less than talkers of a language with a crowded vowel space (such as English with eleven monophthongs). This cross-language comparison would thereby provide additional insight into the principles that guide the production of clear speech. All three of these experimental variables (preceding consonant place-of-articulation, speaking mode, and language) have well-documented effects on vowel production. Of primary interest in this study were their effects in combination.

The specific research questions were: (1) Is coarticulation minimized, maintained or exaggerated in clear speech? And, (2) Does the vowel space expansion effect of clear speech vary across languages with vastly different vowel inventory sizes? As a secondary issue, I was also interested in comparing the English vowel spaces of monolinguals and English-Spanish bilinguals in order to see the extent to which the bilingual vowel spaces showed evidence of the languages in contact.

2. Methods

2.1 Materials

English materials consisted of CV target forms where C = /b/ or /d/, and V = either /i/ or /u/. The target forms were embedded in the following frame sentence, "Simon says [target form] starts with [target form initial letter]". Spanish materials consisted of $C_1V_1C_2V_2$ forms where C_1 = /b/ or /d/, and V_1 = either /i/ or /u/. For the Spanish materials, C_2V_2 varied depending on the target vowel: if V_1 was /u/ then C_2V_2 was /so/; if V_1 was /i/ then C_2V_2 was /fo/. The target forms were embedded in the following frame sentence, "Escribes [target form] siempre con [target form initial letter], which translates as "You write [target form] always with [target form initial letter]". The /fo/ context for the Spanish /i/ materials was originally intended as a means for avoiding an F2 plateau for /i/ in a /d_so/ context. However, this feature of the design placed an unfortunate limit on the subsequent cross-language comparison for the /i/ data. An additional constraint on the cross-language comparison for both the /i/ and /u/ materials was the monosyllabic versus disyllabic target forms in English and Spanish, respectively. (Both of these limitations are a result of the fact that the cross-language comparison was not part of the original conception of the larger project which encompasses the data and analyses present here. Nevertheless, as the project developed suggestive insights began to emerge from the unplanned, and therefore imperfect, cross-language comparison. These limitations will certainly be corrected in a future replication and extension of this study).

2.2 Subjects

Subjects were recruited from the Northwestern University community and included twelve American English monolinguals (six females and six males) and nine Mexican Spanish – American English bilinguals (six females and three males). Ages ranged from 18–33 years. All subjects were paid for their participation, and none reported any speech or hearing impairment at the time of testing. Several of the American English subjects had studied foreign languages, however all had spent the majority of their lives in the United States. All of the Spanish speaking subjects identified themselves as balanced bilinguals who had acquired both English and Spanish well before ten years of age. All were exposed to Spanish in the home and to some extent in their home community, but had received all of their schooling in English.

2.3 Recording procedure

Subjects were seated in a sound-treated room and asked to read the test sentences from a printed list. They spoke into a microphone that fed directly into the sound card (Sound Blaster Live) of a desktop computer running Windows NT. Recording was done on a single channel at a sampling rate of 16 kHz using the PRAAT speech analysis software package. The input level was monitored and adjusted so as to ensure maximum gain without exceeding the dynamic range of the recording system. All subjects produced the sentences in both conversational and clear speaking modes. For the conversational speaking mode, subjects were told to read at their normal pace without any particular attention to clarity. Subjects were told to imagine that the intended listener of these recordings was someone highly familiar with her or his voice and speech patterns. For the clear speaking mode, subjects were told to read the sentences as if speaking to a listener with a hearing loss or from a different language background. Each sentence was read only once in each mode unless there was an error or disfluency, in which case the sentence was repeated at the end of the current set of sentences.

The monolingual American English subjects first recorded all of the English sentences in the conversational speaking mode, and then re-recorded them in the clear speaking mode. The bilingual subjects first recorded all of the Spanish sentences in the conversational speaking mode, followed by all of the Spanish sentences in the clear speaking mode. After a short break, they recorded all of the English sentences in the conversational speaking mode, followed by all of the English sentences in the clear speaking mode. In total, three data sets were recorded: English materials by English monolinguals (Eng-Eng), Spanish materials by Spanish-English bilinguals (Span-Span), and English materials by Spanish-English bilinguals (Span-Eng).

2.4 Acoustic measurements

Using the PRAAT speech analysis software package, target vowel durations and formant frequencies were measured. Vowel durations were measured from the consonant release to the onset of frication for the following /s/. Formant frequencies were measured at points 20%, 50% and 80% into the vowel duration. These measurement points were determined on the basis of the duration measurements. The first three formant measurements were taken from LPC autocorrelation formant tracks which were checked against the formants observed in wide-band spectrograms. The LPC prediction order was adjusted as appropriate to yield accurate formant measurements. For the purposes of all figures and statistical analyses all formant measurements in Hertz were converted to values along the perceptually motivated mel scale (Fant, 1973) according to the following equation: $M = (1000/\log 2) \log ((F/1000) + 1)$, where M and F are the frequencies in mels and Hertz, respectively. Furthermore, for all figures and statistical analyses, F2' (rather than F2) was used in order to take into account the perceptual integration that occurs for two spectral prominences that are separated by less than about 3.5 bark (Chistovich & Lublinskaya, 1979). For the front vowel /i/ where F2 and F3 are very close in frequency (within 3.5 bark of each other), F2' was taken as the mean of F2 and F3; for the back vowel /u/ where F2 is well separated from both F1 and F3, F2' was simply equal to F2.

3. Results

3.1 Confirmation of speech mode difference

Previous studies of the durational characteristics of clear speech (e.g. Picheny et al., 1986; Uchanski et al., 1996) have consistently found increased vowel durations for clear speech relative to conversational speech. Therefore, in order to establish that the instructions to the talkers were successful in eliciting two distinct speaking modes, vowel durations were compared across the conversational and clear speech tokens within each data set. Figure 1 shows a scatter plot of vowel durations in conversational versus clear speech modes for individual subjects from each data set. The data shown in this figure represent averages across the bilabial and alveolar consonantal contexts, and across the two vowels, /i/ and /u/. With one exception, each individual data point in this figure falls above the diagonal, indicating an increase in vowel duration for clear speech relative to conversational speech.

These vowel duration data were submitted to a mixed, four factor ANOVA with one between-groups variable (data set: Eng-Eng vs. Span-Span vs. Span-Eng), and three within-groups variables (consonant: bilabial vs. alveolar, vowel: /i/ vs. /u/, and mode: conversational vs. clear). Results showed that the four-way in-

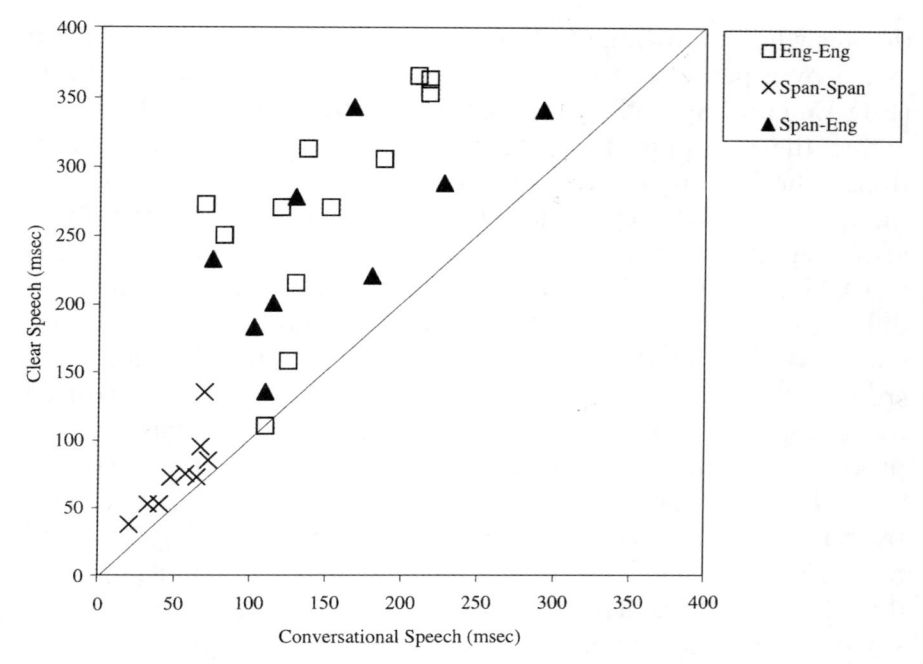

Figure 1: Vowel durations in conversational versus clear speaking modes for individual subjects from each data set, averaged across the bilabial and alveolar consonantal contexts and across /i/ and /u/.

teraction and the three-way interactions were not significant. Furthermore, the main effect of vowel was not significant, and none of the two-way interactions involving this factor were significant. There was a highly significant main effect of data set ($F(2,27) = 22.27$, $p < .0001$). Post-hoc tests showed that while there was no significant duration difference between the two sets of English vowels (Eng-Eng and Span-Eng), the Spanish vowels (Span-Span) were significantly shorter than both sets of English vowels ($p < .0001$ in both cases by Fisher's PLSD). This difference is likely due to the different syllabic contexts in which the vowels were produced. Furthermore, this statistical analysis showed a significant interaction between data set and consonant ($F(2,17) = 4.97$, $p < .05$). Tests of simple effects showed that the Span-Eng vowel durations (averaged across vowel context and speaking mode) varied as a function of the place-of-articulation of the preceding consonant (longer when following /d/ than when following /b/, $t(8) = 2.29$, $p = .05$ by a paired t-test). In contrast, for the other two data sets (Eng-Eng and Span-Span) there was no vowel duration difference across the two preceding consonant place-of-articulation conditions. The reasons for this difference between the Span-Eng and the other two data sets remain to be explained. Finally, there was also a significant interaction between data set and mode ($F(1,27) = 10.96$, $p < .001$). Comparisons of the clear-conversational vowel duration differences (collapsed across vowel and consonant contexts) showed that the increase in vowel duration for clear speech relative to conversational speech was significantly reduced for the Spanish vowels (Span-Span) relative to the English vowels produced by both talker groups (by Fisher's PLSD, $p < .0001$ and $p < .01$ for the comparisons with Eng-Eng and Span-Eng, respectively). There was no significant difference between Eng-Eng and Span-Eng data sets with respect to the conversational-clear vowel duration difference. This data set by mode interaction may reflect some systematic difference between English and Spanish with respect to the role that the duration increase plays in the conversational to clear speech mode transformation, or this may also be a reflection of the different syllabic contexts across the English and Spanish materials. Nevertheless, the consistent duration increase for all three data sets indicates that the talkers did indeed produce two distinct speaking modes.

3.2 Coarticulation and clear speech

Having established that the subjects produced the intended speech mode difference, we can now turn to the main concern of the present study, namely, the interaction between speaking mode and consonantal context on vowel production within each of the three data sets (Eng-Eng, Span-Span, and Span-Eng). Figure 2 shows the effect of consonantal context on F1 and F2' frequency at the vowel midpoint for all three data sets averaged across speaking modes. Data are shown separately for /i/ and /u/. It is evident from these plots that F1 and F2' formant frequencies for /i/ did not

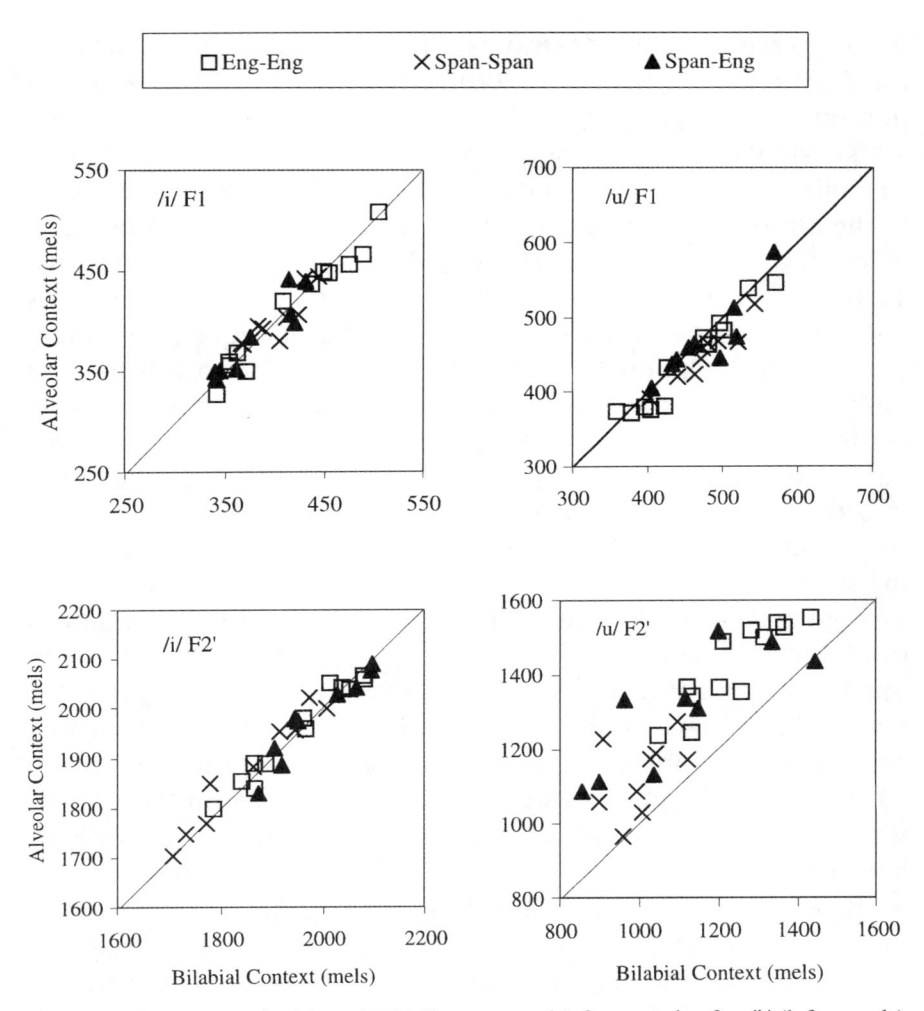

Figure 2: F1 (upper panels) and F2' (lower panels) frequencies for /i/ (left panels) and /u/ (right panels) following /b/ versus /d/. Individual subject data are shown for Eng-Eng, Span-Span and Span-Eng data sets, averaged across conversational and clear speaking modes.

vary as a function of the place-of-articulation of the preceding consonant. This resistance of /i/ to preceding consonant-dependent coarticulation replicates a well-known finding for several languages (e.g. English: Stevens & House, 1963; Catalan: Recasens, 1985), and is presumably due to the fact that the high-front gesture for /i/ places severe constraints on tongue dorsum variability. Furthermore, the effect of preceding consonant place-of-articulation on F1 frequency for /u/ was negligible. However, /u/ F2' varied substantially depending on whether the preceding consonant was bilabial or alveolar. As expected, F2' frequencies were higher in the alveolar context than in the bilabial context, and this effect of context was consistent across subjects in all three data sets. Thus, since significant consonant-dependent vowel variability was only found for /u/ in the F2' dimension, the subsequent investigation of coarticulation in conversational and clear speech focused on /u/ F2' in the two consonantal contexts (i.e. /bu/ and /du/) across conversational and clear speaking modes. Furthermore, the data were examined at points 20%, 50% and 80% into the vowel in order to see whether the CV coarticulatory effect in each of the two speaking modes diminished with distance from the conditioning segment.

Figures 3, 4 and 5 show /u/ F2' frequency in all four conditions (/bu/ and /du/, conversational and clear) for the Eng-Eng, Span-Span, and Span-Eng data sets, respectively. In all three figures, the x-axis shows time in milliseconds where 0 represents the vowel onset after the consonant release. The particular points in time at which the F2' frequencies were plotted were based on the average vowel duration across all subjects in each of the four conditions; however, the F2' frequency value of each data point represents the average across all subjects taken at time points specified on an individual subject basis. Thus, on average, 50% into clear speech vowels for the Eng-Eng data set shown in Figure 3 occurred at approximately 125 milliseconds. However, as shown in Figure 1, clear speech vowels for this data set ranged in total duration from approximately 125–375 milliseconds, giving 50% points ranging from approximately 62.5–187.5 milliseconds. Figure 6 shows scatter plots of the F2' frequency in the bilabial context versus in the alveolar context for individual subjects in the Eng-Eng (top row), Span-Span (middle row) and Span-Eng (bottom row) data sets. These scatter plots are shown for each of three points into the vowel duration: 20% (left column), 50% (middle column), and 80% (right column). It is clear from each of these figures that

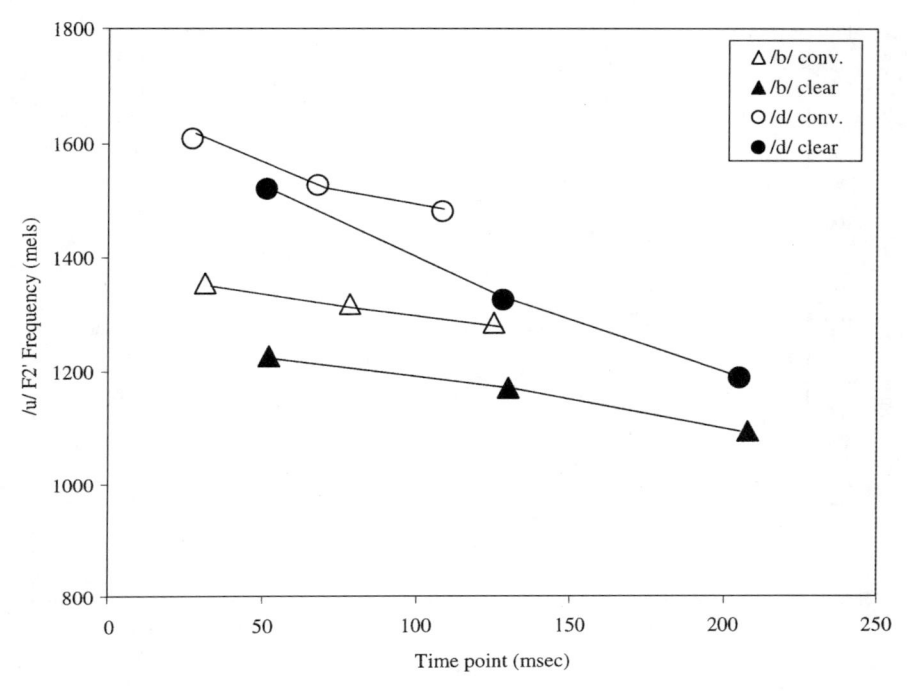

Figure 3: English F2′ frequency for /u/ in conversational (open symbols) versus clear (filled symbols) speech when following /b/ (triangles) versus when following /d/ (circles) as produced by English monolinguals (Eng-Eng). Data are shown on a time scale that represents the average vowel duration across all subjects.

the effect of consonantal context was maintained across speaking modes and throughout the duration of the vowel for each data set. That is, in Figures 3, 4 and 5, there is a consistent F2′ frequency difference between /u/ in a bilabial context versus in an alveolar context regardless of speaking mode or time point (filled and open circles are always higher in F2′ than their respective filled and open triangles). In figure 6, the vast majority of data points are above the diagonal regardless of speaking mode or time point.

Within each data set, a three-factor repeated-measures ANOVA (with mode, consonantal context, and time point as the factors, and F2′ as the dependent variable) supported these observations. For the Eng-Eng data set, there was a highly significant three-way interaction between mode, consonantal context and time point

254 Ann R. Bradlow

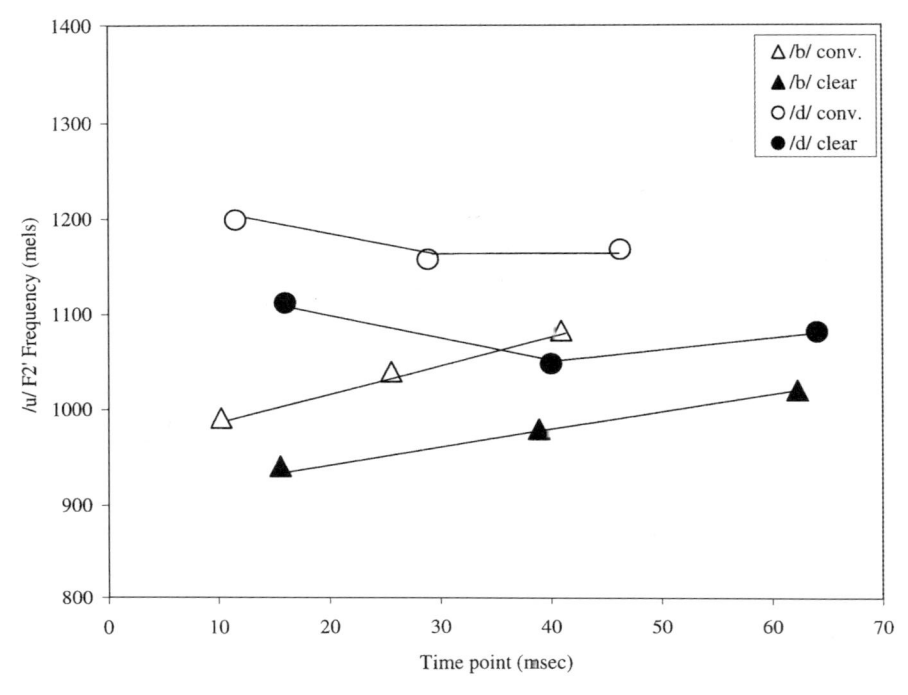

Figure 4: Same as Figure 3, for Spanish data produced by bilinguals (Span-Span).

($F(2,22) = 21.05$, p < .0001). Separate two-factor repeated-measures ANOVAs at each time point (with mode and consonantal context as the factors) showed that at each of the two earlier time points (20% and 50% into the vowel duration), the two-way interaction between mode and consonantal context was not significant. In each of these two cases, there was a highly significant main effect of mode (20% time point: $F(1,11) = 36.49$, p < .0001; 50% time point $F(1,11) = 40.79$, p < .0001), and a highly significant main effect of consonant context (20% time point: $F(1,11) = 80.27$, p < .0001; 50% time point $F(1,11) = 127.38$, p < .0001). At the 80% time point, the interaction between mode and consonantal context was significant ($F(1,11) = 9.52$, p < .05). This interaction resulted from the fact that, at this point in the vowel, the consonantal context effect was diminished for clear speech relative to conversational speech: the mean /u/ F2' difference for clear and conversational speech were 94 and 196 mels, respectively. Never-

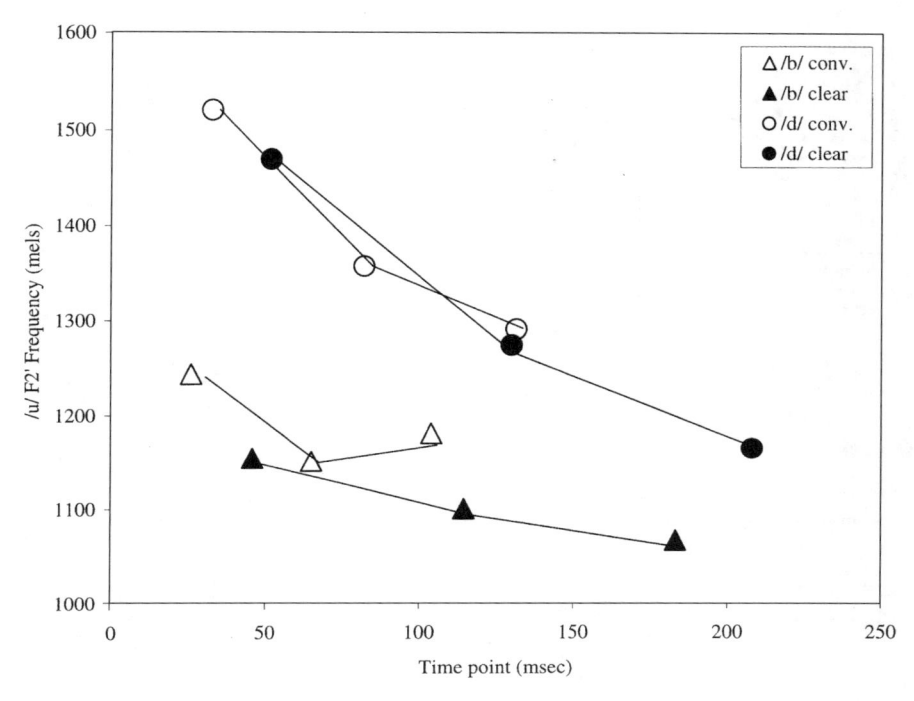

Figure 5: Same as Figure 3, for English data produced by bilinguals (Span-Eng).

theless, post-hoc paired t-tests showed that these context induced vowel formant differences were highly significant for both speech modes (conversational mode: $t(11) = 8.24$, $p < .0001$; clear mode: $t(11) = 5.02$, $p < .001$).

For both the Span-Span and Span-Eng data sets, the three-way interaction between mode, consonantal context and time point was not significant (Span-Span: $F(2,16) = .258$, $p = .78$; Span-Eng: $F(2,16) = .32$, $p < .73$). Furthermore, for both data sets, the two-way mode by time point interaction was not significant (Span-Span: $F(2,16) = .77$, $p = .48$; Span-Eng: $F(2,16) = 1.27$, $p < .31$), whereas time point interacted significantly with consonant context such that the effect of consonant context diminished across the vowel duration (Span-Span: $F(2,16) = 24.15$, $p < .0001$; Span-Eng: $F(2,16) = 17.85$, $p < .0001$). Most importantly, the mode by consonant context interaction was not significant for either data set (Span-Span: $F(1,16) = 1.46$, $p = .26$; Span-Eng: $F(1,16) = .03$, $p = .86$),

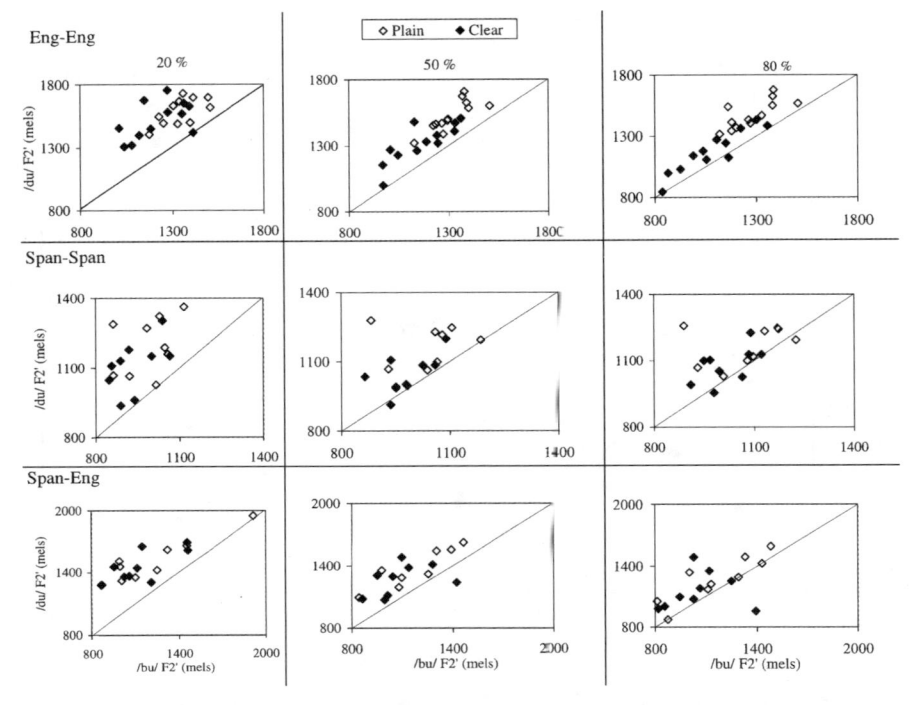

Figure 6: Scatter plots of /u/ F2' frequency in the context of /b/ (x-axis) versus /d/ (y-axis) for conversational (open symbols) and clear (filled symbols) speech. The left, middle and right columns represent measurements at 20%, 50% and 80% into the vowel duration, respectively. The top, middle and bottom rows represent measurement for the Eng-Eng, Span-Span and Span-Eng data sets, respectively.

indicating that the consonant context effect was equivalent across speaking modes. For both data sets, the main effect of mode was highly significant (Span-Span: $F(1,16) = 37.53$, $p < .001$; Span-Eng: $F(1,16) = 5.40$, $p < .05$), as were the main effects of consonant context (Span-Span: $F(1,16) = 19.30$, $p < .01$ Span-Eng: $F(1,16) = 28.17$, $p < .001$) and time point (Span-Span: $F(2,16) = 8.31$, $p < .005$; Span-Eng: $F(2,16) = 16.13$, $p < .0001$). Post hoc paired t-tests showed that the F2' frequency difference for /u/ in the bilabial context versus in the alveolar contexts (collapsed across mode) was significant at all three time points for both data sets (at the $p < .05$ level) with just one exception: for the Span-Eng data set, the consonant context effect at 80% into the vowel was significant at the p = .05 level. Thus the general finding was that, within each data set, variability induced by consonant context in /u/ F2' frequency was maintained across conversational and clear speaking modes, and in general this pattern held throughout the vowel duration.

In summary, this investigation of CV coarticulation across speaking modes showed that the effect of preceding consonant place-of-articulation on /u/ F2' frequency was maintained across conversational and clear speaking modes for all three data sets. Furthermore, this effect of preceding consonant place-of-articulation was typically maintained up until at least 80% into the vowel duration, even for long, clear speech vowels. Thus, these data support the hypothesis that the effects of CV coarticulation are maintained in clear speech. While the results of the present analyses are quite consistent, it is important to acknowledge the limitations of these data. Most notably, the key finding pertains only to /u/ variability following /b/ and /d/. As yet, we have no information on the generalizability of these findings to other vowels, other consonants, other syllabic contexts and under various prosodic conditions.

3.3 Vowel space expansion in English versus Spanish clear speech

The second question that this study sought to address was whether the effect of clear speech on vowel quality varies across languages with vastly different vowel inventory sizes. By comparing the extent of vowel space expansion across two such languages we can see whether the hyper-articulation typical of the clear speech mode is localized to segments that are more likely to be subject to perceptual confusion, or if clear speech is characterized by global hyper-articulation across all segments. Specifically, I wanted to see whether the crowded vowel space of English would show greater expansion in clear speech relative to conversational speech than the sparsely populated vowel space of Spanish. If indeed English clear speech is characterized by a greater degree of vowel space expansion than Spanish clear speech, then this would suggest that talkers economize on the effort spent in producing clear speech by taking into consideration the overall system of contrasts that the listener must access. In other words, this result would suggest that even in the listener-oriented clear speech mode, talkers economize on effort by only hyper-articulating those segments that are most likely to be vulnerable to perceptual confusion. In contrast, if the data show that the amount of clear speech vowel space expansion is independent of vowel inventory size, then this would suggest that talkers generally do all they can to enhance the acoustic-phonetic salience of clear speech and that clear speech is characterized by global hyper-articulation.

Figure 7 shows the location in the F1 by F2' vowel space of /i/ and /u/ in conversational and clear speech for all three data sets. These formant measurements were averaged across the two consonant contexts, and were taken at a point 50% into the vowel duration. The arrows show the direction of change from conversational to clear speech. As seen in this figure, for all three data sets, the clear speech vowels are more peripheral in the vowel space than the conversational speech vowels, giving the overall effect that the clear speech vowel space is expanded relative to the conversational speech vowel space. Note that for visual display purposes, the F1 dimension (x-axis) in Figure 7 is on a larger scale than the F2' dimension (y-axis) giving the (erroneous) impression that the conversational and clear speech vowels differ substantially in both dimensions. In fact, there is far more stylistic variation in F2' than in F1.

In order to quantify the extent of this expansion effect, the Euclidian distance between /i/ and /u/ was calculated for each of the two speaking modes, in each of the two consonantal context conditions, and for each of the three data sets. Scatter-plots of the individual subject data are shown in Figure 8. These /i/–/u/ distance measures were submitted to a mixed three factor ANOVA with data set as the between-groups variable (Eng-Eng vs. Span-Span vs. Span-Eng), and consonant context (bilabial vs. alveolar) and mode (conversational vs. clear) as the within-groups variables. Results showed a highly significant main effect of data set ($F(2,27)$

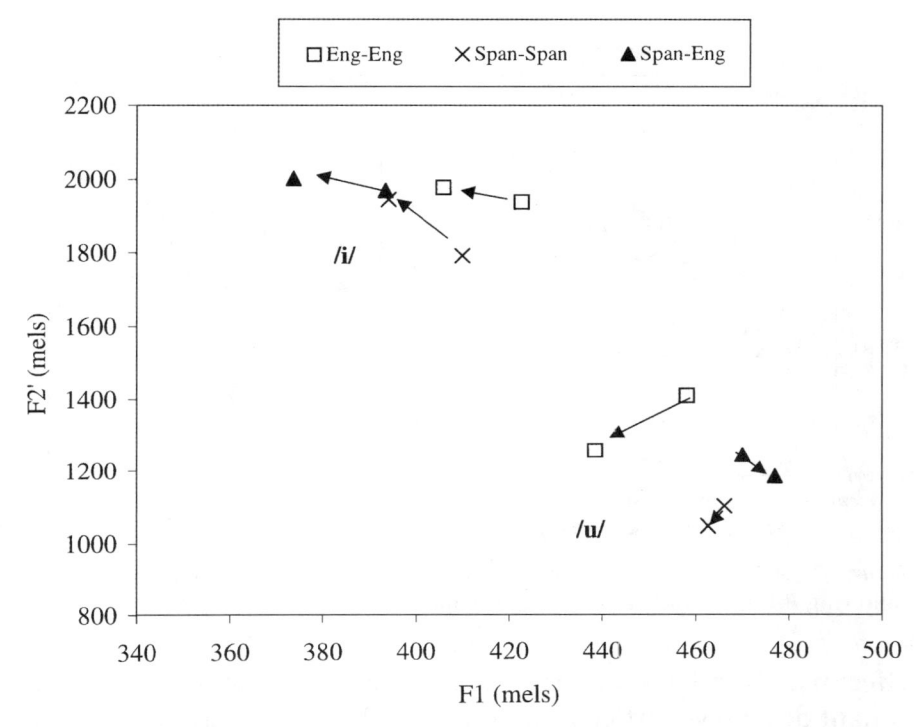

Figure 7: F1 by F2' vowel space plots for /i/ and /u/ in conversational and clear speech, by data set, for the 50% time point, averaged across bilabial and alveolar consonantal contexts. Arrows show the direction of change from conversational to clear speech within each data set.

= 9.760, p < .001). Post-hoc tests showed that there was no significant difference in /i/−/u/ distance between the two sets of vowels produced by the bilingual talkers (Span-Eng and Span-Span); however, the English vowels produced by the monolinguals (Eng-Eng) had significantly shorter /i/−/u/ distances than both sets of bilingual vowels (p < .001 in both cases by Fisher's PLSD.) This effect of talker language background (monolingual versus bilingual) is somewhat surprising and remains to be explained. There were also highly significant main effects of consonant context ($F(1,27) = 86.537$, p < .001) and mode ($F(1,27) = 66.824$, p < .001). The effect of consonant context was due to the greater /i/−/u/ distance for vowels following /b/ than following /d/. This

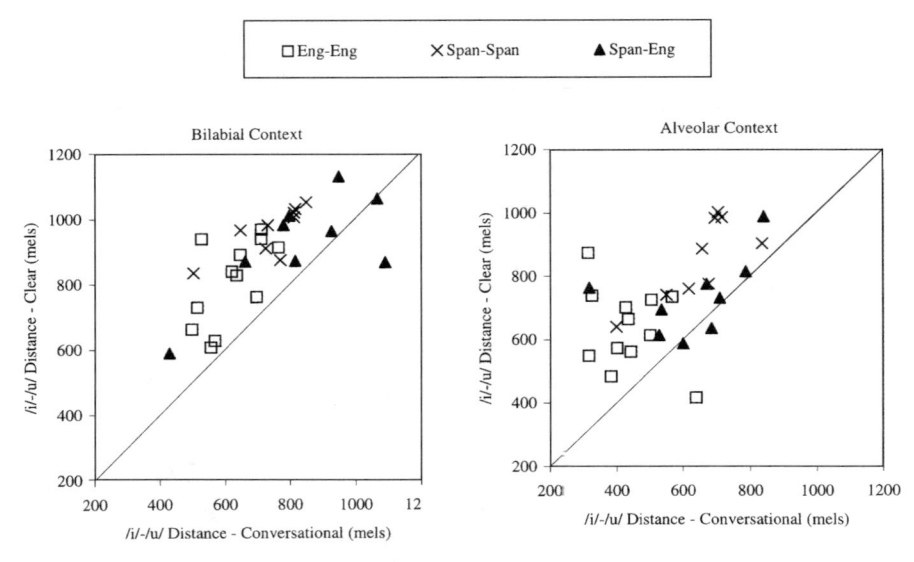

Figure 8: /i/–/u/ distance in conversational versus clear speech for vowels following /b/ (left panel) and /d/ (right panel) for all three data sets.

effect may be related to the greater independence between the consonant and vowel articulators for the /bV/ syllables relative to the /dV/ syllables. The effect of mode was due to the fact that the /i/–/u/ distance was greater in magnitude for clear speech than for conversational speech. Of most interest for this study was the finding of a non-significant two-way interaction between data set and mode ($F(2,27) = 2.873$, p = .0739), indicating that the clear speech high vowel space expansion effect was equivalent across data sets. None of the other two- or three-way interactions were significant.

In summary, this comparison of the high vowel space expansion effect for clear speech across the three data sets in this study yielded two main findings. First, there was a significant difference in /i/–/u/ distance across data sets regardless of speaking mode. Surprisingly, this difference was due to a smaller /i/–/u/ distance for the Eng-Eng data set than for the other two data sets. It is unlikely that this difference is due to differences in the English and Spanish materials, or to structural differences between English and Spanish, because the Span-Eng data patterned with the Span-Span data rather than with the Eng-Eng data. Thus, the source of this difference must be the talkers themselves. Whether this is an effect of bilingualism or of some idiosyncratic feature of this group of nine talkers remains to be resolved. Furthermore, it may be that even for these talkers, when the entire vowel space including low vowels is taken into account, the English vowel space is indeed expanded relative to the Spanish vowel space, as found by Bradlow (1995). This issue will need to be addressed by future studies.

The second main finding of this analysis was the consistent degree of vowel space expansion for clear speech relative to conversational speech across all three data sets, thereby demonstrating that clear speech is characterized by a similar degree of vowel space expansion regardless of vowel inventory size. This finding suggests that under clear speech conditions, talkers will spare no effort in enhancing the acoustic-phonetic salience of the overall vowel space. A close examination of Figure 7 provides further support for this conclusion by showing that for all three data sets, the clear speech high vowel space approached the extremes of the vowel space indicated by the union of their conversational speech vowel spaces. Specifically, for the Eng-Eng data set, the overall /i/−/u/ clear speech expansion effect was due mostly to a lowering of /u/ F2' towards the low /u/ F2' for conversational Span-Span. In contrast, for the Span-Span data set, the overall /i/−/u/ clear speech expansion effect was due mostly to a raising of /i/ F2' towards the high /i/ F2' for conversational Eng-Eng and Span-Eng. Thus, the overall impression is that, in the clear speech mode, the talkers attempted to expand the vowel space as far as possible. While the Spanish clear speech vowel space expanded all the way to the high F2' extreme indicated by English /i/, the English clear speech vowel space did not extend all the way to the low F2' extreme indicated by Spanish /u/. This may be due to an independent constraint on English /u/ backness, and should be further investigated in future work.

In summary, these data suggest that vowel space expansion is a characteristic of clear speech in languages with relatively crowded vowel spaces as well as in languages with relatively uncrowded vowel spaces. This finding suggests further that the focus of the acoustic-phonetic enhancements in clear speech production is not determined by the system of underlying phoneme contrasts of the language. Rather, clear speech is characterized by global hyperarticulation. While the patterns observed in this cross-language comparison are suggestive, there are several limitations of the study which must be overcome before any strong conclusions can be drawn. First, while the Eng-Eng data set represents productions from monolingual speakers, the Span-Span data set represents productions from Spanish-English bilinguals. Thus, it is possible that the vowel space expansion that we observed for the Span-Span data set would not be observed in Spanish productions by monolingual Spanish speakers. Second, as described in section 2.1 above, the English and Spanish materials differed in important ways which may have influenced the extent of vowel space expansion in clear versus conversational speech.

3.4 Bilingual vowel spaces

The third (and somewhat peripheral) question I wanted to address with the present data was related to the nature of the bilingual vowel space. In particular, I wanted to investigate whether the English and Spanish vowel spaces of the bilinguals in this study would show any acoustic-phonetic evidence of the language contact experienced by these subjects. Earlier work has shown that the monolingual English vowel space is generally shifted upward in the F2' dimension relative to the monolingual Spanish vowel space, indicating a fronted "base of articulation" for English relative to Spanish (Bradlow, 1995). In the present study with Spanish-English bilinguals I wondered whether this previously reported English-Spanish difference would be maintained or neutralized for the individual bilingual subjects. A subset of the data collected for this study where the English and Spanish materials were best matched, namely the /u/ materials, allowed for this investigation and could provide some preliminary insights into the bilingual vowel space(s).

As seen in Figure 2 (lower right panel) the general pattern is for /u/ F2' frequency to be highest for the Eng-Eng data set, lowest

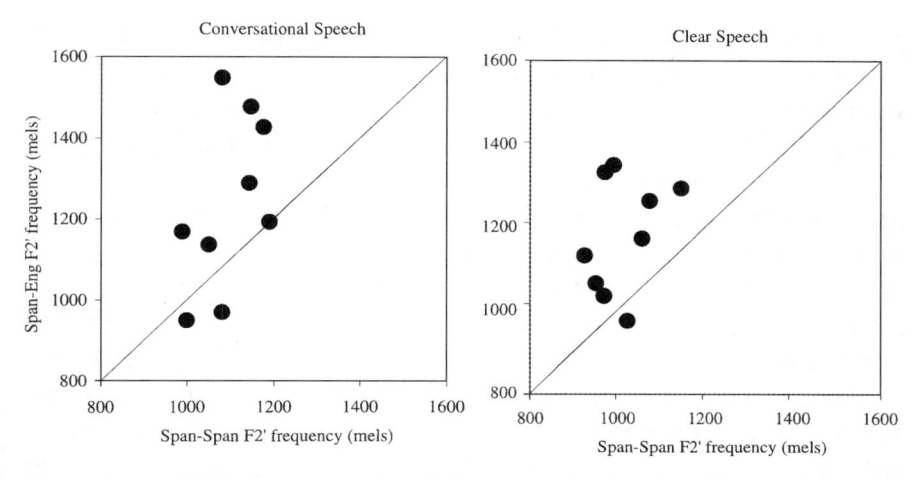

Figure 9: /u/ F2′ frequency at the 50% time point for the bilinguals' Spanish vowels (Span-Span) versus their English vowels in conversational (left panel) and clear (right panel) speech, averaged across the /b/ and /d/ contexts.

for the Span-Span data set, and intermediate for the Span-Eng data set. Furthermore, there is very little overlap in F2′ frequency for the Eng-Eng and Span-Span data sets, but extensive overlap between the Span-Eng data set and both of the other data sets. In other words, the Spanish-English bilinguals produced Spanish /u/ with consistently lower F2′ frequencies than monolingual English /u/. However, this same group of Spanish-English bilinguals produced highly variable English /u/ tokens. Nevertheless, as shown in Figure 9, when we examine the English and Spanish vowels on an individual subject basis we find that most of the individual bilinguals maintained a difference in F2′ frequency between their productions of English and Spanish /u/ in both conversational and clear speaking modes. Furthermore, this difference was in a direction that is consistent with the previously reported English-Spanish difference for monolinguals. That is, the English vowels had higher F2′ frequencies than their Spanish counterparts. Separate ANOVAs for the conversational and clear speech F2′ frequencies at the vowel midpoint averaged across the bilabial and alveolar consonant contexts showed significant main effects of data set (conversational speech: $F(2,57) = 18.403$, $p < .0001$; clear speech: $F(2,57) = 12.457$, p < .0001). Post-hoc comparisons (Fisher's PLSD) showed significant differences (at the p < .02 level) for all two-way comparisons, with the only exception that the F2' difference between the Eng-Eng and Span-Eng clear speech tokens failed to reach significance.

This comparison across monolingual and bilingual subject groups suggests two generalizations regarding the effect of bilingualism on vowel production. First, the significantly lower F2' frequency for the Span-Eng data set relative to the Eng-Eng data set for conversational speech suggests that the English vowel space of Spanish-English bilinguals differs in subtle ways from its monolingual counterpart in a direction that reflects the influence of Spanish. However, this difference was not observed in clear speech, apparently due to F2' lowering for the Eng-Eng data set under clear speech conditions. Second, even though English /u/ produced by bilinguals is somewhat more "Spanish-like" than English /u/ produced by monolinguals, most individual bilingual subjects maintain a clear difference between English /u/ and Spanish /u/. This first generalization suggests that the two linguistic systems of a bilingual are represented in a single, unified mental model to the extent that the presence of each system exerts some influence over the other; however, the second generalization suggests that bilinguals typically do maintain some degree of separation between the two systems.

This situation is in accord with other studies of bilinguals showing clear effects of L1 on L2 speech production and vice versa (e.g. Flege, 1987, 1995; Sancier & Fowler, 1997). However, a notable difference between the bilinguals in the present study and the subjects of most other studies of bilingual speech production is that the present subjects acquired both languages well before puberty, whereas other studies have typically focused on subjects who acquired one of their languages later in life. Obler & Gjerlow (1999, pp. 126–128) cite an exception to this generalization which matched the design of the present study quite closely and led to a similar conclusion. Obler (1982) examined voiced versus voiceless stop consonant production in balanced Hebrew-English bilinguals who had acquired both languages very early in life. She found that the stop consonant voice onset times in each of the two languages clearly reflected an influence of the other language. Furthermore, the data showed that these bilinguals tended to produce stops with voice onset times that maximized the difference across the two languages, suggesting that they had broad, unitary phonetic systems.

While these data are highly suggestive, much further research is needed before they can be taken as conclusive. First, it is important to complete this analysis by including Spanish data from Spanish monolinguals. Since the present data revealed acoustic-phonetic differences between English vowels produced by monolinguals and bilinguals, it is important to also investigate whether there are similar differences between Spanish vowels produced by monolinguals and bilinguals. Specifically, based on the present data, we would predict that the Spanish vowels produced by monolinguals should have even lower F2' frequencies than those produced by Spanish-English bilinguals. Second, as discussed above, there were potentially significant differences between the Spanish and English materials. The present findings need to be confirmed with more closely matched materials across the two languages. Finally, the general pattern of results needs to be replicated with bilinguals with different language acquisition profiles, and across different language pairs. Specifically, the bilingual subjects in this study typically acquired Spanish first in the home, and then acquired English later from teachers and peers in the surrounding English-speaking community. Thus although these subjects can safely be called "balanced" bilinguals, the spheres of life in which the two languages were learned and applied are quite different. To what extent might the present results reflect this functional separation of the two languages? For example, is it possible that the greater F2' frequency variability for the English vowels than for the Spanish vowels from the bilinguals is related to the order of language acquisition for these subjects? Similarly, is it the case that all bilinguals will show similar influences of each language on the phonetic output of the other? That is, to what extent are the intermediate F2' values for the Span-Eng data related to the F2' frequency difference between monolingual English and monolingual Spanish? What other, sociolinguistic factors might be exerting an influence? To answer these questions a more extensive cross-language approach with carefully selected subjects and materials is needed.

4. Discussion

The overall goal of this study was to examine the acoustic-phonetic modifications that characterize a change from a conversational to a clear speech mode with particular attention to features of speech production that are generally taken to reflect the talker-oriented force towards ease-of-articulation. In particular, I wanted to see whether coarticulatory influences were minimized, maintained or exaggerated in clear speech, and whether the hyper-articulation that characterizes clear speech is limited to segments that are likely to be vulnerable to perceptual confusion, or if clear speech is produced with "global" hyper-articulation.

The first main finding was that clear speech involved the maintenance of CV coarticulation for the high vowel /u/ when produced following /b/ and /d/. This result was obtained for monolingual speakers of English, as well as for Spanish-English bilinguals when producing either English or Spanish. Stevens (1998) estimated that a window of about 100 milliseconds is required for the tongue body to move from a front to a back position. As shown in Figures 3–5, the coarticulatory influence in the clear speech vowels in this study extended substantially further into the vowel duration than this time frame. Therefore, it is likely that the observed maintenance of CV coarticulation in clear speech was under talker control, and presumably serves some listener-oriented purpose rather than reflecting a purely talker-oriented concern for economy of effort. (For a similar finding regarding the temporal extent of coarticulatory influences, see Suomi, 1987).

The second main finding of this study was that clear speech in both English and Spanish involved vowel space expansion. Furthermore, the degree of vowel space expansion was comparable across the two languages even though they have vastly different vowel inventory sizes. This cross-language, inventory-independent tendency towards an expanded vowel space indicates that acoustic distinctiveness can, at least to some extent, be defined in absolute terms without reference to the size of the segment inventory in question. Additionally, this finding suggests that talkers spare no effort in producing clear speech and instead "globally" hyperarticulate even for segments that are unlikely to be perceptually confused with their distant neighbors.

Taken together, these two main findings demonstrate that clear speech vowel production involves both maintenance of coarticulation and enhanced acoustic distinctiveness. That is, clear speech vowels occupy peripheral positions in the vowel space relative to conversational speech vowels while still maintaining the coarticulatory effect of the preceding consonant place-of-articulation. Although the data in this study are limited and must be considered preliminary, they present provocative patterns which deserve further interpretation.

It may seem that maintenance of coarticulatory influences and enhanced acoustic distinctiveness are incompatible, opposing forces that represent the tension between the talker-oriented principle of economy of effort and the listener-oriented principle of sufficient contrast, respectively. Under this view, it is odd that clear speech is apparently characterized by both of these features. Manuel (1999) noted a similar oddity in her review of cross-language studies of coarticulation as they pertain to the loss of underlying distinctions, and resolved it as follows: "If coarticulation is in some sense a strategy by which speakers reduce their overall effort, and limiting coarticulation is a way of responding to the need for listeners to get a clear and unambiguous signal ..., then it would seem that sometimes sloth wins out." Rather than resorting to the overwhelming power of sloth, I will argue that maintenance of coarticulation and enhanced acoustic distinctiveness are compatible and expected features of clear speech for both talker- and listener-oriented reasons.

First, let us consider maintenance of coarticulation and enhanced acoustic distinctiveness as they apply to the talker, that is, in terms of speech production. As suggested by the fact that the English and Spanish vowel spaces showed similar amounts of vowel space expansion, it is likely that the force towards enhanced acoustic distinctiveness in clear speech production applies equally to all segments, thereby actually *causing* the apparent maintenance of coarticulation. In the case of a CV syllable, both the consonant and the vowel would be subject to hyperarticulation in clear speech, resulting in more extreme articulatory targets for both the C and the V. Thus, the overall effect on any particular acoustic parameter, such as F2' frequency, is that the trajectory joining the hyperarticulated targets will reflect both the more extreme C and the more extreme V articulations. This will lead to exactly the type of consonant context effect that was observed in the present study where, regardless of speaking mode, /u/ after /b/ had a lower F2' frequency throughout the vowel than /u/ after /d/. For /bu/, the effect of hyperarticulation is to lower both the /b/ and the /u/ targets resulting in a very low F2' trajectory; for /du/ the effect of hyperarticulation is to raise the /d/ target and to lower the /u/ target resulting in a very steep trajectory that will likely be higher than the /bu/ trajectory throughout the vowel. Thus, under this explanation, the maintenance of coarticulation is a direct consequence of the "global" hyperarticulation that characterizes clear speech. (For a somewhat similar idea, see van Son & Pols, 1999).

With respect to the listener, we need to fully understand the perceptual advantages of both enhanced acoustic distinctiveness and maintenance of consonant contextual variability that lead to their being characteristics of clear speech. The perceptual advantage of enhanced acoustic distinctiveness is easily understood in terms of the general theory of adaptive dispersion (Liljencrantz & Lindblom, 1972; Lindblom, 1990). As for maintenance of consonant contextual variability, it can be understood with respect to two properties of speech perception. First, there are clear advantages to having information about individual segments distributed over time. This type of signal redundancy makes speech perception robust and functional even in noisy environments (see Broe & Pierrehumbert, 2000 for some discussion of this point of view), and conditions where talkers produce clear speech are exactly those conditions where signal redundancy is most helpful. Second, numerous studies on perceptual compensation for coarticulation have demonstrated that listeners are quite good at using contextual information to perceptually reduce, or compensate for, acoustic variability (e.g. Mann, 1980; Fowler, 1984; Beddor & Krakow, 1999 and many others). This process of perceptual compensation is plausible because contextual variability is lawful and highly predictable. In this sense then, contextual variability can serve as a rich source of information about the underlying segmental structure without incurring a high processing "cost." In other words, the advantage of distributing segmental information over time is likely to be greater than the (relatively minor) disadvantage of requiring listeners to perceptually compensate for the consequent, but lawful, acoustic variability.

What then is the nature of the relationship between talker- and listener-oriented forces in clear speech production? One possibility is that clear speech is purely listener-oriented to the extent that all talker-oriented forces that are operative in conversational speech have been completely overcome by the listener-oriented requirement for sufficient contrast. Under this view, clear speech is listener-oriented in an absolute sense, and the fact that coarticulation is maintained in clear speech simply implies that coarticulation should not always be taken as a measure of talker effort. As demonstrated by the present study, globally hyper-articulated speech can involve extensive coarticulation in spite of the extra effort expended by the talker. This purely listener-oriented view of clear speech is consistent with theories that view speech communication as a dynamic interaction between the talker-oriented force towards economy of effort and the opposing, listener-oriented force towards sufficient contrast.

An alternative possibility is that clear speech, like conversational speech, reflects confluent talker- and listener-oriented forces. Under this view, clear speech is not listener-oriented at the expense of the talker, but rather clear speech is a mode of speech production in which successful communication is supported by the close link between speech production and perception. The basic idea here is that speech communication is a co-operative activity during which the talker draws on her experience as a listener and does all she can to avoid mis-perceptions on the part of the listener. Similarly, the listener draws on her experience as a talker in interpreting the signal. Since the listener "knows" only too well that the vocal apparatus is controlled by continuously (and not abruptly) changing movements, she expects pervasive coarticulatory influences and is well-equipped to interpret them. In communicative settings that demand clear speech the overriding concern of the talker (guided by her experience as a listener in these conditions) is to enhance acoustic distinctiveness in order to guard against the increased likelihood of perceptual confusion on the part of the listener. This is achieved through the kind of global hyper-articulation identified by the present data. Clearly this "hyper" mode of articulation takes more effort (in the sense that it probably requires more energy) on the part of the talker, however, under the view of confluent talker- and listener-related forces, this extra talker effort is spent in order to match (rather than balance out) the extra listener effort demanded by the situation. In this sense, then, the talker-listener relationship is defined by a close production-perception link rather than by competing demands of production and perception. Independent evidence in favor of confluent, rather than opposing, talker- and listener-related forces comes from a recent demonstration of language specific patterns of perception of coarticulation that match quite closely the language specific patterns of coarticulation production (e.g. Beddor & Krakow, 1999).

Perhaps the most notable point of conflict between these two alternatives is the role that they assign to the listener. Under the view of opposing talker- and listener-oriented forces the burden is placed on the talker, whose speech production varies along a hypo- to hyper-articulation continuum. In contrast, under the view of confluent talker- and listener-oriented forces the hypo-hyper continuum is defined in terms of both production and perception: talkers hypo- or hyper-articulate in concert with listeners who hypo- or hyper-perceive. The present study, like many previous studies, focused on speech production in response to varying communicative situations. However, a potentially fruitful direction for future work on this issue is to investigate both production and perception under various communicative situations in an effort to document hypo-hyper variation in both talker and listener responses.

Acknowledgments

This work was supported by NIDCD grant DC03176. I gratefully acknowledge the assistance of Lyla Miller and Yelena Goretskaya. I am also grateful to an anonymous reviewer for extremely helpful suggestions and comments on an earlier draft. All errors are my own.

References

Beddor, P. S. & Krakow, R. A.
    1999   Perception of coarticulatory nasalization by speakers of English and Thai: Evidence for partial compensation. *Journal of the Acoustical Society of America*, **106**, 2868–2887.

Boersma, P.
    1998   *Functional Phonology: Formalizing the interactions between articulatory and perceptual drives*. The Hague: Holland Academic Graphics.

Bradlow, A. R.
    1995   A comparative acoustic study of English and Spanish vowels. *Journal of the Acoustical Society of America*, **97**, 1916–1924.

Broe, M. B. & Pierrehumbert, J.
    2000   Introduction. In M. B. Broe and J. Pierrehumbert (eds.), *Papers in Laboratory Phonology V: Acquisition and the Lexicon*, (pp. 1–8.) Cambridge: Cambridge University Press.

Cho, T.
    1999   Effect of prosody on vowel-to-vowel coarticulation in English. *Proceedings of the XIVth International Congress of Phonetic Sciences*, 459–462.

Chistovich, L. A. & Lublinskaya, V. V.
    1979   The "center of gravity" effect in vowel spectra and critical distance between the formants: Psychoacoustical study of the perception of vowel-like stimuli. *Hearing Research*, **1**, 185–195.

Cutler, A. & Butterfield, S.
    1991   Word boundary cues in clear speech: A supplementary report. *Speech Communication*, **10**, 335–353.

Duez, D.
    1992   Second formant locus-nucleus patterns: An investigation of spontaneous French speech. *Speech Communication*, **11**, 417–427.

Engstrand, O.
    1988   Articulatory correlates of stress and speaking rate in Swedish VCV utterances. *Journal of the Acoustical Society of America*, **83**, 1863–1875.

Fant, G.
    1973   *Speech Sounds and Features*. Cambridge, MA: MIT Press.

Flege, J. E.
    1987   The production of "new" and "similar" phones in a foreign language: evidence for the effect of equivalence classification. *Journal of Phonetics*, **15**, 47–65.

Flege, J. E.
    1995   Second language speech learning: theory, finding, and problems. In W. Strange (ed.), *Speech perception and linguistic experience: Issues in cross-language research*, (pp. 233–277). Baltimore, MD: York Press.

Flemming, E.
  1995 *Auditory Representations in Phonology*. PhD dissertation, UCLA.
Fowler, C.
  1981 Production and perception of coarticulation among stressed and unstressed vowels. *Journal of Speech and Hearing Research*, **24**, 127–139.
Fowler, C. A.
  1984 Segmentation of coarticulation speech in perception. *Perception & Psychophysics*, **36**, 359–368.
Johnson, K., Flemming, E. & Wright, R.
  1993 The hyperspace effect: Phonetic targets are hyperarticulated. *Language*, **69**, 505–528.
Krause, J. C. & Braida, L. D.
  1995 The effects of speaking rate on the intelligibility of speech for various speaking modes. *Journal of the Acoustical Society of America*, **98**, Pt. 2, 2982.
Krull, D.
  1989 Consonant-vowel coarticulation in spontaneous speech and in reference words. *Speech Transmission Laboratory Quarterly Progress Status Reports, Royal Institute of Technology, Stockholm, Sweden*, **1**, 101–105.
Liljencrants, J. & Lindblom, B.
  1972 Numerical simulation of vowel quality systems: The role of perceptual contrast. *Language*, **48**, 839–852.
Lindblom, B.
  1990 Explaining phonetic variation: A sketch of the H&H theory. In W. J. Hardcastle and A. Marchal (eds.), *Speech Production and Speech Modeling*, (pp. 403–439). Netherlands: Kluwer Academic.
Lively, S. E., Pisoni, D. B., Van Summers, W. & Bernacki, R. H.
  1993 Effects of cognitive workload on speech production: Acoustic analyses and perceptual consequences. *Journal of the Acoustical Society of America*, **93**, 2962–2973.
Mann, V. A.
  1980 Influence of preceding liquid on stop-consonant perception. *Perception & Psychophysics*, **28**, 407–412.
Manuel, S.
  1999 Cross-language studies: Relating language-particular coarticulation patterns to other language-particular facts. In W. J. Hardcastle and N. Hewlett (eds.), *Coarticulation: Theory, Data and Techniques*, (pp. 179–198). Cambridge, UK: Cambridge University Press.
Moon, S.-J. & Lindblom, B.
  1994 Interaction between duration, consonant context, and speaking style in English stressed vowels. *Journal of the Acoustical Society of America*, **96**, 40–55.

Nord, L.
1974 Vowel reduction – centralization or consonant contextual assimilation? In G. Fant (ed.), *Speech Communication,* **II**, (pp. 149–154). Stockholm: Almqvist & Wiksell.

Obler, L. K.
1982 The parsimonious bilingual. In L. K. Obler & L. Menn (eds.), *Exceptional Language and Linguistics*, (pp. 339–346). New York, NY: Academic Press.

Obler, L. K. & Gjerlow, K.
1999 *Language and the Brain*. Cambridge, UK: Cambridge University Press.

Payton, K. L., Uchanski, R. M. & and Braida, L. D.
1994 Intelligibility of conversational and clear speech in noise and reverberation for listeners with normal and impaired hearing. *Journal of the Acoustical Society of America*, **95**, 1581–1592.

Picheny, M. A., Durlach, N. I. & Braida, L. D.
1985 Speaking clearly for the hard of hearing I: Intelligibility differences between clear and conversational speech. *Journal of Speech and Hearing Research*, **28**, 96–103.

Picheny, M. A., Durlach, N. I. & Braida, L. D.
1986 Speaking clearly for the hard of hearing II: Acoustic characteristics of clear and conversational speech. *Journal of Speech and Hearing Research*, **29**, 434–446.

Recasens, D.
1985 Coarticulatory patterns and degrees of coarticulatory resistance in Catalan CV sequences. *Language and Speech*, **28**, 97–114.

Sancier, M. L. & Fowler, C. A.
1997 Gestural drift in a bilingual speaker of Brazilian Portuguese and English. *Journal of Phonetics*, **25**, 421–436.

Stevens, K. N.
1998 *Acoustic Phonetics*. Cambridge, MA: MIT Press.

Stevens, K. N. & House, A. S.
1963 Perturbations of vowel articulations by consonantal context: An acoustical study. *Journal of Speech and Hearing Research*, **6**, 111–128.

Suomi, K.
1987 On spectral coarticulation in stop-vowel-stop syllables: Implication for automatic speech recognition. *Journal of Phonetics*, **15**, 85–100.

Uchanski, R. M, Choi, S., Braida, L. D., Reed, C. M. & Durlach, N. I.
1996 Speaking clearly for the hard of hearing IV: Further studies of the role of speaking rate. *Journal of Speech and Hearing Research*, **39**, 494–509.

van Son, R. J. J. H. & Pols, L. C. W.
1999 An acoustic description of consonant reduction. *Speech Communication*, **28**, 125–140.

Whalen, D.
1990 Coarticulation is largely planned. *Journal of Phonetics*, **18**, 3–35.

Phonological Processing:
Comments on Pierrehumbert, Moates et al., Kubozono, Peperkamp & Dupoux, and Bradlow

Anne Cutler

1. Introduction

Processing is a very general term. Preceded by *phonological* its domain of reference can be located by presumption in the realm of language (if only because the phonological processing of food, or of passport applications, seems rather improbable). But it remains an unsatisfyingly ambiguous expression, allowing either an interpretation in which information of a phonological nature is processed (cf. mathematical instruction), or one in which unspecified information is processed via the application of phonology (cf. mathematical reasoning). Perhaps for this reason psycholinguists, though they are excessively fond of the general term processing, do not standardly use phonological processing to refer to any aspect of their models.

Processing in psycholinguistics covers all mental operations involved in the use of language (and most particularly in listening and speaking). The five papers commented on here all refer in some way to evidence from language performance, and hence imply such operations. But they involve processing of several different kinds: production of words (Pierrehumbert), production of phonemes (Bradlow), perception of words (Moates, Bond and Stockmal), perception of vowels (Kubozono) and perception of stress (Peperkamp and Dupoux).

An introductory overview of the consensus model of word and phoneme production in psycholinguistics is contained in the chapter by Levelt (this volume; for further detail see Levelt, Roelofs & Meyer, 1999). It would be redundant to recapitulate the summary here. The following section offers a matching overview of the consensus model of listening to spoken language (with special reference to the processing levels just mentioned: words, phonemes, stress).

The evidence on which the modelling efforts are based — in production as well as in comprehension research — has been collected in most part from behavioural experiments in the psycholinguistic laboratory. In more than three decades of spoken-language comprehension research, an extensive arsenal of empirical techniques has been developed (see Grosjean & Frauenfelder, 1996, for a review). In some of these techniques task performance is assessed qualitatively, but the majority involve measurement of response time (RT), i.e. the latency with which listeners can perform some simple operation such as repeating a heard input, making a binary decision about it, or signalling detection of a target. RT measures represent the best attempts to investigate processing "on-line", i.e. in the course of its operation. In psycholinguistics, on-line measures are often preferred over less direct measures of performance.

2. Spoken-word recognition

Listening to spoken language involves recognising, in the incoming speech signal, discrete portions which correspond to stored representations in the listener's lexicon. Several facts about spoken-word recognition make it a challenging research area. First, the process takes place in time — words are not heard all at once, but from beginning to end. Second, words are rarely heard in isolation, but rather within longer utterances, and there is no reliable equivalent in speech of the spaces which demarcate individual words in a printed text. Thus listening to speech necessarily involves segmentation, i.e. division of the continuous input into the portions corresponding to individual words. Third, spoken tokens of individual words are highly variable, because speakers' voices differ greatly and background noise and other aspects of the listening situation can affect intelligibility. And fourth, spoken words are not highly distinctive; language vocabularies of tens of thousands of words are constructed from a repertoire of on average only 30 to 40 phonemes (Maddieson, 1984). As a consequence words tend to resemble other words, and may have other words embedded within them (thus *great* contains possible pronunciations of *grey* and *rate* and *eight*, it resembles *grape* and *crate* and *greet*, it occurs embedded within possible pronunciations of *migrate* or *grating* or even *league rating*, and so on). How do listeners know when to recognise *great* and when not?

All current models of spoken-word recognition assume that whatever words are supported by the speech signal, irrespective of whether such support is intended by the speaker, may become active in the listener's recognition system. There is now abundant experimental evidence indicating that words may become activated when they are embedded within other words (such as *grey* in *grating*; Cluff & Luce, 1990; Shillcock, 1990; Gow & Gordon, 1995), or when they are spuriously present across two other words (such as *great* in *league rating*; Tabossi, Burani & Scott, 1995), and that partially overlapping words (*grey, great, grating*) may become simultaneously active (Zwitserlood, 1989; Marslen-Wilson, 1990; Connine, Blasko & Wang, 1994; Vitevich & Luce, 1998; Soto-Faraco, Sebastián-Gallés & Cutler, 2001). Recognition then ensues after a process of competition between the activated candidate words. Again, there is empirical evidence which solidly supports the contribution of competition in word recognition (Goldinger, Luce & Pisoni, 1989; McQueen, Norris & Cutler, 1994; Norris, McQueen & Cutler, 1995; Vroomen & De Gelder, 1995; Soto-Faraco et al., 2001).

Since TRACE (McClelland & Elman, 1986a), models of spoken-word recognition have been computationally implemented, allowing explicit simulation of experimental findings. Of all such models, only Shortlist (Norris, 1994) currently allows simulations with a realistically sized dictionary of tens of thousands of words. In Shortlist, competition involves lateral inhibition between simultaneously active candidates for any part of the speech signal. The more active a candidate word is, the more it may inhibit activation of its competitors. Activated and competing words need not be aligned with one another, and the competition process in consequence offers a potential solution to the segmentation problem. Thus although the recognition of *league rating* may involve competition from *grey, great* and *eight*, this will eventually be overcome by joint inhibition from *league* and *rating*.

Models of spoken-word recognition differ on a number of dimensions, most notably on whether they allow bidirectional or only unidirectional flow of information between processing levels. However, there is widespread agreement on the above outline architecture. In the following section the models are compared with regard to the role they allow to phonological constructs.

3. Phonology in spoken-word recognition

Do phonological constructs define entities which play a necessary role in models of perceptual processing? The answer to this question must be no. Years of psycholinguistic research have been invested in examination of whether various phonological constructs function as "perceptual units", but, as I have argued in a previous contribution to the Laboratory Phonology series and elsewhere (Cutler, 1992a, 1992b), the questions asked by spoken-word recognition researchers have not allowed for answers which might be useful to phonology. In the modelling framework sketched above, the phoneme can certainly be said to have a vital role, insofar as the phoneme is by definition the minimal sequential unit of distinction between two words. Each such minimal distinction between two simultaneously active lexical candidates will influence the process of competition between them. But such influence does not depend on an explicit representation of the phoneme as the means by which the distinction is achieved.

Some current computational models (e.g. TRACE, Shortlist) in fact operate with explicit representations of phonemes; but this is always described as a computational convenience rather than an inherent component of the model. Evidence that listeners effectively exploit coarticulatory cues to upcoming phonemes (e.g. Whalen, 1984, 1991; Streeter & Nigro, 1979; Marslen-Wilson & Warren, 1994; McQueen, Norris & Cutler, 1999) has been interpreted as arguing against an explicit role for phonemes in the lexical access process (e.g. Marslen-Wilson & Warren, 1994), although in reality it is, like the fact that a minimal difference between two words is by definition a difference of one phoneme, neutral with respect to the representational issue.

Similarly, episodic models of word recognition (e.g. Goldinger, 1998) are often held to be incompatible with the notion of obligatory intermediate representations in terms of phonemes or other units; but they too are in fact neutral on this issue. It is true that they offer a framework which can be realised without such representations; but so do non-episodic models. In short, the search for evidence which will settle the issue of "perceptual units" may be a hopeless quest; many psycholinguists have indeed abandoned it as such.

The performance evidence discussed in the papers to which these comments refer correspondingly does not provide evidence concerning the role of phonological constructs in the perception model (or, for that matter, in the production model discussed by Levelt). However, the papers do to a considerable extent address questions which have more to do with processing (and how it should be modelled) than with phonological structure (and its role in the grammar). In particular conjunctions of subsets of the five papers raise a number of interesting questions of importance for the processing model. Five of these questions, of varying degrees of granularity, will be considered in part 4 below; they concern respectively the relation between perception and production, the flexibility of the language processing system, the relative contribution of vowels and consonants in spoken-word recognition, the processing implications of phoneme coarticulation, and the position of language-specificity in the processing system.

4. Processing questions from a phonological perspective

4.1 How close is the relation between perception and production?

Listeners are also speakers; barring impairment, any language user's processing of spoken language includes both perception and production. For this reason alone perception and production must to a substantial extent be considered together. Production is ultimately very dependent on perception, in that we speak the words and structures we have heard. On the other hand, the translation of sound to meaning and of meaning to sound require different types of processing, which, as brain imaging and neurological impairment evidence attests, are to a considerable degree subserved by different mechanisms in the brain (Price, Indefrey & Van Turennout, 1999). Thus the closeness (or otherwise) of the relation between the language input and output systems is a regular object of study, and two traditional types of evidence concerning this issue are addressed in the present set of papers.

Evidence that speakers often cater to the needs of listeners can readily be found (see e.g. Cutler, 1987). The study of clear speech has provided a rich source of relevant data: deliberately or not, speakers adjust their clarity of articulation and other aspects of speaking style when listeners are in difficulty (Picheny, Durlach & Braida, 1985, 1986). Many adjustments they make would be difficult to bring under conscious control — for instance, adaptation of vowel formant structure to compensate for the formant masking in background noise (Van Summers, Pisoni, Bernacki, Pedlow & Stokes, 1988), or selective emphasis on the word boundaries which perceptual processing is most likely to overlook (Cutler & Butterfield, 1990). The vowel production measurements described by Bradlow surely belong in this class, although in her data clear articulation is applied to all segments irrespective of intrinsic intersegment confusability within the vowel inventory of the language. The vowel space expansion in clear speech conditioned by listener difficulty parallels that recently reported for infant-directed speech (Kuhl, Andruski, Chistovich, Chistovich, Kozhevnikova, Ryskina, Stolyarova, Sundberg & Lacerda, 1997). These results suggest close attunement of production and perception systems.

Pierrehumbert also posits a close perception-production relation, though of a different kind. In her proposal, word production is based very directly on aggregated experience of word perception. In fact the evidence which she reviews does not actually include lexeme-specific effects of the kind that the proposal in principle predicts — i.e. idiosyncratic properties of production associated with individual words; rather, she points to talker-repetition advantages in perception, systematic word frequency effects on articulation, and sociolinguistic effects (which are in a way also frequency effects, of a group-specific nature). For further discussion of this issue see Levelt (this volume); it will be interesting to see whether future studies will produce evidence for the truly lexeme-specific production effects which would support Pierrehumbert's position.

Another type of evidence often called upon in discussions of perception-production relations concerns neutralisation effects. If underlying distinctions are masked, i.e. neutralised, are speakers ignoring perceptual exigencies? If phonologically conditioned neutralisation in fact turns out to be incomplete, is this because perceptual needs have prevailed? So far, a simple conclusion for this literature has proved elusive; the picture is complex, with many sources of information contributing to the realisation or nonrealisation of a contrast, systematic differences being produced but below the level at which listeners can profit from them, and differences which listeners are well able to use being unreliably produced (see e.g. Warner, Jongman, Sereno & Kemps, submitted).

Kubozono describes a case of neutralisation which is remarkable in that information available to nonnative listeners is ignored by native listeners. That is, the neutralisation is itself part of the native user's system. This pattern in fact suggests that his finding belongs in the realm of effects which are captured by some other aspect of processing. A parameter of variation which provides information of one kind may thereby become unavailable for use as information of another kind; systematic durational cues to stress may be overlooked by listeners for whom duration is a cue to phonemic quantity distinctions (Berinstein, 1979); systematic palatalisation variation as a function of syntactic structure may be overlooked by listeners for whom palatalisation is sociolinguistically informative (Scott & Cutler, 1984). It is thus not unreasonable to propose that the nonnative listeners in Kubozono's study may have been exploiting a type of information which for the native listeners was already captured by another function.

4.2 How flexible is the language processing system?

To what extent can the operation of the processing system be varied by the language user? This too has been a question which has long aroused research interest (indeed, some of the relevant research is mentioned under the topic of clear speech in section 4.1 above, or under coarticulatory effects in section 4.4 below).

The modulating effects of attention are at issue in contributions in this section. Attention is (like the larger issue of consciousness to which it is very closely connected) a notoriously elusive psychological concept; nonetheless, processing effects reasonably ascribed to attentional variation are widespread. Particularly the type of psycholinguistic experiment in which explicit phonemic decisions are required provides an appropriate environment for such effects to manifest themselves. Thus presence or absence of a secondary task encouraging attention to meaning (Dell & Newman, 1980), or simply varying the relative monotony of stimulus materials (Cutler, Mehler, Norris & Segui, 1987) both affect whether or not lexical characteristics influence listeners' response latencies in a phoneme detection experiment; this is explained as indicating reduced attention to lexical processing when it is not explicitly required for task performance, or even when words and nonwords hardly vary. Implicit direction of attention to target position is also possible in the same task (Pitt & Samuel, 1990; Pallier, Sebastián-Gallés, Felguera, Christophe & Mehler, 1993). Direction of attention to target phoneme location also improves listener performance in distinguishing noise-masked versus noise-replaced phonemes (Samuel & Ressler, 1986).

Pierrehumbert (citing Johnson, 1997) sees a role for attention in explaining speaker normalisation effects in listening. The mental representation of a given word is the aggregate of perceptual episodes involving that word; however, if attention can play the role assigned to it, it is clear that individual episodes must be tagged for origin. Pierrehumbert suggests that listening can selectively refer incoming input from a given speaker to previous exemplars of the same speaker's production, or at least weight those exemplars more highly (it might seem that non-matching exemplars should in fact be ruled out completely; the question of whether or not this is possible is not addressed). This would allow more accurate phonemic classifications, as occurs with speaker normalisation. Pierrehumbert also proposes a more nebulous effect in speech production, whereby selective attention to exemplars of a given speaker can lead to productions which more closely imitate that speaker. Most speakers are of course notoriously bad at imitating other individuals successfully, so the extent of this component of Pierrehumbert's proposal, and its precise role, need to be spelt out in greater detail. One potential function of a mechanism of this kind might be switches in speaking style and register.

A more straightforward role for attention in listening is proposed by Peperkamp and Dupoux. Although the long-term goal of their project is specification of how infants learn the phonology of a native language, their model also delivers predictions about adult listening. In a series of experiments following the earlier work of Dupoux, Pallier, Sebastián-Gallés and Mehler (1997), they have examined the phenomenon that listeners can sometimes correctly perceive a nonnative contrast in a forced-choice discrimination task, but are unable to match tokens varying in the same contrast in an ABX categorisation task. They propose that whether attention can be paid to a stress contrast is determined, analogously to the case of segmental contrasts, by whether it functions to distinguish between words; stress contrasts however obviously differ from segmental contrasts in listeners' relative discrimination success. Peperkamp and Dupoux's account offers a potential explanation for this in a relatively late setting of the Stress Parameter (contrastive vs. non-contrastive) in acquisition: at the time that the parameter is set, language learners already have acquired at least a content/function word opposition.

4.3 Do vowels and consonants differ in their contribution to the recognition of spoken words?

Whether vowels and consonants constitute dichotomous classes is a contentious issue for processing models, as for linguistics. Within the continuous-activation framework sketched in section 2 above, there would seem to be no basis for a categorical distinction; any information which allows a distinction to be made between two words, be it vocalic or consonantal information, should be equally useful to the processor. Consistent with this, Soto-Faraco et al. (2001) demonstrated exactly equivalent effects of single-vowel and single-consonant mismatch on lexical activation; the effect of the vowel signalling a difference between *sardina* and *sardana* (Soto-Faraco et al.'s experiments were conducted in Spanish) was in no way different from the effect of the consonant signalling a difference between *papilla* and *patilla* or (with more features mismatching) between *cinico* and *civico*.

Nevertheless there are a number of robust vowel-consonant differences which have appeared in perceptual experiments. One of the most striking is the consistent finding, from experiments using the word reconstruction task (van Ooijen, 1996), that it is easier to locate a real-word candidate by altering a vowel in the input than by altering a consonant. Listeners presented with *eltimate* or *weddow* find it easier to reconstruct these nonword inputs into *ultimate* and *widow* than *estimate* and *meadow*. As Moates et al. describe, this vowel/consonant asymmetry has been demonstrated in English (van Ooijen, 1996), in Dutch and in Spanish (Cutler, Sebastián-Gallés, Soler Vilageliu & van Ooijen, 2000), and most recently, in a modified variant of the task, in Japanese (Cutler & Otake, 2002).

A difference between vowel and consonant processing has also been observed in the phoneme detection task. Response times to vowels are inversely correlated with the target duration — the longer the vowel token, the faster listeners detect it (van Ooijen, 1994; Cutler, van Ooijen, Norris & Sanchez-Casas, 1996). Again, this effect appears in both English and Spanish (Cutler et al., 1996), and it is not observed with consonants (van Ooijen, 1994).

Both these effects have been explained in terms of learned responses on the part of listeners to contextually induced variability of phonetic segments in speech. Vowels are more variably realised; because of this listeners have built up a history of initially erroneous vowel identifications which have had to be corrected, and they have learned to be cautious when required to make a definite identification (as in the phoneme detection task). However, longer vowel tokens are more likely to approach a canonical realisation, and the longer the token, the more likely listeners are to achieve a confident detection response without additional evidence from post-vocalic context. The experience with correction of an initially inaccurate vowel hypothesis has in turn rendered, in the word reconstruction task, the adjustment of a vowel a much more readily available operation than the adjustment of a consonant. This explanation is fully compatible with the word activation framework described above; in principle all types of phonetic information are equal, but in practice some are more variable than others.

The present papers add usefully to this discussion. Moates et al. present a further demonstration of the vowel advantage in word reconstruction; in addition, they show that responses involving reconstruction of more frequent phonemes are easier to produce than responses requiring production of less frequent phonemes. This finding strengthens the interpretation that patterns of performance in this task reflect listeners' past experience with hypotheses about phonetic identity in speech input. Kubozono's results show that indirect (visual) cues to a vowel length contrast may be ignored, as listeners have never learned (or needed) to rely on them; Peperkamp and Dupoux argue that the type of vowel contrasts which a language makes can modulate listeners' sensitivity to stress distinctions. Again, both results show listeners' processing shaped by past phonetic experience.

Bradlow's claim that coarticulated segments do not suffer from reduced distinctiveness may seem incompatible with the explanation of vowel/consonant processing differences in terms of experience of variability. However, distinctiveness in the utterance context is not necessarily the same as distinctiveness for the fraction of a second which corresponds to a segment's central realisation. Listeners have learned that speakers will give them all the information they need, though this information may be considerably distributed (and perhaps more so for vowels than for consonants). In word recognition all that is required is attention to the output of the lexical processor; incoming phonetic information will act to constrain word-candidate activation as soon as it is available, whether or not its availability can be tied to some particular stretch of the speech signal uniquely corresponding to a given segment. Tasks such as phoneme detection and word reconstruction, on the other hand, require attention to individual segments, and in such tasks, differences in listeners' readiness to make confident identifications of one versus another segment type may more easily be observed.

4.4 Is coarticulation a severe problem for the language processor?

The fact that phonetic evidence which distinguishes one word from another (and thus by definition represents phonemes in the speech signal) is continuous rather than discrete has long been seen as a problem for listeners. Phonemes do not correspond to clearly separable sequential portions of the signal; if they can indeed be said to be present in speech, then at the very least they overlap. Listeners have the task of decoding an encoded representation (Liberman, Cooper, Shankweiler & Studdert-Kennedy, 1967) if they are to extract from speech a percept in terms of a string of phonemes.

There is an enormous literature on the nature of coarticulatory effects (see e.g. Farnetani, 1997; Hardcastle & Hewlett, 1999) and their reflection in listeners' judgements (see e.g. Nygaard & Pisoni, 1995). But the very notion of coarticulation implies some reality to separable segments which in principle might be articulated without reference to one another (see Beckman, 1999, and Kühnert & Nolan, 1999, for discussion of this issue). Only if (a) non-coarticulated segments are easier for listeners to process than coarticulated segments, and (b) segment perception is required of the listener, could one make a strong case that coarticulation complicates the listening process.

Certainly coarticulation leads to variability in the portions of speech which cue identity of any given phoneme, and where phonemic decisions are indeed required, variability may slow decision-making. Thus the greater readiness of listeners to replace vowels than consonants in word reconstruction, as discussed above and as replicated once again by Moates et al., has been attributed to a side effect of coarticulation. Cutler et al. (2000) argued that vowels are more likely to be initially misidentified than consonants, so that listeners are usually more likely to have to revise decisions about vowels than about consonants in lexical processing. This experience translates into greater readiness to try another vowel than another consonant in the reconstruction task. The robustness of the effect across languages argues in favour of this account, given that it has been observed not only in vowel-rich languages like English and Dutch (van Ooijen, 1996; Cutler et al., 2000; Moates et al.) but also in two languages with five-vowel inventories, Spanish (Cutler et al., 2000) and Japanese (Cutler & Otake, 2002).

Explicit phonemic decision-making is however not required in everyday listening, and, despite the undoubted underlying contribution played by the phoneme as the minimal distinction between words, implicit phonemic decision-making may not be part of spoken-word recognition either (see Norris, McQueen & Cutler, 2000 for further discussion). Listeners need to identify words, not the component parts of words; coarticulation may speed this process rather than retarding it.

The type of word processing model which Pierrehumbert argues for, in which stored representations of words directly reflect a history of individual word processing episodes, seems in principle to require no phonemic decision-making. Interestingly, coarticulatory phenomena offer relevant evidence for evaluating this type of model. Studies of coarticulation reveal regularities which are determined by phonemic environment – the gestures which correspond to /k/ are different if the following vowel is high front /i/ rather than low back /ɔ/, for instance. Such studies have not revealed a role for the word itself as a determiner of regularity – high frequency words such as *key* and *cause* and low frequency words such as *kiwi* and *caucus* show the same patterns of variation. Without some expansion of the episodic modelling framework beyond word-specific phonetics, such regularities must presumably be ascribed to chance.

The role of coarticulation in listening is central to Bradlow's contribution; she argues that coarticulation is not at all harmful to the listener's interests, and bases her argument on the fact that speakers do not suppress coarticulatory influences when they are deliberately trying to speak clearly. Word recognition theorists have argued for more than a decade (see e.g. McClelland & Elman, 1986b) that since coarticulatory effects are predictable, they should rather be helpful than harmful for word identification. Indeed, there is abundant evidence that listeners are very adept at extracting information from cross-phonemic coarticulatory influences. Typically, in the kind of experiment which has provided such evidence, listeners are presented with cross-spliced speech. For instance, a token of *slee-* from *sleep* and another token of *slee-* from *sleek* may be judged to have the same phonemic structure, but if the former is spliced to the /k/ of *sleek* and the latter to the /p/ of *sleep*, recognition of those final consonants, and of the whole words, is impaired (Martin & Bunnell, 1981, 1982; Whalen, 1984, 1991; Marslen-Wilson & Warren, 1994; McQueen, Norris & Cutler, 1999). Gating experiments (in which listeners are presented with word fragments, of increasing size, and are asked to guess word identity) also show that listeners make effective use of coarticulatory cues to identify upcoming phonemes (Ellis, Derbyshire & Joseph, 1971; Lahiri & Marslen-Wilson, 1991).

4.5 Where does language-specificity occur in the processing system?

The processing model sketched in part 2 above has no features which limit it to a specific language or group of languages. All listeners will have discrete memory representations of sound-meaning pairings, which will be activated by incoming speech signals; multiple simultaneous activation and inter-word competition presumably form the basis of a universal model of spoken-word recognition.

This is not to claim that all languages provide the same kind of information for lexical activation. Phoneme repertoires differ in their size and in the features which distinguish phonemes; thus in a language which distinguishes dental from retroflex articulation, this difference will affect word-candidate activation, while the same difference might occur in speech in another language but be irrelevant for defining word identity. Similarly, suprasegmental information will be useless for distinguishing words in some languages, but is vital to distinguish words of a tone language. Nevertheless, the basic architecture of activation and competition is assumed to be constant.

The universal architecture includes effects which in principle might have been language-specific. Norris, McQueen, Cutler & Butterfield (1997) showed that the competition process is effectively modulated by a viability filter on the ongoing parse of the signal which would result from putative candidate words. If accepting a potential word would mean that a residue of the speech signal would be left over and could not be parsed as a word, that potential word is reduced in activation. Norris et al. called this effect the Possible-Word Constraint (PWC): it rules out residues which would make it impossible to parse the input as a continuous sequence of words. It is particularly useful as a way of ruling out activated words which are spuriously present via embedding; *ring* in *bring* can be rejected because the leftover *b* is not a viable word candidate.

Interestingly, what counts as an unparseable residue does not seem to differ across languages, although languages differ in what they allow as minimal words. Single consonants without vowels, such as *b*, are always unacceptable residues; but monomoraic syllables do not violate the PWC even in English, a language with a bimoraic minimal word (Norris, McQueen, Cutler, Butterfield & Kearns, 2001), nor does a single syllable violate the PWC in Sesotho, a language in which surface words must be bisyllabic (Cutler, Demuth & McQueen, 2002). The PWC might have tested residues against the vocabulary requirements of the language in question (bimoraic, bisyllabic, etc.), but it appears instead to be universal.

However, the PWC co-operates with language-specific effects in the competition process. Thus segmentation of continuous speech into its component words is sensitive to the boundaries of rhythmic units, but languages differ in rhythmic structure; segmentation in English, a language with stress rhythm, is sensitive to foot boundaries (Cutler & Norris, 1988), but segmentation in Japanese, a language with moraic rhythm, is sensitive to mora boundaries (Otake, Hatano, Cutler & Mehler, 1993). These boundaries also define the domain of operation of the PWC (Norris et al., 1997; McQueen, Otake & Cutler, 2001).

Thus the processing model of word recognition is universal but realised with respect to the features specific to a particular language. The evidence provided in the present papers does not challenge this framework. Bradlow's findings imply that coarticulated information about segmental structure is equivalently available in languages with large or small vowel repertoires; Moates et al.'s results extend the cross-linguistically consistent pattern whereby listeners consider vowel information to be more mutable than consonant information. Peperkamp and Dupoux show that stress contrasts, though realised similarly in a pair of languages, may be salient for word recognition only in one, and Kubozono shows how a temporal distinction, though realised similarly word-medially and word-finally, may be exploited for discriminating between words in only one of these positions. A welcome next step would be experiments in which these effects were investigated in laboratory paradigms specifically designed to study activation and competition.

5. Conclusion

As the above comments suggest, current psycholinguistics is characterised by multiple lines of research which concern, one way or another, the role of phonological constructs in processing. The evidence provided by the five papers discussed fits into several of these themes, confirms and amplifies some conclusions from existing work, and is in turn illuminated by some previous findings.

Those papers which raise perceptual issues do not challenge the generally agreed architecture of the spoken-word recognition system, with its central role for automatic lexical activation and inter-word competition. Nor do the papers which address issues of language production provide direct evidence which would require incorporation in the model described by Levelt (this volume) and variously addressed also by papers on which Levelt comments. (In fact it is tempting to speculate that the methodological mismatch — psycholinguistics prefers on-line procedures, while laboratory phonology rarely uses such methods — might make a direct challenge difficult to mount in any case.)

Finally, consider the observation, pointed out in part 3 above, that psycholinguists have abandoned the issue of whether phonological constructs might serve as obligatory perceptual entities. If the present set of papers is a representative sample of (laboratory) phonological studies of processing topics, we may conclude that this question is a non-issue for laboratory phonologists as well.

References

Beckman, M. E.
    1999   Implications for phonological theory. In W. J. Hardcastle & N. Hewlett (eds.), *Coarticulation: Theory, Data and Techniques,* (pp. 199–225). Cambridge: Cambridge University Press.

Berinstein, A. E.
    1979   A cross-linguistic study on the perception and production of stress. UCLA *Working Papers in Phonetics,* **47**.

Cluff, M. S. & Luce, P. A.
    1990   Similarity neighborhoods of spoken two-syllable words, Retroactive effects on multiple activation. *Journal of Experimental Psychology: Human Perception & Performance,* **16**, 551–563.

Connine, C. M., Blasko, D. G. & Wang, J.
    1994   Vertical similarity in spoken word recognition: Multiple lexical activation, individual differences, and the role of sentence context. *Perception & Psychophysics,* **56**, 624–636.

Cutler, A.
    1987   Speaking for listening. In A. Allport, D. G. MacKay, W. Prinz & E. Scheerer (eds.), *Language Perception and Production: Relationships between Listening, Speaking, Reading and Writing,* (pp. 23–40). London: Academic Press.

Cutler, A.
    1992a   Psychology and the segment. In G. J. Docherty & D. R. Ladd (eds.), *Papers in Laboratory Phonology II: Gesture, Segment, Prosody,* (pp. 290–295). Cambridge: Cambridge University Press.

Cutler, A.
1992b Why not abolish psycholinguistics? In W. U. Dressler, H. C. Luschützky, O. E. Pfeiffer & J. R. Rennison (eds.), *Phonologica 1988*, (pp. 77–87). Cambridge: Cambridge University Press.

Cutler, A. & Butterfield, S.
1990 Durational cues to word boundaries in clear speech. *Speech Communication*, **9**, 485–495.

Cutler, A., Demuth, K. & McQueen, J. M.
2002 Universality versus language-specificity in listening to running speech. *Psychological Science*, **13**, 253–262.

Cutler, A., Mehler, J., Norris, D. G. & Segui, J.
1987 Phoneme identification and the lexicon. *Cognitive Psychology*, **19**, 141–177.

Cutler, A. & Norris, D. G.
1988 The role of strong syllables in segmentation for lexical access. *Journal of Experimental Psychology: Human Perception and Performance*, **14**, 113–121.

Cutler, A., Ooijen, B. van, Norris, D. & Sanchez-Casas, R.
1996 Speeded detection of vowels: A cross-linguistic study. *Perception & Psychophysics*, **58**, 807–822.

Cutler, A. & Otake, T.
2002 Rhythmic categories in spoken-word recognition. *Journal of Memory and Language*, **46**, 296–322.

Cutler, A., Sebastián-Gallés, N., Soler Vilageliu, O. & Ooijen, B. van
2000 Constraints of vowels and consonants on lexical selection: Cross-linguistic comparisons. *Memory & Cognition*, **28**, 746–755.

Dell, G. S. & Newman, J. E.
1980 Detecting phonemes in fluent speech. *Journal of Verbal Learning & Verbal Behavior*, **19**, 609–623.

Dupoux, E., Pallier, C., Sebastián-Gallés, N. & Mehler, J.
1997 A destressing 'deafness' in French. *Journal of Memory and Language*, **36**, 406–421.

Ellis, L., Derbyshire, A. J. & Joseph, M. E.
1971 Perception of electronically gated speech. *Language and Speech*, **14**, 229–240.

Farnetani, E.
1997 Coarticulation and connected speech processes. In W. J. Hardcastle & J. D. M. H. Laver (eds.), *A Handbook of Phonetic Science*, (pp. 371–404). Oxford: Blackwell.

Goldinger, S. D.
1998 Echoes of echoes? An episodic theory of lexical access. *Psychological Review*, **105**, 251–279.

Goldinger, S. D., Luce, P. A. & Pisoni, D. B.
1989 Priming lexical neighbours of spoken words: Effects of competition and inhibition. *Journal of Memory & Language*, **28**, 501–518.

Gow, D. W. & Gordon, P. C.
1995   Lexical and prelexical influences on word segmentation: evidence from priming. *Journal of Experimental Psychology: Human Perception and Performance*, **21**, 344–359.

Grosjean, F. & Frauenfelder, U. H. (eds.)
1996   Spoken Word Recognition Paradigms. *Special issue of Language and Cognitive Processes*, **11**(6).

Hardcastle, W. J. & Hewlett, N. (eds.)
1999   *Coarticulation: Theory, Data and Techniques.* Cambridge: Cambridge University Press.

Johnson, K.
1997   Speech perception without speaker normalization: An exemplar model. In K. Johnson & J. W. Mullennix (eds.), *Talker Variability in Speech Processing*, (pp. 145–166). San Diego: Academic Press.

Kuhl, P., Andruski, J., Chistovich, I., Chistovich, L., Kozhevnikova, E., Ryskina, V., Stolyarova, E., Sundberg, U. & Lacerda, F.
1997   Cross-language analysis of phonetic units in language addressed to infants. *Science*, **277**, 684–686.

Kühnert, B. & Nolan, F. J.
1999   The origin of coarticulation. In W. J. Hardcastle & N. Hewlett (eds.), *Coarticulation: Theory, Data and Techniques*, (pp. 7–30). Cambridge: Cambridge University Press.

Lahiri, A. & Marslen-Wilson, W. D.
1991   The mental representation of lexical form, A phonological approach to the recognition lexicon. *Cognition*, **38**, 245–294.

Levelt, W. J. M., Roelofs, A. & Meyer, A. S.
1999   A theory of lexical access in speech production. *Behavioral and Brain Sciences*, **22**, 1–38.

Liberman, A. M., Cooper, F. S., Shankweiler, D. P. & Studdert-Kennedy, M.
1967   Perception of the speech code. *Psychological Review*, **74**, 431–461.

Maddieson, I.
1984   *Patterns of Sounds.* Cambridge: Cambridge University Press.

Marslen-Wilson, W. D.
1990   Activation, competition and frequency in lexical access. In G. T. M. Altmann (ed.), *Cognitive Models of Speech Processing*, (pp. 148–172). Cambridge MA: MIT Press.

Marslen-Wilson, W. & Warren, P.
1994   Levels of perceptual representation and process in lexical access: words, phonemes, and features. *Psychological Review*, **101**, 653–675.

Martin, J. G. & Bunnell, H. T.
1981   Perception of anticipatory coarticulation effects. *Journal of the Acoustical Society of America*, **69**, 559–567.

Martin, J. G. & Bunnell, H. T.
  1982 Perception of anticipatory coarticulation effects in vowel-stop consonant-vowel sequences. *Journal of Experimental Psychology: Human Perception and Performance*, **8**, 473–488.
McClelland, J. L. & Elman, J. L.
  1986a The TRACE model of speech perception. *Cognitive Psychology*, **18**, 1–86.
McClelland, J. L. & Elman, J. L.
  1986b Exploiting lawful variability in the speech wave. In J. Perkell & D. H. Klatt (eds.), *Invariance and Variability in Speech Processes*, (pp. 360–385). Hillsdale, NJ: Erlbaum.
McQueen, J. M., Norris, D. G. & Cutler, A.
  1994 Competition in spoken word recognition: Spotting words in other words. *Journal of Experimental Psychology: Learning, Memory and Cognition*, **20**, 621–638.
McQueen, J. M., Norris, D. G. & Cutler, A.
  1999 Lexical influence in phonetic decision-making: Evidence from subcategorical mismatches. *Journal of Experimental Psychology: Human Perception and Performance*, **25**, 1363–1389.
McQueen, J. M., Otake, T. & Cutler, A.
  2001 Rhythmic cues and possible-word constraints in Japanese speech segmentation. *Journal of Memory and Language*, **45**, 103–132.
Norris, D. G.
  1994 Shortlist: A connectionist model of continuous speech recognition. *Cognition*, **52**, 189–234.
Norris, D. G., McQueen, J. M. & Cutler, A.
  1995 Competition and segmentation in spoken word recognition. *Journal of Experimental Psychology: Learning, Memory and Cognition*, **21**, 1209–1228.
Norris, D. G., McQueen, J. M. & Cutler, A.
  2000 Merging information in speech recognition: Feedback is never necessary. *Behavioral and Brain Sciences*, **23**, 299–325.
Norris, D. G., McQueen, J. M., Cutler, A. & Butterfield, S.
  1997 The possible-word constraint in the segmentation of continuous speech. *Cognitive Psychology*, **34**, 191–243.
Norris, D. G., Cutler, A., McQueen, J. M., Butterfield, S. & Kearns, R.
  2001 Language-universal constraints on speech segmentation. *Language and Cognitive Processes*, **16**, 637–660.
Nygaard, L. C. & Pisoni, D. B.
  1995 Speech perception: New directions in research and theory. In J. L. Miller & P. D. Eimas (eds.), *Speech, Language and Communication*. Volume **11** of E. C. Carterette & M. P. Friedman (eds.), *Handbook of Perception and Cognition*, (pp. 63–96). NY: Academic Press.

Ooijen, B. van
 1994   *Processing of vowels and consonants.* PhD Dissertation, University of Leiden.
Ooijen, B. van
 1996   Vowel mutability and lexical selection in English: Evidence from a word reconstruction task. *Memory & Cognition,* 24, 573−583.
Otake, T., Hatano, G., Cutler, A. & Mehler, J.
 1993   Mora or syllable? Speech segmentation in Japanese. *Journal of Memory and Language,* 32, 358−378.
Pallier, C., Sebastián-Gallés, N., Felguera, T., Christophe, A. & Mehler, J.
 1993   Attentional allocation within the syllabic structure of spoken words. *Journal of Memory and Language,* 32, 373−389.
Picheny, M. A., Durlach, N. I. and Braida, L. D.
 1985   Speaking clearly for the hard of hearing I: Intelligibility differences between clear and conversational speech. *Journal of Speech and Hearing Research,* 28, 96−103.
Picheny, M. A., Durlach, N. I. and Braida, L. D.
 1986   Speaking clearly for the hard of hearing II: Acoustic characteristics of clear and conversational speech. *Journal of Speech and Hearing Research,* 29, 434−446.
Pitt, M. A. & Samuel, A. G.
 1990   Attentional allocation during speech perception, How fine is the focus? *Journal of Memory and Language,* 29, 611−632.
Price, C., Indefrey, P. & Turennout, M. van
 1999   The neural architecture underlying the processing of written and spoken word forms. In P. Hagoort & C. Brown (eds.), *Neurocognition of Language,* (pp. 211−240). Oxford: Oxford University Press.
Samuel, A. G. & Ressler, W. H.
 1986   Attention within auditory word perception, Insights from the phoneme restoration illusion. *Journal of Experimental Psychology: Human Perception & Performance,* 12, 70−79.
Scott, D. R. & Cutler, A.
 1984   Segmental phonology and the perception of syntactic structure. *Journal of Verbal Learning and Verbal Behavior,* 23, 450−466.
Shillcock, R. C.
 1990   Lexical hypotheses in continuous speech. In G. T. M. Altmann (ed.), *Cognitive Models of Speech Processing: Psycholinguistic and Computational Perspectives,* (pp. 24−49). Cambridge, MA: MIT Press.
Soto-Faraco, S., Sebastián-Gallés, N. & Cutler, A.
 2001   Segmental and suprasegmental mismatch in lexical access. *Journal of Memory and Language,* 45, 412−432.
Streeter, L. A. & Nigro, G. N.
 1979   The role of medial consonant transitions in word perception. *Journal of the Acoustical Society of America,* 65, 1533−1541.

Tabossi, P., Burani, C. & Scott, D.
  1995   Word identification in fluent speech. *Journal of Memory and Language*, **34**, 440–467.
Van Summers, W., Pisoni, D. B., Bernacki, R. H., Pedlow, R. I. & Stokes, M. A.
  1988   Effects of noise on speech production: Acoustic and perceptual analyses. *Journal of the Acoustical Society of America*, **84**, 917–928.
Vitevitch, M. S. & Luce, P. A.
  1998   When words compete, Levels of processing in spoken word recognition. *Psychological Science*, **9**, 325–329.
Vroomen, J. & de Gelder, B.
  1995   Metrical segmentation and lexical inhibition in spoken word recognition. *Journal of Experimental Psychology: Human Perception and Performance*, **21**, 98–108.
Warner, N., Jongman, A., Sereno, J. & Kemps, R.
  submitted   Subphonemic durational differences in production and perception. *Journal of Phonetics*.
Whalen, D. H.
  1984   Subcategorical phonetic mismatches slow phonetic judgments. *Perception & Psychophysics*, **35**, 49–64.
Whalen, D. H.
  1991   Subcategorical phonetic mismatches and lexical access. *Perception & Psychophysics*, **50**, 351–360.
Zwitserlood, P.
  1989   The locus of the effects of sentential-semantic context in spoken-word processing. *Cognition*, **32**, 25–64.

Part II
In the laboratory and in the field: relating phonetics and phonology

Explosives, implosives and nonexplosives: The linguistic function of air pressure differences in stops

G. N. Clements and Sylvester Osu

Abstract

Nonexplosive stops, including implosives and other stops regularly lacking an explosive release burst, occur in roughly 20% of the world's languages, yet their phonological and phonetic properties are still poorly understood. This paper seeks to determine the phonological feature that characterizes this class of sounds. The classical definition of implosives in terms of the ingressive glottalic airstream mechanism raises a number of problems and does not generalize to other types of nonexplosives. It is proposed here instead that the feature underlying the class of nonexplosive stops as a whole is nonobstruence, defined as the absence of positive oral air pressure during occlusion. This definition is shown to extend to a previously undocumented type of nonexplosive stop found in Ikwere, a Niger-Congo language spoken in Nigeria. In this language, the phonemically contrastive nonexplosive bilabial stops [ɓ 'ɓ], though resembling implosives in certain respects, are produced with no lowering of the larynx, nor in the case of [ɓ], any implosion at release. A study of the acoustic, articulatory and aerodynamic properties of these sounds shows that they satisfy the definition of nonobstruent stops. It is finally suggested that apparently contradictory aspects of the phonological patterning of nonexplosive stops across languages can be explained if they are viewed as both nonobstruents and nonsonorants. In this view, phonological feature theory requires both articulatory features such as [± obstruent] and acoustic features such as [± sonorant].

1. Nonexplosive stops

Beside the familiar explosive stops found in all languages, many languages make use of a class of sounds that we shall refer to as *nonexplosive stops*. This class of sounds, defined by their characteristic lack of explosion at release, includes implosives and several related types of stops, as discussed below. Sounds of this class are not uncommon. Implosive, laryngealized or glottalized stops are found in about 20% of the world's languages (Maddieson, 1992), and their virtual absence in Indo-European languages must be regarded as an "exotic" feature of this group. But in spite of their frequency, they are still not well understood. Questions for which clearcut answers are still unavailable include the following:

1. *How many types of nonexplosive stops can be distinguished phonetically?* Linguists have distinguished several types of nonexplosive stops, including voiced and voiceless implosives, laryngealized stops and preglottalized stops, and certain varieties of "lenis" and labial-velar stops.[1] However, these stops have been relatively little studied instrumentally, and it can be extremely difficult to determine exactly what is meant by these labels in a given description, or where the dividing line between one category and another is to be drawn.

2. *How many of these sounds contrast with each other phonologically?* Greenberg (1970), extending earlier observations by Haudricourt (1950) and Ladefoged (1967), stated that no language known to him offered two or more phonemic contrasts among implosive, preglottalized and laryngealized stops. Subsequently, several African languages have been found to have phonemic contrasts between voiced implosives and what are often termed voiceless implosives, produced with complete glottal closure (see §3.2). To our knowledge, however, no further phonation type contrasts within this class have been reported.

3. *How do these sounds pattern phonologically?* Relatively little cross-linguistic research has been carried out on this question, and most of what has been done concerns voiced implosives. There is good evidence that implosives constitute a natural class distinct from explosives, but there is little current agreement on how implosives and other nonexplosive stops pattern with other sounds.

4. *What is their feature analysis?* Consistently with the disagreement concerning phonological patterning, there are competing views as to how implosives and related sounds should be characterized in terms of phonological features. Some linguists have treated implosives as obstruents, others as sonorants, others as neither obstruents nor sonorants, and still others as obstruents in some languages and sonorants in others.

In sum, nonexplosive stops constitute a poorly-understood area of phonetics and phonology in which there is need for new research.

The main objective of this paper will be to define and motivate the class of nonexplosive stops as a phonological category. It will be proposed, following earlier suggestions by Stewart (1989) and Creissels (1994), that the feature which underlies implosives and other nonexplosive stops is *nonobstruence*, defined as the absence of positive oral air pressure during occlusion. Other criteria for defining this class will be shown to be less satisfactory.

The remaining discussion proceeds as follows. Section 2 reviews the classical characterization of implosives in terms of airstream mechanisms, and discusses several respects in which the proposed diagnostics have proven inadequate in the light of more recent research. Section 3 argues that implosives are better characterized in terms of the feature *nonobstruent*, defined by the absence of air pressure buildup in the oral cavity[2] during occlusion, and shows that other types of nonexplosive stops fall under this definition as well. Section 4 documents a previously unreported type of nonexplosive stop found in Ikwere, a Niger-Congo language spoken in Nigeria. Ikwere has a pair of phonemically contrastive nonexplosive stops which, though similar to implosives in many respects, are produced with no lowering of the larynx. An examination of their phonetic properties shows that these stops, though not implosive in the classical sense of this term, satisfy the definition of nonobstruent stops. Section 5 reviews the phonological properties of nonexplosive stops as a whole, and shows that a characterization as [− obstruent] and [− sonorant] sounds explains the apparently contradictory aspects of their phonological behavior. Section 6 summarizes our main results, and suggests that phonological feature theory requires both the articulatory feature [± obstruent] and the acoustic feature [± sonorant].

2. Characterizing implosives

2.1 The classical account

The modern treatment of implosives is due to the work of J. C. Catford (1939, 1977), inspired by Beach's description of

Nama phonetics (1938). In the first of his studies, Catford defined stop consonants in terms of two articulatory parameters: pressure vs. suction, and inner closure point (pulmonic, glottalic, or velaric). These parameters define six airstream mechanisms, of which three are egressive and three are ingressive.[3] Ejectives and implosives are characterized as glottalic stops, that is, stops involving closure at the glottis. Within this class, implosives are described as suction stops in which "the glottis is closed [and] a sudden depression of the larynx, by enlarging the supraglottal cavities, rarefies the imprisoned air, so that an implosion occurs when the outer closure is released" (Catford, 1939: 3).

In Catford's account, then, implosive production involves four characteristics: 1) glottal closure, 2) larynx lowering, 3) rarefaction, and 4) implosive release. This way of describing implosives has been widely followed and forms the basis of most textbook treatments up to the present.

2.2 Problems with the classical account

The classical account of implosives, by acknowledging the fundamental role of air pressure and the mechanisms by which it is controlled, represents an important advance over earlier work. However, subsequent research has shown that such an account fails to distinguish implosives clearly from other stop types. It is now known that just like ordinary voiced stops, implosives may be produced with ordinary ("modal") voicing, with no ingressive airstream, and without rarefaction (negative oral air pressure). Moreover, larynx lowering is not unique to implosives, but is commonly observed in the production of ordinary voiced explosives as well. It is consequently no longer clear in what essential respect implosives differ from other types of stops. These problems are briefly reviewed in the following subsections.

2.2.1 Implosives may be produced with modal voicing[4]

The classical taxonomy of stop types, as just summarized, requires the inner closure point to be the glottis for implosives, but the lungs for ordinary explosive stops. While this view provides a good account of voiceless implosives (see § 3.2), it proves problematical when applied to voiced implosives. More recent research, beginning with Peter Ladefoged's pioneering study of the phonetics of West African languages (1968), has shown that there are several ways of producing voiced implosives, not all of which involve what can be termed glottal closure. In one common way of producing voiced implosives, the vocal folds are held loosely together in a configuration appropriate for modal voicing, as found in ordinary voiced stops. Ladefoged has summarized his observations in the following terms:

> It is perfectly possible to produce ingressive glottalic sounds by a... process in which the closed glottis is rapidly lowered... But this type of sound is rare. The more common airstream process involving the lowering of the glottis does not have the vocal folds held tightly together. Instead, as they descend they are allowed to be set in vibration by the air in the lungs, which is always at a higher than atmospheric pressure during any speech activity. (Ladefoged, 1971: 25−6)

The "inner closure point" in such sounds is the lungs, not the glottis.

The idea that implosives involve a glottal closure point might alternatively be understood to imply that they are produced with a stiffer vocal fold configuration than that found in ordinary voiced stops, creating a higher resistance to airflow across the glottis. This configuration could be expected to result in laryngealization or creaky voice. But while it is true that some voiced implosives are laryngealized, not all are. Summarizing their review of the literature on this point, Ladefoged and Maddieson conclude that implosives can be produced with modal voice, with a more tense voice setting, or with complete glottal closure (1996: 82). Only the last type conforms to the classical definition of implosives.

2.2.2 Implosives need not be produced with an ingressive airstream

Another widely-accepted criterion for distinguishing implosive from explosive stops is the presence of an ingressive airstream (implosion), which is often observed at the implosive release. However, this criterion, too, proves inconclusive. Ladefoged (1968, 1971) found few examples of actual ingressive airflow at the release of the implosive stops in his survey of West African languages. He observed:

> The downward movement of the vibrating glottis tended to lower the pressure of the air in the mouth; but this was usually more than offset by the increase in pressure due to the outgoing lung air. These sounds were seldom ingressive in the sense that on the release of the articulatory closure air flowed into the mouth. (Ladefoged, 1968: 6)

This result has been confirmed by others. Lex, in a phonetic study of implosives in the Fouladou dialect of Fula, found that airflow can be either ingressive or stationary at the implosive release, and proposed that what marks implosives is the *absence* of egressive airflow (Lex, 1994: 137). Assessing the literature, Ladefoged and Maddieson conclude that ingressive airflow provides no categorical distinction between voiced implosives and explosives, and state: "there is a gradient between one form of voiced plosive and what may be called a true implosive, rather than two clearly defined cases" (1996: 82).

2.2.3 Implosives need not involve negative oral air pressure

Several studies, such as Demolin (1995), have confirmed that oral air pressure may indeed be lowered to subatmospheric level during the closure phase of implosives. However, sometimes there is no observable lowering of air pressure. In their phonetic study of Owere Igbo, Ladefoged, Williamson, Elugbe & Uwulaka remark (1976: 154): "it seems that [ɓ] contrasts with [b] simply by having no increase (rather than by having an actual decrease) in oral pressure during the closure". Ladefoged (1971: 26) elsewhere states: "in many of the languages I have observed the pressure of the air in the mouth during an ingressive glottalic stop is approximately the same as that outside the mouth."

2.2.4 Larynx lowering is not unique to implosives

If neither glottal closure, ingressive airflow, nor negative air pressure provide robust diagnostics for identifying implosives, what does? Larynx lowering, required to initiate the glottalic airstream mechanism, is the single most commonly cited property in definitions of implosives in the current literature. However, it has been well established since the study of Ewan & Krones (1974) that larynx lowering is not unique to implosives, but is regularly used to maintain voicing in ordinary voiced pulmonic stops.

The explanation for this is quite straightforward. Consider the production of an ordinary pulmonic voiced stop, such as [b]. Assuming that the vocal folds are kept in a position appropriate for modal voicing and that no other special adjustments are made, air pressure starts to build up in the oral cavity just after the labial closure is formed, and the pressure drop across the glottis decreases by a corresponding amount. When this pressure drops below a certain threshold, vocal fold vibration ceases. The decrease in pressure is sufficiently rapid that only one or two glottal pulses would normally occur after the closure is formed. In order for voicing to be sustained for a longer interval, therefore, supplementary adjustments must be made. These may include increasing subglottal pressure, slackening the vocal folds, or decreasing supraglottal pressure. The latter adjustment can be achieved either by venting the airstream outward through the nasal cavity during part of the occlusion, or by expanding the oral cavity. (See e.g. Stevens, 1997, 1998 for more detailed discussion.)

The last of these adjustments, oral cavity expansion, is of particular interest to the present discussion. It can be achieved by several different but complementary maneuvers, including larynx lowering, tongue root advancement, relaxation of the soft tissues of the vocal tract walls, raising of the velum, shifting of the oral closure forward to expand cavity size longitudinally, and lowering of the jaw (see e.g. Ewan & Krones, 1974; Bell-Berti, 1975; Catford, 1977; Ohala & Riordan, 1979; Westbury, 1983; Ladefoged & Maddieson, 1996; Stevens, 1998). Most of these mechanisms, including larynx lowering, have been observed in the production of "ordinary" voiced obstruents in better-studied languages such as

English and French, often in combination. The combination of larynx lowering and tongue root advancement is illustrated schematically in Figure 1, from Stevens (1998: 467).

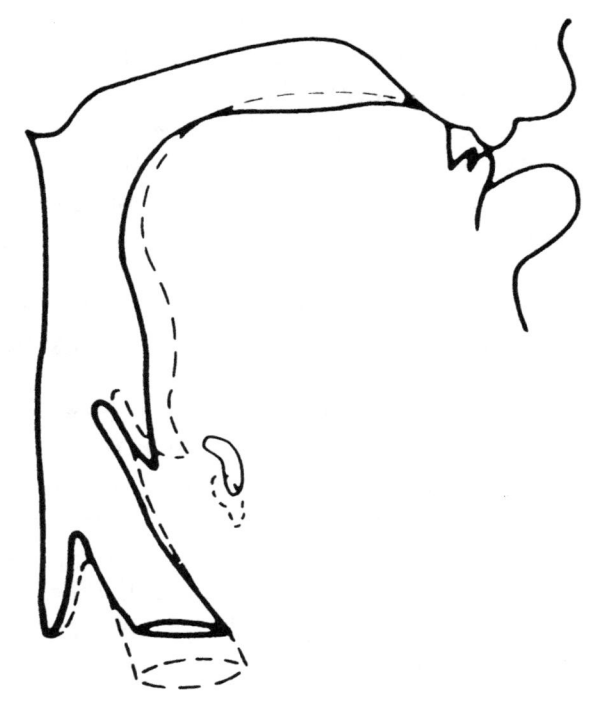

Figure 1: Schematic representation of the midsaggital section of the vocal tract at two points in time during the production of intervocalic [d]: during the consonant closure (solid line); immediately before the consonant is released (dashed line). (After Stevens, 1998, Figure 8.69)

Both of these adjustments, if maintained throughout the stop closure, will tend to sustain voicing.

The effect of relaxing the soft tissues of the walls has been calculated for a labial stop by Westbury (1983, Fig. 3), as shown in Figure 2. This figure shows that we may expect voicing to continue in a stop for only 7 ms if the vocal tract is bounded by rigid walls (dotted line), for about 30 ms if its tension is analogous to that of the neck wall (lower dashed line), for slightly over 60 ms if its tension is similar to that of the tensed cheeks (solid line), and for 80 ms or more (that is, throughout the normal duration of a stop

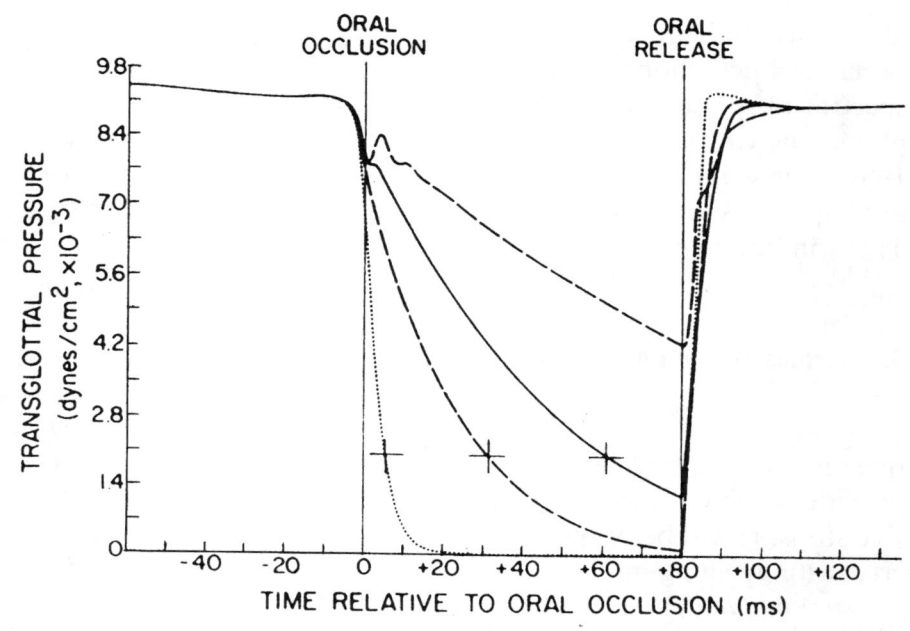

Figure 2: Synthesized time functions of the transglottal pressure gradient during an intervocalic labial stop bounded by rigid walls (dotted line), walls mechanically analogous to the neck wall (lower dashed line), tensed cheeks (solid line), or relaxed cheeks (upper dashed line). Crosses indicate points where the pressure gradient falls below voicing threshold. (After Westbury, 1983, Figure 3)

closure) if its tension is equal to that of the relaxed cheeks (upper dashed line). As Westbury notes, "the cumulative effect of articulatory movements on volume of the cavity above the glottis is more relevant to the problem of voicing maintenance during consonantal closure than are the direction and extent of movements of any single articulator" (Westbury, 1983: 1331).

In sum, larynx lowering and other cavity-expanding adjustments are not unique to implosives, and cannot be used as a discrete criterion to distinguish them from ordinary voiced stops. It might be possible to maintain that the difference between the two stop types is gradient, lying primarily in the comparatively larger and more rapid descent of the glottis in implosives (Ladefoged, 1971: 27). This view, however, would not explain why languages appear to distinguish at most two phonological categories along this gradient. Under the view that articulatory variation between distinct phonemic categories is marked by rapid shifts in spectral properties, while articulatory variation within any single phone-mic category is not (see Stevens' quantal theory of speech, 1989), one would expect to find a categorical property distinguishing implosives and other non-explosive stops from explosive stops. This will be the goal of the next section.

3. Implosives as nonobstruent stops

We have seen that neither glottal closure, ingressive air flow, negative air pressure (rarefaction), nor the presence of larynx lowering provide reliable criteria for distinguishing implosives from explosive stops. It will be proposed here instead that the common property distinguishing implosives from explosives is the *absence of air pressure buildup in the oral cavity*. As will be seen, this property is exactly the correlate of the feature [− obstruent]. This feature provides a categorical basis for distinguishing implosives from explosive sounds. And as the later discussion will show, it generalizes straightforwardly to other kinds of nonexplosive stops, and provides an explanatory account of the phonological patterning of the class of nonexplosive stops as a whole.

This section proposes a definition of the feature [obstruent] (§ 3.1), showing that both voiced and voiceless implosives satisfy this definition (§ 3.2). It then shows that this definition generalizes to other types of nonexplosive stops as well (§ 3.3).

3.1. Approaches to the obstruent/nonobstruent distinction

The attempt to define a binary feature assigning all speech sounds to one of two large classes, obstruents and sonorants, has a long history in phonological research. Such a feature is required to define the natural classes of sounds involved in the statement of many common phonological patterns. Thus, for example, Trubetzkoy proposed to characterize the obstruent/sonorant distinction in terms of degree of obstruction to the airflow (Trubetzkoy 1969: 141); however, he allowed this feature to distinguish sonorants and obstruents only in languages lacking a phonemic contrast between stops and fricatives. Chomsky & Halle (1968: 302) gave the binary feature [± sonorant] a more central place in their feature system. They defined sonorants as sounds produced with a vocal tract cavity configuration in which spontaneous voicing is possible, and obstruents as sounds whose cavity configuration makes spontaneous voicing impossible.[5] Chomsky and Halle did not define this configuration directly, but maintained that it can be created by narrowing the air passage to the point where airflow velocity at the glottis is reduced below the critical level necessary for spontaneous voicing to take place.

These definitions of the obstruent/sonorant distinction were stated in terms of vocal tract configurations. In contrast, Stevens (1983) proposes an aerodynamic definition, which we quote in full due to its importance for the following discussion:

> Another class of consonants, called *obstruent*, is defined in the articulatory domain by the presence of a pressure increase within the vocal tract during production of the consonant. This pressure increase occurs because a complete closure or a sufficiently narrow constriction is made within the vocal tract to contain the air. The acoustic consequence of this pressure increase is that turbulence noise is generated in the vicinity of the constriction at some point during production of the sound. This noise can occur either throughout the constriction interval (as in a fricative consonant) or at the release of a closure (as in a stop consonant), but in any case it will occur in the time interval in the vicinity of the region where the rapid spectrum change for the consonant occurs. Presumably, a listener is sensitive to the presence or absence of this type of noise in the sound, and this attribute, then, defines the natural class of obstruent consonants. (Stevens, 1983: 254)

In contrast, sonorants are produced with no pressure increase, and consequently no audible noise. (Similar accounts have been proposed by Halle & Clements 1983, Halle 1992, and Stevens

1998.) A further attribute of obstruence cited by Stevens (1997: 490) is reduction or cessation of vocal fold vibration during the oral constriction, a mechanical effect of pressure increase as discussed earlier.

One advantage of this definition is that it can be applied to easily obtainable speech data, and readily confirmed, or corrected if need be. To test this definition, one of the authors (GNC) conducted air pressure measurements at the Phonetics Laboratory of the University of Paris 3. Air pressure variation in the anterior oral cavity can be measured by introducing a thin plastic tube into the side of the mouth behind the rear molars so that its open end points toward the center of the oral tract. The other end of the tube is passed through an oral mouth mask and connected to a pressure transducer. The pressure measured is the static pressure behind labial and coronal constrictions. The subject (GNC) read a short passage containing representative English stops, fricatives and sonorants several times into the mouth mask, while simultaneously recording it on the system's audio input. Resulting airflow and air pressure measurements were segmented by examination of spectrograms of the corresponding speech signal and by selective auditory playback of portions of the spectrogram.[6]

Figure 3 presents measurements from a spoken text illustrating obstruents and sonorants in several contexts. Obstruents are labelled to the right of vertical lines aligned with their beginning (onset of closure). The top trace represents the audio signal, the middle trace oral airflow, and the bottom trace oral air pressure.

It can be observed that every sustained rise in oral pressure corresponds to an obstruent. Similarly, every nonvelar obstruent in this phrase is realized with a sustained increase in oral pressure. (Air pressure buildup behind velar stops is not detected by the transducer due to the placement of the tube in the center of the mouth, and so no pressure rise is recorded for the two velar stops in this text.)

The air pressure pattern in Figure 3, which is similar to other pressure traces obtained in the same way, is thus consistent with Stevens' definition of the class of obstruent sounds.

Explosives, implosives and nonexplosives 311

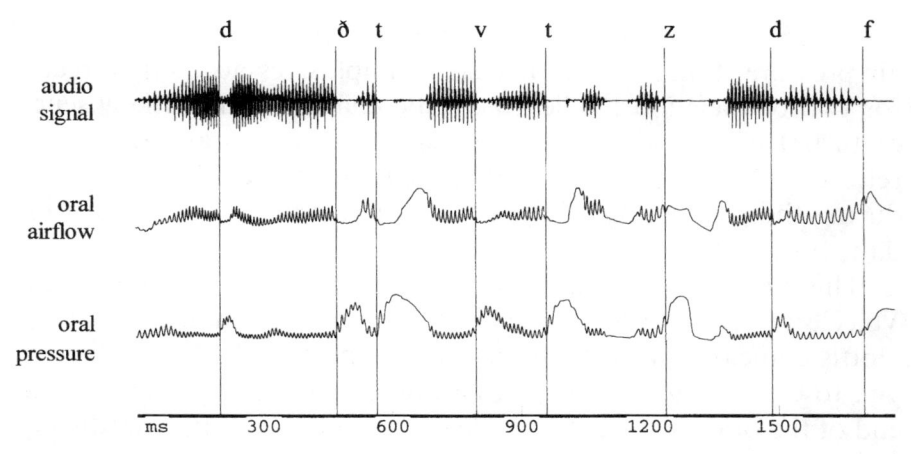

Figure 3: Oral airflow (middle line) and oral air pressure variation (bottom line) during a reading of the passage *right away the traveller took his coat off*. Obstruents are labelled to the right of vertical lines aligned with their beginning (onset of closure).

3.2 Implosives as nonobstruents

Based on this definition of obstruence, we propose that implosives are nonobstruent stops. In contrast, explosive stops, including ejectives and clicks (note 1), will normally qualify as obstruents, because their explosive release implies air pressure buildup.

This analysis of implosives provides an improved basis for understanding their phonetic characteristics. First, although implosives are not always produced with negative air pressure, they are never reported to be produced with positive air pressure; the feature [− obstruent] requires only that they lack positive air pressure. Second, though implosives are not always produced with an ingressive airstream, they are never reported to be produced with an egressive airstream. This, too, follows from their status as nonobstruents, since an egressive airstream requires positive pressure buildup behind the oral closure. Third, the fact that implosives are typically produced by lowering the larynx can be explained by the fact that this gesture increases the volume of the oral cavity and hence, in the absence of any opening, reduces air pressure within. Larynx lowering can thus be understood as a control mechanism for keeping oral air pressure at or below the level of atmospheric air pressure. Finally, this analysis of implosives accounts directly for two of their most salient acoustic characteristics, the absence of turbulence noise (in the form of burst or aspiration) at their release and the steady or rising amplitude of vocal fold vibration during the production of the constriction (for the latter, see Lindau, 1984).

This analysis extends readily to voiceless implosives as well. Voiceless implosives are produced by forming a tight closure at the glottis coinciding with the oral closure and then lowering the larynx to create negative air pressure in the oral cavity. Toward the end of the oral closure, air may leak through the glottis, producing a short voicing interval just prior to release which continues uninterrupted into the vowel. Less commonly, the stop is voiceless throughout, with a voicing lag at its release (see data in Pinkerton, 1986). At release of the oral closure, there is typically a brief period of rapid ingressive airflow. Voiceless implosives were first described in theoretical terms by Catford (1939) and Pike (1943), and were subsequently observed in several African and Mayan languages (see Greenberg, 1970; Campbell, 1973, and references therein). The first published phonetic description of these sounds based on instrumental evidence, to our knowledge, was the study of the stops of Owere Igbo by Ladefoged et al. (1976). This work was followed by phonetic studies of voiced and voiceless implosives in Quichean (Mayan) languages by Pinkerton (1986), in Xhosa by Roux (1991), in Fouladou Fula by Lex (1994), in Ngiti by Kutsch Lojenga (1994), and in the closely related Lendu language by Demolin (1995). Voiceless implosives have also been reported in Seereer-Siin by McLaughlin (1992-4).

3.3 Other types of nonobstruent stops

Other types of nonexplosive stops are expected to qualify as nonobstruents as well, since their lack of explosion normally results from the absence of increased oral cavity air pressure during their closure. These include various types of glottalized stops, whose glottal characteristics tend to impede or eliminate transglottal airflow and thus to maintain a low level of oral air pressure.

The term *glottalized* is generally used to refer to stops which involve some degree of glottal constriction beyond that involved in ordinary modal voicing.[7] This class includes voiceless implosives, laryngealized (or creaky voiced) stops, preglottalized stops, and other types. However, due to the lack of experimental studies as well as to inconsistencies in terminology, the distinction among these categories is not always clear. Ladefoged & Maddieson (1996) propose to distinguish voiceless (i.e., fully glottalized) implosives from laryngealized implosives, laryngealized stops, and various other types of stops with accompanying glottal closure. The distinction among some of these categories is subtle, but is often auditorily detectable. For example, the Xhosa implosives, including their voiceless variants, are typically produced with little or no detectable creak (Roux 1991; Michael Jessen, personal communication), while the glottalized stops of Hausa are typically creaky (Lindau, 1984; Lindsey, Hayward & Haruna, 1992). Such distinctions are not contrastive in any language, as far as we know.

The distinction between voiceless implosives and *preglottalized* stops is especially hard to pin down. This term is subject to widely varying interpretations. Some linguists use the terms "preglottalized stop" and "implosive" synonymously, but most use them differently. For example, Haudricourt (1950) uses the term "preglottalized" for any sound produced with full glottal closure, regardless of how the glottal closure is phased with the supraglottal articulation. Goyvaerts (1988) considers a stop to be preglottalized if it is produced with minimal implosion, as opposed to the strong implosion of true implosives. For Dimmendaal (1986) and many others, preglottalized stops necessarily involve a sequencing of the glottal and oral closures, in that order. As far as is currently known, such segment-internal sequencing is never lexically contrastive or phonologically relevant.[8] Due to these different and largely incompatible usages, the term "voiceless implosive" is used in this study, following common practice, to refer to all voiceless glottalized implosives, regardless of the sequencing of the glottal and oral articulations.

It seems, then, that the feature [− obstruent] provides a categorical basis for distinguishing implosive (and other nonexplosive) stops from explosive stops. As we have noted, however, many other types of glottalized stops as discussed in this section are still poorly understood, and we currently know of no phonetic studies bearing on the aerodynamic properties of, for example, nonimplosive laryngealized stops, preglottalized stops, or the "consonnes douces" often reported in the Francophone literature. It seems likely, however, that at least some varieties of these sounds, to the extent they are nonexplosive, will prove to be nonobstruent stops as we have defined them here.

4. Nonexplosive stops in Ikwere

We now turn to a phonetic study of two further types of nonexplosive stops, neither of which can be easily identified with any of the stop types reviewed up to this point. These sounds do not satisfy the classical definition of implosives, as they do not involve the glottalic airstream mechanism. Though similar to implosives acoustically, neither is produced with any detectable movement of the larynx, neither is auditorily laryngealized, and only one of them involves glottal closure. In some respects they resemble the "lenis" stops sometimes reported by Africanist scholars (Stewart 1989). The evidence summarized in this section shows that they represent further members of the class of nonobstruent stops.

4.1 Ikwere consonants

Ikwere, a Niger-Congo language spoken in Nigeria,[9] has a pair of bilabial stops written *gb* and *kp* in the standard orthography. These sounds are reflexes of older labial-velar stops, and may still have labial-velar realizations in some varieties of Ikwere. However, in the variety described here, they are realized as bilabial sounds with no velar contact at any point in their production. We transcribe them as [b̞] and ['b̞], respectively. Both are relatively common sounds in Ikwere, each having a lexical frequency of over 4% with respect to all consonants. They are phonemically distinctive, contrasting with *p* and *b* as shown in Figures 4 and 5.[10]

Obstruents:					
explosive voiceless stops	p	t	tʃ	k	kʷ
explosive voiced stops	b	d	dʒ	g	gʷ
voiceless fricatives	f	s			
voiced fricatives	v	z			
Nonobstruents:					
nonexplosive voiced stop	ḅ				
nonexplosive glottalized stop	'ḅ				
lateral approximant			l		
central approximants			r	y ɣ w	
laryngeals					h hʷ

Figure 4: Consonant phonemes in Ikwere

The classification of ḅ and 'ḅ as nonobstruents will be justified below. The nonobstruent consonants of the last five rows have oral realizations before oral vowels and nasal realizations before nasal vowels, giving the pairings [ḅ]/[m], ['ḅ]/['m], [l]/[n], [r]/[r̃], etc. Each of these pairs constitutes a single phoneme in which nasality is nondistinctive (Clements & Osu, in preparation).

Figure 5 gives examples of lexical contrasts between the nonexplosive stops ḅ, 'ḅ and the explosive stops *p*, *b* (´ = high tone, ` = low tone, ˆ = falling tone).

Nonexplosive ḅ, 'ḅ		Explosive b, p	
àḅá (ɛ́fɔ́)	'to run'	àbá (ézè)	'to become rich'
èḅê	'to prepare food'	èbê	'to touch'
à'ḅá	'to sow'	àpá (ólú)	'to climb'
áḅà [ámà̰]	'machete'	àbà	'jaw'

Figure 5: Minimal contrasts involving /ḅ, 'ḅ, p, b/

Due to the uncertainty regarding their classification, a phonetic study was conducted to determine how the Ikwere sounds ḅ and 'ɓ are distinguished phonetically from the "ordinary" bilabials b and p. All phonetic data were obtained from one of the authors (SO). The main results of this study are presented below. The following questions will be considered in turn: Are ɓ and 'ɓ obstruents? If not, are these sounds implosives? If not, are they glottalized stops? What evidence do their f_0 characteristics provide? Can they be regarded as "lenis" stops? And finally, how is air pressure regulated in the production of ɓ and 'ɓ?

4.2 Are ɓ and 'ɓ obstruents?

It will be recalled that the main auditory correlate of obstruence, in Stevens' account, is turbulence noise in the vicinity of the constriction. Neither ɓ nor 'ɓ display any such noise, whether in the form of a release burst or of post-release frication noise. Spectrograms comparing the words àbá and àɓá are shown in Figure 6.[11]

In these examples, which are typical of our data, a weak transient of about one glottal pulse in length can often be observed at the release of b (top spectrogram) but none at the release of ɓ (bottom spectrogram). Neither stop is followed by a noise burst or frication.

Spectrograms comparing àpá 'to climb' and à'ɓá 'to sow' appear in Figure 7. In these examples, p (top spectrogram) shows a voiceless post-release transient of about 20 ms, followed by voicing. The duration of this transient varies a good deal in our data, a few tokens being heavily aspirated, and others unaspirated. (Explosive stops at other places of articulation typically show a more pronounced burst and a longer post-burst transition filled with noise and aspiration.) 'ɓ (bottom spectrogram) shows no burst, but a prevoicing segment of about 40 ms in length.

These spectrograms also confirm that we are dealing with bilabial sounds, not labial-velars. Labial-velar stops typically show velar-like transitions on their left (Ladefoged & Maddieson, 1996: 334-6). In Figures 6 and 7, however, F2 transitions on the left of ɓ and 'ɓ fall, just as they do before b and p. This pattern contrasts

Explosives, implosives and nonexplosives 317

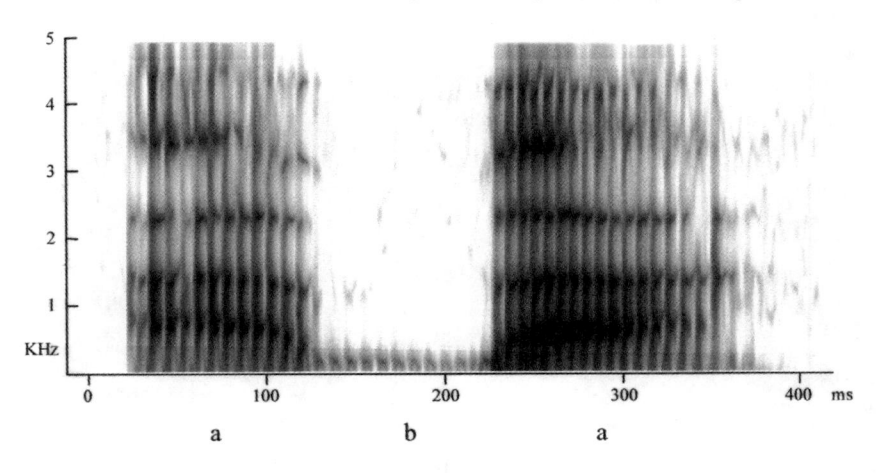

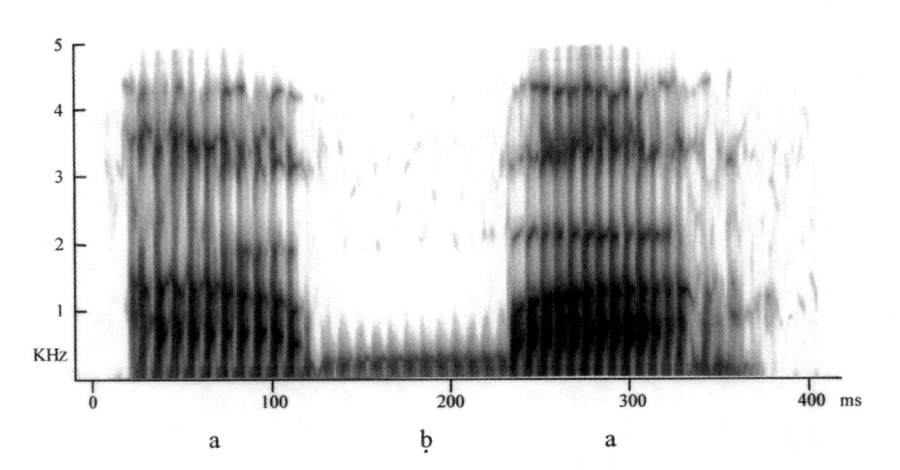

Figure 6: Spectrograms of the words *àbá* (top) and *àḅá* (bottom).

with that in words like *àká* 'to fast' and *àgâ* 'to walk' (not shown here), in which F2 rises at the left edge of the velar stops.

A further acoustic property of voiced obstruents is the tendency for voicing to decay or cease altogether during occlusion (Lindau, 1984). Both *b* and *ḅ* are fully voiced in all our data. However, *b* often shows some decay in voicing amplitude toward the end of the occlusion, while *ḅ* often shows an increase in voicing amplitude. The voice bar patterns in Figure 6 are typical in this respect. This distinction does not constitute a reliable criterion for distin-

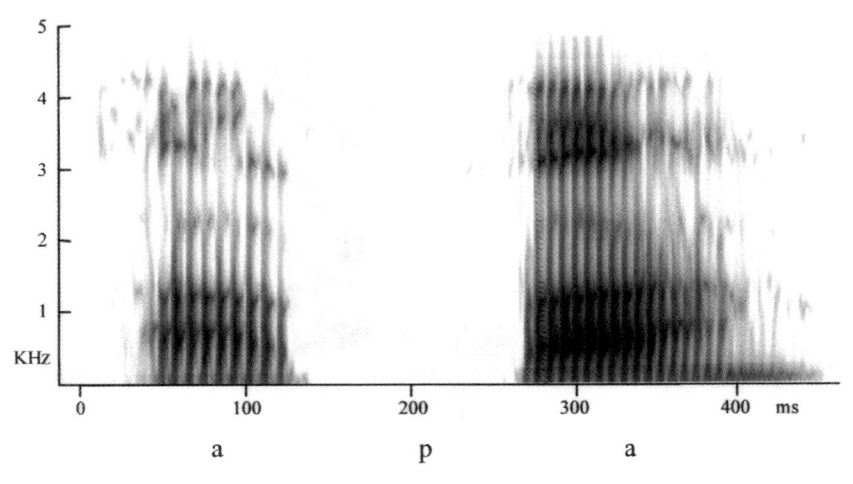

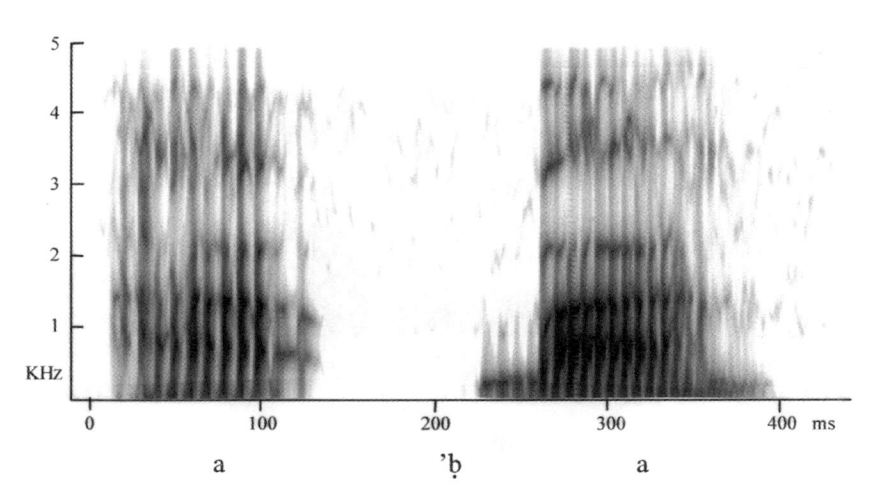

Figure 7: Spectrograms of *àpá* (top) and *à'ḫá* (bottom).

guishing *b* from *ḫ*, however, as both stops sometimes show level voicing amplitude throughout their duration.

Airflow and air pressure measurements were also conducted for selected utterances spoken by SO using the methodology described in section 3.1. Figures 8 and 9 show results for representative productions of *b*, *ḫ*, *p*, and *'ḫ*. Egressive airflow is shown by a rise of the airflow trace above the median line, and ingressive airflow

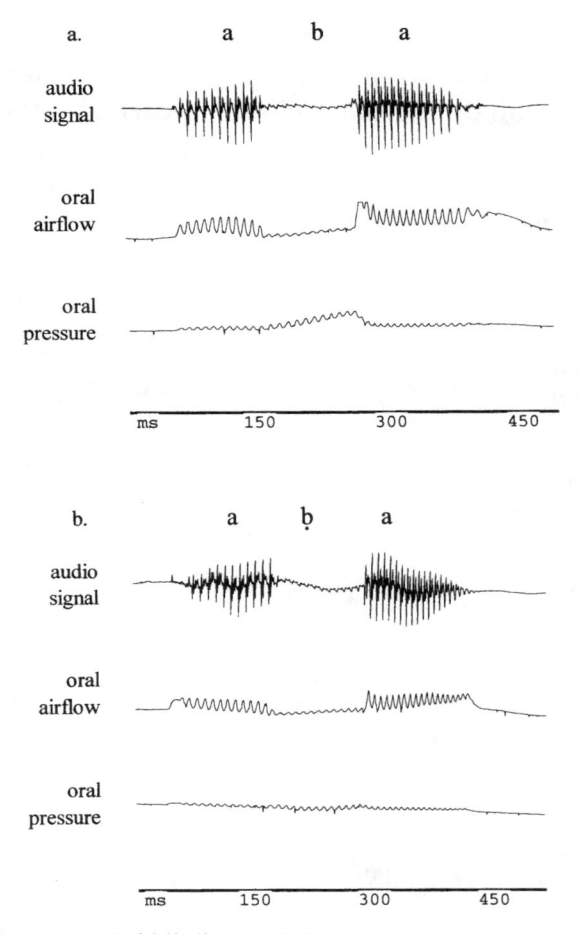

Figure 8: Airflow traces (middle line) and air pressure traces (bottom line) for *b* and *ḅ* in the words *àbá* and *àḅá*. Egressive airflow is shown by a rise of the airflow trace (middle line) above the baseline. Increase in air pressure is shown by a rise in the air pressure trace above the baseline.

(present only in Figure 9b) by a fall. An increase in oral air pressure is shown by a rise in the air pressure trace above the median line, and a decrease (again present only in Figure 9b) by a fall. The top line shows the synchronized audio signal. We now examine Figures 8 and 9 in turn.

Figure 8 presents data for *b* and *ḅ* in the words *àbá* and *àḅá*, spoken in isolation.

The explosive stop *b* (Figure 8a) shows a brief burst of egressive airflow at its release, lasting for two or three glottal pulses. Air pressure builds up during the occlusion, peaks at release and then drops quickly at the onset of the vowel. In contrast, *ɓ* (Figure 8b) shows no release burst, nor does it show any increase in oral air pressure during occlusion.[12]

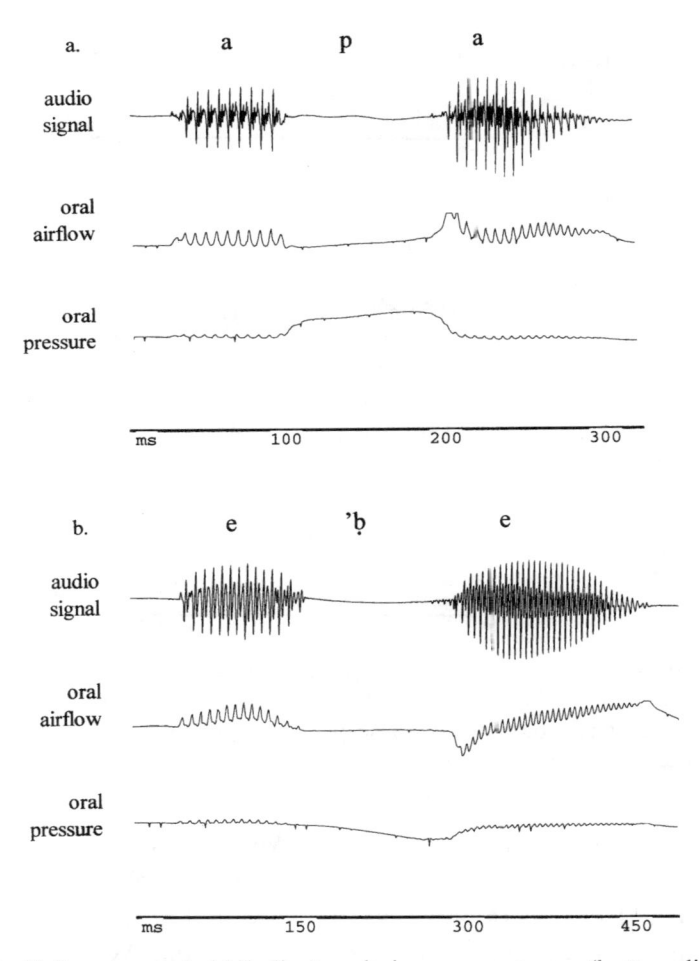

Figure 9: Airflow traces (middle line) and air pressure traces (bottom line) for *p* in *àpá* (a) and *'ɓ* in *è'ɓé* (b). Egressive airflow is shown by a rise of the airflow trace above the baseline, and ingressive airflow by a fall. An increase in oral air pressure is shown by a rise in the air pressure trace, and a decrease by a fall.

Figure 9 presents traces for p and $'ḅ$ in the words àpá and è'ḅé, spoken in isolation. As with $ḅ$, the voiceless stop p (Figure 9a) shows a burst of egressive air at its release and a buildup of oral air pressure during occlusion, peaking just before release. In contrast, $'ḅ$ (Figure 9b) presents a pattern similar to that often found in implosive sounds: an ingressive airstream at release, and a sharp drop in oral air pressure culminating just before release.[13]

Following the definition of obstruence proposed by Stevens (1983), then, Ikwere $ḅ$ and $'ḅ$ are nonobstruents: neither shows the acoustic properties of obstruence (turbulence noise), and both lack oral air pressure increase during occlusion.

4.3 Are $ḅ$ and $'ḅ$ implosives?

We have just seen that some instances of $'ḅ$ display two typical properties of implosives, negative air pressure and ingressive airflow. An obvious question, then, is whether either $ḅ$ or $'ḅ$ are produced with a glottalic airstream mechanism, which requires a lowering of the larynx.

External observation of many of SO's productions of $ḅ$ and $'ḅ$ failed to show visible larynx lowering on any occasion. To study this question more systematically, videotapes were made of Ikwere words containing $ḅ$, $'ḅ$ and other stops in intervocalic position. Film speed was 25 frames/sec, yielding one image every 40 ms. These images were viewed in frame-by-frame mode on a large-screen television monitor, and selected sequences were traced onto transparencies. Representative productions of àḅá and à'ḅá are shown in Figure 10.

These tracings show overlays of three consecutive points at the release of the labial stop into the vowel: (a) shortly after mid-point in the labial closure, (b) just prior to release, and (c) just after release. The protrusion of the larynx (thyroid cartilage) is clearly visible along the profile of the neck, as shown by the arrows. There is no visible descent or rise of the larynx at any point in the production of either sound, either in the frames shown here or in adjacent frames; all movement is located in the region extending from the lips to the chin.

a.   a'ba   b.   aba

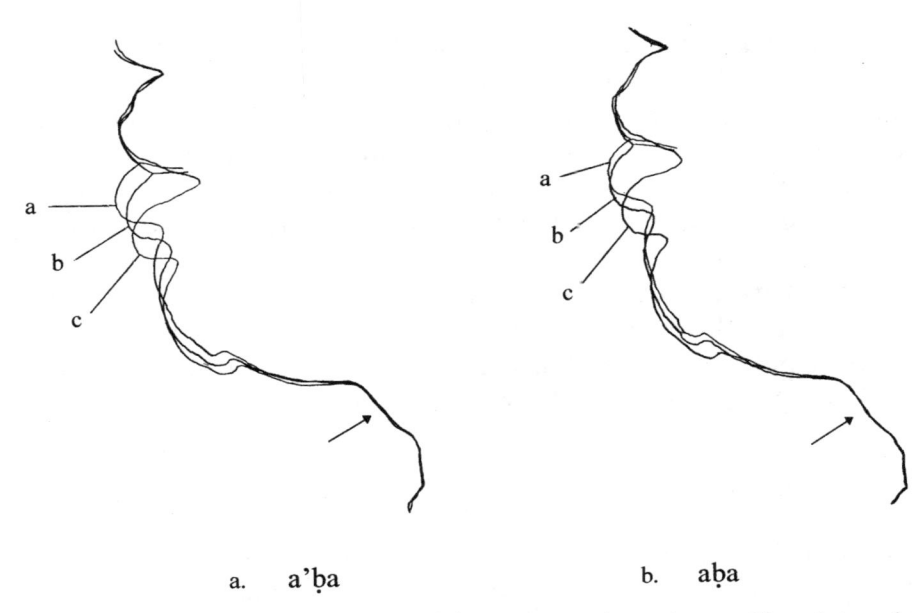

Figure 10: Overlaid profile tracings of three consecutive points at 40 ms intervals during the release of the labial stop into the following vowel in the words *à'bá* and *àbá*: (a) shortly after mid-point in the labial closure, (b) just prior to release, and (c) just after release. The protrusion of the larynx is clearly visible along the profile of the neck, as shown by the arrows.

In summary, neither ɓ nor 'ɓ are implosive stops, in the usual definition of this category. Neither sound is produced with detectable larynx lowering, and thus neither can be said to make use of a glottalic airstream mechanism.[14]

4.4   Are ɓ and 'ɓ glottalized stops?

Let us next consider the nature of the glottal closure in these two sounds, beginning with 'ɓ. Glottalization is auditorily detectable at the left edge of 'ɓ, where it sounds rather like the *p* in *cap* as pronounced by English speakers who preglottalize their word-final voiceless stops. Traces of glottalization can be observed toward the end of the vowel preceding 'ɓ in the spectrogram in Figure 7. In contrast, no glottalization is heard when voicing resumes at the end of the stop, or in the following vowel.

To check for visual evidence of a special glottal configuration in ɓ or 'ɓ, a fiberoptic study of SO's production of several words containing the four bilabial stops and other sounds was conducted at the Hôpital Laennec, Paris, under the supervision of Dr Lise Crevier-Buchman. The fiberscope was connected to a camera with a time resolution of 25 frames per second. The images were recorded on a Umatic videocassette recorder and transferred to VHS format. After preliminary viewing in frame-by-frame mode, selected sequences were digitized for closer study. Laryngeal views mid-way through the occlusive phases of 'ɓ, p, ɓ, and b are reproduced in Figure 11.[15]

The base of the epiglottis is visible at the bottom of each image, and the posterior wall of the pharynx at the top. Prominent structures include the arytenoid cartilages, the aryepiglottic folds which join them to the sides of the epiglottis, the vocal folds, and the ventricular bands (or false vocal folds) lying just above them, sometimes partly concealing them.

The first image shows the occlusion of 'ɓ toward its beginning. We observe an anterior-posterior compression of the aryepiglottic sphincter in which the arytenoids are drawn forward to approach (but not touch) the base of the epiglottis, while the ventricular bands are drawn laterally together to nearly cover the closed vocal folds. This configuration, found in all tokens of 'ɓ, also characterizes the glottal stops which are regularly inserted before utterance-initial vowels by this speaker, and is similar to fiberscopic images of glottal stops in other languages published elsewhere in the literature (e.g. Harris, 1999). It confirms that 'ɓ is formed with a tight glottal closure.

The second image shows p for comparison. During the occlusive phase of this sound, the vocal folds are momentarily spread apart, as shown in the image. This configuration is typical of voiceless stops in other languages (e.g. Sawashima & Hirose, 1983). Thus though both 'ɓ and p are acoustically voiceless, their voicelessness results from two different articulatory mechanisms, glottal closure in the first case and glottal opening in the second.

The last two images show the closures of ɓ and b. The glottal configurations in these sounds are virtually indistinguishable. Both

324 G. N. Clements and Sylvester Osu

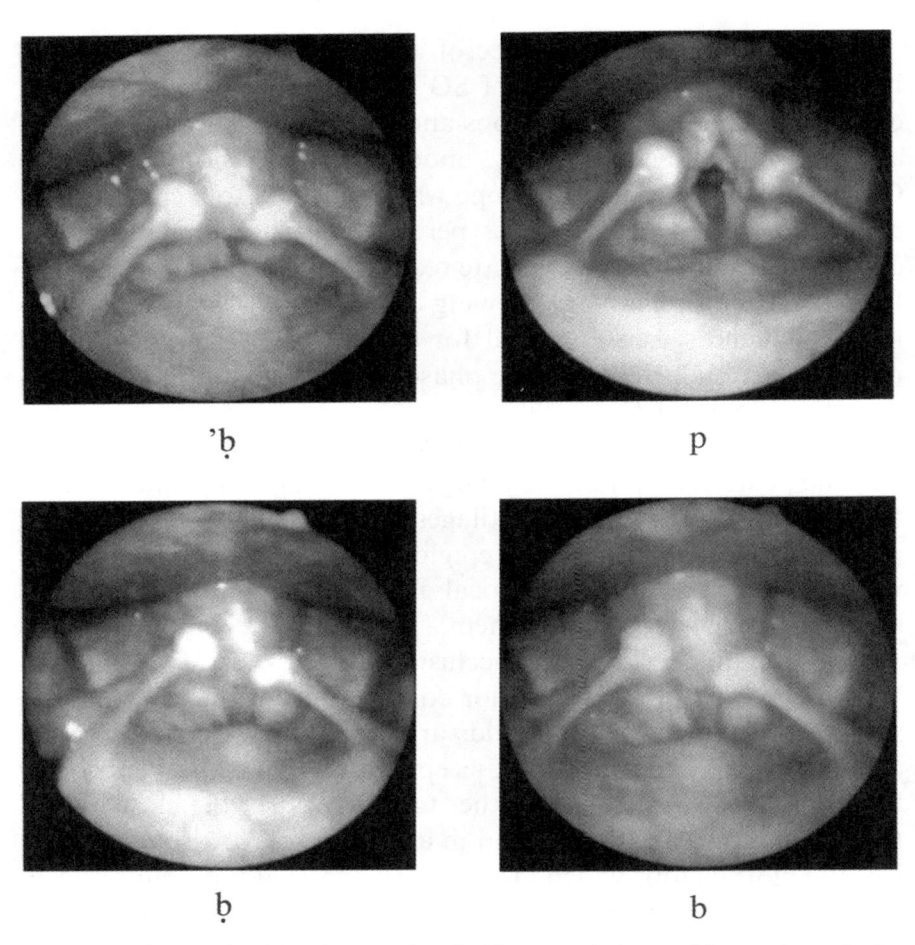

'ɓ̰   p

ɓ̰   b

Figure 11: Fiberoptic video frames showing laryngeal views mid-way through the occlusive phases of 'ɓ̰ (upper left), *p* (upper right), ɓ̰ (lower left), and *b* (lower right). The base of the epiglottis is visible at the bottom and the posterior wall of the pharynx at the top.

involve a loose approximation of the vocal folds as is observed in modal voicing. These images are similar to those of *m* (not shown), as well as to those of other sonorant sounds we have examined. They support the auditory impression that both ɓ̰ and *b* are produced with modal voice, similar to that used in sonorants.

Of further interest is what the fiberoptic images did *not* show: there was no evidence of larynx lowering at any point during the

Explosives, implosives and nonexplosives 325

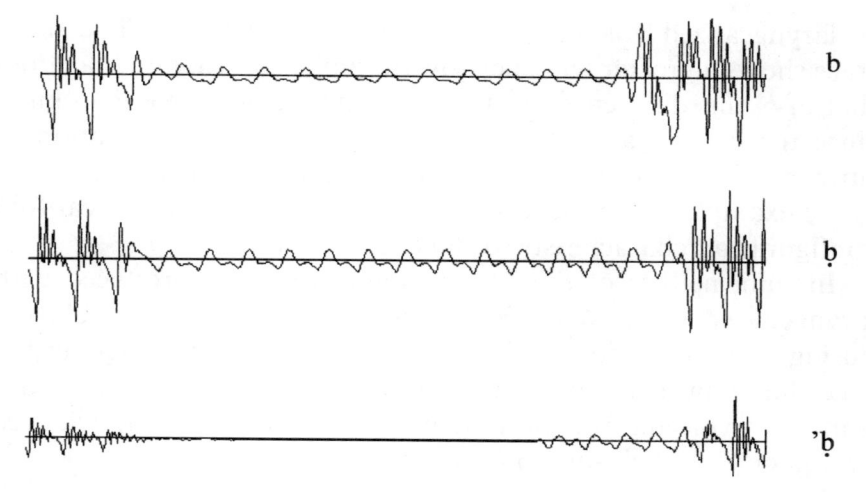

Figure 12: Acoustic waveforms of the occlusive phase of intervocalic *b* (top), *ḅ* (middle), and '*ḅ* (bottom).

closure phases of '*ḅ* or *ḅ*. Larynx lowering appears in fiberoptic films as a "zoom out" effect as the larynx moves downward, with a concomitant decrease in brightness of the arytenoids (Kagaya, 1974: 177, n. 11). While evidence of such lowering could conceivably have been missed in any individual sequence due perhaps to the 40-ms interval between successive images or the counteracting effect of sporadic camera movements, it is unlikely that it could have been missed in all images.[16]

We were unable to find any evidence that *ḅ* (or '*ḅ* during the prevoiced portion preceding release) are laryngealized. Auditorily, we were unable to hear any phonatory quality distinguishing the voicing in these sounds from that of the modally voiced *b*. Neither one sounds "creaky", either during its voiced portion or in the transition to the following vowel.

This auditory impression is supported by the acoustic data. Waveforms of the occlusive phase of intervocalic *b* (top), *ḅ* (middle), and '*ḅ* (bottom) are shown in Figure 12.

The waveforms of both *ḅ* and '*ḅ* (in its prevoiced portion) resemble that of *b*. These voicing patterns are quasiperiodic throughout, with no aperiodic intervals, increase in period, dips in amplitude, or other irregularities such as are found in typical examples of laryngealized voicing published in the literature. While the ɓ trace shows a greater tendency toward biphasic structure than does that of b, this difference seems more a matter of degree than kind, since the b trace also shows a double peak. An examination of fiberoptic images of ɓ and b, of which Figure 11 provides representative examples, also failed to reveal any evidence of a vocal fold configuration characteristic of laryngealization.

In sum, neither of these sounds appears to be produced with laryngealized voice. While 'ɓ is produced with full glottal closure during its first portion, which may induce some creakiness in the preceding vowel, voicing is modal in its prevoiced portion, and ɓ is modally voiced throughout. Nor is there any observable evidence of tighter glottal closure in ɓ than in b.

4.5 How do ɓ and 'ɓ influence f_0?

Although our data failed to reveal any direct evidence of a special laryngeal state in the Ikwere nonexplosive stops, indirect evidence for such a state might theoretically come to light from a study of f_0 effects at the consonant release. Greater vocal fold tension or stiffness in these sounds, by increasing resistance to airflow at the glottis (Rg), would tend to increase f_0 at the beginning of the following vowel. Conclusive evidence for such increased tension would suggest that the mechanism underlying the nonexplosive stops of Ikwere might be situated in the larynx, and would undermine the evidence for a feature [− obstruent]. This subsection first reviews phonetic studies of the tonal effects of implosive sounds in other languages, and then examines f_0 effects at the release of Ikwere stops.

Implosives are usually observed not to have the tone-depressing effects widely found after other voiced stops (an exception is Xhosa, as discussed by Jessen & Roux, 2000). This trend is not yet well understood. Theoretically, the reduction in vocal fold stiffness resulting from larynx lowering[17] should have a tone-lowering effect in implosives, just as it does in ordinary voiced obstruents.

To understand why implosives do *not* normally depress tone, it must be assumed that this factor is overridden by others. Addressing this question, Hombert et al. (1979: 48) suggest that the rapid lowering of the larynx during implosive production might generate such a high rate of glottal airflow that f_0 is raised above its normal level; however, as they point out, this explanation could account only for f_0 raising during the implosive closure itself. More recent studies have shown that f_0 raising can continue into the vowel as well. Thus, Wright & Shryock (1993) have shown that the pitch-raising effect of the Siswati voiced implosive ɓ on high-tone vowels perseveres well into the vowel. Similar effects are reported for voiceless implosives. Kutsch Lojenga's (1994) f_0 tracings of Ngiti show that the raised f_0 characterizing the final prevoiced portion of voiceless implosives continues into the vowel,[18] and Demolin (1995) reports analogous effects in the closely-related Lendu language.

To see what f_0 effects are present in the Ikwere nonexplosive stops, a study was conducted of f_0 patterns at the consonant-vowel transition. The consonants examined were [p 'ḅ b ḅ m]. Ten recordings were made of words containing these consonants embedded in a sentence frame.[19] In all test words, the consonants of interest are released into a high-tone vowel, either *a* or *e*. The lengths of the three glottal periods just preceding consonant release and of the seven following release were measured directly from the signal and converted into f_0 values. Averaged values for the ten tokens were plotted on graphs.

The results are shown in Figure 13. This figure overlays f_0 traces for *p* and 'ḅ (Figure 13a) and *b*, *m*, and ḅ (Figure 13b). In these graphs, glottal pulses −2 to 0 represent the final f_0 values of the consonant (absent in the case of voiceless *p*), and glottal pulses 1 to 7 represent the f_0 values of the following vowel.

Figure 13a shows high f_0 values at the release of *p* (dashed line), as expected after a voiceless consonant. By the third glottal pulse, 20 ms into the vowel, however, f_0 has reached a value appropriate for the following high tone vowel. The f_0 trace of 'ḅ (solid line) includes the three final values of its prevoiced portion (points −2 to 0), which was present in six of the ten tokens. This trace shows a

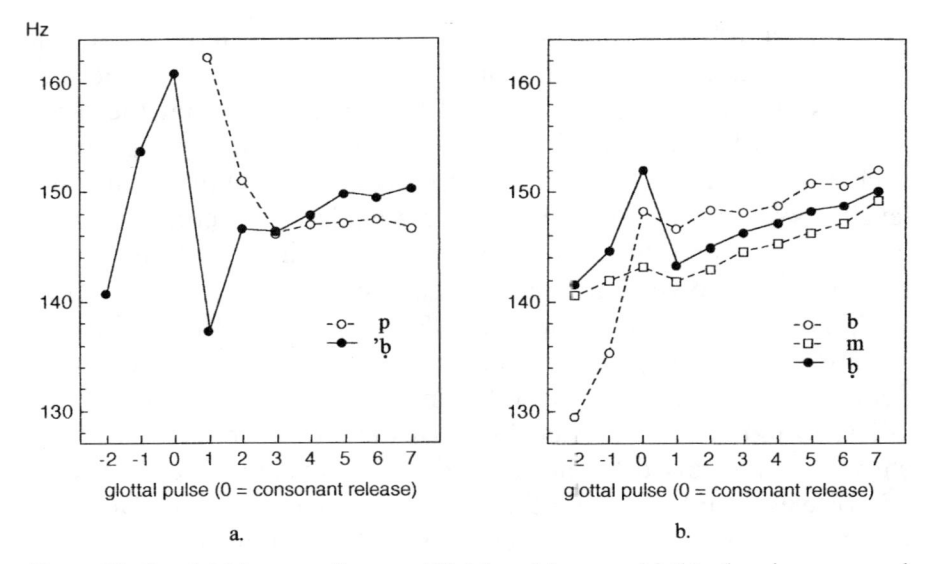

Figure 13: Overlaid f_0 traces for p and $'\underset{.}{b}$ (a) and b, m, and $\underset{.}{b}$ (b), showing averaged f_0 values of ten glottal pulses preceding and following the consonant release. In these graphs, glottal pulses -2 to 0 represent the final f_0 values of the consonant (absent in the case of voiceless p), and glottal pulses 1 to 7 represent the f_0 values of the following vowel. N = 10.

sharp rise-fall-rise pattern which can be explained by the expected variations in air pressure and airflow. F_0 values first rise sharply during the prevoiced portion of the stop (points -2 to 0), reflecting a high rate of airflow across the glottis just after the glottal closure is released. F_0 drops sharply at the release of the labial closure as air rushes into the oral cavity, reducing transglottal air pressure (point 1), and then quickly rises to a value appropriate for the following high tone vowel as the pulmonic airstream increases subglottal air pressure again and the vocal folds adjust to the configuration required for high tone production (points 2–7). These traces are different from those reported by Kutsch Lojenga and Demolin, who, as noted above, found higher f_0 values to persevere into the vowel. This perseverance may be an effect of the rise of the larynx from its lowered position in Ngiti and Lendu, which takes place during the initial part of the vowel. No similar perseverance would be expected in Ikwere, which, as discussed above, has no detectable larynx lowering.

Figure 13b presents comparable data for b, $ɓ$, and m. The f_0 traces of these sounds show variants of the rise-fall-rise pattern observed with '$ɓ$, though to a lesser extent. Thus, f_0 values peak just prior to consonant release (point 0), drop at release (point 1), and then climb along a gradually rising high tone ramp (point 2 onward). However, the explosive b starts at a much lower f_0 value than do $ɓ$ and m (point -2), in agreement with the inherently lower pitch usually observed in voiced obstruents.

What do these data show us, then, about the nature of the contrast between nonexplosive '$ɓ$, $ɓ$ and the explosives p, b? The f_0 peak at point 0, immediately preceding release, is especi-ally revealing in this regard: it is highest in '$ɓ$, next highest in $ɓ$, and lowest in b. These differences correlate directly with observed differences in pressure drop across the glottis, which, assuming constant subglottal pressure, should be highest in '$ɓ$ due to its negative air pressure, next highest in $ɓ$ in which oral air pressure is equal to atmospheric pressure, and lowest in b, due to its positive oral air pressure. Theoretically, greater pressure drop is expected to increase transglottal airflow and thus to raise f_0.[20]

In sum, the f_0 data can be fully explained on the view that $ɓ$ and '$ɓ$ are nonobstruent stops characterized by negative or zero air pressure during occlusion. This explanation requires no special assumptions regarding vocal fold stiffness. Given the absence of any independently observable evidence of such stiffness, it can be concluded that such a state, if present at all, is minimal and unlikely to be responsible for the aerodynamic properties of these sounds.

4.6 Are $ɓ$ and '$ɓ$ lenis stops?

Could $ɓ$ and '$ɓ$ be alternatively viewed as lenis stops, as have occasionally been reported in African languages? If this proved to be the correct analysis, their reduced oral air pressure could be considered a secondary effect of a more basic feature [+ lenis]. In that case the feature [− obstruent] would be redundant, and possibly unnecessary.

The terms "fortis" and "lenis" (or "tense" and "lax") have been used in a variety of senses in the literature. Most commonly, they are employed as broad terms to cover a variety of realizations. In the case of fortis sounds these include voicelessness, aspiration, longer duration, greater air pressure, and greater muscular tension; in the case of lenis sounds, they include voicing, lack of aspiration, shorter duration, lower pressure, and weaker tension. In a recent, comprehensive review of this feature, Jessen (1998) suggests that the most widely-accepted common denominator of the fortis/lenis distinction is duration: in most accounts, fortis sounds differ from lenis sounds in having relatively greater duration. Other properties associated with this feature can, Jessen argues, be best understood as contributing to, or resulting from, these durational differences.

The distinction between *p* and '*ḅ* on the one hand and *b* and *ḅ* on the other shows some of the secondary characteristics of the fortis/lenis distinction. The first member of each pair is produced with positive oral air pressure and greater muscular tension around the lips, and the second with zero or negative air pressure and a general laxing of lip tension. The differences in muscular tension are easily confirmed by external examination of the lips and surrounding tissues (see further discussion below). In addition, while *p* may sometimes be realized with aspiration, '*ḅ* never is.

To determine whether '*ḅ* and *ḅ* might be distinguished from *p* and *b* by the feature fortis/lenis, 10 repetitions of words containing each were recorded in a carrier sentence, and the durations of the stops (including burst and voicing lag, when present) were measured. Values for *m* (the nasal allophone of *ḅ*) are given for comparison. Results are shown in Figure 14.[21]

	p	b	'ḅ	ḅ	m
duration (ms)	110.8	90.5	102.4	103.9	96.1
s. d.	9.9	7.4	6.3	7.0	5.5

Figure 14: Average durations and standard deviations of *p b 'ḅ ḅ m* in words spoken in the frame *kă_ṁḅá lâ* 'say X twice' (N = 10).

These results show that *p* and *b* are not both longer than '*ḅ* and *ḅ*, as the fortis/lenis feature would require. Though *p* averages about 8 ms longer than '*ḅ*, there is considerable overlap in their values.

Moreover, the voiced explosive b is about 13 ms *shorter* than its nonexplosive counterpart ḅ. Indeed, b is shorter than m, which would normally be considered a lenis sound.

It seems, then, that the two sets of stops 'ḅ/ḅ and p/b are not reliably distinguished by the feature fortis/lenis. It is possible, instead, that some of the fortis/lenis stop contrasts reported in the literature may actually reflect a more basic obstruent/nonobstruent distinction, as Stewart (1989) has already suggested. The fact that ḅ and 'ḅ share a lax articulation can be understood as a strategy for allowing passive expansion of the vocal tract walls during occlusion, facilitating realization of the feature [− obstruent].[22]

4.7 How is air pressure regulated in the production of ḅ and 'ḅ?

We have so far seen that 'ḅ and ḅ are not produced with larynx lowering, and that while 'ḅ is glottalized, ḅ shows no clear evidence of any special glottal state. The obvious question is, then: how is air pressure regulated in these sounds? Several possibilities can be considered. We have already pointed out (section 2) that air pressure is regulated in ordinary voiced stops by a variety of cavity-expanding mechanisms, including, but not limited to, larynx lowering. As far as implosives are concerned, Maddieson has suggested: "No measurements have been done to confirm the occurrence of oral cavity expansion by tongue movement, jaw lowering or use of the cheeks in production of implosives... Nonetheless, the theory that such expansion occurs is plausible and appealing" (1984: 119).

Let us consider, then, some of the other mechanisms that might be employed in the Ikwere nonexplosives. As noted earlier, oral cavity expansion can be achieved by either passive or active means. *Passive* oral cavity expansion involves the relaxation of the soft tissues of the vocal tract walls, including those of the lips, cheeks, and/or throat. If these tissues are relaxed, any air pressure increases in the oral cavity will tend to distend them, increasing vocal tract volume and thus tending to keep oral air pressure constant. The importance of this effect in the production of a labial stop was demonstrated in the model shown in Figure 2, and there is evidence of this mechanism in Ikwere. In the production of 'ḅ and ḅ, as shown clearly in the videos, the lips are rounded and held loosely together in a poutlike configuration, with no visible evidence of muscular tension; in the production of *p* and *b*, in contrast, the lips are spread and pressed firmly together in a "smirk", with evident tensing of the surrounding musculature, as revealed in the characteristic vertical creases visible along the sides of the spread lips. These differences in muscular tension, easily visible in normal speech, are consistent from utterance to utterance, and correspond to differences in lip protrusion, and hence in vocal tract length. They can be best appreciated by examining overlaid profile views of comparable points in the production of these sounds. Figure 15 show representative examples of the stops 'ḅ (solid line) and *p* (dashed line) as produced in the words à'ḅá and àpá. Each trace shows the maximally protruded lip position for each sound, occurring about halfway through the closure. The lips are visibly more protruded in 'ḅ than in *p*.

Active vocal tract expansion is achieved by increasing the volume of the oral cavity along one or more dimensions. Apart from lip protrusion as just noted, we have found some evidence that jaw lowering may contribute to regulating air pressure in Ikwere. Figure 10 showed that the mandible is lowered toward the end of the closure portions of 'ḅ and ḅ (compare points a and b). Since the oral cavity is closed during this period of time (apart from leakage at the vibrating glottis), such lowering will tend to lower oral air pressure.[23]

What other factors might be involved in regulating air pressure in Ikwere? We have found no direct evidence of tongue root advancement, velum raising, or any other mechanism of pharyngeal expansion that might distinguish the nonexplosives from the explosives.[24] One suggestion is that strong velarization (i.e., tongue body retraction) may somehow increase oral cavity volume sufficiently to create an ingressive airstream at release (Catford 1977: 36). In fact, a number of languages have been reported in which

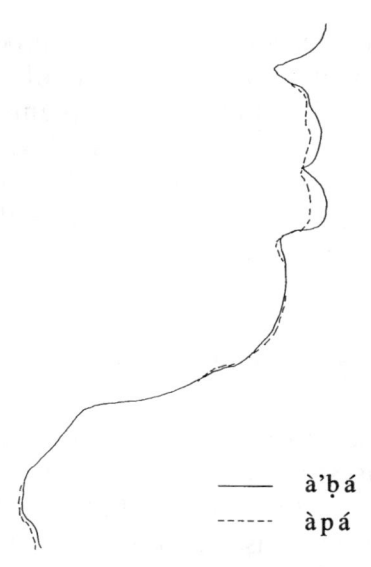

Figure 15: Overlaid profile views of comparable points in the production of the stops 'ɓ (solid line) and p (dashed line) as produced in the words à'ɓá and àpá.

implosives are produced, at least in part, by tongue retraction with or without larynx lowering:

- In Mbatto (Ngula), implosives are said to be produced by larynx lowering and/or the retraction of the base of the tongue (Grassias, 1983: 479)
- In Ebrié, the implosives [ɓ] and [ɗ] are said to be produced by retracting the tongue (Bole-Richard, 1983b: 331)
- In one Igbo dialect, it has been reported that the labial implosive is produced by jaw lowering or tongue retraction rather than by lowering the glottis (De Boeck, 1948, cited by Anyawu, 1998: 27)

These are admittedly impressionistic reports. However, MRI tracings of the bilabial implosive in Mangbetu reproduced by Demolin (1995: 378) show this sound to be strongly velarized, even though it does not, according to Demolin, arise from a labial-velar sound historically. Velarization is not a necessary accompaniment of implosives; for example, Ladefoged (1968: 7) states that implosives are not velarized in Degema and Ijo. It appears, however, that velarization accompanies the production of implosives in some languages, though it still remains to be explained whether and how it can be used to expand oral cavity volume. We have not obtained MRI tracings or other direct evidence of velarization in Ikwere, but auditory and acoustic evidence suggests that 'ḅ and ḅ are at least somewhat velarized.

4.8 Summary: Ikwere nonexplosive stops as nonobstruents

We conclude that the Ikwere stops 'ḅ, ḅ are members of a natural class of [− obstruent] stops, characterized (among other properties noted in this section) by the absence of air pressure buildup behind the oral closure and the consequent absence of noise turbulence at their release. As observed in §4.1, these stops pattern as a natural class with sonorants in that they take nasal allophones before nasal vowels. It is perhaps remarkable that 'ḅ and ḅ form any kind of natural class at all, given the dramatic difference in their glottal articulations. That they do suggests that the feature [− obstruent] may play a central role in phonological patterning.

5. Nonexplosive stops as [− obstruent], [− sonorant] sounds

Let us now consider the phonological behavior of nonexplosive stops. If all such sounds are [− obstruent], as we have proposed, we expect them to behave like other nonobstruent sounds. We first review several respects in which nonexplosive stops pattern with sonorants. We then consider other respects in which they pattern instead with obstruents, and suggest how this apparent contradiction can be resolved in a feature analysis.

Nonexplosive stops pattern with sonorant consonants, notably nasals and laterals, in many respects. First of all, nonexplosive stops, like sonorants, show a wide tendency to be nasalized in nasal vowel contexts. In Ebrié (Bole-Richard, 1983b), for example, /ɓ/ and the sonorants /l y w/ are nasalized to [m n ɲ ŋ], respectively, before and after nasal vowels. In Gbaya (Moñino, 1995), /ɓ/ and /ɗ/ are realized as glottalized implosives before oral vowels but as glottalized nasals before nasal vowels: compare [ɓàà] 'dismember' with ['màà] 'rainy season'. In Ikwere, as will be recalled, the nonobstruent consonants, including /ḅ 'ḅ/ and all sonorants, are realized as oral before oral vowels and nasal before nasal vowels. Such examples can be easily multiplied. In these and many other languages, nonobstruents are nasalized in the context of nasal vowels while obstruents are not. The resistance of obstruents to nasalization is explained by the incompatibility of the increase in air pressure required for obstruent production with the velum lowering required for nasalization (Ohala & Ohala, 1993: 227−231).

Secondly, and for similar reasons, nonexplosive stops, as well as sonorants, are widely disfavored in nasal-stop clusters, where in many languages only explosive stops may appear. This constraint is especially strong in tautosyllabic clusters (i.e., pre- and postnasalized stops). A few examples will suffice. Implosives and liquids are excluded in prenasalized stops in Ngiti (Kutsch-Lojenga, 1994) and Seereer-Siin (McLaughlin, 1992−4). In Gwari, the implosive stop /ɓ/ and liquids are excluded in postnasalized stops (Hyman & Magaji, 1970). Maddieson's cross-linguistic database of 451 phoneme systems (1992) includes 57 languages with pre- or post-nasalized explosive stops, 53 languages with implosive stops, but no languages with pre- or post-nasalized implosives. In Fula (Pulaar), implosives do not occur in prenasalized stops, though they do occur after nasals in a preceding syllable (Paradis, 1992). There is much evidence, then, that implosives are strongly disfavored in nasal clusters, especially when they are tautosyllabic. The same is true of sonorant consonants: nasal + consonant clusters such as *nr*, *nl*, *ny*, *nw* tend to be absent in languages that admit prenasalized stops.[25]

Thirdly, as discussed in section 4.6, nonexplosive stops, as well as sonorants, are widely excluded from the class of "depressor consonants" which in many languages have a tone-lowering effect on adjacent vowels (see Bradshaw, 1999, for a review). In many West African languages, consonants fall into two classes depending on their tonal influence, voiced obstruents having a tone-lowering effect, while other consonants do not. Implosives, when present, usually fall into the non-lowering class, and occasionally raise tone. For example, in Ega, a language with implosives at five places of articulation, voiced obstruents lower high tones and prevent the rise of low tones to mid, while implosives do not (Bole-Richard, 1983a). In Chadic languages, low tones often occur predictably after initial voiced obstruents except for glottalized sounds, including implosives (Wolff, 1987). Some, such as Masa, have a third class of "tone raisers" including implosives and voiceless consonants which exclude low tones on a following vowel. The exclusion of implosives and other nonexplosive stops from the class of tone-depressors can be explained by their aerodynamic properties, as discussed in §4.5.

Fourthly, as noted by Kaye (1981) and others, nonexplosive stops are often in complementary distribution with liquids, and may alternate with them. In Ebrié, for example, the phoneme otherwise realized as [l] in oral contexts is realized as [ɖ] before high vocoids (Bole-Richard, 1983b). Nonexplosive stops and liquids are commonly cognate in closely-related languages, where e.g. [ɖ] in one language may correspond to [l] in another.

Fifthly, as pointed out by Creissels (1994), the usual value of voicing in nonexplosives, as in sonorants, is [+ voice]. As noted in the earlier discussion, this fact is related to the absence of pressure buildup during the occlusion. Although a few languages have voiceless nonexplosives, these sounds, like Ikwere 'ḅ, typically have a brief period of prevoicing before release.

All these examples of the patterning of nonexplosive stops with sonorants can be related to the fact that both types of sounds lack a buildup of oral air pressure, consistent with their characterization as [− obstruent] sounds.

Given this patterning, one might also be tempted to conclude that nonexplosive stops are members of the class of *sonorants*. This would follow from the commonly-held view that [− obstruent] is strictly equivalent to [+ sonorant]. However, there are significant respects in which nonexplosive stops fail to pattern with sonorants, suggesting that this conclusion may be incorrect.

For example, unlike true sonorants (vowels, liquids, nasals), nonexplosive stops such as the implosives ɓ and ɗ do not appear to function as syllabic sounds in any language. In contrast, not only vowels but liquids and nasals commonly assume the function of syllable peak. Moreover, we know of no languages in which nonexplosive stops bear tone or pitch-accent, even in the syllable coda. These properties may be related to the fact that nonexplosive stops, like most obstruents, are low-amplitude sounds, bearing very little "sonority" in whatever sense we might wish to give this term.

Indeed, nonexplosive stops tend to pattern with obstruents in terms of most of their sonority-related distributional properties. Thus, like other obstruents, they favor syllable onsets and disfavor syllable codas. In some languages, they may precede liquids in syllable-initial clusters, a position in which sonorants are disallowed; in Lendu, for example, implosives, like explosives, cluster with liquids in the syllable onset in words like *blŭ* 'put on heaps', *ɓlŭ* 'have an empty stomach', and *'ɓlŭ* mellow' (Dimmendaal, 1986). In other languages, obstruents and implosives are excluded as the first member of word-internal consonant clusters, where only sonorants are allowed. In Hausa, for example, underlying C_aC_b sequences whose first member is an obstruent or implosive commonly simplify to a geminate C_bC_b: *zàaf-záafáa* → *zàzzáafáa* hot', *káɗ-kàɗáa* → *kákkàɗáa* 'keep beating', while sonorants stay in place: *fàrkáa* 'paramour' (Newman, 1987). In Fula, the first member of a coronal cluster must be more sonorous than the second. Liquids and nasals may therefore precede stops (*ld, nd*), but stops, including implosives, may not (*ɗd, *ɗt). Phoneme sequences violating this generalization are subject to repair operations such as gemination, as in the example *mɔɗ-t-a* → *mɔtta* 'to swallow again' (Paradis, 1992).

In view of such facts, taking up a suggestion by Stewart (1989),[26] it seems appropriate to view nonexplosive stops as neither obstruents nor sonorants, but an intermediate class of [− obstruent, − sonorant] sounds. In this view, [± obstruent] and [± sonorant] are two separate features, which combine to yield a three-way classification of explosive stops (A), nonexplosive stops

(B), and true sonorants (C, including nasal stops and laterals) as shown in Figure 16.

	A	B	C
obstruent	+	−	−
sonorant	−	−	+

Figure 16: Feature classification of stops

For such a proposal to be tenable, the two features must have separate definitions, consistent with the phonetic and phonological properties of the sounds they designate. It has already been suggested that [± obstruent] should be defined in terms of air pressure buildup in the oral cavity. But what about [± sonorant]? Here an acoustic definition appears more appropriate, in keeping with the fact that implosives are observed to pattern with obstruents in terms of sonority-related generalizations. Ladefoged has argued that the class of sonorants can be given a unified definition only at the auditory level: sonorant sounds, in his proposal, are those having a periodic, well-defined formant structure (1997: 615). This definition applies to voiced nasals and approximants, while excluding both oral stops (which lack a formant structure) and voiceless sounds (which lack periodicity, i.e. voicing). While nonexplosive stops are usually voiced, they lack the formant structure required by the definition of [± sonorant]. If sonority rank is defined by the sum of sonority-related features borne by a segment, as proposed by Clements (1990), the low rank of nonexplosive stops on the sonority scale, as discussed above, receives a direct explanation: nonexplosives are identical to obstruents in terms of all sonority-related feature specifications.[27]

Should the feature combination [+ obstruent, +sonorant] be universally excluded, as Stewart (1989) suggests? Unlike other mutually exclusive feature values such as [spread glottis] and [constricted glottis], such sounds are physically possible: laxly-articulated voiced fricatives such as *z* and *v* often combine the clearly-marked formant structure characteristic of sonorants with the turbulence noise component characteristic of obstruents, and thus qualify as "sonorant obstruents" under the proposed definitions of these features. However, we have so far been unable to find examples of minimal three-way phonemic contrasts among obstruents, sonorants, and a third term which is both of these, such as one between a fully fricative [β$_1$], a fully sonorant (i.e. approximant) [β$_2$], and a "sonorant fricative" [β$_3$]; indeed, even two-way contrasts within this set seem to be unattested. Nor have we found crucial cases in which voiced fricatives pattern with sonorants to the exclusion of obstruents, as such a feature characterization would also predict to be possible (but see Rice, 1993, for possible cases in Athapaskan languages). Unless evidence to this effect is forthcoming, it would seem appropriate to retain Stewart's constraint.

A further question is whether the three-way distinction proposed for stops in Figure 16 is required for continuant sounds as well. Do we ever find a three-way distinction within the class of continuants among obstruents, sonorants and a third type of sound which is *neither* of these? Such sounds would theoretically be produced with no buildup in oral air pressure and without voicing, or without a clearly-marked formant structure. The obvious candidates to fill this slot are the so-called voiceless sonorants, including the laryngeals *h* and *ʔ*. These sounds have been notoriously difficult to classify in feature terms in the past, due to their behavior in some respects as obstruents, in others as sonorants. An analysis of these sounds as [− obstruent, −sonorant] sounds might go some way toward explaining this ambiguity.

6. Summary and discussion

This paper has proposed that the class of nonexplosive stops, that is, implosives and several related sounds including the nonexplosive pulmonic stops of Ikwere, is characterized by the features [− obstruent] and [− sonorant]. What characterizes the class as a whole phonetically is the absence of air pressure buildup during the occlusion phase combined with a lack of well-defined formant structure. This feature characterization explains a wide range of phonetic and phonological properties of these sounds. We are now in a position to return to the questions raised at the outset of this paper:

How many types of nonexplosive stops can be distinguished phonetically? The number of *phonetic* distinctions that can be drawn within the class of nonexplosive stops is large and perhaps openended, as Ladefoged & Maddieson (1996) suggest. It includes not only implosives in the classical sense — sounds produced with a glottalic ingressive airstream — but many other sounds, including the nonexplosive stops ɓ, 'ɓ of Ikwere described above.

How many of these sounds ever contrast with each other phonologically? Within this large and diverse class, at most a two-way phonological distinction has been documented within any single language, one of whose terms is voiced and the other of which is fully glottalized, that is, produced with complete glottal closure. Other imaginable phonation type contrasts within this class, such as voiced implosive vs. laryngealized, or laryngealized vs. preglottalized, appear to be unattested.

How do these sounds pattern phonologically? Nonobstruent stops exhibit two types of behavior: in some respects, they pattern like sonorants, and in others, like obstruents. Their sonorant-like behavior appears related to their aerodynamic properties (lack of air pressure buildup), while their obstruent-like behavior may be related to their auditory properties (lack of sonority).

What is their feature analysis? The dual phonological behavior of nonexplosive stops supports an analysis characterizing the class as a whole as both [−obstruent] and [−sonorant]. Within this class, voiced and voiceless nonexplosives may be distinguished by the features [constricted glottis], and perhaps [−voice], depending on their status in the system. We conclude that no special features such as [suction], [glottalic airstream mechanism], [lowered larynx], and the like are required to distinguish nonexplosive stops from other stops, or to account for other aspects of their phonological patterning.

We conclude by pointing out a more general consequence of our study for phonological feature theory. The results presented here cannot be easily reconciled with versions of feature theory which hold that phonological primes are defined only in articulatory terms, or only in acoustic-auditory terms, as some current views maintain. The feature [± obstruent] is most easily interpreted as an aerodynamically-based articulatory feature based on the presence vs. absence of increased oral air pressure, as its major acoustic correlate, turbulence noise, is often found to be weak or lacking in voiced obstruents.[28] In contrast, [± sonorant] is most easily defined in the acoustic-auditory domain, since it is difficult to find any unique articulatory definition of the class of sonorants as a whole. This result is consistent with the view that phonological features are best understood as couplings of articulatory and acoustic properties (Lieberman, 1970; Halle, 1983; Stevens, 1983, 1989). In some cases it is simpler to define a given feature in terms of its articulatory correlates, and in other cases an acoustic definition may be more straightforward, but we should be careful to avoid the mistake of extrapolating from a few instances of one case or the other to feature theory as a whole. Phonological features link the abstract representations of phonology to physical continua in both the articulatory and acoustic-auditory domains, and both seem to be essential to a complete understanding of phonology/phonetics relations.

Acknowledgements

We would like to thank Dr Lise Crevier-Buchman of the ORL Service 2, Hôpital Européen Georges Pompidou, Paris, for her valuable assistance in helping us to film and interpret the fiberoptic images discussed in section 4. We have also benefited from many valuable questions and suggestions received from participants at LabPhon 7 and other meetings, including Mary Beckman, Bruce Connell, Didier Demolin, Ian Maddieson, Shinji Maeda and Janet Pierrehumbert, as well as the useful comments of an anonymous reviewer. Naturally, all responsibility for the content of this paper remains our own.

Notes

1 Two further types of "nonstandard" stops are not discussed in this paper, since they are fully or partly explosive: ejectives, produced with complete glottal closure and an egressive airstream following the glottal and oral re-

leases, and clicks, produced with a double closure in the oral cavity and an egressive airstream following the release of the posterior closure.

2   The term "oral cavity" is used in this paper to refer to the portion of the vocal tract extending from the larynx to the lips, excluding the nasal cavity.

3   The term "airstream mechanism" is due to Pike (1943). Catford, though using the term "mechanism" in his 1939 paper, later preferred to speak of "initiator types" (1977: 247−8).

4   In modal voicing, the glottis closes completely during part of the cycle, but the vocal folds are not pushed tightly together during the closed phase (Stevens 1998: 59).

5   Chomsky and Halle held that voicing is "spontaneous" when the vocal cords are placed so as to vibrate spontaneously in response to an unimpeded airflow. When the airflow is impeded, as in obstruents, air pressure builds up behind the constriction in the oral cavity, reducing airflow velocity across the glottis. Under this condition, supplementary adjustments must be made if vocal cord vibration is to be maintained. Chomsky and Halle speculated that vibration may be facilitated by increasing the size or duration of the glottal opening on each glottal cycle; however, this speculation has not been confirmed in subsequent work (see e.g. Ladefoged, 1971: 109−110).

6   The device used for obtaining air pressure measurements was PCQuirer, a pressure and airflow measurement apparatus manufactured by SciCon, Los Angeles, CA. Speech produced with an oral face mask tightly fitted over the mouth is not entirely natural. However, pressure variation over different types of speech sounds proves to be relatively constant from one reading to another, and is assumed here to be representative of more natural speech in relevant respects.

7   Maddieson (1984) draws a distinction between *glottalized* sounds, in which a glottal constriction is superimposed on a pulmonic airstream mechanism, and *glottalic* sounds, produced with the glottalic airstream mechanism. As Catford notes (1977: 248, note 2), it is often useful to extend the term "glottalized" to both types of sounds in phonological descriptions, since they frequently pattern together and are rarely if ever contrastive. This practice is followed here, except when the difference between "glottalic" and "glottalized" sounds is relevant to the discussion.

8   However, Dimmendaal (1986) argues that preglottalized stops represent a genuine phonetic and phonological category distinct from voiceless implosives, citing arguments such as their auditory distinctiveness, the presence of an independent glottalized sonorant series in some languages (such as Lendu), and, assuming them to be basically voiced sounds, their general conformity with the generalization that voiced consonants favor front places of articulation.

9   Ikwere [ik^{w}éré] is spoken by a people of the same name inhabiting the Rivers State in Southeast Nigeria (Osu, 1998). It is classified among the Delta Igboid languages of the Benue-Congo subgroup of Niger-Congo (Williamson, 2000).

The present study is based on the speech of one of the authors (SO), from Ogbakiri [ɔ̀ḅàkìrì].

10 We use a non-IPA symbol (the subscript dot) to transcribe the nonexplosive pulmonic stops 'ḅ and ḅ, as no existing IPA symbol seems completely appropriate for these sounds.
11 Spectrograms and waveforms were made with the CSRE42 speech analysis package (Avaaz Innovations, Inc., Ontario).
12 Some of our traces for ḅ show a small amount of oral air pressure increase, always well below values for b.
13 While these tokens of 'ḅ are typical of most that we have seen of deliberate citation-form utterances, other tokens, especially in utterance-medial position, show a flat air pressure trace and no ingressive (or egressive) airflow.
14 It is possible, as Ian Maddieson suggests to us, that further laboratory tests using specialized equipment might reveal small larynx movements that we were unable to detect in the videos. We do not know whether such minute movements could account for the air pressure and airflow differences we have observed in Ikwere, though they might well contribute to them. It is unlikely, in any case, that field reports of larynx lowering in implosives in other languages are based upon movements undetectable by eye, and it seems reasonable to conclude that the Ikwere stops are produced by a different mechanism than the canonic implosives reported in the descriptive literature.
15 These sounds occurred in the words è'ḅé 'to pray', èpérú 'to take a liquid', èḅê 'to fry', and èbé 'weevil'.
16 Fiberscopic evidence for larynx movement is indirect and must be interpreted with caution. Since the fiberscope rides on the velum, lowering of the velum moves the objective lens closer to the larynx, giving a "zoom in" effect similar to that resulting from larynx raising, and conversely for velum raising. We have noted such effects at transitions between oral and nasal sounds and have excluded them in interpreting our data.
17 The tone-depressing effect of ordinary voiced obstruents is usually attributed to the reduced vocal fold tension associated with larynx lowering (Hombert et al. 1979). According to Stevens (1998: 466–7), larynx lowering tends to shorten the vocal folds by about 2–3 percent, which theoretically decreases vocal fold stiffness in the range of 9–15 percent. This reduction in stiffness facilitates voicing during the closure phase of a stop, and when carried over into an adjacent vowel should lower its fundamental frequency by an estimated 5–7 percent. (See Ewan & Krones, 1974; Ohala, 1978; Traill et al., 1987, and Maddieson, 1997 for further discussion.)
18 Kutsch Lojenga found no clear raising or lowering effects after voiced implosives. She suggests that the greater f_0 rise in voiceless implosives might be due to their full glottal closure, which creates a greater transglottal pressure buildup.
19 The words were àpá 'to climb', à'ḅá 'to sow', èbê 'to touch', èḅê 'to prepare food', and àmá 'to show wisdom', and the frame sentence was kǎ‿ḿḅá lâ 'say X twice'. The lexical falling tones of èbê and èḅê were realized as high tones in this context.

20 In the case of *m*, the small spike at point 0 probably has another cause, since sonorants produced with a continuous airstream passing through the mouth or nose are expected to perturb f_0 minimally or not at all (Hombert et al., 1979: 40).

21 Test words were the same as those given in note 19.

22 We also exclude an analysis in which 'ḅ and ḅ are treated as distinctively rounded stops, as opposed to spread *p* and *b*, for two main reasons. First, our videotapes show that the lips are maximally protruded at the mid-point of 'ḅ and ḅ, rather than at their release. In distinctively rounded sounds, such as Ikwere k^w, g^w, h^w, maximum protrusion coincides with release and is typically prolonged into the vowel, creating a *w*-like transitional sound which provides a cue to the rounding of the consonant. These effects are not present in Ikwere 'ḅ, ḅ. Second, while the feature [obstruent] accounts for a full range of phonetic and phonological properties of 'ḅ and ḅ, including but not limited to the fact that they are produced with lip protrusion (which, by lengthening the vocal tract, tends to reduce oral air pressure), a feature [round] would not account for the other properties of these sounds.

23 Our videotapes show that *p* and *b* are also produced with some jaw lowering before release of the lip constriction. However, a frame-by-frame examination of the data suggests that 'ḅ and ḅ are produced with a faster descent of the lower lip than are *p* and *b*, perhaps due to the fact that the lower lip drops to a lower position after the release of 'ḅ, ḅ than it does after *p* and *b* over the same period of time, creating a larger lip aperture at the beginning of the following vowel. These differences, together with differences in lip protrusion at release, may be responsible for the rapidly rising formant transitions observed at the release of 'ḅ and ḅ (see Figures 6 and 7), which provide one of the main auditory cues distinguishing 'ḅ and ḅ from their explosive counterparts.

24 Our fiberoptic images show that the epiglottis moves forward during the stop phase of 'ḅ and ḅ, but it is also advanced during the stop phase of *p* and *b*.

25 Some West African languages, such as Igbo and Ikwere, appear to contradict this generalization. However, in these languages the sounds written *n*, *m*, etc. before liquids, glides and other consonants are tone-bearing and probably represent nasal vowels, rather than true consonants. In some other languages allowing *n*, *m* before liquids and glides, such as Ganda (Luganda), the nasal constitutes a tone-bearing mora. As these cases do not involve true consonant clusters, they do not constitute exceptions to the above statement.

26 Stewart's discussion pertains primarily to what he calls "lenis" stops, but he takes these sounds to be comparable to implosives in relevant respects (1989: 232−3).

27 The sonority-defining features, in Clements' proposal, are [+ sonorant], [+ approximant], and [+ vocoid], the latter corresponding to the more familiar [− consonantal].

28 Recall, for example, the spectrogram of Ikwere [b] in Figure 6, showing a weak transient at the stop release but no noise burst as such.

References

Anyawu, R.-J.
    1998   *Aspects of Igbo Grammar.* Hamburg: Lit Verlag.

Beach, D. M.
    1938   *The Phonetics of the Hottentot Language.* Cambridge: Heffer.

Bell-Berti, F.
    1975   Control of pharyngeal cavity size for English voiced and voiceless stops. *Journal of the Acoustical Society of America*, **57**, 456−61.

Bole-Richard, R.
    1983 a   Ega. In G. Hérault (ed.), *Atlas des langues kwa de Côte d'Ivoire*, Tome **1**: Monographies, (pp. 359−401). Abidjan: ILA.

Bole-Richard, R.
    1983 b   Ebrié. In G. Hérault (ed.), *Atlas des langues kwa de Côte d'Ivoire*, Tome **1**: Monographies, (pp. 307−57). Abidjan: ILA.

Bradshaw, M.
    1999   A crosslinguistic study of consonant-tone interaction. PhD dissertation, Ohio Sate University.

Campbell, L.
    1973   On glottalic consonants. *International Journal of American Linguistics*, **39**, 44−6.

Catford, J. C.
    1939   On the classification of stop consonants. *Le Maître Phonétique* (3rd series), **65**, 2−5. Reprinted in W. E. Jones & J. Laver (eds.), *Phonetics in Linguistics: A Book of Readings*, London: Longmans, 1973.

Catford, J. C.
    1947   Consonants produced with a closed glottis. *Le Maître Phonétique*, 3rd series 87.

Catford, J. C.
    1977   *Fundamental Problems in Phonetics.* Edinburgh: Edinburgh University Press and Bloomington: Indiana University Press.

Chomsky, N. & Halle, M.
    1968   *The Sound Pattern of English.* New York: Harper & Row.

Clements, G. N.
    1990   The role of the sonority cycle in core syllabification. In J. Kingston & M. E. Beckman (eds.), *Papers in Laboratory Phonology 1: Between the Grammar and the Physics of Speech*, (pp. 283−333). Cambridge: Cambridge University Press.

Clements, G, N. & Osu, S.
    in preparation   Nasals and nasalization in Ikwere. Paper read at the 3rd World Conference on African Linguistics (WOCAL 3), Lome, August 2000.

Creissels, D.
  1994   Aperçu sur les structures phonologiques des langues négro-africaines. 2nd edition. Grenoble: ELLUG, Université Stendhal.
De Boeck, P. L. B.
  1948   Kp et gb dans les langues bantou septentrionales. *Zaire*, **2**.
Demolin, D.
  1995   The phonetics and phonology of glottalized consonants in Lendu. In B. Connell & A. Arvaniti (eds.), *Phonology and Phonetic Evidence: Papers in Laboratory Phonology* **4**, (pp. 368–385). Cambridge: Cambridge University Press.
Dimmendaal, G, J.
  1986   Language typology, comparative linguistics, and injective consonants in Lendu. *Afrika und Übersee*, **69**, 161–192.
Ewan, W, G. & Krones, R.
  1974   Measuring larynx movement using the thyroumbro-meter. *Journal of Phonetics*, **2**, 327–35.
Goyvaerts, D.
  1988   Glottalized consonants: a new dimension. *Belgian Journal of Linguistics*, **3**, 97–102
Grassias, A.
  1983   Le m'batto (ngula). In G. Hérault (ed.), *Atlas des langues kwa de Côte d'Ivoire*, Tome **1**: Monographies. (pp. 465–490). Abidjan: ILA.
Greenberg, J, H.
  1970   Some generalizations concerning glottalic consonants, especially implosives. *International Journal of American Linguistics*, **36**, 123–145.
Halle, M.
  1983   On distinctive features and their articulatory implementation. *Natural Languages and Linguistic Theory*, **1**, 91–105.
Halle, M.
  1992   Features. In W. Bright (ed.), *Oxford international encyclopedia of linguistics*, Vol. 3, (pp. 207–212). New York: Oxford University Press.
Halle, M & Clements, G, N.
  1983   *Problem Book in Phonology*. Cambridge, MA.: MIT Press.
Harris, J. G.
  1999   States of the glottis for voiceless plosives. In J. J. Ohala, Y. Hasegawa, M. Ohala, D. Granville, & A. C. Bailey (eds.), *Proceedings of the XIV International Congress of Phonetic Sciences*, (pp. 2041–2044). Berkeley: University of California.
Haudricourt, A. G.
  1950   Les consonnes préglottalisées en Indochine. *Bulletin de la Société de Linguistique de Paris*, **46**, 172–182.

Hombert, J.-M., Ohala, J. J. & Ewan, W. G.
1979 Phonetic explanations for the development of tones. *Language*, **55** Vol **1**, 37–58.

Hyman, L. M. & Magaji, D. J.
1970 *Essentials of Gwari grammar* (Occasional Publication **27**). Ibadan: Institute of African Studies, University of Ibadan.

Jessen, M.
1998 *Phonetics and Phonology of Tense and Lax Obstruents in German.* Amsterdam: John Benjamins.

Jessen, M. & Roux, J. C.
2002 Voice quality differences associated with stops and clicks in Xhosa. *Journal of Phonetics*, **30**, 1–52.

Kagaya, R.
1974 A fiberscopic and acoustic study of the Korean stops, affricates, and fricatives. *Journal of Phonetics*, **2**, 161–180.

Kaye, J.
1981 Implosives as liquids. *Studies in African Linguistics*, Supplement 8, 78–81.

Kutsch Lojenga, C.
1994 *Ngiti: a Central-Sudanic language of Zaire.* Cologne: Rüdiger Köppe.

Ladefoged, P.
1967 Linguistic phonetics. *UCLA Working Papers in Phonetics*, **6**.

Ladefoged, P.
1968 *A Phonetic Study of West African Languages.* 2nd edition. Cambridge: University Press.

Ladefoged, P.
1971 *Preliminaries to Linguistic Phonetics.* Chicago: The University of Chicago Press.

Ladefoged, P.
1997 Linguistic phonetic descriptions. In W. J. Hardcastle & J. Laver (eds.), *The Handbook of Phonetic Sciences*, (pp. 589–618). Oxford: Blackwell.

Ladefoged, P. & Maddieson, I.
1996 *The Sounds of the World's Languages.* Oxford: Basil Blackwell.

Ladefoged, P., Williamson, K, Elugbe, B. & Uwulaka, A.
1976 The stops of Owerri Igbo, *Studies in African Linguistics*, Supplement 6, 147–63.

Lex, G.
1994 *Le dialecte peul du Fouladou (Casamance - Sénégal): Étude phonétique et phonologique.* Thèse pour le nouveau doctorat, Université de Paris 3 (Sorbonne-Nouvelle). (Published by Lincom, Munich)

Lieberman, P.
1970 Towards a unified linguistic theory. *Linguistic Inquiry*, **1**, 307–22.

Lindau, M.
    1984   Phonetic differences in glottalic consonants. *Journal of Phonetics* **54**, 147−55.
Lindsey, G, Hayward, K. & Haruna, A.
    1992   Hausa glottalic consonants: a laryngographic study. *Bulletin of the School of Oriental and African Studies*, **LV 3**, 511−527.
Maddieson, I.
    1984   *Patterns of Sounds*. Cambridge: Cambridge University Press.
Maddieson, I.
    1992   UCLA Phonological Segment Inventory Database, version 1.1. Los Angeles: Dept. of Linguistics, UCLA.
Maddieson, I.
    1997   Phonetic universals. In W. J. Hardcastle & J. Laver (eds.), *The Handbook of Phonetic Sciences*, (pp. 619−39). Oxford: Blackwell.
McLaughlin, F.
    1992−4   Consonant mutation in Seereer-Siin. *Studies in African Linguistics*, **23**, 279−313.
Moñino, Y.
    1995   *Le proto-gbaya: Essai d'application de la méthode comparative à un groupe de 21 langues oubangiennes*. Paris: Peeters.
Newman, P.
    1987   Hausa and the Chadic languages. In B. Comrie (ed.), *The World's Major Languages*, (pp. 705−723). New York: Oxford University Press.
Ohala, J. J.
    1978   The production of tone. In V. A. Fromkin (ed.), *Tone: a Linguistic Survey*, (pp. 5−39). New York: Academic Press.
Ohala, J. J. & Ohala, M.
    1993   The phonetics of nasal phonology: theorems and data. In M. K. Huffmann & R. A. Krakow (eds.), *Phonetics and phonology, Volume 5: Nasals, nasalization, and the velum*, (pp. 225−249). New York: Academic Press.
Ohala, J. J. & Riordan, C. J.
    1979   Passive vocal tract enlargement during voiced stops. In J. J. Wolf & D. H. Klatt (eds.), *Speech Communication Papers*, (pp. 89−92). New York: Acoustical Society of America.
Osu, S.
    1998   *Opérations énonciatives et problématique du repérage: cinq particules verbales ikwéré*. Paris: L'Harmattan.
Paradis, C.
    1992   *Lexical Phonology and Morphology: The Nominal Classes in Fula*. New York: Garland Publishing, Inc.
Pike, K.
    1943   *Phonetics*. Ann Arbor: University of Michigan Press.

Pinkerton, S.
   1986   Quichean (Mayan) glottalized and nonglottalized stops: A phonetic study with implications for phonological universals. In J. J. Ohala & J. J. Jaeger (eds.), *Experimental Phonology*, (pp. 125–139). Orlando: Academic Press.
Rice, K.
   1993   A re-examination of the feature [sonorant]: the status of 'sonorant obstruents'. *Language*, **69**, 308–344.
Roux, J.
   1991   On ingressive glottalic and velaric articulations in Xhosa. *Proceedings of the XII International Congress of Phonetic Sciences,* Vol **3**, (pp. 158–161). Aix-en-Provence: Université de Provence.
Sawashima, M. & Hirose, H.
   1983   Laryngeal gestures in speech production. In P. F. MacNeilage (ed.), *The Production of Speech*, (pp. 11–38). New York: Springer.
Stevens, K. N.
   1983   Design features of speech sound systems. In P. F. MacNeilage (ed.), *The Production of Speech*, (pp. 247–261). New York: Springer.
Stevens, K. N.
   1989   On the quantal nature of speech. *Journal of Phonetics*, **17**, 3–46.
Stevens, K. N.
   1997   Articulatory-acoustic-auditory relationships. In W. J. Hardcastle & J. Laver (eds.), *The Handbook of Phonetic Sciences*, (pp. 462–506). Oxford: Blackwell.
Stevens, K. N.
   1998   *Acoustic Phonetics*. Cambridge, MA: MIT Press.
Stewart, J. M.
   1989   Kwa. In J. Bendor-Samuel (ed.), *The Niger-Congo Languages*, (pp. 217–245). New York: Lanham.
Traill, A., Khumalo, J. S. M. & Fridjhon, P.
   1987   Depressing facts about Zulu, *African Studies*, **46** Vol **2**, 255–74.
Trubetzkoy, N.
   1969   *Principles of Phonology*. English translation of *Grundzüge der Phonologie* (1939). Berkeley: University of California Press.
Westbury, J. R.
   1983   Enlargement of the supraglottal cavity and its relation to stop consonant voicing. *Journal of the Acoustical Society of America*, **73**, 1322–1336.
Williamson, K.
   2000   Reconstructing Proto-Igboid obstruents. In V. Carstens & F. Parkinson (eds.), *Advances in African Linguistics* (Trends in African Linguistics, **4**). Trenton, N. J.: Africa World Press.

Wolff, E.
    1987   Consonant-tone interference in Chadic and its implications for a theory of tonogenesis in Afroasiatic. In D. Barreteau & L. Sorin-Barreteau (eds.), *Langues et cultures dans le bassin du lac Tchad*, (pp. 193–216). Paris: Editions de l'Orstom.

Wright, R. & Shryock, A.
    1993   The effects of implosives on pitch in SiSwati, *Journal of the International Phonetic Association*, **23**, 16–23.

Assimilatory processes and aerodynamic factors

Maria-Josep Solé

Abstract

This paper explores the role of aerodynamic factors in some assimilatory processes, focussing specifically on the assimilation of lingual fricatives to following tongue-tip trills in a variety of languages. It tests the hypothesis that the extensive anticipatory movements for the trill, directed to attain its highly constrained production requirements, override the aerodynamic conditions for frication. Articulatory, acoustic and aerodynamic analyses of sequences of fricatives plus trills were made for three Catalan speakers. Gradient and complete assimilation of lingual fricatives to trills was found in the articulatory data. Palatal fricatives proved to be more resistant to assimilation than alveolars. Phrasal boundaries proved to have an effect on fricative to trill assimilation. Aerodynamic analysis showed that trills are more constrained aerodynamically than voiced fricatives. The time required to achieve the pressure drop at the oral constriction for audible frication was in the range of 50 ms for voiced and 30 ms for voiceless fricatives. Hence, if onset of articulatory movements for the trill reach the articulator within 50 ms from onset of the movements for the voiced fricative, audible friction will not be achieved. Thus the early onset of movements for the trill bleed the postural and aerodynamic requirements to generate frication.

1. Introduction

In the search for the phonetic basis of assimilatory processes, a number of factors have been investigated, including articulatory (Browman & Goldstein, 1990; Recasens, Pallarès & Fontdevila, 1997), auditory (Hume, Johnson, Seo & Tserdanelis, 1999) and perceptual (Ohala, 1990) factors. The work presented here explores the role of aerodynamic factors in some assimilatory processes. Pioneering work by Ohala (1976, 1981) has shown that some assimilatory processes may originate from aerodynamic factors. For example, coarticulatory devoicing of high vowels and glides following voiceless stops results in the affrication of stops (e.g., tea[tˢiː], *venture* [tʃ] < [tj]), due to increased airflow through the open glottis resulting in a higher particle velocity across the narrow oral constriction for high vowels and glides, thus generating audible frication. The higher incidence of velar palatalization (i.e., velar stops becoming palatoalveolar affricates) in voiceless than voiced segments cross-linguistically can also be attributed to the increased airflow through the glottal resistance for voiceless segments (Guion, 1998). Despite evidence of this type, the effect of aerodynamic conditions on assimilation has been little addressed and available assimilatory models do not incorporate an aerodynamic component (but see McGowan & Saltzman, 1995).

This paper reports on a series of experiments directed to ascertain the articulatory and aerodynamic requirements of tongue-tip trills and how such requirements may lead to assimilation of neighboring segments. In particular, we address sequences of lingual fricatives and trills produced with the same articulator, in order to account for the common assimilation of fricatives to following apical trills (e.g., /z, s, ʒ, ʃ/ + /r/ > [rː]), where the fricative disappears in normal, colloquial speech in a variety of languages (such as Catalan, Spanish, and Portuguese).

Tongue-tip trills involve a complex production mechanism requiring finely tuned neuromotor adjustment of various parameters – positioning of the articulators, shape, articulator mass, stiffness and aerodynamic conditions[1] – which accounts for the difficulties lingual trills present to inexperienced (e.g., foreign learners) and immature (e.g., children) speakers, and even to adult native speakers. Such precise requirements make trills very sensitive to variations in the articulatory and aerodynamic conditions, which may result in lack of tongue-tip vibration. Thus, trills are often realized as non-trilled variants, as in Spanish (Blecua, 1999), Toda (Spajic, Ladefoged & Bhaskararao, 1996) and Italian (Ladefoged & Maddieson, 1996), and they often alternate historically, dialectally and allophonically with fricatives, approximants and taps (Solé, in press). The precise articulatory and aerodynamic requirements of lingual trills allow little coarticulation and overlap with conflicting lingual configurations if trilling is to be preserved.

It has been observed that sequences such as Spanish *dos-reales* 'halfpenny' or Catalan *les Rambles* 'the Rambles' are assimilated to a single trill, a long trill [rː] or a sequence [ɹr] ([ɹ] = fricative r) (Navarro Tomás 1980; Recasens 1993). Other examples are presented in (1a, b) (Only the single trill realization is exemplified here, but [rː] and [ɹr] realizations are also possible). The fricative portion of affricates also disappears before a trill, (1b). In dialects of Portuguese with an alveolar trill, final lingual fricatives disappear before [r] (Vázquez & Mendes, 1971), as illustrated in (1c). In a similar vein, varieties of Portuguese with a uvular trill, [ʀ], – involving the tongue dorsum – assimilate dorsal fricatives before trills. In Italian, on the other hand, the fricative is preserved, most probably due to the widespread insertion of epenthetic sounds at consonant release which allows the sequencing (i.e., lack of overlap) of the gestures for the fricative and the trill, as illustrated in (1d). In words such as *Israel*, where the /r/ is coproduced with an epenthetic [d], the trill is commonly detrilled into a tap. Note that in these languages coda fricatives, if they are realized, are voiced before a trill due to regressive voice assimilation.

(1). a. Iberian Spanish
/s (#) r/ *las rojas* [laˈroxas] 'the red ones', *Osram* [ˈoram]
/θ # r/ *voz ronca* [ˌboˈroŋka] 'hoarse voice', *Cruz Roja* [ˌkruˈroxa] 'Red Cross'
b. Catalan
/ʃ # r/ *mateix rotllo* [məte̯(j)ˈrɔλλu] 'same story'
/s # r/ *has rebut* [ə rəˈβut̪] 'you received'
/dʒ # r/ *boig rematat* [ˌbɔ(j)d̪ rəməˈtat̪] 'real crazy'
c. Portuguese
/ʃ # r/ dois requerimentos [ˌdoj rəkriˈmentuʃ] 'two requests'
/ʃ # ʀ/ *dos reis* [du ˈʀɐjʃ] 'of the kings', *Israel* [iʀɐˈɛɫ]
d. Italian
/s # r/ *autobus rosso* [ˌautobusᵊˈrɔsɔ] 'red bus', *Israele* [izᵈraˈɛle], [izᵈraˈɛle]

It should be noted that lingual fricatives assimilate exclusively to following trills involving the same articulator, and are preserved (i.e., retain their fricative quality) in all other contexts.[2] Thus, no fricative assimilation occurs if the two segments involve independent articulators (*e.g.*, Catalan *tuf rar* /f # r/ > [vr] 'funny smell'), since the labiodental constriction for [v] and the movements towards the lingual constriction for [r] can take place simultaneously. There is also no defrication if C2 is not /r/, e.g., *les liles* /s # l/ > [zɫ] 'the purple ones', *les té* /s # t̪/ > [st̪] 'she has them'. C1 other than fricatives accommodates to the constriction location of the trill but remains stable otherwise, e.g., *pot remenar* /t̪ # r/ >[dr] 'he can stir'. The question is then why only lingual fricatives disappear, and why they only disappear before trills. This paper argues that articulatory and aerodynamic competition between these two segments accounts for the trill overriding the requirements for the generation of turbulence for the fricative.

Whereas fricative to trill assimilation is probably an articulatorily gradient process, due to varying amounts of consonant overlap, the perceptual result is mostly categorical, that is, no frication is produced and the percept is commonly that of a trill or a long trill. Indeed, this process has led to reinterpretation in some place-names in Catalan, where the fricative has disappeared in the lexical form, e.g., *Purroi* < etym. *Puigroig* /tʃ + r/ (Alcover & Moll, 1979), *Puigreig* [pu'retʃ] < /tʃ + r/.

In autosegmental phonology, fricative-trill assimilation could be represented as linking the coronal and manner nodes of [z] to the feature specifications of [r], say [−distributed] and [+interrupted] (Jakobson, Fant & Halle, 1952). The long trill would result from delinking the coronal and manner nodes for [z] from its original specifications. This formal representation does not explain why the assimilation should affect only these particular segments, or in what direction and degree it should apply, and falls short of representing reduced articulations, such as the single trill (e.g., /sr/ > [r]), as well as residual or intermediate articulations.

In gestural phonology (Browman & Goldstein, 1986, 1990), the assimilatory process may be described as perturbation of the articulatory trajectory for the fricative due to temporal overlap of the competing configuration for the trill and/or reduction in the temporal and spatial domain of the fricative gesture. Again, why only fricatives disappear, and why they only disappear before trills, remains to be explained. Furthermore, the predicted articulatory blending or intermediate articulation of the two target gestures in cases of same-tier articulations is not found.

In the next section it will be argued that existing models of degree and direction of assimilation cannot account for the assimilatory patterns observed unless aerodynamic factors are considered. In section 3 the articulatory and acoustic result of the assimilation of lingual fricatives to trills and the prosodic factors affecting them are described. The constrained aerodynamic requirements of trills and fricatives are explored in section 4. Finally, it is argued that the extensive anticipatory movements for the trill override the aerodynamic and postural requirements for the acoustic event of frication.

2. Factors affecting assimilatory processes

Sequences of consonants involving the same articulatory structure, the tongue, exhibit various degrees of accommodation depending on a variety of factors interacting in complex ways: compatibility of the lingual configurations, degree of tongue dorsum involvement, constriction degree, time constraints and syllable position. In the present paper it is argued that aerodynamic factors also play a role in assimilatory processes, in particular in fricatives and trills, which are aerodynamically driven sounds.

2.1 Application of these factors to lingual fricative-trill sequences

Sequences of lingual fricatives and trills may have problems with compatibility of the gestures, since two conflicting configurations must overlap. In the case of alveolar fricatives, a raised and advanced tongue dorsum for /s/ (passively raised due to coupling effects with tongue-blade raising), conflicts with predorsum lowering and postdorsum retraction for the trill to allow for the vertical vibration of the tongue-tip (Recasens & Pallarès, 1999). The tongue-tip/blade shape is convex for the fricative (forming a medial groove) and concave for the trill. Lingual fricatives and trills also involve antagonistic stiffness requirements: muscular activation of the tongue tip-blade is required for alveolar fricatives whereas a relaxed articulator is required to vibrate. Overlap of motor commands for the two segments may affect the tongue-tip tension and impair tongue-tip vibration. Conflicting gestures directed to the same articulator may be solved through sequencing the gestures, if there is sufficient time, or adjustments in the articulatory characteristics of the segments.

Adjustment of segments to the context is a function of their degree of articulatory constraint. Both lingual fricatives and trills have been shown to exhibit very narrow postural requirements. Work on coarticulatory resistance (Bladon & Nolan, 1977) and tongue dorsum variability (Hoole, Nguyen & Hardcastle, 1993) has shown that the fricative /s/ involves severely constrained production characteristics which limit allowable articulatory variability and account for fricatives exerting important coarticulatory influence on adjacent segments (Recasens et al., 1997). Tongue-tip trills, however, exhibit more highly constrained articulatory requirements than fricatives. First, trills have stronger coarticulatory effects on neighboring vowels than fricatives, and themselves are less affected by surrounding vowels (Recasens et al., 1997; Recasens & Pallarès, 1999). Second, trills accommodate less to (and are less overlapped by) adjacent consonants involving the same articulator than fricatives (Recasens, 1995, 1999). Third, trills involve antagonistic stiffness conditions for adjacent articulators (active tongue sides and predorsum and relaxed tongue-tip and blade to allow vibration) which require fine neuromotoric control. Such antagonistic stiffness requirements are not present in lingual fricatives.

Syllable position also plays a role in assimilatory effects since the articulatory properties of consonants differ with position in the syllable. Coda consonants involve a larger gestural reduction in time and magnitude (Browman & Goldstein, 1995; Krakow, 1989, 1993; Sproat & Fujimura, 1993) and are more overlapped by following consonants (Byrd, 1996), vis-à-vis onset consonants. Perceptual factors, such as the greater availability of auditory cues and greater auditory salience of onset consonants vis-à-vis coda consonants (Ohala & Kawasaki, 1984; Redford & Diehl, 1999) may also contribute to onset consonants dominating the assimilatory result, as is the case for lingual fricative to trill assimilation.

Syllable position alone, however, does not account for the assimilation of lingual fricatives to trills since onset consonants involving a comparably high degree of constraint as [r], e.g., [ʃ], pull preceding consonants to their place of articulation (i.e., /sʃ/, /rʃ/ > [s̠ʃ], [r̠ʃ] for Catalan (Recasens, 1999), or /sʃ/ > [sʃ, ss̠ʃ, ʃʃ] for English (Holst & Nolan, 1995)), but do not cause coda consonants to disappear. Similarly, competing coda consonants other than fricatives accommodate to the constriction location of C2 = [r] but remain stable otherwise, e.g. [d̠r, l̠r, n̠r] (Recasens, 1999). The test for syllable position effects would be to observe the behaviour of trill + /s, z, ʃ, ʒ/ sequences. However, trills exhibit a limited distribution and pattern of contrast and do not occur in syllable codas contrastively; coda /r/ is realized as a tap (or a fricative).

Time constraints and phrasal boundaries have also been shown to affect degree of assimilation, with tighter time constraints and weaker boundaries resulting in more assimilated forms (Browman & Goldstein, 1990; Holst & Nolan, 1995; Hardcastle, 1985; MacClean, 1973).

2.2 Articulatory models

The 'Degree of Articulatory Constraint' (DAC) model (Recasens et al., 1997, Recasens & Pallarès, 1999) predicts the degree to which a particular segment is likely to affect neighboring segments and the direction of assimilatory effects, on the basis of degree of tongue dorsum involvement and compatibility of the lingual configurations. This model predicts more prominent coarticulatory and assimilatory effects of highly gesturally constrained segments. According to this model, lingual fricatives and trilled /r/s have the highest DAC value, 3, indicating that they are highly constrained and unyielding segments. They also involve conflicting gestures directed to the same articulator. Along the same lines, Dembowski & Westbury (1999) posit a hierarchy of postural constraints among segment articulations, such that those which are more highly constrained and allow lesser variability exert the greatest contextual influence.

Such models correctly predict that the trill would dominate the assimilatory result, due to a higher degree of gestural constraint for the trill. If trills and fricatives have, in fact, similar degrees of articulatory constraint, as in the 'DAC' model, the gesture for the onset consonant, /r/, would prevail (due to articulatory reduction of coda consonants and perceptual factors referred to above). What remains unexplained, however, is why only fricatives disappear whereas other same-articulator segments (e.g., [l, t, d, n]) simply accommodate to the constriction location of the trill. Unless aerodynamic factors are taken into account, a satisfactory explanation for the assimilation of fricatives to trills cannot be provided.

Degree of coarticulation and assimilation is also dependent on aerodynamic factors, in particular in fricatives and trills, which are aerodynamically driven sounds. Both sound types require an articulatory setting for the laryngeal (vocal fold adduction/abduction and tension) and supralaryngeal configurations (tongue positioning, bracing and stricture), and an aerodynamic setting: sufficient pressure drop across the glottis for voiced segments, and across the lingual constriction for frication or tongue-tip vibration. Perturbation of the critical articulatory or aerodynamic requirements for these sounds, due to coproduction with other sounds, may result in lack of frication or tongue-tip trilling. This paper argues that the narrowly constrained positional and aerodynamic requirements for initiating a trill bleed the postural and time requirements for the generation of turbulence for competing fricatives.

3. Articulatory data

Experiment 1 investigates the articulatory and acoustic result of the assimilation of fricatives to trills across different prosodic boundaries to explore the effect of time constraints and syntactic structure on assimilation. Experiment 2 examines the effect of degree of gestural constraint in alveolar vs. palatal fricatives on assimilation.

3.1 Experiment 1: Effect of time constraints on fricative to trill assimilation.

This experiment involved collection of simultaneous electropalatographic (Reading EPG system) and acoustic data for three Catalan

Table 1: Experimental and control materials with boundary type for the first occurrence, (1), and second occurrence, (2), of the target sequences (underlined). Presence (S = stressed) or absence (U = unstressed) of stress on the syllable containing the fricative is also indicated.

Experimental	Stress	Boundary (1)	Boundary (2)
1. A: Què li has recomanat que fés? B: Res (*A: What did you recommend that she do? B: Nothing*)	US	Word +	Sentence //
2. Què li has recomanat que fés? Res? (*What did you recommend that she do? Nothing?*)	US	Word +	Sentence #
3. Que li has recomanat que fés res? (*Did you recommend that she do anything?*)	US	Word +	Phrase /
4. La carta la vas redactar i la vas revisar, oi? (*You wrote and checked the letter, right?*)	SS	Word +	Word +
5. Els 'dos-reals' encara existeixen, oi? (*Half-pennies still exist, right?*)	S	Syllable $	
Control			
1. A: Què li ha recomanat fer [fe]? B: Res (*A: What did he recommend that she do? B: Nothing*)	US	Word +	Sentence //
2. Què li ha recomanat fer [fe]? Res? (*What did he recommend that she do? Nothing?*)	US	Word +	Sentence #
3. Que li ha recomanat fer [fe] res? (*Did he recommend that she do anything?*)	US	Word +	Phrase /
4. La carta la va redactar i la va revisar, oi? (*He wrote and checked the letter, right?*)	SS	Word +	Word +
5. Quan diu borra-ho, ho diu de debó? (*When he says delete it, does he mean that?*)	S	Syllable $	

speakers (DR, MJ and AF) reading a list of meaningful sentences. Materials included /sr/ (the environment for assimilation) between non-high vowels, with prosodic boundary strength and stress manipulated (Table 1). These were contrasted with intervocalic /r/ in matched control utterances. Subjects read the list of sentences five times each. Details appear in Solé (1999). The assimilatory behaviour of fricatives to trills was analyzed auditorily, articulatorily and acoustically.

3.1.1 Analysis technique

The EPG data were converted to Contact Anteriority (CA), Contact Posteriority (CP) and Contact Centrality (CC) index values. Contact indices are the weighted sum of activated electrodes along selected areas of the palate (Fontdevila, Pallarès & Recasens, 1994). Indices of linguopalatal contact activation were calculated at the first contact for the trill. Trill duration was measured for all tokens from onset of the first complete contact for the trill to release of the last contact (e.g., from frame 177 to frame 183, top of Fig. 2), or from point of maximum constriction to release of the constriction for fricative realizations. Duration of the lingual movement toward the consonant in /sr/ and /r/ sequences was measured from the first indication of buildup in the number of tongue-palate contacts towards the alveolar region to the first full closure for /r/. Trill realization in test and control sequences as one-contact, two-contact, three-contact, four-contact or fricative trill was analyzed from the EPG and acoustic data.

3.1.2 Results. Assimilation types by prosodic boundary.

All /sr/ sequences were classified as one of four types based on acoustic and EPG data. Type 1 consisted of assimilated forms with a single or a long trilled /r/ [r, rː] and no fricative or residual frication. Type 2 had no frication for [z], and had /r/ realized as a weak postalveolar fricative ([ɹ̝, ɹ̝ː]) rather than trilled. Cases with a single apicoalveolar contact followed by a fricative, reflecting failing vi-

/sr/ sequences

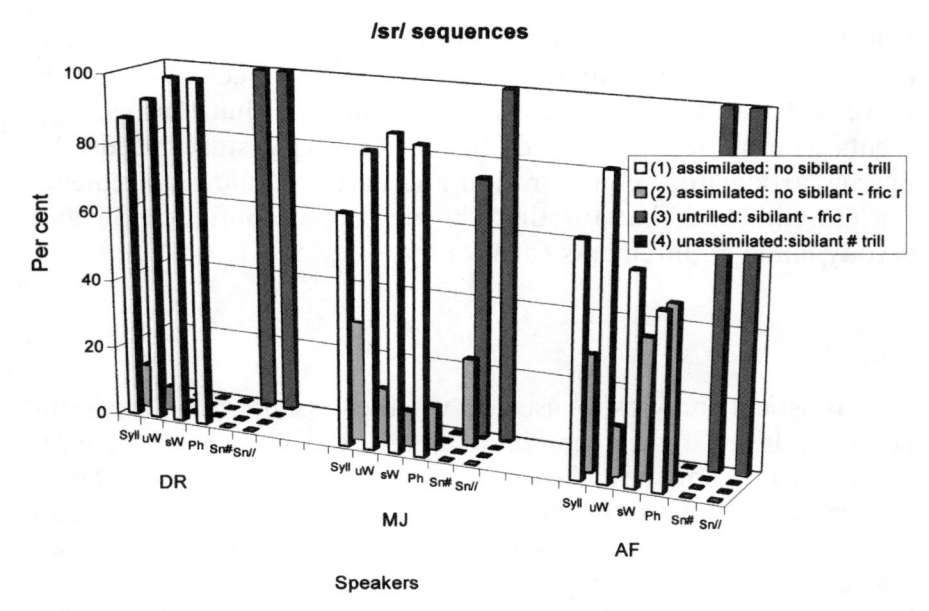

Figure 1: Distribution of assimilation types (z axis) in percentages by boundary conditions (x axis) for each speaker.

bratory motion of the tongue tip, were also classified as Type 2. (This realization most probably corresponds to what is found in the literature as [ɹr].) Type 3 was defined as untrilled sequences with a sibilant present but with the /r/ not trilled ([zɹ]). As will be seen in the next section, fricative [ɹ] is a common realization of both an underlying trill and a trill arising from a sequence /sr/. It should be noted, however, that presence of [z] is associated with lack of trilled /r/, unless there is an intervening pause. Type 4 was defined as unassimilated sequences with the fricative and trill sequenced ([z # r]). All tokens of Type 4 had pauses longer than 70 ms. The distribution of the four types is shown in Fig. 1 by boundary condition and speaker. Types 1 and 2 occur only at weak boundaries, while Type 3 was found only at a pauseless major boundary, and Type 4 only at major boundaries with a pause.

It can be noted that whenever frication for [z] is present, the /r/ is not trilled (type 3), except if there is an intervening pause (type 4), which allows resetting the articulatory configuration for the trill. In turn, whenever a trill is produced, frication is not present (type 1), unless there is an intervening pause. The lack of co-occurrence of frication and trilling seems to indicate that the two segments cannot be coproduced, that is, the [z] gesture bleeds the narrow articulatory configuration and aerodynamic requirements for the trill, and that for the trill bleeds the configuration and aerodynamic requirements for friction.

3.1.3 EPG results

The statistical analyses focused on whether assimilation across minor boundaries was categorical or gradient. The analyses were restricted to minor boundaries since major sentence boundaries showed no assimilation of the fricative to the trill. The hypotheses to be tested were (1) that trills arising from assimilated /sr/ sequences differed from underlying single lexical /r/ (i.e., that assimilation was not complete), and (2) that degree of assimilation in /sr/ sequences across minor boundaries varied with boundary strength (i.e., that assimilation was gradient). These hypotheses were tested by comparing assimilated /sr/ to underlying /r/ across minor boundaries. Two factor ANOVAS with sequence type (/sr/ vs /r/) and boundary type (syllable boundary, unstressed word boundary, stressed word boundary, phrase boundary) as independent variables were performed. The number of observations for the various boundary conditions varied (unstressed word boundary: 6 sentences × 5 repetitions, stressed word boundary: 4 × 5, phrase and syllable boundary: 2 × 5, see Table 1). The tests were performed across items for each condition for each individual speaker (DR, MJ, AF). The dependent variables were trill duration, preceding vowel duration, and indices of alveolar contact activation (CA), posterior contact activation (CP) and central contact activation (CC).

For all speakers and all dependent variables the ANOVAS revealed significant main effects of boundary type at the $p < .01$ level, except in the following cases: CP for speakers DR and AF, and CC for speaker DR were non-significant. This indicates that vowel duration, trill duration, and EPG contact indices vary with the strength of the boundary. Phrase boundaries had longer trills

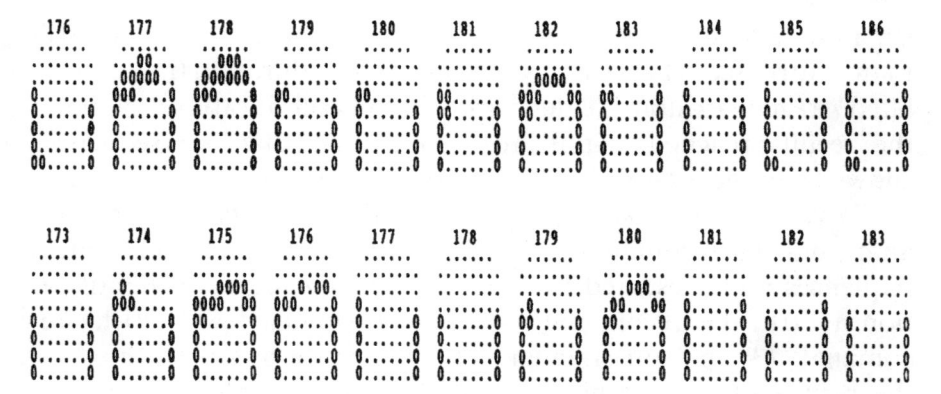

```
176       177       178       179       180       181       182       183       184       185       186
......    ......    ......    ......    ......    ......    ......    ......    ......    ......    ......
          ..00..    ..000..                                            ..0000.
          ..00000.  ..000000.                                          .000...
0.......  000....0  000.....0 00......0 00......0 00......0 000...00  00......0 0.......0 0.......0 0.......0
0.......0 0.......0 0.......0 0.......0 0.......0 00......0 00......0 0.......0 0.......0 0.......0 0.......0
0.......0 0.......0 0.......0 0.......0 0.......0 0.......0 0.......0 0.......0 0.......0 0.......0 0.......0
0.......0 0.......0 0.......0 0.......0 0.......0 0.......0 0.......0 0.......0 0.......0 0.......0 0.......0
00......0 0.......0 0.......0 0.......0 0.......0 0.......0 0.......0 0.......0 0.......0 00......0 00......0

173       174       175       176       177       178       179       180       181       182       183
......    ......    ......    ......    ......    ......    ......    ......    ......    ......    ......
          .0.....   ..0000.   ..0.00.                                  ...000.
          000....   0000..00  000....0  0.......                       .00...00
0.......  0.......0 00......0 0.......0 0.......0 0.......0 0.......0 00......0 00......0 0.......0 0.......0
0.......0 0.......0 0.......0 0.......0 0.......0 0.......0 0.......0 0.......0 0.......0 0.......0 0.......0
0.......0 0.......0 0.......0 0.......0 0.......0 0.......0 0.......0 0.......0 0.......0 0.......0 0.......0
0.......0 0.......0 0.......0 0.......0 0.......0 0.......0 0.......0 0.......0 0.......0 0.......0 0.......0
```

Figure 2: Linguopalatal contacts for assimilated /sr/ (top) and /r/ sequences (bottom) across phrase boundary. Speaker DR.

and shorter vowels than others, but trill duration and vowel duration did not increase or decrease with boundary strength. EPG contact indices, on the other hand, increased with boundary strength. The main effect of sequence type (/r/ vs /sr/) did not reach significance except for speaker MJ, who showed a longer trill in assimilated /sr/ sequences than in lexical /r/ sequences ($F(1, 66) = 9.24$, $p < 0.001$). Significant interactions between sequence type and boundary type were only found for CA indices for speaker DR ($F(3, 66) = 3.4$, $p<0.01$). For this speaker, sequence type affected CA significantly only at phrase boundaries ($F(1, 10) = 35.86$, $p<0.001$, using a Scheffé test), with a more anterior alveolar contact for /sr/ than for intervocalic /r/. This is compatible with residual movements toward /s/ in the /sr/ sequences. The effect was not significant for any other type of prosodic boundary, suggesting complete assimilation of the lingual fricative to the trill in these conditions.

Other dependent variables were analyzed in an attempt to find articulatory differences between the assimilated /sr/ and control /r/ sequences: duration of lingual movement toward the consonant (i.e., /sr/ sequences may involve an earlier onset of lingual movements to form the critical constriction for /s/ than control sequences), distribution of trill realization as one-contact, two-contact, three-contact, four-contact or fricative trills (i.e., assimilated

/sr/ may be associated with more fricative realizations of the trill than control sequences), and variability of trill duration (i.e., assimilated /sr/ may exhibit greater variability in trill duration). None of the results reached significance, suggesting that /sr/ sequences showed complete assimilation to a trill across minor boundaries.

To validate the results perceptually, the sequences 'has recomanat' and 'ha recomanat' were excised from the test and control sequences and presented to eight Catalan speakers for identification as '(tu) has recomanat' (2nd person singular) or '(ell) ha recomanat' (3rd person singular). A Chi-square test performed on the results of the listening test showed that speakers could not reliably tell /sr/ and /r/ apart (χ^2 (1) = 0.315, p = 0.580). Listeners exhibited a bias toward identifying fricative realizations of the trill, i.e., [ɹ̝], as /sr/ sequences, although fricative realizations were no more common for /sr/ than /r/.

3.1.4 Discussion

The results show evidence of categorical as well as gradient assimilation. The assimilation is categorical in the great majority of cases. In cases with a weak boundary, there is complete assimilation (a trill is found with no trace of a sibilant, type 1 in Fig. 1). In cases with a strong boundary, no assimilation is present (sibilant-pause-trill sequences are found, type 4). Intermediate-type articulations (types 2 and 3, [ɹ̝] and [zɹ̝] respectively) could be argued to represent a categorical process as well, with complete assimilation /sr/ > /r/ in (2), and without assimilation in (3), the strong-boundary context. Reduction of the trill to a fricative [ɹ̝] would be a separate process unrelated to overlap, to which both derived and underlying trills are subject. Fricative [ɹ̝] could also plausibly arise from a blend of a sibilant and a trill — neither configuration is perfectly attained but some compromise between the two is reached. However, since trills often reduce to fricatives in other contexts, the first interpretation is favoured.

The results show weaker evidence of gradient assimilation across phrase boundaries: residual movements for /s/ for speaker DR, and a longer duration of the resulting trill for speaker MJ, though there is no audible frication. This suggests that the fricative has been planned by the speaker but the postural and/or aerodynamic requirements for generating turbulence are not achieved. Evidence for both gradient and categorical assimilation across different phrasal boundaries has also been reported by other investigators (e.g., Holst & Nolan, 1995).

3.2 Experiment 2: Effect of postural constraint on fricative to trill assimilation

Experiment 1 addressed temporal constraints on fricative to trill assimilation by comparing /sr/ to intervocalic /r/ across different prosodic boundaries. In a second experiment, I investigated the effect of degree of postural constraint on assimilation by comparing assimilation of the two fricatives /s/ and /ʃ/ to /r/. Alveolopalatals have been shown to be more severely constrained articulations than alveolars due to the larger involvement of the tongue dorsum in their articulation (Recasens et al., 1997). Simultaneous EPG and acoustic data were obtained for the same three Catalan speakers described above. The speakers read a list of meaningful sentences involving word final /s, ʃ/ followed by word initial /r/, as shown below. Control sequences involving [r], [z], and [ʒ] were also recorded for comparison.

Experimental

1. Fes rodolar el feix rodonet   [zr], [ʒr]   *(Roll the round bundle)*
2. Vull peix rostit, però   [ʒr], [zr]   *(I want the roasted fish,*
   més rostit   *but more roasted)*

Control

1. Va fer [fe] rodolar el   [VrV], [VʒV]   *(He rolled the scented*
   feix olorós   *bundle)*
2. Vull fer [fe] rostit, però   [VrV], [VzV]   *(I will roast some meat*
   més aviadet   *but a bit earlier)*

Frication was not present in /sr/ sequences, which apparently assimilate to [r] in all speakers. Alveolopalatal fricatives do not lose

366 *Maria-Josep Solé*

their frication as readily as alveolars do and they exhibit more variability in their realization within and across speakers. /ʃ + r/ sequences show varying degrees of assimilation which can be categorized into four groups, as shown in Figure 3. In type (1), there is apparent complete palatal fricative to trill assimilation (i.e., no frication but residual palatal contacts in the preceding vowel and in the trill). Type (2) shows an assibilated trill, (i.e., some frication during the first contact for the trill). Type (3) shows no fricative but a transitional front glide (e.g., *peix rostit* [ˌpej ɹusˈtit])[3]. Type (4) represents unassimilated sequences (speaker AF). In the latter two categories, i.e., when a palatal glide or fricative is present, tongue-tip trilling is not achieved – the trill is a weak postalveolar fricative– suggesting that the two antagonistic segments cannot be coproduced. Speaker AF showed a categorical assimilatory behaviour: /sr/ sequences assimilated to [r], but no assimilation was present in /ʃr/ sequences, which were produced as [ʃr]. Thus, the rest of the discussion will focus on the articulatory data for the other two speakers.

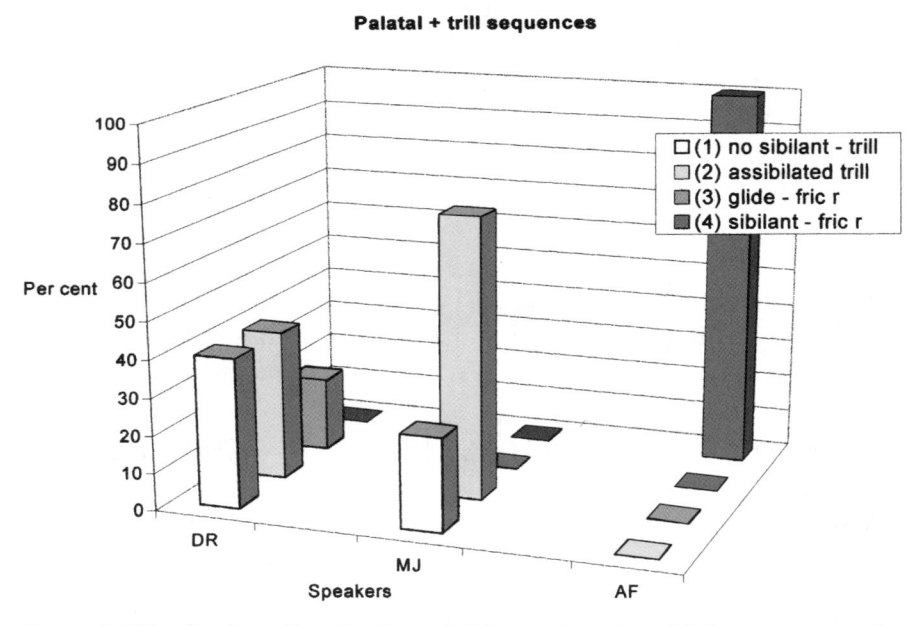

Palatal + trill sequences

Figure 3: Distribution of realization of /ʃr/ sequences (z axis) in percentages for each speaker (x axis).

One-way analyses of variance were performed with sequence type (/r/, /sr/, /ʃr/) as the independent variable, and indices of alveolar (CA), central (CC) and posterior (CP) contact activation at the first contact for the trill, duration of the trill in /r/ and assimilated /sr/,/ʃr/ sequences, duration of the preceding vowel, and contact coefficients in the middle of the preceding vowel, as dependent variables. The results for the ANOVAS and the post-hoc pair-wise comparisons are presented in Table 2. The ANOVAS showed a significant effect of sequence type on the CP index for the trill and on CC for the vowel in both speakers, as well as on the other contact indices for the preceding vowel and on trill duration for speaker MJ. Pair-wise comparisons using a Scheffé test showed that all significant differences were between /ʃr/ and the other two sequences. Trills derived from assimilated /ʃr/ sequences exhibited a longer trill (speaker MJ) and a higher CP for the trill (but same CA and CC) than /sr/ and control sequences, the latter indicating that the tongue dorsum is making some more palatal contact during the production of the trill. Vowels preceding palatal sequences exhibited a significantly higher elevation of the tongue dorsum (higher CP and CC) and tongue-tip/blade (higher CA) than control sequences, reflecting the early movements of the tongue towards the palatal constriction for [ʃ]. Such early lingual elevation was not found in /sr/ sequences, indicating that the movements for the palatal start earlier than those for the alveolar fricative due to the tongue dorsum being a more sluggish articulator, which results in more prominent coarticulatory effects. The transitional front glide between the vowel and the palatal fricative (found in type 3, Fig. 4) reflects the tongue dorsum movement towards the palatal before the pressure drop necessary to create audible friction is achieved (cf. data for Catalan in (1b) above).

Table 2 shows no difference between control /r/ and /sr/ sequences, suggesting complete assimilation of the alveolar fricative to the trill for the two speakers. The higher resistance of palatal fricatives, vis-à-vis alveolars, to assimilation is in accord with the notion that segments with a high degree of articulatory constraint are less likely to be overlapped, thus supporting the claim that degree of assimilation is related to postural constraint.

There is some evidence for gradient assimilation in /ʃr/ sequences. Though some cases show apparent complete assimilation

Table 2: Significant differences for the ANOVAS and post-hoc pair-wise comparisons (Scheffé test) for control /VrV/ and assimilated /VsrV/, /VʃrV/ sequences for speakers DR and MJ. Dependent variables are shown on the left. Asterisks indicate significant differences (Scheffé, p < 0.05).

	ANOVAS		Scheffé	
	DR	MJ	DR	MJ
	r -sr-ʃr	r-sr-ʃr	r-sr r-ʃr sr-ʃr	r-sr r-ʃr sr-ʃr
Trill duration		$F_{(2,14)}= 8.03$, $p < 0.01$		* *
Vowel duration				
CA r				
CP r	$F_{(2,14)} = 7.41$, $p < 0.01$	$F_{(2,14)} = 29.55$, $p < 0.0001$	* *	* *
CC r				
CA mid vowel		$F_{(2,14)} = 41.01$, $p < 0.0001$		* *
CP mid vowel		$F_{(2,14)} = 26.54$, $p < 0.001$		* *
CC mid vowel	$F_{(2,14)} = 7.342$, $p < 0.01$	$F_{(2,14)} = 5.517$, $p < 0.001$	* *	* *

of the palatal fricative to the trill, anticipatory palatal contacts in the preceding vowel and residual palatal contacts in the trill, indicate motor commands for the fricative /ʃ/, though there is no audible trace of it. The type (3) articulation may also evidence gradient assimilation: /ʃ/ reduces to a palatal glide and /r/ to a fricative, but neither disappears completely.

4. Aerodynamic data

In this section the aerodynamic requirements of tongue-tip trilling and frication are analyzed. The first experiment explores the allowable range of aerodynamic variation in lingual fricatives and trills, in order to determine which segment type is more highly constrained. Since fricatives and trills are aerodynamically driven sounds, it can be hypothesized that those segments which allow lesser variability in their aerodynamic conditions are more severely constrained and will exert greater contextual influences over neighboring segments, similar to the effect of postural constraint on assimilation described in section 2.2. In the second experiment, the time requirements for frication are considered. It is argued that the narrowly constrained positional and aerodynamic requirements for initiating a trill bleed the postural and time requirements for the generation of turbulence for competing fricatives.

4.1 Aerodynamic features of voiced fricatives and trills

Previous work (Ohala, 1983; Solé, 1998) has shown that voiced fricatives and trills have very strict aerodynamic requirements. Both segment types require a high oral pressure (P_o) and a pressure difference (ΔP) across the oral constriction sufficient to generate turbulence for fricatives, and to set the tongue-tip into vibration for trills. A high oral pressure, however, tends to impair the transglottal flow required for voicing. Thus, voiced fricatives and trills involve very finely tuned aerodynamic conditions so that a pressure drop is maintained across both the glottal and the supraglottal constrictions.

The allowable range of aerodynamic variation for voiced trills and fricatives can be estimated from aerodynamic data. Solé (1998) estimated a subglottal pressure (P_s) of 7.6 cmH$_2$O during trill and fricative production. If transglottal flow for voicing requires a pressure drop across the glottis (P_s-P_o) of at least 2−3 cmH$_2$O, that leaves a P_o of at most 5.6 cmH$_2$O, as schematically shown in Fig. 4. A minimum pressure drop of 4cmH$_2$O across the oral constriction is required to sustain the tongue-tip vibration, and a higher P_o is required to initiate it (Solé, Ohala & Ying, 1998), which means that P_o may vary between a rather narrow range of 5.6−4 cmH$_2$O in order to sustain voicing and trilling. Similarly,

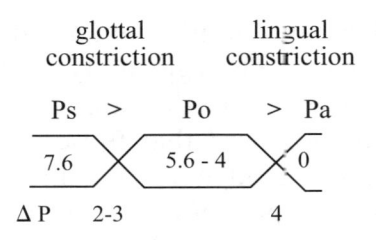

```
              glottal          lingual
           constriction     constriction

           Ps      >    Po       >   Pa
              ╲       ╱    ╲       ╱
           7.6    ╳    5.6 - 4  ╳    0
              ╱       ╲    ╱       ╲
           ΔP       2-3              4
```

Figure 4: Estimated P_o range for voiced trills for speaker MJ.

generation of turbulence for voiced fricatives ceases when the translingual pressure drops to about 3cmH$_2$O (Ohala, Solé & Ying, 1998; Catford, 1977: 124; Stevens, 1998: 480), resulting in a similarly narrow range of P_o variation, between 5.6 and 3cmH$_2$O. Thus, the P_o range for voiced fricatives and trills is very narrow and unforgiving, and small pressure variations may lead to devoicing or cessation of trilling/frication, as evidenced synchronically and diachronically (Solé, 1998).

4.2 Experiment 3: Variations in oral pressure

The following experiment was designed to find out which segment type – voiced fricatives or trills – was more highly constrained aerodynamically, that is, allowed lesser aerodynamic variability.

4.2.1 Experimental Method

Two trained phoneticians produced steady state and intervocalic voiced and voiceless trills and fricatives (the intervocalic in /aCa/ and /iCi/ environments), as well as prolonged trills and fricatives with maximum exhalatory effort (i.e., until speakers ran out of breath). Audio was recorded by a high quality microphone. Oropharyngeal pressure (P_o) and airflow were recorded simultaneously. Oral pressure was sampled by a catheter inserted into the pharynx via the nasal cavity and connected to a pressure transducer. Airflow was collected with a Rothenberg mask. The oral Pressure and airflow signals were low-pass filtered at 50 Hz.

Oral pressure during trill and fricative production was intermittently vented with catheters of varying cross-sectional areas (7.9, 17.8, 31.6, 49.5 mm^2), all 25 cm long, inserted into the speaker's mouth via the buccal sulcus and the gap behind the back molars (Solé, in press). The impedance[4] (i.e., resistance to exiting air) of the catheters for the range of flow used in fricatives and trills was calculated, as well as the vocal tract impedance during the production of these segments for each speaker. These are shown in Figure 6. The catheters venting the P_o were intended to simulate variations in oral pressure present in speech due to contextual and prosodic factors, e.g., coarticulation with sounds of varying impedance, stress, speaking rate, phrasal position, etc. Oral pressure and airflow were measured for the different conditions and the variation, impairment or extinction of trilling/frication, as a function of varying intraoral pressure was analyzed acoustically.

Masking noise was presented to the speaker over headphones during data acquisition to minimize auditory feedback. Kinaesthetic feedback could not be eliminated and measurements were made during the first 60 ms after P_o was varied to avoid the effect of compensatory maneuvers.

4.2.2 Variations in oral pressure. Results

Figure 5 illustrates the effects of the reduction in P_o associated with a 7.9 mm^2 vent. The first panel displays an intervocalic voiced trill under normal pressure conditions (left), and with a vent area of 7.9 mm^2 (right), where the reduced P_o impairs tongue-tip vibration resulting in a non-sibilant voiced fricative. Tongue-tip vibration was extinguished into a fricative as the reduction in P_o diminished the rate of flow through the oral constriction and the magnitude of the Bernoulli effect, which was not sufficient to suck the tongue-tip back to the contact position. A reduction in Po of 2.5–3.5 cmH$_2$O impaired trilling. Voiced fricatives, on the right panel, show a slight increase in amplitude of periodic energy in the vented condition (right), and a decrease in the amplitude of the high frequency noise, but they retain their fricative nature. Thus, trills are more severely affected by changes in oral pressure than fricatives.

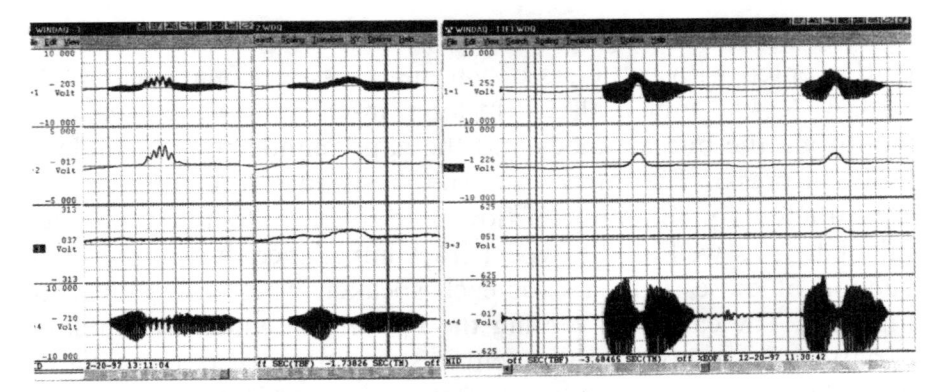

Figure 5: (1) Unfiltered P$_o$, (2) low-pass filtered P$_o$, (3) airflow escaping through the catheter when unblocked, (4) audio signal for unvented and vented [i'ri] (left panel) and [i'zi] (right panel).

Figure 6 exhibits the values for impedance at the oral constriction (dashed lines) for various intervocalic fricatives (6a) and the voiced and voiceless trill (6b). It also shows the impedance of the catheters at the flowrates used in fricatives and trills (e.g., the rates of flow used in the production of intervocalic fricatives ranged from 0.124 to 0.406 lit/sec, the impedance of the catheters at these two extremes of flowrate was calculated and the values are shown in the bars). The figure also includes the effect of venting the P$_o$ with the various catheters. Figure (6a) shows that venting the fricative with catheters with a higher impedance (7.9 mm^2 area catheter) than that at the oral constriction did not affect the quality of the fricative, it just sightly attenuated the fricative noise. Catheters with values for impedance similar (17.8 mm^2 area) to those at the oral constriction had noticeable effects on fricatives: they lost much of their high-frequency aperiodic energy. Sibilant fricatives sounded non-sibilant. Voiced fricatives became frictionless continuants, with increased energy of voicing (i.e., a lower C/V energy ratio). Larger area catheters ($\geq$ 31.7 mm^2), with a lower impedance than that in the vocal tract, extinguished frication, since airflow exited through the aperture with lower impedance, thus reducing the required pressure drop across the oral constriction to generate turbulence. Voiced fricatives were more seriously affected than voiceless fricatives, becoming vowel-like. This is partly due to the

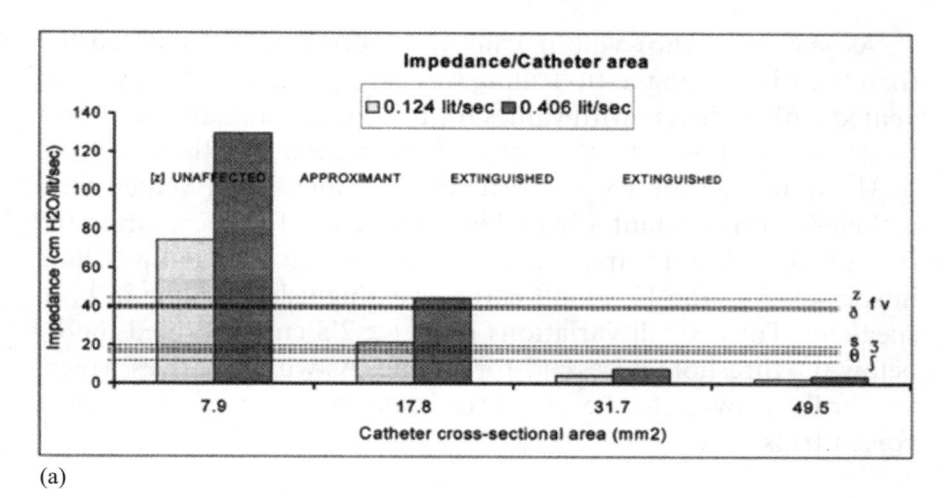

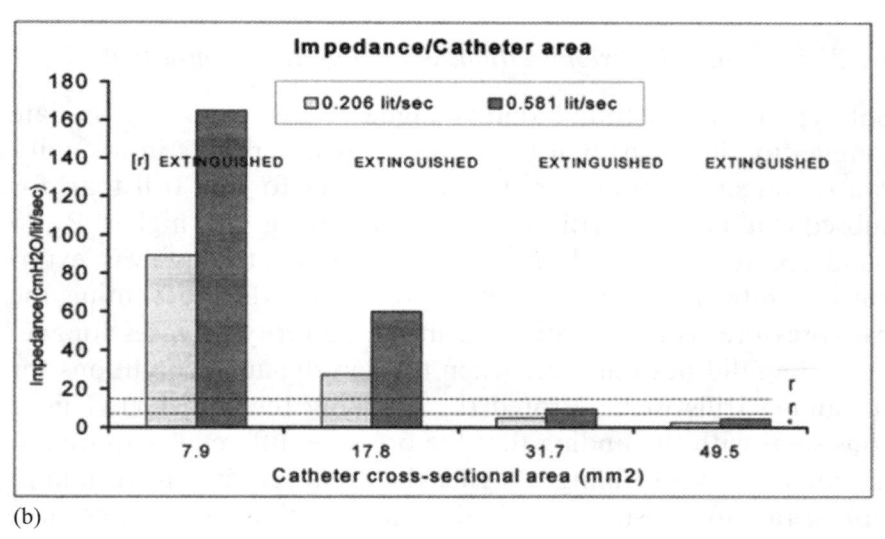

Figure 6: Impedance (ordinate) for catheters of varying cross-sectional area (abscissa) at the flowrates (in lit/sec) used in intervocalic fricatives (a) and trills (b). Values of measured vocal tract impedance for the various fricatives and trills have been overlayed on the graph (Speaker MJ).

fact that a catheter of a given area reduced the oropharyngeal pressure of voiced fricatives more than that of voiceless fricatives, due to the open glottis for the latter allowing the vented air to be more readily resupplied from the lungs.

As shown in (6b) voiced trills were adversely affected earlier than fricatives. Tongue-tip trilling was extinguished not only when vented with catheters with values for impedance similar to or lower than impedance at the oral constriction (catheter areas $\geq 31.7\,\text{mm}^2$), as for voiced fricatives, but also when vented with catheters with substantially higher impedance. That is, venting the P_o with the 7.9 mm^2 area catheter extinguished tongue-tip trilling in speaker MJ; the 17.8 mm^2 catheter extinguished trilling in both speakers. Thus, small variations in P_o ($\geq 2.5\,\text{cmH}_2\text{O}$) bled the P_o below the threshold necessary for trilling. As with fricatives, voiceless trills proved to be more resistant to P_o variations than voiced trills.

4.2.3 Trill and fricative initiation, extinction and reinitiation

Solé et al. (1998) found that a higher P_o is needed to initiate tongue-tip vibration than to sustain it, which results in a significantly longer duration for the first contact for the trill than for subsequent contacts (Blecua, 1999), allowing the higher P_o to build-up. It was found that when sustained trilling was extinguished into a fricative or an approximant, due to venting the backpressure with the catheters, in the majority of cases tongue-tip trilling did not reinitiate when the aerodynamic conditions for sustaining trills were restored (by blocking the catheter). This is consistent with the finding that the pressure difference required to initiate tongue-tip trilling is higher than that required to sustain it. In contrast, for sustained voiced fricatives, high energy noise *was* restored when the catheter was blocked. This may reflect differences in the initial tongue positioning or bracing for trills and fricatives. Thus there is a narrow region of values of the aerodynamic parameters where tongue-tip vibration cannot be initiated, but once started, can be maintained. In the cases where lingual vibration did reinitiate (usually when the venting period was very short) it generally did so through a transitional fricative, most likely reflecting the increase in P_o and in volume velocity before the Bernoulli force closed the alveolar channel.

In prolonged trills, tongue-tip vibration was sustained as long as sufficient airflow was available. When P_s (and consequently P_o) diminished, thus endangering trilling, two possible outcomes were found: frication and/or devoicing. In the great majority of cases, the trill decayed into a fricative as airflow through the lingual constriction dropped, due to diminished P_s. In a few cases, the trill or the resulting fricative were further devoiced. Devoicing can be seen as a manoeuvre to directly access P_s by removing the resistance at the glottis in order to prolong trilling. The extinction and reinitiation of trills into a fricative suggests that the aerodynamic range of variation for trills is narrower than for fricatives.

4.2.4 Discussion.

The results indicate that trills allow a narrower range of P_o and P_s variation than fricatives, and thus have more highly constrained aerodynamic requirements. Thus trills are more sensitive to changing aerodynamic conditions (i.e., they decay earlier) than fricatives, and they decay into (and reinitiate through) fricatives or approximants. Moreover, trills show stricter postural and aerodynamic requirements for initiating, as opposed to sustaining, tongue-tip trilling. Such tight requirements allow little coarticulation and overlap with conflicting lingual configurations if trilling is to be preserved. Thus, the more severely constrained requirements of trills over those of fricatives account for trills dominating the assimilatory process. Next we turn to how the requirements for tongue-tip trilling affect the conditions for generating frication.

4.3 Experiment 4: Aerodynamic requirements for fricatives

Production of lingual fricatives involves not only articulatory positioning, but also creating sufficient *pressure drop* (ΔP) across the oral constriction to generate audible frication. This requires sufficient volume velocity (rate of flow) and sufficient time to build up oro-pharyngeal pressure behind the oral constriction. In addition, the *cross-sectional area* of the oral constriction has to be within a certain range for audible friction. That is, the rate of flow (U) needed to generate turbulent noise depends on the area (A) of the constriction and the difference in the pressures (ΔP) of the cavities on both sides of the constriction, $U = A(\Delta P)^{0.5}$ (such that the larger the difference in pressure and the smaller the aperture area, the larger the rate of flow and the higher the amplitude of the resulting friction).

4.3.1 Time requirements for fricatives

Given sufficient rate of flow, a certain time is required to achieve the pressure drop across the constriction for audible frication. We propose that fricative to trill assimilation may result from the anticipatory movements for the trill bleeding the time required to achieve the difference in pressure (from 5–10cmH$_2$O) across the alveolar constriction required for frication. In order to determine the time needed to achieve the pressure drop at the oral constriction for audible frication (TΔP$_{frication}$), in a fourth experiment oropharyngeal pressure (P$_o$) and airflow were recorded simultaneously in two subjects (the same as in experiment 3) producing intervocalic voiced and voiceless fricatives, [v, f, ð, θ, z, s, ʒ, ʃ]. Bordering vowels were /a/_/a/ and /i/_/i/. Audio was recorded by a high quality microphone, oral pressure was sampled by a catheter inserted into the pharynx via the nasal cavity and connected to a pressure transducer, and airflow was collected with a Rothenberg mask as described above. EPG and acoustic data were collected in a separate session for one of the speakers reading the same material. Alignment of the EPG and aerodynamic data at crucial points on the waveform allowed us to observe the interaction between articulatory movements, aerodynamics, and acoustic result, although not for identical items.

The time from the onset of the P$_o$ rise to onset of audible frication was measured. Fig. 7 shows the measuring procedure. The continuous vertical lines show the onset of P$_o$ rise (*i.e.*, onset of sufficient oral constriction to create a difference in pressure, which roughly coincides with the onset of reduction in airflow for voiced fricatives[5]). The small vertical lines extending below the unfiltered

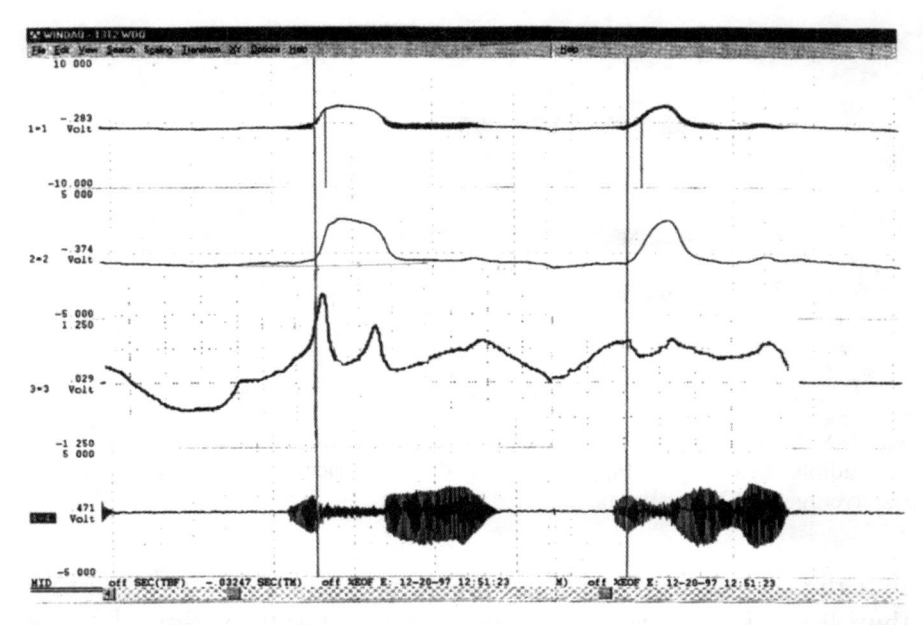

Figure 7: Unfiltered P$_o$, filtered P$_o$, airflow and audio signal for ['asa] (left) and ['aza] (right).

P$_o$ trace are located at the onset of audible friction (which coincides with the lowest values for airflow for voiced fricatives), as seen on the waveform. Onset of audible friction was determined from auditory and spectrographic analysis.

The results are presented in Fig. 8, which shows the mean T ΔP$_{frication}$ (the difference in time between these two points) for the different fricatives. Two-way ANOVA with place of articulation and voicing as factors showed that place did not have a significant effect on the time needed to reach audible frication (most probably due to differences in cavity volume being compensated by differences in articulator's velocity). The effect of voicing was significant ($F(1, 62) = 55.87$, p = 0.0001) and no interaction effects were found. The mean T ΔP$_{frication}$ was in the range of 50 ms for voiced and 30 ms for voiceless fricatives. Voiced fricatives take approximately 66% longer, vis-à-vis voiceless fricatives, to achieve a pressure drop at the constriction sufficient for audible turbulence, due to glottal impedance and reduced transglottal flow. Fig. 7 shows

378 *Maria-Josep Solé*

Time to achieve ΔP for friction

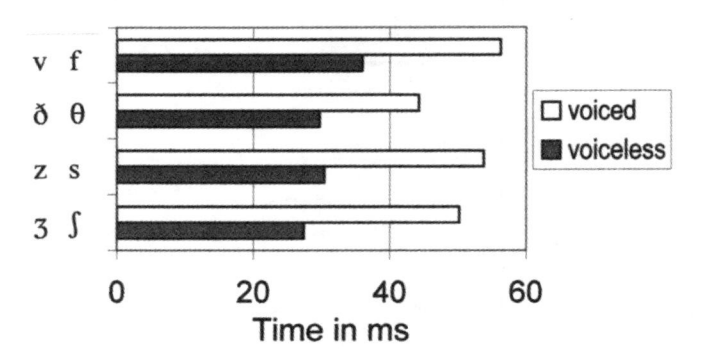

[Bar chart showing voiced vs voiceless fricatives:
- v f
- ð θ
- z s
- ʒ ʃ
Time in ms, axis 0 to 60]

Figure 8: Mean time needed to achieve the pressure drop at the oral constriction for audible frication (T ΔP$_{frication}$) for the different fricatives. Each bar represents the average of 12 measurements.

that the rise in oropharyngeal pressure is much slower for voiced than for voiceless fricatives, due to a lower rate of flow through the adducted vocal folds for the former.

Thus, voiced fricatives take around 50 ms to achieve the pressure drop required for audible frication. If onset of articulatory movements for the trill reach the articulator within 50 ms from onset of P_o build up, the pressure drop necessary for creating audible friction will not be achieved. Voiceless fricatives are more resistant to overlapping movements for the trill since the time required for generating friction is shorter (i.e., overlap of motor commands within 40ms from onset of the P_o rise would bleed frication in voiced but not in voiceless fricatives). Thus, the aerodynamic requirements of voiced fricatives are more constrained in *time* than those for corresponding voiceless fricatives, and thus are more likely to be affected by overlapping gestures. Spectra at different points in time in the voiced fricative showed that, in accordance with aerodynamic events, the amplitude of high frequency noise is weaker during the first half of the fricative constriction (as the oral pressure gradually increases) and then reaches a stable value over the last part of the constriction (due to the higher rate of flow as air accumulates behind the constriction). The asymmetry in P_o build up (and noise amplitude) for voiced, but not for voiceless, fricatives can be observed in the filtered P_o trace in Fig. 7 (in accordance with data in Stevens, 1998, Fig. 8.75). Thus if movements for the trill overlap the second half of the voiced fricative, the initial low amplitude turbulence may not be heard. Moreover, the reduced transglottal flow for voiced fricatives is responsible for a lower particle velocity across the lingual constriction, and a lower *intensity* of friction, vis-à-vis voiceless fricatives, which may contribute to decreased audible friction. Thus, the aerodynamics of voicing (i.e., regressive voicing assimilation) affects the likelihood of fricative assimilation.

4.3.2 Postural requirements

Early onset of articulatory movements for the trill may reach the articulator before the tongue-tip (or tongue-blade and dorsum for alveolopalatals) attains the critical cross-sectional area to create sufficient ΔP to generate friction. In order to quantify the duration of the tongue-tip/dorsum closing gesture, the time from onset of lingual movement for the fricative (i.e., the first EPG frame showing a buildup in the number of tongue-palate contacts toward the alveolar/palatal area) to the first steady state fricative contact (which approximately coincides with onset of P_o rise) was measured on the EPG data. The mean duration was 33 ms for alveolar and 59.5 ms for palatal fricatives. These values agree with data on velocity of tongue-tip and dorsum movement (Stevens, 1998: 47, 382): If we assume the rate of change of cross-sectional area for an alveolar fricative to be 30 cm^2/sec, then the time taken for the tongue-tip to form a fricative constriction (0.1 cm^2) is around 30ms, assuming an initial area of 1.0 cm^2 for the vowel. Thus, if instructions for /r/ reach the articulator within 30 ms from onset of the movement for the alveolar fricative they will bleed the postural and aerodynamic (area of aperture) requirements for frication. The rate of movement of the tongue dorsum is slower than that for the tongue-tip, approximately 15 cm/s, thus it takes longer to form a palatal constriction, around 60 ms. The slower rate of movement of the tongue dorsum accounts for the earlier onset of movements to form the palatal constriction, the residual palatal glides and the more prominent coarticulatory effects, vis-à-vis alveolars.

5. General discussion

The results show that lingual trills exhibit highly constrained articulatory and aerodynamic requirements and small variations result in lack of tongue-tip vibration. In order to preserve spectral identity (i.e., trilling), aerodynamic and articulatory variation must remain within very narrow bounds. In /s, ʃ + r/ sequences early onset of the lingual movements for the trill to attain the constrained positioning, tongue configuration and aerodynamic requirements for tongue-tip vibration affect the articulatory and aerodynamic conditions to generate audible turbulence for the fricative, resulting in fricative to trill assimilation.

The data seem to show that fricative to trill assimilation may sometimes be an articulatorily gradient process, as shown by residual articulatory contacts for the fricative and a longer duration of the resulting trill, though frication is not achieved. In the great majority of cases, however, assimilation is either absent (strong boundaries) or complete and categorical (weak boundaries).

The gradient nature of lingual fricative to trill assimilation can be accounted for by Gestural Phonology if aerodynamic factors are incorporated: overlap of conflicting segments affects the articulatory configuration and time required for the aerodynamic event of frication. In cases of extreme overlap, early onset of movements for the /r/ — within 30 ms from onset of lingual movements for the fricative — perturbs the articulatory trajectory and the critical constriction area required for friction. In cases of lesser overlap, motor commands for the trill arrive shortly after the articulator attains the cross-sectional area for frication, but within the time needed to build up the sufficient pressure difference to create audible frication, i.e., within 50 ms from onset of P_o rise. In such cases turbulent noise will not be generated.

Cases of complete assimilation, resulting in a trill indistinguishable from lexical single trills, may result not only from extreme overlap between the two gestures. Alternatively, trills arising from assimilation may reflect higher level restructuring of consecutive motor commands for /s/ and /r/ in a single articulatory gesture, that is, complete assimilations may result from an optional phonological rule. Such a rule may allow speakers to scan ahead in an utterance and plan a number of conventionalized articulatory simplifications.

Thus the range of assimilatory phenomena may originally stem from the same source (gestural overlap and time constraints on aerodynamic requirements) but may reflect two synchronically different processes. At one end of the range, mechanical gestural overlap may result in varying degrees of articulatory assimilation (though the aerodynamic and perceptual result is mostly categorical, that is, no audible frication results) or in complete assimilation in cases of extreme overlap. At the other end, these phonetic tendencies may have been encoded in a higher reorganization of motor commands or a categorical phonological process, giving rise to complete assimilation. Sound change would result from historically lexicalized results of such effects, such as etym. *Puigroig* /tʃ + r/ > *Purroi* /r/.

The assimilation of fricatives to following trills can partly be modeled as a duration dependent effect along the lines of Lindblom's (1963) undershoot model: As the time to attain the critical cross-sectional area of constriction and to build up the oral pressure for frication becomes shorter, due to anticipatory movements for the trill, the pressure drop required for frication is not achieved. This results in both aerodynamic and acoustic lack of turbulence. In summary, the data indicate that the acoustic requirements (audible turbulence) for voiced fricatives impose relatively strict aerodynamic and time constraints (rate of flow, size and duration of constriction) which may be adversely affected by competing overlapping gestures, resulting in lack of frication or, alternatively, in lack of tongue-tip trilling if frication *is* achieved.

The results are in agreement with Recasens' 'Degree of Articulatory Constraint' model, which predicts a higher resistance to coarticulatory and assimilatory effects of highly gesturally constrained segments. The results further suggest that degree of aerodynamic constraint — with trills being more narrowly constrained than voiced fricatives which, in turn, have tighter aerodynamic and time requirements than voiceless fricatives — also play a role in assimilatory processes.

The flowrate and time constraints on fricative production account for several observed phonological phenomena in addition to fricative-trill assimilation: gliding of final fricatives (e.g., Italian *noi* < Latin *nos* 'we', Roussillon Catalan *mateix* [mə'tej] 'same', cf. Central Catalan [mə'teʃ]), reflecting failure to achieve the pressure drop necessary for frication, due to the reduction in time and magnitude of the gesture for the coda fricative. Aspiration of coda /s/ in many dialects of Spanish (e.g., *los niños* [lɔʰ 'niɲɔʰ] 'the kids'), with glottal frication but not sufficient translingual pressure drop for supraglottal frication is another such case. Furthermore, intervocalic fricatives becoming approximants (e.g., Spanish, Catalan *cada* [ð] 'each'), may reflect time rather than aperture constraints (Romero, 1996), since fricatives require a longer constriction than approximants in order to build up sufficient oral pressure for turbulence.

Acknowledgments

Earlier versions of parts of this work were presented at the XIV International Conference of Phonetic Sciences and the 5th Speech Production Seminar and appear in the proceedings of those conferences. This research was funded by grants BFF2001-2498, BFF2000-0075-C02-01 from the Ministry of Education, Spain and by the research group 1999SGR 00256 of the Catalan Government. My thanks go to an anonymous reviewer for insightful remarks on a previous version of this manuscript.

Notes

1   The mechanics of tongue-tip vibration have been described by Catford (1977), Ladefoged & Maddieson (1996), Spajic, Ladefoged & Bhaskararao (1996), Barry (1997) and modeled by McGowan (1992). These authors describe trills as the vibration of certain supralaryngeal articulators (tongue-tip, uvula, lips) caused by aerodynamic forces, as opposed to taps and flaps, which involve active muscular movements of the tongue. The conditions for initiating lin-

gual trilling involve (i) muscle contraction of the tongue to assume the position, shape and elasticity requirements, and (ii) sufficient pressure difference across the lingual constriction. Once trilling is initiated, tongue-tip vibration is maintained as a self-sustaining vibratory system.

2   Though /s/ in coda position is aspirated in many dialects of Spanish, the dialects described here do not aspirate coda /s/. In Catalan coda /s/ is always pronounced.

3   The transitional glide has been reinterpreted as a separate segment in the NW and Valencian dialects of Catalan, *e.g.*, *peix* /pejʃ/, Caixa ['kajʃə] vs Central Catalan /peʃ/, Caixa ['kaʃə], Latin *pisce, capsa*.

4   Impedance is a function of the area of the aperture, the properties of the channel through which the air passes (length, compliance, surface) and the rate of flow; so that the smaller the aperture, the longer the channel and the larger the amount of flow, the higher the impedance.

5   The two peaks of flow at the VC and CV boundaries are commonly found in fricatives and reflect abduction of the glottis before the supraglottal constriction is formed. Some glottal abduction is also present in voiced fricatives in order to provide sufficient airflow to generate frication at the supraglottal constriction (Stevens, 1998: 382, 479).

References

Alcover, A. M. & Moll, F.
  1979   *Diccionari Català-Valencià-Balear*. Mallorca: Moll.
Barry, W. J.
  1997   Another R-tickle. *Journal of the International Phonetic Association*. **27**, **2**, 35–45.
Bladon, R. A. W. & Nolan, F.
  1977   A videofluorographic investigation of tip and blade alveolars in English. *Journal of Phonetics*, **5**, 185–193.
Blecua, B.
  1999   Características acústicas de la vibrante múltiple del español en habla espontánea. *Proceedings of the 1st Congress of Experimental Phonetics*, Tarragona, 119–126.
Browman, C. P. & Goldstein, L. M.
  1986   Towards and articulatory phonology. *Phonology Yearbook*, **3**, 219–252.
Browman, C. P. & Goldstein, L. M.
  1990   Tiers in articulatory phonology, with some implications for casual speech. In J. Kingston & M. E. Beckman (eds.), *Papers in Laboratory Phonology I: Between The Grammar and Physics of Speech*, (pp. 341–376). Cambridge: Cambridge University Press.

Browman, C. P. & Goldstein, L. M.
  1995   Gestural syllable position effects in American English. In F. Bell-Berti & L. J. Raphael (eds.), *Producing Speech: Contemporary Issues. For K. S. Harris*, (pp. 19−34). Woodsbury, N.Y: American Institute of Physics.
Byrd, D.
  1996   Influences on articulatory timing in consonant sequences. *Journal of Phonetics*, **24**, 263−282.
Catford, J. C.
  1977   *Fundamental Problems in Phonetics*. Edinburgh: Edinburgh University Press.
Dembowski, J. & Westbury, J. R.
  1999   Contextual influences on stop consonant articulatory postures in connected speech. *Proceedings of the XIV International Congress of Phonetic Sciences*, San Francisco, Vol **3**, 2419−2422.
Fontdevila, J., Pallarès, M. D. & Recasens, D.
  1994   The contact index method of EPG data reduction. *Journal of Phonetics*, **22**, 141−154.
Guion, S. G.
  1998   The role of perception in the sound change of velar palatalization, *Phonetica*, **55**, 18−52.
Hardcastle, W.
  1985   Some phonetic and syntactic constraints on lingual coarticulation during /kl/ sequences. *Speech Communication*, **4**, 247−263.
Holst, T. & Nolan, F.
  1995   The influence of syntactic structure on [s] to [ʃ] assimilation. In B. Connell & A. Arvaniti (eds.), *Phonology and Phonetic Evidence: Papers in Laboratory Phonology IV*, (pp. 315−333). Cambridge: Cambridge University Press.
Hoole, P., Nguyen, N. & Hardcastle, W.
  1993   A comparative investigation of coarticulation in fricatives: EPG, electromagnetic and acoustic data. *Language and Speech*, **36**, 3, 235−260.
Hume, E., Johnson, K., Seo, M. & Tserdanelis, G.
  1999   A cross-linguistic study of stop place perception. *Proceedings of the XIV International Congress of Phonetic Sciences*, San Francisco, 2069−2072.
Jakobson, R., Fant, C. G. M. & Halle, M. J.
  1952   *Preliminaries to Speech Analysis*. Cambridge, Mass.: MIT Press.
Krakow, R. A.
  1989   The articulatory organization of syllables: A kinematic analysis of labial and velar gestures. PhD Dissertation, Yale University.
Krakow, R. A.
  1993   Nonsegmental influences on velum movement patterns: Syllables, sentences, stress, and speaking rate. In M. K. Huffman & R. A.

Krakow (eds.), *Phonetics and phonology, Volume 5: Nasals, nasalization, and the velum*, (pp. 87−116). San Diego, CA: Academic Press.
Ladefoged, P. & Maddieson, I.
1996   *The Sounds of the World's Languages*. Oxford: Blackwell.
Lindblom, B.
1963   A spectrographic study of vowel reduction. *Journal of the Acoustical Society of America*, 35, 1773−1781.
MacClean, M.
1973   Forward coarticulation of velar movement at marked junctural boundaries. *Journal of Speech and Hearing Research*, 16, 286−296.
McGowan, R. S.
1992   Tongue-tip trills and vocal tract wall compliance. *Journal of the Acoustical Society of America*, 91 (5), 2903−2910.
McGowan, R. S. & Saltzman, E. L.
1995   Incorporating aerodynamic and laryngeal components into task dynamics. *Journal of Phonetics*, 23, 255−269.
Navarro Tomás, T.
1980   *Manual de Pronunciación Española* (20th edition). Madrid: CSIC.
Ohala, J. J.
1976   A model of speech aerodynamics. *Report of the Phonology Laboratory*, 1, 93−107. Berkeley.
Ohala, J. J.
1981   Articulatory constraints on the cognitive representation of speech. In T. Myers, J. Laver & J. Anderson (eds.), *The Cognitive Representation of Speech*, (pp. 111−122). Amsterdam: North Holland.
Ohala, J. J.
1983   The origin of sound patterns in vocal tract constraints. In P.F. MacNeilage (ed.), *The Production of Speech*, (pp. 189−216). New York: Springer.
Ohala, J. J.
1990   The phonetics and phonology of aspects of assimilation. In J. Kingston & M. E. Beckman (eds.), *Papers in Laboratory Phonology I: Between The Grammar and Physics of Speech*, (pp. 258−275). Cambridge: Cambridge University Press.
Ohala, J. J. & Kawasaki, H.
1984   Phonetics and prosodic phonology. *Phonology Yearbook*, 1, 113− 127.
Ohala, J. J., Solé, M. J. & Ying, G.
1998   The controversy of nasalized fricatives. *Proceedings of the 135th Meeting of the ICA/ASA*. Seattle, Washington, 2921−2922.
Recasens, D.
1993   *Fonètica i Fonologia*. Barcelona: Enciclopèdia Catalana.
Recasens, D.
1995   Coarticulació i assimilació en fonologia. Dades de moviment lingual sobre els grups consonàntics amb C2 = /d/ en català. *Caplletra* 19, Revista Internacional de Filologia, 11−26.

Recasens, D.
1999 Theoretical and methodological issues on coarticulation. *Proceedings of the 1st Congress of Experimental Phonetics*, Tarragona, 67–75.
Recasens, D., Pallarès, M. D. & Fontdevila, J.
1997 A model of lingual coarticulation based on articulatory constraints. *Journal of the Acoustical Society of America*, **102** Vol 1, 544–561.
Recasens, D. & Pallarès, M. D.
1999 A study of /ɾ/ and /r/ in the light of the 'DAC' coarticulation model, *Journal of Phonetics*, **27**, 143–169.
Redford, M. A. & Diehl, R. L.
1999 The relative perceptual distinctiveness of initial and final consonants in CVC syllables. *Journal of the Acoustical Society of America*, **106** (3), 1555–1565.
Romero, J.
1996 Articulatory blending of lingual gestures. *Journal of Phonetics*, **24**, 99–111.
Solé, M. J.
1998 Phonological universals: trilling, voicing and frication. *Proceedings of the Berkeley Linguistics Society*. University of California, Berkeley, 403–416.
Solé, M. J.
1999 Production requirements of apical trills and assimilatory behaviour. *Proceedings of the XIV International Congress of Phonetic Sciences*. San Francisco, 487–490.
Solé, M. J.
in press Aerodynamic characteristics of trills and phonological patterning, *Journal of Phonetics*.
Solé, M. J., Ohala, J. J. & Ying, G.
1998 Aerodynamic characteristics of trills. *Proceedings of the 135th Meeting of the ICA/ASA*, Seattle, Washington, 2923–2924.
Spajic, S., Ladefoged, P. & Bhaskararao, P.
1996 The trills of Toda, *Journal of the International Phonetic Association*, **26**, 1–21.
Sproat, R. & Fujimura, O.
1993 Allophonic variation in English /l/ and its implications for phonetic implementation. *Journal of Phonetics*, **21** 291–311.
Stevens, K.
1998 *Acoustic Phonetics*. Cambridge, Mass.: MIT Press.
Vázquez Cuesta, P. & Mendes de Luz, M. A.
1971 *Gramática Portuguesa* (3rd edition). Madrid: Gredos.

Tonal association and target alignment in European Portuguese nuclear falls

Sónia Frota

Abstract

Intonational phonology analyses of nuclear falls often treat the tones that make up falling contours either as separate tonal events, i.e. as a single-tone pitch accent and an edge tone of some sort, or as part of a bitonal accent. This work evaluates the competing phonological analyses for the broad and narrow focus nuclear falls in European Portuguese declaratives. By exploring the factors that may affect the alignment of the H(igh) and L(ow) targets, such as proximity to prosodic edges and distance between word stresses, evidence is presented in support of the bitonal hypothesis for both the neutral and the focus falls. Subsequently, the relation between the H and L targets is shown to differ in the two bitonal accents, supporting a leading/trailing tone distinction whereby the leading tone is timed independently of the T* and the trailing tone is timed with reference to the T*. Besides bringing phonetic data to bear on the phonological organisation of pitch contours, the results have consequences for the view of intonation primes as tonal targets (rather than configurations) and bitonal accents as structured (rather than flat) tonal units.

1. Introduction

Phonological analyses of nuclear falls in various languages have disagreed on the organisation of the tones that make up such contours. The main dispute is between the proposal to capture the falling movement by means of separate tonal events and the proposal of a bitonal accent of the H+L type: the former position has been maintained by Pierrehumbert (1980) for English, Benzmüller & Grice (1998) for German, D'Imperio (1999) for Neapolitan Italian, Grønnum & Viana (1999) for European Portuguese; the latter has been supported by Ladd (1983) and Gussenhoven

(1984) for English, Grabe (1997) for German, D'Imperio & House (1997) for Neapolitan Italian, Frota (1997) for European Portuguese. The issue is naturally intertwined with the typology of pitch accents and edge tones assumed in the different accounts, as well as with their phonetic interpretation.

This paper investigates the f_0 contours of nuclear falls in European Portuguese declarative sentences with a broad focus or a narrow focus reading. The analysis of the falling patterns developed here follows the autosegmental metrical theory of intonational phonology, according to which intonation has a phonological organisation, and intonational features relate to other features of the phonological organisation of speech established on the basis of prosodic structure (Beckman & Pierrehumbert, 1986; Pierrehumbert & Beckman, 1988; Hayes & Lahiri, 1991; Grice, 1995a,b; Prieto, van Santen & Hirschberg, 1995; Jun, 1996; Ladd, 1996; D'Imperio, 1996; Hirschberg & Avesani, 1997; Arvaniti, Ladd & Mennen, 1998, 2000; Sosa, 1999; Gussenhoven & van der Vliet, 1999; Grice, Ladd & Arvaniti, 2000, among others).

One of the basic assumptions of the approach to intonation followed here is the view that the intonation contour is formed by a string of tones. In languages like English and European Portuguese, the events of the tonal string are either pitch accents (T*) or edge-related tones. The former are tonal events associated with prominent elements in the segmental string. The latter are tonal events linked to prosodic domain edges. Edge-related tones comprise two categories, boundary tones and phrase accents (respectively, T% and T⁻ in Pierrehumbert's notation). Between the local tonal events, the intonation contour is phonologically unspecified.

In languages such as Bengali and European Portuguese (see, respectively, Hayes & Lahiri 1991 and Frota 2000), the prosodic structure relevant to intonation is that provided under the Prosodic Hierarchy Theory, as developed in Selkirk (1984), Nespor & Vogel (1986), and Hayes (1989), among others. The phonological phrase (φ) and the intonational phrase (I) will thus be the prosodic constituents used in the description of European Portuguese intonation structure that follows.

1.1 Nuclear falls in European Portuguese declaratives

There are two indisputable facts that come out of the literature on European Portuguese declarative intonation: first, the declarative contour consists of an initial rise and a sharp final fall, between which there is a plateau; second, the falling movement occurs in the last stressed syllable of the intonational phrase (Delgado Martins & Lacerda, 1977; Martins, 1986; Viana, 1987; Frota, 1991, 1993; Falé, 1995; Vigário, 1998; Grønnum & Viana, 1999). Both the sparseness of tonal events and the nuclear fall that characterise neutral declaratives are illustrated in Figures 1—2 (panel A).

This contour is typical of sentences uttered out-of-the-blue or in response to 'what-happened' questions, that is sentences with a broad focus reading. In addition, the same type of nuclear fall has also been found in the pitch contour of topicalised phrases (*in situ* or dislocated phrases that express what the sentence is about — Frota, 2000).

Despite the coincident phonetic descriptions, different authors have proposed different analyses of the falling movement. In Viana (1987), it is accounted for by a H* L tonal sequence associated with the final stressed syllable (the nature of the L is not discussed by the author). In the analyses of Frota (1993, 1997), Falé (1995) and Vigário (1998), on the other hand, a bitonal pitch accent involving a High and Low tone (H+L*) is assumed. Finally, in Grønnum & Viana (1999) the neutral declarative fall is analysed as comprising a L* accent preceded by a tonal target explained by a prior H* tone.

The neutral declarative (and the topic) contour can be compared with the contours of sentences in which a particular constituent is focalised, and thus the broad focus reading is lost in favour of a narrow/contrastive focus reading. Although the literature on focus intonation is much more limited than that on its neutral counterpart, there are two salient properties in the available descriptions: a falling pitch movement is present in the vicinity of the stressed syllable of the focalised element, regardless of its position in the intonational phrase; if the syllable bearing the focus nuclear fall is neither the last stressed syllable of the intonational phrase

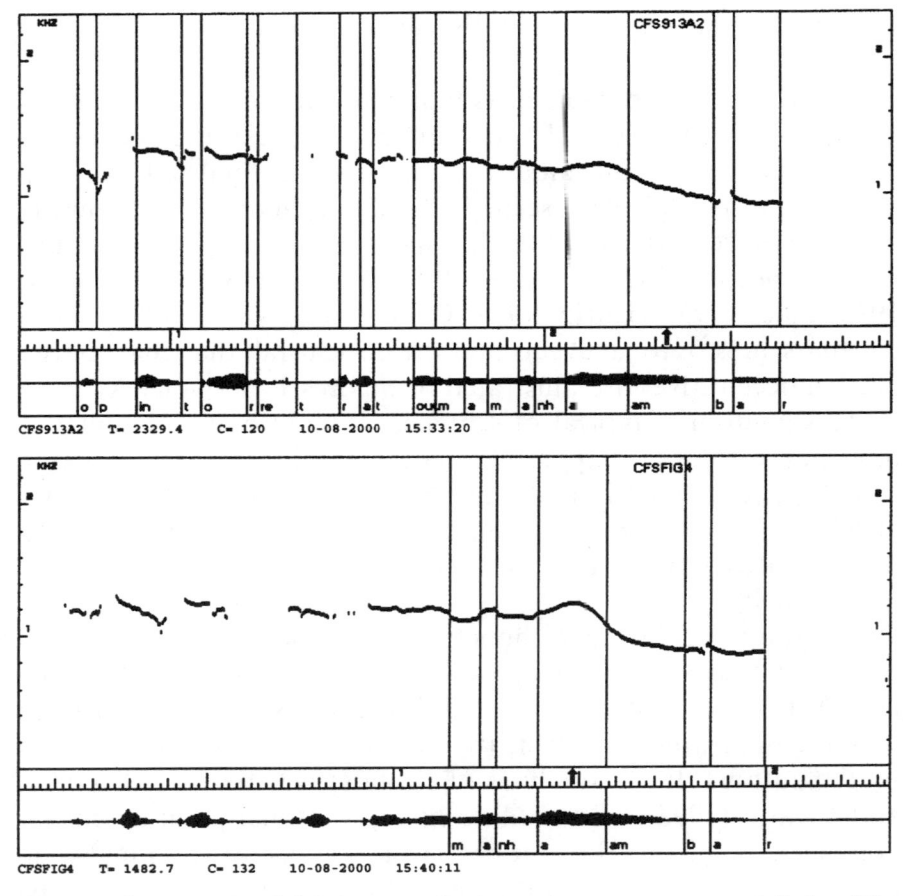

Figure 1: f₀ contours of the sentence *O pintor retratou uma maNHÃ ÂMbar* 'The artist painted an amber morning': panel A, neutral contour; panel B, focus on maNHÃ. Both utterances are phrased into one intonational phrase. The relevant stressed syllables are indicated in capitals.

nor adjacent to the last stressed syllable, a post-focal fall occurs in the final stressed syllable (Frota, 1997, 2000; Vigário, 1998). Figures 1–2 (panel B) and Figure 3 illustrate these properties.

The focus falling movement looks different from the neutral one. This difference is reflected in the analyses of the focus nuclear fall, which have all assumed a bitonal pitch accent (H*+L). This proposal, however, has never been systematically confronted with alternative analyses of nuclear falls, such as those proposed for

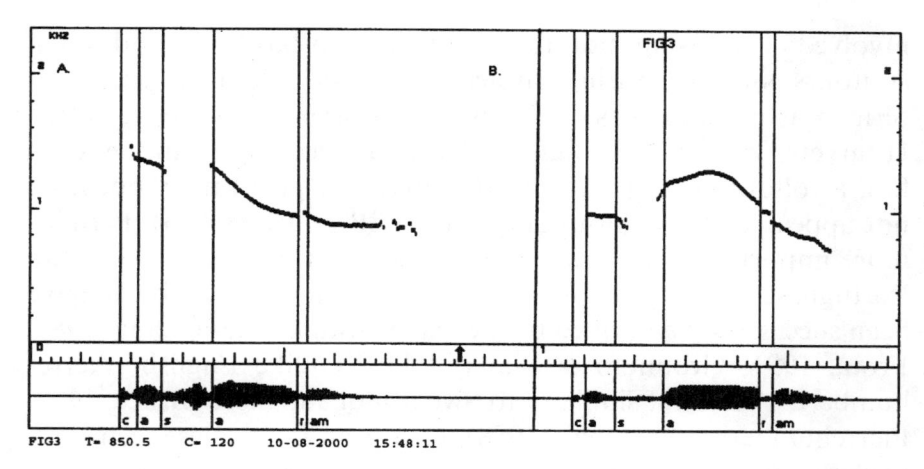

Figure 2: f₀ contours of *CasAram* 'They got married': (A) neutral contour; (B) focus contour. The stressed syllable is in capitals.

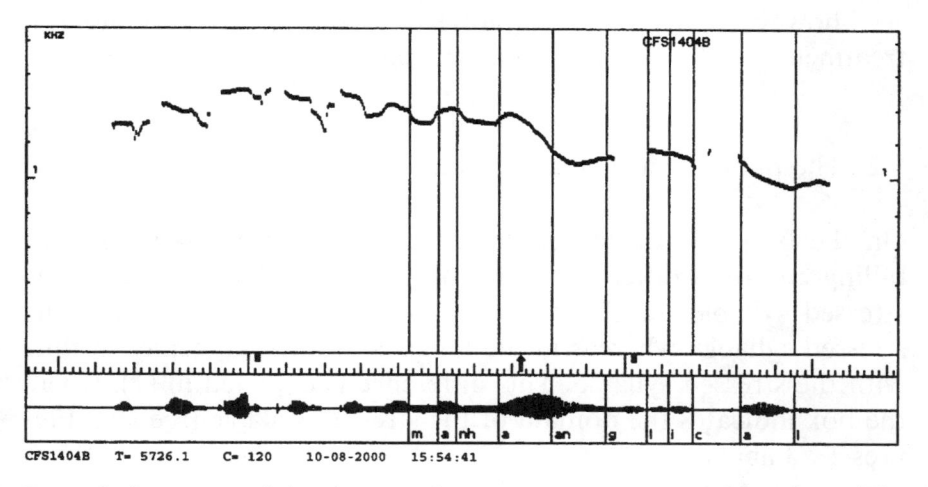

Figure 3: f₀ contour of the sentence *O poeta cantou uma maNHÃ angeliCAL* 'The poet sang an angelic morning'. The sentence is phrased into one intonational phrase. The relevant stressed syllables are indicated in capitals. Narrow/contrastive focus is indicated in bold.

Bengali or German (Hayes & Lahiri, 1991 and Benzmüller & Grice, 1998, respectively).

It should be noted that in all the previous descriptions of both the neutral nuclear fall and the focus nuclear fall a HL melody is involved. The assumption that there are two targets in both pitch contours is not surprising. In neither case can the L target be described as a consequence of "sagging" interpolation between two H targets: in the neutral fall, there is no succeeding H; in the focus fall, a following H (pronounced with a low peak) may, but need not appear in the contour (Figures 1−2B and Figure 3). Perhaps more importantly, the transitions between H targets in European Portuguese, such as the prenuclear plateau mentioned above, have been successfully described by means of straight lines (Viana, 1987; Frota, 1991; Grønnum & Viana, 1999). Unlike English (Pierrehumbert, 1980), but similarly to Swedish or Japanese (Bruce, 1977; Pierrehumbert & Beckman, 1988), European Portuguese seems not to show sagging transitions.

In accordance with the previous literature, we will consider that the nuclear falls involve a HL melody. Contrary to the prior analyses, however, this paper explores the alternative phonological treatments of the two HL tonal sequences.

1.2 The phonological status of nuclear falls

On the basis of the earlier descriptions, it is clear that the two falling contours differ in the location of the peak relative to the stressed syllable. In the neutral contour, the peak precedes the stressed syllable, whereas in the focus contour it coincides in time with the stressed syllable. This difference is depicted in (1), where the box indicates the domain of the stressed syllable (see also Figures 1−3 above).

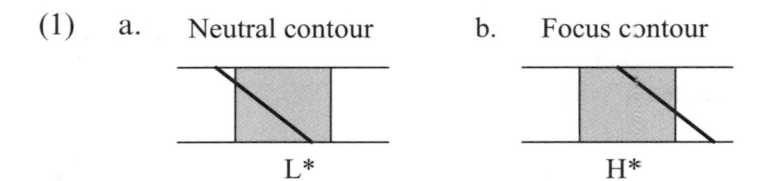

(1) a. Neutral contour   b. Focus contour

                L*   H*

It can thus be hypothesised that the neutral fall includes a starred low tone, while the focus fall includes a starred high tone. Similar timing contrasts involving peaks have been found in other languages and have been argued to express different lexical or semantic-discourse meanings (e.g. HL contrast in Swedish word accents, Bruce, 1977; LH contrasts in English, Pierrehumbert & Steele, 1989; LH/HL contrasts in Neapolitan Italian, D'Imperio & House, 1997 and D'Imperio, 1999; accent-lending falls in Dutch, Verhoeven, 1994, Caspers, 1999).

As to the status of the unstarred tones and the relationship between the two tones in each of the HL sequences, the possible alternatives are listed in (2)–(4).

(2) *The neutral HL sequence*
    a. Edge tone and monotonal accent
       (i.e. a word or φ-initial tone, realised in the first syllable of the relevant domain, followed by a T*)

$$[\,[\sigma\,'\sigma\,\sigma\,]\omega\,\ldots\,]\phi$$
$$\quad\;|\quad\;|$$
$$\quad\,H\quad L^*$$

    b. Preaccentual target explained by a preceding accent via spreading

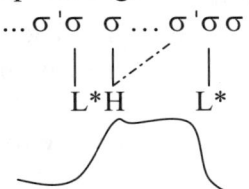

$$\ldots\sigma\,'\sigma\quad\sigma\,\ldots\,\sigma\,'\sigma\,\sigma$$
$$\quad\;|\;\;|\quad\quad\;|$$
$$\;\;L^*H\quad\quad L^*$$

('substainted pitch', Ladd 1983, Grice 1995b, for English)

    c. Complex pitch accent
       Ex: declaratives in Italian, H+L* (Grice, 1995a; D'Imperio, 1996; Hirschberg & Avesani, 1997)

(3) *The focus HL sequence*
    a. Monotonal accent and boundary tone
       Ex: focus in Bengali, L* Hp (Hayes & Lahiri, 1991)
    b. Monotonal accent and phrase accent
       Ex: Wh-questions in Greek, H* L⁻ (Grice et al., 2000)

c. Complex pitch accent
   Ex: focus in Palermo It. , H*+L;
   yes-no questions in Palermo and Neap.It., L*+H
   (Grice, 1995a; D'Imperio, 1999)

In the phonological representations hypothesised in (2a, b) and (3a, b), the falling movement is conceived as a transition between two independent tonal events. The representations hypothesised in (2c) and (3c), by contrast, treat the fall as a bitonal pitch accent.

If the testing of the hypotheses in (2) and (3), turns out to support one or both of the bitonal representations, then the hypotheses in (4) about the phonology and phonetics of bitonal accents will also have to be examined.

(4) $T+T$
   a. Both leading T and trailing T are timed with reference to T*
      (a head-initial/head-final difference, as in Pierrehumbert & Beckman 1988)
   b. Only trailing T is timed with reference to T*
      (a leading/trailing tone difference, as in Grice 1995b)
   c. Neither leading T nor trailing T is timed with reference to T*
      (independent targets, aligned with reference to some segmental landmark)
      Ex: prenuclear rises in Greek (L H)
      ... V C 'V C V ...
           | |
           L   H
      (Arvaniti et al., 2000)

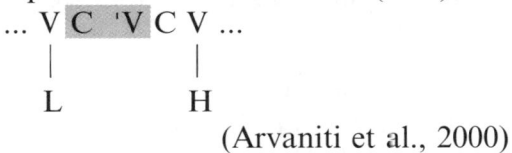

In the framework of intonation analysis adopted here, the choice among the alternatives in (2)–(4) should be empirically based. It is thus crucial to look for phonetic criteria to decide which is the starred tone and determine the relationship between the tones in each of the HL sequences. If target alignment is a reflection of phonological association, as generally assumed in the intonational phonology approach (e.g. Pierrehumbert & Beckman, 1988; Pierrehumbert & Steele, 1989; Hayes & Lahiri, 1991; Grice, 1995a; Arvaniti et al., 1998; Benzmüller & Grice, 1998; Grice et al., 2000), then the following is expected: tonal anchoring relative to (i) a prominent element indicates a T*, while tonal anchoring relative to (ii) a prosodic edge indicates a boundary tone. Furthermore, tonal anchoring conditioned by both (i) and (ii) indicates a phrase accent. Although not all phrase accents necessarily show these properties, this kind of tonal event has been described as combining a phonological edge affiliation with a secondary association to a stressed syllable in many cases (Ladd, 1996: ch. 6; Grice et al., 2000). In regard to bitonal pitch accents, the duration and slope properties of the accent are expected to indicate the kind of relationship that holds between the two tones (Arvaniti et al., 1998; D'Imperio, 1999).

In what follows, phonetic data will be examined in the light of the hypotheses in (2)–(4). We will present evidence in support of one of the competing phonological analyses for the European Portuguese nuclear falls. Implications of the results for the tonal targets view and the status of unstarred tones in intonational phonology will be subsequently discussed.

2. Methods

2.1 Speech materials

Read speech materials were designed to contain pairs of tokens with the same segmental string and the different nuclear falls in the same position, or the same type of nuclear fall in different positions. These were obtained by setting up a felicitous context (by means of a previous paragraph/question – see example (5e) below) that would elicit a neutral reading, a topic reading, or a focus reading. As the two nuclear falls had been shown to express different meanings (Vigário, 1998; Frota, 2000), it was expected that the neutral contour would be produced in the case of the neutral and topic readings, and the focus contour in the case of the focus reading. This is illustrated in (5) (capitals signal the nuclear accented syllable; the focused constituent is in bold; expected intonational phrasing is indicated).

(5)   Example from Dataset 1
As angolanas ofereceram especiarias
aos jornalistas
'The Angolans gave spices to the journalists'

   a. [As angolanas ofereceram especiarias   (neutral reading)
aos jornaLIstas]I
neutral contour

   b. [As angolanas ofereceram especiarias]I (topic reading)
[aos jornaLIstas]I
neutral contour

   c. [As angolanas ofereceram especiarias   (focus reading)
aos jornaLIstas]I
focus contour

   d. [As angoLAnas]I [ofereceram especiarias (topic reading)
aos jornalistas]I
neutral contour

   e. Context: Sabe-se que os jornalistas   (focus reading)
receberam especiarias: quem lhas
ofereceu?
'It is known that spices were given to the
journalists: who gave them?'
[**As angoLAnas** ofereceram especiarias
aos jornalistas]I
focus contour

In the corpus, the distance of the nuclear accented syllable from various prosodic edges, and the number of postnuclear syllables before the next word stress varied. The nuclear accented syllable was preceded by between zero and three prenuclear syllables up to the left-edge of the nuclear word (ω), and by between two and five syllables up to the left-edge of the phonological phrase (φ) that contains the nuclear word. The distance in syllables to the right-edge of ω and φ varies, respectively, from zero to two and zero to three postnuclear syllables. Finally, the interval between the nuclear accented syllable and the next word stress may consist of zero to three syllables. Examples of the different conditions are provided in (6)–(7), with indication of prosodic phrasing (the postnuclear word stress is underlined).

(6)   Example from Dataset 2
    a. [[O galã]φ [anda]φ [de PORsche]φ]I   (neutral contour)
    b. [[**O gaLÃ**]φ [anda]φ [de porsche]φ]I   (focus contour)
    c. [[**O gaLÃ**]φ [andava]φ [de porsche]φ]I   (focus contour)
       'The romantic lead drives/used to drive a Porsche'

(7)   Example from Dataset 2
    a. [[O pintor]φ [retratou]φ [uma manhã   (neutral contour)
       angeliCAL]φ]I
    b. [[O pintor]φ [retratou]φ [uma **maNHÃ**   (focus contour)
       angelical]φ]I
    c. [[O pintor]φ [retratou]φ [uma   (focus contour)
       maNHÃ âmbar]φ]I
       'The artist painted an amber/angelic morning'

Due to the need to obtain specific prosodic configurations, such as the ones in (5)–(7) above, a number of additional factors had to be controlled for in the corpus: syntactic structure, constituent weight, and the presence of contexts for the application of prosodically conditioned sandhi rules and rhythmic processes. Within the limits of these constraining factors, an attempt was made to choose words with sonorants in the intonationally relevant syllables and sentences that were natural sounding. The materials illustrated in (5) and (6–7) will be respectively referred to as Dataset 1 and Dataset 2.

All the materials are related to the hypothesis that there is a L* in the neutral contour and a H* in the focus contour (see (1) above). The examination of the alignment of the low target in the neutral fall and the high target in the focus fall should provide an answer as to the starred status of the L and H tones, respectively.

Materials such as those illustrated in (6)–(7) allow the testing of the hypotheses put forward in (2) and (3) regarding the status of the unstarred tones. To examine the alternative analyses of the nuclear falls, we are interested in the effects on the alignment of the HL targets of both the distance relative to prosodic edges and the next word stress. Specifically, if the contours involve an edge tone (hypotheses 2a–3a), it is predicted that target alignment should be affected by the distance relative to a given prosodic edge. If target alignment shows dual behaviour in that it is both constrained by a prosodic edge and a stressed syllable, this would constitute evidence for the phrase accent analysis (hypothesis 3b). If the presence of a preceding accent turns out to be crucial for deriving the alignment of a specific target, this would support the spreading account (hypothesis 2b). Finally, the complex pitch accent analysis (hypotheses 2c–3c) predicts that the alignment of the HL targets should show a strict relationship between the two tones, irrespective of the factors mentioned above.

The alternatives in (4) can be assessed by means of materials such as those in (5). These materials allow a direct comparison between the two falling contours produced in exactly the same segmental string. If one of the targets is timed with reference to the other in both HL sequences (hypothesis 4a), then a constant duration of the interval between targets and/or a constant slope is expected to characterise both nuclear falls. Conversely, the absence of any timing dependence between targets in either case (hypothesis 4c) would predict the opposite result. If such timing dependence is a property of only one of the sequences (hypothesis 4b), a contrast in the timing relation between targets and in the slope values is expected to set the two nuclear falls apart.

2.2 Procedure

A total of 15 test-sentences (9 from set 1 and 6 from set 2) were randomly included in a larger corpus of sentences, which contained three repetitions of each test-sentence. The materials were recorded by three female native speakers of European Portuguese (Lisbon variety). A total of 135 utterances (15 test-sentences × 3 repetitions × 3 speakers) were produced.

The speakers, all graduate students at the University of Lisbon at the time of the recordings, were instructed to read the sentences as naturally as possible in response to a previously given context. They were free to repeat the sentences in case they considered their reading not fluent or unnatural. The three best repetitions of each sentence were included in the data, with two exceptions: one of the speakers did not produce the intended nuclear fall in two of the three repetitions of one sentence, and thus this sentence was not considered for this speaker; for three other test-sentences, four repetitions of each sentence by one speaker were found to be equally acceptable and were all included in the data.

The recordings were made on audiotape in the phonetics room of the Centre of Linguistics of the University of Lisbon. The materials were later digitised at 16kHz, using the Sensimetrics Speech Station package for speech analysis. In the f_0 contours plotted using the pitch tracker facility of the Speech Station, the location of the targets involved in each nuclear fall was labelled. Identification of the H and L targets was according to the following criteria: the H was defined as the *local maximum* in the vicinity of the stressed syllable immediately before the fall (this includes both the end of a sequence uttered at the same pitch (not precluding declination) and the highest point of locally higher pitch); the L was defined as the *local minimum* also in the vicinity of the stressed syllable right before the ensuing low stretch. Examples of target identification are provided in Figure 4.

While the identification of the H was unproblematic, in some cases the L target was difficult to locate consistently. In such cases, a decision was made with the help of the Pitch ASCII facility of the Speech Station, which produces a text file with every f_0 value. This file can then be edited and used to plot a contour where regression lines are fitted to the falling region and to the low stretch after the fall. The point where the two lines intersect is taken to define the L target. A similar methodology to find a low has been used by Pierrehumbert & Beckman (1988) and D'Imperio (1996).

Two locations in the segmental string were marked with the help of zoomed waveforms in combination with spectrograms: the

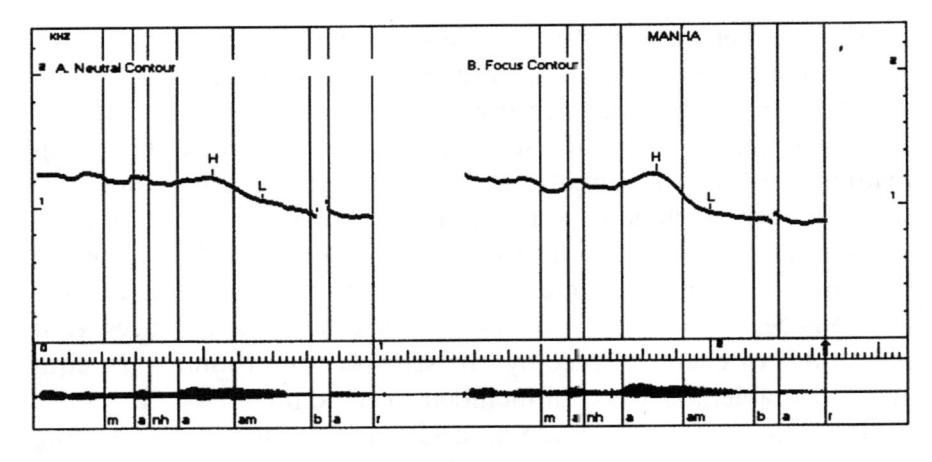

Figure 4: Waveform and f₀ traces for one neutral rendition (A: manhã âMbar) and one focus rendition (B: maNHÃ âmbar), showing the points at which the H and L targets were measured.

onset of the nuclear accented syllable (S0) and the offset of the nuclear vowel (V1). Standard criteria of segmentation were followed (Peterson & Lehiste, 1960). However, the segmentation of the vowel-vowel sequences found in the materials (see the examples in (6−7) above) requires some comment, due to its inherent difficulty. In these cases, energy curves were also used in addition to waveforms and spectrograms. The fluctuations in the location of V1 that could result from segmentation difficulties were assessed on a sample of 15 cases that were segmented three times (each time in different orders, and on different days). The results showed an average fluctuation of 5.23 ms, which did not undermine the judgements of target location as preceding or following V1.

2.3 Measurements

The data was first examined for syllable alignment. Information on the location of the targets inside or outside the nuclear syllable domain was obtained. The alignment of the targets not located within the nuclear syllable was expressed in number of syllables from the nuclear syllable (-1, -2, $-N$ for prenuclear syllables and $+1$, $+2$, $+N$ for postnuclear syllables). This observation of syllable alignment provided a primary test to the hypotheses in (1), (2) and (3), as it scrutinises the timing of the tonal targets with respect to the nuclear syllable, and the effects of both the distance from prosodic edges and a following word stress.

Additionally, several timing and f_0 measurements were obtained. They are schematically indicated in (8): the duration of the distance between S0 and the H and L targets (HtoS0 and LtoS0, respectively); the duration of the interval between H and L (DHL); the f_0 difference between H and L (f_0HL); the slope of the falling contour, measured as the relation between f_0HL and DHL.

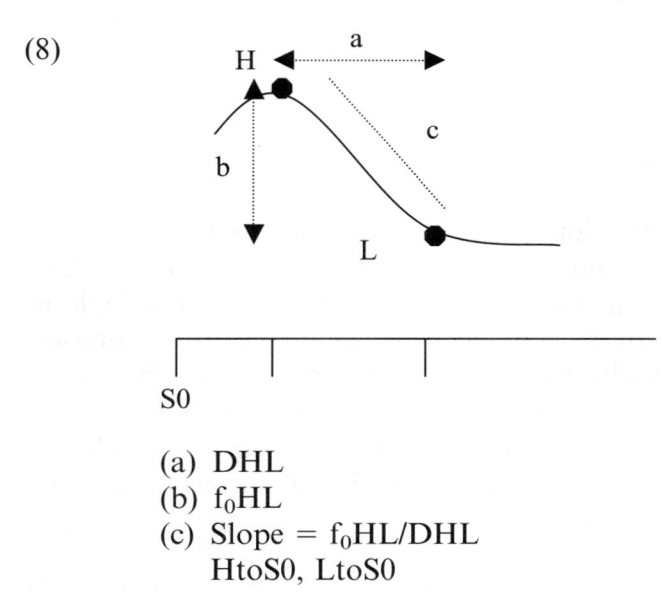

(8)

(a) DHL
(b) f_0HL
(c) Slope = f_0HL/DHL
HtoS0, LtoS0

In the materials where the two nuclear falls occur at the same position in the segmental string (see the examples in (5) above), a further measurement was considered: the duration of the distance between V1 and the L target (LtoV1).

The measurements HtoS0 and LtoV1 bear on the starred status of the H and L tones hypothesised in (1). DHL, slope, and the relation between HtoS0 and LtoS0 are particularly helpful in investigating the different alignment effects predicted by the competing hypotheses in (3), especially those related to the phrase accent analysis which may be more subtle and thus harder to disclose.

If the data support the bitonal accent hypothesis in either the neutral contour or the focus contour, or both, the alternatives put forward in (4) will require examination. The relations between DHL and f_0HL, on the one hand, and HtoS0 and LtoS0, on the other, should provide the answer: a correlation between DHL and f_0HL indicates a tendency towards a constant slope of the fall; a correlation between HtoS0 and LtoS0 indicates a tendency towards a constant duration of the interval between targets; the absence of such correlations indicates the absence of any timing dependence between targets.

3. Results

3.1 Evidence for the starred tone

Table 1 shows the position of the H and L targets relative to the nuclear syllable. The contrast between the two contours is clear. In the neutral contour, the peak precedes the nuclear syllable in 83% of the cases contra zero occurrences in the focus contour. Conversely, the low always aligns with the nuclear syllable in the neutral contour and never occurs in this position in the focus contour. These results support hypothesis (1), according to which L is a starred tone in the neutral fall, while H is a starred tone in the focus fall.

Table 1: Syllable alignment of H and L relative to the nuclear syllable (−N/+N respectively indicate the number of syllables before/after the nuclear syllable). Number of cases observed and percentages (in parenthesis). Data from sets 1 and 2.

Nuclear Fall		>−2	−2	−1	Nuclear syllable	+1	+2	>+2	Total
Neutral Contour	H	0	0	70(83)	14(17)	0	0	0	84(100)
	L	0	0	0	84(100)	0	0	0	84(100)
Focus Contour	H	0	0	0	33(65)	18(35)	0	0	51(100)
	L	0	0	0	0	32(63)	19(37)	0	51(100)

However, the peak may also occur one syllable after the syllable it is typically aligned with in both contours. In the neutral fall this pattern of alignment characterises the topic sentences where the peak is I-initial (like (5d) above), as can be seen in Figure 5. In the focus fall the initial position of the peak (as in (5e) and (6b, c)) also accounts for the cases of peak displacement. Similar cases of late alignment of the first peak in the utterance have been described for European Portuguese in Vigário (1998), Grønnum & Viana (1999) and Frota (2000), and parallel a tendency for late peak placement found in other languages (e.g. Silverman & Pierrehumbert, 1990; Prieto et al., 1995; Wichman, House & Rietveld, 1997).

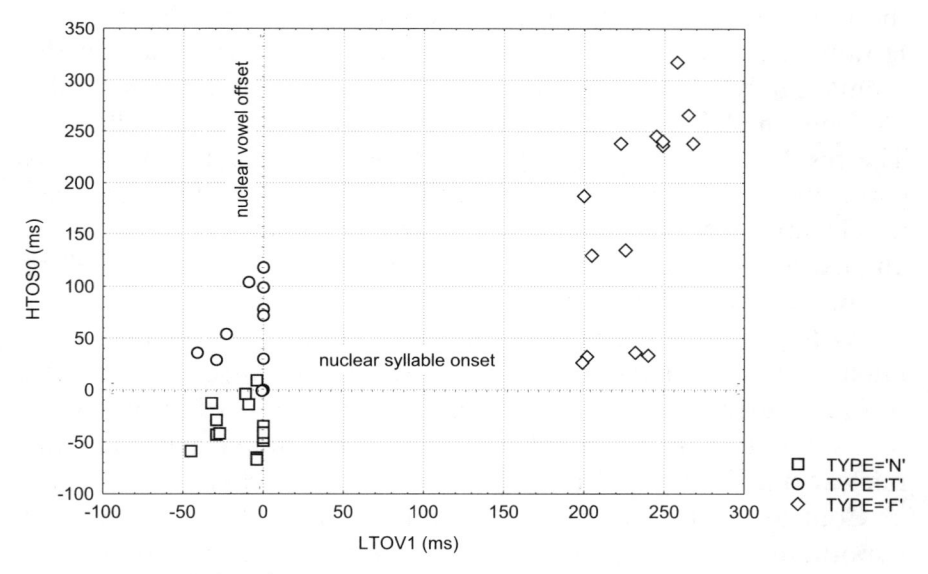

Figure 5: The intervals HtoS0 and LtoV1 for the neutral fall ('N'eutral and 'T'opic) and the focus fall ('F'ocus). Data from set 1 for speakers MV and SF, who show very similar speech rates. Equivalent contrasts are shown by the data from the third speaker.

It should further be noticed that peak displacement has different consequences for the alignment of the L target in the two contours (Table 1). In the neutral fall, the L aligns with the nuclear syllable whether the peak has been displaced or not; in the focus fall, peak displacement is largely coincident with later alignment of the following L as well (35% of late peaks and 37% of late lows). Again, this is consistent with the starred status of the low in the neutral contour, but not in the focus contour. Overall, the syllable alignment results clearly set the two nuclear falls apart, as illustrated in Figure 5.

3.2 The neutral contour

The results in Table 1 also bear on the hypothesis put forward in (2a) regarding the status of the peak in the neutral fall. If the peak were an edge tone as hypothesised in (2a), its location in the prenuclear string relative to the nuclear syllable should vary. However, it was found that the peak typically occurs within the prenuclear syllable, irrespective of the distance of the nuclear syllable from the left-edge of ω (0 to 3 syllables) or φ (2 to 5 syllables). The results thus failed to support hypothesis (2a). This finding is confirmed by the alignment patterns of the neutral fall described in Grønnum & Viana (1999), according to which the peak is aligned just before the nuclear accented syllable and never before the prenuclear syllable.

As to the hypothesis that the peak derives from a preceding pitch accent (2b), it can be straightforwardly dismissed on the basis of the occurrence of the neutral contour in one-word intonational phrases, that is in strings where the only accentable syllable is the nuclear one. Figure 2(A) illustrates one of such cases.

Contrary to the edge-tone or prior accent analyses, the bitonal hypothesis in (2c) is confirmed by the data. The peak closely precedes the low, whether located in the prenuclear or the nuclear syllable (Table 1 and Figure 5), as expected from a leading H tone of a bitonal H+L* accent.

3.3 The focus contour

Unlike in the neutral fall, the syllable alignment results of the focus fall show more variation in the position of the unstarred tone in the postnuclear string (Table 1). Although the location of the L target one or two syllables after the nuclear one is apparently related with the absence or presence of peak displacement (section 3.1), this variation may also be consistent with the alignment effects predicted by the hypotheses in (3a) and (3b).

According to hypothesis (3a), the alignment of the low should be affected by the distance to a following prosodic edge. The results in Table 2, however, show that proximity to the nuclear syllable preponderates over proximity to the prosodic edge: on the one hand, the +2 alignment is not driven by proximity to the prosodic edge, as it may occur whether the second postnuclear syllable is or is not adjacent to a prosodic boundary; on the other hand, the +1 alignment dominates even when the location of the L in the second postnuclear syllable would make it closer to a prosodic boundary.[1] Hypothesis (3a) is thus not supported by the data.

Table 2: Syllable alignment of the L target in the focus contour relative to the ω and φ boundaries. _]_ = 1 syllable at either side of the boundary; _σ]σ_ = 2 syllables before/after the boundary. Percentages relative to the possible number of cases (given in parenthesis) for each boundary description. Data from sets 1 and 2.

Boundary	]ω		]φ	
Postnuclear σ	_]_	_σ]σ_	_]_	_σ]σ_
+1	63% (51)	100% (9)	46% (35)	100% (25)
+2	35% (26)	29% (34)	21% (42)	56% (18)
Totals	53% (77)	44% (43)	33% (77)	81% (43)

The phrase accent hypothesis in (3b) predicts a composite set of alignment effects. If the phrase accent is simply characterised by a phonological edge affiliation (as in Cypriot Greek question intonation — Grice et al., 2000), the kind of effect expected would be the same as that described in the previous paragraph, which was already shown not to hold. If the phrase accent combines the former property with stress-seeking properties (as in German nuclear falls — Benzmüller & Grice, 1998), then the alignment of the low should be affected by the distance to a following word stress. Before examining whether this kind of effect is present in the data, a clarifying remark is needed regarding stress clashes in European Portuguese. As mentioned in section 1.1, European Portuguese is characterised by a sparse distribution of pitch accents whereby only the first stressed syllable and the nuclear stressed syllable of an intonational phrase are pitch accented in the typical case. Thus, a stress clash in this language does not induce the tonal crowding situation characteristic of adjacent accented syllables, which is known to affect the behaviour of tonal targets (e.g. Arvaniti et al., 1998). As a result, the behaviour of targets in stress clash sequences is not different from the cases where two or more syllables intervene between word stresses (Frota, 2000: chap. 3).

Table 3 presents the syllable alignment results of the interstress interval effect. It can be seen that contrary to expectations the occurrence of +2 alignment does not increase with the size of the interstress interval.

Table 3: Syllable alignment of the L target in the focus contour relative to the number of syllables in the interstress interval. Data from sets 1 and 2.

Interval Postnuclear σ	0 (n = 16)	1 (n = 9)	2 (n = 9)	3 (n = 17)
+1	75%	44%	100%	47%
+2	25%	56%	0	53%

Although these results do not support hypothesis (3b), it may well be the case that the stress-seeking effects have remained undisclosed by an examination based on syllable counts. Grice et al. (2000) suggest that these effects may be rather subtle and require detailed instrumental research. The testing of hypothesis (3b) was thus pursued by examining how the interstress interval affects the variation of the DHL and slope values in Dataset 2, where the distance between stresses ranges from zero to two syllables. It was expected that larger intervals yield longer DHLs and shallower slopes.

DHL values for the different interval sizes are shown in Figure 6. It can be seen that the distance between targets either remained unaffected (this is the dominant pattern), or was affected in conflicting ways contrary to our predictions (for MV it decreases when the interval gets larger, in the 'galã' subset; for CF it increases with the interval, in the 'manhã' subset).

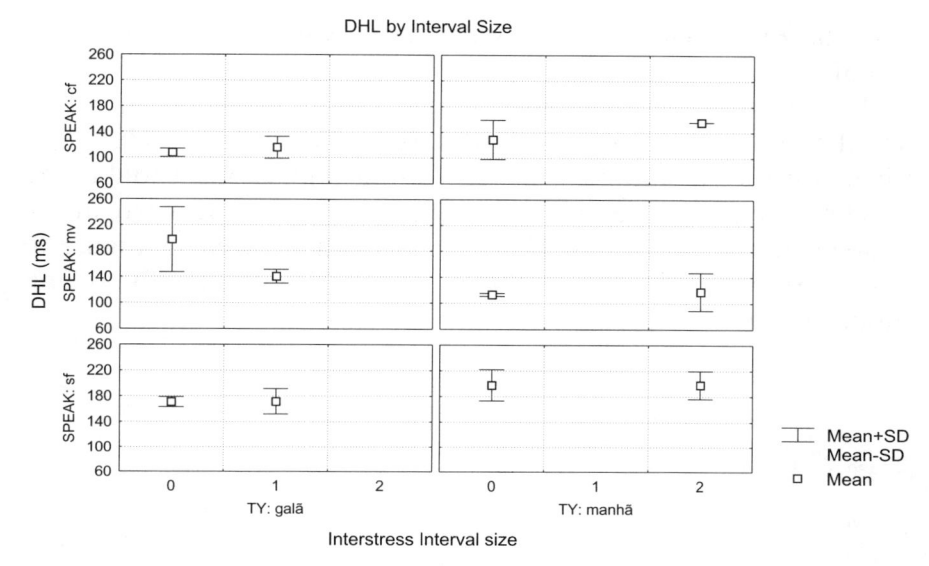

Figure 6: Whiskers plot for DHL values by interstress interval size. Data from set 2 ('**galÃ** ANda/anDAva'; **maNHÃ** âMbar/ang(e)liCAL) for each speaker separately.

These data were tested through a two-way ANOVA on pooled data for all speakers, with speaker and interval size as factors. The latter variable had two levels in each of the two subsets of data analysed: 0,1 for 'galã', and 0,2 for 'manhã' (the two subsets were illustrated in (6) and (7), respectively; in all the analyses performed, the results that yield $p \le .01$ are considered statistically significant).[2] There was no significant effect of interval size and no significant interaction, while speaker was significant [For the 'galã' set—INTERVAL SIZE: $F(1,12) = 2.569, p > .05$; SPEAKER: $F(2,12) = 15.305, p = .0005$; INTERACTION: $F(2,12) = 3.934, p = .05$. For the 'manhã' set—INTERVAL SIZE: $F(1,10) = 0.835, p > .05$; SPEAKER: $F(2,10) = 23.044, p < .0005$; INTERACTION: $F(2,10) = 0.362, p > .05$]. Post hoc comparisons of means between groups (Scheffé) showed no significant effect of INTERVAL SIZE within each speaker's data.

The examination of the effect on slope of interval size yields similar results: INTERVAL SIZE did not affect the speed of the focus fall [For the 'galã' set—INTERVAL SIZE: $F(1,12) = 0.002, p > .05$; SPEAKER: $F(2,12) = 0.082, p > .05$; INTERACTION: $F(2,12) = 2.488, p > .05$. For the 'manhã' set—INTERVAL SIZE: $F(1,10) = 1.609, p > .05$;

SPEAKER: $F(2,10) = 3.771, p > .05$; INTERACTION: $F(2,10) = 0.755, p > .05$].

The relation between HtoS0 and LtoS0 provides an additional test to hypothesis (3b). If target alignment is indeed affected by the interstress interval, HtoS0 and LtoS0 should not be correlated. The results, however, show a strong correlation between the alignment of H and L, as can be seen in Figure 7 [$r = 0.767$, $r^2 = 0.588$, $p < .0001$]. Again, hypothesis (3b) is not supported by the data.

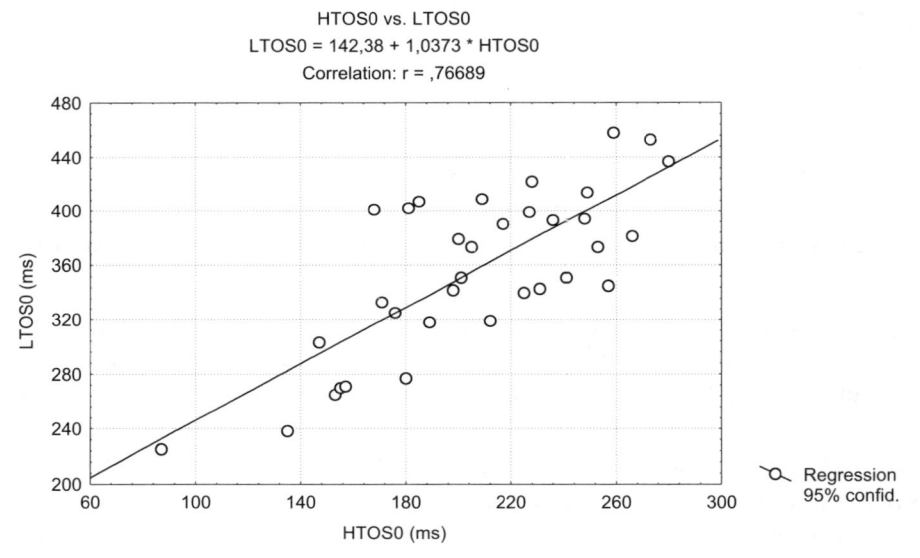

Figure 7: The interval LtoS0 as a function of the interval HtoS0 in the focus fall. Data from set 2 (all speakers together).

Overall, the results indicate that the location of the low is independent of the position of the following stress, while it is dependent on the location of the peak. In other words, the results show a tight timing relationship between the H and L targets. This finding is certainly consistent with the bitonal hypothesis in (3c). There is, however, a third version of the phrase accent analysis that is also consistent with the data: the possibility that the phrase accent may show a secondary association not to a postnuclear stressed syllable but to the nuclear accented syllable (as in English nuclear falls — Grice et al., 2000). In the two alternative treatments the timing dependence of the low on the peak is expected. The phrase accent alternative, nevertheless, must be rejected for independent reasons. Phrase accents are defined as final in a phrase, that is they follow the last pitch accent (Beckman & Pierrehumbert, 1986). In European Portuguese, an early focus fall is followed by a post-focal accent in the last stressed syllable of the phrase (as mentioned in section 1.1; see also Frota, 2000: ch. 5). As the focus fall is not always phrase-final, the low cannot be explained by a phrase accent that has a secondary association with the nuclear syllable across the last accented syllable of the same phrase.

Note that an analysis in which desequencing is allowed for, as proposed in Gussenhoven (2000) for Roermond Dutch, would not provide an adequate account of the European Portuguese data either. Under such analysis, a right-edge tone may appear to the left of an accentual tone which is final in its phrase, where the two tones compete for the final position. In the Portuguese case, however, we can see no reason why an ordering of the edge tone before the final pitch accent should arise, as the same contour is found irrespective of the number of syllables after the last stressed syllable of the phrase or the length of the intervening stretch between the early focus fall and the post-focal accent.

Consequently, only the bitonal analysis, according to which the low is a trailing tone of a H*+L accent, may account for the focus fall.

3.4 The characterisation of bitonality

We have reached the conclusion that both nuclear falls should be treated as bitonal pitch accents. We are thus compelled to examine the three alternative descriptions of bitonality put forward in (4) above. The three alternatives distinguish among a timing dependence between targets in all bitonal accents (4a), in some of them (4b), or in none of them (4c). Crucially, only in possibility (4b) are leading and trailing tones expected to show different properties.

These possibilities were tested by examining slope and interval duration in both nuclear falls in Dataset 1.

As can be seen in Table 4, a significant correlation between DHL and f₀HL was found only in the focus fall. This is a first indication of a contrast between the two bitonal accents, suggesting that slope is a relevant property only for H*+L.

Table 4: Summary of the correlation results for DHL/f₀HL. Pearson *r* values. ** = $p \leq .005$; *** = $p \leq .001$. Data from set 1.

DHL/f₀HL	H+L* (angolanas)	H*+L (angolanas)	H+L* (jornalistas)	H*+L (jornalistas)
r	−0.307	0.953***	−0.086	−0.974**

The results, however, also indicate that there is more to the timing of the targets in the focus fall than a tendency to achieve a constant slope. First, the direction of the correlation is different if the focus fall occurs in the last stressed syllable of the phrase, as in 'jornalistas', or earlier in the phrase, as in 'angolanas', indicating that time pressure will prompt speakers to produce steeper slopes. More importantly, as Figure 8 shows, HtoS0 and LtoS0 are more strongly correlated in H*+L than in H+L*. Furthermore, the difference between the two correlation coefficients is highly significant [H*+L: $r = 0.932$; H+L*: $r = 0.659$; Difference: $p < .005$]. Clearly, then, a tendency towards a constant duration of the interval between targets prevails in the focus fall. That is, H*+L has both a more constant slope and a more constant timing interval between its targets than H+L*. The second result, in particular, suggests that the relation between targets is different in the two accents.

The finding that the two accents contrast does not support alternatives (4a) and (4c), while it is consistent with alternative (4b). Besides the head-initial/head-final difference that characterises H*+L and H+L*, the results show a leading/trailing tone difference in which the leading H tone is timed independently of the T*, whereas the trailing L tone is timed with reference to the T*.

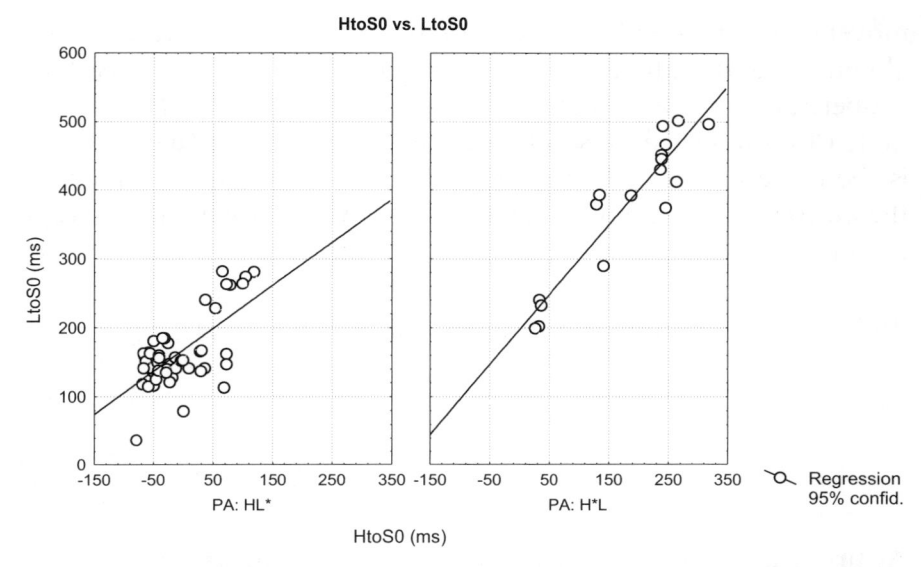

Figure 8: The interval LtoS0 as a function of the interval HtoS0, for each kind of nuclear fall. Data from set 1 (all speakers together).

4. Discussion

4.1 Primitives of intonation: targets or configurations?

This paper was motivated by issues that spring from the autosegmental metrical approach to intonational phonology, in particular the need to provide evidence for the appropriate phonological analysis of European Portuguese nuclear falls. Evidence was provided for treating the nuclear falls as bitonal pitch accents, instead of transitions between a single-tone accent and an edge-tone of some sort. In addition, the bitonal accents were shown to display different properties as to the kind of relationship that holds between the two tones of each accent. These findings, however, are also relevant to the targets versus configurations debate around the nature of intonation primes. For the present purposes, the relevant trait of the two positions boils down to the following: if configurations are primitives, then slope and/or duration of the pitch movement should be the consistent properties of pitch accents, and the local f_0 targets would be determined by the properties of the movements; if levels are what tonal events consist of, then the alignment and scaling of local f_0 targets should be the consistent properties of pitch accents, and 'rises' or 'falls' would be determined by the transitions between tonal targets. The first position is the more traditional one, whereas the latter is that assumed by the autosegmental approach. The two views are schematically represented in (9).

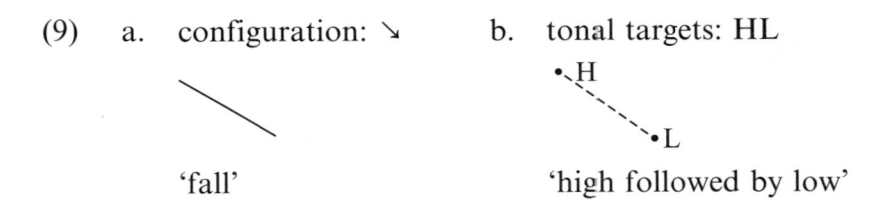

(9) a. configuration: ↘   b. tonal targets: HL

  'fall'   'high followed by low'

At first glance, the evidence provided by the contrast between the two bitonal accents looks inconclusive: the properties of H*+L apparently favour (9a), whereas the properties of H+L* favour (9b). A closer observation, however, shows that this contrast offers an argument for the tonal targets view. We have seen that the unstarred tone of the neutral accent is not timed with reference to the starred tone, but with a particular position in the segmental string (i.e. the pre-accented syllable). Therefore, in the neutral fall both tones are aligned with specific segmental positions. Such regular patterns of alignment are what defines H+L*, and not the duration or slope of the fall. Accents like H+L* are thus not expected under the configurations view. As to the focus fall, it looks like a configuration, especially due to the importance of interval duration as a consistent property of H*+L. However, the 'configuration' effect is derived from regular patterns of alignment as well: the peak aligns with the stressed syllable and the low is timed with reference to the peak. Consequently, the interval between the high and the low tends to be constant. In other words, the same mechanisms that underlie the tonal targets view are also capable of accounting for accents like H*+L. Contrasts between unstarred tones timed independently of the starred tone or with reference to it are only possible within a theory that treats tonal targets as primitives.

The EP findings, however, do not support the strong version of the "segmental anchoring" claim proposed by Ladd, Faulkner, Faulkner & Schepman (1999), which takes the tonal target view to its extreme by disallowing accents with the properties of H*+L.

4.2 Leading and trailing tones and pitch accent structure

A complete account of the contrast between the two bitonal accents should deal with the difference in the phonetics of leading and trailing tones described in section 3.4. In the spirit of the intonational phonology approach, such a systematic difference should be taken to reflect a difference in their phonological representation. The standard distinction that characterises bitonal accents is a head-initial/head-final difference, as depicted in (10a) (Pierrehumbert, 1980; Beckman & Pierrehumbert, 1986). The European Portuguese accents, however, show that leading and trailing tones cannot be simply seen as the unstarred element of a bitonal accent: besides either closely preceding or following the accent's head, the unstarred element may lean on the head or be independent of the head. Along the lines of proposals in Grice (1995a,b), such a difference can be naturally captured in terms of the structural relations that may hold between tones, as depicted in (10b). This makes the internal organisation of pitch accents similar to that of other phonological entities, such as the prosodic word (as noted by Grice) or the tune (according to proposals in Ladd, 1996).

(10) a. standard linear view

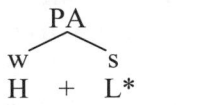

```
        PA                    PA
       /  \                  /  \
      W    S                S    W
      H  + L*               H* + L
```

b. structured view

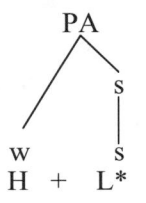

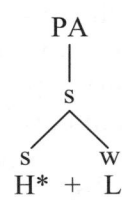

```
        PA                    PA
       / \                    |
      /   S                   S
      |   |                  / \
      W   S                 S   W
      H + L*                H* + L
```

If bitonal pitch accents are structured entities, the realisational difference found would follow from a *dominance* contrast: the independence of H, the leading tone, follows from its projection outside the scope of the accent's head, whereas the dependence of L, the trailing tone, follows from its projection inside the head's scope.

The hypothesis of pitch accent structure, which is empirically motivated by findings such as those presented in this paper, opens a new line of research devoted to exploring the theoretical and empirical consequences of the proposal. Issues like the independence of precedence and dominance relations or the potential asymmetry between leading and trailing tones are among the topics for future cross-linguistic research in this area of intonational phonology.

5. Conclusion

In this paper, the various competing phonological analyses for the nuclear falls that characterise European Portuguese declarative sentences with a broad or a narrow focus reading have been tested. Evidence was provided for treating both the neutral and the focus nuclear falls as bitonal pitch accents, instead of transitions between phonologically independent tonal events. In addition, the examination of the different alternatives that might account for the relationship between the two tones of a bitonal accent provided evidence for a contrast in the timing of unstarred tones relative to the accent's head. It was shown that the leading tone is timed independently, whereas the trailing tone is timed with reference to the starred tone. Implications of the results for the conception of intonation primes as tonal targets and bitonal accents as structured entities have been discussed.

To the extent that the present investigation has succeeded, we have been able to bring phonetic data to bear on the phonological organisation of pitch contours. In future research, we hope to extend this approach to the yet largely unstudied rising contours of European Portuguese.

Acknowledgements

I would like to thank Martine Grice, Bob Ladd, Marina Nespor, Lisa Selkirk, Marina Vigário and an anonymous reviewer for their helpful comments on earlier versions of this work. I gratefully acknowledge financial support from *Fundação Calouste Gulbenkian* for my participation in Labphon7.

Notes

1 In the materials, there are cases where the ω and φ boundaries coincide (e.g. [as angolanas]φ). These cases count for both the ω and φ boundary cells in Table 2.
2 Due to the relatively small n per cell, two of the main assumptions underlying the use of ANOVA have been tested and checked for violations, for all sets of data analysed: the normal distribution fit of the dependent variable and the non-correlation between means and standard deviations. No violations that could yield a misleading F statistic were found. The level of significance selected ($p \leq .01$) was also chosen to reduce the probability of error involved in accepting the observed values as representative.

References

Arvaniti, A., Ladd, D. R. & Mennen, I.
    1998   Stability of tonal alignment: the case of Greek prenuclear accents. *Journal of Phonetics*, **26**, 3−25.
Arvaniti, A., Ladd, D. R. & Mennen, I.
    2000   What is a starred tone? Evidence from Greek. In M. Broe & J. Pierrehumbert (eds.), *Papers in Laboratory Phonology*, **V**: *Acquisition and the Lexicon* (pp. 119−131). Cambridge: Cambridge Universty Press.
Beckman, M. & Pierrehumbert, J.
    1986   Intonational structure in Japanese and English, *Phonology Yearbook*, **3**, 255−310.
Benzmüller, R. & Grice, M.
    1998   The nuclear accentual fall in the intonation of Standard German. *ZAS Papers in Linguistics: Papers on the conference "The word as a phonetic unit"*, (pp. 79−89). Berlin.
Bruce, G.
    1977   *Swedish Word Accents in Sentence Perspective*. Lund: Gleerup.
Caspers, J.
    1999   The early versus late accent-lending fall in Dutch: phonetic variation or phonological difference? Paper presented at HILP4, Amsterdam.

Delgado Martins, M. R. & Lacerda, F.
1977   Para uma gramática da entoação. Paper given at the *Congresso de Filologia e Linguística*, Rio de Janeiro.

D'Imperio, M.
1996   Caratteristiche di timing degli accenti nucleari in parlato italiano letto. *Associazione Italiana di Acustica, XXIV Convegno Nazionale*, 55–60. Trento.

D'Imperio, M.
1999   Tonal structure and pitch targets in Italian focus constituents. *Proceedings of the XIV International Congress of Phonetic Sciences*, **99**, Vol **3**, 1757–1760. San Francisco.

D'Imperio, M. & House, D.
1997   Perception of questions and statements in Neapolitan Italian. *Eurospeech '97*, 251–254.

Falé, I.
1995   Fragmento da prosódia do Português Europeu: as estruturas coordenadas, MA thesis, University of Lisbon.

Frota, S.
1991   Para a prosódia da frase: quantificador, advérbio e marcação prosódica, MA thesis, University of Lisbon.

Frota, S.
1993   On the prosody of focus in European Portuguese. *Proceedings of the Workshop on Phonology*, (pp. 45–66). Lisboa: APL.

Frota, S.
1997   On the prosody and intonation of focus in European Portuguese. In F. Martínez-Gil & A. Morales-Front (eds.), *Issues in the Phonology and Morphology of the Major Iberian Languages*, (pp. 359–392). Washington, D.C.: Georgetown University Press.

Frota, S.
2000   *Prosody and focus in European Portuguese. Phonological phrasing and intonation.* New York: Garland Publishing.

Grabe, E.
1997   Comparative intonational phonology: English and German. In A. Botinis et al. (eds.), *Intonation: Theory, Models and Applications*, (pp. 157–160). Athens: ESCA/University of Athens.

Grice, M.
1995a   *The Intonation of Interrogation in Palermo Italian: Implications for Intonation Theory.* Tübingen: Niemeyer.

Grice, M.
1995b   Leading tones and downstep in English. *Phonology*, **12**, 183–233.

Grice, M., Ladd, D. R. & Arvaniti, A.
2000   On the place of phrase accents in intonational phonology. *Phonology*, **17**, 143–185.

Grønnum, N. & Viana, M. C.
1999 Aspects of European Portuguese Intonation. *Proceedings of the XIV International Congress of Phonetic Sciences*, Vol 3, (pp. 1997–2000). San Francisco.

Gussenhoven, C.
1984 *On the Grammar and Semantics of Sentence Accents*. Dordrecht: Foris.

Gussenhoven, C.
2000 The boundary tones are coming: on the nonperipheral realisation of boundary tones. In M. B. Broe & J. B. Pierrehumbert (eds.), *Papers in Laboratory Phonology V: Acquisition and the Lexicon*, (pp. 132–151). Cambridge: Cambridge Universtity Press.

Gussenhoven, C. & van der Vliet, P.
1999 The phonology of tone and intonation in the Dutch dialect of Venlo. *Journal of Linguistics*, **35**, 99–135.

Hayes, B.
1989 The prosodic hierarchy in meter. In P. Kiparsky & G. Youmans (eds.), *Phonetics and Phonology. Rhythm and Meter*, (pp. 201–260). New York: Academic Press.

Hayes, B. & Lahiri, A.
1991 Bengali Intonational Phonology. *Natural Language and Linguistic Theory*, **9**, 47–96.

Hirschberg, J. & Avesani, C.
1997 The role of prosody in disambiguating potentially ambiguous utterances in English and Italian. In A. Botinis et al. (eds.), *Intonation: Theory, Models and Applications*, (pp. 189–192). Athens: ESCA/ University of Athens.

Jun, S.-A.
1996 *The Phonetics and Phonology of Korean Prosody: Intonational Phonology and Prosodic Structure*. New York: Garland Publishing.

Ladd, D. R.
1983 Phonological features of intonational peaks. *Language*, **59**, 721–759.

Ladd, D. R.
1996 *Intonational Phonology*. Cambridge: CUP.

Ladd, D. R., Faulkner, D., Faulkner, H. & Schepman, A.
1999 Constant "segmental anchoring" of F0 movements under changes in speech rate. *Journal of the Acoustical Society of America*, **106**, 1543–1554.

Martins, F.
1986 Entoação e Organização do Enunciado, MA dissertation, University of Lisbon.

Nespor, M. & Vogel, I.
1986 *Prosodic Phonology*. Dordrecht: Foris.

Peterson, G. E. & Lehiste, I.
1960　　Duration of syllable nuclei in English. *Journal of the Acoustical Society of America*, **32**, 693−703.
Pierrehumbert, J.
1980　　The phonology and phonetics of English intonation, Ph.D. dissertation, MIT.
Pierrehumbert, J. & Beckman, M.
1988　　*Japanese Tone Structure*. Cambridge, Mass.: MIT Press.
Pierrehumbert, J. & Steele, S. A.
1989　　Categories of tonal alignment in English. *Phonetica*, **46**, 181−196.
Prieto, P., van Santen, J. & Hischberg, J.
1995　　Tonal alignment patterns in Spanish. *Journal of Phonetics*, **23**, 429−451.
Selkirk, E.
1984　　*Phonology and Syntax: The Relation between Sound and Structure*. Cambridge, Mass.: MIT Press.
Silverman, K. & Pierrehumbert, J.
1990　　The timing of prenuclear high accents in English. In J. Kingston & M. Beckman (eds.), *Papers in Laboratory Phonology I: Between the Grammar and the Physics of Speech*, (pp. 72−106). Cambridge: Cambridge University Press.
Sosa, J. M.
1999　　*La entonación del Español. Su estructura fónica, variabilidad y dialectologia*. Madrid: Cátedra.
Verhoeven, J.
1994　　The discrimination of pitch movement alignment in Dutch. *Journal of Phonetics*, **22**, 65−85.
Viana, M. C.
1987　　Para a síntese da entoação do Português, Dissertação para acesso à categoria de Investigador Auxiliar. Lisboa: CLUL-INIC.
Vigário, M.
1998　　*Aspectos da Prosódia do Português Europeu: estruturas com advérbio de exclusão e negação frásica*. Braga: CEHUM.
Wichmann, A., House, J. & Rietveld, T.
1997　　Peak displacement and topic structure. In A. Botinis et al. (eds.), *Intonation: Theory, Models and Applications*, (pp. 329−332.) Athens: ESCA/University of Athens.

Gestural overlap and recoverability: Articulatory evidence from Georgian

Ioana Chitoran, Louis Goldstein and Dani Byrd

Abstract

According to previous investigations of gestural patterning, consonant gestures exhibit less temporal overlap in a syllable/word onset than in a coda or across syllables. Additionally, front-to-back order of place of articulation in stop-stop sequences (labial-coronal, coronal-dorsal, labial-dorsal) exhibits more overlap than the opposite order. One possible account for these differences is that substantial overlap of obstruent gestures may threaten their perceptual recoverability, particularly word/utterance-initially and in a back-to-front sequence. We report here on a magnetometer study of gestural overlap, investigating the role of perceptual recoverability. We focus on Georgian, which allows stop sequences in different positions in the word. C1C2 sequences were examined as a function of position in the word, and the order of place of articulation of C1 and C2. The predictions were borne out: more overlap was allowed in positions where recoverability of C1 is less easily compromised (word-internally and in front-to-back sequences). Similar recoverability requirements are proposed to account for consonant sequencing phenomena violating sonority. Georgian syllable onsets violate sonority, but are apparently sensitive to gestural recoverability requirements as reflected in overlap patterns. We propose that sonority sequencing allows gestures to overlap while still allowing recoverability, but this function can apparently be filled in other ways.

1. Introduction

Linguistic phonetics has long been motivated, or perhaps plagued, by the search for articulatory and acoustic invariance. However, the discovery of invariant aspects of speech has proven elusive. In fact, one of the aspects of speech which has been long recognized as highly variable is its temporal patterning (Gaitenby, 1965; Klatt, 1976). In response to this fact, research has been developed along two directions: (i) pursuing more abstract methods of expressing timing relations in terms of dynamics and phasing, as part of a general theoretical framework that characterizes the systematic articulatory patterns occurring in speech (Kelso, Saltzman & Tuller, 1986; Browman & Goldstein, 1990; Saltzman & Byrd, 2000); (ii) attempting to identify different linguistic factors which systematically determine surface variation, and to account for the variation in terms of the interaction of multiple constraints, possibly reflecting different levels of phonological structure (Byrd, 1996b; Byrd & Saltzman, 1998). For example, parameter values such as constriction location and degree (traditional, place and manner) of gestures and their position in the larger structures of the syllable, word and phrase have been found to exert systematic influences on gestural timing — both within and between gestural units.

It has also become clear that many of these linguistic effects on the speaker's coordination of gestures are likely to be motivated either diachronically or synchronically (or both) by the need to ensure the best chance at successfully completing the communicative act. That is to say, that the temporal variability shown in speakers' coordination of articulatory movements appears to be sensitive to the necessity of recovering the intended linguistic units from the acoustic signal.

In the present study, we investigate two phonological properties which have been suggested to systematically influence multi-gesture coordination. These are place of articulation and position in the word. These parameters are of particular interest, as the influence they have been hypothesized to exert on intergestural timing seems to reflect the needs of the listener in terms of perceptual recoverability of the coordinated gestures. Specifically, our study focuses on the articulatory patterning of consonant sequences in Georgian, a South Caucasian, Kartvelian language.

Consonants, and particularly the consonants of Georgian, are of special interest for such work. Landmarks in consonant (constriction) articulatory trajectories are reasonably well understood and amenable to analysis. Georgian provides an excellent test bed for questions of intergestural timing as it allows complex sequences of adjacent stop consonants in both word initial and word internal positions — a combination which is rare in the world's languages.

Stop sequences are an important multi-gesture complex to study, as recoverability of these gestures is at particular risk when there is a large amount of gestural overlap. Finally, no articulatory data has been available on Georgian, that we are aware of, apart from X-ray data discussed in Zhgenti (1956).

In this study we use movement tracking data to ascertain the degree of articulatory coproduction (or overlap) in stop-stop sequences as a function of two linguistic factors:

- order of place of articulation (front preceding back versus back preceding front) in the consonant sequences
- position of the consonant sequence in the word (word-initial versus word-internal)

We propose that perceptual recoverability requirements account for consonant sequencing phenomena in Georgian, which violate the sonority sequencing generalization.

We begin in Section 2 with an overview of previous work on the effect of place of articulation and word position on the timing, or gestural overlap, of consonant sequences. The method for the articulatory experiment on Georgian is presented in section 3. Section 4 contains the results; and a discussion is presented in section 5.

2. Background

2.1 Effects of word position

Recent investigations of gestural patterning (e.g., Hardcastle, 1985; Byrd, 1996a) have found that sequences of consonant gestures exhibit less temporal overlap in a word onset than when they occur elsewhere. One possible account for this difference is that substantial overlap of obstruent gestures may threaten their perceptual recoverability, and this may be particularly problematic in utterance-initial position. The proposal that recoverability-related issues guide the coordination of gestures has previously been formulated by Byrd (1994; 1996a, b), Silverman & Jun (1994), Silverman (1995), and Wright (1996). We argue here for a similar approach.

There are two reasons why word onset position might be well protected against a high degree of gestural overlap; both relate to issues of perceptual recoverability. Word onsets are potential utterance onsets and, as such, sequences of stop consonant gestures in this position provide the listener with no acoustic information during their formation. That is, no formant transitions from a preceding vowel into either C1 or C2 are available. Transitions are present only during the release of C2 into a following vowel, but not during the release of C1, since there is no vowel following (for discussion, see Redford & Diehl, 1999). Because the acoustic information for C1 is limited in this way, the degree to which the two consonants may overlap each other might be consequently restricted so as to preserve as much acoustic information as possible about each of the consonants. In this case it becomes crucial for the first consonant in the sequence to be acoustically released if it is a stop, since in word-/utterance-initial position the acoustic release is the only available information as to the presence and nature of that consonant. Furthermore, it is well known that word onsets are important in lexical access (Marslen-Wilson, 1987). This factor might further encourage limits on articulatory overlap in this position to ensure recoverability of the important initial segments.

Several previous studies have contributed to our understanding of the effect of word position on consonant sequence timing. An electropalatographic study of stop-stop and s-stop clusters by Byrd (1996a) indicates that consonant gestures exhibit less temporal overlap in a syllable/word onset than in a coda or across syllables/words. Similarly, for stop-liquid clusters, Hardcastle (1985) found less overlap in onset #kl than in k#l. Byrd (1996a) also demonstrated that an s-stop sequence occurring as an onset cluster is not only less overlapped, but also less variable in its timing than the same sequence as a coda cluster or a heterosyllabic sequence.

Acoustic data on consonant overlap is available from two languages, Tsou (spoken in Taiwan) and Georgian. Wright (1996) shows acoustic evidence from Tsou stop-stop sequences, suggesting that the timing between articulations is governed by recoverability requirements. In Tsou word-initial stop-stop sequences, a smaller degree of overlap is allowed than in word-internal sequences. The same is found to be true in an acoustic study of Georgian (Chitoran, 1999). The acoustic signal, however, is not directly informative as to the amount of overlap, nor as to whether the absence of an acoustic release is due to the fact that the respective stop is not released articulatorily, or to the fact that its release is hidden, overlapped by the following stop. It generally can only tell us whether sufficient overlap exists to obscure an acoustic release burst of C1. In both Tsou and Georgian, C1 is always released in word-initial position, and is less systematically released when the stop-stop sequence occurs word-internally. This suggests that overlap is more constrained word-initially.

In summary, the articulatory study we present below will test the hypothesis:

H1: Word-initial stop-stop sequences will be less overlapped than like word-internal sequences.

2.2 Effects of order of place of articulation

Just as perceptual recoverability is argued to be a factor in the word position effect on timing in stop-stop sequences, recoverability considerations may also constrain the patterns of articulatory overlap that occur as a function of the places of articulation of the consonants. In particular, a front-preceding-back order of place of articulation in stop-stop sequences (such as labial-coronal, coronal-dorsal, or labial-dorsal) is expected to allow more overlap than the back-preceding-front order. (In the following we will use the phrase "back-to-front" to refer to a sequence where the more posterior constriction is that of C1 and the more anterior constriction is that of C2; and the reverse for "front-to-back" sequences.) Back-to-front sequences are expected to allow less overlap because, just in the case when the second stop constriction is more anterior than the first, the release of the constriction for the first stop will produce no acoustic manifestation if the constriction for the second consonant is already in place. At a high degree of overlap, the second constriction lies ahead of the first constriction, which is yet to be released. If, however, the second consonant has a place of articulation more posterior than that of the first, then at least some acoustic information will be generated on release of C1 (even if it does not generate the substantial release burst associated with venting a high-pressure chamber to the atmosphere). Even at a high degree of overlap, because the second constriction lies behind the first constriction, it is less likely to obscure the first consonant's release. The loss of the release information useful in recovering the first consonant in the back-to-front order would be a detriment to perceptual recoverability. Consequently, a more limited degree of overlap would be predicted for such a back-to-front sequence, where C1 gestures are more easily hidden by C2 gestures.

These recoverability considerations may account for several previous experimental results that show that a front-to-back order of place of articulation (labial-coronal, coronal-dorsal, labial-dorsal) allows more overlap than the opposite order, and is more effective in the recoverability of C1 gesture. C1 is more systematically correctly perceived, for example, in labial-coronal than in coronal-labial sequences, even at a higher degree of overlap. Byrd (1992) finds that in the speech stimuli [b#d] and [d#b] synthesized with an articulatory synthesizer, as the amount of overlap is increased, identification of C1 is significantly reduced in [d#b], more so than in [b#d]. This suggests an effect of ordering of the two gestures, and Byrd proposes that a tongue tip gesture is more easily hidden by a following labial gesture than vice-versa. Surprenant & Goldstein (1998) obtained similar results with natural speech [p#t] and [t#p] in English. The tokens used in the perception experiment exhibited the same considerable amount of overlap. C1 in [p#t] was correctly identified significantly more often than C1 in [t#p].

As for other places of articulation, articulatory data from English in Hardcastle & Roach (1979), Zsiga (1994), Byrd (1996a) show that coronal-dorsal sequences ([t#k], [d#g]) allow more overlap than the opposite order ([k#t], [g#d]). Peng (1996) presents results from a perceptual study of place coarticulation in Taiwanese which suggest that a similar overlap pattern is present in this language (a coronal-dorsal sequence is more overlapped than a dorsal-coronal one). This suggests that a tongue tip gesture is more easily overlapped by a following tongue body gesture than vice versa. However, these studies do not provide articulatory data that include the labial stops.

The effect of order of place is observed in acoustic studies by Wright (1996) for Tsou, and by Chitoran (1999) for Georgian. The acoustic parameter measured in both studies is the inter-burst interval between C1 and C2. The interval was found to be significantly shorter in front-to-back than in back-to-front sequences, suggesting a higher degree of overlap in the former. However, these acoustic findings are again limited in interpretability given that gestural overlap cannot be directly inferred from acoustics alone.

The articulatory movement tracking study reported below evaluates the following hypothesis:

H2: Stop-stop sequences with a back-to-front order of constriction location (coronal-labial, dorsal-labial, dorsal-coronal) will evidence less gestural overlap than stop-stop sequences with a front-to-back order.

We turn in the next section to the description of the experiment, and some information on the phonology of Georgian.

3. Method

Two native speakers of Georgian served as subjects.

3.1 Data

We begin by presenting the stop inventory of Georgian:

(1)   b   d   dz   dʒ   g
                pʰ   tʰ   tsʰ   tʃʰ   kʰ
                p'   t'   ts'   tʃ'   k'   q

The stimulus sentences each have a target word containing a stop-stop sequence. The target words were embedded in the frame sentence: **Sit'q'va ___ gamoitʰkʰmis ordʒer.** *'word ___ is pronounced twice.'* Although more data were collected and analyzed, we report here the results for a subset of the forms, selected for a balanced factorial design. These stimuli are listed in Table 1, with their glosses.

Table 1: Stimuli and glosses in IPA transcription (- indicates a morpheme boundary).

Consonants C1	C2	Word-initial sequences		Word-internal sequences	
front-to-back					
b	g	bgera	'sound'	abga	'saddle bag'
pʰ	tʰ	pʰtʰila	'hair lock'	apʰtʰar-i	'hyena'
d	g	dg-eb-a	's/he stands up'	a-dg-eb-a	's/he will stand up'
back-to-front					
g	b	g-ber-av-s	's/he is inflating you'	da-gbera	'to say the sounds'
tʰ	b	tʰb-eb-a	'it is warming up'	ga-tʰb-a	'it has become warm'
g	d	gd-eb-a	'to be thrown'	a-gd-eb-a	'to throw smth. in the air'

All of the stop-stop sequences are tautomorphemic, with the exception of *g-ber-av-s*, a verb form where *g-* is a person marker. The vowels preceding and following the stop sequences are, as often as possible, the low central [a]. This vowel is preferred because it minimally interferes with the trajectory of the consonantal gestures evaluated here. However, not all combinations of consonants occur in lexical items where they are flanked by low central vowels; therefore in some of the stimuli the consonant sequences are followed by the vowels [e], [o], or [i]. The tokens were randomized in stimulus blocks that include other stimuli not analyzed here, and seven repetitions of each block were recorded.

The syllabification of the word-internal stop-stop sequences is not clear, therefore we cannot tell for sure that these sequences span a syllable boundary. Reports from five native speakers (Chitoran, 2000) show that their intuitions on syllabification are very clear only concerning word-initial clusters and single intervocalic consonants. Word-initial clusters are systematically reported to be tautosyllabic, and single intervocalic consonants are syllabified as onsets (e.g. *k'a.la.mi* 'pen'). Intuitions regarding word-internal clusters are, on the contrary, very mixed. The location of the syllable boundary could not be consistently marked. The only pattern unacceptable to the speakers is *VCC.V, where both consonants are syllabified in the coda of the first syllable, leaving the second syllable onsetless. Morphological boundaries also do not seem to play a role in syllabification, with the exception of compounds, which are not included here.

We should also point out that some of the stop-stop sequences in our list are those referred to in traditional grammars as "harmonic clusters". They are characterized by three properties: (i) the two members of these clusters always share the same laryngeal specifications (voiced, aspirated, or ejective, the three-way laryngeal distinction in the Georgian consonant system); (ii) the order of the place of articulation is always labial-dorsal or coronal-dorsal (e.g. *bg, dg, $t^h k^h$, $ts^h k^h$*); (iii) harmonic clusters have been impressionistically described as being single segments, with only one closure and one release. However, acoustic evidence (Chitoran, 1998; McCoy, 1999) indicates that they are sequences of two stops, each with its own closure and release. There is therefore no structural difference between them and the other stop sequences investigated here.

3.2 Data collection

Each frame sentence containing the stimuli was typed in the Georgian alphabet, one sentence per page. The speaker was instructed to read each sentence aloud, at a normal, comfortable pace. The experimenter cued the speaker for each sentence by the word "Go." If the speaker paused or had a false start, he was asked to re-read the sentence. The 12 stimuli were read 7 times, therefore a total of 84 stimuli were recorded. In spite of the careful data collection, a few stimuli were lost due to technical problems (e.g. transducers came loose). Thus, three stimuli were lost from the first speaker (one of each: $p^h t^h ila$, $ap^h t^h ari$, $abga$), and four from the second speaker (one of each: $dgeba$, $gdeba$, $p^h t^h ila$, $adgeba$).

Data were collected using the EMMA (Electromagnetic Midsagittal Articulometer) magnetometer system. The technical specifications of the EMMA magnetometer system are outlined in Perkell, Cohen, Svirsky, Garabieta & Jackson (1992) (see also Gracco & Nye, 1993; Löfqvist, 1993). Receivers were attached to three midsagittal points on the subject's tongue. One, (TD) was positioned as posterior as possible, another (TT) was attached approximately 1 cm from the tongue tip, and a third was positioned at an intermediate location. In addition, receivers were placed on the upper and lower lip, the lower and upper teeth (maxilla & jaw, respectively) and the nose bridge, the latter two for correction of head movement. Both acoustic and movement data were obtained. The movement data were sampled at 500Hz (after low-pass filtering before voltage-to-distance conversion) and the acoustic data were sampled at 20kHz. The data were corrected for head movement and rotated to the occlusal plane of the subject such that the x-axis is parallel to the occlusal plane and the y-axis lies perpendicular to it. Voltages were low-pass filtered at 15 Hz, using a 9th-order Butterworth filter. After voltage to distance conversion, correction for head movement (using the nose and maxillary reference transducers), and rotation to the occlusal plane, the position signals were also low-pass filtered at 15 Hz.

Movement trajectories of the receivers attached to the tongue tip (TT), tongue dorsum (TD), upper lip (UL) and lower lip (LL) were evaluated. For coronal stops ([t^h], [d]) the tangential velocity (xy) minima of the tongue tip receiver were used to delimit the gestures' temporal location. This was calculated as follows:

$$tvel = \sqrt{((V_x)^2 + (V_y)^2)}$$

where: $tvel$ = tangential velocity of the tongue tip transducer
V_x = velocity in the x-coordinate of the tongue tip transducer

V_y = velocity in the y-coordinate of the tongue tip transducer

For velar stops ([g]) the velocity zero-crossings of the vertical (y) movement of the tongue dorsum receiver was employed. For labial stops ([b], [pʰ]) both the upper lip and lower lip receiver vertical (y) trajectories were evaluated. Both speakers showed considerable displacement of the upper lip during the closure phase of bilabial stops, and of the lower lip during the release phase. We therefore employed the movement of the two lips separately, rather than as a single variable (lip aperture), representing the vertical distance between the two lips. Upper lip velocity zero-crossings were used to identify the onset and achievement of the labial constriction, and lower lip movement was used to identify the constriction release.

3.3 Analysis

The data were analyzed using MATLAB to algorithmically identify important landmarks in the movement trajectories. For each gesture the following three points were identified and labeled: movement onset (labeled *On*), target achievement (point at which constriction is achieved, labeled *Off*), and target release (point at which constriction is released, labeled *On*). Onsets of motion were defined algorithmically as the points in time at which the velocity exceeded some specified threshold above zero velocity. Offsets were defined as the points where velocity fell below that same threshold. Thresholds were set as a percentage of the effective maximum speed that each receiver dimension exhibited over all utterances. The effective maximum speed was calculated by finding the maximum speed (absolute value of velocity) observed in the middle 1/3 of each utterance, and then averaging across all utterances. Percentages were as follows: for TT, 15% of the effective maximum tangential velocity (xy); for TD, 15% of the effective maximum vertical (y) speed; for UL, 20% of the effective maximum vertical (y) speed to identify the onset of movement and the constriction achievement; for LL, 15% of the effective maximum vertical (y) speed to determine the constriction release.

As an index of the temporal overlap between the two sequential stop gestures, the following measure was evaluated in the quantitative analyses: the percentage of the interval between target achievement and release for the first stop at which movement onset for the second stop is initiated. That is, how early does C2 movement onset occur within the constriction 'plateau' interval of C1? This measure will be referred to as overlap. A small value indicates a large degree of overlap, that is, C2 movement starts quite early in C1's constriction, and a large value indicates little or no (if >100%) overlap, that is, C2 movement starts quite late in C1's constriction, or after it. A sample data panel is shown in Figure 1:

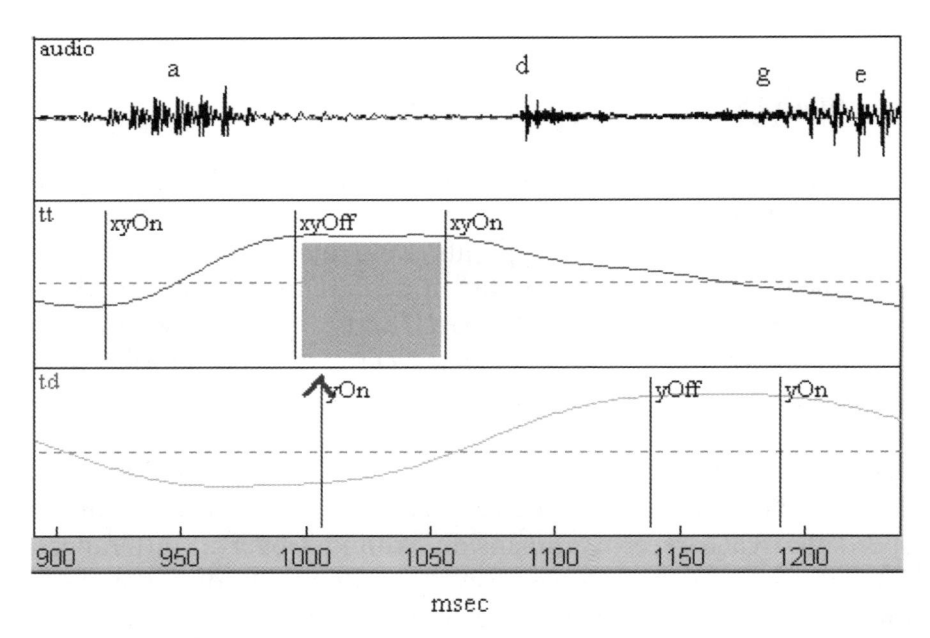

Figure 1: The sequence **[a#dge]** in **[sit'q'va#dgeba]**
Top panel: audio; Middle panel: tongue tip y with events labeled; Bottom panel: tongue dorsum y with events labeled. Labels: **On** indicates onset of movement, toward and away from target. **Off** indicates offset of movement, target achievement. Note that in this token C2 initiates shortly after C1 constriction is achieved.

4. Results

The overlap measure is evaluated as the dependent variable in a 3-factor full-interaction ANOVA model for each speaker separately. The three independent variables for the non-repeated measures ANOVA are:
(i) POSITION (2 levels: word-initial, word-internal)
(ii) ORDER (2 levels: front-to-back, back-to-front)
(iii) PLACES (3 levels: labial & coronal, coronal & dorsal, labial & dorsal; irrespective of order of occurrence)

Table 2: Summary of results (significant effects in bold).

Effect	Speaker 1	Speaker 2
POSITION	**$F(1,69)=51.48, p<.001$**	$F(1,68)=.06, p>.05$
ORDER	**$F(1,69)=52.91, p<.001$**	**$F(1,68)=8.37, p<.01$**
PLACES	**$F(2,69)=17.03, p<.001$**	**$F(2,68)=8.63, p<.001$**
POSITION x ORDER	$F(1,69)=.23, p>.05$	**$F(1,68)=8.07, p<.01$**
POSITION x PLACES	$F(2,69)=.81, p>.05$	$F(2,68)=3.41, p>.01$
ORDER x PLACES	$F(2,69)=.16, p>.05$	**$F(2,68)=7.95, p<.01$**
POSITION x ORDER x PLACES	$F(2,69)=1.5, p>.05$	$F(2,68)=3.56, p>.01$

Table 2 shows that all main effects are significant, with the exception of the POSITION effect for the second speaker. No two-way or three-way interactions are significant for the first speaker. For the second speaker, two two-way interactions are significant: POSITION x ORDER and ORDER x PLACES. While the first interaction, to be discussed below, is relevant to our hypotheses, the second one is not. We did not predict an effect of PLACES, and we do not have at present an explanation for this significant interaction in the case of only one speaker.

4.1 Effects of POSITION

An effect of POSITION was found for both speakers, with some individual differences. The data of the first speaker show a significant effect of POSITION, and no significant interactions. The second speaker shows no main effect of POSITION, but the interaction between POSITION and ORDER is significant.

The main effect of POSITION obtained for the first speaker indicates that stop-stop sequences in word-internal position have a significantly greater amount of overlap than like sequences in word-initial position. This finding confirms hypothesis H1 and is consistent with similar findings for English outlined in section 2.1. Furthermore, the results also show that in word-internal sequences, C2 onset occurs on average soon after the achievement of C1 target, after only 5% of the C1 constriction interval, whereas in word-initial sequences C2 onset occurs much later (after an average of 82% of the interval). The results for the first speaker are summarized in Table 3, and illustrated in Figure 2, further below.

While the lack of a main effect of position for the second speaker fails to support H1 as it is stated, the pattern of this speaker's results is consistent with the reasoning behind H1. The results show that in word-initial position, where release is hypothesized to be critical to recoverability, front-to-back sequences are more overlapped than back-to-front ones (as predicted by H2). In the word-initial front-to-back stop sequences, C2 onset occurs on average even before the constriction for C1 is achieved (−42% of the C1 constriction interval). In back-to-front sequences, on the other hand, there is a long delay for the C2 onset, which occurs on average after 62% of the C1 constriction interval. Word-medially, however, where more information is available to support recoverability, the amount of overlap is comparable, as discussed further in section 4.2. The results for the second speaker are summarized in Table 4, and illustrated graphically in Figure 3, further below.

4.2 Effects of ORDER

The data of the first speaker show a significant main effect of ORDER, and no significant interactions. In the front-to-back stop-stop sequences, C2 onset occurs on average after 3% of the C1 constriction interval, as opposed to back-to-front sequences, where C2 onset occurs after 82% of the interval. The second speaker also shows a significant main effect of ORDER, but, as discussed above, a significant interaction is also found between POSITION and OR-

DER. The simple main effect of ORDER is significant in word-initial position, but not word-medially. For both orders of place, C2 onset occurs on average after 17% of the C1 constriction interval.

Overall, these results confirm our hypothesis H2: stop-stop sequences with a front-to-back ordering of place of articulation show significantly more overlap than sequences with the reversed order of place of articulation. This result is also consistent with previous findings summarized in section 2.2.

4.3 Effects of PLACES

Finally, a significant main effect of PLACES (the types of gestures involved — labial, coronal or dorsal) was found for both speakers. This effect was not one that we had predicted. For the first speaker the highest degree of overlap was found for dorsal-coronal/coronal-dorsal sequences, where C2 onset occurs on average after only 4% of the C1 constriction interval. The next most overlapped sequences are labial-dorsal/dorsal-labial. C2 onset occurs on average after 46% of the C1 constriction interval. The least overlapped sequences are labial-coronal/coronal-labial. C2 onset occurs on average after 85% of the C1 target-release interval.

For the second speaker, as for the first, the least overlapped sequences are those combining labials and coronals. C2 onset occurs on average after 60% of the C1 constriction interval. The other two place combinations have higher degrees of overlap: -24% for labial-dorsal/dorsal-labial, and 7% for coronal-dorsal/dorsal-coronal.

4.4 Summary of results by speaker

The results for each speaker are summarized in Tables 3 and 4, respectively. Those specific to Hypotheses 1 and 2 are shown graphically in Figures 2 and 3, for each speaker. The results will be further discussed in section 5.

Table 3: Summary of overlap means for Speaker 1 (C2 onset relative to C1 constriction interval). Lower numbers indicate greater overlap.

	n	Mean (%)	S.D. (%)
POSITION			
word-initial	41	82%	75
word-internal	40	5%	63
ORDER			
front-to-back	39	3%	54
back-to-front	42	82%	80
PLACES			
labial & coronal			
labial & dorsal	26	85%	84
coronal & dorsal	27	46%	75
POSITION x ORDER (ns)	28	4%	59
word-initial			
front-to-back	20	39%	31
back-to-front	21	124%	82
word-internal			
front-to-back	19	−34%	47
back-to-front	21	41%	54

The interaction between POSITION and ORDER is plotted in the graph in Figure 2, below.

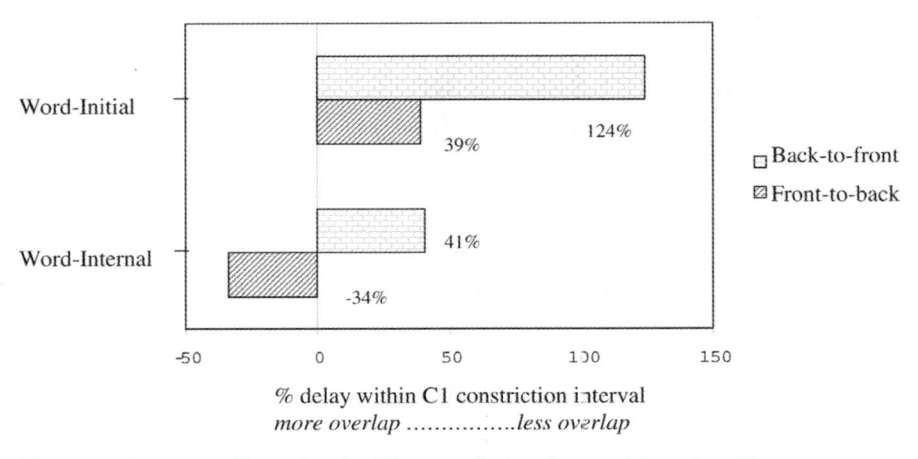

Figure 2: Amount of overlap in C1 constriction interval (speaker 1)

The graph indicates very little overlap in the back-to-front word-initial sequences, as expected from the main effects. A mean overlap measure greater than 100% indicates C2 onset occurs on average after the release of the C1 constriction. The most overlapped sequences are the front-to-back word-internal sequences. A negative mean overlap measure indicates C2 onset occurs before the target achievement for the C1 constriction.

Table 4: Summary of overlap means for Speaker 2 (C2 onset relative to C1 constriction interval)

	n	Mean (%)	S.D. (%)
POSITION (ns)			
word-initial	39	10%	130
word-internal	41	17%	52
ORDER			
front-to-back	39	−12%	127
back-to-front	41	39%	47
PLACES			
labial & coronal	27	60%	37
coronal & dorsal	25	7%	48
labial & dorsal	28	−24%	145
POSITION × ORDER			
word-initial			
front-to-back	19	−42%	172
back-to-front	20	62%	21
word-internal (ns)			
front-to-back	20	17%	52
back-to-front	21	17%	54

The interaction between POSITION and ORDER is plotted in the graph in Figure 3. The graph indicates that a much greater amount of overlap is allowed in word-initial front-to-back sequences than in back-to-front ones, in keeping with Hypothesis 2. In word-internal position, however, the same amount of overlap is found, regardless of order of place.

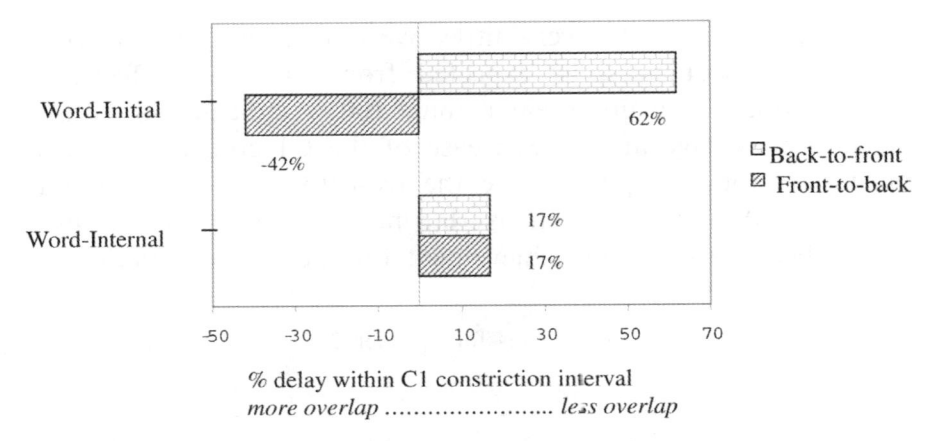

Figure 3: Amount of overlap in C1 constriction interval (speaker 2)

5. Discussion

5.1 Patterns of gestural overlap

The results of this movement tracking study of the articulation of Georgian consonant sequences confirm both of the original hypotheses regarding degree of overlap as a function of position in the word and of order of place of articulation. Specifically:

- More gestural overlap is found word-internally than word-initially (H1);
- More gestural overlap is found in sequences with a front-to-back order of place of articulation than in back-to-front sequences (H2).

The data of the first speaker supports both hypotheses: word position and constriction order both affect the relative timing among gestures. The data of the second speaker confirm the order hypothesis, but only in word-initial position. For both speakers, an additional, unpredicted effect of place combination was also found, such that combinations of labial and coronal stops are the least overlapped. The PLACES effect can be readily interpreted, however, since labial and coronal sequences are in fact the ones which are not usually described as "harmonic" in Georgian, and not claimed to be single segments. It is possible that their relatively reduced degree of overlap may in fact be responsible for their perception as a clear sequence of consonants. It is also significant to note that cross-linguistically, double articulations of labials and coronals are not attested. Closure gestures can be nearly synchronous in combinations of labials and velars, and in combinations of coronals and velars in clicks. Labials and coronals, though, do not seem to display a high degree of overlap. The implications of degree of overlap for the status of "harmonic" clusters in Georgian will be further discussed in section 5.3.

Our original hypotheses concerning word position and order of place of articulation were both motivated by the view that listeners' needs for perceptual recoverability play a role in determining the spatiotemporal patterning of gestures produced by speakers (Mattingly, 1981; Silverman, 1995). Less gestural overlap between consonants in sequences helps preserve the information that serves to specify the identity of the first consonant, in particular the release burst of C1 and the specificity of the VC and CV formant transitions for each of the consonants. With regard to the gestural overlap (or phase relations) among gestures, the experiment results provide preliminary evidence that timing patterns reflect constraints of perceptual recoverability in at least two different respects. First, less overlap (or better preservation of information on consonant identity) is found in a prosodic position which is critical for lexical access — the word onset. Second, less overlap is observed when C1 is especially vulnerable to being obscured by C2.

Of course, recoverability, while a primary concern for both speaker and listener, is not the only influence on spatio-temporal variability in speech. Efficiency is a parallel concern. Gestural overlap or coproduction presents an advantage from the point of view of transmitting information simultaneously about several linguistic units — what has been called *parallel transmission* (Liberman, Cooper, Shankweiler & Studdert-Kennedy, 1967). Thus, it seems that there are competing influences on intergestural timing; the first is the need to ensure recoverability of linguistic units from the signal, and the second is the need to encode and transmit information at a high rate.

Theories of speech production must have some way of incorporating these competing influences on speech timing. One approach is outlined in Byrd (1996b) in which she views influences on phase relations as interacting probabilistically. Another approach has been offered by Browman & Goldstein (2000). They note that gestural parameters and phase relations may be quantitatively scaled as a function of speaking conditions. One step toward accomplishing this is to allow phase relations between gestures to have different degrees of cohesion or bonding strength (Browman & Goldstein, 2000). Sources of variation in gestural overlap influence a given pair of gestures in inverse proportion to their bonding strength. The surfacing temporal pattern is taken to be the result of competing phase relations such that the surface timing maximizes the satisfaction of the competing constraints as weighted by their bonding strength (Browman & Goldstein, 2000). The specific example sketched by Browman & Goldstein in their presentation includes a C-V relation that defines syllable onsets, and a C-C relation between two adjacent consonants. According to the C-V relation, each consonant gesture in a complex onset bears the exact same phase relation to the vowel. If each consonant gesture is coordinated in the same way with respect to the nuclear vowel gesture, the consonants tend to synchronize. However, the second relation (the C-C relation) phases the consonant gestures with respect to each other in a way which allows them to be recoverable. According to this relation, the consonants tend to be sequential. Browman and Goldstein describe these competing constraints as being able to account for the observation that in #CC(C)V sequences the temporal center of the consonant interval ("C-center") maintains a fixed temporal relation to the vowel. In more general terms, they view these constraints as characterizing the desirability of simultaneous parallel transmission (the C-V relation) *and* of perceptual recoverability (the C-C relation). These two tendencies are both accommodated in speech, and furthermore, can be explicitly incorporated into their model of intergestural timing.

Within this model, the results of our study can be interpreted as follows. For both speakers, the bonding strength of the C-C relation varies as a function of ORDER and POSITION. For the first speaker they combine linearly, giving the independent contribution of the two factors. The data of the second speaker can be explained with the same kinds of constraints, but simply under the assumption that the word-medial consonants are not tautosyllabic. If this is the case, the C-V constraint does not come into play in this context. The remaining C-C constraint does not compete against anything, and thus differences in weights do not have any effect on the observed timing patterns.

If this analysis is correct, it makes a number of predictions about the C-center relations: both speakers should show a C-center effect in word-initial position (we have vowel duration measurements showing that this is the case for the second speaker), but word-medially only the first speaker should show a C-center effect. The results are in fact consistent with the native speakers' mixed intuitions about syllabification in word-medial clusters.

5.2 Implications for sonority sequencing violations

The two potentially opposing tendencies presented above have implications for understanding consonant sequencing in Georgian and other languages that violate the sonority sequencing principle. The sonority principle states the cross-linguistic tendency for complex onsets to rise in sonority toward the syllable nucleus, and complex codas to fall in sonority away from the syllable nucleus. The sonority scale based on this principle contains vowels at the most sonorous end, and obstruents at the least sonorous end:

Obstruents < Nasals < Liquids < Glides < Vowels

The sonority principle is thus primarily a generalization capturing the observation that certain types of onset consonant sequences are the most common cross-linguistically. No consistent phonetic (acoustic or articulatory) correlate of sonority exists, but most attempts to define sonority phonetically relate it to the notion of increased perceptibility of segments. Some of the definitions that we find most intuitive (Mattingly, 1981; Ohala, 1990) refer to perceptibility as the ease with which individual segments or gestures are correctly identified in a sequence.

Mattingly's (1981) proposal is based on the notion of parallel transmission as an important organizing principle for speech communication. Phonetic elements, although perceived as ordered, are not produced in strict succession. There is a clear many-to-many relationship between phonological units and acoustic cues to these units. The simultaneous availability of information for multiple segments is claimed to facilitate higher information rates for speech. Sonority is one way of achieving this goal of parallel transmission. He treats the traditional sonority ranking as a ranking of manner classes according to degree of "closeness." The scale is argued to follow an ordering that crucially depends on the degree to which information is available during the release or application of the constriction, and during the constriction itself.

> "The general articulatory prerequisite for parallel transmission would appear to be that the constriction for one or more closer articulations must be in the process of being released or applied in the presence of constrictions for one or more less close articulations. In terms of this formulation, the conventional ranking of manner classes...corresponds to a ranking according to the degree to which information can be encoded during the release or application of the constriction, and the inverse of this ordering, to the degree to which information can be encoded during the period of maximal constriction...[T]he articulations of speech must be scheduled so that periods during which constrictions are released in rank order alternate with periods during which constrictions are applied in inverse rank order. This is of course exactly what is accomplished by the syllabic organization of speech." [Mattingly, 1981, p. 418]

This view does indeed define a ranking very similar to the sonority scale, if we consider how much and what kind of acoustic information is available from different segments. For stops (both oral and nasal), acoustic information for place is present primarily at the application and release of the constriction, and only manner information is present during the closure interval. In the case of liquids, place information is also available during the constriction itself. The same is true of fricatives, although perhaps less so of non-sibilant fricatives, which have lower energy. For glides and vowels, both place and manner information is present throughout the constriction formation and release process. In a complex onset structured according to this scale, articulations are released into more open constrictions, thereby allowing a relatively high degree of overlap. Overlap in turn allows more acoustic information to be transmitted for more than one phonetic element at the same time. This provides an elegant foundation for the generalization captured traditionally by the sonority scale and, more generally, for the syllabic organization of speech.

Such an approach to sonority is also consistent with the views held by Ohala & Kawasaki (1984) and Ohala (1990), who propose that the salience of an acoustic signal may be given by maximal modulations in several acoustic parameters varying simultaneously (e.g. amplitude, periodicity, spectral shape, fundamental frequency). Preferred sequences of segments would be characterized by large modulations in acoustic parameters. The more acoustic information is present simultaneously, the more successful the identification of the component segments is by the listener. For these modulations to be available to the listener, however, the sequencing must also follow the patterns of intergestural timing we proposed, which best ensure that the relevant acoustic information will not be obscured.

We would like to suggest that such patterns of gestural coordination that satisfy both parallel transmission of information and recoverability are "attractors" towards which phonological structures evolve (through talker-listener interaction), and that these "attractors" underlie the traditional sonority principle. Stop-liquid sequences, for example, are so common cross-linguistically because they allow substantial overlap while maintaining recoverability. A number of languages evolve uncommon sequences ("sonority plateaus" or "reversals"). These less common sequences are not ideal for the transmission of gestural information, unless their gestural timing is tightly controlled. We have seen that Georgian syllable onsets violate the sonority sequencing generalization, but appear to be sensitive to gestural recoverability requirements as reflected in overlap patterns. The articulatory patterning of Georgian onsets can be explained by the same opposing tendencies at work in the more common patterns of sonority sequencing: the tendency for gestures to overlap so as to allow parallel transmission, and the tendency to limit the amount of overlap in order to ensure perceptual recoverability. Languages which obey sonority sequencing may also demonstrate effects of perceptual recoverability on intergestural timing.

We propose, therefore, that cross-linguistically syllable structure adheres to a particular ordering or temporal patterning that allows for maximum overlap with minimal loss of information. We would expect the more common sequences to exhibit relatively less sensitivity to gestural coordination. For example, a velar-liquid onset cluster should exhibit a comparable place effect to a bilabial-liquid onset cluster. The order effect should be negligible here, because acoustic release of either stop is equally unlikely to be obscured by the following liquid, produced with a more open vocal tract. On the other hand, in sonority plateaus and sonority reversals, such as the sequences found in Georgian, intergestural timing is expected to play a crucial role, and the magnitude of the order of place effect should be greater.

5.3 Implications for the status of "harmonic" clusters

The account presented here can be extended to explain the impressionistic descriptions of "harmonic" clusters in Georgian as being single segments. Recall that "harmonic" clusters are front-to-back C1C2 sequences where C2 is dorsal, and C1 and C2 share the same laryngeal specification (i.e. voiced, voiceless, or ejective). Such sequences are common in Georgian. Of the four logically possible combinations of consonants in terms of order of place and laryngeal homogeneity, three are attested in the language (the third being the "harmonic" type):

- homogeneous, back-to-front: gdeba   'to throw'
- non-homogeneous, back-to-front: q'ba   'jaw'
- homogeneous, front-to-back: dgoma   'standing'
- non-homogeneous, front-to-back: *unattested*   *(*dk^h, *p^{h}k', *p'g)*

We argue that the large amount of overlap in front-to-back sequences is responsible for the absence of front-to-back sequences that do not agree in laryngeal features.

We hypothesize that in Georgian a consonant cluster licenses at most a single laryngeal gesture: glottal abduction (for aspirated consonants) or a laryngeal raising/closing gesture (for ejectives). Voiced stops are hypothesized to result from no active laryngeal maneuver at all (i.e. the speech-default position of the vocal folds is that of adduction appropriate for vibration). Voiced obstruents in Georgian have very weak voicing, and are not necessarily voiced throughout the closure.

We also hypothesize that in Georgian the laryngeal gesture, if present, is coordinated in such a way that its target (opening or closing) is achieved during the first of the two stops. This means that in the case of the more overlapped front-to-back sequences the time between the laryngeal event (coordinated with the first consonant) and the second consonant will be relatively short. Therefore, the laryngeal gesture will still have its characteristic effect (opening or closure) at the time of the release of the second consonant. This would explain why front-to-back clusters *in particular* always agree in voicing since the laryngeal gesture extends through both of them due to their high degree of overlap.

If any laryngeally heterogeneous sequences ever existed, they would be predicted to undergo voicing assimilation. A proposal by Gamkrelidze & Ivanov (1995) supports this prediction from a diachronic perspective. They argue that harmonic clusters in Proto-Kartvelian were complex consonants that later segmented into clusters. (They were probably velarized consonants, which would explain why in the modern languages the second consonant is always dorsal, a velar or uvular stop or fricative.) The authors suggest that non-homogeneous, front-to-back sequences did exist, but have undergone voicing assimilation, merging with "harmonic" clusters.

As for the non-harmonic back-to-front sequences that have less overlap, there will be a greater delay between the laryngeal gesture (coordinated with the first consonant) and the release of the second consonant. This accounts for the mixed voicing found in back-to-front (non-harmonic) sequences. This delay may be sufficient for the larynx to return to its default state, resulting in a weakly voiced or voiceless unaspirated stop. This is in fact what is observed for C2 in such clusters (Chitoran, 1999).

Of course, this account of Georgian harmonic clusters still remains to be tested, ideally with instrumentation that will allow us to evaluate laryngeal behavior and its coordination with supralaryngeal articulation.

6. Conclusions

This study contributes to our understanding of cross-linguistic patterns of gestural overlap, and of the types of factors influencing them. We tested the effects of two linguistic factors (position in the word and order of place of articulation) on the amount of overlap allowed between consonantal gestures in Georgian stop-stop sequences. Both were found to systematically affect the temporal coordination of linguistic units. We discussed the implications of the results for the theoretical conceptualization of articulatory timing. We proposed to account for the results in terms of the weighting of constraints that ensures the perceptual recoverability of gestures, while allowing efficiency through overlap.

We outlined a proposal as to how sonority sequencing may evolve from the same competing constraints, reflecting the desirability of efficient patterns of information transmission to listeners while ensuring that perceptual recoverability is possible for the listener.

Finally, we argued that the substantial amount of overlap found in Georgian front-to-back stop sequences may be responsible for the so-called "harmonic" clusters in Georgian, in which the two members of the clusters always agree in laryngeal specification.

Acknowledgements

The authors gratefully acknowledge the support of NIH grant DC-03172 and NSF grant SBR-951730. We would like to thank the LabPhon7 participants, the reviewer, and Alice Harris for their useful comments.

References

Browman, C. & Goldstein, L.
  1990   Tiers in articulatory phonology, with some implications for casual speech. In J. Kingston & M. E. Beckman (eds.), *Papers in Laboratory Phonology I: Between the Grammar and Physics of Speech*, (pp. 341–376). Cambridge: Cambridge University Press.

Browman, C. & Goldstein, L.
  in press Competing constraints on intergestural coordination and self-organization of phonological structures. *Bulletin de la Communication Parlée*, **5**, 24–34.

Byrd, D.
  1992   Perception of assimilation in consonant clusters: a gestural model. *Phonetica*, **49**, 1–24.

Byrd, D.
  1994   *Articulatory Timing in English Consonant Sequences*. PhD dissertation, UCLA, published as UCLA Working Papers in Phonetics 86.

Byrd, D.
  1996a Influences on articulatory timing in consonant sequences. *Journal of Phonetics*, **24**, 209–244.

Byrd, D.
  1996b A phase window framework for articulatory timing. *Phonology*, **13** Vol **2**, 139–169.

Byrd, D. & Saltzman, E.
  1998   Intergestural dynamics of multiple phrasal boundaries. *Journal of Phonetics*, **26**, 173–199.

Chitoran, I.
  1998   Georgian harmonic clusters: phonetic cues to phonological representation. *Phonology*, **15**, 121–141.

Chitoran, I.
  1999   Accounting for sonority violations: the case of Georgian consonant sequencing. *Proceedings of the XIV International Congress of Phonetic Sciences*, San Francisco, 1999, 101–104.

Chitoran, I.
  2000   Some evidence for feature specification constraints on Georgian consonant sequencing. In O. Fujimura, B. Joseph & B. Palek (eds.), *Proceedings of LP '98*, 185–204.

Gaitenby, J.
  1965   The elastic word. *Haskins Laboratories Status Report on Speech Research*, **2**.

Gamkrelidze, T. V. & Ivanov, V.
  1995   *Indo-European and the Indo-Europeans: A reconstruction and historical analysis of a Proto-Language and a Proto-Culture*. (English version by Johanna Nichols). Berlin, New York: Mouton de Gruyter.

Gracco, V. L. & Nye, P. W.
   1993   Magnetometry in speech articulation research: Some misadventures on the road to enlightenment. *Forschungsberichte des Instituts für Phonetik und Sprachliche Kommunikation der Universität München*, **31**.
Hardcastle, W. J.
   1985   Some phonetic and syntactic constraints on lingual coarticulation during /kl/ sequences. *Speech Communication*, **4**, 247–263.
Hardcastle, W. J. & Roach, P.
   1979   An instrumental investigation of coarticulation in stop consonant sequences. In H. Hollien & P. Hollier (eds.), *Current Issues in the Phonetic Sciences*, (pp. 531–540). Amsterdam: John Benjamins.
Kelso, J. A. S., Saltzman, E. & Tuller, B.
   1986   The dynamical perspective on speech production: data and theory. *Journal of Phonetics*, **14**, 29–59.
Klatt, D. H.
   1976   Linguistic uses of segmental duration in English: Acoustic and perceptual evidence. *Journal of the Acoustical Society of America*, **59**, 1208–1221.
Liberman, A., Cooper, F. S., Shankweiler, D. & Studdert-Kennedy, M.
   1967   Perception of the speech code. *Psychological Review*, **74**, 431–461.
Löfqvist, A.
   1993   Electromagnetic transduction techniques in the study of speech motor control. Reports from the Department of Phonetics, University of Umeå, PHONUM, **2**, 87–106.
Marslen-Wilson, W. D.
   1987   Functional Parallelism in Spoken Word-Recognition. *Cognition*, **25**, 71–102.
Mattingly, I. G.
   1981   Phonetic representation and speech synthesis by rule. In T. Myers, J. Laver & J. Anderson (eds.), *The Cognitive Representation of Speech*, (pp. 415–420). North Holland Publishing Company.
McCoy, P.
   1999   Harmony and sonority in Georgian. In *Proceedings of the XIV International Congress of Phonetic Sciences*, San Francisco, 1999, 447–450.
Ohala, J. J.
   1990   Alternatives to the sonority hierarchy for explaining segmental sequential constraints. *Papers from the Chicago Linguistic Society*, **26**, Vol **2**, *The parasession on the syllable in phonetics and phonology*, 319–338.
Ohala, J. J. & Kawasaki, H.
   1984   Prosodic phonology and phonetics. *Phonology Yearbook*, **1**, 113–127.
Peng, Shu-Hui
   1996   *Phonetic Implementation and Perception of Place Coarticulation and Tone Sandhi*. PhD dissertation, Ohio State University.

Perkell, J., Cohen, M., Svirsky, M., Matthies, M., Garabieta, I. & Jackson, M.
   1992   Electromagnetic midsagittal articulometer (EMMA) systems for transducing speech articulatory movements. *Journal of the Acoustical Society of America,* **92**, 3078–3096.

Redford, M. A. & Diehl, R. L.
   1999   The relative perceptual distinctiveness of initial and final consonants in CVC syllables. *Journal of the Acoustical Society of America,* **106**, 1555–1565.

Saltzman, E. & Byrd, D.
   2000   Demonstrating effects of parameter dynamics on gestural timing. May 2000 Meeting of the ASA, Atlanta, GA. *Journal of the Acoustical Society of America,* **107**, Vol **5**, **2**, 2904.

Silverman, D. & Jun, J.
   1994   Aerodynamic evidence for articulatory overlap in Korean. *Phonetica,* **51**, 210–220.

Silverman, D.
   1995   Phasing and Recoverability. UCLA Ph.D dissertation, published by Garland Publishing, 1997.

Surprenant, A. M. & Goldstein, L.
   1998   The perception of speech gestures. *Journal of the Acoustical Society of America,* **104**, Vol **1**, 518–529.

Wright, R.
   1996   Consonant clusters and cue preservation in Tsou. PhD dissertation, UCLA. Dissertations in Linguistics, **20**.

Zhgenti, S.
   1956   *Kartuli enis ponetika (Phonetics of the Georgian language).* Tbilisi.

Zsiga, E. C.
   1994   Acoustic evidence for gestural overlap in consonant sequences. *Journal of Phonetics,* **22**, 121–140.

The Phonetics-Phonology Interface: Comments on Clements & Osu, Solé, Frota, and Chitoran et al.

Bruce Hayes

Research in how phonology relates to phonetics has followed diverse lines, and the papers in this section illustrate three of the different paths that have been taken. The contributions of Solé and of Chitoran and her colleagues follow a classic route, showing how many phonological phenomena can be better understood by attributing them to phonetic causes, and studying those causes with sophisticated methods and equipment. Frota follows a research tradition associated with Pierrehumbert and her colleagues: the pitch movements of an intonational system — varying, gradient, and often hard to come to grips with — can be brought into an orderly pattern by tying them to an intonational phonology, which provides the structural basis on which the raw pitch data can be understood, as well as relating the pitch contours to other structural entities like syllables, stress, and boundaries. Broadly, we can see Solé and Chitoran et al.'s papers as attempts to use phonetics to illuminate phonology, and Frota's paper as an attempt to use phonology to illuminate phonetics.

Clements and Osu's paper follows a long-standing phonological tradition from Jakobson and Trubetzkoy through Chomsky and Halle and much of Clements's own earlier work. The guiding idea, as I interpret it, is that it is possible for the theorist to examine the chaotically diverse world of phonetic phenomena and extract from it a fairly small set of truly essential phonetic features; the ones that play a role in phonological structure. Clements and Osu show, I think, the right way to pursue this program: with full attention to phonetic detail, and careful consideration of rival hypotheses.

As the papers are all clear and defend their positions well, I have little to add to what they have to say. However, Chitoran, Goldstein and Byrd's paper (hereafter CGB) on Georgian harmonic clusters raises a couple of questions that are worth pursuing further.

To review: a harmonic cluster in Georgian can be defined as one that requires agreement in laryngeal features. The phonological question at hand is to explain, on a phonetic basis, why only certain clusters in Georgian are harmonic. CGB's explanation ultimately hinges on patterns of articulatory overlap and the distribution of acoustic cues that are found in various overlap configurations.

To start, I will compare CGB's paper with Chitoran's earlier treatment (1998) of the harmonic clusters. Chitoran sought to use acoustic measurements to determine whether these clusters are actually "complex segments"; i.e. single segments with two simultaneous places of articulation. Her evidence suggested a negative answer; in particular, she observed salient **release bursts** in the middle of these clusters. Chitoran interpreted these bursts as evidence for fully-nonoverlapped articulation: "simultaneity of closure ... can be eliminated from the list of properties characterizing harmonic clusters" (p. 140).[1]

Electromagnetic articulography, however, appears to indicate otherwise: in the experiments for CGB, the authors found that the harmonic clusters do indeed have extensive articulatory overlap. What, then, are we to make of the medial release bursts?[2]

CGB have a nice answer for this: they note that it is possible to release a stop and produce a burst even while another stop is being articulated. All that is necessary is that the released stop have a fronter place of articulation than the "covering" stop (otherwise, the acoustic consequences of the release would be confined within a closed vocal tract).

Applying this idea to the harmonic clusters, the prediction is that they should occur only in front-to-back sequences, and this turns out to be true. Thus, CGB's idea not only solves a phonetic mystery, but it also provides a phonetic explanation for phonological patterning. Here is the explanation laid out all in one place:

– Languages favor overlapped consonant sequences, for reasons of speed and efficiency (CGB, sections 1 and 5.1).

- However, overlap is avoided when cues for consonant place would be obscured (CGB 1).
- A major cue for place of articulation occurs at consonant release (CGB 2.1).
- Release is totally inaudible when a consonant is overlapped by a fronter closure, but is moderately audible when it is overlapped by a backer closure (CGB 2.2).
- Georgian accordingly assigns a greater degree of overlap to front-to-back clusters, where doing so does not radically damage perceptibility of place (CGB 2.2).
- Heterogeneous laryngeal specifications can be executed more easily if sufficient time is available to them; i.e. in non-overlapped clusters (CGB 5.3).
- Thus, Georgian requires front-to-back clusters, which are heavily overlapped, to be harmonic (CGB 5.3).

This elegant account shows that phonetic explanation in phonology can involve quite nontrivial chains of reasoning. I think it is likely to be correct in its outlines. However, two important mysteries remain.

First, while it is true that all heavily overlapped clusters in Georgian are front-to-back, it is *not* true that all front-to-back clusters are heavily overlapped. As CGB's experiment showed (see Tables III and IV), **labial-coronal** sequences receive *non*-overlapped articulation. Moreover, this anomaly is reflected at the phonological level: the harmonic clusters of Georgian do not include labial-coronal sequences (CGB, section 3.1).

Another mystery involves differences in **intensity** between the bursts produced under various situations of articulatory overlap. Chitoran's (1998) acoustic study includes a spectrographic comparison between the true harmonic cluster of [**dg**oma] 'standing' (her Fig. 3) and the "accidental" /d#g/ cluster that arises from word concatenation in [sa**d g**ip'ovo] 'where do I find you?' (Fig. 6). In [dgoma], the burst of [d] is quite robust; whereas in [sad gip'ovo], the burst is (as Chitoran puts it) "quite weak, not clearly visible on the spectrogram." This is despite the fact that /dg/ is a front-to-back cluster; i.e. the /d/ burst is not obscured by the /g/ closure.

Puzzled by this difference, I checked spectrographically for bursts in several tokens of front-to-back clusters in my own (American English) speech, making sure I pronounced them with articulatory overlap. I found that the bursts I produced for the fronter consonant were like those in Georgian [sad gip'ovo]: acoustically present, but very weak. Henderson & Repp (1982) studied overlap bursts in a systematic experiment, and most of the bursts they found were also weak – so weak that experimental subjects did hardly better than chance in trying to detect them.

In contrast, the burst found in Georgian harmonic clusters (as distinguished from "accidental" clusters like [sad gip'ovo]), is apparently rather strong, indeed, it is strong enough to serve as the principal cue for a phonological contrast (/dg/ vs. /g/). I conjecture, then, that there must something about harmonic clusters per se, going beyond a simple consonant release, that gives special prominence to the C1 burst.

A clue for what this might be is given in CGB, section 2.2. Discussing the idea of a release generated in overlap conditions, the authors note: "if ... the second consonant has a place of articulation more posterior than that of the first, then at least some acoustic information will be generated on release of C1 (even if it does not generate the substantial release burst associated with venting a high-pressure chamber to the atmosphere)." The lack of high pressure in the chamber formed between two simultaneous articulations explains why the bursts in [sad gip'ovo], and in English, are so weak. But we also need an explanation for why the bursts in harmonic clusters are so strong.

I conjecture, then, that harmonic clusters actually *do* involve "venting a high-pressure chamber to the atmosphere." My guess is that Georgian achieves this with an **egressive velaric** airstream mechanism; i.e. the opposite of what happens in clicks.[3] A slight pressure buildup is effected between the front (labial/coronal) and back (dorsal) closures, probably through forward and upward motion of the tongue dorsum, and the release of this pressure gives rise to a more robust burst at the front closure than would otherwise occur. The egressive velaric mechanism permits a strong burst for both members of a cluster, even under conditions of heavy overlap.

At the level of phonetic introspection, I find it rather easy to produce strong bursts for [d] and [b] in syllables like [dga] or [bga] by using an egressive velaric airstream mechanism. Of course, it is an empirical question whether Georgian speakers do the same thing in speaking their language.

If correct, my hypothesis would explain the other mystery noted above, namely the absence of labial-coronal harmonic clusters. Specifically, the *ingressive* velaric airstream mechanism, as used in click languages, is known to be limited to labial-dorsal and coronal-dorsal combinations (cf. CGB 5.1), and does not occur for labial-coronal sequences (indeed, this is why the mechanism is called "velaric," and why phonetic taxonomies do not include an "alveolic" airstream mechanism). All else being equal, we would expect the counterpart egressive mechanism to be limited to dorsal combinations. Introspectively, I find that it is far easier to produce acoustically robust egressive releases in coronal-dorsal and labial-dorsal combinations than in the labial-coronal combination. Lastly, since it is impossible to produce a velaric egressive consonant without front-to-back order and heavy articulatory overlap, all of CGB's reasoning about overlap and its phonological consequences would carry over under this theory.

My conjecture could be tested by making oral pressure measurements. If the anticipated inter-closure pressure build-up does not occur, then some other explanation for the robust bursts of Georgian harmonic clusters, and for why labial-coronal clusters are not harmonic, will have to be found.

Notes

1   Chitoran was not alone in holding this opinion. Robins & Waterson (1952) transcribed the harmonic cluster in *dgoma* 'stand' with a superscript schwa ([d̥ᵊgoma]), indicating that they perceived a fully non-overlapped pronunciation.
2   A crucial assumption here, which seems plausible but for which I have no data, is that the consultants for the two experiments did not differ in how they pronounced the harmonic clusters. In other words, a single speaker measured both articulatorily and acoustically would be shown to produce release bursts under conditions of heavy overlap.

3   According to Catford (1977), there are four airstream mechanisms found in ordinary languages: egressive pulmonic, egressive glottalic, ingressive glottalic, and ingressive velaric. He notes the existence of bilabial egressive velaric stops used (a) as gestural sounds by French speakers; (b) in Damin, the ritual language of the Lardil (Australia). If I am correct about Georgian it would count as the first observed instance of egressive velaric sounds in ordinary language.

References

Catford, J. C.
 1977   *Fundamental Problems in Phonetics*. Edinburgh: Edinburgh University Press.
Chitoran, I.
 1998   Georgian harmonic clusters: phonetic cues to phonological representation. *Phonology*, **15**, 121–41.
Henderson, J. B. & Repp, B. H.
 1982   Is a stop consonant released when followed by another stop consonant? *Phonetica*, **39**, 71–82.
Robins, R. H. & Waterson, N.
 1952   Notes on the phonetics of the Georgian word. *Bulletin of the School of Oriental and African Studies*, **14**, 54–72.

The search for primitives in phonology and the explanation of sound patterns: The contribution of fieldwork studies

Didier Demolin

Abstract

The search for an adequate set of primitives in phonology and the explanation of sound patterns is a major issue for the discipline. This paper discusses the contribution of fieldwork studies to such a goal. The focus will be on the ways in which phonological theory is shaped by empirical data. It begins by briefly outlining what is meant by fieldwork and sketching the theoretical framework adopted, which follows the lines of the emergent phonology hypothesis proposed by Lindblom (1986, 1990). Phonological problems related to aerodynamic principles, principles relating vocal tract shape to acoustic output, principles relating acoustic output to auditory representation and cognition will be addressed for different languages.

1. Introduction

The average number of sound segments in human languages is a little over 33, even though considerable variation exists, with Hawaiian having only 11 and !Kung 151 segments. One of the questions facing phonologists is why this is so. On the basis of UPSID (Maddieson, 1984) and on what we know of historical linguistics, it does not appear to be the case that the sound systems of human languages evolve from simple to more complex or the other way around. The UPSID data do show, however, that there are a number of restrictions or even prohibitions on the co-occurrence of segments. An explanation of this state of affairs can be approached both from first principles and from a more typological point of view, as inspired by fieldwork studies. There is currently no consensus among phonologists on what the set 'first principles' is which explain the widely observed patterns in sound systems. Fieldwork studies can contribute towards the answer by providing new data, by examining the (co-)occurrence of common speech sounds in languages, and by understanding how uncommon sounds arise. Our conceptions of fieldwork and of phonological theory are first discussed in separate sections.

1.1 Fieldwork

A definition of fieldwork can be approached from two viewpoints. The broader perspective considers any kind of data collection outside the laboratory to be fieldwork. This would include studies in socially stratified communities, for instance, as well as pathological studies among specific groups of patients. In the narrower perspective, fieldwork amounts to data collection from undescribed or poorly described languages. The latter view is traditional among 'linguistic fieldworkers' in remote areas. One of the concerns in a recent collection of papers (Newman & Ratliff, 2000) relates to sites and informants. Dimmendaal (2000) emphasizes that linguists and phonologists should do fieldwork with numerous informants if they wish to achieve a full description, and of course representativeness is a crucial consideration at the start of any investigation. In the same volume, Hyman (2000) considers two situations: going into the field to carry out research on questions that could have been studied in the laboratory if the right speakers had been available, and doing research that can only be done on location. The first situation is typical of linguistic fieldwork, the second of ethnographic linguistics. However, whatever the situation, the field site or the informants, it is crucial to define appropriate goals. These can be descriptive, historical or theoretical. The particular setting of the fieldwork may not be so important, as long as one agrees that this part of the investigation is concerned with data collection and that this activity is related to some theory.

Our perspective on the issue of the relation between fieldwork and phonological theory follows Ohala (1990) in assuming that there is no interface between phonetics and phonology. The same point has recently been emphasized by Kohler (2000), who argues that the time-honoured division of the field of phonetic science into phonetics and phonology has outlived its usefulness, and the integration of phonetics and phonology has been a guiding principle in recent OT-based work (Flemming 1995, Boersma 1998). Ohala (1990: 168) also claims that phonology is the superordinate discipline, because it seeks answers to a much broader range of phenomena involving speech behaviour. The discussion on cognition and symbolization in the last section of this paper will illustrate this point.

The paper assumes that the description of the sound structure of a language is largely determined by phonetic parameters. This does not mean that phonetic parameters are purely descriptive. Deductive phonetics, such as adopted in the work of Lindblom (1986), offers phonology an opportunity to go beyond merely observational and descriptive data and accords phonetics a more predictive role in linguistic theory. This way of considering the phonetic content of phonology also hypothesizes a reversal of the doctrine of the priority of linguistic form (Chomsky, 1964). This hypothesis can be illustrated by addressing questions about the role of phonetic constraints on segmental inventories. For example, why is there a tendency in the world's languages to have 33 phonemes? Why not more or less? Why does 10 seem to be the maximum number for plain oral vowels? What is the origin of featural and segmental structure? The data to be presented below will address some of these questions. As shown by Lindblom (1990), another crucial task concerns the explanation of the behaviour of phonological systems, and the primitives and principles underlying such explanations. In this respect, the aim of fieldwork studies and their relation with phonology is to help to produce a suitable theory which incorporates phonological and phonetic phenomena. The claim that phonetic facts observed in languages must be included in a complete grammar is exemplified by Ladefoged & Traill (1984) in their linguistic description of clicks in Nama, which shows that the segments they study require specific accounts of the relative timing of articulatory movements. These specifications are plainly not in a one-to-one relation with the phonological features, and the question arises how to incorporate these in a descriptive grammar of the language. Ladefoged and Traill show that the relation between phonetic facts and phonological descriptions is more complex than is generally assumed. The issues they raise and the facts they describe are typical of the contribution of fieldwork studies to phonological theory.

The data presented in this paper fall within the narrower definition of 'fieldwork', not because it is felt that the concept must be restricted in this way, but because they adequately illustrate the relevance of phonetics to phonology. Whatever the viewpoint adopted, the result of fieldwork should provide reliable data and observations which contribute towards new hypotheses, and which can be tested by adducing new evidence and adequate experiments.

1.2 Phonological theory

1.2.1 Emergent phonology

Phonological theory is not given 'a priori'. Rather, the underlying primitives and principles must be found by careful observation and hypothesis-directed experimental research. As argued by Lindblom (2000), this means that the priority of form over substance must be rejected and a new paradigm be adopted. Phonology can be seen as an emergent phenomenon, with phonemic and featural coding emerging from optimizing discriminability within a bounded articulatory space, reflecting physical or biological constraints and evolutionary factors, both in ontogeny and in phylogeny. Theoretical phonology must explain how sounds are made, and how they change and evolve, i.e. explain the dynamics of sound patterns. This approach is in accordance with Lindblom's (1984 : 78) claims that phonologists should derive fundamental units and processes deductively from independent premises anchored in physiological and physical realities.

Traditionally, phonology has been seen as a level of abstract form which is largely independent of phonetics (see for example Anderson, 1981; Kenstowicz, 1994; Goldsmith, 1999; Hale & Reiss, 2000). Halle (1990), for instance, emphasizes that sounds are complexes of features that reflect phonetic capabilities of the independently movable portions of the vocal tract, and that certain phonological regularities must be expressed by means of rules, assuming that this knowledge is part of the human genetic endowment. The emergent phonology approach is diametrically opposed to this view. It does not in fact challenge the notion that humans have a genetic endowment accounting for the process of language acquisition, but it does challenge the balance between innateness and acquisition. As stated by Elman et al. (1996), the term 'innate' is often used in linguistics in a simplistic way. To say that a behaviour is innate is sometimes taken to mean that there is a single genetic locus or set of genes which have the specific function of producing the behaviour in question. To say that some behaviour is innate is thus seen as tantamount to explaining the ontogeny of that behaviour (Elman et al., 1996: 357). There can be no question about the major role played by our biological inheritance determining our physical form and our behaviour, but in order to argue for innateness, a specific link between genetic variation and some grammatical outcome must be first demonstrated (Elman et al., 1996: 372). What is at issue here is the interaction between nature and nurture. Fieldwork studies on human speech and languages provide the seeds for a study of the principles grounding such a hypothesis and show that linguistic behaviour can be understood by examining how languages give rise to uncommon sounds.

1.2.2 The principle of maximum dispersion

As emphasized by MacNeilage & Davis (2000: 284), a central claim of the emergent phonology approach is that segment inventories are structured, among other things, to enhance auditory distinctiveness among speech sounds (see also Lindblom 1986, 1990, 2000). This point is stated as the principle of maximal dispersion, which refers to the hypothesis that the distinctive sounds of a language tend to be positioned in phonetic space so as to maximize perceptual contrast (Liljencrants & Lindblom, 1972; Lindblom & Engstrand, 1989; Lindblom, 1990). Evidence for adaptive dispersion is not abundant, but recent experiments by Johnson et al. (1993) have shown that when listeners are asked to choose between different English categories from an array of synthetic vowels, they choose vowel qualities that are more disperse in the acoustic vowel space (the perceptual hyperspace) than the vowel qualities produced in normal speech. Johnson (2000) carried out a second experiment which confirmed that the hyperspace effect is very robust and that this perceptual preference for a large acoustic vowel space supports the theory of adaptive dispersion. The robustness of the hyperspace effect is important because it provides direct psycholinguistic support for adaptive dispersion. Listeners do in fact prefer maximal contrast. Observations made by Vallée (1994) about the regularities found in the vowel systems of the world's languages confirm that languages obey such a rule more often than they violate it. Diachronic data from Nilo-Saharan languages (Demolin, 1988; Denning, 1989; Dimmendaal, 1996) show that vowel systems follow this principle when they evolve from inventories of 10 vowels to a smaller number of vowels and that there seems to be a perceptual preference for systems obeying the principle of maximal dispersion. Most work in this framework deals with vowels, but de Jong & Obeng (2000) have shown that the principle of maximum dispersion (which they call the adaptive dispersion theory) explains the combinations of constriction location and degrees of rounding found in Twi labio-palatalization by a common acoustic function of both articulations of lowering the timbre of consonantal noise.

This approach to phonology as an emergent phenomenon of course has its limitations. For example, Diehl (2000) observes that the principle of maximal dispersion does not make detailed predictions about the likely locations of perceptual boundaries between categories. For Studdert-Kennedy (2000), what seems to be missing in this conception of phonology is an explicit mechanism by which auditory patterns make contact with the neuroanatomical machinery that produces them. These are of course fundamental questions which can be addressed, since their assumed physical basis can be falsified.

1.2.3 Speech ontogeny and sound patterns

When discussing how speech can be derived from non-speech, MacNeilage & Davis (2000a,b) suggest that aspects of the structure of speech produced by infants were probably the building blocks of the first spoken words. Their findings show that proto-word forms share four sequential sound patterns with the word forms occurring in actual languages and the first words of infants. These patterns involve intra-syllable CV co-occurrence. Labial consonants associate with central vowels, coronal consonants with front vowels and dorsal consonants with back vowels. A further pattern is an intra-syllabic preference for initiating words with a labial consonant/vowel/coronal consonant sequence. These findings concur with the Frame/Content theory proposed by MacNeilage (1998). According to this theory, simple bio-mechanical properties of the vocal apparatus and their interactions with the contingencies of movement initiation have played a fundamental role in both the acquisition and evolution of speech. Again, this way of considering phonology, relying on principles derived from self-organization (Lindblom et al., 1983; Demolin & Soquet, 2000), contrasts with the view that speech results from a specific genetic substrate.

1.2.4 First principles

As stated by Ohala (1990), whatever the model of phonology adopted, phonological theory must incorporate parameters from the sub-systems involved in speech communication, such as principles relating vocal tract shape and acoustic output, aerodynamic principles, and principles that explain how our auditory system extracts information from the acoustic signal. In addition, information from feedback on articulatory control, such as those proposed by Perkell (1981) and MacNeilage (1981), should be included in such a theoretical framework. With respect to perception, an approach recently proposed by Schwartz et al. (2000) holds that speech perception amounts to the set of perceptual processes which allow, at the segmental level, the recovery and specification of the timing and targets of speech gestures, supplying a set of representations for the control of one's own action and the specification of the speaker's actions.

1.2.5 Cognition and knowledge

The cognitive dimension of phonological systems involves issues such as phonetic knowledge and levels of representation (Elman et al., 1996). One interesting hypothesis about phonetic knowledge has recently been proposed by Kingston & Diehl (1994), who argue that the phonetic interpretation of phonological representations may be controlled as well as automatic. In their view, contextual variation in the realization of distinctive feature values is a flexible and adaptive response to variation in the demands on the production or perception of these values in different contexts (1994: 419). Therefore, all co-varying articulations must be considered to be part of a controlled strategy. Variation in the phonetic realization of speech sounds between contexts or languages involves a reorganization into distinct phonetic categories. Kingston & Diehl (1994) have provided extensive evidence of such reorganization for the feature [voice]. The most important point of Kingston & Diehl's study is that the realization of speech sounds is not exclusively determined by their phonological specification or by constraints imposed by the speech production apparatus. Rather, the implementation of phonological contrasts requires a complex intermediate mechanism to control sets of articulators which produce arrays of mutually enhancing acoustic effects. Kingston and Diehl have shown that the output of this device for [voice] contrasts is distinct phonetic categories. Evidence for this has also been presented in Kingston & MacMillan (1995), who have shown that F1 and nasalization interact strongly in isolated and contextualized vowels. The perceptual explanation for co-variation of voice quality and tongue root position presented in Kingston et al. (1997) is consistent with this independent control even if the evidence presented by the authors leaves some unanswered questions about the perceptual interactions between the acoustic correlates of voice quality and tongue root position. However, what is important to note here is that by integrating the perceptual interaction between the acoustic properties of phonological features, this approach allows the issue of categorization to be addressed in a way which is different from the categorical perception model, in addition to showing that the categorization issue cannot be addressed in phonology separately from perception.

1.2.6 Self organization

Lindblom et al. (1983) have argued that segmental and featural structure seems to incorporate the phylogeny and ontogeny of speech as a statistical bias, and arises implicitly in a self-organizing manner. The emergence of phonological structure can be modeled as arising as a consequence of self-organization and interaction among the neuro-muscular, articulatory, aerodynamic, and acoustic subsystems involved in speech production and perception. Emerging systems such as phonological systems provide adaptive and flexible responses to changing conditions in the environment or to the changing needs of the system (Demolin & Soquet, 2000). It is important to note that the multiplicity of interactions that characterize self-organizing systems means that they are dynamic; an ongoing process of interaction is required to produce and maintain structure.

1.2.7 Phonology as a laboratory science

Speech production and perception offer models a good opportunity to test phonological hypotheses if phonological problems are stated in terms of physical primitives. Models are usually formulated in mathematical terms, which make explicit the relevant parameters involved in particular domains of speech. A reasonable definition of what constitutes a model is given by Bender (2000): 'a mathematical model is an abstract, simplified, mathematical construct related to a part of reality and created for a particular purpose'. This means that the use of models in phonology will not give a global explanation of a system, but will rather help to formulate a particular problem, discard unimportant details and specify the interactions between the variables. Using a model can help to make predictions that can be checked against data or common sense; using a model will also allow simulations of observed facts to be made. This last point is crucial when considering how the shift from fieldwork data to theory and laboratory testing is made. Indeed, many facts arising from fieldwork cannot always be tested right in the field. The construction of a model from observed facts and based on known first principles therefore provides a useful way to test hypotheses. The use of models to treat phonological problems is not new; for example Ohala (1978) and Kingston (1984) have proposed models based on aerodynamic principles to handle phonological problems; Browman & Goldstein's (1989, 1992) model of articulatory phonology is based on task dynamics which is based on a rigorous mathematical formulation. This model, the first to explicitly introduce a dynamic component into phonology, has now become an important framework within the discipline. In acoustics, a theory has been available since Fant (1960) which has provided a framework for handling and treating a number of problems from principles independent of speech. In the domain of speech perception, there are a number of models that can be very useful for treating phonological problems; for example, phoneme monitoring (Foss, 1969; Segui & Frauenfelder, 1986), phoneme restoration (Warren, 1970; Samuel, 1981), and phonetic categorization (Lieberman et al.. 1957), to cite only a few, provide important information that can be used to introduce a perceptual component into phonology.

The development of portable computers and the miniaturization of laboratory equipment has given a new dimension to data collecting and offers a way to do laboratory work in the field (cf. Ladefoged, 1997). The fieldwork data of the type presented in this chapter typically come from carefully-made observations using a variety of tools, from palatography to acoustic and aerodynamic measurements. Such data can form the basis of hypotheses to be tested in the laboratory or in the field. A typical fieldwork experiment in the perceptual domain is provided by Traill (1994), who tested two hypotheses about the phonetic structure of clicks. Traill was able to establish that clicks fall into two classes on the basis of the relative prominence of high and low frequencies in the spectrum. A second important point established by Traill's experiments is that clicks are intensified variants of pulmonic and glottalic sounds. Such results illustrate the establishment of linguistic categorizations in a way which cannot be achieved without experiments relying on acoustic primitives.

The following sections will examine how sound patterns are shaped in response to specific problems related to the three principles (aerodynamic principles, principles relating vocal tract shape and acoustic output, and principles relating acoustic output to auditory representation) proposed by Ohala (1990). Fieldwork data from various languages will be discussed for each point.

2. Aerodynamic principles

The aerodynamic principles examined here come from ejective fricatives (singleton and geminate) in Amharic and from bilabial trills in Central Sudanic languages. The aim of this section is show how aerodynamic constraints and principles contribute to the shaping of sound patterns.

2.1 Ejectives in Amharic

Ejectives in Amharic demonstrate the interplay between aerodynamic requirements, articulatory control and coordination, and the acoustic output. Ejectives are not uncommon (Ladefoged & Maddieson, 1996), but there are considerable acoustic differences among the ejectives in different languages (Lindau, 1984; Kingston, 1984; Pinkerton, 1986; Warner, 1996). Amharic has five ejective consonants, [p', t', k', s', tʃ'], all of which have a corresponding geminate: [pː', tː', kː', tʃː', sː']. Geminate ejectives are quite rare. Ejective fricatives, both singleton and geminate, will be examined in some detail.[1] For an ejective, the speaker makes an oral closure, with an almost simultaneous closure of the glottis, and then raises the larynx (Catford, 1977). This upward movement of the larynx causes an unusually high pharyngeal air pressure. At the release of the oral closure, air rushes out of the mouth. In Amharic, the glottal closure is released after the oral closure. Thus the distinctive aspects of ejectives are the raising of the larynx and high oral air pressure.

The aim of this study was to obtain data on Amharic ejectives, and particularly on the articulatory coordination of ejective fricatives. The second point was to understand how it is possible to produce an ejective geminate alveolar fricative [s:'], since for aerodynamic reasons (the air supply between a closed glottis and the alveolar constriction is limited) it seems difficult, if not impossible, to produce such a sound.

2.1.1 Methods and material

The subjects were three native speakers of Amharic with no voice problems. The data were recorded at the Phonology Laboratory of the Université Libre de Bruxelles. A recording was made of intra-oral pressure as well as of oral airflow, with simultaneous acoustic and electroglottographic (EGG) recordings. A small flexible plastic tube (ID 2 mm) was inserted through the nasal cavity into the oro-pharynx, for the measurement of intra-oral pressure. Oral airflow was measured with a flexible silicone rubber mouthpiece. The tube and rubber mouthpiece were connected to a Physiologia workstation (Teston & Galindo, 1990, 1995) consisting of a PC computer and an acquisition system equipped with various transducers and the Phonédit signal editing and processing software. For one speaker, sub-glottal pressure was also recorded by direct tracheal puncture, as well as EPG (Reading system) in another recording session. EGG recordings were made using the Fourcin laryngograph. The subjects' task was to pronounce and repeat 5 times the words in (1), which include the relevant fricatives.

(1) kasa   'compensation'
     s'ɨs'ɨt   'regret'
     bəs:a   'he pierced'
     k'ɨs:'ɨl   'adjective'
     kəsəl   'charcoal'

2.1.2 Measurements and results

Results of acoustic and aerodynamic measurements, given in Table 1, consist of the duration, intra-oral pressure (Iop) presented for three subjects (12 repetitions), and sub-glottal pressure (Sgp) for one subject (5 repetitions). Duration measurements were made in intervocalic position, from the last cycle of the preceding vowel to the first cycle of the next vowel.

Table 1: Mean duration and intra-oral pressure [three subjects (n = 12)], sub-glottal pressure [one subject (n = 5)].

	Duration (ms)	Sgp (hPa)^2	Iop (hPa)
[s]	112	11	9
[sː]	173	10	9
[s']	88	10	21
[sː']	134	11	29

These measurements show that there is a significant difference in duration between singleton and geminate fricatives in Amharic, both for plain and ejective fricatives. In addition, ejectives are always shorter compared to their plain counterparts. At first sight it is hard to understand how the geminate ejective is produced because the air chamber between the sealed glottis and the alveolar constriction cannot be extended in time. However, when comparing the audio waveforms and spectrograms of plain and ejective fricatives, it appears that the frication noise for the singleton and geminate plain fricatives has a more or less constant amplitude, with the noise of the geminate being often more intense. Frication noise for the ejectives is very different in two ways. The first is a gradual increase in amplitude towards the constriction release, the second is a short period of silence after the turbulent noise of the ejective alveolar fricative (the glottal lag) before the beginning of the next vowel (see audio waveform and spectrograms in Figures 1, 2, 3, 4). This last fact suggests that the vocal fold vibration begins some time after the constriction release. No exceptions to the latter point were found in our data. The glottal lag is always shorter after a geminate ejective fricative. These data are summarized in Table 2.

Figures 1 and 2 show that Iop raising is very different when comparing plain and ejective fricatives. The Iop raising of ejectives fricatives is rapid, with the decrease beginning right after the peak,

468 Didier Demolin

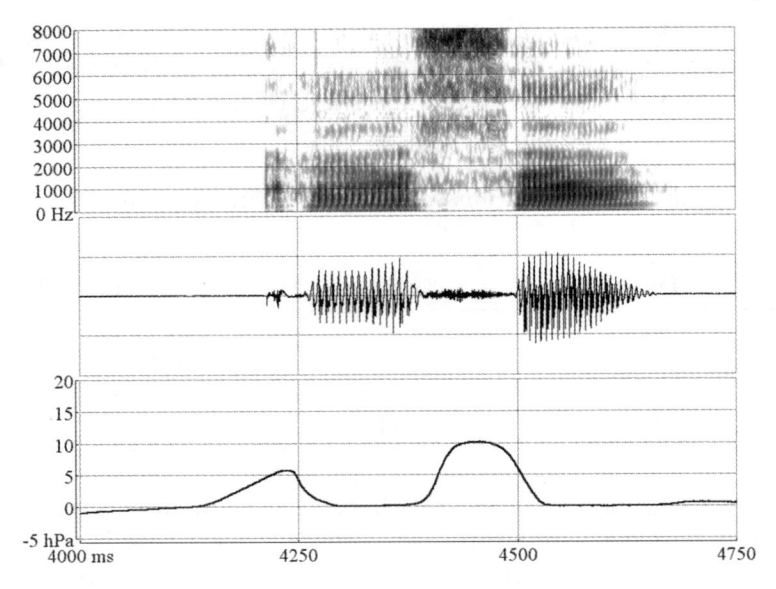

Figure 1: Spectrogram, audio waveform and intraoral pressure of the word kasa 'compensation'.

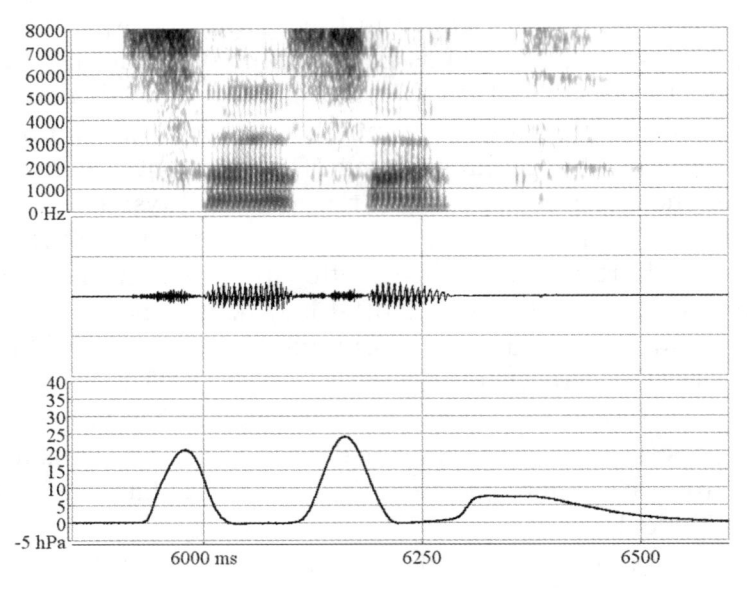

Figure 2: Spectrogram, audio waveform and intraoral pressure of the word s'ɪs'ɨt 'regret'.

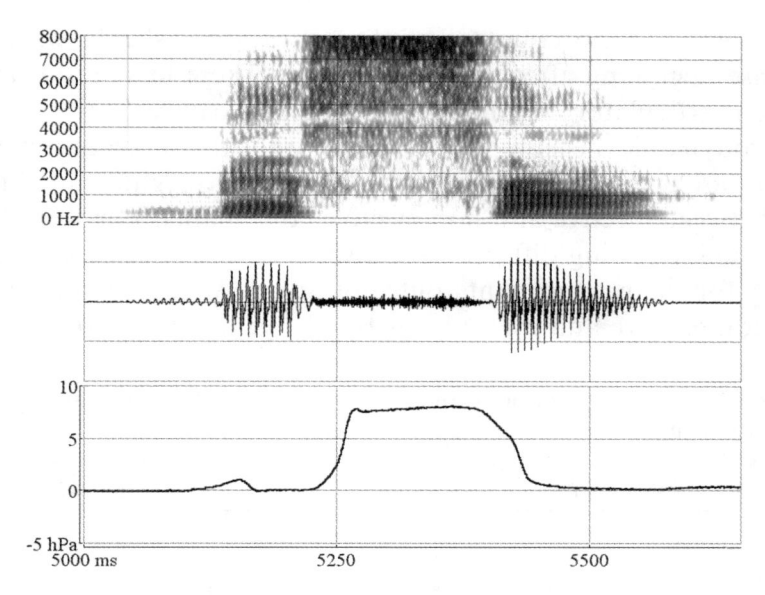

Figure 3: Spectrogram, audio waveform and intraoral pressure of the word bəsːa 'he pierced'.

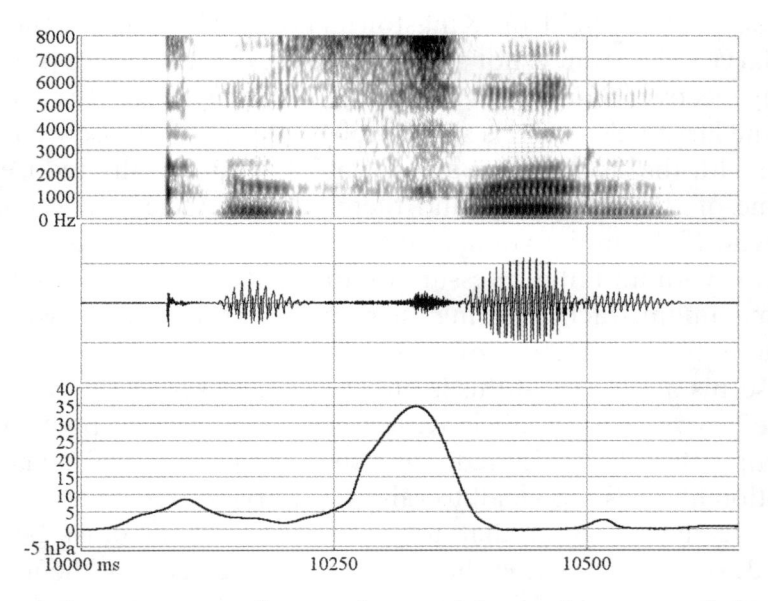

Figure 4: Spectrogram, audio waveform and intraoral pressure of the word k'ɨsː'ɬ 'adjective'.

while for the plain counterpart, Iop rises more slowly with the decrease beginning after a small 'plateau'. These facts result from different articulatory manoeuvres in the oral cavity.

Aerodynamic measurements show that for the subject for whom sub-glottal pressure was measured, there is no significant difference between ejective and non-ejective consonants. For Iop, there are some interesting differences between the four fricatives. Iop is similar for plain consonants but more than twice as high for the singleton ejective and even higher for the geminate ejective.

Table 2: Maximum value of noise amplitude (in dB) and glottal duration (in ms) for fricatives in Amharic

	Noise amplitude (RMS) dB	Glottal lag (ms)
[s]	53	0
[s:]	52	0
[s']	52	30
[s:']	58	12

This sheds more light on Kingston's (1984) claims about the fact that larynx elevation is not sufficient to explain the rise in pressure during ejectives. Kingston's modeling of Tigrinya ejectives showed that the larynx elevation is simply too slow and too loosely coordinated with the stop closure and release to dramatically reduce the volume of the oral cavity, and thereby make the Iop rise during ejectives. If the initial volume of the vocal tract is estimated to be 100 cm^3 with an initial pressure of 1030 hPa, the value of 42 hPa (the maximum reached during the recordings for ejective fricatives) accounts for a reduction of about 4 cm^3 in the oral cavity size.[3] This seems quite large if this is only accounted for by the elevation of the larynx. This parallels Kingston's (1984) second point when he claims that the cavity reduction that can be obtained by larynx elevation alone is too small to raise Iop to the observed levels. The Amharic data suggest that additional maneuvers must be employed, such as retracting the tongue root or extending the magnitude of the contact in the oral cavity. Kingston also suggested an additional tensing of the walls of the vocal tract.

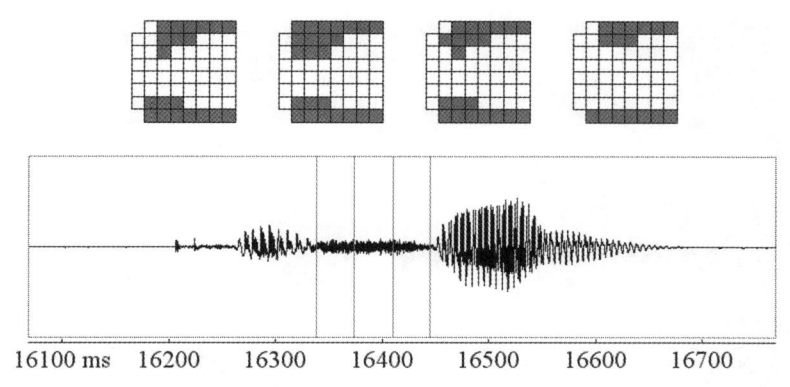

Figure 5: Audio waveform and EPG frames for the word kasa 'compensation'.

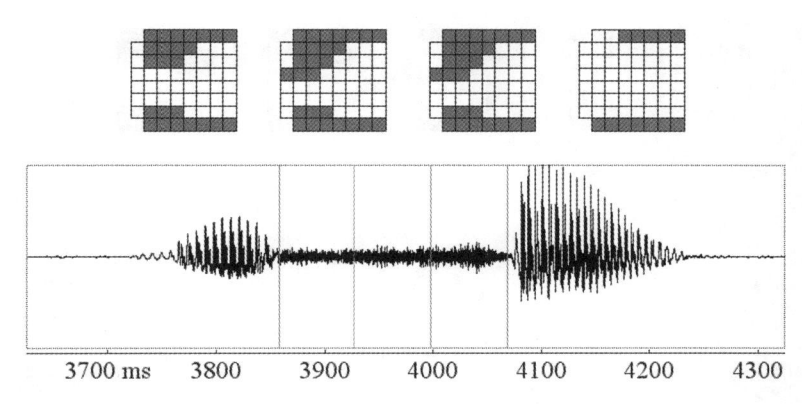

Figure 6: Audio waveform and EPG frames for the word bəsːa 'he pierced'.

Data obtained in EPG and 'classic' palatography give more indications about additional maneuvers and particularly about a bigger contraction of the cavity. Figures 5, 6, 7, 8 show the audio waveform of the words kasa 'compensation' (5), bəsːa he pierced' (6), s'ɨs'ɨt 'regret' (7), k'ɨsːˈɨl 'adjective' (8) and an EPG representation taken at 4 different moments. For each word, the first frame is taken at the start of the fricative, the second and the third are placed after setting a frame (the fourth) at the end of the fricative, in order to place a constant time interval between each frame.

EPG frame comparison between [s] and [sː] (Figures 5 and 6) shows that the constriction is narrower and slightly more fronted

472 *Didier Demolin*

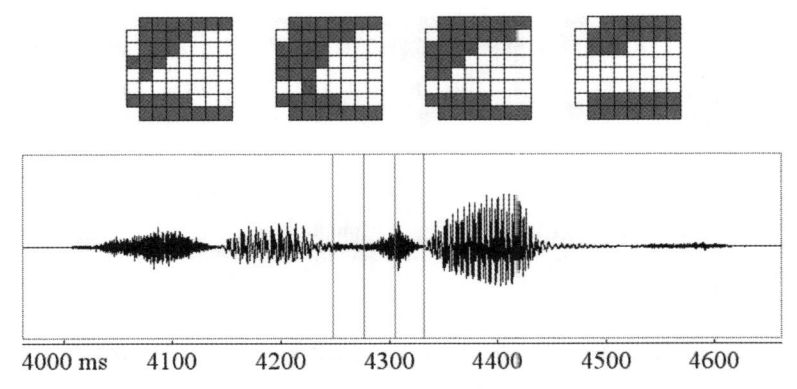

Figure 7: Audio waveform and EPG frames for the word s'ɪs'ɨt 'regret'.

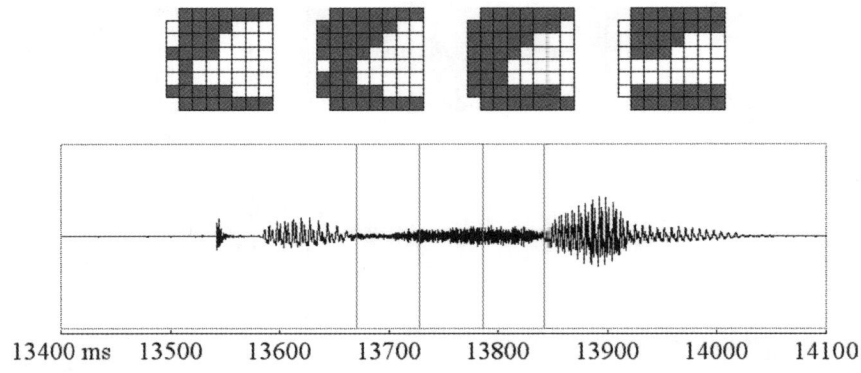

Figure 8: Audio waveform and EPG frames for the word k'ɪsː'ɨl 'adjective'.

for the geminate at frames 2 and 3. The ejectives [s'] and [sː'] show a wider contact in the alveolo-palatal regions, implying a reduction in the size of the oral cavity. For the singleton ejective (Figure 7), a closure seems to occur at frame 2, but even if there is a contact, there is likely to be leakage of air at this point. EPG does not measure the pressure of the contact; indeed, a light contact should be enough to make the closure, but with some leakage as shown by the noise on the audio waveform. Frames 1 and 3 show the size and the length of the constriction which is narrower and wider compared to [s] and [sː]. Figure 8 shows that there is a wider contact for [sː'] and a similar impression of closure in the alveolar and

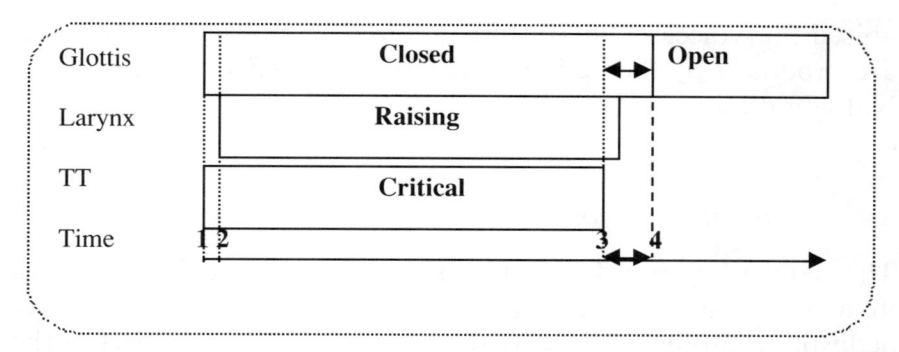

Glottis	Closed	⟷	Open
Larynx	Raising		
TT	Critical		
Time	1 2		3 4

Figure 9: Temporal coordination of tract variables for Amharic ejective fricatives.

palatal regions. However, the audio waveform shows once again that there must be some leakage, the noise amplitude increasing from frame 2 to frame 3. Frame 4 shows the size of the constriction before the vowel, which is narrower and has greater duration compared to other alveolar fricatives in Amharic. These data also suggest that there is a difference in the magnitude of the contacts between singleton and geminate ejectives, but this effect seems less obvious for the non-ejectives.

The data presented on ejective fricatives suggest the following temporal coordination of articulators: glottal closure and oral constriction are almost simultaneous (see Figure 4) and the oral constriction is crucially released before the glottal closure. The way in which native speakers control this coordination must be studied in further experiments and compared with ejectives in other languages, for example Tigrinya (Kingston, 1984; Fre Woldu, 1985) and Tlingit (Maddieson et al., 1996).

2.2 Bilabial trills in Mangbetu

An explanation of the production of bilabial trills interestingly shows the role of aerodynamic, articulatory and acoustic parameters in speech production. Bilabial trills are found in the Moru-Mangbetu group, a sub-phylum of the Central Sudanic language family (Demolin, 1988, 1992). Mangbetu, has three bilabial trills:

voiced [ʙ], voiceless [ʙ̥] and prenasalized [mʙ]. These consonants are produced by the action of the Bernoulli effect producing labial vibration.

2.2.1 Material and method

The data were recorded in two separate sessions. The first was made in Congo at Nangazizi, with five subjects, and included only acoustic recordings. The second was made with one subject at the Phonetics Laboratory of the Université de Provence. In this session, aerodynamic data were obtained by measuring intra-oral pressure as well as of oral airflow, with simultaneous acoustic and electroglottographic (EGG) recordings using the method described in 2.1.1. Articulatory data were also collected during this session. They involved a simultaneous recording of face and profile images using a high speed video camera. Profile images were obtained by putting a mirror against the cheek of the speaker, at a 45° angle to the sagittal plane. These data, some of which are given in (2), were intended to study the relative lip movements during the Mangbetu bilabial trills [ʙ], [ʙ̥], [mʙ].

(2) naaʙu   'dead body'
     naaʙ̥u   'war'
     nemʙo   'cooking pot'

2.2.2 Measurements and results

The spectrograms in Figure 10 show that bilabial trills typically exhibit two or three bursts, very rarely four, followed by short formant structures due to the vowel. The spectrograms also show that the closure is realized with noise, as for glottal fricatives, which is true both for voiced and voiceless consonants. From an articulatory point of view, the setting favouring bilabial trills is that of a voiced bilabial consonant followed by a high back vowel, thus [b] + [u], but it is not restricted to this setting (see Ladefoged & Maddieson, 1996). Such articulatory settings are found in

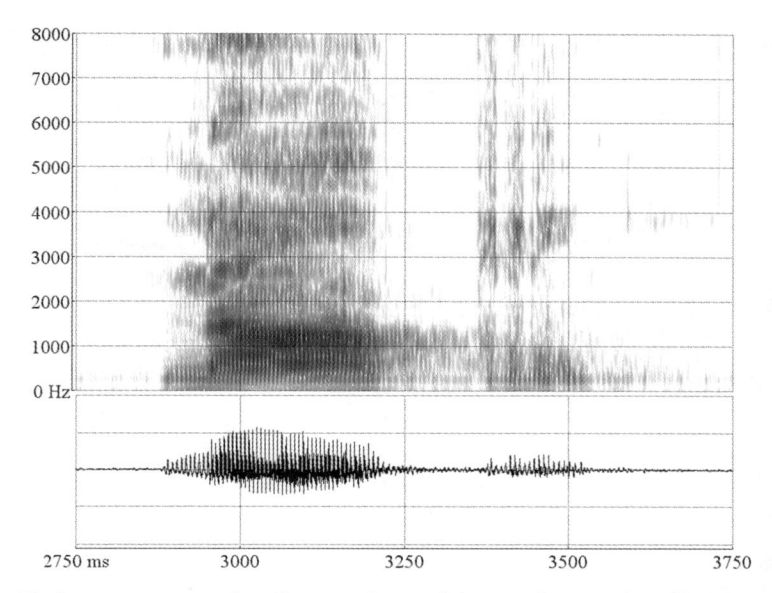

Figure 10: Spectrogram and audio waveform of the word naaʙo 'war' in Mangbetu.

many of the world's languages, but bilabial trills are nevertheless quite rare due to the unfavourable aerodynamic and articulatory conditions necessary to produce them. Aerodynamic measurements (see Figure 11) show that pharyngeal pressure rises more during a closure preceding a bilabial trill than before a bilabial stop. In addition, Iop does not decrease sharply as expected, but insttead falls very gradually, thus maintaining a sufficient difference with atmospheric pressure for the Bernoulli effect to have significant influence on the lips. Electroglottographic measurements additionally show that the vocal folds have a higher amplitude of vibration before a bilabial trill than before a bilabial stop, creating a higher transglottal airflow. Thus, if pressure is maintained above a certain critical level during a period of about 60 ms to 100 ms (the average duration of trills), a trill will be realized. However, in order to generate a trill, there must in addition be a relaxation of the lips, for otherwise affricates [pf] or [bv] are realized, as is shown by comparative data on Central Sudanic languages (Demolin, 1992). Figure 12 shows front and profile video images of the lips during the trill in a pronuciation of naabu 'dead

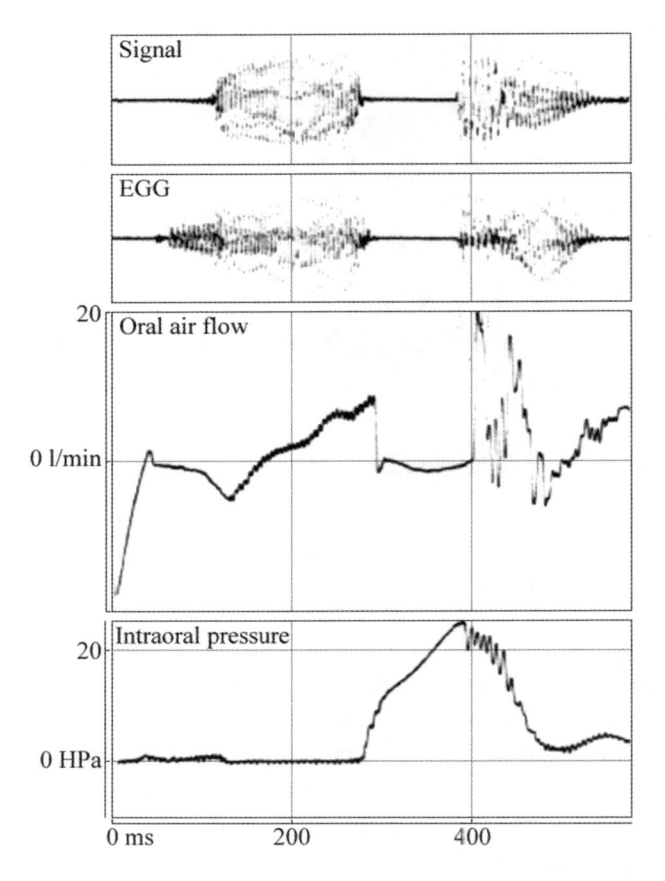

Figure 11: Audio waveform, EGG signal, oral airflow and intra-oral pressure for the word naaɓu 'war' in Mangbetu.

body'. The images show (1) lips during closure, (2) lip closure 20 ms before closure release, (3) lips opening 20 ms after closure release, (4) the closing gesture 40 ms after closure release, (5) the following closure and (6) the reopening 20 ms after this closure. The lighter part of the lips before closure release probably accounts for reduction in stiffness and for the deformation typically observed. Note that lip opening shows a 'spread' opening instead of the expected roundish opening because of the deformation due to the Bernoulli effect. Lip opening for voiced bilabial stops does not show this effect.

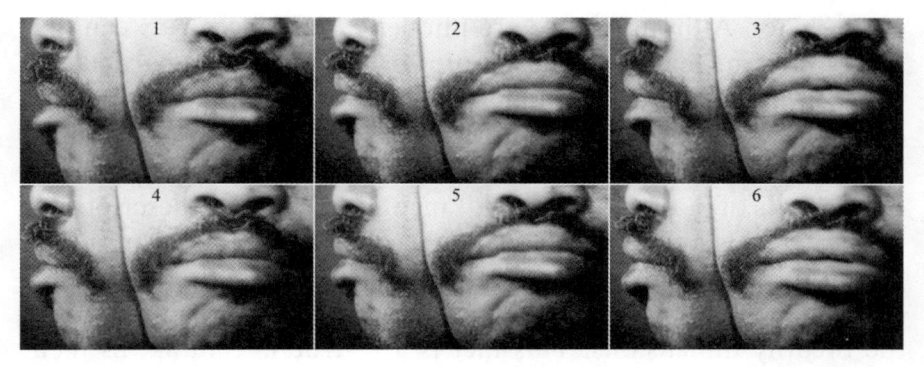

Figure 12: Lip movements of a Mangbetu speaker producing a bilabial trill [ʙ] during the word naaʙu 'dead body' in Mangbetu.

The production of bilabial trills is thus linked to aerodynamics. The seeds of these sounds are to be found in basic aerodynamic constraints in the relation between pressure, volume and the maintenance of a high pressure difference for some time. These can be taken into account by the phonology of a language and interpreted as a symbolic element of the system.

These observations and experiments can be tested by, for instance, a two-mass model or one of the models for simulating vocal fold vibration (Titze, 1994).

3. Principles relating vocal tract shape and acoustic output

3.1 Nuer vowels and the principle of maximum dispersion

Nuer is a Nilotic language spoken in Sudan and Ethiopia (Greenberg, 1963). The vowel system of this language exhibits a set of modal and breathy vowels. Yigezu (1995) describes the system as having a set of 16 vowels, seven of which are plain and nine breathy, / i, e, ɛ, a, ɔ, o, u/ and /i̤, e̤, ɛ̤, a̤, ɔ̤, o̤, ɨ̤, æ̤, ʌ̤/. In addition, length is contrastive. Yigezu's description is different from that given in previous works on Nuer made by Crazzolara (1933), Tucker (1936, 1975) and Denning (1989) which took into account Nuer dialects from Sudan. Yigezu's work and the present data concern the Ethiopian variety of Nuer. Although there are phonetic differences between dialects, a striking feature of the Nilotic vowel systems and particularly of Nuer and neighboring languages (Dinka and Shilluk) consists of differences between the inventories described so far. For example, Tucker (1975) noted the existence of two centralized high vowels [ɪ, ʊ] (variants of [i, u]) which are not mentioned in other descriptions. These variants are quite interesting because they can be variants of [i] and [u] but also of [e̤] and [o̤] in our data. There are also differences in the number of central vowels, which are more numerous in the breathy dimensions. This fact is also true in Shilluk, as mentioned by Denning (1989), who also notes that in Dinka and Shilluk, [æ] is sometimes heard as [ɛ].

Vowel systems such as Nuer offer phonology a way to test and refine some basic principles, for example the dispersion principle and the principle of maximal (or sufficient) contrast. Since these principles claim that the phonetic space is identical to the articulatory space × the perceptual space (Lindblom, 1986), the accurate description of such a system offers a good opportunity to increase our understanding of how the different phonetic parameters are taken into account. Claiming that there are two disjoint vowel spaces because there is a different source mechanism (or another feature) is not a satisfactory explanation. In fact there is only one vowel space, and the explanation of its dispersion requires acoustic, articulatory and auditory data. The combination of some of these parameters, at least in production, allows a good representation of the vowel space. An additional question is to know if there is any reason why in the breathy vowel system [ṳ] is missing in the inventory, and why there are more breathy central vowels in this system.

3.1.1 The Nuer vowel system: material and method

The vowel contrasts in Table 3 have been recorded and analyzed for five subjects from the Ethiopian variety of Nuer (Gambella region). For all speakers, audio and EGG recordings were simultaneously made for each word. The dimensions involved in these contrasts are the contrast between: plain and breathy vowels;

length contrasts for plain and breathy vowels; and finally contrasts involving the three breathy central vowels.

Table 3: Nuer vowel contrasts inluding in the experiment

Plain/breathy		Short/long		Short/long breathy		Central vowels	
tìt	to remember	jì̤t	scorpion	bì̤	you (sg) will		
tì̤t	magicians	jì̤ìt	stopping of the rain	bì̤ì	cloth	kɛɛ	with
tɛ̀t	hand	kèk	dam	tɛ̤̀t	to dig	kɛ̤ɛ̤	first-born child
tɛ̀t	to dig	kéèk	ruler	tɛ̤́ɛ̤̀t	to take it back	kæ̤æ̤	divorced woman
tɛ̄t	reclaim	tɛr	conflict	rɛ̤l	sunrise	pàt	to clap
tɛ̱̄t	branch	tɛɛr	september	r̤ɛ̱̄ɛ̱̄l	downhill	pà̤t	cook
tát	buttock	gàk	to quarrel	láŋ	praying	pɨt	tray
tà̤t	erection	gààk	flower	làáŋ	golden colors	lɔk	rinsing the mouth
tɔt	waste	kɔ́r	after	kɔ̤c	climbing	lɔ̤k	umbilical cord
tɔ̤t	summer	kɔ́ɔ́	homosexual	kɔ̤̄ɔ̤̄c	something dry	lʌk	refusal
tót	to bend	tók	sound of a broken object	kór	war		
tót̮	lifting up	tóòk	calabash	kò̤ò̤r	stream		
tút	bulls	kùk	beside				
tʌt	pair of buttocks	kúùt	fiancé				
kʌr	'war'						

3.1.2 Explaining the system

Yigezu's (1995) description of the Nuer vowel system shows that there is no high back vowel [u̱] but instead there is a central [ɨ].

This fact is also true in Crazzolara's (1933) Nuer description and in Dinka as described by Malou (1988). In addition there are two central vowels in the breathy dimension [æ̤, ʌ̤]. A possible explanation of the existence of these central vowels of the breathy type and of the absence of a high back breathy [ṳ], lies in the acoustic coupling with the subglottal cavities which can modify the spectrum of the sound output from the vocal tract by introducing perturbations in the vicinity of the subglottal resonances. Stevens (1998) claims that the amount of perturbation depends on the size of the glottal opening. Since breathy vowels are produced with a separation between the arytenoids that extends back from the vocal processes, it is imaginable that while producing breathy vowels, Nuer speakers introduce such coupling with the subglottal cavities. The acoustic effect is that spectral peaks become less prominent and additional peaks and valleys are superimposed on the spectrum. Additional peaks arise in the vicinity of 600, 1550 and 2200 Hz, with bandwidths in the range of 200 to 400 Hz. An additional spectral peak between F2 and F3 in the spectrum of the high back vowel [u] can create the spectrum of the central breathy vowel [ɨ]. The existence of centralized [æ̤] and [ʌ̤] can be explained in the same way, but the correspondence with plain vowels is less easily established.

Figures 13 and 14 show the F1/F2 distribution of plain and breathy vowels from data from five speakers. Plain vowels appear to be more peripheral than breathy vowels. Subglottal resonances occur around 200, 1550 and 2200 Hz, which are superposed on the vowel's spectrum. The first and third resonances probably contribute towards (upward or downward) formant shifts for breathy vowels compared to their plain counterparts. However, there are more factors involved in the way the perceptual system integrates these subglottal resonances. One of these is the bandwidth, which tends to be larger for breathy vowels. This is comparable to what happens in coupling for nasal vowels (Beddor et al., 1986), the difference being that for breathy vowels the coupling is made with fixed resonances of the tracheal system. It is therefore less variable than in the case of nasal vowels.

The Nuer example shows that there is a multiplicity of factors which converge to account for the dispersion of vowels in the

Primitives in phonology 481

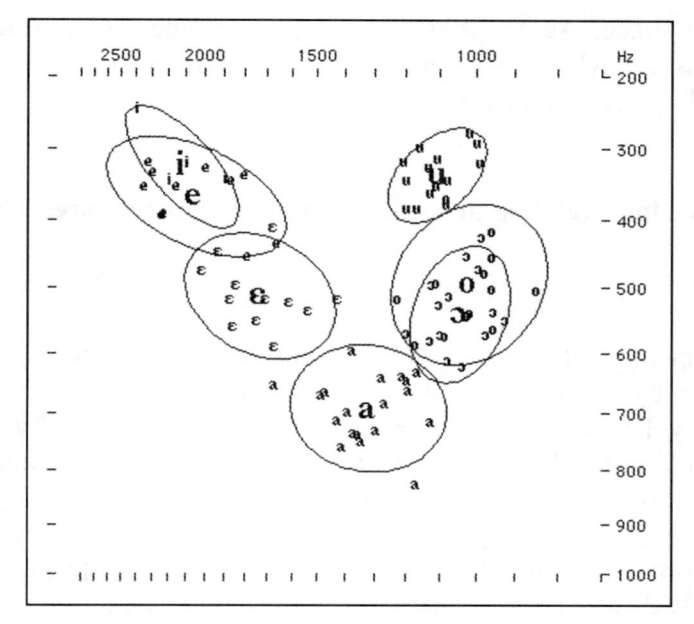

Figure 13: F1/F2 dispersion of Nuer oral vowels.

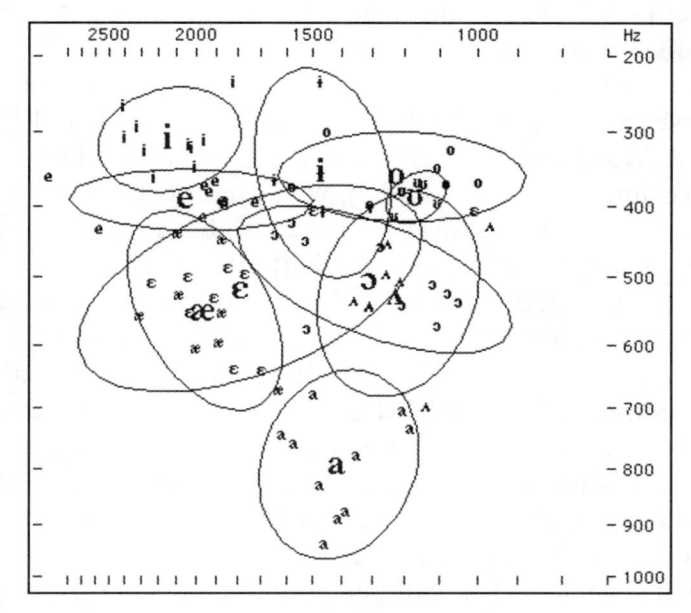

Figure 14: F1/F2 dispersion of Nuer breathy vowels.

acoustic space. Again physical and physiological constraints are the basis on which phonological systems are organized and by which they are universally constrained.

4. Principles relating acoustic output to auditory representations

4.1 Lendu vowelless syllables

The relevance of auditory processing to phonology may be illustrated by vowelless syllables of Lendu, which were first mentioned by Tucker (1940) and recently received attention by Kutsch Lojenga (1989). The case illustrates how the overlap of articulatory gestures can be interpreted perceptually. Lendu vowelless syllables either contain an alveolar fricative or a trill as the nucleus. Data come from three sources, Mertens (1978), Kutsch Lojenga's (1989) and from three Lendu speakers. Lendu (ɓāθà), the language of the ɓālē, is spoken by about 500,000 people in various areas of the Ituri Province west of Lake Albert, north-eastern Congo. This language belongs to the Central Sudanic subgroup of the Nilo-Saharan language family.

Lendu is not the only language with these syllabic consonants. They have been reported for other languages by Bell (1978), Jakobson & Waugh (1982), who quote data from Krejnovic (1958) in Korjak, and by Christol (1988), who presents facts from several Indo-European languages. Theys have also been reported for Bella Coola by Newman (1947) and Hockett (1955). There are similarities between the facts observed in Lendu and other languages. Bell (1978: 183) described [z]-like syllabic fricatives in some Sino-Tibetan languages; Ladefoged & Wu (1984) and Dimmendaal (1986) have examined comparable data in Pekinese fricatives. Laver (1994) also mentions and examines cases similar to that of Lendu.

There are several questions about these syllables. How can the syllabic structure of Lendu be defined? How can these syllables be accounted for in a phonological model? What is the phonetic reality of such syllables? How can perceptual factors contribute to our understanding of phonological phenomena? Both Mertens (1978) and Kutsch Lojenga (1989) have shown that vowelless syllables occur with voiced and voiceless alveolar fricatives [s, z] and trills [r], which can be preceded by labial, alveolar and velar stops, whether complex or not. The data in Table 4 illustrate this for fricatives; trills will not be examined here. The methods used to process the data were described in sections 2.1.1 and 2.2.1.

Table 4: Lendu words used in the experiments.

ss̀	to prepare beer	tss̀	to eat
ss̄	black wasp	tss̄	banana
sš	to move quickly	tsš	to shave
sś	shoe	tss̀tss̄	banana
sšsś	black snake		
zz̄	target	dzz̀	tree from the forest
zz̀	to lay	dzz̄	to weep
zž	to milk	dzž	to mould
zz̀zź	drink		
zźzz̀	loss		

4.1.1 Acoustic analysis

Words may consist of one or two consecutive vowelless syllables, as illustrated in the data presented in Table 3. Spectrograms of Lendu vowelless syllables containing an alveolar fricative show obvious resonances following the initial fricative, which are located in the nuclei of these syllables and represent a kind of vocoid. However, perceptually their quality is not easy to identify. Inspection of the spectrogram in Figure 15 of the word zz̀ 'to lay' shows that noise is concentrated between 3000 and 5000 Hz, with a low peak between 3000 and 4000 Hz. This peak starts 150 ms from the beginning and lasts 200 ms. The resonances at 500 Hz and 1200 Hz might be due to a vowel: such resonances have been found with all the so-called vowelless syllables having an alveolar frica-

484   *Didier Demolin*

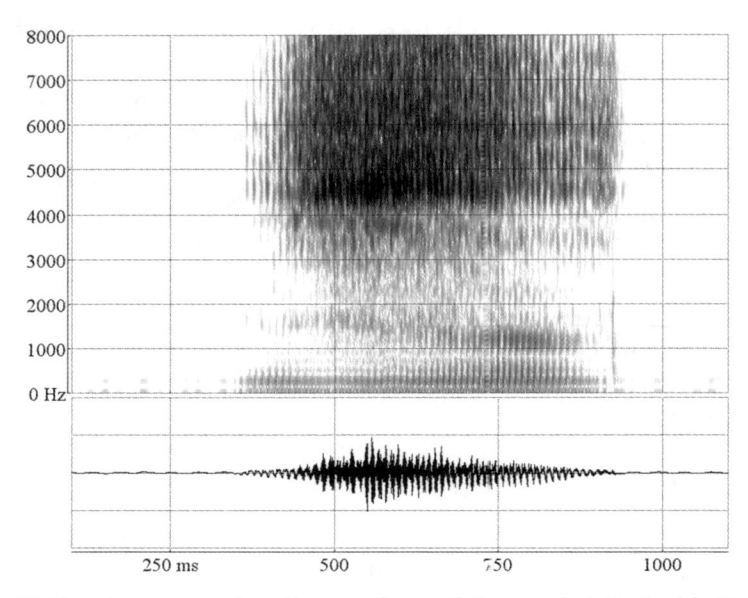

Figure 15: Spectrogram and audio waveform of the word zż 'to lay' in Lendu.

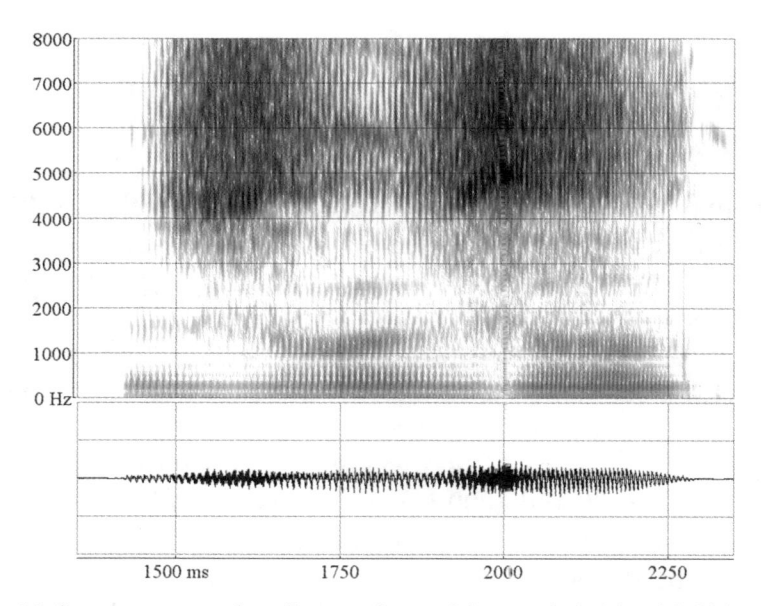

Figure 16: Spectrogram and audio waveform of the word zżzź 'to drink' in Lendu.

Primitives in phonology 485

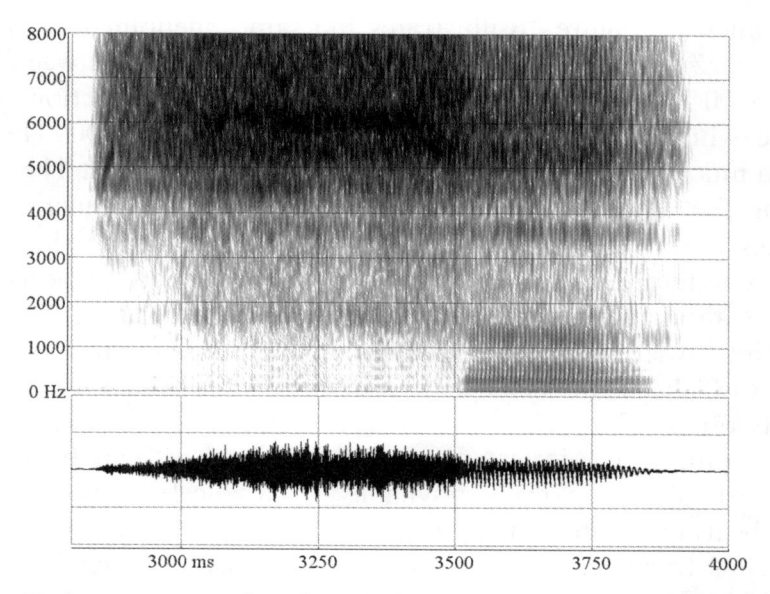

Figure 17: Spectrogram and audio waveform of the word sś̀ 'to prepare beer' in Lendu.

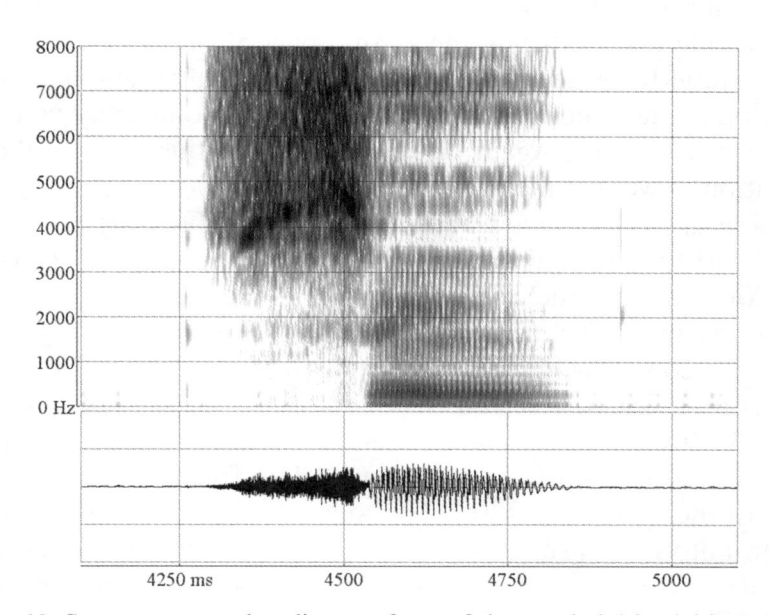

Figure 18: Spectrogram and audio waveform of the word sè 'slowly' in Lendu.

tive nucleus. Figure 16 illustrates the same phenomenon for the word zżzź 'to drink'. Here also, noise is concentrated between 3000 and 5000 Hz. There is nevertheless a considerable reduction of the noise, which remains concentrated between 4000 and 5000 Hz, and has a much weaker intensity during the syllabic nucleus. The interesting fact about these syllables is that the air turbulence that makes the alveolar fricative is not interrupted during the vowel but is reduced in frequency and in intensity. This suggests that consonantal and vocalic gestures are superposed or that there is a multiple stricture during the syllabic nucleus. This fact explains why the nucleus of such syllables is so difficult to identify.

As observed by Kutsch Lojenga (1989), syllables that apparently contain a voiceless fricative in the nucleus can bear tone. Figure 17 shows a vowelless syllable with a voiceless alveolar fricative bearing a low tone. The first part of the spectrogram, the voiceless fricative, shows noise at frequencies between 1500 and 8000 Hz. These frequencies continue into the syllabic nucleus but with less amplitude. The nucleus has formant frequencies around 500 Hz and 1200 Hz. This syllable is transcribed as [sŝ] by Mertens (1978) and Kutsch Lojenga (1989). Kutsch Lojenga (1989) states that voicing occurs during the second part of the syllable in order for the tone to be realized. What is unsatisfactory about this description is that a consonant identified as phonologically voiceless co-occurs with tone. Again we can understand this segmental configuration if we assume that the nucleus and the onset are partly overlapping. The tone is realized during (and phonologically associated with) the vocoid nucleus. It is the continuation of the onset frication into the nucleus, although at a reduced intensity level, that gives the voiceless quality to the entire syllable. Figure 18 shows the comparison with the word sè 'slowly', where the consonant is followed by a 'clean' vowel. Noise is mainly concentrated above 3000 Hz, but also at frequencies as low as 1500 Hz during the voiceless alveolar fricative onset, and no frication noise continues into the following vowel. This suggests that noise spreading is not an automatic process in Lendu, but is contrastive. The same phenomenon can be observed when the fricative is preceded by a stop.

4.1.2 Aerodynamic and articulatory analysis

A close examination of the aerodynamic data allows us to understand the process of co-occurrence of vocoid and consonantal gestures. They also confirm the acoustic findings. This is illustrated in Figures 19, 20, 21, 22 for the words zż 'to lay', zżzż 'to drink', sś 'to prepare beer' and sè 'slowly'. Plots 1, 2, 3, show respectively: audio signal (1), electroglottograph (2), and intra-oral pressure (3). Figures 19 and 20, containing words with voiced fricatives in the syllabic nucleus, show that voicing, which is present throughout the word, is different during syllabic onset and nucleus, the amplitude being greater during the nucleus. The pharyngeal pressure in (3) shows that after an increase of pressure corresponding to the narrowing of the vocal tract, pressure decreases gradually up to the end of the syllable. This latter fact is crucial, since it confirms that the narrowing of the oral tract in the alveolar region is not abruptly released, as is normally the case when a vowel follows. It also shows that there is an important overlap between the gestures made for syllabic onset and nucleus. The importance of the gradual release of the constriction can be understood by comparing the pharyngeal pressure plot (3) in Figure 22 (where the vowel following the initial fricative is not accompanied by a sustained constriction gesture) with the pharyngeal pressure plots in Figures 20 and 21, where pressure decreases gradually up to the end of the syllable. Plot 3 in Figures 20 and 21 shows that pressure increases are followed by gradual decreases. Every pressure increase corresponds to a syllable onset and every gradual decrease corresponds to a nucleus. Pharyngeal pressure is maintained well above the level expected for a vowel during the pressure decreases. This confirms that some narrowing of the oral tract is maintained during the vowel, and that both an alveolar fricative and a second gesture are articulated at the same time.

The spreading of frication onto the following nucleus observed on the spectrograms is due to articulatory factors. Both the initial consonant and the following gesture accounting for the resonances are articulated in the front part of the mouth. The consonant onset is alveolar and the second gesture is more palatal. The articulatory movement between the alveolar and the palatal regions allows the

488 *Didier Demolin*

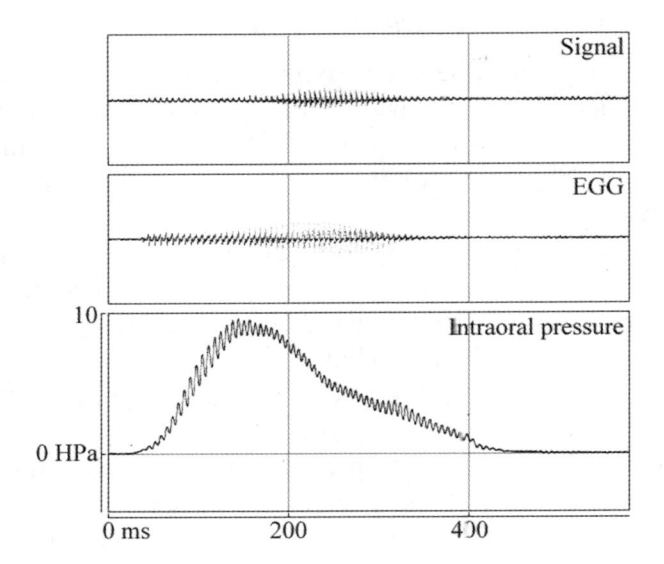

Figure 19: Audio waveform waveform, EGG signal and intra-oral pressure of the word zz̀ 'to lay' in Lendu.

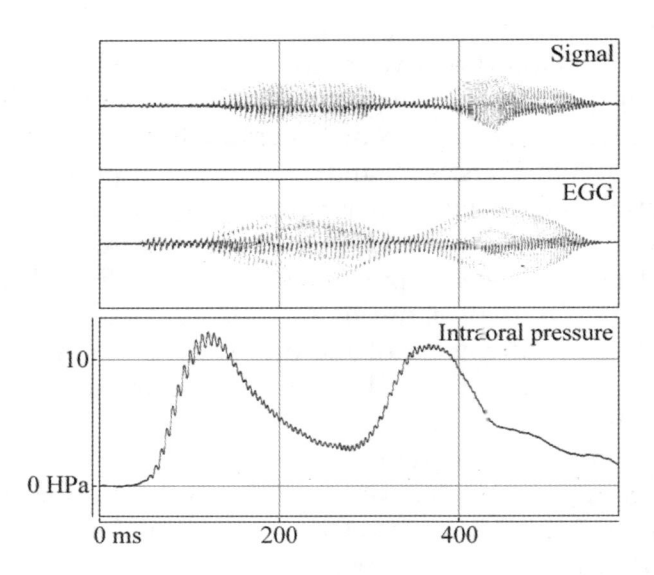

Figure 20: Audio waveform waveform, EGG signal and intra-oral pressure of the word zz̀zź 'to drink' in Lendu.

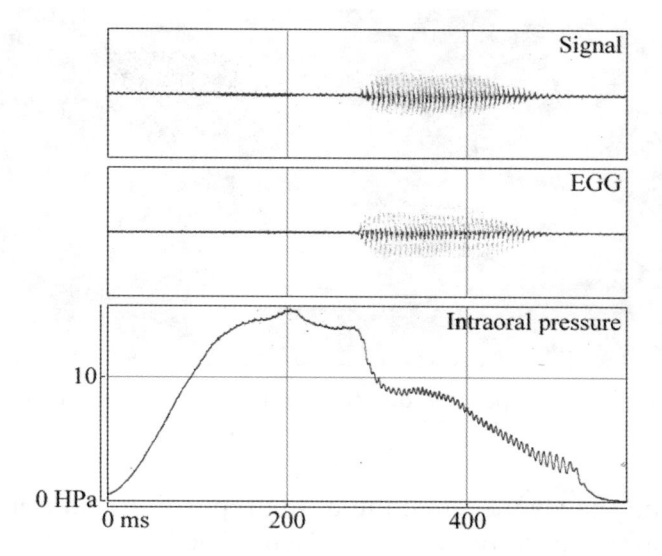

Figure 21: Audio waveform waveform, EGG signal and intra-oral pressure of the word sṣ̀ 'to prepare beer' in Lendu.

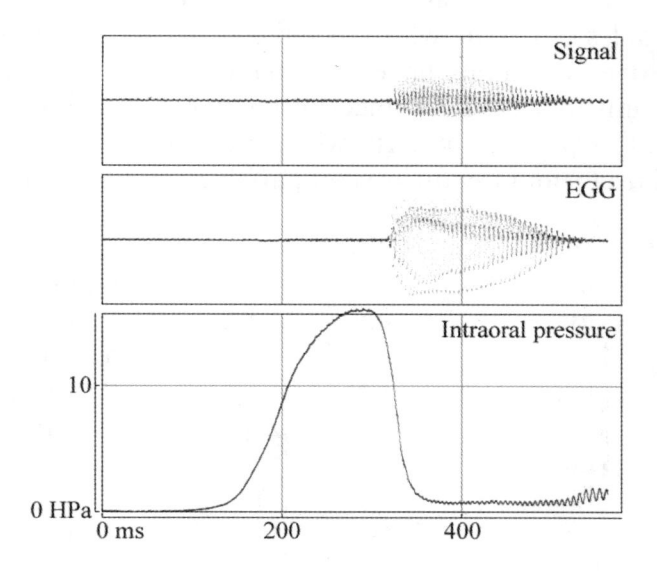

Figure 22: Audio waveform waveform, EGG signal and intra-oral pressure of the word sè 'to lay' in Lendu.

490 Didier Demolin

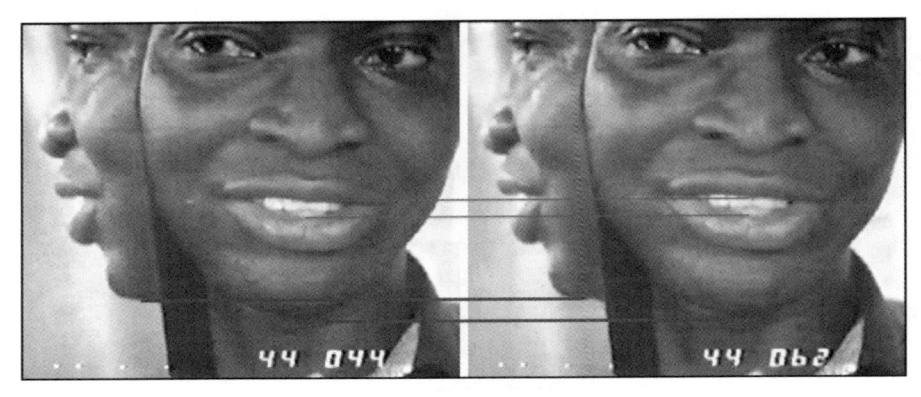

Figure 23: Lip and jaw position during syllabic onset and nucleus for the word zz̀ 'to lay' in Lendu.

tongue and the jaw to remain in a (high) position and noise turbulence to spread onto the vocoid nucleus. The high jaw position can be observed on video images (Figure 23) which show front and profile frames recorded simultaneously. The data suggest that the overlap between the onset and the nucleus of the syllable is probably due to the static position of the jaw. Thus, the so-called vowelless syllables of Lendu, whose syllabic nuclei are represented alveolar fricatives, do in fact have a resonant nucleus. Kutsch Lojenga (1989) claims that the resonances of the nuclei account for a "hidden" front vowel, particularly when Ngiti (one of the two main Lendu dialects) and Lendu are compared, as in the examples in (3).

(3) | Ngiti | Lendu | | |
|---|---|---|---|
| izǎ | zǎ | | 'animal' |
| ıdza | dza | | 'house' |
| adzi | dzz | | 'earth' |
| ıtsi | tsṡ | [tsż] | 'laziness' |
| azi | zi | [zz] | 'brother-in-law' |
| àtsǐ | tsǐ | [tsž] | 'red kaolin' |
| idzi | ìdzz̀ | [ìdzż] | 'drum' |
| ɔ̀tsi | tss | [tsz] | 'to crackle' |

Although more research is required, it seems reasonable to conclude from the acoustic, aerodynamic and comparative data that

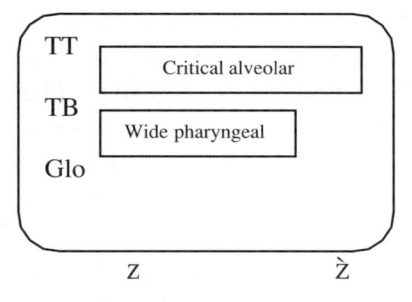

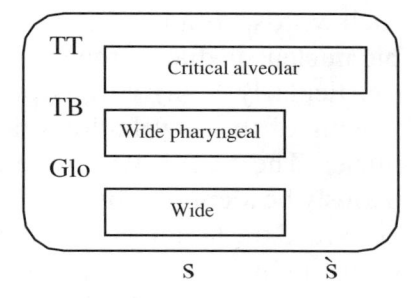

```
┌─────────────────────────┐         ┌─────────────────────────┐
│ TT  ┌─────────────────┐ │         │ TT  ┌─────────────────┐ │
│     │ Critical alveolar│ │         │     │ Critical alveolar│ │
│ TB  └─────────────────┘ │         │ TB  └─────────────────┘ │
│     ┌──────────────┐    │         │     ┌──────────────┐    │
│     │ Wide pharyngeal│  │         │     │ Wide pharyngeal│  │
│ Glo └──────────────┘    │         │ Glo └──────────────┘    │
│                         │         │           ┌──────┐      │
│                         │         │           │ Wide │      │
│                         │         │           └──────┘      │
└─────────────────────────┘         └─────────────────────────┘
     z              ż                     s              s̀
```

Figure 24: Schematic gestural scores for the syllables zż 'to lay' and ss̀ 'to prepare beer' in Lendu.

Lendu vowelless syllables are apical dorsal vocoids. Laver (1994) notes that these sounds are relatively rare, but the Szechuanese example he quotes from Scott (1947) suggests that the Lendu syllabic consonants might be similar. Indeed, Scott states that in 'the prononciation of *si, dzi, tsi* and *zi* the fricative part of these articulations 'is followed by a voiced sound made with the tip and blade of the tongue in approximately the position for [z], little or no friction being produced. The sound has some resemblance to a retracted [i]' (in Lendu there is always clear friction).[4]

Using the gestural scores proposed by Browman & Goldstein (1989, 1992), the phonological representation of Lendu syllabic consonants, based on these phonetic observations, can be gievn as in Figures 24ab for the syllables zż, ss̀. These schematic gestural scores show values for the following tract variables: tongue tip (TT), tongue body (TB) and glottis (Glo). This analysis suggests that the important gestures are tongue tip and tongue body. Tongue tip has critical value during the whole syllable for fricatives. The difference between voiced and voiceless fricatives is that for a syllable such as the glottis has a wide value corresponding to the syllabic onset. Tongue body has a wide pharyngeal value corresponding to the syllabic onset. This wide pharyngeal value disappears as soon as the vowel occupying the syllabic nucleus is realized.

In summary, a consonant identified as phonologically voiceless can co-occur with a low tone in words such as ss̀ 'to prepare beer' and words such as zż 'to lay' are identified phonologically as having a fricative in the nucleus. Acoustic, aerodynamic and diachronic data show that vocoid and consonant gestures overlap in such words. As a result, the identification of a fricative in the syllabic nucleus is due to the spreading of turbulent noise during front (particularly high) vowels preceded by an alveolar fricative. The voicing of the vowel allows distinctive pitch to be realized on such nuclei. The reason why tone and voiceless fricatives can simultaneously be identified by Lendu speakers (and the linguists who have described the language) is that voiceless fricatives are identified categorically by low frequency frication noise (present in the nucleus at low intensity levels) and tone by a specific pitch (present in the nucleus thanks to vocal cord vibration contributed by the vowel).

4.2 !xóõ sound change

If a case study were needed to show the contribution of fieldwork to theoretical problems in phonology, !xóõ would with little doubt provide the best example. The papers by Traill (1985, 1994, 1995), Ladefoged & Traill (1984, 1994) and Traill & Vossen (1997) are important contributions to problems that have occupied a central place of phonological research over the last twenty or thirty years. As mentioned in the introduction, phonological descriptions are aimed at classifying segments and accounting for sound patterns. The study of !xóõ has highlighted the way in which phonologists should attempt to incorporate all the linguistically-significant phonetic facts into a formal grammar. Ladefoged & Traill (1984) have shown that binary features do not reveal the crucial properties of segments: !xóõ segments show that the relative timing of articulatory movements can be a defining property. In addition, the specifications of timing do not lie in a one-to-one relation with phonological features. Ladefoged & Traill's (1984) work has shown how a complex, language-specific relationship exists between the phonological specification and the phonetic facts of a language: there is no way in which phonological features can be associated with simple phonetic facts.

A case of sound change in Khoisan languages shows how important the acoustic factors are that underlie the processes of click replacement and click loss. Traill (1995) and Traill & Vossen (1997) have shown that in order to reveal the essential relationships be-

Primitives in phonology 493

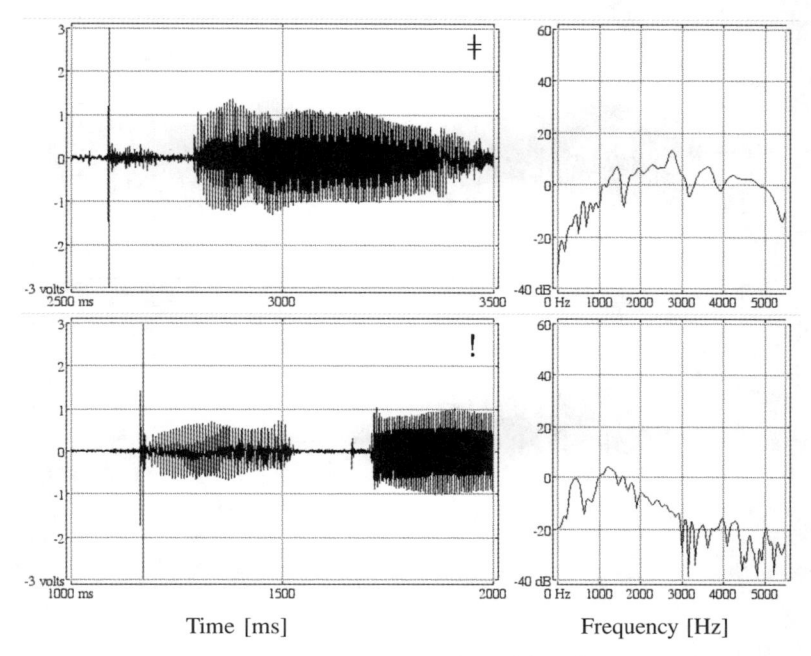

Figure 25: Waveform and spectra showing the two abrupt clicks [!, ǂ] in different !xóõ words.

tween clicks and non-clicks, the generalizations for clicks cannot be stated in terms of articulatory features, which obscure these relationships, but instead require perceptually-defined features. Specifically, !xóõ clicks fall into two classes, depending on whether their burst noises are either abrupt and short or noisy and long. The former have very fast rise times of about 1 ms and are about 8ms long, whereas the latter have a crescendo-like onset of acoustic energy lasting about 25 ms. This allows clicks to be classified according to the acoustic features of abruptness and spectral tilt (Table 5, Figure 25 and Figure 26).

Table 5: Click classification according to burst properties.

	bilabial ⊙	dental |	lateral ||	palatal ǂ	alveolar !
abrupt	−	−	−	+	+
high frequency	−	+	−	+	−

494 Didier Demolin

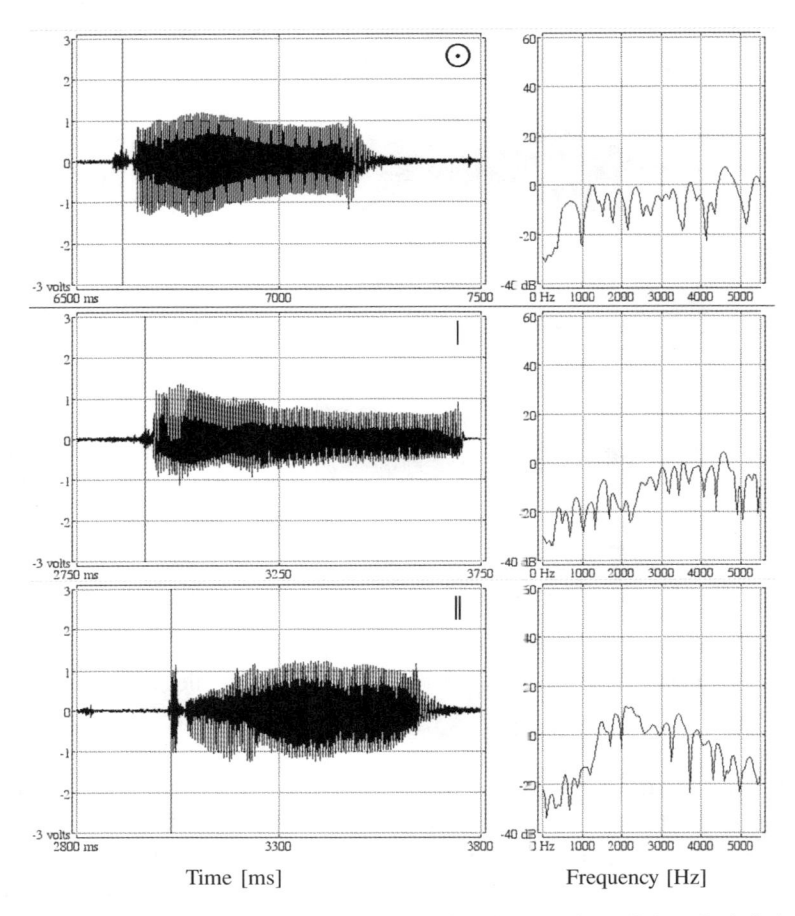

Figure 26: Waveform and spectra showing the three noisy clicks [☉, |, ‖] in different !xóõ words.

Another important point about clicks is made by Sands (1999), who claims that they are immune to all forms of co-articulation except that of anticipatory rounding. The variability seen in the click spectra must therefore be internal to the articulation of the click itself. Thus, the role of spectral emphasis is not trivial and makes clicks an ideal object to refer to perceptual factors involved in sound change.

Click loss is defined by Traill & Vossen (1997) with reference to languages where a click influx has been replaced with a non-click consonant. Click replacement is applied to cases where one influx is replaced by another. The progression from click to (acoustically) weakened click and to non-click shows how sound change is manifested in Khoisan languages and how important perceptual factors are in this process. The data in (5) show some examples of click loss in Khoe (Traill & Vossen, 1997). These data indicate that the alveolar and palatal clicks [!, ǂ] have a lower frequency emphasis in their spectra and give rise to cognate forms sharing acoustic features with those clicks, i.e. energy of the burst, which is intense and long, and concentrated in a narrow band of the spectrum. In the light of these data, the process of click loss can be considered as the endpoint of click weakening.

(5)   Alveolar influx !   palatal influx ǂ

!go   go   antbear   ǂgeu   ɟiu   bustard
!ae   kae   tie   ǂxoa   cxoa   enter
!xan   kxan   sew   ǂnuam   ɲum   whistle
!nu   ŋu   country   ǂkx'oa c'oa   come out

Traill & Vossen (1997) show how the weakening and loss of a click is a response to co-articulatory pressure from phonetic contexts where abrupt clicks require extreme distortions of tongue body trajectories. Weakening these clicks involves articulatory undershoot, but because the result is a noisiery, weaker, and more diffuse click, there is an auditory cost, which amounts to a reduction in the dispersion of clicks in the acoustic space. Traill & Vossen (1997) suggest that this may explain why click loss leads to acoustically-similar non-clicks which re-establish saliency among the contrasts. This example shows that by looking at details in the phonetics of languages and by relying on acoustic and perceptual principles it is possible to explain why sound patterns are what they are.

5. Cognition and symbolization

5.1 Phonological awareness and word games

Phonologists have speculated at length on how sound patterns are represented in the human mind. Claims regarding the psychological mechanisms underlying language use are often difficult to validate because the choice between competing hypotheses is not always easy to test. This section will consider a remarkable case study of number of word games by Ngonga (2001), from a Bantu language spoken in Congo, Hendo. In this language, word games create derived languages, which manipulate and rearrange a variety of phonological unit, permitting a number of phonological claims to be tested, in the cognitive and symbolic domains. The Hendo case is particularly interesting because it allows us to discuss at what level of analysis speakers operate and shows that the patterns generated by word games are purely not conventional, but derive from the speakers' representation and processing of words. It also illustrates the importance of controlled observation in the field, outside the laboratory. Careful observation of Hendo word games not only reveals important facts about the language and the way it is processed but also show how phonological awareness can emerge among speakers of an unwritten language.

5.2 Hendo word games

Hendo is spoken in Western Kasaï within the Kole area of the Democratic Republic of Congo. There are 7 vowels /i, e, ɛ, a, ɔ, u/, 16 consonants /b, p, d, t, k, m, n, ŋ, f, s, ʒ, ʃ, w, l, h, ʄ/ (the last of these being a palatal unexploded implosive), 18 complex consonants /tʃ, dʒ, pf, bv, mp, mb, nt, nd, ŋk, ŋg, mf, ns, ʃʷ, tʃʷ, nh, mpf, mbv, dʒʷ/, and two tones, high (H) and low (L), in the phonemic inventory. Ngonga's (2000) study has identified 18 different word games that are learned during initiation, in reclusion camps. Until Ngonga's work these word games remained a secret of Hendo society. Each of these word games creates a new derived language which exploits at least one phonological unit of the language. Broadly speaking, there are two main types of derived languages: simple and compound. The following tables illustrate the processing for 2 examples in each of the 18 word games.

Table 6: Additive languages 1.

Hendo	Gloss	L1	L2	L3
tʃɔ́ká	Go	tʃɔ́ŋgɔ́kaŋgá	tʃísɔkísa	tʃɔnákaná
ota	Weapon	oŋgótaŋgá	óʃitîsa	onɔ́taná

Table 7: Additive languages 2.

Hendo	Gloss	L4	L5	L6
tʃɔ́ká	Go	tʃɔsɔ́kánga	tʃɔkánga	tʃɔkádʒa
ota	Weapon	osótala	otala	otaládʒa

Table 8: Simple derived languages 1: mutative languages.

Hendo	Gloss	L7	L8	L9
tʃɔ́ká	Go	kátʃɔ́	tʃáko	kɔ́tʃá
ota	Weapon	tao	ato	toka

Table 9: Simple derived languages 2: substitutive languages.

Hendo	Gloss	L10	L11	L12
tʃɔ́ká	Go	tʃɔ́ŋgá	tʃɔ́ŋgjá	tʃéké
ota	Weapon	ola	okja	ɛtɛ

Table 10: Compound derived languages.

Hendo	Gloss	L13	L14	L15
tʃɔ́ká	Go	mákátʃɔ́	tʃáŋgɔ́	wɔ́kálá
ota	Weapon	matao	alo	owala

Table 11: Prosodic derived languages.

Hendo	Gloss	L16	L17	L18
tʃɔ́ká	Go	katʃɔ	tʃɔ̀kà	ka:katʃɔ
ota	Weapon	ta:o	ótá	ta:tao

5.2.1 Processes

Tables 6 to 11 show processes that involve the behaviour of six different kinds of word games which are in fact derived languages (Ngonga, 2000). Of course, each type of word game could be described and discussed in much more detail, but here the focus will only be on the description of the various processes.

L1 to L4 add a new syllable after each syllable of the original word; L5 to L6 add one syllable after the last syllable of a word. Because of this principle of syllable addition, L1 to L6 are considered as additive languages. L7 to L12 present two types of simple derived languages, i.e. mutative and additive. Mutative languages can permute a syllable (L7), a vowel (L8) or a consonant (L9). Substitutive languages may permute features such as voicing (L10 and 11), vowel height, or may show vowel harmony processes (L12). Compound derived languages (L13 to L15) combine various processes of additive and simple derived languages. Prosodic derived languages involve tone erasure and/or length addition (L16 and L18) and tone permutations (L17).

5.2.2 Analysis

The striking feature of these word games is that they involve all phonological units, syllables, tones, lengths (moras or X-slots), segments and features in an unwritten language. This fact challenges Morais & Mousty (1992), who claim that phonological awareness of segments or phonemes comes from an intermediary alphabetic script. L8 and L9 show clear examples of consonant and vowel permutations and L10 to L12 even show manipulations of features. In L10 the word tʃɔ́ká 'go' changes to tʃɔ́ŋgá where the voiceless velar stop /k/ is changed into a voiced velar prenasalized stop /ŋg/; the word ota 'weapon' is changed into ola where the voiceless alveolar stop /t/ is changed into a voiced alveolar lateral /l/ (which is a voiced allophone of /t/). L11 substitutes a palatalized velar stop at the onset of the second syllable. In L12, the principle

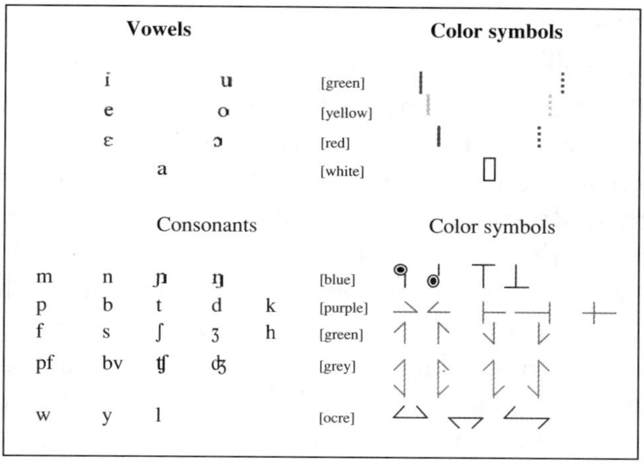

Figure 27a: Hendo vowels and consonants phonemes and their representation as colored symbols. Colors for the vowels are: green for i and u, yellow for e and o, red for ɛ and ɔ, white for a. Colors for the consonants are: blue for nasals, red for stops, green for fricatives, grey for affricates and ocre for approximants.

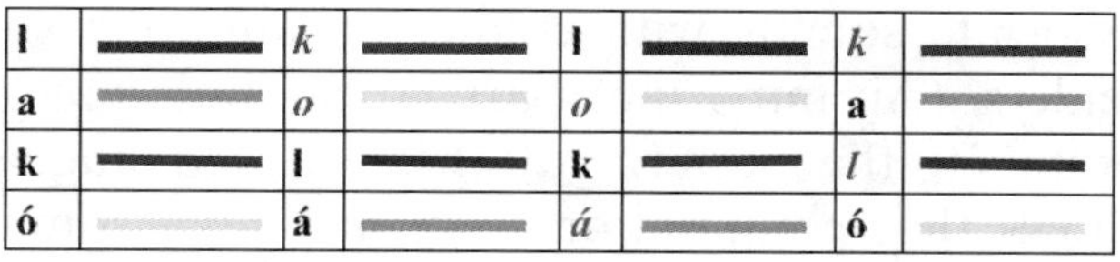

l		k		l		k	
a		o		o		a	
k		l		k		l	
ó		á		á		ó	

Figure 27b: Example of manipulations associating colors and sounds in Hendo word games. The left most form lako 'nothing' is the starting form. The next forms show manipulations of syllables, vowels and consonants (l is brown, a is white, k is purple and o is yellow).

is the following: first permute back vowels with front vowels (or the contrary when it happens) i.e. /ɔ/ to /ɛ/ and /o/ to /e/ in this case; then raise the height of the second vowel by one level (feature) i.e. /a/ to /ɛ/, while keeping the same front/back dimension for this vowel compared to the first (/a/ becomes /ɛ/ in both cases because of the shift /ɔ/ → /ɛ/ and /o/ → /e/ in the first syllable). The second word ota is not changed into etɛ but ɛtɛ because of the Hendo rule of vowel harmony, which requires all consecutive mid-vowels to be harmonized with the lowest mid-vowel (/e/ → /ɛ/ and /o/ → /ɔ/).

5.2.3 Discussion

The discussion could be extended at length with numerous examples from Ngonga (2001), but will be restricted to two main questions. First, how is it that, in an unwritten language, speakers can manipulate every phonological unit? Second how are these word games learned? In other words, if the claim that the mediation of an alphabetic script is necessary to create phonological awareness is correct, what is the equivalent of alphabetic script for Hendo speakers? The answer is that these word games are learned through the mediation of a special kind of writing, which associates each phoneme of the language to a color symbol, usually represented by a line drawn on a piece of wood. Figure 25 shows how vowels and consonants are represented in this quasi-alphabetic writing system.

The way colors are manipulated and the way word games are thought up can be summarized in the examples presented in Figure 26, which show how, by making permutations of colored lines associated with sounds, children or adults participating in initiation learn to associate sounds with colors, by imitating stimuli proposed by elders. (An important part of the initiation among the Hendo amounts to the mastering of these derived languages). This example shows that permutation from an initial stimulus which associates color lines with phonemes of a bisyllabic word allows syllable, consonant and vowel metathesis to be carried out.

This suggests that imitation and repetition acting at a basic cognitive level (Donald, 1990) play a crucial role in creating phonological awareness. The Hendo example also raises a number of important questions, such as the psychological reality of phonological units and their mental representations and the status of tacit knowledge of phones and features among illiterate speakers. The case also provides data bearing on the status of phonological units and processes. Why is an alphabetic system necessary for phonological awareness, instead of a syllabary or a feature writing system? These data, when compared with results from experimental psycholinguistics, allow cognitive processes and symbolic aspects of phonology to be evaluated. For example, on the basis of these word games, one could think of phonological units such as segments as emerging from the combination of more basic elements or, as claimed by Bertoncini & Mehler (1981), that phonological units develop from the global to the specific. Hendo word games are a perfect example of the benefit of fieldwork studies in understanding the phonological properties of natural languages. One might consider such studies as merely butterfly collecting or the accumulation of details, but these aspects of phonological research provide data and observations which contribute towards building strong hypotheses about sound patterns and how they might be represented in the human mind.

6. Conclusion

The data presented in this paper were intended to illustrate how one of the aims of fieldwork studies is to contribute to the production of a suitable phonological theory which incorporates phonological and phonetic phenomena of languages. Data obtained from fieldwork studies allow primitives to be discussed and phonological hypotheses to be refined. The growing body of such data allows improved answers to a number of fundamental questions. What information and what physical constraints are taken into account by phonology? How variable are these? How do they contribute to theory formation? What are the phonetic details which must be included in the phonetic output of the grammar of a language?

At the beginning of the paper it was outlined that phonological theory should be based on aerodynamic principles, principles relating vocal tract shape and acoustic output and principles relating acoustic output to auditory representation. Fieldwork studies based on instrumental observations provide an essential way to validate or contest these claims. First, the Amharic and Mangbetu data provide good examples of the relevance of aerodynamic primitives. Amharic geminate alveolar ejective fricatives show that the classical view of ejectives as being produced by raising the larynx and compressing the air in the oral cavity should be refined, because the very high intra-oral pressure achieved by Amharic speakers is unlikely to occur because of this single articulatory movement. What is relevant is a global reduction of the cavity between the closed glottis, the place of the constriction and a fine control of articulatory movements. This has already been shown in a model proposed by Kingston (1984) but on a more limited set of data and for a different language. The way speakers of different languages control articulatory maneuvers and their acoustic consequences (glottal lag, burst, duration and noise intensity) is likely to account for the variation found in the features of ejectives between languages. Such claims should be tested in the future by running perceptual experiments in order to verify how speakers control the features for ejectives. Second, bilabial trills in Mangbetu demonstrate the relevance of the Bernoulli effect as an independent principle explaining how these sounds are made. No feature analysis can account for this phenomenon. To explain how the Bernoulli effect is applied at the lips and therefore how the acoustic effect of a trill is obtained, aerodynamic principles and specific articulatory movements are necessary. Third, the Nuer example provides an excellent way to show the relevance of the principle of maximal dispersion set forward by the emergent phonology approach. The acoustic principles involved in an explanation of the existence of plain and breathy vowels in the same vocalic system also accounts for the existence of gaps and additions in the inventory of breathy vowels. Indeed the additional resonances of the tracheal tract explain these phenomena in a natural way which can furthermore be tested by doing perceptual experiments in the future. Fourth, Lendu provides a good example of the importance of both the timing of gestures and of co-articulation processes. This also shows the role played by perceptual categorization in sound change. The comparison of two Lendu dialects has shown that it is the superposition of two gestures which accounts for the realization of alveolar fricative consonants as syllabic nuclei in this language. The almost simultaneous realization of the tongue tip and tongue body gestures necessary to produce syllabic consonants such as [s] or [z] is possible because of some inhibition of jaw movement. The simultaneous realization of a voiceless alveolar fricative and a tone can be accounted for because speakers may simultaneously categorize two different acoustic events, i.e. noise frequency for the voiceless fricative and voice for the tone. Fifth, data from !xóõ illustrated how perceptual factors affect sound change. The importance of identifying good acoustic cues in understanding sound change is perfectly illustrated by this example.

Lastly, the Hendo example illustrated that phonological theory must account for the way in which what are described as speech features or phonological units are represented in the human mind and can be accessible after training. The Hendo data offer a natural experiment allowing a number of issues related to cognitive aspects of phonology to be discussed. It is not only the role of the phoneme in perception and awareness in phonological processing which is at play but also the approach to levels-of-processing in the study of mental representations. The emergence of phonological categories at the meta-phonological level is illustrated by the way Hendo speakers learn their word games. At first sight Hendo word games, performed in a society where language is transmitted orally, contradict a number of psycholinguistic studies showing that literacy contributes to the awareness of phones (e.g. Morais et al., 1979; Morais, 1985; Morais & Kolinsky, 1994). The way Hendo speakers learn their word games shows that the principles outlined in these studies are valid.

Pierrehumbert et al. (2000) remark that an observation made in a few minutes in the field might suggest a hypothesis whose evaluation requires months of work in the laboratory. While this is clearly true, it is good to remember that fieldwork is not just data collection. To be able to make a contribution to the understanding and explanation of sound patterns, descriptions must be formalized, i.e. made explicit. This issue is crucial in the systematization of observed structural facts in language. Indeed, phonological theories have laid great emphasis on this in the last 40 years. Emergent phonology can contribute to such a goal by looking at the relevance of features and constraints necessary to describe sound patterns from independent principles. The focus of this paper has been on an illustration of the hypothesis that phonology must be derived from phonetics and that it should be based on a limited set of first principles. Fieldwork data provide a source of examples that can be used to study and challenge this hypothesis and these principles.

Acknowledgements

This paper owes much to discussions with John and Manjari Ohala, John Kingston, Björn Lindblom, Ian Maddieson, Peter Ladefoged, Anthony Traill, Gerrit Dimmendaal, Larry Hyman, José Morais and my colleagues of the Phonology Laboratory at the University of Brussels: Caroline Corneau, Véronique Delvaux, Moges Yigezu, and Hubert Ngonga. I would like to thank particularly Alain Soquet and Gordon Ramsay for many stimulating exchanges on various aspects of this work. Data were collected during several fieldwork trips in Congo and Ethiopia. This research has been supported by FNRS grants and by a ARC convention 98−02 n°226 of the Belgian ministry of scientific research.

Notes

1   Hayward & Hayward (1999) also mention that in Amharic there are labialized consonants [k^w, g^w, $k^{w'}$]. The labialized ejective will not be discussed in this paper.
2   The data are described in hPa (the Pascal being the international unit for pressure), 1 hPa = 1 Cm H_2O.
3   V2 = P1 X V1/P2, where P1 = initial volume, V1 = initial pressure, P2 second pressure and V2 second volume. (See Catford, 1977, for details).
4   Following Laver's (1994: 319) comments on Norman's (1988) description of Mandarin Chinese, the nuclei of Lendu vowelless syllables could also be described as weak syllabic fricatives [z̞] and [s̞] bearing in mind that they are apical dorsal vocoids.

References

Anderson, S.
    1982   Why phonology isn't natural. *Linguistic Inquiry*, **12**, 493−539.
Beddor, P. M., Krakow, R. A. & Goldstein, L. M.
    1896   Perceptual constraints and phonological change: a study of nasal vowel height. *Phonology Yearbook*, **3**, 197−217.
Bell, A.
    1978   Syllabic consonants. In J. Greenberg (ed.), *Universals of Human Language, Volume 2: Phonology*, (pp. 153−202). Stanford: Stanford University Press.

Bender, E. A.
2000   An Introduction to Mathematical Modeling. New York: Dover.
Bertoncini, J. & Mehler, J.
1981   Syllables as units in infant speech perception. *Infant Behaviour and Development*, **4**, 247–260.
Bladon, R. A. W. & Lindblom, B.
1981   Modeling the judgment of vowel quality differences. *Journal of the Acoustical Society of America*, **69**, 1414–1422.
Boersma, Paul
1998   *Functional Phonology: Formalizing the Interactions between Articulatory and Perceptual Drives.* The Hague: Holland Academic Graphics.
Broe, M. & Pierrehumbert, J. (editors)
2000   *Papers in Laboratory Phonology V: Language Acquisition and the Lexicon.* Cambridge: Cambridge University Press.
Browman, C. & Goldstein, L.
1989   Articulatory gestures as phonological units. *Phonology*, **6**, 201–251.
Browman, C. & Goldstein, L.
1992   Articulatory Phonology: an overview. *Phonetica* **49**, 155–180.
Catford, J. C.
1977   *Fundamental Problems in Phonetics.* Edinburgh: Edinburgh University Press.
Cho, T. & Ladefoged, P.
1999   Variation and universals in VOT: Evidence from 18 languages. *Journal of Phonetics*, **27**, 207–229.
Chomsky, N.
1964   Current trends in linguistic theory. In J. Katz & J. Fodor (eds.), *The Structure of Language*, (pp. 50–118). New York: Prentice Hall.
Christol, A.
1988   From phonetics to phonology: the case of laryngeals. *Belgian Journal of Linguistics*, **3**, 17–37.
Connell, B. & Arvaniti, A.
1995   *Phonology and Phonetic Evidence. Papers in Laboratory IV.* Cambridge: Cambridge University Press.
Crazzolara, J. P.
1933   *Outlines of Nuer Grammar.* Vienna: Anthropos.
De Jong, K. & Obeng, S. G.
2000   Labio-palatalization in Twi: Contrastive, quantal, and organizational factors producing an uncommon sound. *Language*, **76**, 682–703.
Demolin, D.
1988   Some problems of phonological reconstruction in Central Sudanic. *Belgian Journal of Linguistics,* **3**, 53–95.
Demolin, D.
1992   *Le Mangbetu: etudes phonétique et phonologique.* Thèse de doctorat Université Libre de Bruxelles.

Demolin, D. & Soquet, A.
    2000   The role self-organization in the emergence of phonological systems. *Evolution of Communication*, 3, 21–48.
Denning, K.
    1989   *The Diachronic Development of Voice Quality*. PhD Dissertation. Stanford University.
Diehl, R.
    2000   Searching for an auditory description of vowel categories. *Phonetica*, 57, 267–274.
Dimmendaal, G. J.
    1986   Language typology, comparative linguistics and injective consonants in Lendu. *Afrika und Übersee*, 69, 161–192.
Dimmendaal, G. J.
    2000   Places and people: field sites and informants. In P. Newman and M. Ratliff (eds.), *Linguistic Fieldwork*, (pp. 73–98). Cambridge University Press.
Docherty, G. J. & Ladd, D. R. (editors)
    1992   *Papers in Laboratory Phonology II: Gesture, Segment, Prosody*. Cambridge: Cambridge University Press.
Donald, M.
    1990   *The Origins of Modern Mind*. Harvard.
Elman, J., Bates, E. A., Johnson, M. H., Karmiloff-Smith, A., Parisi, D., & Plunkett, K. (editors)
    1996   *Rethinking Innateness. A Connectionist Perspective on Development*. Cambridge, MA: MIT Press.
Fant, G.
    1960   *Acoustic Theory of Speech Production*. The Hague: Mouton.
Flemming, E.
    1995   Auditory Representations in Phonology. PhD dissertation, UCLA.
Flemming, E., Ladefoged, P. & Thomason, S.
    1994   Phonetic structures of Montana Salish. *Fieldwork of Targeted Languages II, UCLA Working papers in Phonetics*, 87, 1–34.
Foss, D. J.
    1969   Decision processes during sentence comprehension: Effects of lexical item difficulty and position upon decision times. *Journal of Verbal Learning and Verbal Behaviour*, 8, 457–462.
Fre Woldu, K.
    1985   The perception and production of Tigrinya stops. *Reports from Upsala University Department of Linguistics*, 13.
Goldsmith, J.
    1999   Harmonic Phonology. In J. Goldsmith (ed.), *Phonological Theory: The Essential Readings*, (pp. 91–101). Oxford: Blackwell.
Greenberg, J.
    1963   *The Languages of Africa*. Bloomington: Indiana, University Press.

Hale, M. & Reiss, C.
2000 "Substance Abuse" and "Dysfunctionalism": Current Trends in Phonology. *Linguistic Inquiry*, **31**, 157–169.
Halle, M.
1990 Phonology. In D. N. Osherson & H. Lasnik (eds.), *An Invitation to Cognitive Science*, Vol **1**, (pp. 43–68). Cambridge, Mass: MIT Press.
Hayward, K. & Hayward, R. J.
1999 Amharic. In *Handbook of the International Phonetic Association*, (pp. 45–50). Cambridge: Cambridge University Press.
Hockett, C. F.
1955 A manual of phonology. *International Journal of American Linguistics Memoir*, **11**.
Hyman, L.
2000 Fieldwork as a state of mind. In P. Newman & M. Ratliff (eds.), *Linguistic Fieldwork*, (pp. 18–43). Cambridge University Press.
Jakobson, R. & Waugh, L.
1979 *The Sound Shape of Language*. Bloomington: Indiana University Press.
Johnson, K.
2000 Adaptive dispersion in vowel perception. *Phonetica*, **57**, 181–188.
Johnson, K., Flemming, E. & Wright, R.
1993 The hyperspace effect: Phonetic targets are hyperarticulated. *Language*, **69**, 505–528.
Keating, P. (editor)
1995 *Papers in Laboratory Phonology III: Phonological Structure and Phonetic Form*. Cambridge: Cambridge University Press.
Kenstowicz, M.
1994 *Phonology in Generative Grammar*. Oxford: Blackwell.
Kingston, J. & Beckman, M. (editors)
1990 *Papers in Laboratory Phonology I: Between the Grammar and the Physics of Speech*. Cambridge University Press.
Kingston, J. and MacMillan, N. A.
1995 Integrality of nasalization and F1 in vowels in isolation and before oral and nasal consonants: A detection-theoretic application of the Garner paradigm. *Journal of the Acoustical Society of America*, **97**, 1261–1285.
Kingston, J. & Diehl, R.
1994 Phonetic knowledge. *Language*. **40**, 419–454.
Kingston, J., MacMillan, N. A., Dickey, L. W., Thorburn, R. & Bartels, C.
1997 Integrality in the perception of tongue root position and voice quality in vowels. *Journal of the Acoustical Society of America*, **101**, 1696–1709.

Kingston, J. C.
> 1984   The phonetics and phonology of the timing of oral and glottal events. University of California Berkeley. Ph D. dissertation.

Kohler, K. J.
> 2000   Investigating unscripted speech: Implications for phonetics and phonology. *Phonetica*, **57**, 85−96.

Krejnovic, E. A.
> 1958   Opyt issledovanija struktury sloga v korjakskom jazke. Doklady i soobscenija instituto jazykoznznija, Akad. nauk SSSR, **11**, 151−167.

Kutsch Lojenga, C. K.
> 1989   The secret behind vowelless syllables in Lendu. *Journal of African Languages and Linguistics*, **II**, 115−126.

Kutsch Lojenga, C. K.
> 1991   Lendu: a new perspective on implosives and glottalized consonants, *Afrika und Übersee*, **74**, 77−86.

Ladefoged, P.
> 1997   Linguistic phonetic descriptions. In W. J. Hardcastle & J. Laver (eds.), *The Handbook of Phonetic Sciences*, (pp. 589−618). Oxford: Blackwell.

Ladefoged, P. & Traill, A.
> 1984   Linguistic phonetic descriptions of clicks, *Language*, **60**, 1−20.

Ladefoged, P. & Traill, A.
> 1994   Clicks and their accompaniments, *Journal of Phonetic*, **22**, 333−64.

Ladefoged, P. & Maddieson, I.
> 1996   *The Sounds of the World's Languages*. Oxford: Blackwell.

Ladefoged, P. & Wu, Z.
> 1984   Places of articulation: an investigation of Pekingese fricatives and affricates. *Journal of Phonetics*, **12**, 267−278.

Laver, J.
> 1994   *Principles of Phonetics*. Cambridge: Cambridge University Press.

Lieberman, A. M., Harris, K. S., Hoffman H. S. & Griffith, N. C.
> 1957   The discrimination of speech sounds within and across phonemic boundaries. *Journal of Experimental Psychology*, **53**, 358−368.

Liljencrants, J. & Lindblom, B.
> 1972   Numerical simulations of vowel quality systems: the role of perceptual contrast. *Language*, **48**, 839−862.

Lindau, M.
> 1984   Phonetic differences in glottalic consonants. *Journal of Phonetics*, **12**, 147−155.

Lindblom, B.
> 1984   Can models of evolutionary biology be applied to phonetic problems? In M. P. R. van den Broecke & A. Cohen (eds.), *Proceedings of the 10th International Congress of Phonetic Sciences.*, (pp. 67−81). Dordrecht: Foris.

Lindblom, B.
1986   Phonetic universals in vowel systems. In J. J. Ohala & J. J. Jaeger (eds.), *Experimental Phonology*, (pp. 13–44). Orlando: Academic Press.

Lindblom, B.
1990   Role of phonetic content in phonology. In W. U. Desssler, H. C. Luschützky, O. E. Pfeiffer & J. R. Renisson (eds.), *Phonologica 1988*, (pp. 181–196). Cambridge: Cambridge University Press.

Lindblom, B.
2000   Developmental origins of adult phonology: The interplay between phonetic emergents and the evolutinary adaptations of sound patterns. *Phonetica*, **57**, 297–314.

Lindblom, B. & Engstrand, O.
1989   In what sense is speech quantal? *Journal of Phonetics*, **17**, 3–45.

Lindblom, B. & Maddieson, I.
1988   Phonetic universals in consonant systems. In L. Hyman and C. Li (eds.), *Language, Speech and Mind*, (pp. 62–78). London: Routledge.

Lindblom, B., MacNeilage, P. F. & Studdert-Kennedy, M.
1983   Self-organizing processes and the explantion of phonological universals. In B. Butterworth, B. Comrie & O. Dahl (eds.), *Explanation for Language Universals*, (pp. 180–201). Amsterdam: Mouton.

MacNeilage, P. F.
1981   Feedback in speech production: an ecological perspective. In T. Myers, J. Laver & J. Anderson (eds.), *The Cognitive Representation of Speech.*, (pp. 39–44). Amsterdam: North-Holland.

MacNeilage, P. F.
1998   The Frame/Content theory of evolution of speech production. *Brain and Behavioural Sciences*, **21**, 499–548.

MacNeilage, P. F. & Davis, B. L.
2000a   On the origin of internal structure of word forms. *Science*, **228**, 527–531.

MacNeilage, P. F. & Davis, B. L.
2000b   Deriving speech from nonspeech: a view from ontogeny. *Phonetica*, **57**, 284–296.

MacNeilage, P. F.
1994   Prolegomena to a Theory of the Sound Pattern of the First Spoken Language. *Phonetica*, **51**, 184–194.

MacNeilage, P. F. & Davis, B. L.
1990   Acquisition of speech production: The achievement of segmental indpendence. In W. J. Hardcastle & A. Marchal (eds.), *Speech Production and Speech Modelling*, (pp. 55–68). Dordrecht: Kluwer.

Maddieson, I.
1984   *Patterns of Sounds*. Cambridge: Cambridge University Press.

Maddieson, I., Bessel, N. & Smith, C.
    1996   A preliminary report of the sounds in Tlingit. *UCLA Working Papers in Phonetics*, **93**, 125−148.

Maeda, S.
    1978   Une analyse statistique sur les positions de la langue: étude préliminaire sur les voyelles françaises, *Actes des 9èmes journées d'étude sur la parole*, 59−63.

Malou, J.
    1988   *Dinka vowel system*. Arlington: SIL and University of Texas.

McDonough, J. & Ladefoged, P.
    1993   Navajo stops. *UCLA Working Papers in Phonetics*, **84**, 151−164.

Mertens, F.
    1987   *Dictionnaire Bba-dhà français*. Mimeicgraphed, Drodro, Congo.

Morais, J.
    1985   Literacy and awareness of the units of speech: implications for research on the units of perception. *Linguistics*, **23**, 707−724.

Morais, J., Cary, L., Alegria, J. & Bertelson, P.
    1979   Does awareness of speech as a sequence of phones arise spontaneously? *Cognition*, **7**, 322−331.

Morais, J. & Mousty, P.
    1992   The causes of phonemic awarness. In J. Alegria, D. Holender, J. Junca de Morais & M. Radeau (eds.), *Analytic Approaches to Human Cognition* (pp. 193−212). Amsterdam: North-Holland.

Morais, J. & Kolinsky, R.
    1994   Perception and awareness in phonological processing: The case of the phoneme. *Cognition*, **50**, 287−297.

Myers, T., Laver, J. & Anderson, J. (editors)
    1981   *The Cognitive Representation of Speech*. Amsterdam: North-Holland.

Nettle, D.
    1999   *Linguistic Diversity*. Oxford: Oxford University Press.

Newman, P. & Ratliff, M. (editors)
    2000   *Linguistic Fieldwork*. Cambridge: Cambridge University Press.

Newmann, S. S.
    1947   Bella Coola, I: Phonology. *International Journal of American Linguistics*, **13**, 129−134.

Ngonga, H.
    2001   *Phonologie et metaphonologie des langues dérivées initiatiques Ohendo*. Thèse de doctorat. Université Libre de Bruxelles.

Norman, J.
    1988   *Chinese*. Cambridge: Cambridge University Press.

Ohala J. J.
    1983   The origin of sound patterns in vocal tract constraints. In P. F. MacNeilage (ed.), *The Production of Speech*, (pp. 189−216). New York: Springer.

Ohala J. J.
1989   Sound change is drawn from a pool of synchronic variation. In L. E. Breivik & E. H. Jahr (eds.), *Language Change: Contributions to the Study of Its Causes*, (pp. 173–198). New York: Mouton De Gruyter.
Ohala J. J.
1990   There is no interface between phonology and phonetics: A personal view. *Journal of Phonetics*, **18**, 153–171.
Ohala J. J.
1992   The segment: Primitive or derived? In G. J. Docherty & D. R. Ladd (eds.), 166–183.
Ohala, J. J.
1981   Articulatory constraints on the cognitive representation of speech. In Myers et al. (eds.), 113–124.
Ohala, J. J.
1990   The phonetics and phonology of aspects of assimilation. In Kingston & Beckman (eds.), 258–275.
Ohala, J. J. and Jaeger, J. J. (editors)
1986   *Experimental Phonology*. Orlando: Academic press.
Perkell, J.
1981   On the sue of feedback in speech production. In Myers et al. (eds.), 45–57.
Pierrehumbert, J., Ladd, R. D. and Beckman, M.
1996   Laboratory Phonology. In J. Durand and B. Laks (eds.), *Current Trends in Phonology: Models and Methods*, (pp. 535–548). Paris CNRS ESRI, Paris X.
Pierrehumbert, J., Ladd, R. D. & Beckman, M.
2000   Conceptual Foundations in Phonology as a Laboratory Science. Oxford University Press.
Pinkerton, S.
1986   Quichean (Mayan) glottalized and nonglottalized stops. In Ohala & Jaeger (eds.), 125–139.
Rousselot, A.
1924   *Principes de Phonétique Expérimentale, 2 vol.* Paris. Didier.
Samuel, A. G.
1981   Phonemic restoration: Insights from a new methodology. *Journal of Experimental Psychology: General*, **110**, 474–494.
Sands, B.
1999   *Evaluating claims of distant linguistic relationships: The case of Khoisan.* Rudiger Köppe Verlag. Cologne.
Schwartz, J. L., Abry, C. & Boë, L.-J.
2000   Phonology in a theory of Perception-for-Action-Control. In J. Durand & B. Laks (eds.), *Phonology: from Phonetics to Cognition* (pp. 255–280). Oxford: Oxford University Press.

Scott, N. C.
  1947 The monosyllable in Szechuanese. *Bulletin of the School of Oriental and African Studies*, **12**, 197–213.
Segui, J. & Frauenfelder, U.
  1986 The effect of lexical constraints on speech perception. In F. Klix & H. Hagendorf (eds.), *Human memory and Cognitive abilities: Symposium in memoriam Hermann Ebbinghaus*, (pp. 795–808). Amsterdam: North-Holland.
Stevens, K.
  1998 *Acoustic Phonetics*. Cambridge, Mass: MIT Press.
Studdert-Kennedy, M.
  1998 The origins of generativity. In J. Hurford, C. Knight & M. Studdert-Kennedy (eds.), *The Evolutionary Emergence of Language*, (pp. 169–176). Cambridge: Cambridge University Press.
Studdert-Kennedy, M.
  2000 Imitation and the emergence of segments. *Phonetica*, **57**, 275–283.
Teston, B.
  1991 Station de travail ORL-phoniâtrie: Caractéristiques techniques. *Phonologia*. Marseilles: IIRIAM Technopole de Château Gombert. Europarc.
Teston, B. & Galindo, B.
  1990 Design and development of a work station for speech production analysis. *Proceedings VERBA 90. International Conference on Speech Technologies*, Rome, 400–408.
Teston, B. & Galindo, B.
  1995 A diagnostic and rehabilitation aid workstation for speech and voice pathologies. *Proceedings of Eurospeech,* **4**. Madrid: European Speech Communication Association.
Titze, I.
  1994 *Principles of Voice Production*. Prentice Hall. New Jersey: Englewood Cliffs.
Traill, A.
  1985 *Phonetic and phonological studies of !xoo Bushman*. Hamburg: Helmut Buske Verlag.
Traill, A.
  1994 *A !xoo Dictionnary*. Cologne: Rudiger Köppe Verlag.
Traill, A.
  1995 The perception of clicks in !xoo. *Journal of African Languages and Linguistics*, **15**, 161–174.
Traill, A. & Vossen, R.
  1997 Sound change in the Khoisan languages: New data on click loss and click replacement. *Journal of African Languages and Linguistics*, **18**, 21–56.

Tucker, A.
1936   The function of voice quality in the Nilotic languages. In D. Jones & B. D. Fry (eds.), *Proceedings of the Second International Congress of phonetic Sciences*, (pp. 125–128). London: Cambridge University Press.

Tucker, A.
1940   *The Eastern Sudanic Languages.* Oxford: Oxford University Press.

Tucker, A.
1975   Voice quality in African Languages. In S. H. Hurreiz & H. Bell (eds.), *Directions in Sudanese Linguistics and Folklore*, (pp. 293–308). Khartoum: Sudanese library 4. I.A.S.S.

Vallée, N.
1994   *Systèmes vocaliques: de la typologie à la prédiction.* PhD dissertation, Université de Grenoble.

Warner, N.
1996   Acoustic characteristics of ejectives in Ingush. *Proceedings of the IV International Congress of Spoken Language Processing*, Philadelphia. 1525–1528.

Warren, R. M.
1970   Perceptual restoration of missing speech sounds. *Science*, **167**, 392–393.

Yigezu, M.
1995   The Nuer vowel system. *Journal of African Languages and Linguistic*, **16**, 157–170.

Durational variability in speech and the Rhythm Class Hypothesis

Esther Grabe and Ee Ling Low

Abstract

We provide evidence for rhythmic classifications of speech from duration measurements. Our investigation differs from previous studies in two ways. First, we do not relate speech rhythm to phonological units such as interstress intervals or syllable durations. Instead, we calculate durational variability in successive acoustic-phonetic intervals using *Pairwise Variability Indices*. Second, we compare measurements from languages traditionally classified as stress-, syllable- or mora-timed with measurements from hitherto unclassified languages. The values obtained agree with the classification of English, Dutch and German as stress-timed and French and Spanish as syllable-timed: durational variability is greater in stress-timed languages than in syllable-timed languages. Values from Japanese, a mora-timed language, are similar to those from syllable-timed languages. But previously unclassified languages do not fit into any of the three classes. Instead, their values overlap with the margins of the stress-timed and the syllable-timed group.

1. Introduction and Background

In this paper, we investigate the acoustic-phonetic basis of speech rhythm. In speech production, rhythm has been defined as an effect involving the isochronous recurrence of some type of speech unit, a view made popular by Pike (1946) and Abercrombie (1965, 1967). Pike and Abercrombie suggested that all spoken languages exhibit isochronous units of speech, and that languages are either stress-timed or syllable-timed. In stress-timed languages, intervals between stresses or rhythmic feet are said to be near-equal, whereas in syllable-timed languages, successive syllables are said to be of near-equal length. In Pike and Abercrombie's view, the distinction between stress- and syllable-timing was strictly categorical; languages could not be more or less stress- or syllable-timed. Abercrombie (1965) based his categorical distinction on the physiology of speech production. All spoken languages were said to have two types of pulses, chest-pulses and stress-pulses. Chest pulses were pulse-like puffs of air from the lungs, resulting from alternate contractions and relaxations of the breathing muscles. Stress-pulses were less frequent, more powerful contractions of the breathing muscles which reinforce some of the chest-pulses. Rhythm, Abercrombie suggested, was a product of the way in which the two pulse-systems combined. Two categorically different combinations were possible (Abercrombie, 1965). In syllable-timing, chest-pulses were in isochronous sequence, but stress-pulses were not. In stress-timing, stress-pulses reinforced chest pulses in isochronous sequence.

A third type of rhythm, mora-timing, was proposed by Bloch (1942), Han (1962), and Ladefoged (1975). Mora-timing was exemplified by Japanese. Traditionally, morae are sub-units of syllables consisting of one short vowel and any preceding onset consonants. In mora-timing, successive morae are said to be near-equal in duration. Thus, mora-timed languages are more similar to syllable-timed languages than to stress-timed languages.

1.1 Evidence for stress- and syllable-timing from duration measurements

The empirical basis of the rhythm class hypothesis has been investigated extensively, but experimental support for isochrony in speech is lacking (Beckman, 1992; Laver, 1994). In stress-timed languages, interstress intervals are far from equal, and interstress-intervals do not pattern more regularly in stress-timed than in syllable-timed languages (Shen & Peterson, 1962; Bolinger, 1965; Delattre, 1966; Faure, Hirst & Chafcouloff, 1980; Pointon, 1980; Wenk & Wioland, 1982; Roach, 1982; Dauer, 1983; Manrique & Signorini, 1983; Nakatani, O'Connor & Aston, 1981; Dauer, 1987; Eriksson, 1991). Nor are syllables or morae of roughly equal length in syllable-timed languages (Pointon, 1980; Wenk & Wioland,

1982; Roach, 1982; Dauer, 1983, 1987). Roach (1982), for instance, compared interstress intervals in languages classified as stress-timed and languages taken to be syllable-timed. He investigated two claims made by Abercrombie (1967) about the difference between stress-timed and syllable-timed rhythm: (i) there is considerable variation in syllable length in a language spoken with stress-timed rhythm, whereas in a language spoken with syllable-timed rhythm, syllables tend to be equal in length, and (ii) in syllable-timed languages, interstress intervals are unevenly spaced. Roach's findings did not support either claim. The syllable-timed languages in his sample exhibited greater variability in syllable durations than the stress-timed languages. Roach also observed a wider range of percent deviations in interstress intervals in stress-timed than in syllable-timed languages. Roach concluded that measurements of time intervals in speech could not provide evidence for rhythm classes. Roach's view has been supported by Dauer's (1983) study. Dauer compared interstress intervals in English, Thai, Spanish, Italian and Greek. She found that interstress intervals were no more regular in English, a stress-timed language, than in Spanish, a syllable-timed language. Dauer concluded that the search for acoustic phonetic correlates of stress- and syllable-timing was futile.

Isochrony in mora-timing was investigated by Han (1962), Port, Al-Ani & Maeda (1980), and Port, Dalby & O'Dell (1987). Port et al. (1987) argue that these studies provide some preliminary support for the mora as a constant time unit. But other researchers have questioned the acoustic basis for mora-timing (Oyakawa, 1971; Beckman, 1982; Hoequist, 1983a,b). Beckman (1982)'s data, for instance, did not show that segments vary in length in Japanese in order to compensate for intrinsic durations of adjacent segments so that morae are equal in length.

In short, although popular among linguists, the rhythm class hypothesis has been contradicted by numerous empirical studies. Abercrombie's view of speech rhythm as a combination of chest and stress-pulses has long been disproven (e.g. Ladefoged, 1967), destroying the physiological basis of a strict categorical distinction into stress- and syllable-timed languages. The predictions for speech timing arising from the rhythm class hypothesis have suffered a similar fate. Researchers have not provided support from duration measurements for isochronous timing, on any absolute basis (Laver, 1994). This failure has obliged some researchers to retreat from 'objective isochrony' to 'subjective isochrony'. These researchers describe the physical regularity of isochrony as a tendency (Beckman, 1992; Laver, 1994). True isochrony is assumed to be an underlying constraint, and the surface realisation of isochronous units are perturbed by phonetic, phonological and grammatical characteristics of the language. Other researchers have concluded that isochrony is primarily a perceptual phenomenon (e.g. Lehiste, 1977; Couper-Kuhlen, 1990, 1993). Proponents of the 'isochrony-as-perception' view argue that the differences in duration measured between interstress-intervals or syllable durations are well below the threshold of perception. Consequently, isochrony may be accepted as a concept that relates to speech perception.

1.2 Other views of rhythm in speech

The weak empirical evidence for isochrony led Dauer (1983, 1987) to propose a new system for rhythmic classification. In Dauer's view, speakers do not attempt to equalise interstress or intersyllable intervals. Instead, all languages are more or less stress-based. Dauer suggests that prominent syllables recur at regular intervals in English, a stress-timed language, but also in Spanish, a syllable-timed language. But in English, prominent syllables are perceptually more salient than in Spanish. Consequently, rhythmic diversity results from the combinations of phonological, phonetic, lexical and syntactic facts associated with different languages. Syllable-structure, the presence or absence of vowel reduction, and word stress are especially relevant to rhythmic differences. In stress-timed languages, syllable structures are more varied than in syllable-timed languages. In syllable-timed languages, vowel reduction is rarely found. Dauer's account is similar to a proposal published a year earlier by Dasher & Bolinger (1982). Dasher and Bolinger suggested that the rhythm of a language is the result of specific phonological phenomena such as variety of syllable types, the presence or absence of phonological vowel length distinctions, and vowel reduction.[1] Dasher and Bolinger argued that rhythm type is not a phonological primitive but results from the phonological structure of a given language.

Nespor (1990) offered another view of speech rhythm that differs from the continuous system proposed by Dauer. Nespor argued against traditional rhythmic categories on the basis of rhythmically intermediate languages. Intermediate languages exhibit some properties associated with stress-timing and some associated with syllable-timing. Nespor held that neither a dichotomous view nor a continuous classification system can adequately account for the rhythmic properties of such languages. The languages she cited to support her proposal were Polish, which has been classified as stress-timed but does not exhibit vowel reduction, and Catalan, which has been described as syllable-timed but has vowel reduction.

1.3 Evidence for rhythm classes from durational variability

The present study concerns the relationship between speech timing and rhythmic classifications of languages. We depart, however, from the search for isochrony.[2] We did not measure interstress intervals or syllable durations which are phonological units. Some of their phonetic correlates can be disputed. Instead, we followed Low, Grabe & Nolan (2000) and took a direct route from impressionistic observations of rhythmic differences between languages to the acoustic signal. We measured the durations of vowels, and the duration of intervals between vowels (excluding pauses) in a passage of speech. Then we computed a Pairwise Variability Index for each type of measurement. The index expresses the level of variability in successive measurements. The raw Pairwise Variability Index (rPVI) is given in equation (1).

(1) $$rPVI = \left[\sum_{k=1}^{m-1} \left| d_k - d_{k+1} \right| / (m-1) \right],$$

where *m* is number of intervals, vocalic or intervocalic, in the text and *d* is the duration of the *k*th interval. Notice that *rPVI* is not normalised for speech rate.

Low et al. used a normalised version of the Pairwise Variability Index in their measurements on vowel durations. The equation for this version, the normalised Pairwise Variability Index (*nPVI*), is

$$(2) \quad nPVI = 100 \times \left[\sum_{k=1}^{m-1} \left| \frac{d_k - d_{k+1}}{(d_k + d_{k+1})/2} \right| / (m-1) \right],$$

where *m* is number of items in an utterance and *d* is the duration of the *k*th item.

Equation (2) shows that the *nPVI* is compiled by calculating the difference in duration between each pair of successive measurements, taking the absolute value of the difference and dividing it by the mean duration of the pair. Equation (1) for the *rPVI* differs only in omitting the third step. The differences are then summed and divided by the number of differences. The output is multiplied by 100, because the normalisation produces fractional values.

In previous studies (Low & Grabe, 1995; Low, 1998; Grabe, Post & Watson, 1999; Low, Grabe & Nolan, 2000), we applied the *nPVI* to vowel durations.[3] This followed work by authors such as Beckman & Edwards (1994) who showed that vowels constitute the lowest level of the prosodic hierarchy (at least in English). Our studies revealed that so-called stress- and syllable-timed languages differ in the durational variability encountered in vowels. Stress-timed languages such as English exhibit more vocalic variability than syllable-timed languages such as French (Grabe, Post & Watson, 1999). We related this finding to vowel quality. English has full as well as spectrally reduced and shortened vowels. The consequence is a high level of variability in vowel durations. French does not have vowel reduction, and the level of vocalic variability is significantly lower. Low et al. (2000) applied the *nPVI* to data from ten speakers of British English (stress-timed) and ten speakers of Singapore English (syllable-timed). The data provided an acoustic basis for the impression of syllable-timing in Singapore English. Statistical analyses showed that vowel durations are significantly more variable in British English than in Singapore English. Deterding (1994) obtained similar results in an investigation of spontaneous speech data from British English and Singapore English.

In a related study, Ramus, Nespor & Mehler (1999) set out to provide acoustic evidence for the traditional stress-timing/syllable-timing dichotomy. Ramus and colleagues argued that a viable account of speech rhythm should not rely on complex and language-dependent phonological concepts but on purely phonetic characteristics of the speech signal. These authors segmented speech into vocalic and consonantal intervals. In other words, they measured vowel durations and the duration of intervals between vowels. Ramus et al. computed three acoustic correlates of rhythm from the measurements: (a) %V, the proportion of time devoted to vocalic intervals in the sentence, disregarding word boundaries; (b) ΔV: the standard deviation of vocalic intervals; (c) ΔC: the standard deviation of consonantal intervals, the sections between vowel offset and vowel onset.

On the basis of their findings, Ramus et al. argued that a combination of %V and ΔC provided the best acoustic correlate of rhythm classes. In English, which has full and reduced vowels, %V was smaller than in French, which does not have vowel reduction. On the other hand, ΔC was larger in English and reflected the more complex syllable options available in that language.

Low et al. (2000) compared the *nPVI* with the standard deviation measures ΔV and ΔC. The authors concluded that a Pairwise Variability Index may be a better indicator of rhythmicity than ΔV or ΔC. Ramus and colleagues measured duration in a set of tightly controlled sentences from eight languages (5 sentences each produced by four speakers). In less tightly controlled data, Low and colleagues argued, the standard deviation would reflect spurious variability introduced by changes in speaking rate within and across sentences and between-speaker differences in speaking rate. Consider a language where three successive long vowels follow three successive short vowels and another where long and short vowels alternate. Both would give the same standard deviation, although the pattern of vowel durations differs radically between the two.

Low et al. (2000) concluded their paper by suggesting an addition to the vocalic *nPVI*. The standard deviations published by

Ramus et al. (1999) showed that rhythmically mixed languages such as Catalan and Polish exhibit complementary levels of vocalic and intervocalic variability. In Polish, the standard deviation of vocalic intervals was relatively low, making Polish similar to the syllable-timed languages in the sample. But the standard deviation of intervocalic intervals was comparatively high. The reverse applied to Catalan. Low and colleagues suggested that a combination of their vocalic *nPVI* with a measure of intervocalic interval variability would provide a better indicator of rhythmic class than the vocalic *nPVI* alone. This combination would capture the rhythmic characteristics of stress-timed, syllable-timed and mixed languages. Low and colleagues predicted that English (stress-timed) should exhibit relatively high variability index values for vocalic and intervocalic intervals. Some English syllables are relatively complex and we find consonant clusters in the onset and in the coda. Others have a very simple structure. Consequently, intervocalic variability is likely to be high. Spanish (syllable-timed) should have low values in both types of interval. Successive vowels are similar in length, and a large proportion of syllables have a simple CV structure (Dauer, 1983). Polish (mixed) would be low on the vocalic axis and high on the intervocalic axis. Catalan (mixed) would be high on the intervocalic axis, and low on the vocalic axis.

In the present paper, we have tested the predictions made by Low, Grabe and Nolan. We also have added measurements on a range of rhythmically unclassified languages. Our aim was to establish whether the unclassified languages would pattern with the stress-timed or the syllable-timed group or whether some or all of them would be intermediate.

2. Method

2.1 Languages

We made duration measurements on comparable passages of speech from eighteen languages (one speaker per language). The subjects read 'The North Wind and the Sun', a standard text from phonetic research. Translations of this text into Catalan, Dutch, English, French, German, Japanese, and Thai are available in the Handbook of the International Phonetic Association (1999), accompanied by brief phonetic and phonological analyses. Translations not available in the handbook were made by the subjects and by colleagues. In Table 1, we list the languages investigated and, where possible, their rhythmic classification.

Table 1: Traditional rhythmic classifications of languages investigated in the present study.

Language	Classification
British English	Stress-timed (Classe, 1939; Pike, 1946; Abercrombie, 1967)
German	Stress-timed (Kohler, 1982)
Dutch	Stress-timed (Ladefoged, 1975; Smith, 1976)
Thai	Stress-timed (Luangthongkum, 1977)
Tamil	Syllable-timed (Corder, 1973; Asher, 1985)
Spanish	Syllable-timed (Pike, 1946; Hockett, 1958)
French	Syllable-timed (Abercrombie, 1967; Catford, 1977)
Singapore English	Syllable-timed (Tongue, 1979; Platt & Weber, 1980)
Japanese	Mora-timed (Bloch, 1942; Han, 1962)
Polish	Mixed (Dauer, 1987; Nespor, 1990)
Catalan	Mixed (Dauer, 1983; Nespor, 1990)
Estonian	Unclassified
Greek	Unclassified
Luxembourg	Unclassified
Malay	Unclassified
Mandarin	Unclassified
Rumanian	Unclassified
Welsh	Unclassified

2.2 Recording procedure

We recorded one speaker from each language. The British English, French, German, Greek, Polish, Rumanian, and Welsh subjects were recorded in a sound-treated booth in the Oxford Phonetics Laboratory. Dutch, Estonian, Japanese, Luxembourg, and Thai subjects were recorded in a comparable booth in the Cambridge Phonetics Laboratory. The Catalan data were recorded in a sound-treated room at University College London. Tamil, Malay, and Singapore English were recorded in a quiet room at the National Institute for Education in Singapore. The Mandarin data were also recorded in Singapore and represent the variety of Mandarin spoken in Singapore. The Spanish data were provided by Anders Eriksson (University of Stockholm). Subjects were asked to read the text once, at their own pace. They were given time to read the text before the recordings were made.

2.3 Acoustic analysis

Duration measurements were made by the first author, with assistance from a colleague. Vocalic intervals were defined as the stretch of signal between vowel onset and vowel offset, characterised by vowel formants, regardless of the number of vowels included in the section (a vocalic section could contain a monophthong, a diphthong, or, in some cases, two or more vowels spanning the offset of one word and the onset of the next). Intervocalic intervals were defined as the stretch of signal between vowel offset and vowel onset, regardless of the number of consonants included. The duration of vocalic and intervocalic intervals was measured left-to-right, using wide-band spectrograms generated by xwaves™. Vowels were identified using generally accepted criteria (Peterson & Lehiste, 1960; Fischer-Jørgensen & Hutters, 1981). For instance, in fricative-vowel sequences, the onset of the vowel was taken to be the onset of the second formant. In vowel-voiceless fricative sequences, the vowel was considered terminated where the noise pattern began. In vowel-voiced fricative sequences, we considered the vowel terminated at the onset of high frequency energy. Nasal-vowel sequences were segmented by observing the fault transitions between nasal and vowel. Our approach to glides was based on acoustic, not phonetic or phonological criteria. In initial glides, the formant movements continue seamlessly from glide to vowel. We excluded initial glides from vocalic portions if their presence was indicated by clearly observable changes in formant structure or in the amplitude of the signal. Otherwise, glides were included in the vocalic portion.

Pauses between intonation phrases, as well as hesitations, were excluded from the analysis. One consequence of this approach is that some intervals taken to be continuous are, in fact, split by a pause. Although this approach is not ideal, it allows us to calculate *PVI* values from longer samples of speech. In earlier work, we calculated *PVI* values for individual intonation phrases (Low & Grabe, 1995; Grabe et al., 1999; Low et al., 2000). In the present paper, we have departed from our earlier approach for three reasons. First, we wished to distance ourselves from as many subjective or intuitive linguistic decisions as possible when taking measurements. The location of intonation phrase boundaries is debatable, and native speakers of a language can disagree on where a boundary should be placed. In the present study, we investigated some languages that we do not speak. Consequently, we could not determine the location of intonation phrase boundaries in these languages with any certainty. Second, in earlier work on British English and Singapore English, we excluded intonation phrase-final syllables from the index, because we knew that Singapore English is characterised by relatively more phrase-final lengthening than British English. In the present study, we have no information on the relative degree of phrase-final lengthening or shortening in the languages investigated, and therefore we include phrase-final syllables. Third, the number of intervals separated by a pause is relatively small and is not likely to change the results greatly.[4]

Finally, a note on vowel devoicing: English and Japanese, for instance, exhibit devoiced vowels. In spectrograms, devoiced vowels do not exhibit the formant patterns which characterise voiced vowels. Consequently, as our approach to measuring is acoustic, not phonological, we have measured the duration of a vowel only if there was evidence of a voiced vowel in the acoustic signal.

2.4 Normalisation

In previous work, we applied the *nPVI* to vocalic intervals, normalising for changes in speaking rate. In the present paper, we have investigated intervocalic as well as vocalic intervals, so we have reconsidered the question of normalisation. A significant correlation between interval variability and speaking rate would support the application of normalisation. For our purposes, we defined speaking rate as the average vocalic or intervocalic interval duration produced by a speaker. We examined the effect of speaking rate on interval variability across speakers using data from (a) the twenty speakers who provided data for Low et al., and (b) data from the present study (one speaker of each of eighteen languages). The effect of speaking rate on the *rPVI* (*PVI* before normalisation) was tested across speakers and across languages. In British English, vocalic and intervocalic *rPVI* values increased significantly as the average interval duration increased across speakers (Pearson's r, vocalic intervals: $r = 0.867$, $p < 0.01$, intervocalic intervals: $r = 0.801$, $p < 0.01$, 2-tailed). The data from the present study (one speaker per language) showed similar results (vocalic intervals: $r = 0.613$, $p < 0.01$, intervocalic intervals: $r = 0.808$, $p < 0.01$, 2-tailed).

These results confirm that normalisation is desirable for vocalic intervals. The results for intervocalic intervals suggested that we may also need to normalise for intervocalic interval duration. However, this is not a necessary conclusion. Vocalic and intervocalic intervals differ in one respect which affects the rate normalisation question. An intervocalic interval is compositional. It can contain several different segmental units, and these may be subject to different speech rate effects. But the majority of our vocalic intervals consists of a single vowel that is stretched or compressed when speech rate changes. If we consider that intervocalic units can hold roughly one to five segments in Polish but only one to two segments in Japanese, we can account for part of the correlation between intervocalic intervals and speech rate across languages. The correlation arises from (a) an increase in the intervocalic *rPVI* as the duration of intervocalic intervals increases, and (b) cross-language differences in syllable structure. Languages that exhibit a greater number of syllable-structure options may be associated with a greater intervocalic *rPVI*. The correlation between the duration of intervocalic intervals and language may be due to the combined effects of speaking rate and cross-language differences in syllable-structure. These effects are not easy to tease apart.

An investigation into the details of rate normalisation in intervocalic intervals goes beyond the scope of the present paper. In what follows, we continue to normalise vocalic intervals for speech rate, as in previous work.[5] For intervocalic intervals, we do not apply the normalisation, using the *rPVI*.[6]

2.5 Predictions

We predicted that stress-timed languages would exhibit high vocalic *nPVI* and high intervocalic *rPVI* values. Syllable-timed languages would have low vocalic *nPVI* and low intervocalic *rPVI* values. Polish, a mixed language with complex syllable structure and no vowel reduction was predicted to exhibit a lower vocalic *nPVI* value than stress-timed languages but a relatively high intervocalic *rPVI* value. Catalan, another mixed language, was expected to have a relatively high vocalic *nPVI* value combined with a low intervocalic *rPVI*, possibly similar to the intervocalic *rPVI* of Spanish. We did not make any predictions for Estonian, Greek, Luxembourg, Malay, Mandarin, Rumanian or Welsh. Japanese (mora-timed) has a relatively simple syllable structure. As there is no vowel reduction in Japanese, we predicted that the vocalic *nPVI* would be similar to the vocalic *nPVI* values of syllable-timed languages (e.g. French or Spanish). The relatively simple syllable-structure led us to expect a low intervocalic *rPVI* also. However, between voiceless consonants, vowels are often devoiced and not associated with formant patterns. In our measurements, devoiced vowels were included in intervocalic intervals, and intervocalic intervals containing a devoiced vowel were longer than intervocalic intervals separated by voiced vowels. This approach necessarily raises the intervocalic *rPVI* value for Japanese.

3. Results

3.1 PVI Results

Figure 1 shows the data on languages that have often been cited as prototypical examples of stress-, syllable- and mora-timing: British

English, Dutch and German (stress-timed), French and Spanish (syllable-timed) and Japanese (mora-timed). Vocalic *nPVI* values are plotted on the vertical axis against intervocalic *rPVI* values on the horizontal axis.

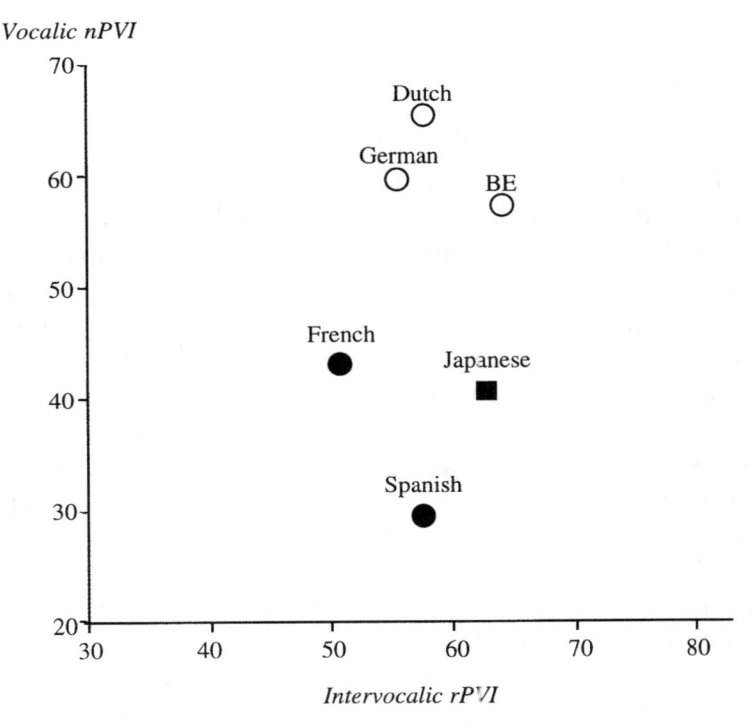

Figure 1: *PVI* profiles from prototypical stress-timed languages English, Dutch and German, syllable-timed languages French and Spanish, and mora-timed language Japanese. Vocalic variability is plotted on the vertical axis against intervocalic variability on the horizontal axis. ○ = stress-timed, ● = syllable-timed, ■ = mora-timed.

The *PVI* profiles provide acoustic evidence for rhythmic differences between English, Dutch and German on the one hand, and French and Spanish on the other. English, Dutch and German have been described as stress-timed and exhibit high vocalic *nPVI* values. French and Spanish have been described as syllable-timed and exhibit low vocalic *nPVI* values. This finding supports the rhythmic classification suggested by Pike (1946) and Abercrombie

(1967), even if the evidence does not come from isochronous interstress-intervals or syllable-durations. There is no support, however, for a strict categorical distinction between languages with high vocalic and intervocalic *PVI* values and languages with low vocalic and intervocalic *PVI* values. Rather, it appears that languages can be more or less 'stress-timed' or 'syllable-timed'.

Figure 1 also shows that our predictions for the intervocalic *rPVI* are supported by the contrast between French (syllable-timed), and British English, Dutch and German (stress-timed). French, which has a relatively simple syllable structure, appears to have a lower intervocalic *rPVI* than English, Dutch and German, which have more complex syllable-structures. Spanish, however, exhibits a lower intervocalic *rPVI* than English but does not seem to be very different from Dutch or German, contrary to our prediction. Future research using more speakers needs to be done in order to validate the role of the *rPVI* in capturing rhythmic patterning of different languages.

Our findings support the prediction for Japanese. Japanese is mora-timed, and it patterns with the syllable-timed languages. A mora is a linguistic unit that is often smaller than a syllable, but in terms of speech timing, mora-timing is more similar to syllable-timing than to stress-timing. The comparable vocalic *nPVI* values for Japanese and French agree with this observation. Neither language has vowel reduction. In contrast, the intervocalic *rPVI* values for Japanese are in the region of those exhibited by the stress-timed languages English, Dutch and German. Initially, this is surprising, since Japanese has a relatively simple syllable structure. Vowels between voiceless consonants are often devoiced in Japanese, however, and are not associated with formant patterns in a spectrogram. As stated above, we have taken devoiced vowels to be part of an intervocalic, not a vocalic, interval. Potentially devoiced vowels constitute 16% of the vowels in the Japanese North Wind passage (cf. IPA Handbook, 1999). Our approach to measuring intervocalic intervals probably raised the intervocalic *rPVI* value for Japanese.

Figure 2 contains the results for all languages in our corpus. Table 1 in the appendix gives the normalised vocalic and the raw intervocalic values for the complete set of data. Consider first the *PVI* values from the rhythmically mixed languages Polish and Catalan.

Nespor (1990) argued that Polish is rhythmically mixed because the language does not have vowel reduction, but can have very complex syllable-structures. Catalan was said to be mixed because it resembles syllable-timed languages in syllable-structure, but does have vowel reduction, unlike syllable-timed Spanish.

Our data provide an acoustic basis for Nespor's claims. The vocalic *nPVI* value for Polish is similar to that for syllable-timed French. But on the intervocalic axis, the two languages are some considerable distance apart. In fact, the intervocalic *rPVI* value for Polish is the highest in our set.

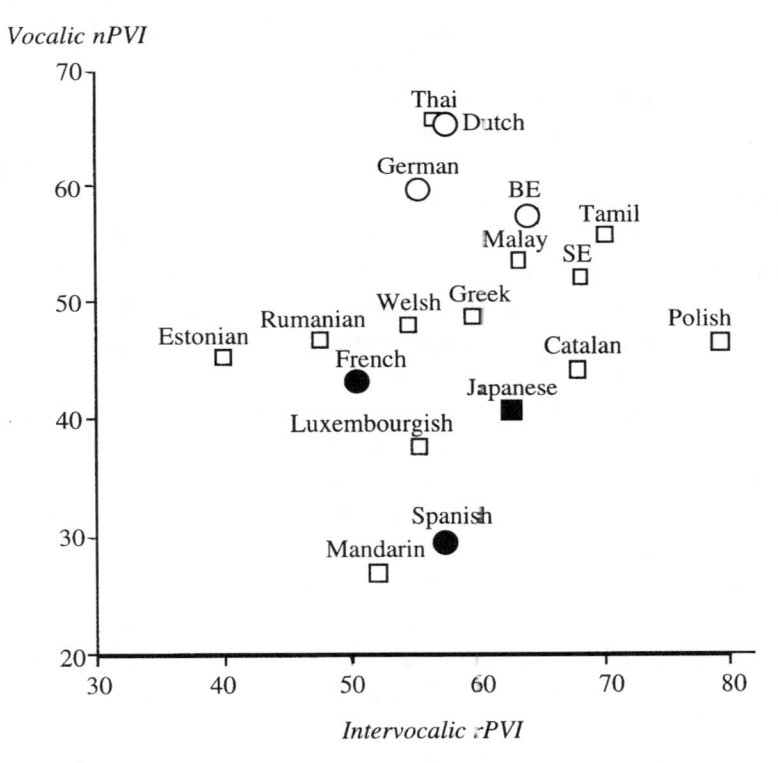

Figure 2: PVI profiles for data from eighteen languages.
Prototypical ○ = stress-timed, ● = syllable-timed, ■ = mora-timed, □ = mixed or unclassified

Figure 2 also supports for Nespor's (1990) observations on vocalic differences between Spanish and Catalan. These languages are separated on the vocalic *nPVI* axis. But the vocalic *nPVI* from Catalan, which has vowel reduction, is similar to that obtained from French, which does not. This finding illustrates a point made by Low et al. (2000) who compared spectral patterns of reduced vowels in Singapore English and British English. Significant differences appeared in the way vowels are reduced in these varieties of English. From a phonological point of view, Singapore English has vowel reduction, but reduced vowels are less centralised in the F1/F2 space than reduced vowels in British English. Reduced vowels in Singapore English are also longer than their counterparts in British English. These findings suggest that we may be able to account for our vocalic *nPVI* data from French, Spanish, and Catalan on the basis of differences in vowel quality and vowel reduction.

We will discuss the remaining findings beginning with Thai. This language patterns with the stress-timed group (Dutch, German, British English). Thai was classified as stress-timed by Luangthongkum (1977). Our findings support his view. Singapore English, marked SE in Figure 2, was classified as syllable-timed by Tongue (1979), Platt & Weber (1980) and Yeow (1987). Our data show that Singapore English exhibits slightly less vocalic variability than British English. However, Singapore English is not at all close to the traditional syllable-timed languages French or Spanish.

Luxembourg and Mandarin pattern with the syllable-timed group. Our Mandarin data provide the lowest vocalic *nPVI* of all languages investigated in the present study. Overlapping with the edges of the stress-timed and the syllable-timed group, we find the unclassified languages Welsh, Greek, Malay, Tamil and Rumanian. Estonian exhibits the lowest intervocalic *rPVI* value. Apparently, with respect to intervocalic variability, Estonian is the opposite of Polish. Finally, the findings for Tamil go against Corder's (1973) and Asher's (1985) classification of Tamil as syllable-timed. We found high vocalic *nPVI* and high intervocalic *rPVI* values for Tamil.

3.2 Further analyses

Since we have data from only one speaker per language, we investigated the stability of *PVI* values within each speaker. We split the vocalic and intervocalic values from each of our eighteen speakers into three equal subsections. This procedure supplied three pairs of values from each speaker. The data are given in Table 2 in the appendix.

Then we carried out statistical analyses on the data. Since we have data from only one subject per language, the results of the analyses are preliminary. First, we tested whether the values from the three vocalic and the three intervocalic sections correlate across languages. All correlations were highly significant (vocalic intervals: sections 1 and 2: $r = 0.926$, $p < 0.01$, sections 1 and 3: $r = 0.844$, $p < 0.01$, sections 2 and 3: $r = 0.788$, $p < 0.01$; intervocalic intervals: sections 1 and 2: $r = 0.673$, $p < 0.01$, sections 1 and 3: $r = 0.816$, $p < 0.01$, sections 2 and 3: $r = 0.624$, $p < 0.01$, 2-tailed). The stability of our measurements seems quite satisfactory.

Second, we performed an analysis of variance on the data (SPSS, General Linear Model, repeated measures) with the dependent variables vocalic $nPVI$ and intervocalic $rPVI$ and the within-subjects factor Section (1,3). Between-subjects effects were highly significant, but the factor Section was not (vocalic $nPVI$ $F[1,17] = 729.6$, $p < 0.001$, intervocalic $rPVI$ $F[1,17] = 347.8$, $p < 0.001$; NB: our between subject-effects are equivalent to between-language effects). Then we carried out post hoc tests on the data (SPSS, General Linear Model, multivariate analysis, Tukey).

Table 2 shows which of the vocalic $nPVI$ and the intervocalc $rPVI$ differences between languages were significant (Tukey, $p < 0.05$).

The upper half of the matrix in Table 2 shows the results for the vocalic $nPVI$, while the lower half shows the results for the intervocalic $rPVI$. The number of significant differences for the $nPVI$ measure was twice as large as the number of differences for the $rPVI$ measure. Apparently, the $nPVI$ provides a better separation of languages than the $rPVI$. Table 2 shows that the $nPVI$ values from the prototypical stress-timed languages German, English and Dutch differ from the $nPVI$ values of the prototypical syllable-timed languages French and Spanish. But the languages whose values are located between those from the prototypical stress-timed and the prototypical syllable-timed group are not sig-

Table 2. Post-hoc multiple comparisons for *rPVI* values, x = significant vocalic *nPVI* difference, p<0.05; o = significant intervocalic *rPVI* difference, p < 0.05.

		1	2	3	4	5	6	7	8	9	10	11	12	13	14	15	16	17	18
		Th.	Du.	Ge.	BE	Ta.	Mal	SE	Gr.	We.	Ru.	Po.	Es.	Ca.	Fr.	Ja.	Lu.	Sp.	Man
1	Thai					x	x	x	x	x	x	x	x	x	x	x	x	x	x
2	Dutch					x	x	x	x	x	x	x	x	x	x	x	x	x	x
3	German							x	x	x	x	x	x	x	x	x	x	x	x
4	BE												x	x	x	x	x	x	x
5	Tamil		o										x	x	x	x	x	x	x
6	Malay												x		x		x	x	x
7	SE														x	x	x	x	x
8	Greek														x		x	x	x
9	Welsh				o													x	x
10	Rumanian				o		o											x	x
11	Polish	o	o	o		o		o	o	o								x	x
12	Estonian	o	o		o	o	o	o	o			o						x	x
13	Catalan													o				x	x
14	French					o		o				o							
15	Japanese					o							o						x
16	Luxemb.					o							o						
17	Spanish					o													
18	Mandarin					o	o					o							

nificantly different from either (see Figure 2). Fewer differences emerged for the intervocalic measure: basically, Polish and Estonian differ from each other and from most of the other languages in the sample. The so-called rhythmically mixed language Catalan differs from Spanish on the vocalic but not on the intervocalic axis. Polish, also classified as mixed, is significantly different from most other languages on the intervocalic axis. The vocalic *nPVI* values from Polish differ from the German and Dutch *nPVI* values, but not from the British English values.

Finally, we compared our measures with those developed by Ramus et al. for rhythmic classification. Ramus and colleagues suggested that the best measure of rhythmic diversity is provided by %*V*, the proportion of time in an utterance devoted to vowels, and Δ*C*, the standard deviation of intervocalic intervals. We calculated these measures from our data. The results appear in Figure 3. We have plotted %*V* on the y-axis in descending order, to allow a direct comparison with our vocalic *nPVI* findings. Table 3 in the appendix gives the %*V* and Δ*C* values.

Figure 3 shows that the %*V*/Δ*C* measure provides results similar to those provided by the combined *PVI* for Estonian, Polish, and

534   *Esther Grabe and Ee Ling Low*

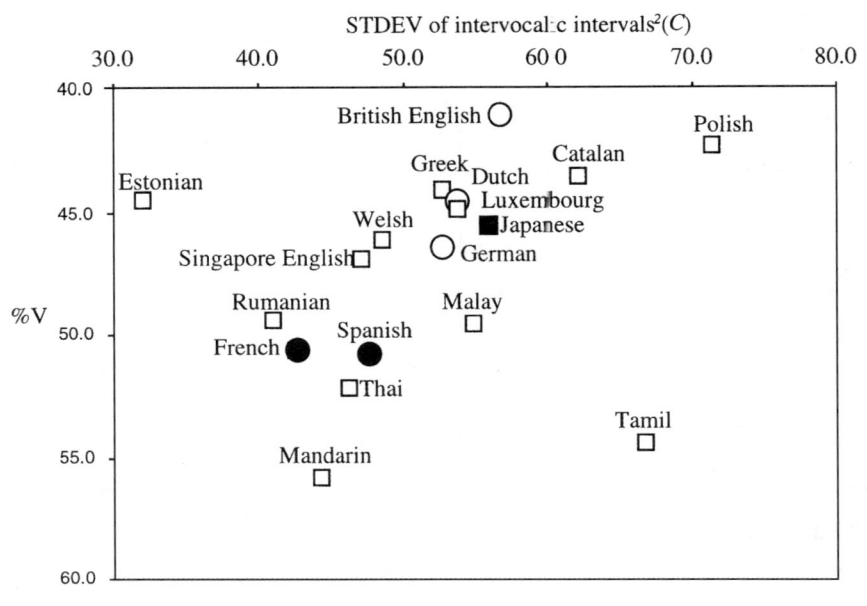

Figure 3: The measure %V is plotted on the y-axis, in reverse order. The standard deviation of intervocalic intervals ΔC is given on the x-axis.

Mandarin. The *rPVI* places Estonian and Polish at the extremes of the intervocalic axis, and so does the ΔC. Mandarin is the language with the highest %V value, and it has the lowest vocalic *nPVI*.

The results for German, Dutch and English are similar on both sets of measures. These languages exhibit relatively low %V values, and mid-range ΔC values. But Greek, Catalan, Welsh, and Luxembourg appear in the stress-timed area in Figure 3. They exhibit lower %V values than German and appear to be more stress-timed than German.

Two languages move from the stress-timed group in Figure 2 to the syllable-timed group in Figure 3. Thai, which is supposedly stress-timed and has the highest vocalic *nPVI*, moves into the syllable-timed area. Tamil, another language with a high vocalic *nPVI*, also moves there. Corder (1973) and Asher (1985) suggested that Tamil is syllable-timed, but Thai was said to be stress-timed (Luangthongkum, 1977). The results for Thai and Tamil show that languages which exhibit a high proportion of vowels in utterances may also exhibit a high level of variability in vocalic intervals. Note that this is not the case for English (high vocalic *nPVI*, low *%V*) or Spanish (low vocalic *nPVI*, high *%V*).

The %V measure places Japanese between German and Dutch, within the stress-timed group. Polish exhibits a %V value between those of German and British English. This finding does not support Nespor's suggestion that Polish patterns with syllable-timed languages with respect to vowels.

4. Discussion

4.1 Rhythm classes: categorical or gradient?

On the vocalic axis, the prototypical stress-timed languages German, English and Dutch are well separated from the syllable-timed languages French and Spanish. On the basis of this result, one could offer a categorical distinction between stress- and syllable-timing (for want of better terms for the rhythmic groupings in question). But the data also show that languages can be more or less stress-timed or syllable-timed. Therefore, a strict categorical distinction between stress-timing and syllable-timing cannot be defended. In some areas of linguistics, strict categorical distinctions exist, for instance, in syntax. Either a word is a member of a syntactic category, or it is not. The nature of the rhythm class distinction is different: we find degrees of stress- or syllable-timing. Distinctions which are similar in nature to the one between rhythmic groupings in our data are found in speech perception. The studies by Samuel (1977) and by Carney, Widen & Viemeister (1977) and colleagues showed that although certain speech continua were perceived categorically by naive subjects, the labelling function became less distinct with practice while discrimination performance improved. Categorically perceived continua are not necessarily perceived in an absolute or discrete manner (Harnad, 1987). We will refer to this effect as 'weak categorical'. Our data show that there is a weak categorical distinction between the group of languages that has been described as stress-timed, and the group of languages that have been described as syllable-timed.

Second, the results show that there is overlap between the stress-timed and the syllable-timed group and unclassified languages, and that Japanese is not in a rhythm class of its own. Therefore, although we find a weak categorical distinction between stress- and syllable-timing, it is clear that not all languages of the world fit into that distinction.

Third, the results show that the vocalic *nPVI* separates languages into a stress-timed and a syllable-timed group, but the intervocalic *rPVI* does not. Instead, the intervocalic *rPVI* shows why Polish does not fit into either of the prototypical rhythm classes, and why Estonian may be difficult to classify. Polish is different because the intervocalic *rPVI* is very high. Estonian is different because the *rPVI* is very low.

Finally, the data show that languages that exhibit an extreme level of durational variability in one dimension have non-extreme variability in the other. The plot in Figure 2 has a distinct diamond shape. A definition of rhythm in speech as the recurrence of similar acoustic units at relatively regular intervals may account for this finding. If vocalic as well as intervocalic intervals were extremely variable, and independent, then there would be no recurrence of similar acoustic units, and hence no impression of rhythmicity.

4.2 Measures of rhythm class: The vocalic PVI and %V

We have found comparable results for the extremes of the *PVI* space and the %*V*/Δ*C* space proposed by Ramus, Nespor & Mehler (1999). The locations of Estonian, Polish, Mandarin and British English are similar in both spaces. But in the centre of the space, we find differences. The %*V* values show that the proportion of vowel time in Greek, Catalan, Welsh, Luxembourg and Japanese is lower than in German. Accordingly, these languages should be more stress-timed than German. Our data contradict this assertion: the vocalic *nPVI* is lower in Greek, Catalan, Welsh, Luxembourg and Japanese than in German. Hence, the *nPVI* suggests that these languages are less, not more stress-timed than German.

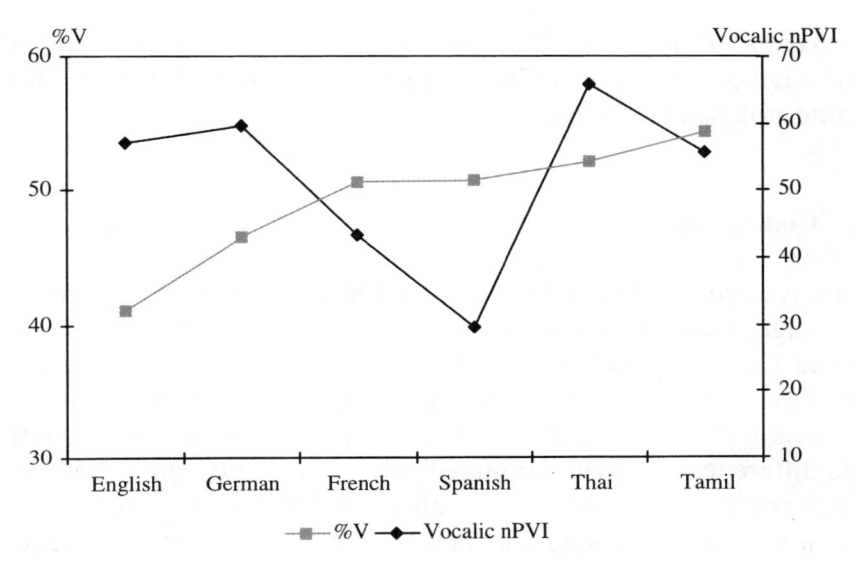

Figure 4: Left y-axis: %V; right y-axis: vocalic *nPVI* values. The variety of English is British English.

The switch of Tamil and Thai from the stress-timed group to the syllable-timed group was particularly noticeable under the %V/ ΔC measure. Thai is associated with a very high vocalic *nPVI*, but %V also is high. The same observation holds for Tamil, although vocalic *nPVI* values for Thai are more extreme. The relationship between %V and the vocalic *nPVI* in traditional stress- or syllable-timed languages is different. In British English and Spanish %V and vocalic *PVI* values seem complementary. Figure 4 illustrates our point. The figure shows that British English and German have low %V values and high vocalic *nPVI* values. French and Spanish have high %V values, but low vocalic *PVI* values. In Thai and Tamil, %V values are higher than in French and Spanish. But unlike in French and Spanish, the vocalic *nPVI* is high also.

This complementarity of overall vowel time and vocalic variability in English and German on the one hand, and French and Spanish on the other may contribute substantially to impressions of stress- or syllable-timing. If the relationship between the two measures provides the acoustic basis for an impression of stress-

or syllable-timing, then Thai would be classified as stress-timed. Although %V is high, the vocalic $nPVI$ is even higher. But Tamil would not be classifiable.

5. Conclusion

We have provided acoustic evidence for rhythmic diversity among languages from duration measurements. Unlike other researchers in the field of speech timing, we did not measure interstress intervals or syllable durations which are phonological units. Instead, we took a direct route from impressionistic observations of rhythmic differences between languages to the acoustic signal. We measured the durations of vowels, and the duration of intervals between vowels in a passage of speech. Then we computed an acoustic variability index which expresses the level of variability in vocalic and intervocalic intervals. Our data support a weak categorical distinction between stress-timing and syllable-timing. But the distinction does not encompass all of the world's languages. There is considerable overlap between the stress-timed and the syllable-timed group and hitherto unclassified languages.

Acknowledgements

For comments and suggestions, we are grateful to John Coleman, Anders Eriksson, Brechtje Post, Burton Rosner, Andrew Slater, Ian Watson and Briony Williams. We would also like to thank an unnamed reviewer for their help. For translations and assistance with recruiting subjects we would like to thank Eva Liina Asu, Eva Estebas-Vilaplana, Eric Fixmer, Keiko Masuda, Elinor Reynolds, Catherine Sangster, Nancy Waugh and Paula West. Finally, we are grateful to Andrew Slater for IT assistance. The research reported here was supported by the U.K. Economic and Social Research Council (ESRC) through grant no. R000237145.

Notes

1   The contribution of vowel reduction to the impression of stress- and syllable-timing was investigated more generally in studies by Wenk & Wioland (1982)

and by Brakel (1985). These authors suggested that the basis for stress- or syllable-timing may rest on vowels rather than syllables. In British English, there is vowel reduction and the effect of this is that the duration of each foot is nearly isochronous. Syllable-timed languages like French do not have reduced vowels and as such, do not seem to achieve foot isochrony.
2. For an investigation of rhythm which also departs from isochrony, but in a different direction, see Cummins & Port (1998). Cummins and Port define rhythm in speech as the hierarchical organization of temporally coordinated prosodic units.
3. We did not apply this index to a mora-timed language.
4. A further consequence of our approach to measuring in the present paper is that we do not include the hold phase of intonation-phrase-initial stops after a silence interval.
5. Note that we could have normalised by dividing by the average interval duration. We have retained the normalisation procedure suggested by Deterding (1994) as it is more sensitive to local changes in speech rate. Local changes may be especially relevant in languages like French, which, crudely, have rhythmic structures consisting of very similar intervals within rhythmic groups, with considerable phrase-final lengthening at the end of each group. For a prosodic analysis of French intonation, see Post, 2000.
6. A further reason not to apply the normalisation procedure for vocalic intervals to intervocalic intervals arises from research on speech rate effects on vowels and consonants. Gay (1978) has shown that increases in speaking rate in English lead to a shortening of both consonantal and vocalic portions of syllables, but most of the change results from a shortening of the vocalic portions. Changes in the duration of initial and final formant transitions in CVC sylllables accounted for about one third of the total shortening.

References

Abercrombie, D.
    1965   *Studies in Phonetics and Linguistics*. London: Oxford University Press.
Abercrombie, D.
    1967   *Elements of General Phonetics*. Edinburgh: Edinburgh University Press.
Asher, R. E.
    1985   *Tamil*. London: Croom Helm.
Beckman, M. E.
    1982   Segment duration and the 'mora' in Japanese. *Phonetica*, **39**, 113–135.

Beckman. M. E.
- 1992 Evidence for speech rhythms across languages. In Y. Tohura, E. Vatikiotis-Bateson and Y. Sagisaka (eds.), *Speech Perception, Production and Linguistic Structure*, (pp. 457–63). Tokyo: Omsha and Amsterdam: IOS Press.

Beckman, M. E. & Edwards, J.
- 1994 Articulatory evidence for differentiating stress categories. In P. Keating (ed.), *Phonological structure and phonetic form. Papers in Laboratory Phonology III*, (pp. 7–33). Cambridge: Cambridge University Press.

Bloch, B.
- 1950 Studies in colloquial Japanese IV: Phonemics. *Language*, 26, 86–125.

Bolinger, D. L.
- 1965 *Forms of English: Accent, Morpheme, Order*. Cambridge, MA: Harvard University Press.

Brakel, A.
- 1985 Towards a morphophonological approach to the study of linguistic rhythm. *Chicago Linguistic Society*, 21, 15–25.

Carney, A. E., Widen, B. & Viemeister, N.
- 1977 Non-categorical perception of stop consonants differing in VOT. *Journal of the Acoustical Society of America*, 62, 961–970.

Catford, J. C.
- 1977 *Fundamental Problems in Phonetics*. Edinburgh: Edinburgh University Press.

Classe, A.
- 1939 *The Rhythm of English Prose*. Oxford: Blackwell.

Corder, S. P.
- 1973 *Introducing Applied Linguistics*. Harmondsworth, Middlesex: Penguin.

Couper-Kuhlen, E.
- 1990 Discovering rhythm in conversational English: Perceptual and acoustic approaches to the analysis of isochrony, *KontRI Working Paper No. 13*, University of Konstance, Fachgruppe Sprachwissenschaft.

Couper-Kuhlen, E.
- 1993 *English Speech Rhythm. Form and Function in Everyday Verbal Interaction*. Amsterdam: Benjamins.

Cummins, F. and Port, R. F.
- 1998 Rhythmic constraints on stress timing in English. *Journal of Phonetics*, 26, 145–171.

Dasher, R. & Bolinger, D.
- 1982 On pre-accentual lengthening. *Journal of the International Phonetic Association*, 12, 58–69.

Dauer, R. M.
 1983 Stress-timing and syllable-timing re-analysed. *Journal of Phonetics*, **11**, 51−62.
Dauer, R.
 1987 Phonetic and phonological components of language rhythm. *Proceedings of the XIth International Congress of Phonetic Sciences*, Tallinn, Estonia, 447−450.
Delattre, P.
 1966 A comparison of syllable length conditioning among languages. *International Review of Applied Linguistics in Language Teaching*, **IV** Vol **3**, 183−198.
Deterding, D. H.
 1994 The rhythm of Singapore English. Paper presented at the Fifth Australian International Conference on Speech Science and Technology. December 6−8, 1994.
Eriksson, A.
 1991 *Aspects of Swedish speech rhythm*. Gothenburg Monographs in Linguistics, **9**, University of Göteborg.
Faure, G. Hirst, D. J. & Chafcouloff, M.
 1980 Rhythm in English: Isochronism, pitch, and perceived stress. In L. R. Waugh & C. H. van Schooneveld (eds.), *The Melody of Language*, (pp. 71−79), Baltimore: University Park Press.
Fischer-Jørgensen, E. & Hutters, B.
 1981 Aspirated stop consonants before low vowels, a problem of delimitation, its causes and consequences. *ARIPUC*, **15**, 77−102.
Gay, T.
 1978 Effects of speaking rate on vowel formant transitions. *Journal of the Acoustical Society of America*, **63**, 223−230.
Grabe, E., Post, B. & Watson, I.
 1999 The acquisition of rhythm in English and French. *Proceedings of the Intonational Congress of Phonetic Sciences*, **2**, 1201−1204. San Francisco, August 1999
Handbook of the International Phonetic Association.
 1999 Cambridge: Cambridge University Press.
Harnad, S.
 1987 *Categorical Perception*. Cambridge: Cambridge University Press.
Han, M. S.
 1962 The feature of duration in Japanese. *Onsei no kenkyuu*, **10**, 65−80.
Hockett, C. F.
 1958 *A Course in Modern Linguistics*. New York: Macmillan.
Hoequist, C. J.
 1983a Durational correlates of linguistic rhythm categories. *Phonetica*, **40**, 19−31.

Hoequist, C. J.
1983b Syllable duration in stress-, syllable- and mora-timed languages. *Phonetica*, **40**, 203−237.
Kohler, K.
1982 Rhythmus im Deutschen, *Arbeitsberichte, Institut für Phonetik der Universität Kiel*, **19**, 89−106.
Ladefoged, P.
1967 *Three Areas of Experimental Phonetics*. London: Oxford University Press.
Ladefoged, P.
1975 *A Course in Phonetics*. New York: Harcourt Brace Jovanovich.
Laver, J.
1994 *Principles of Phonetics*. Cambridge: Cambridge University Press.
Lehiste, I.
1977 Isochrony reconsidered. *Journal of Phonetics*, **5**, 253−263.
Low, E. L.
1998 Prosodic prominence in Singapore English. PhD Thesis, University of Cambridge.
Low, E. L. & Grabe, E.
1995 Prosodic patterns in Singapore English. *Proceedings of the Intonational Congress of Phonetic Sciences*, **3**, 636−639, Stockholm 13−19 August.
Low, E. L., Grabe, E. & Nolan, F.
2000 Quantitative characterisations of speech rhythm: 'syllable-timing' in Singapore English. *Language and Speech*, **43**, 377−401.
Luangthongkum, T.
1977 Rhythm in Standard Thai. PhD thesis. University of Edinburgh.
Manrique, A. M. B. & Signorini, A.
1983 Segmental reduction in Spanish. *Journal of Phonetics*, **11**, 117−128.
Nakatani, L. H., O'Connor, J. D. & Aston, C. H.
1981 Prosodic aspects of American English speech rhythm. *Phonetica*, **38**, 84−105.
Nespor, I.
1990 On the rhythm parameter in phonology. In I. Roca, (ed.), *Logical issues in Language Acquisition*, (pp. 157−175). Dordrecht: Foris.
Oyakawa, T.
1971 On the directionality of segmental conditioning in Japanese. Monthly Internal Memo, Department of Linguistics, University of California at Berkely, 81−103.
Peterson, G. E. & Lehiste, I.
1960 Duration of syllable nuclei in English. *Journal of the Acoustical Society of America*, **32**, 693−703.
Pike, K.
1946 *The Intonation of American English*. 2nd edition. Ann Arbor: University of Michigan Press.

Platt, J. T. & Weber, H.
 1980 *English in Singapore and Malaysia: Status, Features and Functions.* Kuala Lumpur: Oxford University Press.
Pointon, G. E.
 1980 Is Spanish really syllable-timed? *Journal of Phonetics*, **8**, 293–304.
Port, R. F., Al Ani, S. & Maeda, S.
 1980 Temporal compensation and universal phonetics. *Phonetica*, **37**, 235–252.
Port, R. F., Dalby, J. and O'Dell, M.
 1987 Evidence for mora-timing in Japanese. *Journal of the Acoustical Society of America*, **81**, 1574–85.
Post, B.
 2000 *Tonal and Phrasal Structures in French Intonation.* Thesus: The Hague.
Ramus, F., Nespor, M. & Mehler, J.
 1999 Correlates of linguistic rhythm in the speech signal, *Cognition*, **72**, 1–28.
Roach, P.
 1982 On the distinction between 'stress-timed' and 'syllable-timed' languages. In D. Crystal (ed.), *Linguistic Controversies*, (pp. 73–79), London: Arnold.,
Samuel, A. G.
 1977 The effect of discrimination training on speech perception: noncategorical perception. *Perception & Psychophysics*, **22**, 321–330.
Shen, Y. & Peterson, G. G.
 1962 Isochronism in English. *University of Buffalo Studies in Linguistics, Occasional Papers*, **9**, 1–36.
Smith, A.
 1976 Syllable-structure and rhythm in Japanese. *Work in Progress*, Department of Linguistics, University of Edinburgh, **8**, 1–8.
Tongue, R. K.
 1979 *The English of Singapore and Malaysia.* Singapore: Eastern Universities Press.
Wenk, B. & Wioland, F.
 1982 Is French really syllable-timed? *Journal of Phonetics*, **10**, 193–216.
Yeow, K. L.
 1987 Stress, Rhythm and Intonation in Educated Singapore English. Unpublished Masters Thesis, National University of Singapore.

Appendix

Table 1: Normalised vocalic *nPVI* and intervocalic *rPVI* values. The table is sorted in ascending order by vocalic *nPVI* values.

Languages	Normalised Vocalic *nPVI*	N	Raw Intervocalic *rPVI*	N
Thai	65.8	161	56.5	164
Dutch	65.5	132	57.4	136
German	59.7	155	55.3	153
BE	57.2	124	64.1	124
Tamil	55.8	149	70.2	150
Malay	53.6	205	63.3	204
SE	52.3	118	68.2	118
Greek	48.7	177	59.6	179
Welsh	48.2	152	54.7	150
Rumanian	46.9	183	47.6	182
Polish	46.6	124	79.1	128
Estonian	45.4	162	40.0	158
Catalan	44.6	144	67.8	139
French	43.5	146	50.4	142
Japanese	40.9	176	62.5	177
Luxembourg	37.7	131	55.4	139
Spanish	29.7	173	57.7	156
Mandarin	27.0	141	52.0	135

Table 2: Vocalic *nPVI* and intervocalic *rPVI* data subdivided into three sections. Sorted as Table 1. above to allow for comparisons. i.e. by mean vocalic *nPVI* in ascending order.

	Vocalic *nPVI*	Intervocalic *rPVI*	N
Thai	52.6	69.5	53
	63.0	71.1	53
	53.3	56.4	53
Dutch	60.6	66.6	44
	41.8	70.8	44
	55.2	59.4	44
German	52.1	57.6	51
	57.0	65.3	51
	55.9	58.7	51

Table 2: (continued)

	Vocalic nPVI	Intervocalic rPVI	N
BE	65.6	55.2	40
	65.0	53.6	40
	54.4	56.1	40
Tamil	70.1	56.1	50
	67.8	53.9	50
	72.8	56.4	50
Malay	55.1	53.1	68
	60.4	60.0	68
	63.0	48.2	68
SE	70.6	49.9	39
	69.8	45.3	39
	64.5	58.7	39
Greek	57.2	51.5	59
	58.0	43.9	59
	61.5	54.7	59
Welsh	50.9	43.6	50
	50.6	48.2	50
	59.2	46.5	50
Rumanian	42.1	52.2	60
	47.4	46.1	60
	49.7	39.0	60
Polish	71.6	48.6	42
	77.8	46.3	42
	80.3	43.2	42
Estonian	37.0	49.6	53
	39.0	49.4	53
	38.7	41.1	53
Catalan	66.0	46.0	47
	52.8	47.9	47
	62.1	38.5	47
French	49.3	39.4	46
	49.7	38.7	46
	44.3	42.0	46
Japanese	56.3	39.9	58
	71.3	42.9	58
	47.0	40.3	58
Luxembourg	52.3	30.1	43
	58.2	39.4	43
	54.0	37.5	43

Table 2: (continued)

	Vocalic nPVI	Intervocalic rPVI	N
Spanish	60.3	30.5	52
	56.9	28.0	52
	54.7	31.2	52
Mandarin	52.0	26.4	45
	55.0	27.7	45
	44.2	26.0	45

Table 3: Comparison of our findings with data from Ramus et al. (1999). NB. Ramus and colleagues investigated Italian, but Italian was not investigated in the present paper.

	%V	%V Ramus et al.	ΔV	ΔV Ramus et al.	ΔC	ΔC Ramus et al.
British English	41.1	40.1	46.6	46.4	56.7	53.5
Polish	42.3	41.0	44.9	25.1	71.4	51.4
Catalan	43.6	45.6	33.9	36.8	62.1	45.2
Greek	44.1		49.1		52.7	
Estonian	44.5		39.6		31.9	
Luxembourg	44.7		31.1		53.7	
Dutch	44.9	42.3	48.4	42.3	53.7	53.3
Japanese	45.5	53.1	53.0	40.2	55.8	35.6
Welsh	46.1		39.4		48.5	
German	46.4		44.5		52.6	
Singapore English	46.9		41.0		47.0	
Rumanian	49.4		49.5		40.9	
Malay	49.5		56.7		54.8	
French	50.6	43.6	35.5	37.8	42.4	43.9
Spanish	50.8	43.8	20.7	33.2	47.5	47.4
Thai	52.2		74.8		46.1	
Tamil	54.4		76.4		66.6	
Mandarin	55.8		36.2		44.1	

From pitch-accent to stress-accent in Basque

José Ignacio Hualde, Gorka Elordieta, Iñaki Gaminde and Rajka Smiljanić

Abstract

The prosodic system found in Northern Bizkaian (NB) Basque dialects shares a number of properties with Japanese (a lexical distinction between accented and unaccented words, phrase-initial rise, no durational correlates of accent). In this paper we examine and explore the geographical distribution of the features that make these Basque dialects different from stress languages, on the basis of experimental data. The results of this investigation indicate that within the western Basque area there is a continuum between pitch-accent and stress-accent. We draw two major conclusions for the typology of accentual systems. First of all, the striking coincidence between NB Basque and Tokyo Japanese in a number of important prosodic properties suggests that this set of common properties can be used to characterize an accentual prototype. On the other hand, the existence in the Basque territory of varieties presenting a range of intermediate points between this system and stress systems shows that there is no absolute distinction between stress-accent languages and pitch-accent languages of the type considered here.

1. Our current understanding of the Basque pitch-accent system

The term "pitch-accent language" has been used to refer to a heterogeneous set of languages – including, for instance, Japanese, Swedish, Serbo-Croatian and Ancient Greek (see van der Hulst & Smith, 1988, for an overview) – which appear to share some features with, but differ from, both tone languages and stress languages. One language to which this label would seem clearly to apply is Basque, or rather, some western Basque dialects. Our own fieldwork over the years, as well as that of other researchers (Hualde, 1991, 1999a; Hualde & Bilbao, 1993; Hualde, Elordieta & Elordieta, 1994; Elordieta, 1997, 1998; Jun & Elordieta, 1997; Gaminde, 1994, 1998, among others) has revealed that some

Basque dialects, spoken along the Bizkaian coast and in the immediate hinterland, possess an accentual system with the following characteristics:

a) Lexical accented/unaccented distinction.
b) Invariable realization of accents as H*L.
c) Non-accentual phrase-initial rise % L H-: In all phrases, the pitch invariably rises on or around the second syllable (% LH-) and remains high up to the accented syllable, immediately after which there is a steep fall (H*L). The accented syllable may have approximately the same or a slightly higher pitch than preceding syllables.
d) No durational correlates of accentual prominence (tentatively established in Hualde, Smiljanić & Cole, 2000).

From this description it should be apparent that this system bears a strong resemblance to the well-known Tokyo Japanese accentual system (for which, see Beckman & Pierrehumbert, 1986; Pierrehumbert & Beckman, 1988). The resemblance is all the more striking given the genetic and geographical separation, the two languages. We may use the features shared by these languages to define an accentual type, which we will call T(okyo)-type pitch-accent language. We suggest the notion of "prosodic prototype" to refer to a combination of prosodic features that seems particularly stable or likely to arise independently. In this sense, the four features listed above appear to define a prosodic prototype.[1]

Other Basque dialects, by contrast, present prosodic systems that do not appear to differ greatly from those employed by their Romance neighbors, Spanish and Gascon, which are rather typical stress languages.

Some early work on Basque accentuation (Hualde, 1991) assumed a binary distinction between "tonal" (= pitch-accent) dialects and "stress" dialects of Basque. Such simple classification, however, raises some fundamental questions. From a synchronic, dialectological, point of view it implies that, to the extent that these are two distinct prosodic types, it should be a straightforward matter to classify every local Basque dialect as belonging to one or the other of these two groups and to find a well-defined isogloss between pitch-accent and stress-accent systems within the Basque territory. From a diachronic perspective, it suggests that some specific sound change would result in a pitch-accent dialect becoming a stress-accent dialect or vice versa.

Notice that to the extent that these assumptions are not realistic the very possibility of neatly classifying the accentual systems of the languages of the world as either "stress-accent" or "pitch-accent" systems must be seriously questioned, unless one particular feature is chosen over the others for these purposes.

In this paper we examine two of the features listed above, the presence of the accented/unaccented contrast and the presence of a phrase-initial tonal rise, in a number of dialects covering the whole geographical area where we could reasonably expect these features to be present. The picture that emerges is one where local dialects have lost these features to different degrees, probably under the influence of Spanish. Within the western Basque area we have what looks like a continuum between T-type pitch-accent and stress-accent.

2. The accented/unaccented contrast

2.1 Properties of accented and unaccented words

An essential feature in the accentual system of Northern Bizkaian Basque (henceforth NB Basque) is the existence of a contrast between lexically accented and lexically unaccented words, where the latter represent the majority class (Hualde, 1991, 1999).

In phrases composed entirely of lexically unaccented words, there is no accentual prominence on any syllable, except that the final syllable of the phrase receives accentual prominence if the phrase is in focus position (immediately preceding the verb, when the verb itself does not bear focus) or is pronounced in isolation (i.e. when the utterance consists of a single focalized phrase). We will refer to this phrasal-accent borne by lexically unaccented words as "derived accent" (following Jun & Elordieta, 1997).[2]

Lexically accented words, on the other hand, have an accentually prominent syllable and surface with prominence on this syllable in all sentential contexts (represented here with an acute accent on the vowel of the accented syllable). The accent may fall on any syllable, except that lexical accent on the final syllable is very rare (in some local dialects there are strong restrictions on the position of accents, see Hualde, 1999a, 2000a). The class of accented words includes all words bearing plural inflectional suffixes (a fact which gives rise to many singular/plural minimal pairs); e.g.: unaccented *laguneri* 'to the friend, DATsg' vs. accented *lagúneri* 'to the friends, DATpl'. A couple of nonplural inflectional suffixes, including ablative *-tik,* also induce lexical accent; cf., eg.: *basótik* 'from the forest' vs. *basora* 'to the forest' (In Basque only the last word in the noun phrase bears inflection; i.e., inflection is phrasal in scope; e.g. *gure lagun on-ari* 'to our good friend' = 'our friend good-DATsg'). In addition, certain stems are always accented regardless of inflection. These include many derived and compound stems (e.g. *begígorri* 'red-eyed' < *begi* 'eye' + *gorri* 'red', *amáma* ~ *amúma* 'grandmother', cf. *ama* 'mother'). A considerable number of loanwords, both ancient and recent, are also lexically accented. For the productive adaptation of borrowings from Spanish there are some very specific patterns (see Hualde, 1999b). In particular, in the case of proper names, normally an accent appears in the position of the penultimate and antepenultimate stress in the Spanish word, and final-stressed Spanish words are adapted as unaccented; e.g.: Sp. *Fidél* → *Fidel, Fideleri* 'to Fidel' (unaccented) vs. Sp. *Fidéla* → *Fidéla, Fidélari* 'to Fidela'.[3]

To be sure, in a language like Spanish as well there is a class of lexically unstressed and unaccented words, but this class is limited to function words such as definite articles and prepositions (see Quilis, 1993: 390—395). All other words have lexical prominence on one syllable or another and can bear a pitch-accent. Furthermore, lexically unstressed articles and prepositions can also receive stress and bear a pitch-accent under contrastive focus. In NB Basque, on the other hand, most words are lexically unaccented and can only receive a pitch-accent if they occupy the syntactic position to which a derived accent can be assigned. It is thus impossible to place an accent on a lexically unaccented word which is not in the syntactic position where it could receive a derived accent. As an answer to (1a) we may have (1b), but not (1c), because the word *txakur* 'dog', which is lexically unaccented and is not phrase-final in the preverbal constituent, cannot receive accentual prominence, even if the pragmatics would appear to strongly require it:

(1) a. *katu baltza ikusi dozu?*   'Did you see the black cat?'
    cat black see AUX
  b. *ez, txakur baltzá ikusi dot.* 'No, I saw the black dog'
    no dog black see AUX
  c. **ez, txakúr baltza ikusi dot*

On the other hand, lexically accented words bear a H*L accent in every utterance where they appear, although lexical accents after the main sentential accent (the one normally borne by the preverbal phrase) can be very reduced. This accent is part of the lexical make-up of the words in question. Again, this can be compared with the situation in stress-accent languages like Spanish and English, where it is not the case that certain words will necessarily carry a pitch-accent; rather a given word may or not bear a pitch-accent depending on pragmatic factors.

Our previous fieldwork indicates that some western Basque dialects outside of the NB area may possess a more restricted accented/unaccented contrast. In Hualde (1992, 1999a), the claim is made, based on impressionistic analysis, that in the dialect of Zeberio, in Southern Bizkaia, all inflected words are accented but the accented/unaccented distinction is preserved with uninflected words.

2.2 Acoustic investigation of the accented/unaccented contrast: methods

We take the existence of a robust lexical contrast between accented and unaccented words to be an important characteristic of a T-type accentual system. To determine whether indeed this can be taken as the defining feature of this type of accentual system, we decided to investigate to what extent this contrast is made in

Basque dialects in and around the NB area and whether it correlates with other prosodic features.

The strategy, thus, is starting from dialects for which the existence of a lexical accented/unaccented distinction has been documented (in our previous research), 1) to find a quantifiable acoustic feature that corresponds to the lexical distinction, and 2) to examine a group of dialects from a larger area and differing in other prosodic respects, for the existence and distribution of this feature.

To establish the accented/unaccented distinction empirically, we need, then, to find an acoustic feature in the signal that correlates strongly with the putative distinction. As mentioned above, our observations indicate that accent is consistently manifested in NB Basque by a fall in pitch immediately after the accented syllable. The accented/unaccented contrast is shown schematically in (2) and in Figure 1 with a minimal pair:

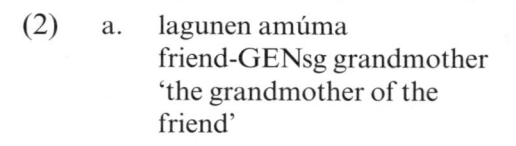

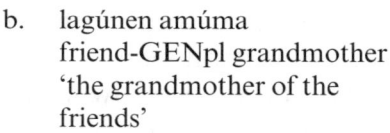

(2) a. lagunen amúma
     friend-GENsg grandmother
     'the grandmother of the friend'

   b. lagúnen amúma
      friend-GENpl grandmother
      'the grandmother of the friends'

As said, the unaccented character of certain words is revealed when they are placed in non-phrase-final position. In principle, in order to investigate whether a given dialect possesses an accented/unaccented distinction of this sort, one could examine whether in examples like (2) there is a fall somewhere in the first word. The presence of a medial fall in both (2a) and (2b) would indicate that in both cases the first word has an accent. In practice, however, reliably determining what counts as an accentual fall can be difficult, mainly because a prosodic boundary could be introduced between the two words, inducing a shallow dip in the contour.

We thus needed to identify a more reliable acoustic correlate of the accented/unaccented distinction. From the inspection of f_0 contours and based on the literature on other languages (for Japanese see Poser, 1984; Pierrehumbert & Beckman, 1988), we hy-

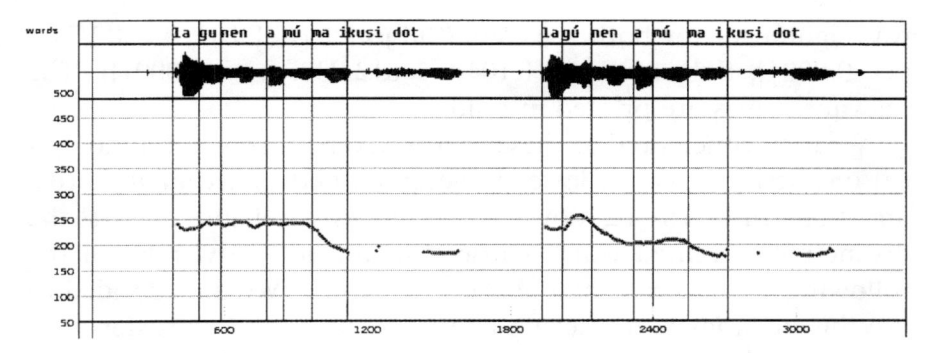

Figure 1: Speech wave form and F0 track of *lagunen amúma ikusi dot* 'I saw the grandmother of the friend' (left) and of *lagúnen amúma ikusi dot* 'I saw the grandmother of the friends' (right). Speaker Lekeitio-1.

pothesized that the presence vs. absence of downstep on following accents would be such a correlate.

In a pilot experiment, reported in Hualde, Smiljanić & Cole (2000), it was found that, for two speakers (5 repetitions of 26 randomized sentences per speaker), the downstepping of the accentual peak on a following word did provide a very reliable cue for the presence of an accent in two-word sequences where the first word could be either accented or unaccented. The results of this pilot experiment are summarized in Table 1.

Table 1: Means and standard deviations of f_0 (Hz) on accentual peaks after accented and unaccented words for two speakers of NB Basque

			Mean	sd	N
IS, Markina	U/A	Accent Peak (W2)	**262 Hz**	13.06 Hz	64
	A/A	Accent Peak W1	268.83 Hz	12.49 Hz	65
		Accent Peak W2	**213.92 Hz**	11.54 Hz	65
MB, Bermeo	U/A	Accent Peak (W2)	**197.83 Hz**	7.28 Hz	65
	A/A	Accent Peak W1	204.85 Hz	7.34 Hz	65
		Accent Peak W2	**172.08 Hz**	9.55 Hz	65

An ANOVA showed that the difference in the height of the Accent Peak in Word2 between Context U/A (Word1 Unaccented/ Word2 Accented) and Context A/A (Word1 Accented/Word2 Accented)

was significant for both speakers (Subject 1 [$F(1,103) = 582.742$, $p < 0.0001$], Subject 2 [$F (1,104) = 612.930$, $p < 0.0001$]). The relevant values are printed in bold.

We may conclude that these two speakers possess a phonological distinction between lexically accented and unaccented words, and that, furthermore, downstep provides a reliable clue to the distinction: accented words cause a significantly lower F0 of the following accent peak than unaccented words. We thus decided to use this phenomenon to examine the existence and consistency of the accented/unaccented distinction in a number of local western dialects.

To obtain data for our dialectal survey we constructed 10 sentences forming 5 minimally contrasting pairs. An example of a contrasting pair is given in (4) (the complete list is in the appendix, first ten sentences).[4] The list was repeated three times by each subject (for a total of 30 tokens per speaker). The 10 sentences are all of the form [$_{NP}$ W1 W2] V + AUX, and constitute 5 contrasting pairs. In NB dialects that we have investigated in some detail, W1 is unaccented in odd-numbered sentences (Condition U/A) and accented in even-numbered sentences (Condition A/A). W2 is always accented. Two pairs (3–4 and 5–6) represent contrasts between accented and unaccented stems; the other three pairs of sentences illustrate the singular/plural contrast with unaccented stems. The accent on W2 is lexical in some examples and derived in other examples. This circumstance is of no significance, since our pilot experiment showed that downstep after a lexical accent obtains in both cases. The test sentences for downstep are given in (3).

(3) a. *abadien   líbrue ikusi dot*   (U/A)
       W1   W2
       priest.GENsg   book   see   AUX
       'I have seen the book of the priest'

   b. *abádien   líbrue ikusi dot*   (A/A)
       W1   W2
       priest.GENpl   book   see   AUX
       'I have seen the book of the priests'

The two conditions, U/A and A/A, were established according to our expectation for 'core' NB Basque systems. Under the assumption (supported by our pilot experiment) that downstep in W2 consistently indicates the presence of an accent in W1 and, conversely, absence of downstep in W2 shows that W1 is unaccented, we may expect to find the following three situations:

1) Downstep in condition A/A utterances vs. absence of downstep in condition U/A utterances, in dialects with the lexical distribution of accented and unaccented words for which these two conditions were established.

2) Downstep in both condition A/A and condition U/A utterances, in dialects lacking a lexical class of unaccented words.

3) Downstep in condition A/A utterances and also in a subset of condition U/A utterances in dialects with a smaller class of lexically unaccented words, as claimed for Zeberio in Hualde (1992, 1999a). In particular, if all words inflected for number are accented, the only utterances where we may expect absence of downstep are those corresponding to sentences 3 and 5 in the Appendix.

For this experiment we obtained data from speakers of western Basque dialects, concentrating on northern Bizkaia which, from our fieldwork, appeared to be the core pitch-accent zone. In total, we analyzed data from 21 speakers. Speakers are identified by the name of the town whose local dialect they speak, followed by a number if there are more speakers from the same town. For the NB area these are Arteaga, Arratzu, Bermeo, Gatika, Larrabetzu-1, Larrabetzu-2, Larrabetzu-3, Lekeitio-1, Lekeitio-2, Markina, Ondarroa-1 and Ondarroa-2. For the Southern Bizkaian area, these are (SB) Artea, Dima-1, Dima-2, Igorre and Zeanuri, while Western Gipuzkoa (WG) is represented by Bergara-1, Bergara-2, Bergara-3, Bergara-4. Figure-2 shows the geographical locations of these towns. Three speakers, Lekeitio-1, Dima-1 and Bergara-1, were tested twice, under somewhat different conditions. The data corresponding to the second test will be presented together with the rest, identified with the label exp 2 after the name.[5]

Excluded from our investigation are local western dialects in which, as a consequence of a historical change discussed below, the accent regularly falls on the second syllable of the word and

556 *José Ignacio Hualde, Gorka Elordieta, Iñaki Gaminde and Rajka Smiljanić*

Figure 2: The geographical locations of the towns whose dialects were represented by our subjects

which have thus lost the unaccented class of words. Some towns with accentual systems of this type are indicated on the map, with the notation [+2] (meaning accent on the second syllable) to show the limits of the area under investigation.

2.2.1 Experimental results

The results of the experiment are shown in the form of a scatter graph for each subject, where black circles represent tokens in Condition U/A and white triangles tokens in Condition A/A. The X-axis shows the highest f_0 value in W1 (which may or may not correspond to an accent) and the Y-axis shows the highest value around the accented syllable in W2. Axis sections have been chosen such that if we trace a diagonal through the origin, points below this line have a downstepped accent in W2. The data are discussed by geographical area.

2.2.1.1 Northern Bizkaian. All speakers from this area appear to behave uniformly, with the exception of the three Larrabetzu

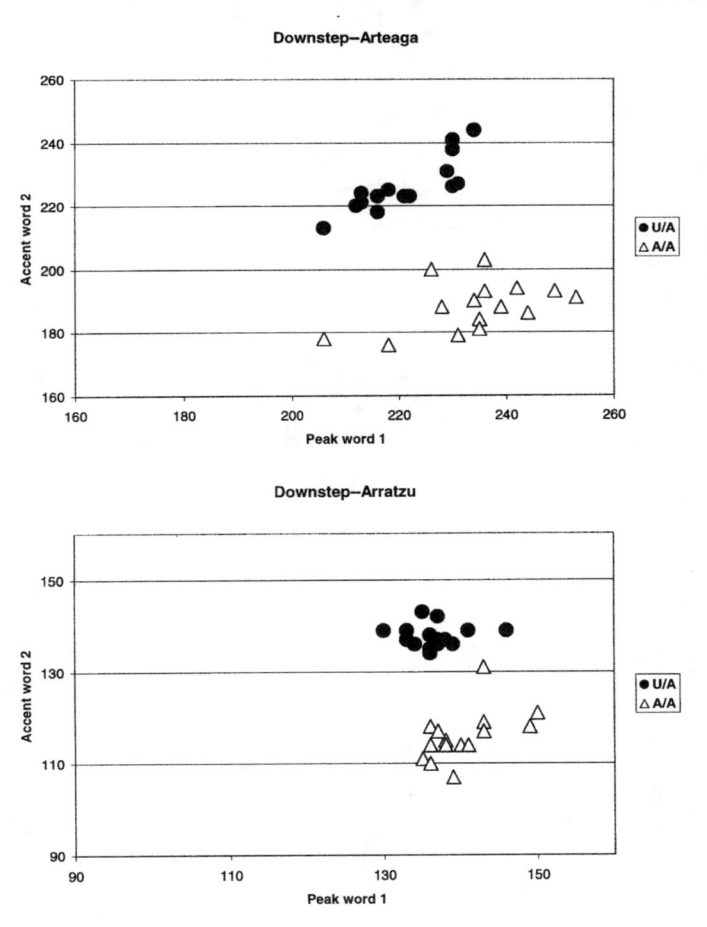

Figure 3: Downstep effects for Northern Bizkaian speakers. The x-axis shows the highest f_0 value in W1 (which may or may not correspond to an accent). The y-axis shows the highest value around the accented syllable in W2. Black circles represent Condition A tokens (W1 hypothesized unaccented, W2 accented) and white triangles are Condition B tokens (both W1 and W2 accented).

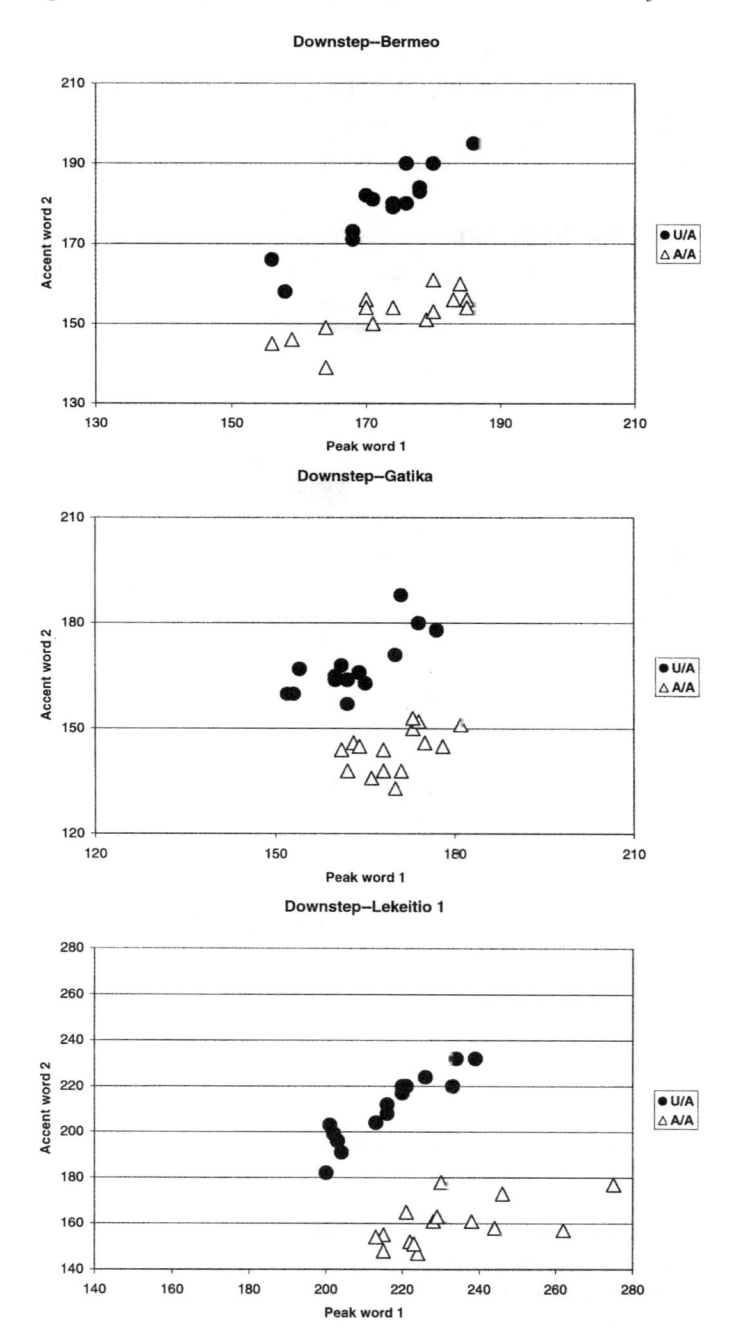

Figure 3: (continued)

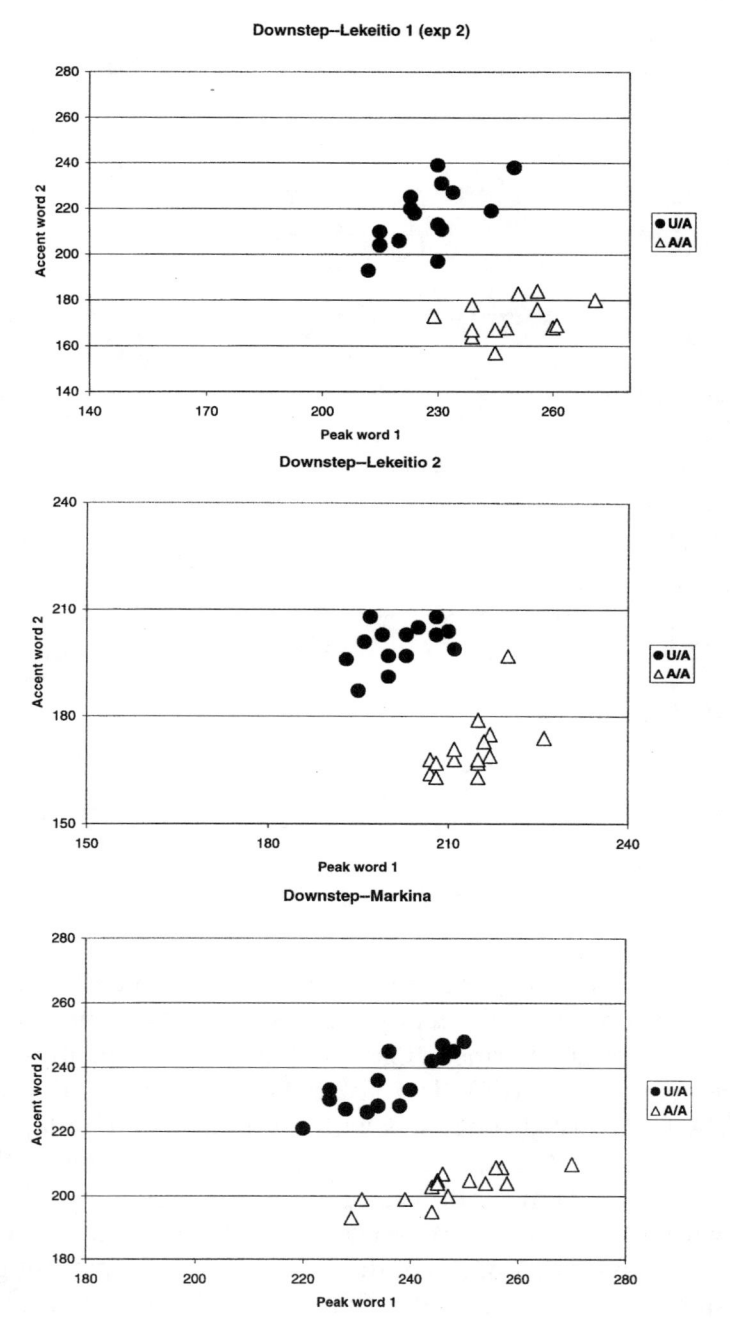

Figure 3: (continued)

Downstep—Ondarroa 1

Downstep—Ondarroa 2

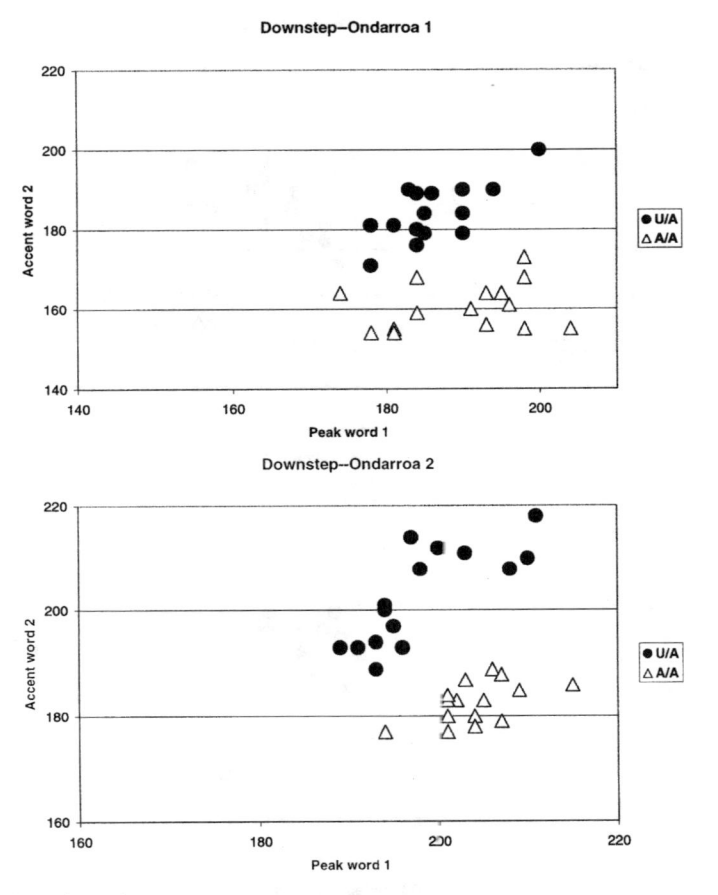

Figure 3: (continued)

speakers. We will postpone the discussion of the data for the three Larrabetzu subjects until section 3.2.3. For the other nine speakers (Arteaga, Arratzu, Bermeo, Gatika, Lekeitio-1, Lekeitio-2, Markina, Ondarroa-1 and Ondarroa-2), the data for conditions U/A and A/A form two distinct sets with essentially no overlap.

In condition U/A, the accent in W2 has a lower value than in condition A/A. That is, downstep in W2 is systematically correlated with the postulated presence of a lexical accent in W1. For all speakers in this group, hypothesized A/A tokens present greater downstep of the accent in W2 than U/A tokens, where phonetic lowering is minimal or absent. (In addition, for some speakers we notice a tendency for the two conditions to segregate along the horizontal dimension, indicating higher f_0 values in W1 when this word bears an accent.)

From these results, we can now establish with confidence that NB Basque possesses a contrast between lexically accented and unaccented words, as claimed in Hualde (1999a) and other work. This is a major feature that differentiates this accentual system from those of perhaps all other languages spoken in Europe. Whether or not a non-phrase-final word bears a pitch accent is a lexically contrastive property.

2.2.1.2 Southern Bizkaian. The results for the SB subjects (Artea, Dima-1, Dima-2, Igorre and Zeanuri) are clearly different from those just discussed for NB, as shown by a comparison between Figures 3 and 4. First of all, the graphs show overlap between U/A and A/A utterances for these five speakers (see Figure 4), indicating downstep under both conditions. The degree of overlap is substantial for Artea, Igorre and Zeanuri, less for the two Dima speakers (a fact to which we will return).

Second, however, all five speakers have a few tokens with no downstep; that is, where W2 is higher than W1 (above the diagonal). Inspection of our data sheets shows that these are not random tokens. They include all realizations of sentence 5 by all five speakers (for Igorre 5−3 is missing). For three of the speakers, some or all repetitions of sentence 3 are also included in this group. What these two sentences have in common is that they are the only ones in the set of ten sentences where W1 is not inflected for either singular or plural and has an unaccented stem. The relevant phrases are 3. *alaba argála* 'skinny daughter', where W1, *alaba* 'daughter' is uninflected and 5. *Fidelen alabéa* 'Fidel's daughter', where *Fidel* carries genitive inflection but is unmarked for number (proper names do not carry number inflection in Basque). For instance, in Figure 6, produced by Zeanuri, it can be readily observed that the phrase *alaba argalá* 'the skinny daughter' contains a single accent, on W2.

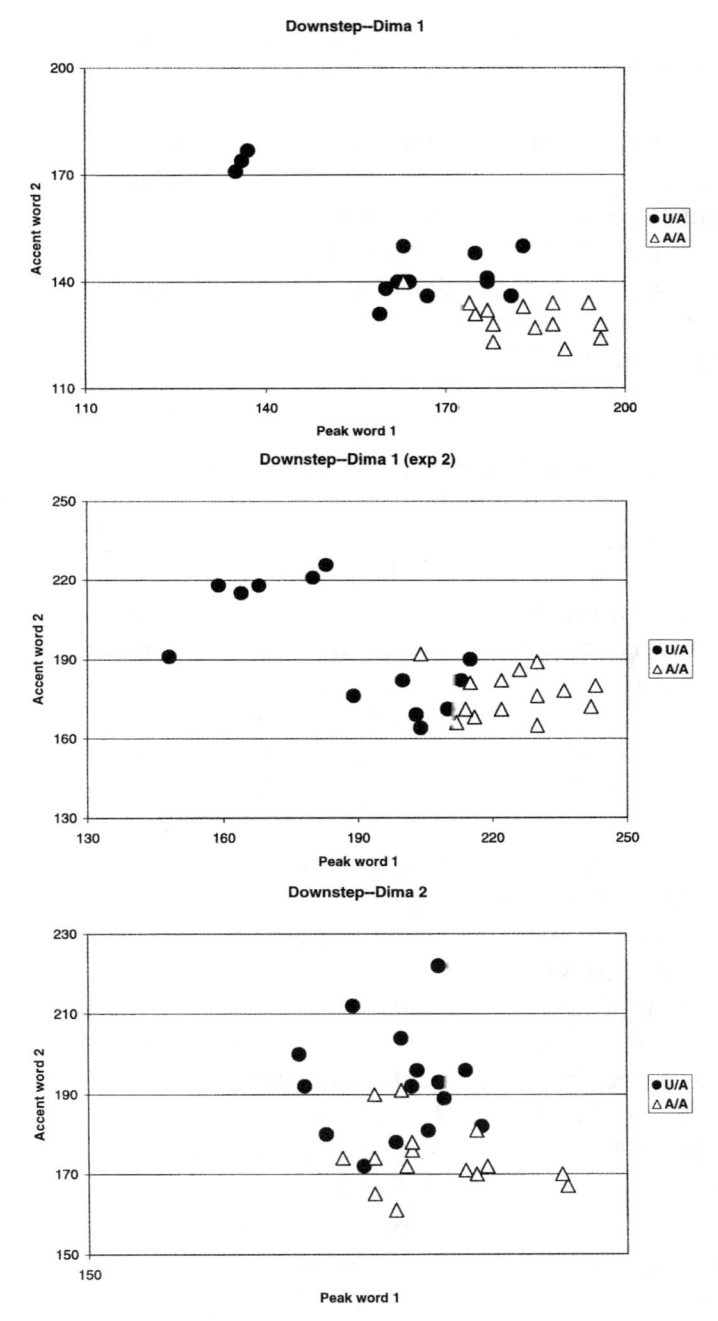

Figure 4: Downstep for Southern Bizkaian speakers. See also caption Figure 3.

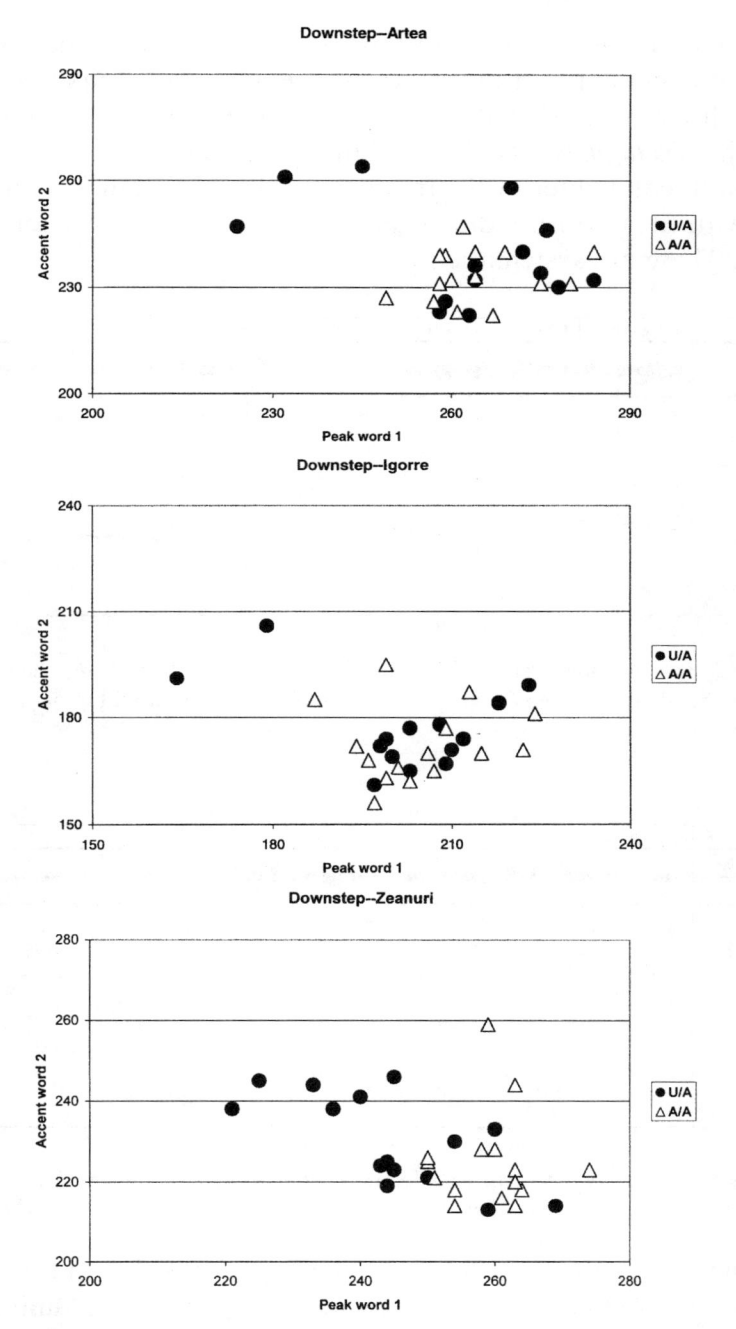

Figure 4: (continued)

Turning to the accented instances of W1, the data show that in SB both singular and plural words are accented (unlike NB), but have different accentual patterns. Compare Figure 5, containing the phrases *lagunén alabéa* 'the daughter of the friend' and *lagúnen alabéa* 'the daughter of the friends', produced by our Zeanuri subject with the corresponding examples above in Figure 1 for Lekeitio-1. These are systematic facts.

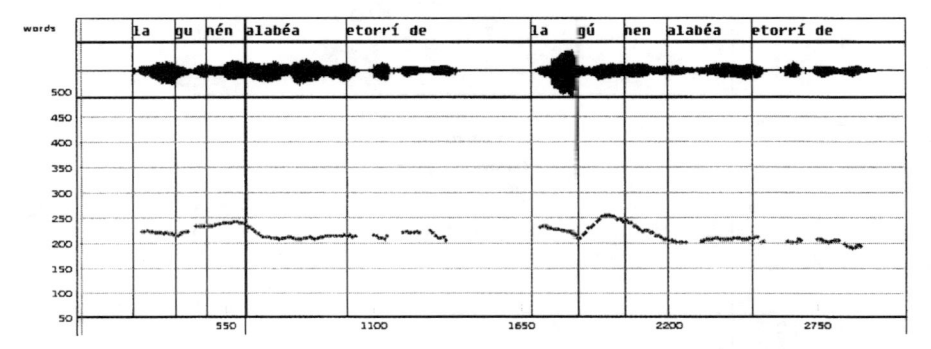

Figure 5: Speech wave form and f₀ track of *lagunén alabéa etorrí de* 'the daughter of the friend has arrived'/ *lagúnen alabéa etorrí de* 'the daughter of the friends has arrived'. Speaker Zeanuri.

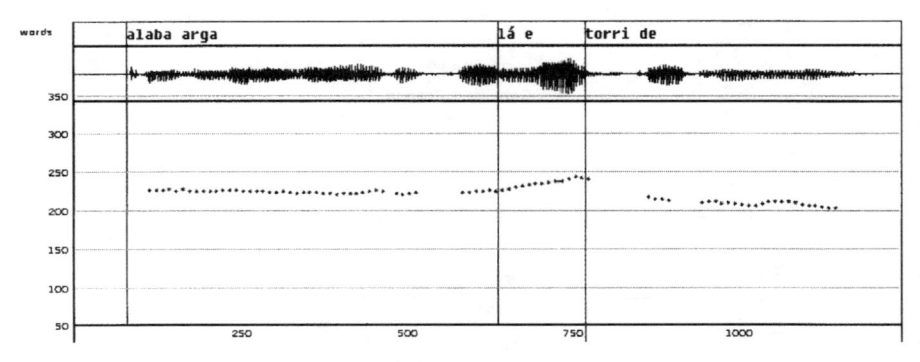

Figure 6: Speech wave form and f₀ track of *alaba argalá etorri de* 'the skinny daughter has arrived'. Speaker Zeanuri.

These data are consistent with the hypothesis that in this dialect all number-inflected words are accented but some uninflected words (e.g. *alaba* 'daughter' in the example in Figure 6) are lexically unaccented. The instrumental data that we have now obtained thus appear to confirm the observation regarding the distribution of accents in Zeberio made in Hualde (1992, 1999a) and allow us to extend it to a larger dialectal area.[6]

Now, even leaving aside those tokens produced without an accent on W1, for the two Dima subjects the overlap between U/A and A/A tokens is less than complete. The separation is especially clear for Dima1. The accent on W1 tends to be higher under condition A/A than under condition U/A. This fact cannot be dismissed as an experimental effect, since Dima1 was retested with essentially the same results. Most likely, the explanation for this fact is that singular forms used to be unaccented, as they still are in NB. At some historical point they acquired an accent on the syllable bearing the inflectional suffix, but this accent has been kept phonetically distinct to some degree from the preexisting accent of plural forms, and not only in its location. This point requires further research.

2.2.1.3 Larrabetzu. The data from our three speakers from Larrabetzu show a different pattern from all other speakers in the NB area, as shown in the scatter plots in Figure 7.[7]

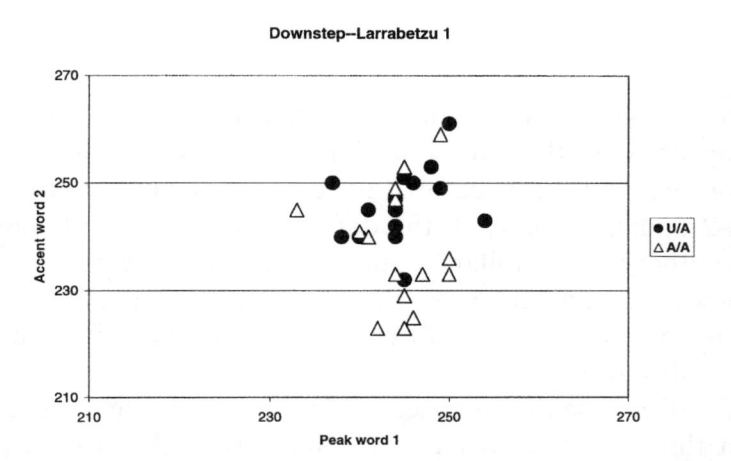

Figure 7: Downstep in Larrabetzu. See also caption Figure 3.

Downstep–Larrabetzu 2

Downstep–Larrabetzu 3

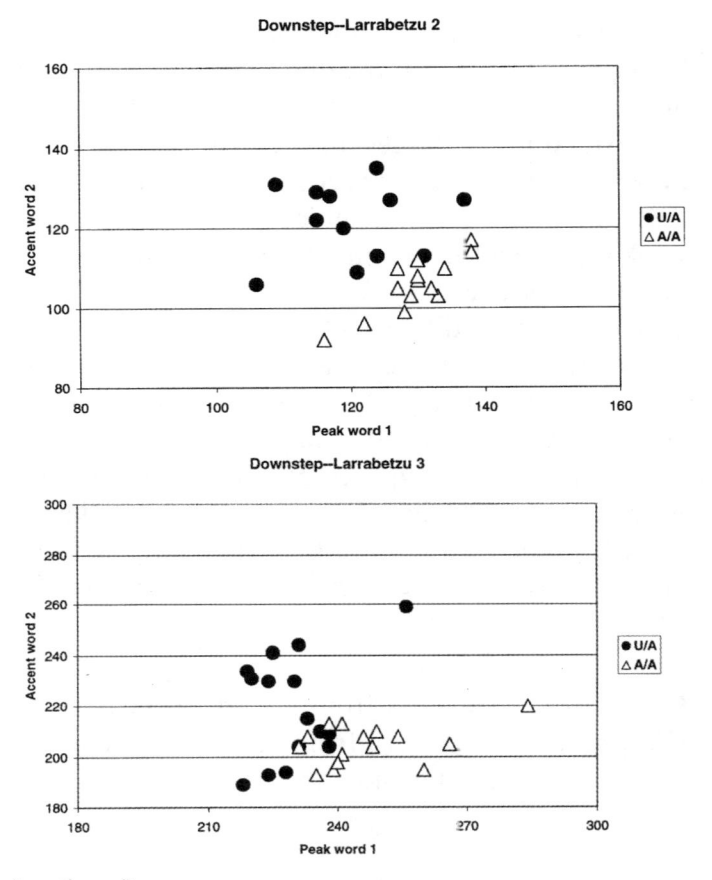

Figure 7: (continued)

Starting with Larrabetzu-1, this speaker shows considerable overlap between the two conditions. We may conclude that this speaker has no lexical accented/unaccented distinction. For Larrabetzu-2 and Larrabetzu-3, the data are somewhat different, and, on the other hand, similar to our findings for SB, especially Dima. In a few tokens, all corresponding to hypothesized U/A sentences, there is no downstep (Larrabetzu-2 has 8 tokens and Larrabetzu-3 has 7 in this group). Inspection of the data sheets reveals that these include all tokens of sentences 3 and 5 for both speakers, coinciding in this with the SB pattern.[8] Auditory and visual inspection of the data confirms that whereas these two speakers consistently pronounced sentences 3 and 5 without an accent on the first word, they are inconsistent in the production of other U/A sentences. Thus, to give an example, for 'the daughter of the friend' in sentence 1, Larrabetzu-2 produced both *lagunen alábia*, with no accent on the first word, and *lagúnen alábia*, with two accents (sentence 2, 'the daughter of the friends' is always *lágunen alábia* for this speaker). This type of inconsistency is not found in the data for any of the other NB dialects. Geographically, Larrabetzu is slightly further south than all other towns that we had initially included in the NB group, but the evidence suggests that it must be placed south of the isogloss. Although more research on this dialect is clearly required, a possible interpretation of the data is that Larrabetzu has unaccented words in the same instances as SB, but optionally other words that in NB are lexically unaccented can also be realized without an accent. Some speakers, such as Larrabetzu-1, however, may have lost the accented/unaccented distinction altogether.

2.2.1.4. Bergara (Western Gipuzkoan). When compared with the data for NB speakers, it is clear that the Bergara dialect does not have a lexical distinction between accented and unaccented words.

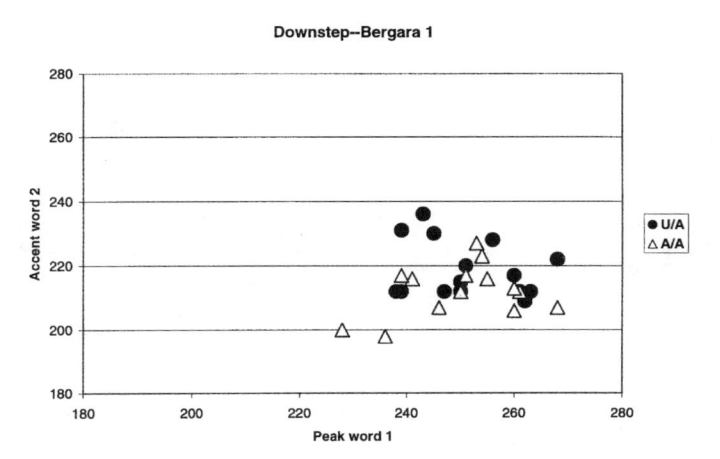

Figure 8: Downstep in Basque. See also caption Figure 3.

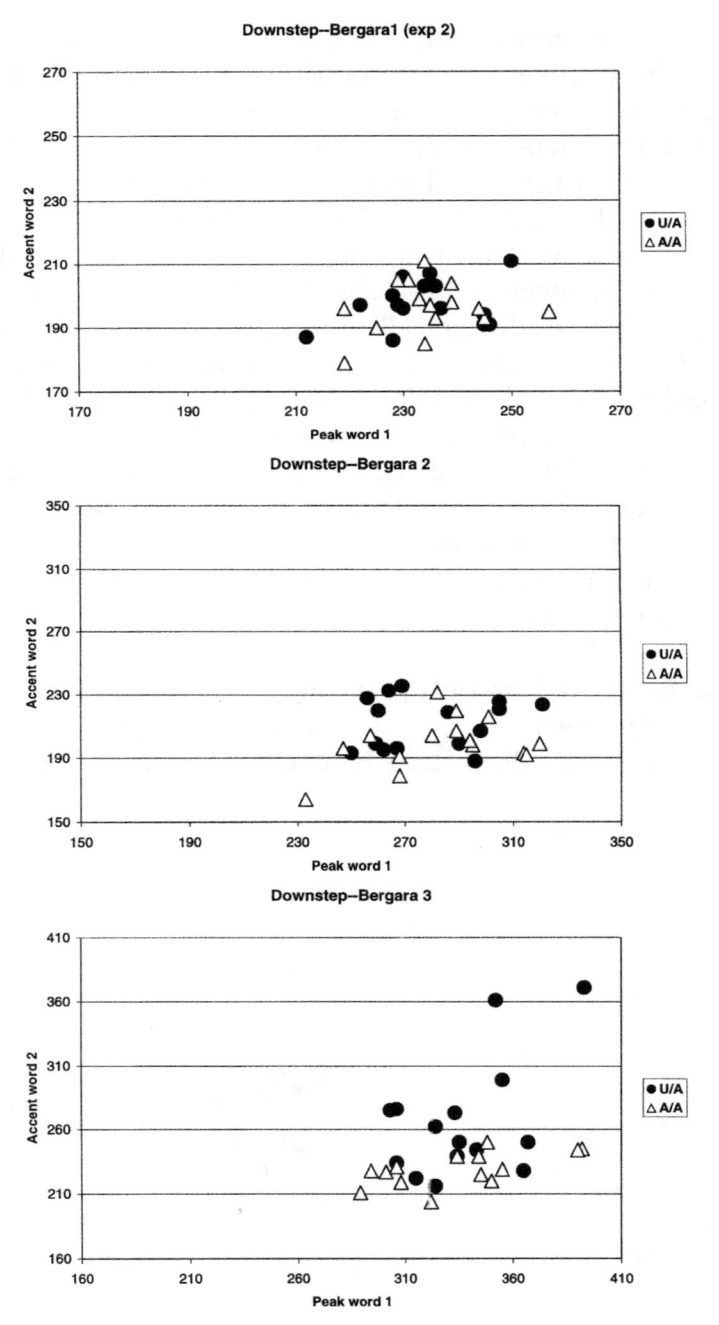

Figure 8: (continued)

Downstep—Bergara 4

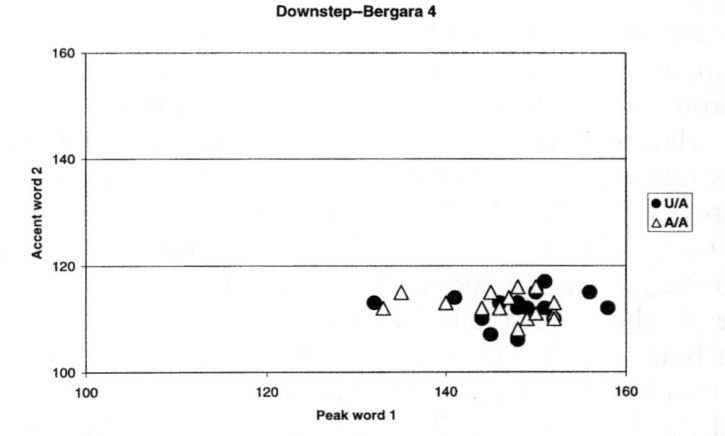

Figure 8: (continued)

Auditory and visual inspection of the data in Figure 8 shows that the singular/plural contrast is, in fact, preserved in this dialect, but as a contrast in the position of the accent; e.g. *lagunán alabía* 'the daughter of the friend' vs. *lágunen alabía* 'the daughter of the friends' (similar but not identical to SB). Unlike what was found for SB, sentences 3 and 5 do not result in a distinct pattern. That is, there are no words in our experimental set that systematically fail to cause downstep of an accent on a following word.

For Bergara3 only, the scatter graphs show a tendency for A/A sentences to be realized with somewhat greater downstep on W2 than U/A sentences, but further inspection of the data does not reveal any systematicity attributable to a phonological contrast.

Of course, the results of this experiment do not by themselves demonstrate that Bergara lacks an accented/unaccented distinction. In principle, it could be the case that even though the experimental words are all accented in Bergara, the dialect has a class of unaccented words that we have failed to identify. However, from our knowledge of accentual patterns in Basque, this seems very unlikely to us.

2.2.3 Conclusions regarding the accented/unaccented distinction in western Basque dialects

Our data fall into three patterns: 1) Complete separation of tokens into the two hypothesized groups, indicating a phonological contrast between accented and unaccented words 2) Some degree of overlap, but with a subset of condition U/A tokens forming a separate group, also revealing a phonological contrast and 3) Substantial overlap between the two hypothesized groups. The first situation is found in the data for all NB speakers, except those from Larrabetzu. The second situation is found in the data for all SB and two Larrabetzu speakers. Finally, the third situation characterizes the Bergara (Western Gipuzkoan) data.

We conclude that the lexical accented/unaccented distinction is found both in NB and in SB varieties, although the contrast is more robust in NB, since in this dialectal area there are more unaccented words (in NB the distinction affects both inflected and uninflected words; in SB only words uninflected for number). If the existence of an accented/unaccented lexical distinction is used as a defining property for T-type accentual systems, both NB and SB would fall under this definition. On the other hand, the Western Gipuzkoan variety of Bergara appears to lack lexically unaccented words and, consequently, could not be defined as a T-type pitch-accent language using this criterion.

These findings are somewhat surprising since, in other respects, the accentual systems of Bergara and SB are rather similar. Although the existence of unaccented words had been previously claimed for the SB variety of Zeberio and not explicitly for any Western Gipuzkoan varieties, the assumption until now has been that both dialectal areas possessed similar accentual systems (see Hualde, 1993b).

3. Initial rise

Besides the lexical accented/unaccented contrast, another distinctive trait which the NB Basque prosodic system has in common with Japanese is a pitch rise at the beginning of the phrase, inducing a preaccentual high-pitch plateau. This phenomenon, which results in high-pitched stretches of speech, has been noticed for several local dialects of this area in Azkue (1931–32), Basterrechea (1974–75), Rotaetxe (1978a,b), Hualde (1991), and more recent work, and different interpretations for it have been proposed. On the other hand, this pitch pattern has not been noted for SB varieties, although the facts have not been systematically studied for these dialects.

Schematically we may characterize the pattern that has been described as typical of some NB varieties as a rise towards the beginning of the phrase continued by a high plateau up to the accented syllable and followed by a fall, as in (4a). If we focus on the realization of the syllables up to the accented syllable, we may contrast this contour with another pattern, typical of Spanish rising accents (see Hualde, 2000b, and references therein), where the tone remains low up to the pretonic (i.e. the syllable immediately preceding the accented one) and the rise starts at the beginning of the tonic (or accented) syllable, as in (4b):

(4) a. o o o o ó   b. o o o o ó

As a first approximation to the characterization of a language or dialect in this respect, we may compare the difference in Hz from the first syllable to the highest point up to the pretonic with the difference between the pretonic and the tonic. The first quantity will be larger than the second in languages with the pattern in (4a) and the opposite will be true in languages with the pattern in (4b).

For 13 of our Bizkaian speakers, we measured F0 values at mid points in all syllables preceding the accented one and at the peak on the accented syllable in a number of utterances where the preverbal constituent contains a single accent. We calculated both the difference in Hz between the initial syllable and the highest point in the preaccentual portion, up to and excluding the accented or tonic syllable, and the difference in Hz between the pretonic and the tonic. Additionally, we calculated the difference between tonic and posttonic syllables.

The sentences used for this purpose are a subset of those listed in the appendix as sentences 3, 5 and 11−15, of which three repetitions per speaker were obtained. Although all subjects recorded this complete list, the usefulness of particular sentences depends on the patterns of accent placement and vowel deletion in each dialect. For this reason the numbers of tokens analyzed differs from subject to subject (e.g. sentence 3 and 5 have not been used for those SB speakers who have an accent on the first word of these sentences, and sentences 14 and 15 have not been used for dialects with final accent in these examples). (A few examples have also been eliminated because of difficulties in taking the relevant measurements).

3.1 Results

The mean F0 values for all 13 speakers are summarized in the histograms in Figure 9, where preH-1st represents the mean difference between the initial syllable and the highest point up to the pretonic syllable, and pret-T is the mean difference between pretonic and the tonic. An initial rise will be revealed by a higher value for the first difference.

3.1.1 Northern Bizkaian Leaving aside Larrabetzu 1 for the moment, for all NB subjects (Arteaga, Bermeo, Gatika, Lekeitio-1, Lekeitio-2, Markina, Ondarroa-1 and Ondarroa-2) the difference between the initial syllable and the pretonic is much greater than that between the pretonic and the tonic. In fact, for most of these speakers there is hardly any rise from the pretonic to the tonic. For Bermeo, Lekeitio-1, Lekeitio-2, Ondarroa-1 and Ondarroa-2 the rise between the pretonic and the tonic is on average just 1 or 2 Hz, and sometimes there is a small decline (because the peak is reached towards the end of the pretonic). The data from the Larrabetzu speaker are again different from the others, with approximately equal F0 increases in both preH-1st and pret-T.

In the NB data, there is a rise early in the phrase, although there appear to be some variation in its shape. Whereas for some speakers there is a slow rise up to the accented syllable, for other speakers, in phrases with three or more syllables preceding the accented syllable, the general pattern shows a high point towards the beginning of the phrase and a very flat contour slowly declining from that point on. The latter pattern is illustrated in Figure 10.

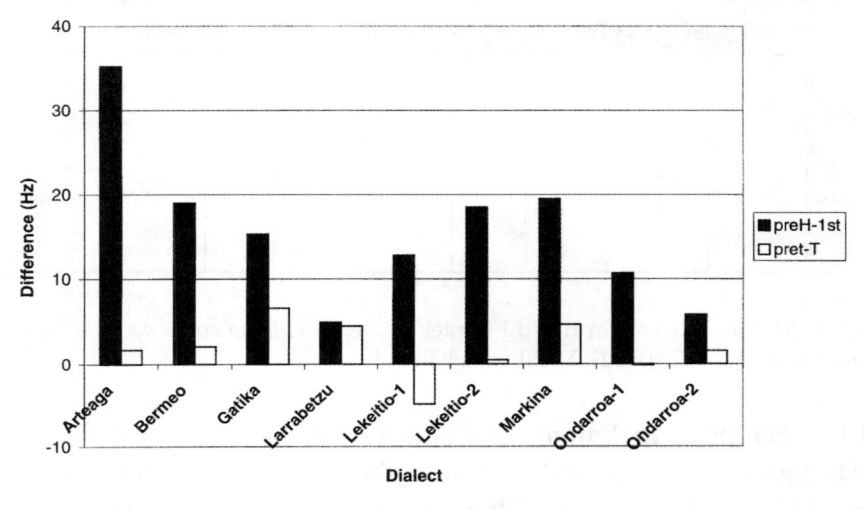

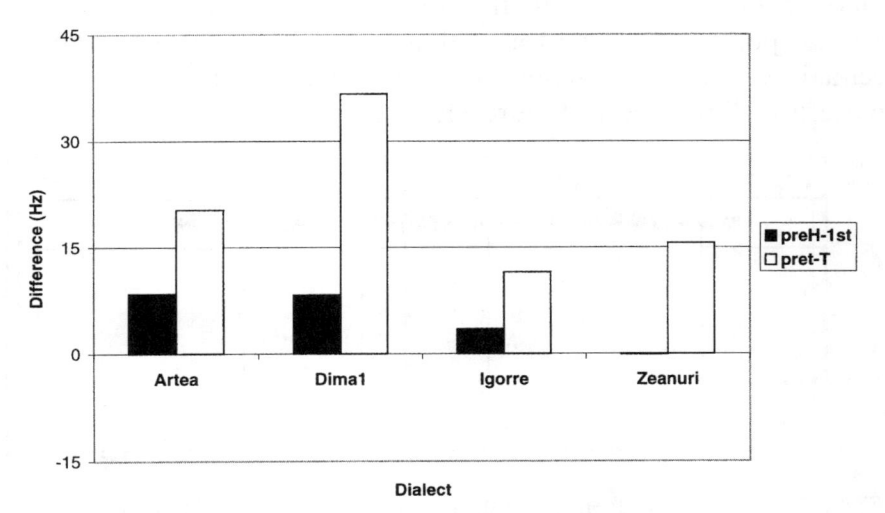

Figure 9: Initial rise for NB (upper panel) and SB speakers (lower panel), shown by comparing the difference in f_0 between the first syllable and the highest point in the portion up to but not including the tonic syllable on the one hand (black bars) and that between the tonic syllable and the immediately preceding syllable on the other (white bars). preH-1st = mean difference between the initial syllable and the highest point up to and including the pretonic syllable, pret-T = mean difference between pretonic and the tonic syllable. N = 24 for Markina, Ondarroa-1 and Ondarroa-2, 21 for Zeanuri, and 18 for all other speakers.

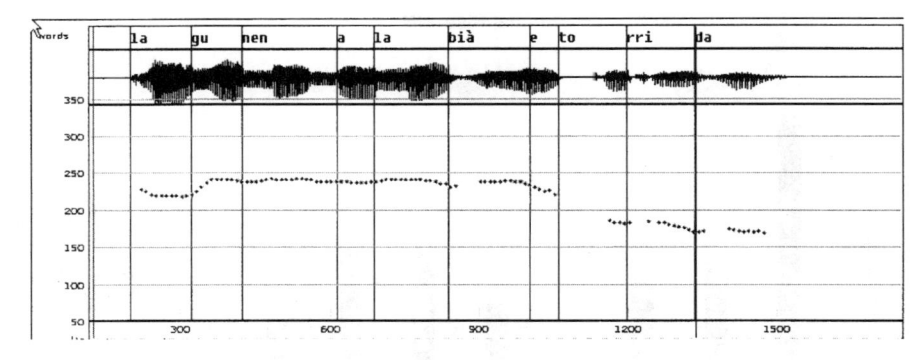

Figure 10: Speech wave form and F0 track of *lagunen alabiá etorri da* 'the friend's (sg) daughter has arrived'. Speaker Lekeitio-1.

3.1.2. Southern Bizkaian The data for the four SB speakers (Artea, Igorre, Dima-1 and Zeanuri) show a very different pattern from that shown by the NB speakers, with a greater rise taking place from the pretonic to the tonic than from the initial to the highest point before the tonic; that is, for these speakers the accented syllable is normally characterized by a salient rise.[9] This pattern is illustrated in Figure 11.

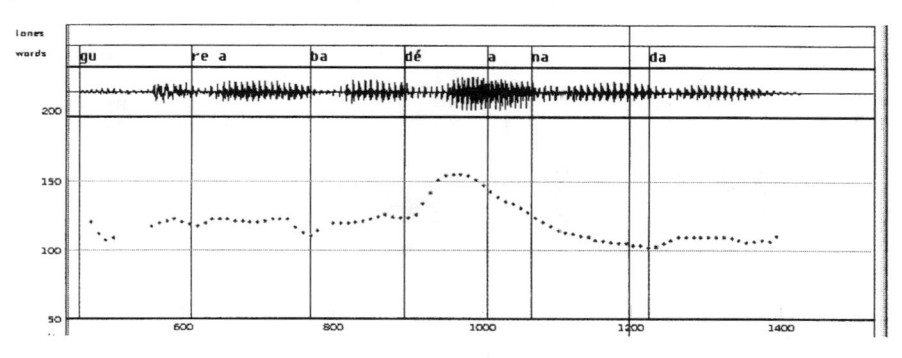

Figure 11: Speech wave form and F0 track of *gure abadéana da* 'it is the one of our priest'. Speaker Dima-1.

3.2 Discussion

In NB the presence of a tone rise is not an indication of accentual prominence in that syllable; rather it only indicates an initial phrase boundary. What cues accentual prominence is the presence of a fall immediately after the peak, on the next syllable (or, in the case of word-final accents, on the same syllable).

The initial rise and high plateau from the second syllable to the accented syllable can be analyzed as deriving from an initial tonal boundary specification %LH$^-$. This is in contrast with the situation in Spanish, where a rise from a valley near the beginning of the syllable, that is, a LH contour, is the tonal configuration most typically associated with accented syllables, at least in prenuclear accents. Typically the peak is reached on the posttonic in non-final words (Navarro Tomás, 1945: 49; Mota, 1995, 1997; Garrido et al., 1993; Llisterri et al., 1995; Prieto et al., 1995; Sosa, 1999; Face, 2000; Nibert, 2000).

NB Basque and Castilian Spanish thus differ radically in the use of rises from valleys and falls from peaks to convey lexical prominence. In Spanish the pitch rises from a valley on the accented syllable and may or may not fall on the posttonic, depending on pragmatic factors and phrasal structure. In Basque, the pitch rises from a valley at the beginning of the phrase and falls right after the accented syllable. In presenting non-accentual rises at the beginnings of phrases, the NB prosodic system is incompatible with that of Spanish. It is reasonable to assume that SB has lost this feature under the influence of Spanish.

In principle, there would be two ways to solve this conflict in the interpretation of rises in a situation of language contact where Spanish is the socially dominant language: either the non-accentual initial rise is eliminated, or it is reinterpreted as indicating accentual prominence on the second syllable. Both paths appear to have been taken in different areas. The reinterpretation of the initial rise as accentual prominence has resulted in systems with accent on the second syllable, (5a).[10] The SB dialects that have been examined here, on the other hand, have eliminated the rise on the second syllable without changing the position of the accent. This may have been a gradual process, in which we can distinguish two stages. At first, there may have been a slow rise with interpolation from a low at the beginning of the word or phrase to the accented syllable. Next, the pitch would be kept low up to the beginning of the accented syllable, as in Spanish, (5b).[11]

(5) a. Initial rise re-interpreted as accent

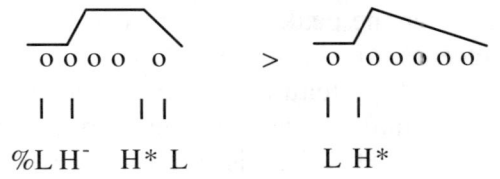

```
  ___                  ___
 /   \                /   \
o o o o  o    >    o  o o o o o
| |   | |              | |
%L H⁻  H* L            L H*
```

b. Deletion of H-

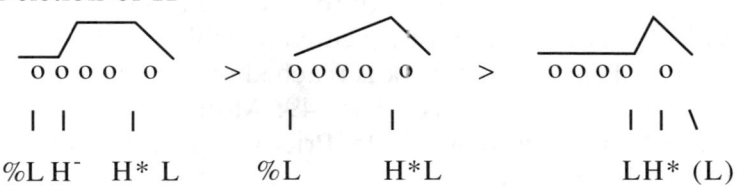

```
  ___                ___                ___
 /   \              /   \              /   \
o o o o  o   >   o o o o  o   >   o o o o  o
| |    |         |      |              | | \
%L H⁻  H* L      %L     H*L            LH* (L)
```

Here we have not been concerned with the evolution in (5a), which has radical effects on the accentual system but is rather straightforward from the typological point of view adopted in this paper. Those dialects that have undergone this change have consequently lost the accented/unaccented distinction (i.e. all words now have lexical accent).

The evolution in (5b), on the other hand, has resulted in systems that are more difficult to classify. Impressionistically, the SB dialect "sounds" much more like Spanish than the NB dialects. It is clear that an important factor that contributes to this auditory impression is the fact that SB Basque lacks the high-toned preaccentual plateaux of NB. Instead, as in Spanish, the pitch remains low up to the beginning of the accented syllable.

4. Summary

The two accentual properties that we have studied allow us to recognize three accentual systems, as shown in Table 2.

Table 2: Three accentual systems in Basque

	NB	SB	WG
Unaccented words	Yes	Yes	No
Initial rise	Yes	No	No

When these properties are taken into consideration we see that whereas NB coincides with Tokyo Japanese, WG does not differ from Spanish. SB occupies an intermediate situation, since it possesses lexically unaccented content words (although fewer than NB) but lacks the preaccentual high plateau that we find in NB and Japanese.

Beckman (1986) proposes that an important feature that distinguishes pitch-accent languages of the Japanese type ('non-stress-accent languages' in her terminology) from stress-accent languages is that accentual prominence is conveyed primarily or even exclusively by means of pitch, whereas in stress languages other features such as duration and intensity play a much more important role.

In a study reported in Hualde, Smiljanić & Cole (2000) the duration of corresponding accented and unaccented syllables was measured in minimal or near-minimal pairs of sentences. The analysis revealed that accented and unaccented syllables had very similar durational values. A summary of the findings is offered in Table 3.

Table 3: Mean durations (ms) and standard deviations in accented and unaccented syllables for two speakers of NB Basque

	IS, Markina		MB, Bermeo	
	unaccented	accented	unaccented	accented
Mean(sd)	79.19 (16.47)	84.78 (15.81)	87.95 (22.03)	85.39 (20.95)
N	69	69	71	75

An ANOVA showed that accent did not significantly affect syllable duration for one of the two subjects, Subject 2, MB [$F(1,116) = 0.037$, $p = 0.848$], but did for the other speaker, Subject 1, IS [$F(1,110) = 17.014$, $p < 0.0001$]. However, although the issue requires further investigation, the differences are so small even for Subject 1 that we can tentatively conclude that duration does not play a role in the perception of the NB accent.

These results for NB are in contrast with those reported by Etxebarria (1991) for the SB dialect of Zeberio. Etxebarria (1991: 71) finds a consistent difference in the duration of accented and unaccented vowels in the dialect of Zeberio for all five vowel phonemes. The average difference that he reports is about 20 ms, based on measurements of 105 accented and 186 unaccented vowels).

In future work, we intend to determine to what extent the accentual role of duration correlates with the other T-type properties discussed in this paper in Western Basque varieties. At this stage in our research it appears at least likely that this feature will also present its own isogloss, different from the other two that we have examined here.

7. Basque and other pitch-accent languages

We draw two major conclusions for the typology of accentual systems. First of all, the striking coincidence between some Basque varieties (NB) and Tokyo Japanese in a number of important prosodic properties suggests that this set of common properties can be used to characterize a prosodic prototype: T-type pitch-accent. By prosodic prototype we understand a combination of prosodic features that may be particularly stable and be likely to develop independently.[12] On the other hand, we have shown that the four properties that we have used to define this prosodic type are to some degree mutually independent. The existence in the Basque territory of varieties presenting intermediate situations between T-type pitch-accent and Spanish-like stress shows that it is not fruitful to impose a clear-cut distinction between stress-accent languages and pitch-accent languages. Rather, a typology in terms of focal types (i.e. cross-linguistically preferred combinations of prosodic features) agrees better with the facts.

In the case of other European pitch-accent languages the situation might be rather different. Languages like Swedish (Bruce, 1999), some Dutch and German dialects (Gussenhoven & van der Vliet, 1999), and Serbo-Croatian appear to be stress-accent languages (where all content words have word stress on a particular syllable) with an added lexical contrast in terms of pitch configurations or alignment of accentual peaks. That is, there is a single added feature that separates these systems from stress languages.

For instance, Serbo-Croatian has a lexical contrast between words with an early accentual peak and words with a late accentual peak (in the posttonic), limited to words stressed on the initial syllable (Smiljanić & Hualde, 2000). Slovenian also appears to have a very similar early vs. late peak lexical contrast (Srebot-Rejec, 1988). The loss of this contrast results in more typical stress-accent languages, without necessarily any intermediate situations, as has happened in Swedish dialects spoken in Finland and Texas (see Salmons, 1992: 39) and also in some Serbo-Croatian and Slovenian dialects.

Acknowledgements

We are very grateful to E. Wayles Browne, Jennifer Cole, Ken de Jong, Khalil Iskarous and Tomas Riad for comments on earlier versions of this paper and help of various kinds.

Notes

1 For a different approach to prosodic prototypes and typology, see Hyman (forthcoming).
2 In the Markina-Ondarroa area, the derived accent falls on the penultimate of the phrase, instead of falling on the last syllable (see Hualde, 2000a, for the diachronic shift of the accent from the final to the penultimate and related changes). In some varieties of this area this produces neutralization between accented and lexically unaccented words in phrase-final position.
3 The accented class also includes other words that are more difficult to classify, although, from a historical point of view, most of the time it is possible to explain why a given word bears a lexical accent (cf. Hualde, 1993a).
4 The actual texts present some differences for each dialect tested. In the case of Bergara, the word *argala* 'skinny' in sentences (4) and (5), which is not used in this dialect, was replaced by *zabala* 'wide'. One speaker from Artea used *makarra* instead of *argala*.
5 For the pilot study, which involved two subjects, the test sentences were written each on an index card in the corresponding dialect (Bermeo or Markina) and in a Spanish translation. The index cards were presented in an arbitrary order and were reshuffled between repetitions. For the dialectal survey, including 21 speakers, given our insufficient prior knowledge of all the local dialects involved, subjects were given the sentences only in Spanish and were asked to translate them orally into their local Basque dialect. The 15 sentences in the appendix were recorded in the order given (of which the first 10 were

used for this experiment) and the list was repeated three times. This mode of presentation would tend to emphasize the phonological contrast between contrasting pairs. About a month later, 3 speakers (one for each major dialectal area) were retested. This time, the test sentences were written on separate index cards, which were reshuffled between repetitions and interspersed with an equal number of distractor sentences. Speakers were told not to put special emphasis on any word. The results were substantially the same under both test conditions, as can be seen in the graphs.

6 Regarding the unaccented character of W1 in sentence 3 (*Fidelen alabéa ikusi dot* 'I have seen Fidel's daughter') for some of the speakers (consistently for Zeanuri and for Dima-1 in the second test and in two of three repetitions for Dima2) it would appear that optionally words can be unaccented not only if they are uninflected but also if they are case-marked (at least in certain grammatical cases, including the genitive) as long as they do not carry number features. Tokens with no downstep also include one condition A/A token: one repetition of sentence 4 for the Zeanuri speaker. This is a completely isolated token, which could be attributed perhaps to a performance error.

7 For the town of Larrabetzu three subjects were chosen (as opposed to one or two for other NB towns) precisely because casual observation of the dialect led us to suspect that it might be prosodically different from other dialects in the NB area.

8 The remaining tokens correspond to one repetition of sentence 7 for each speaker and one repetition of sentence 1 for Larrabetzu-3.

9 For two of these speakers (Igorre, Zeanuri), however, a closer examination of the F0 patterns shows that the rise sometimes includes both the tonic and the pretonic.

10 This evolution is considered in some detail in Hualde (to appear). Jansen (1992) analyzes the intonational system of a dialect with post-initial accent, that of Elorrio.

11 The pattern found in dialects like Gatika in the western part of the NB area, where the pitch steadily rises up to the accented syllable, would represent a point in this evolution.

12 Another language that may belong in this group is Central Carrier (Athapaskan), as described in Pike (1986).

References

Azkue, R. M. de
 1931–32 Del acento tónico vasco en algunos de sus dialectos. *Euskera*, **4**, 282–318 & **6**, 3–50.
Basterrechea, José
 1974–75 Estudios sobre entonación vasca según el habla de Guernica. *Fontes Linguae Vasconum*, **18**, 353–393 & **21**, 289–338.

Beckman, M.
1986 *Stress and Non-Stress accent*. Dordrecht: Foris.
Beckman, M. & Pierrehumbert, J.
1986 Intonational structure in Japanese and English. *Phonology Yearbook*, **3**, 255–309.
Bruce, G.
1999 Scandinavian languages. In H. van der Hulst, (ed.), *Word Prosodic Systems in the Languages of Europe*, (pp. 605–633). Berlin: Mouton de Gruyter.
Elordieta, G.
1997 Accent, tone and intonation in Lekeitio Basque. In Fernando Martínez-Gil & Alfonso Morales-Front (eds.), *Issues in the Phonology and Morphology of the Major Iberian Languages*. (pp. 3–78). Washington, DC: Georgetown Univ. Press.
Elordieta, G.
1998 Intonation in a pitch-accent variety of Basque. *Anuario del Seminario de Filología Vasca Julio de Urquijo*, **32**, 511–569.
Etxebarria Manuel, J.
1991 *Zeberio haraneko euskararen azterketa etno-linguistikoa*. Bilbao: I.K.A.
Face, T.
2000 A phonological analysis of rising pitch-accents in Castilian Spanish. Peper presented at *LSRL*, **30**, Gainsville, Florida, February 2000.
Gaminde, I.
1994 Urduliz eta Gatikako azentu ereduez. *Uztaro*, **11**, 55–88 & **12**, 88–110.
Gaminde, I.
1998 *Euskaldunen azentuak*. Bilbao: Labayru Ikastegia.
Garrido, J. M., Llisterri, J., de la Mota, C. & Riós, A.
1993 Prosodic differences in reading style: isolated vs. contextualized sentences. *Eurospeech*, **93**, 573–576.
Gussenhoven, C. & van der Vliet, P.
1999 The phonology of tone and intonation in the Dutch dialect of Venlo. *Journal of Linguistics*, **35**, 99–135.
Hualde, J. I.
1991 *Basque Phonology*. London: Routledge.
Hualde, José I.
1992 Notas sobre el sistema acentual de Zeberio. *Anuario del Seminario de Filología Vasca Julio de Urquijo*, **27**, 767–776.
Hualde, J. I.
1993 a On the historical origin of Basque accentuation. *Diachronica*, **10**, 13–50.
Hualde, J. I.
1993 b Observaciones acerca de los sistemas acentuales de la zona occidental de Gipuzkoa. *Anuario del Seminario de Filología Vasca Julio de Urquijo*, **27**, 241–263.

Hualde, J. I.
1999 a   Basque accentuation. In H. van der Hulst (ed.), *Word prosodic systems in the languages of Europe*, (pp. 947−993). Berlin: Mouton de Gruyter.

Hualde, J. I.
1999 b   Patterns of correspondence in the adaptation of Spanish borrowings in Basque. In *Proceedings of the 25th Annual Meeting of the Berkeley Linguistics Society. General Session and Parasession on loan word phenomena*, (pp. 348−358). Berkeley, CA: BLS.

Hualde, J. I.
2000 a   On system-driven sound change: Accent shift in Markina Basque. *Lingua*, **110**, 99−129.

Hualde, J. I.
2000 b   Intonation in Spanish and the other Ibero-Romance languages: status questionis. In C. Wiltshire & J. Camps (eds.), *Romance phonology and variation. Selected papers from the 30th Linguistic Symposium on Romance Languages, Gainesville, Florida, February 2000*. To appear.

Hualde, J. I.
to appear   From phrase-final to post-initial accent in western Basque. In Fikkert, Paula & Haike Jacobs, eds., *Development in prosodic systems*. Berlin: Mouton de Gruyter.

Hualde, J. I. & Bilbao, X.
1993   The prosodic system of the Basque dialect of Getxo: a metrical analysis. *Linguistics*, **31**, 59−85.

Hualde, J. I., Elordieta, G. & Elordieta, A.
1994   The Basque dialect of Lekeitio. Bilbao & Donostia/San Sebastián: Univ. del País Vasco & Supplements of *Anuario del Seminario de Filología Vasca Julio de Urquijo*.

Hualde, J., Smiljanić, R. & Cole, J.
2000   On the accented/unaccented distinction in Western Basque and the typology of accentual systems. *Berkeley Linguistics Society* 26. To appear.

Hulst, H. van der & Smith, N.
1988   The variety of pitch accent systems: Introduction. In Harry van der Hulst & N. Smith (eds.), *Autosegmental Studies on Pitch Accent*, **ix−xxiv**. Dordrecht: Foris.

Hyman, L.
forthcoming   Tone systems. In M. Haspelmath, E. König, W. Oesterreicher & W. Raible (eds.), *Language Typology and Language Universals: An International Handbook*, 2 vols. Berlin & New York: Walter de Gruyter.

Jansen, W.
1992   Acento y entonación en Elorrio. *Anuario del Seminario de Filología Vasca Julio de Urquijo*, **26**, 391−440.

Jun S.-A. & Elordieta, G.
1997   Intonational structure of Lekeitio Basque. In A. Botinis, G. Kouroupetroglou & G. Carayiannis (eds.), *Intonation: Theory, models and applications. Proc. ESCA Workshop*, 193–196.

Llisterri, J., Marín, R., Mota, C. de la & Ríos, A.
1995   Factors affecting F0 peak displacement in Spanish. *ESCA, Eurospeech'95. 4th Conference on Speech Communication and Technology*, 2061–2064.

Mota, C. de la
1995   *La representación gramatical de la información nueva en el discurso.* PhD dissertation, Univ. Autònoma de Barcelona.

Mota, C. de la
1997   Prosody of sentences with contrastive new information in Spanish. *ESCA Worskshop on intonation: Theory, models and applications*, 75–78.

Navarro Tomás, T.
1944   *Manual de entonación española.* New York: Hispanic Institute of the United States.

Nibert, H.
2000   *Phonetic and phonological evidence for intermediate phrasing in Spanish intonation.* PhD dissertation, Univ. of Illinois at Urbana-Champaign.

Pierrehumbert, J.
1980   *The phonetics and phonology of English intonation.* PhD dissertation, MIT.

Pierrehumbert, J. & Beckman, M. E.
1988   *Japanese Tone Structure.* Cambridge, Mass.: MIT Press.

Pike, E.
1986   Tone contrasts in Central Carrier (Athapaskan). *International Journal of American Linguistics*, **52**, 411–418.

Poser, W.
1984   *The phonetics and phonology of tone and intonation in Japanese.* PhD dissertation, MIT.

Prieto, P., Santen, J. van & Hirschberg, J.
1995   Tonal alignment patterns in Spanish. *Journal of Phonetics*, **23**, 429–451.

Srebot-Rejec, T.
1988   *Word accent and vowel duration in Standard Slovene: An acoustic and linguistic investigation.* München: Otto Sagner.

Quilis, A.
1993   *Tratado de fonología y fonética españolas.* Madrid: Gredos.

Rotaetxe, K.
1978a   L'accent basque: observations et hypothèses. *La Linguistique*, **14**, 55–77.

Rotaetxe, K.
1978 b   *Estudio estructural del euskara de Ondárroa*. Durango: L. Zugaza.
Salmons, J.
1992   *Accentual change and language contact*. Stanford: Stanford University Press.
Smiljanić, R. & Hualde, J. I.
2000   Lexical and pragmatic functions of tonal alignment in two Serbo-Croatian dialects. *Chicago Linguistic Society*, **36**. To appear.
Sosa, J. M.
1999   *La entonación del español*. Madrid: Cátedra.

Appendix

Experimental materials. Gernika area version of sentences

1. lagunen alabiè etorri de — 'our friend's (sg) daughter has arrived'
2. lagúnen alabiè etorri de — 'our friends' (pl) daughter has arrived'
3. Fidelen alabiè ikusi dot — 'I have seen Fidel's daughter'
4. Fidélan alabiè ikusi dot — 'I have seen Fidela's daughter'
5. alaba argalà etorri de — 'the skinny daughter has arrived'
6. amúma argalà etorri de — 'the skinny grandmother has arrived'
7. lagunen amúma ikusi dot — 'I have seen the grandmother of the friend'
8. lagúnen amúma ikusi dot — 'I have seen the grandmother of the friends'
9. abadien líbrue ikusi dot — 'I have seen the book of the priest'
10. abádien líbrue ikusi dot — 'I have seen the book of the priests'
11. lagunerì emon dotzat — 'I have given it to the friend'
12. gure lagunerì emon dotzat — 'I have given it to our friend'
13. gure lagunenarì emon dotzat — 'I have given it to the one of our friend'
14. gure abadiena dà — 'it is the one of our priest'
15. gure alabiena dà — 'it is the one of our daughter'

Condition U/A: 1, 3, 5, 7, 9
Condition A/A: 2, 4, 6, 8, 10

Lexically contrastive stress accent and lexical tone in Ma'ya

Bert Remijsen

Abstract

Until now, no language has been demonstrated to feature both lexically contrastive stress accent and lexical tone as independent factors in its word-prosodic system. This papers argues that such an analysis is appropriate for the Austronesian language Ma'ya. This analysis is supported by a phonological analysis of the word prosodic system, and by an acoustic analysis of the hypothesized stress accent feature.

1. Introduction

The Austronesian language Ma'ya features a combined word prosodic system, with both lexically contrastive stress accent and lexical tone. But since terms like 'tone', 'stress' and 'accent' are used with a variety of meanings, I will first make clear how they are used in this chapter (Section 1.1). The discussion then moves on to combinations of word prosodic features (Section 1.2), the actual focus of this paper.

1.1 A typology of word-prosodic features: Beckman, 1986

In a lexical tone system, fundamental frequency marks a paradigmatic contrast. This means that one toneme contrasts with other tonemes that could have been marked on the same domain – most often the syllable. Iau, for example, is an 8-toneme language used in New Guinea (Bateman, 1990). A Low level tone on *be* 'fire' encodes a lexical contrast with other tones that could have been marked on the same syllable (see Table 1). Because tone contrasts

Table 1: A classification of word prosodic features, after Beckman (1986). Iau example from Bateman (1990: 35); Una example from Donohue (1997: 367).

Lexical tone: paradigmatic contrast (e.g. Iau)		Accent: syntagmatic contrast			
		Non-stress accent (e.g. Una)		Stress accent (e.g. English)	
Tone	Example	Accent	Example	Accent	Example
Low level	be 'fire'	penult	'bita 'truly'	penult	'pervert
High rise	be 'snake'	final	bi'ta 'frogs'	final	per'vert
Low rise	be 'path'	ante-penult	'kʉnkalya 'joint'		
Mid fall	be 'flower'	penult	kʉn'kalya 'pimple'		
Encoding: f_0				Encoding: parameters other than f_0	

are paradigmatic, tone languages can – and often do – feature more than two tonemes.

Lexical accent systems are structurally different from lexical tone systems, since for accent systems, prosodic parameters mark a syntagmatic contrast within the word domain, rather than a paradigmatic one. This means that lexically accented syllables stand out relative to unaccented syllables to their left and/or to their right. The examples in Table 1 from the Una language of New Guinea and English, both accent systems, illustrate this point. The distinction between lexical tone and lexical accent systems as it is made here, following Beckman (1986), is based entirely on the structure of the prosodic contrast (paradigmatic vs. syntagmatic, respectively). As for the phonetic marking of the contrast, tone is encoded by a specific acoustic correlate, i.e. fundamental frequency (f_0). For accent systems, on the other hand, we have to make a further distinction between pitch- or non-stress accent systems, where the syntagmatic contrast in prominence is encoded by f_0, and stress accent systems, where it is encoded by other prosodic parameters, such as duration, vowel quality and spectral balance.

In non-stress accent languages, it is possible for words with a lexical accent to contrast with unaccented words. In Una, this contrast is limited to monosyllabic words – e.g. the minimal pair *kál* (with high f_0) 'tree species' vs. *kal* (without high f_0) 'marsupial species' (Donohue, 1997: 367). Likewise, Japanese, a well-known non-stress accent language, features unaccented words that can be minimally contrastive with accented words, and here polysyllabic words too can be unaccented: e.g. *'kaki* 'oyster' vs. *ka'ki* 'fence' vs. *kaki* 'persimmon' (McCawley, 1978: 114). However, even when we take into account the possibility of a contrast between unaccented and accented words, non-stress accent systems are distinct from tone systems. In the latter, the prosodic contrast is too complex to be analyzed in terms of (the presence/absence of) a syntagmatically variable prominence feature. Also, tonal systems with more than two contrasting elements preclude a non-stress accent analysis, because accent is by definition a binary feature.

1.2 Combined word-prosodic systems

Can languages combine two of these word-prosodic contrasts, as independent factors? I.e., can a language feature stress accent and also non-stress accent, or both tone and stress accent or non-stress accent? The combination of tone and non-stress accent is unlikely, because these two features are encoded by the same prosodic parameter, namely f_0. Instead of languages with both tone and non-stress accent as independent factors, we find word-prosodic systems that seem hard to classify as either type, with a lexical tone contrast that is syntagmatically constrained (McCawley, 1978; van der Hulst & Smith, 1988; Donohue, 1997).

Combinations of stress accent and non-stress accent are more likely, as are combinations of tone and stress accent. In such combined systems, the prosodic features differ in their phonetic encoding. The creole language Papiamentu most probably features both stress accent and non-stress accent. Papiamentu features hundreds of disyllabic minimal pairs distinguished by a Low-High vs. High-Low tone contrast, and many disyllabic verbs, with the

Low-High pattern and penultimate stress, derive the participle by accent shift to the final syllable (Römer, 1991; Kouwenberg & Murray, 1994).

As for the combination of tone and stress accent, languages like Swedish (Bruce, 1977) and some Limburg dialects of Dutch (Gussenhoven & Bruce, 1998) feature a lexical tone contrast that is limited to syllables carrying a stress accent. Obviously, lexical tone and stress accent are not independent factors in these languages: a syllable can only be marked with one of the lexical tones if it has a stress accent. As far as I know, however, no language has been demonstrated to feature stress accent and lexical tone as independent factors in its word prosodic system.[1] In a way this is surprising, because stress accent and tone differ both structurally and in terms of their encoding, so that the risk of ambiguity is low for this particular combination. However, there would still be a potential source of ambiguity in a language that features stress accent and tone as independent factors. In a simple stress accent language (i.e., one without lexical tone or non-stress accent), focus is typically marked intonationally, i.e., by paradigmatic f_0-contrasts associated with the lexically accented syllable of the word in focus. In a tone system, on the other hand, paradigmatic f_0-contrasts have a lexical rather than a pragmatic meaning. Instead, a tone language like Chinese, for example, marks focus by executing the lexical tone patterns of focused constituents with greater f_0-excursion (Xu & Wang, 1997). So here we find a conflict between stress accent and tone: while stress accent involves f_0 patterns with pragmatic meaning, tone does not. If there exists a language with both stress accent and lexical tone as independent factors in its word prosodic system, it seems likely that the lexical tone feature would preclude intonational f_0-contrast, just like it does in a simple tone language.

In this chapter, I argue that the Austronesian language Ma'ya features a word-prosodic system with both stress accent and tone as independent factors: it has a three-way lexical tone contrast, and lexically contrastive stress accent. This hypothesis is supported by a phonological study of Ma'ya word prosody (Section 2), and a phonetic investigation into the acoustic properties of the hypothesized stress accent feature (Section 3).

1.3 Ma'ya

Ma'ya is an Austronesian[2] language. It is spoken in the Raja Ampat archipelago, off the West Coast of New Guinea, in Indonesia's Papua Barat province. Ma'ya-speaking villages are spread out all over the archipelago, and dialectal variation is considerable (Remijsen, 2001, in press). On the basis of geographical spreading, we can distinguish the variants spoken on the three big islands Salawati, Misool and Waigeo. Anthropological research by van der Leeden (1993 and other references there) indicates that the Ma'ya people have their origins on Waigeo, and spread southwards to Salawati and Misool. Our knowledge of Waigeo and Misool Ma'ya is limited to wordlists. No published data are available on any of the other languages of the Raja Ampat archipelago – we don't even know how many there are (Remijsen, 2001).

I estimate the current number of native speakers of the Salawati dialect of Ma'ya to lie between 500 and 1000, and the total number of Ma'ya-speakers between 4000 and 5000. Because of Indonesia's national language policy, and because of the presence of migrants from other part of Indonesia, language use in Ma'ya villages is shifting towards Standard Indonesian and the local Malay dialect. This is clearest among children and young adults. The situation is worst on Waigeo and best on Misool, where the presence of a few large villages guarantees continuity for the next decades. Clearly, the Ma'ya language is threatened with extinction.

2. The phonology of Ma'ya word prosody

2.1 Van der Leeden's analysis

Van der Leeden (1993) is a descriptive study of Ma'ya phonology, based on the Salawati dialect as it is spoken in the village of Samate. The author distinguishes four tonemes, namely High /3/,

Rising /12/, Falling /21/, and Low /1/.[3] Examples on monosyllabic words are listed in Table 2.

Table 2: Tonemes in monosyllabic words.

Toneme	Examples					
High	'sa³ 'to climb'	'na³ 'sugar palm'	'ga³ 'wood'	'tol³ 'three'		
Falling	'sa²¹ 'one'	'na²¹ 'belly-3sg'	'ga²¹ 'cracked'	'lon²¹ 'heart-3pl'		'be²¹ 'to give'
Rising	'sa¹² 'to sweep'	'na¹² 'sky'	'lon²¹ 'ladder'	'tol¹² 'egg'	'de¹² 'k.o. kinship term'	'mat¹² 'to die'
Low (?)				'de 'still'	'mat 'person'	'be 'for'

Monosyllabic content words with a High, Rising, or Falling toneme are frequent, and there are many minimal pairs between them. Van der Leeden's list of minimal pairs involving toneme Low (1993: 66 – listed in Table 2), on the other hand, is exhaustive, and each of these minimal pairs is debatable.[4] As van der Leeden (1993: 66) himself admits, monosyllabic words offer little evidence for the distinction between Falling and Low tonemes.

Van der Leeden's (1993: 66) main argument for the Low toneme comes from a contrast between two disyllabic tone patterns, illustrated by the minimal pair between *ma²¹'na³* 'light of weight' and *ma¹'na³* 'grease'. Both of these patterns (/21−'3/ and /1−'3/) occur frequently, and in van der Leeden's analysis lexical contrast is maintained by the tonemes of the unaccented first syllables.

Most content word roots are either monosyllabic or disyllabic. The latter are marked by one out of a small set of prosodic patterns (i.e., combinations of tonemes and lexical accent), listed in Table 3. In polysyllabic content roots with more than two syllables, the last two syllables have the patterns in Table 3; all preceding syllables have the Low toneme.

Table 3: Word prosodic patterns in disyllabic words.

Word prosodic pattern		Examples		
/1−'12/	ga'nan^{12}	ta'mep^{12}	ka'tem^{12}
	'small'	'to spill out'	'one'
/1−'21/	ka'wat^{21}	ka'lun^{21}	sa'gul^{21}
	'root'	'feather'	'nose-3sg'
/1−'3/	ma'na^{3}	ta'la^{3}	ma'ya^{3}
	'grease'	'k.o. plant'	'the Ma'ya'
/21−'3/	ma^{21}'na^{3}	ta^{21}'la^{3}	wi^{21}'nim^{3}
	'light of weight'	'banana'	'to drink'

The regularly attested disyllabic word patterns are /1−'12/, /1−'21/, /1−'3/ and /21−'3/. We see that, in each pattern, at least one syllable has a non-Low tone. Apart from /'21−3/, the distribution of non-Low tonemes is limited to the final syllable of the root. Accent appears to be a redundant feature: in non-derived content words, it is invariably marked on the final syllable of the root, which also carries a non-Low toneme.

Both the High and the Rising tonemes can be replaced by the Falling toneme (see Table 4). This occurs in a number of lexical, morphological and syntactic processes. The nature of these processes varies widely: e.g. compound noun formation (4a), noun phrase formation (4b), and comparative formation (4e)). Van der Leeden (1993, 1997) analyzes this phenomenon as morphological tone. That is, toneme /21/, apart from being a lexical tone, can function as a suprafix, and the meanings encoded by this morpheme are collectively labeled, 'permanent relation' (van der Leeden, 1993: 79).

In all but one of the mono- and disyllabic patterns in Table 4, accented High and Rising tonemes are replaced by the Falling toneme. This replacement process actually decreases lexical distinctiveness by reducing lexical contrast, because both /21/ and /1−'21/ also occur in non-derived roots. The only exception to this replacement process is pattern /21−'3/ − already anomalous, as we saw above, because it has a non-Low tone on the penultimate syllable.

Table 4: The effect of morphological tone replacement on word prosodic patterns. Examples a) to d) from van der Leeden (1993: 80).

Morphological tone replacement	Word form before tone replacement	Example – word form under tone replacement
a) /12/ → /21/	'ga^{12} 'place'	'lap^{12} 'ga^{21}-o fire place 'fireplace'
b) /3/ → /21/	'sop^3 'to bathe'	'sop^{21} kalwa^{21} 'nat^3 bathe naked 'to bathe nakedly'
c) /1–'12/ → /1–'21/	ma'le^{12} 'evening'	ma'le^{21} fana evening past_time_marker 'yesterday evening'
d) /1–'3/ → /1–'21/	wa'gul^3 'to shave'	'nik 'syen^{12} te ya'gu^{21}lo pos.pron._1sg knife rel.pron. shave-1sg 'the knife with which I shave'
e) /21–'3/ → /'21–1/	ma^{21}'na$^{'3}$ 'light of weight'	'ma^{21}na 'nyet^3 light_of_weight comparative_ marker 'lighter of weight'

For this disyllabic pattern, the replacement process has a different outcome, the only case of its kind. Specifically, content words of the type /21–'3/ (with lexical accent on the root-final syllable) have /'21–1/, with accent on the penult, as a result of the tone replacement process. In summary, content words have lexical accent on the final syllable of the root. Penultimate accent only occurs when pattern /21–'3/ becomes /'21–1/, in an exception to the tone replacement process. The addition of suffixes to bare content word roots does not trigger a shift in the location of the lexical accent. This implies that accent is part of the lexical form of the word, rather than being determined in relation to the edge of the word domain.

In function words, on the other hand, accent is variable (van der Leeden, 1993: 57–59) – see examples in (1). Function words do not feature variation in tonal patterns: in van der Leeden

(1993), syllables of function words are marked with the Low toneme.

(1) 'ene   'kisa   'gimana
     'I'   'almost'   'over there'

2.2 An alternative analysis

Van der Leeden's analysis of Ma'ya word prosody, outlined above, has some features that are functional only in distinguishing one specific word prosodic pattern. In the tonal system, there is little evidence for the Low toneme /1/: there is not one unquestionable minimal pair involving the Low toneme in monosyllabic words. Van der Leeden's crucial argument for the Low toneme comes from the existence of disyllabic pattern /21−'3/, where toneme /21/ on the first syllable apparently contrasts with the /1/ in the first syllable of pattern /1−'3/ (see examples in Table 3). This pattern /21−'3/ is exceptional in three ways. First, it is the only non-derived pattern with a toneme other than /1/ in the penultimate syllable. If it were not for /21−'3/, we could limit paradigmatic tonal contrast to the final syllable of the root, rather than assuming that every syllable of each word is marked for tone.

Second, under the process of tone replacement discussed above, the final High /3/ is replaced by toneme /1/ rather than by toneme /21/, as is the case for the final-syllable tonemes in all other patterns (see Table 4e). This makes it the only word-prosodic pattern with the Low toneme in the final syllable of the root. Third, the result of this process is the only pattern for content roots involving accent on the penultimate. Everywhere else, accent in content words is marked on the final syllable of the root in van der Leeden's analysis.

Clearly, van der Leeden's treatment of pattern /21−'3/ − and its derived form /'21−1/ − has determined his analysis considerably: if it were not for this pattern, Ma'ya can be analyzed as a three-tone language, with tonal contrast limited to the final syllable of content roots. I will now demonstrate that such a less complex analysis is indeed possible, and show that the pattern that van der Leeden analyzes as /21−'3/ can be accounted for in a more insightful way. An interesting starting point for this alternative analysis is van der Leeden's comment on the contrast between /1−'3/ and /21−'3/:

(2)   /1−'3/ and /21−'3/ are the most suspicious of all toneme patterns. It took a long time before I became aware of, and was able to hear, the difference between them. Forms with the latter pattern differ from those with the first pattern because their initial syllable vowel becomes lengthened by the down-glide, which also lowers the pitch of toneme /3/ of their final syllable. [Van der Leeden, 1993: 71]

Apparently, duration is a major factor distinguishing the first syllables of pattern /1−'3/ and pattern /21−'3/ from one another. This perceived duration can not be interpreted as an indication of lexically contrastive vowel length, since there are no minimal vowel length pairs for monosyllabic content words. Instead, this perceived length could be an indication of stress accent. In the introduction, I argued that it is unlikely for a syllable carrying a stress accent in a tone language to be marked by an intonational f_0-feature, because this would be precluded by the presence of lexical tone. Consequently, we would expect duration to stand out most clearly as an accent cue, unaccompanied by intonational f_0. Therefore, I hypothesize that the contrast between /1−'3/ and /21−'3/ is in fact a contrast in accent location − i.e., /n−'3/ vs. /'n−3/.[5]

This hypothesis is supported by a reinterpretation of what van der Leeden analyzed as morphological tone replacement. In van der Leeden's analysis, this process involves a replacement of tonemes /12/ and /3/ by toneme /21/, with a morphological function. This analysis has a number of weak points. First, if /21/ is a tonal morpheme, it has a number of very different functions. Inspection of the examples in Table 4 reveals that the debatable tonal morpheme encodes comparative formation of adjectives (4e); compounding of nouns (4a), verbs (4b) and adverbs (4c), and instrumental marking on verbs (4d). These and other meanings are proposed in van der Leeden (1993, 1997). Secondly, we would expect a tonal morpheme to distinguish all words within a class; instead two tonemes are merged with a third, existing lexical toneme. Finally, there is the exception for the pattern van der Leeden's analyzes as /21−'3/: for this pattern, van der Leeden's analysis postulates accent shift to the first syllable, and an irregular tone change: /21−'3/ becomes /'21−1/.

Under the reanalysis proposed above, van der Leeden's /'21−3/ is reanalyzed as /'n−3/. There is thus no need for a rule that shifts accent to the first syllable, because accent is penultimate in the first place. In the reanalysis, the final syllable simply loses its toneme: /'n−3/ becomes /'n−n/. Importantly, this tone loss scenario is sufficient to account for all the phonological changes which van der Leeden attributed to morphological tone replacement. Both analyses of the phenomenon are contrasted in Table 5. In the alternative analysis, van der Leeden's toneme /21/ is reinterpreted as accent. Accent remains when tonemes /3/ and /12/ or lost. This implies that accent functions both paradigmatically and syntagmatically. On the one hand, it stands in paradigmatic contrast to tonemes /12/ and /3/, both in monosyllabic and in polysyllabic words. Also, it is the default paradigmatic element to which the /12/ and /3/ tonemes are reduced under tone loss. On the other hand, it functions as syntagmatically contrastive prominence (see Table 5). In fact, tone loss does not come unexpected in Ma'ya: lexical tone is already limited to one syllable per content root, and absent in function words. The tone loss phenomenon further restricts tones in higher constituents, such as compounds and phrases. The output of this phenomenon appears to be that no more than one lexical toneme remains within some phrase-level domain.

In summary, the prosodic phonology of Ma'ya becomes less complex under the above reanalysis, which crucially depends on exploiting lexically contrastive accent.

- The morphological tone proposed by van der Leeden was shown to be vulnerable both because of its representation and because of its unclear meaning. It was reanalyzed as a matter of domain- or phrase-sensitive tone loss. In contrast to van der Leeden's analysis, this tone loss process is without exception: in all cases, the toneme in the final syllable of the root is lost (see Table 5).

Table 5: Overview of word prosodic patterns, both according to van der Leeden's (1993) analysis and according to the reanalysis proposed here. Each prosodic pattern is illustrated by an example. For each prosodic pattern it is specified how it changes under the influence of what van der Leeden analyzes as morphological tone replacement and what is reanalyzed here as tone loss. Low tone is marked in all examples.

Analysis by van der Leeden (1993)			Reanalysis proposed here		
Example	Prosodic patterns	Morph. Tone replacement	Example	Prosodic patterns	Tone loss
'sa^{12} 'to sweep'	'12	'21	'sa^{12} 'to sweep'	'12	'n
'sa^{3} 'to climb'	'3	'21	'sa^{3} 'to climb'	'3	'n
'sa^{21} 'one'	'21	'21	'sa 'one'	'n	'n
'de^{1} 'still'	'1	not reported	de 'still'	n	n
ga^{1}'nan^{12} 'small'	1–'12	1–'21	ga'nan^{12} 'small'	n–'12	n–'n
ma^{1}'na^{3} 'grease'	1–'3	1–'21	ma'na^{3} 'grease'	n–'3	n–'n
ka^{1}'wat^{21} 'root'	1–'21	1–'21	ka'wat 'root'	n–'n	n–'n
ma^{21}'na^{3} 'light'	21–'3	'21–1	'mana^{3} 'light'	'n–3	'n–n

- The distinction between van der Leeden's /1–'3/ and /21–'3/ patterns is reanalyzed as a difference in accent (so /n–'3/ vs. /'n–3/). As a consequence, we no longer need to postulate the Low toneme /1/. Syllables with van der Leeden's Low toneme are unaccented and toneless in the reanalysis.
- Van der Leeden's Falling toneme (/21/) can be reinterpreted as accent /'n/ without tonemes /12/ or /3/. Accent functions as the unmarked paradigmatic tonal element, in contrast with tonemes /12/ and /3/. So, in agreement with the evidence from monosyllabic minimal pairs, Ma'ya has three paradigmatically contrastive tones. One of these, accent, is the default, to which the other two are reduced under tone loss.
- In van der Leeden's analysis every syllable of every word is marked for tone. Under the reanalysis, paradigmatic tonal con-

trast is limited to the final syllable of the root of content words. Pattern /21−'3/ − reanalyzed as /'n−3/ − was the only exception to this rule.

2.3 Conclusion

The reanalysis proposed above can be summarized as follows. Ma'ya features three paradigmatically contrastive tones. First, there are the High and the Rising tonemes (/3/ and /12/, respectively). The distribution of these tonemes is limited to the final syllable of content word roots. Second, accent functions as a third paradigmatically contrastive element, in contrast with the High and Rise tonemes. The following analysis in terms phonological features illustrates how accent can be the unmarked toneme. A word like *'ban* 'to seek shelter' is distinct from *'ban¹²* 'k.o. tree', because *'ban* has [+accent], while *'ban¹²* has [+accent] and [+Rise toneme].[6] Under tone loss, the High and the Rise tonemes are lost leaving accent. Accent is contrastive in polysyllabic words, either on the penultimate or on the final syllable.

As compared with van der Leeden (1993), this reanalysis requires two tonemes less, is more constrained with respect to the domain of lexical tone, is less redundant regarding accent, involves no accent shift rule, and does not postulate morphological tone. Consequently, the reanalysis is less complex: it analyzes the same data with less phonological primitives and postulates less tone marking in the lexicon. In the next section we will look at the phonetic support for the reanalysis.

3. A phonetic account of Ma'ya accent

3.1 Introduction

According to the reanalysis of Ma'ya word prosodic phonology presented above, Ma'ya features lexically contrastive stress accent. If this is true, then the prosodic contrast in minimal pairs such as

/'mana³/ 'light of weight' vs. /ma'na³/ 'grease' is marked by acoustic parameters such as duration, intensity and vowel quality. The hypothesis predicts that f_0, on the other hand, does not mark the accented syllables, because Ma'ya's lexical tone feature precludes intonational f_0-marking. A first support for these predictions comes from van der Leeden's statement – quoted in (2) – that the first syllable of /'mana³/ sounds longer than the corresponding syllable in /ma'na³/. Van der Leeden accounted for this difference by assuming that the longer syllable is marked by a falling contour tone, which would take more time to realize. However, the reanalysis proposed above additionally predicts that the accented second syllable of /ma'na³/ will be longer relative to the corresponding unaccented syllable in /'mana³/. In van der Leeden's analysis, on the other hand, these syllables are word-prosodically identical (both with accent and High tone), and as a consequence, his analysis predicts that there is no difference in duration. Clearly, the duration of the second syllable is an important criterion to evaluate which hypothesis is the better one. Additional support can come from other prosodic parameters. In well-studied stress accent systems such as English (Beckman, 1986; Sluijter, 1995) and Dutch (Sluijter & van Heuven, 1996), vowel quality and spectral balance are important correlates of accent, in combination with duration. Therefore, if duration, vowel quality and spectral balance single out the first syllable in words like /'mana³/ and the second syllable in words like /ma'na³/, this supports the hypothesis that this lexical contrast is one of stress accent. Section 3.3 reports the results of an acoustic analysis of accent parameters in minimal accent pairs. Before that the data collection and analysis procedures are presented.

3.2 Data collection and analysis[7]

3.2.1 Speakers

Recordings were made with eight native speakers of Ma'ya (5 male, 3 female). All speakers had spent most of their lives in the village of Samate on Salawati Island – the village where van der

Leeden collected most of the data for his analysis of Ma'ya phonology. They were between 20 and 70 years old, and all used Ma'ya daily. The informants were paid a fee.

3.2.2 Elicitation procedure

The lexical items on which this analysis is based were recorded as part of a larger wordlist, with members of the same minimal pair at least fifteen minutes apart. The procedure for each item was as follows. The native speaker was presented with a lexical item in Indonesian, the Ma'ya translation of which she or he was to utter out loud. This response, a lexical item in Ma'ya, was recorded in three contexts (see 3): (i) in isolation; (ii) embedded sentence-finally in a carrier sentence; (iii) embedded sentence-medially in a carrier sentence. One to three repetitions were recorded for each context.

(3)
Researcher [in Indonesian]: *te'lur* 'egg'
Informant [in Ma'ya]: *'tol^{12}* 'egg' [citation form]
'sia 'bas 'tol^{12} [sentence-final]
pronoun_3pl say egg
'They say egg'
'sia 'bas 'tol^{12} sa'po^{12} [sentence-medial]
pronoun_3pl say egg not
'They don't say egg'

The recordings were made using a Sony WM-D6C tape recorder (featuring user-controlled input level and a constant-speed mechanism) and a Shure directional close-talking microphone (head mounted). All utterances were digitized.

3.2.3 Materials used in the analysis

This analysis is based on six lexical items, constituting three minimal accent pairs (see Table 6). This approach allows for a paradigmatic analysis of accent. For example, we compare the acoustic parameters of the (arguably accented) first syllable of $'mana^3$ with the same parameters of the (arguably unaccented) first syllable of $ma'na^3$. Both members of the minimal pairs have the High toneme on the final syllable. In all three minimal pairs, both syllables have the vowel /a/ in nucleus.

Only the realizations in sentence-medial context were analyzed, in order to avoid phrase-final effects on the acoustic parameters. The target words are preceded by a low target and followed by a syllable unspecified for tone.

Table 6: The minimal accent pair stimuli, by accent location.

Penultimate accent /'n−3/	Final accent /n−'3/
$'tala^3$	$ta'la^3$
'banana'	'k.o. plant'
$'kaya^3$	$ka'ya^3$
'rich' (loan word)	'machete'
$'mana^3$	$ma'na^3$
'light (of weight)'	'grease'

3.2.4 Data analysis

Two hundred and sixteen cases were analyzed (8 speakers * 3 minimal pairs * 1 to 3 repetitions[8] * 2 target syllables [penultimate/final]). After manual segmentation of the target words, all further measurements were made automatically using the procedures available in the speech analysis package Praat (Boersma & Weenink, 1996). The following measurements were made of each of the vowels in the target words.

- Duration of the vowel (in ms).
- Fundamental frequency (f_0). f_0-mean and standard deviation. Data points were expressed in Hertz (Hz) and in terms of the psychoacoustic ERB-scale.
- Vowel quality. The mean Hz values of the first and second formants (F1 and F2, respectively), were computed for each vowel.

Measurements were made over a 32-ms window symmetrically centered on the temporal mid point of the vowel.
- Spectral balance. Work by Sluijter (1995) on accent in Dutch and subsequent work on other languages, demonstrates that the loudness perceived in accent prominence is related to the proportion of high-frequency energy in the spectrum. The intensity measure used here is based on that conclusion. First, the spectrum of energy distribution was computed over the same 32-ms window used for the formant measures. Mean intensity, expressed in decibel (dB), was measured in the frequency band of 1000 to 1750 Hz. This range (B3) was chosen so as to include the second formant (F2). The B3 measure was normalized for variation in vowel quality between accent conditions, for each syllable separately. This was done using the formula of Fant (1960, in Sluijter & van Heuven, 1996), leading to the derived measure B3*. Because recording sensitivity varied throughout data elicitation, the intensity measure B3* was divided by the overall utterance intensity mean (dB), resulting in a normalized relB3*. In summary, relB3* is a measure of the intensity in the frequency band between 1000 and 1750 HZ, normalized for variation in vowel quality and for variation in recording sensitivity.

3.2.5 Statistical analysis

The descriptive statistics presented below are based on raw measures, and so are the inferential statistics for duration and spectral balance (relB3*). The inferential statistics for f_0 and formants, expressed in ERB and Hz respectively, were standardized per speaker in order to normalize for between-speaker variation in acoustic register and range.

Repeated measures style analyses of variance (ANOVA) (Loftus & Loftus, 1988) were carried out with fixed factors accent (accented/unaccented) and syllable (penultimate/final), and random factor speaker. So all analyses reported below are 'over speakers'. As a criterion to determine significance, alpha was set at the value of 0.01.

Linear discriminant analyses (LDA) were carried out to investigate the relative success of potential accent correlates at discriminating between accented and unaccented syllables. These analyses were carried out over all syllables, and by syllable position (penultimate/final).

3.3 Results and discussion

3.3.1 Duration

The statistics for duration, listed in Table 7, feature two additive effects. First, accented syllables are longer than unaccented syllables [$F(1,7) = 189.5; p < 0.01$]. Importantly, this is also true for the final syllable, where the two competing hypotheses make markedly different predictions. Second, final syllables are significantly longer than penultimate syllables [$F(1,7) = 23.27; p < 0.01$]. This difference between penultimate and final syllables (33 ms on average) is considerably smaller than between accented and unaccented syllables (72 ms on average). To some extent, the effect of syllable position may be due to anticipatory shortening of the penultimate syllable. Finally, there is a significant interaction between accent and syllable [$F(1,7) = 13.54\ p < 0.01$], because the difference in duration between the final and the penultimate syllable is greater for accented than for unaccented syllables.

Table 7: Mean duration in milliseconds (in bold), standard deviation (s.d.), and number of cases (#) by syllable and accent, over speakers and items.

Accent	Penultimate syllable			Final syllable			Penult. & final syllables		
	Mean	s.d.	#	mean	s.d.	#	mean	s.d.	#
Accented	**130**	29	53	**180**	34	55	**156**	40	108
Unaccented	**78**	18	55	**91**	22	53	**84**	21	108
Accented & unaccented	**103**	36	108	**136**	52	108	**120**	48	216

The LDA confirms that duration is a reliable accent cue: 88.9 percent of the syllables can be classified correctly on the basis of their raw duration only. Separate analyses for penultimate and final syllable give correct accent classification results of 87 and 93.5 percent respectively. This means that duration is a reliable accent cue irrespective of syllable position.

3.3.2 Vowel quality

Ma'ya features a five vowel system (/i,u,e,o,a/) with no schwa. All three minimal pairs have the vowel /a/ in both syllables. Centralization of the vowel /a/ in unaccented syllables would affect the first formant (F_1), which reflects vowel height, but not the second (F_2), which reflects the front-back dimension and does not distinguish /a/ from central schwa. Consequently, if the contrast in the minimal pairs in Table 6 is one of stress accent, we predict an effect of accent on F_1, but not on F_2. This is indeed the case (see Table 8): F_1 is significantly lower (i.e. more centralized) for unaccented than for accented vowels [$F(1,7) = 62.26; p < 0.01$]. The effect of syllable on F_1 is not significant [$F(1,7) = 0.658$; ns], and neither is the correlation between accent and syllable [$F(1,7) = 3.985$; ns]. As expected, accent has no significant effect on F_2 [$F(1,7) = 0.341$; ns]. Neither does syllable [$F(1,7) = 0.249$; ns], nor the interaction between syllable and accent [$F(1,7) = 0.247$; ns].

Table 8: Mean first formant expressed in Hz (in bold) and Barks, standard deviation (s.d.), and number of cases (#) by syllable and accent, over speakers and items.

Accent			Penultimate syllable			Final syllable			Penult. & final syllables		
			mean	s.d.	#	mean	s.d.	#	mean	s.d.	#
Accented	Hz		**653**	115	53	**667**	92	55	**660**	104	108
	Bark		6.155	.917		6.278	.719		6.217	.82	
Unaccented	Hz		**577**	97	55	**540**	77	53	**559**	90	108
	Bark		5.572	.806		5.275	.637		5.426	.74	
Accented &	Hz		**614**	112	108	**605**	106	108	**609**	109	216
unaccented	Bark		5.858	.907		5.785	.844		5.822	.874	

The LDA results for correct accent classification on the basis of F1 are 80.6 (both syllables), 77.8 (penultimate syllable) and 84.3 (final syllable). In summary, accented and unaccented syllables can be successfully distinguished on the basis of F1, irrespective of syllable position.

3.3.3 Spectral balance

RelB3* is a corrected measure of mean intensity in the frequency band between 1000 and 1750 Hz (see above). Table 9 shows that relB3* is higher in accented syllables than in unaccented syllables. This effect is significant [$F(1,7) = 18.5$; $p < 0.01$]. RelB3* does not vary significantly in function of the factor syllable [$F(1,7) = 0.003$; ns], and the interaction between syllable and accent is almost significant [$F(1,7) = 8.18$; ns].

Table 9: Mean values for the spectral balance measure relB3* (in bold), standard deviations (s.d.), and number of cases (#) by syllable and accent, over speakers and items. Also the raw decibel values for B3*, before division by the utterance mean.

Accent		Penultimate syllable			Final syllable			Penult. & final syllables		
		mean	s.d.	#	mean	s.d.	#	mean	s.d.	#
Accented	relB3*	**42.0**	4.8	53	**45.9**	6.5	55	**43.9**	6.0	108
	B3*	27.2	3.4		30.1	4.4		28.7	4.2	
Unaccented	relB3*	**39.7**	7.8	55	**35.7**	9.5	53	**37.7**	8.9	108
	B3*	26.0	5.2		23.1	6.1		24.6	5.8	
Accented &	relB3*	**40.8**	6.6	108	**40.9**	9.6	108	**40.8**	8.2	216
unaccented	B3*	26.6	4.4		26.6	6.3		26.6	5.5	

The above results indicate that relB3* varies systematically between accented and unaccented syllables. The almost significant effect of the interaction between accent and syllable reflects that relB3* distinguishes accented from unaccented syllables more clearly in final syllables.

Over all syllables, the LDA correct classification result is 67.6. With 61.1 percent correct classification, the LDA result for the penultimate syllable considerably lower than for the final syllable (74.1 percent). We can conclude that some effect of accent on spectral balance is present in both syllable positions, but the size of the effect is not the same.

3.3.4 Fundamental frequency (f_0)

Table 10 shows accented vowels to be slightly higher than unaccented vowels, but this effect is not consistent over syllables: while in final position accented syllables are higher than unaccented syllables, in the penultimate syllable it is the unaccented that are slightly higher. The effect of accent on f_0 is not significant [$F(1,7) = 9.28$; ns].

Considerably larger and more consistent is the mean difference between penultimate and final syllables (16 Hz on average). This is to be expected, as the final syllable is marked with the High tone in both members of the minimal pairs. This effect is significant [$F(1,7) = 708.05$; $p < 0.01$]. Also, there is a significant interaction between accent and syllable [$F(1,7) = 14.624$; $p < 0.01$]: the final syllable, marked with the High toneme, is relatively higher when accented.

Table 10: Mean f_0 in Hertz (Hz - in bold) and ERB, standard deviations (s.d.), and number of cases (#) by syllable and accent, over speakers and items.

Accent		Penultimate syllable			Final syllable			Penult. & final syllables		
		mean	s.d.	#	mean	s.d.	#	mean	s.d.	#
Accented	Hz	**133**	34	53	**156**	35	55	**145**	36	108
	ERB	3.816	.83		4.362	.81		4.094	.86	
Unaccented	Hz	**137**	31	55	**145**	35	53	**141**	33	108
	ERB	3.925	.75		4.116	.82		4.019	.79	
Accented &	Hz	**135**	33	108	**151**	35	108	**143**	35	216
unaccented	ERB	3.871	.79		4.241	.82		4.056	.82	

The LDA correct classification result for accent is 55.6 percent. Per syllable the LDA result is very variable. Of penultimate syllables, 65.7 percent were correctly classified for accent. The result for the final syllable (78.7 percent) reflects the large difference between accented and unaccented final syllables. The overall LDA result is lower than the by-syllable results because the relation of f_0 between unaccented and accented vowels is not consistent over syllables (see Table 10), and this hinders overall correct classification. We can conclude that f_0 mean is not a reliable correlate of lexical accent.

3.3.5 Interpretation of the results

The results can be summarized as follows. The effect of accent (accented vs. unaccented) and syllable position (penultimate vs. final) was investigated for four acoustic parameters: duration, vowel quality, spectral balance and f_0. While duration, vowel quality and spectral balance values varied significantly in function of accent, f_0 did not. Effect size in ANOVA was greatest for duration, followed by vowel quality and spectral balance. This variation in effect size between acoustic parameters is faithfully reflected in the LDA successful discrimination scores observed for the acoustic parameters. Figure 1 shows that successful discrimination was highest for duration, followed by vowel quality, spectral balance and f_0, in that order. Syllable position, on the other hand, was found to have an unmistakable effect on f_0. Syllable position also had a much smaller effect on duration.

According to the hypothesis argued for here, the lexical contrast between the words in the first and second column of Table 6 is one of accent. Accent is hypothesized to be penultimate in *'mana³* 'light of weight' (pattern /'n−3/), but final in *ma'na³* 'grease' (pattern /n−'3/). This hypothesis is confirmed. Prosodic parameters set apart the first syllable of pattern /'n−3/ and the second syllable of pattern /n−'3/ from the second syllable in /'n−3/ and the first syllable in /n−'3/. In other words, this is a syntagmatic contrast: the accented syllable is distinguished from the unaccented syllable in the word. Secondly, the acoustic parameters marking this syntagmatic contrast are well-known accent correlates: duration, vowel quality and spectral balance. The relative importance of these

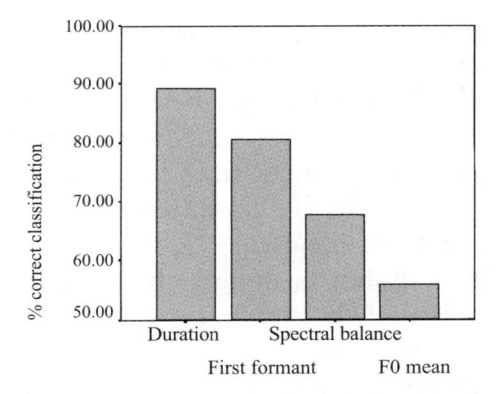

Figure 1: Percentage correct accent discrimination in LDA for each of the acoustic parameters (over syllables).

parameters as correlates of stress accent is similar to their relative importance in well-known stress accent languages such as English (Beckman, 1986; Sluijter, 1995) and Dutch (Sluijter & van Heuven, 1996). The effect of accent on f_0 is inconsistent. For the penultimate syllable, there is hardly any difference in mean f_0 in function of accent. In final position, on the other hand, accented syllables are considerably higher than unaccented syllables. This situation is in agreement with the stress accent hypothesis. For the penultimate syllable, the absence of a difference in f_0 in function of accent follows from the fact that lexical tone precludes focus-marking on accented syllables by means of f_0. The only kind of intonational focus-marking found in tone languages is the realization of lexical tone patterns with greater range (see e.g. Xu & Wang, 1997 on Chinese). This is what we find for the final syllable, which features a High tone, when it is accented.

The contrast analyzed here as one of accent – /'n-3/ vs. /n-'3/ –, was analyzed by van der Leeden (1993) as a tone contrast: /21−'3/ vs. /1−'3/. In van der Leeden's analysis, accent is on the final syllable in both words, and lexical contrast is maintained by lexical tone. Because the first syllable of pattern /21−'3/ carries a contour tone and the first syllable of pattern /1−'3/ does not, his hypothesis can account for the difference in duration between the first syllable of both words (see Table 7 'penultimate syllable'). However, it cannot explain the difference in duration between the second syllables of the two patterns (see Table 7 'final syllable'), because, phonologically, both syllables have the same features in his analysis (accent and toneme /3/). Also, if the difference between penultimate syllable durations is attributed to the contour tone, then the first syllable in /21−'3/ should also be longer than the second syllable for the same reason. Alternatively, if this difference is attributed to the accent on the second syllable of 21−'3, then the second syllable of pattern /1−'3/ also should be longer than the first syllable with contour tone in /21−'3/. In summary, van der Leeden's analysis cannot account for the syntagmatic nature of the difference in syllable duration between the two word prosodic patterns. The same is true for the effect of vowel quality and spectral balance. Van der Leeden's analysis cannot account for the differences in vowel quality and spectral balance between the first syllable of /21−'3/ and the first syllable of /1−'3/, and ditto for the difference between second syllable of /21−'3/ and the second syllable /1−'3/. As for f_0, the /21−'3/ vs. /1−'3/ analysis predicts that the first syllable with tone /21/ is higher than the first syllable with tone /1/. This is not the case.

3.3.6 *Comparing accent correlates with tone correlates*

We can further support the alternative analysis by demonstrating that the prosodic parameters that encode the stress accent contrast do not distinguish between the three paradigmatically contrastive tones (High, Rising and default/accent). Figure 2 presents the LDA correct toneme classification results based on eight monosyllabic three-way pseudo-minimal sets. The nucleus vowel is always /a/, just as in the minimal accent pairs. Since these words are monosyllables, they can only vary paradigmatically, i.e., in terms of lexical tone. The target words were embedded sentence-medially in the same context sentence as the accent items. Data were elicited from eight native speakers.[9] Whenever possible two but otherwise one repetition of each word was analyzed, using the analysis procedure of the above accent analysis. The total number of cases is 381. The only difference in the data analysis procedure has to do with the normalization of the spectral balance measure.[10]

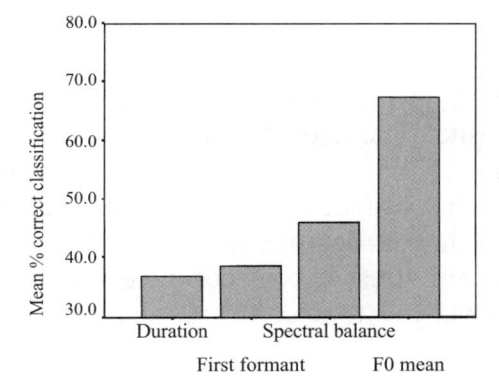

Figure 2: Percentage correct tone discrimination in LDA for each of the acoustic parameters.

Duration and vowel quality (F1) do not really distinguish between the three tones. With correct classification results of 36.7 and 38.6 respectively, they hardly raise discrimination above the 33 percent chance-level baseline. For spectral balance, the correct tone classification result is better – at 45.9 percent. The explanation for this well-above chance result may be that, to some extent, spectral balance is correlated with mean f_0. Table 11 shows that as a tone's mean f_0 is higher, so is the spectral balance value. The highest correct classification result is found for mean f_0 (67.2 percent). This value may still seem low, for a tone language. The reason is that the Falling (= accent) and the Rising tones are similar in terms of this f_0 parameter. An LDA of mean f_0 in combination with a parameter reflecting f_0 slope gives 81.6 percent correct classification.

Table 11: Mean values and standard deviations (s.d.) for duration (in milliseconds), F_1 (in Hz), spectral balance (relB3*−indB), and mean f_0 (in Hz), by factor toneme.

Toneme	Duration		F1		Spectr.bal.		Mean f_0	
	mean	s.d.	mean	s.d.	mean	s.d.	Mean	s.d.
High	**155**	35	**704**	81	**53.7**	6.1	**179**	45
Falling	**143**	35	**682**	96	**49.4**	6.8	**160**	39
Rising	**157**	34	**693**	102	**48.0**	6.4	**154**	37
All tonemes	**152**	35	**693**	93	**50.4**	6.9	**165**	42

When we compare the LDA results for tone discrimination in Figure 2 with the corresponding results for accent discrimination in Figure 1, we find that the relative importance of acoustic parameters is the opposite. The acoustic parameters most important in the encoding of accent are least important in the encoding of tone, and vice versa. This supports the hypothesis that Ma'ya features stress accent, because it demonstrates that the acoustic encoding of the hypothesized stress accent contrast differs markedly from the encoding of Ma'ya's tone contrast.

4. Conclusion

There is compelling evidence that Ma'ya features both lexically contrastive stress accent and lexical tone, as independent factors in its word-prosodic system. Ma'ya has been reported to be a tone language by van der Leeden (1993). Its tonal system was reanalyzed in this paper as a three-way lexical tone contrast, limited to the final syllable of content roots.

The objective of this paper was to present evidence in support of the hypothesis that, in addition to and independent of the lexical tone feature, Ma'ya features lexically contrastive stress accent, a hitherto unknown combination of word-prosodic features. First, a phonological analysis of the word prosodic system revealed that, by postulating contrastive stress accent, a number of phenomena can be described in simpler terms. Second, an acoustic analysis of disyllabic minimal pairs showed that the contrast under investigation is of a syntagmatic nature, and that it is encoded by the configuration of prosodic parameters stress accent tends to be encoded by (Beckman, 1986; Sluijter, 1995; Sluijter & van Heuven, 1996).

Ma'ya's word prosodic system is exceptional, with stress accent and lexical tone as independent factors. It is unclear whether this reflects a typological scarcity of such word prosodic systems, or just a lack of relevant data. More combined phonological-phonetic research is needed into the word prosodic systems of tone and non-stress accent languages in order to determine whether the word prosody of Ma'ya is as unique as it seems.

Acknowledgements

I am very grateful to Lex van der Leeden. Through his detailed descriptive work I got to know the Ma'ya language. I also acknowledge his useful advice in preparing for fieldwork. Many thanks to Hud Arfan and Thahir Arfan for help and advice in the Raja Ampat archipelago.
The following people have provided assistance during data analysis and write-up. Helen Hanson gave advice on how to measure spectral balance. With Cecilia Odé, Harry van der Hulst, Alice Turk, Mitsuhiko Ota and Stefanie Shattuck-Hufnagel I have had thought-provoking discussions on the issues involved in this paper. Ellen van Zanten and Vincent van Heuven proofread earlier versions. I gratefully acknowledge their help. I thank audiences at a seminar of Holland Institute of Linguistics (HIL), at a postgraduate conference at the Department of Theoretical and Applied Linguistics of the University of Edinburgh, and the audience at the Laboratory Phonology conference in Nijmegen. Finally, I thank an anonymous reviewer for helpful comments. This research was carried out under the supervision of Vincent van Heuven, as part of a cooperation project between Leiden University (the Netherlands) and the University of Indonesia (Indonesia), funded by the Netherlands Academy of Arts and Sciences (KNAW).

Notes

1 Potisuk, Gandour & Harper (1996) argue for a lexical accent analysis in the tone language Thai. It is debatable, however, whether the phenomenon involved is a lexical rather than a domain-sensitive prosodic feature. The stress feature investigated by Potisuk et al. is marked only on word-final syllables, and, as a consequence, cannot be investigated in minimal word pairs. As an alternative, the authors analyzed minimal pairs, one of the members of which is a disyllabic compound noun, consisting of a noun root followed by a verb root. In such a compound, the final syllable carries stress. The authors compared the acoustic realization of the less prominent first syllable of such compounds with the same root in a noun-verb sequence, where both syllables carry accent as independent words. The authors find the single noun root word to feature a longer duration than the same noun root in the compound, and interpret this as marking of accent. But because one of the members of the minimal pair was followed by a word boundary, this durational marking can alternatively be explained in terms of word-final lengthening (of the one-root noun), and/or anticipatory shortening (of the noun in the compound).
2 Ma'ya's genetic classification is the following: Austronesian, Eastern Malayo-Polynesian, South Halmahera-West New Guinea (van der Leeden, 1993: 15).
3 I use van der Leeden's transcription system for Ma'ya word prosody. Tonemes are transcribed after the syllable on which they are realized by one or two digits. In this way, the language user's f_0-range is represented by the range

from 1 (lowest) to 4 (highest). A single digit implies the tone is level, double digits imply it is a contour. Syllables not transcribed for toneme have the Low tone /1/ in van der Leeden's analysis, and no tone in my analysis. Accent is marked by ' preceding the lexically accented syllable. Accent is also marked in monosyllables whenever relevant.

4 Two of these items do not constitute independent phonological words: *de* can only appear as an affix on a predicate, and *be* is a prepositional affix. *mat* 'person' can be transcribed alternatively as *mat^{21}*, without loss of lexical contrast.

5 In this alternative analysis, tone is only contrastive on the final syllable. Therefore, non-final syllables are not marked for tone. For example, the minimal pair that van der Leeden transcribed as *ma^{21}'na^3* vs. *ma^1'na^3* becomes *'mana^3* vs. *ma'na^3* respectively. In abstract discussion of tonal patterns, syllables not marked for tone are transcribed 'n'. For example, the above minimal pair illustrates the contrast between /'n−3/ and /n−'3/ respectively.

6 Alternatively, the tonemes can be analyzed in terms of L(ow) and H(igh) tonal targets. Then the rising contour tone is represented phonologically as /LH/, and the level high toneme as /H/.

7 I collected these data during two fieldwork trips to the village of Samate (Papua Barat province, Indonesia): April, 1999, and February, 2000.

8 One to three repetitions were initially recorded for each item. Whenever possible, all repetitions were analyzed. Realizations of poor quality (e.g. because of a hesitation, background noise, etc.) were not included.

9 Four male, four female. Four of these speakers (three male, one female) were part of the group of speakers for the minimal pairs for accent.

10 The calculation of spectral balance (relB3) is slightly different from the way it was calculated for the accent minimal pairs. The normalization for the effect of the shift of formants in function of accent (formula of Fant, 1960, in Sluijter & van Heuven, 1996) was not carried out, because we are dealing with a three-way rather than a two-way distinction. This is not problematic, though, because the formant values are only marginally different in function of tonemes (see F1 values in Table 11).

References

Bateman, J.
　1990　　Iau segmental and tone phonology. In Bambang Kaswanti Purwo (ed.), *Miscellaneous Studies of Indonesian and Languages in Indonesia Pt. X*. NUSA, **32**. Jakarta. Atma Jaya.

Beckman, M.
　1986　　*Stress and Non-stress Accent*. Dordrecht: Foris Publications.

Berinstein, A. E.
　1979　　A cross-linguistic study on the perception and production of stress. *UCLA Working Papers in Phonetics*, **47**.

Boersma, P. & Weenink, D.
  1996   *PRAAT: A system for doing phonetics by computer.* Report of the Institute of Phonetic Sciences of the University of Amsterdam, **132**.
Bruce, G.
  1977   *Swedish Word Accents in Sentence Perspective.* Travaux de l'institut de linguistique de Lund vol. XII. CWK Gleerup – Lund.
Donohue, M.
  1997   Tone systems in New Guinea. *Linguistic Typology*, **1**, 347–386.
Gussenhoven, C. & Bruce, G.
  1998   Word prosody and intonation. In H. van der Hulst (ed.), *Word Prosodic Systems in the language of Europe*, (pp. 233–271) Berlin: Mouton de Gruyter.
Hulst, H. van der & Smith, N.
  1988   The variety of pitch-accent systems – Introduction. In H. van der Hulst & N. Smith (eds.), *Autosegmental studies on pitch-accent.* Dordrecht: Foris Publications.
Kouwenberg, S. & Murray, E.
  1994   *Papiamentu.* Languages of the world / Materials, **83**. Muenchen-Newcastle: Lincom Europe.
McCawley, J.
  1978   What is a tone language? In V. Fromkin (ed.), *Tone: A Linguistic Survey*, (pp. 113–131). Academic Press.
Leeden, A. C. van der
  1993   *Ma'ya: A language study: A Phonology.* Jakarta: Lembaga Ilmu Pengetahuan Indonesia & Rijksuniversiteit Leiden.
Leeden, A. C. van der
  1997   A tonal morpheme in Ma'ya. In C. Odé & W. Stokhof (eds.), *Proceedings of the Seventh International Conference on Austronesian Linguistics.* Amsterdam-Atlanta, GA: Rodopi.
Loftus, G. R. & Loftus, E. F.
  1988   *Essence of Statistics* (2nd edition). New York: Knopf.
Potisuk, S., Gandour, J. & Harper, M. P.
  1996   Acoustic correlates of stress in Thai. *Phonetica*, **53**, 200–220.
Remijsen, B.
  2001   *Word-prosodic systems of Raja Ampat languages.* Nr 49, Netherlands Graduate School of Linguistics, Utrecht. LOT Dissertation Series.
Remijsen, B.
  in press   Dialectal variation in the lexical tone system of Ma'ya. *Language and Speech.*
Römer, R.
  1991   (eds. N. H. Smith & J. M. Stewart) *Studies in Papiamentu tonology.* Caribbean Culture Studies, **5**. Amsterdam and Kingston: Amsterdam Centre for Caribbean Studies

Sluijter, A. M. C.
　1995　　*Phonetic correlates of stress and accent*. PhD Dissertation Holland Institute of Generative Linguistics (Leiden, the Netherlands).
Sluijter, A. M. C. & Heuven, V. J. van
　1996　　Spectral balance as an acoustic correlate of linguistic stress. *Journal of the Acoustic Society of America*, **100**, Vol **4**, 2471−2485.
Xu, Y. & Wang, Q. E.
　1997　　What can tone studies tell us about intonation? In A. Botinis, G. Kouroupetroglou & G. Carayiannis (eds.), *Intonation: Theory, Models and Applications*, Proceedings of the ESCA Workshop (Athens, Greece, Sept. 18−20, 1997), 337−340.

Fieldwork and phonological theory: Comments on Demolin, Grabe & Low, Hualde et al., and Remijsen

W. Leo Wetzels

1. Introduction

Around 85% of the estimated 6,000 languages of the world are spoken in only 22 countries. Nine of these countries are home to more than 200 different languages: Papua New Guinea (850 languages), Indonesia (670), Nigeria (410), India (380), Cameroon (270), Australia (250), Mexico (240), Zaire (210) and Brazil (210). Between 100 and 160 languages are spoken in the Philippines, the former Soviet-Union, the United States, Malaysia, China, Sudan, Tanzania, Ethiopia, Chad, the New Hebrides, the Central-African Republic, Burma and Nepal. In all of these countries, and also in many others, a large number of the non-official languages are threatened by extinction.[1]

The value of documenting endangered languages is sometimes described in the literature against a background of the general value of preserving existing diversity, both in genetic (flora and fauna) and in cultural areas. Language, besides being part of a people's cultural heritage, is at the same time a rather complete and complex reflection thereof. In the course of their history, peoples shape, each in their own manner, the existential, social and practical matters with which their society is faced: the sense of mysticism and the supernatural, death and forefathers, social organization including partnership and leadership, child rearing, medicine, technology, etc. Every culture thus represents a unique and alternative way of organizing the entities that constitute its material and spiritual world.

More often than not, cultural disintegration goes hand in hand with the loss of the traditional language. This is to be expected, since both language and culture are the exponents of a people's identity and equally sensitive to self-depreciation and feelings of inferiority caused by the cultural arrogance of the dominating society. Indeed, the psychologist Lambert and his associates have shown that the oppressed community easily comes to share the negative view of its language with the dominant group that promotes it (see Lambert, 1992).

More often than not, language loss creates a social group that cannot express itself fully in the majority language and assumes an inferior position in the margins of the dominant culture. The existence of a description of a language offers the possibility of setting up programmes for bilingual education. Especially for the peoples that are in regular contact with the dominant culture, the availability of a standard transcription of their language will permit them to acquire literacy in their own language, fortifying group identity and self-esteem, and also allow a solid bilingual education. It is indeed the conviction of a growing group of linguists and anthropologists that bilingual education has become a necessary condition for the cultural and linguistic survival of the minority peoples. Even if indigenous peoples take over the contempt for their language and culture from condescending outsiders and no longer pass it on to their children, it may happen that, at a later stage, they start searching for their cultural roots again. Describing languages that are at the point of extinction is therefore not only important for theoretical linguistics and cultural or cognitive anthropology, but also for the indigenous peoples themselves, so that they can fall back, when the time comes, on documents in which the details of the their language and culture are described.

Describing endangered languages of course also has a strictly scientific value. The ability to develop a language is regarded as one of the most characteristic and complex achievements in man, not only by linguists, but also by psychologists, evolutionists, and neurologists. The relation and interaction between the universal biological basis of the language and the more general cognitive abilities which together enable man to acquire a specific language system (or grammar) and to use it is the subject of a discussion, which is as passionate as it is interesting. To explain the phenomenon of language and to decide which part is grounded in biological predisposition and which in the general cognitive abilities of the human brain, it is obviously necessary to know how languages are structured and in which ways the different languages construe the relation between form (sound shape, word form, sentence structure) and meaning. Consequently, an important question linguists must address is what the 'constants' are in language, and what the possible variations are upon them. In Bernard Comrie's words: "The languages of the world provide us with a rich variety of data on the basis of which we can study the general properties of the human language potential."(1989: x). To the generative grammarians, who tend to understand linguistic primitives and structures and also their constraining principles as determined primarily by a highly specific cognitive module, comparative linguistics is a way of discovering what are the common principles of human language, which in turn should give us insight in the properties of the language faculty. Researchers agree that the identification of facts of substance and principles of structural organization are important for all branches of scientific linguistics. As Ken Hale puts it: "In many cases data from a 'new' language forces changes in the developing theory, and in some cases, linguistic diversity sets an entirely new agenda" (1998: 194).

2. Fieldwork and Phonological Theory Session

In a paper published in 1929 in the *Travaux du Cercle Linguistique de Prague*, Trubetzkoy states: "A comparative investigation of the phonological systems of all the languages of the world is the most urgent task of today's linguistic science." Some fifteen years later Jakobson closes his probably most famous linguistic study in a similar vein: "The more data linguistics makes available, from different peoples, on the speech of children and aphasics, the more significantly and thoroughly can it handle the structural laws of particular languages and of languages in general." (1968: 94). To date, Trubetzkoy and Jakobson's messages have lost nothing of their urgency.

Phonological theory aims to account for the shapes of the sound structures of the world's languages. What is the phonetic composition of contrastive segments, how do phonological segments combine into segmental systems, what metrical, tonal and prosodic structures do languages have, how do they combine linearly and hierarchically, and why are segments, systems, and structures statistically distributed the way they are across languages? Each of the contributions to the *Fieldwork and Phonological Theory* session addressed one or more of these issues.

Didier Demolin rightly draws our attention once more to the fact that a fully-fledged linguistic theory should not only deal with issues regarding distinctive phonological features and their organization in abstract structural units but also address questions regarding subphonemic phonetic detail. Phonetic structure is to a large extent systematic, categorical and language-specific, and the only way to understand these characteristics is to assume that it has become part of the speaker's linguistic knowledge in much the same way phonological structure has (see Clements & Hertz, 1996). According to Demolin, phonological primitives and principles should be strongly rooted in phonetics in order for us to understand why phonological segments and systems are the way they are, and, equally important, why they sometimes are different from the way we would expect them to be. As a matter of fact, Demolin's paper is not primarily concerned with the question how complex and uncommon phonetic facts relate to more abstract phonological entities, such as, for example, the universal set of distinctive features. In this respect, the paper sharply contrasts with the study by Clements & Osu (this volume), but shares with it the concern for careful (experimental) phonetic analysis. Probably the point of view most forcefully sustained by Demolin is that a thorough understanding of "the principles relating vocal tract shape and acoustic output, aerodynamic principles, and principles that explain how our auditory system extracts information from the acoustic signal" will eventually prove the correctness of Lindblom's hypothesis of phonology as an emergent phenomenon and consequently allow us to dispense with a strong version of the innateness hypothesis. Since I consider Lindblom's view a serious alternative to the postulate of a very specific 'black box' responsible for 'substantive' aspects of phonological segments and systems, I can only sympathize with the author's unrelenting concern with phonetic detail. Guided by phonetics, Demolin concentrates upon explaining uncommon sounds or unexpected gaps in phonological systems and shows how the nature of aerodynamic principles and the needs of production and perception may be at the origin of a complex relation between phonemic and subphonemic properties of sounds. At the end of his study, Demolin turns his attention away from phonetics, towards more abstract questions regarding the representation of sound patterns in the human mind and the awareness in speakers of the existence of abstract entities posited by phonologists, such as distinctive features, phonemes, moras, and syllables. A number of interesting word games show that Hendo speakers are capable of manipulating such linguistic units, despite the fact that Hendo is not a written language. Yet, according to Demolin, the Hendo word games do not as such invalidate the idea held by some that phonological awareness of the type under discussion can only be awakened by the mediation of an alphabetic writing system. This is because these games are being taught on the basis of a special kind of mediating system, which associates phonemes with colour symbols. To be sure, it is not entirely clear to me what exactly the intended implication is of the question that Demolin phrases at the beginning of section 5.2.3 with regard to the Hendo word games: "how is it that, in an unwritten language, speakers can manipulate every phonological unit?". There are perhaps two issues here. One is the indirect proof that linguists can gather from the nature of word games for the 'psychological validity' of abstract phonological units, the other is the actual *awareness* in speakers that a phonetic sequence, say a 'word', is of a composite nature, involving building blocks such as features, segments, and syllables. If phonological awareness were necessary to be able to do word games, and if that awareness presupposes an alphabetic writing system, which is apparently what some researchers suggest, word games could never exist in unwritten languages. Although I have not informed myself on this issue, it would come as a surprise to me if the existence of word games in some language could be taken as proof for the phonological awareness of its speakers. This is because at least some of the operations typical of word games, such as syllable reduplication, consonant reduplication (plus default vowel insertion), or infixation do exist as grammatical operations in natural languages, written or unwritten. The claim that phonological awareness is a prerequisite for the creation of word games but not for the existence of similar operations that play a role in a language's expression of meaning seems to me to be in need for some principled explanation. Until that explanation is provided, I would guess that the type of operation under discussion does not necessarily involve phonological awareness, whatever its status in the language. Regarding the specific issue of the implication between the availability of an alphabetic writing system and the existence of wordgames, it seems important to observe that even phonology-based writing systems often do not provide direct evidence for syllable structure (much less, internal syllable structure), moras, or features (tones!). To the extent that systems are more or less explicit with regard to expressing such entities, one would be led to expect that the word-games occurring in a given language manipulate exclusively the entities that are part of the written code of that language, including the learned rules of written syllabification.[2] Again, I would consider it a sensational discovery if such a detailed correlation were shown to be universally valid.

Since Sapir's famous footnote (see chapter 2 of his *Language*), we know that in speakers the awareness of the word is much greater than that of phonemes and syllables. The striking efficiency of alphabetic writing systems for encoding spoken language and the relative easy with which these systems are learned indeed stands in contrast with the lack of awareness of segment-sized units in speakers, especially of unwritten languages. Logically, at least the person(s) who invented some sound-based writing system must have acquired the awareness of the segmentability of a sound sequence, without the prior availability of such a system. An awareness of (abstract) segments must have been present also in the mind of the person(s) who created the intermediate Hendo system based on color symbols. These 'originals', of course, directly challenge the claim that segmental awareness can only be obtained through the mediation of an alphabetical writing system and one wonders what other kind of conditions or circumstances could contribute, in the absence of such a system, to the awakening of phonological awareness. First of all, there must be the availability of a set of data in the language of the type that phonologists use to defend the psychological validity of some posited theoretical entity. Secondly, there must be a motive to reflect upon these data. For example, segmental awareness may well originate in bilingual speakers, especially when the languages they master are close enough for there to exist a systematic set of sound correspondences between the ('same') words of the languages or dialects they know. Relatively small children are capable of noting such systematic differences[3] and so do bilingual (or bidialectal) speakers of unwritten languages. A motive for reflecting upon these correspondences[4] could trigger the awareness that some elements in the sequences compared are interchangeable and, consequently, that these sequences are made up of smaller units. If there is some truth to this suggestion, it naturally takes us back to the Hendo situation. If (at least) the simpler games existed before the colour code was developed, elders intending to teach the 'secret' variants of their language to adolescents will have been forced to reflect on the relations between the 'real' language and the game versions in their search for a method of instruction. Apparently, their study of the phenomenon has been successful, because they found the units that are actually involved in the 'derivations' as well as the systematic nature of the relations in which these were involved. Thus, their awareness of words being composed of smaller units of sound was created by the availability of sound correspondences between words with the same meaning created by 'spontaneous' words games, in addition to the need to reflect on the nature of these correspondences.

Constellations of linguistic facts are often presented in the form of typologies. Typologies group languages in classes that share sets of properties. Each typology embodies the implicit claim that the observed patterning of properties is non-arbitrary and therefore requires a principled explanation. Of course, proposed typologies can be wrong. For example, the rhythm class hypothesis, which classifies languages in stress timed and syllable timed, represents a tenacious but inadequate typology for the classification of rhythmic diversity among languages. According to this hypothesis, in stressed timed languages *metrical feet* tend to be of equal length whereas in syllable timed languages *syllables* have roughly equal length. Moreover, vowel reduction is claimed to be a consequence of stress timing and typically occurs in stress-timed languages. However, as **Esther Grabe** and **Ee Ling Low** point out, this typology is inadequate[5]. Vowel reduction may occur in languages classified as syllable-timed, while languages that are considered stress timed may have no vowel reduction. More dramatically, acoustic evidence for the proposed stress versus syllable-timed dichotomy is lacking. Esther Grabe and Ee Ling Low propose instead that rhythmic diversity can be derived from acoustic variability in two kinds of interval in the speech signal: the vocalic interval, the stretch of speech between the vowel onset and the vowel offset and the intervocalic interval: the stretch of speech between the offset of one vowel and the onset of the next. The measurements of vocalic and consonantal durations are fed into a rhythm-scaling index, which expresses the level of variability in successive measurements. The index is called the Pairwise Variability Index, the normalized (n) version of which I repeat as in (1) below:

$$(1) \qquad nPVI = 100 \times \left[\sum_{k=1}^{m-1} \left| \frac{d_k - d_{k+1}}{(d_k + d_{k+1})/2} \right| / (m-1) \right]$$

In (1) m is the number of items in a sequence and d_k is the duration of the kth item (vocalic or intervocalic interval). Since the numerator will move closer to zero to the extent that successive vocalic intervals have more equal durations, it follows that, the lower the index, the more 'syllable-timed' the language is. The denominator is a scaling parameter, which divides the absolute value of the difference in duration between each pair of successive measurements by the mean duration of the pair. Since the summation does not include the last item in the sequence ($m-1$), the index eliminates the influence of the common phenomenon of 'final lengthening'.

Indeed, the authors claim that the proposed vocalic and intervocalic *PVI*'s offer an empirical basis for cross-linguistic comparison of rhythmic structure, and at the same time account for the stress-timing/syllable timing distinction, albeit not in terms of isochronous interstress-intervals or syllable durations. Typical 'stress-timed' languages exhibit relatively high vocalic variability, combined with mid or high intervocalic variability, whereas syllable-timed languages show low vocalic variability, combined with mid to high intervocalic variability. Mixed languages like Polish and Catalan show high to very high levels of intervocalic variability. Different from what is suggested by the stress timed/syllable timed distinction, measurement of rhythmic variability shows a continuum along the *PVI* profiles proposed by Grabe and Low.

There is one observation repeatedly encountered in the literature that seems of some interest in the light of Grabe and Low's findings, which is the one that Vowel Harmony languages tend to have no vowel reduction. To the extent that 'syllable-timed' languages often do not show vowel reduction either, it would be interesting to know how harmony languages would emerge from the *PVI* tests. Impressionistically, languages like Turkish or Hungarian have always struck me as being rhythmically much more like Spanish and French than like English or Dutch. The interesting fact here would be to establish if indeed syllable-timing correlates with the Vowel Harmony parameter, and, if so, whether directly, or indirectly, on the basis of another phonological property these systems happen to share (such as, maybe, syllable complexity).

A more important comment concerns the comparison with Grabe and Low's work with rather similar but independent work on linguistic rhythm by Ramus (1999). Ramus (1999) segments an utterance into vocalic and consonantal intervals, where a vocalic interval is any uninterrupted sequence of vowels and a consonantal interval any uninterrupted sequence of consonants. Aside from wanting to provide acoustic evidence for the traditional stress-timing/syllable-timing distinction, Ramus advances the interesting hypothesis that a specific rhythm type might provide the newborn child with a cue for other phonological properties of his language, such as the complexity of syllable structure. His motive for measuring vocalic and consonantal intervals derives directly from this further objective. He takes the hypothesis for granted that newborn children have access to the distinction between consonants and vowels, but not to distinctions within these categories (see 1999: 46). As Ramus realizes, the possibility for children to derive other properties from rhythm is more obvious if languages can be classified in a limited number of rhythmic classes, and much less obvious if there are as many rhythm classes as there are different languages. From the measurements of vocalic and consonantal intervals three variables are computed, which will each take a given value per sentence:

%V: the proportion of vocalic intervals in a sentence calculated as the sum of the durations of the vocalic intervals divided by the total duration of the sentence

ΔV: the standard deviation of the vocalic intervals durations in a sentence

ΔC: the standard deviation of the consonantal intervals durations in a sentence

Since syllables in stress-timing languages are of different complexity, sentences will contain more consonantal intervals of variable duration, expressed as ΔC. One thus expects a greater consonant to vowel duration to correlate with a lower %V and a higher ΔC.

Interestingly enough, the results of Ramus' measurements show that the combination of %V and ΔC rather forcefully reflects the traditional rhythm classes, clearly setting apart stress-timed, syllable-timed and mora-timed languages. This raises the question how the results of Ramus' method are so different from those of Grabe and Low. The use of different measures and derived indexes can hardly provide a convincing explanation. This is because one would expect the results of the computation of ΔC not to be very different from the values computed by the intervocalic *PVI*, nor the values for ΔC, which is strongly correlated with %V, to be very different from the values provided by the vocalic *PVI* [6]. If this is correct, the differences can only be explained by the nature of the corpora used by the different authors (Ramus: controlled for differences in speech rate, Grabe and Low: uncontrolled for differences in speech rate), the number of languages tested (Ramus: 8, Grabe and Low: 18), and the number of speakers per language

(Ramus: 4, Grabe and Low: 1). As a matter of fact, Grabe and Low did apply Ramus' method to their data and, as we have seen in their paper, the results are partly similar and partly different from the ones obtained by the vocalic and intervocalic *PVI*, but no clear-cut classification of languages in a limited number of rhythm classes results. A possible problem with the computation of Ramus' indexes over the Grabe and Lowe corpus resides in the fact that standard deviation (ΔV, ΔC) reflects variability in speech rate, which was not controlled for in the Grabe and Low corpus, but which was controlled for in the Ramus' corpus. Consequently, the ΔC values obtained from the Grabe and Low corpus could be polluted by differences in speech rate. On the other hand, the Ramus' corpus being controlled for speech rate, computation of the *PVI* values over his corpus should give results that allow a direct comparison. To conclude, it would be interesting to know what the result would be of a computation of the vocalic and intervocalic *PVI* over the Ramus corpus, especially if this corpus were enlarged with some more languages.

Remijsen's contribution intends to fill a gap in the typology of word-prosodic systems, by showing that the Austronesian language Ma'ya features both stress accent and lexical tone as independent contrastive categories, and, as such, represents, according to the author, an as yet unattested language type. Remijsen starts his discussion of the Ma'ya prosodic system with Beckman's (1986) classification of word-prosodic features, his table I, from which I repeat the basic types on the first row in Table (1) below:

Table 1:

Contrastive category	Lexical Tone	Non-stress Accent	Stress Accent
Contrast type	Paradigmatic	Syntagmatic	Syntagmatic
Acoustic correlates	Fundamental frequency	Fundamental frequency	Duration Vowel quality Spectral balance
Other features	No intonational f_0 contrast	No intonational f_0 contrast	Intonational f_0 contrast
Example	Yoruba, Igbo	Japanese, Basque	English, Dutch

Usually a language chooses its word prosody among the three basic types provided above. However, more complex systems do occur. Logically, we expect complex systems of the following type to exist:

(3) 1. Lexical tone plus non-stress accent
    2. Lexical tone plus stress accent
    3. Non-stress accent plus stress accent
    4. Lexical tone plus non-stress accent plus stress accent

According to Remijsen, the combination of lexical tone and non-stress accent is unlikely to occur for functional reasons. Since both lexical tone and non-stress accent systems rely upon fundamental frequency as the primary acoustic correlate for syllable prominence, their simultaneous implementation would embody the risk of ambiguity. This eliminates the systems in (3)1 and (3)4 as possible word-prosodic systems. System (3)3, the combination of non-stress accent and stress accent, is apparently attested in the Creole language Papiamentu. There are also languages in which lexical tone and lexical stress are coupled, as in Swedish, and some variants of Limburg Dutch, for instance. These languages, which are not particularly rare, may be considered representatives of the mixed system in (3)2. According to Remijsen, the system of Ma'ya is different from the latter languages in that it allows contrastive tone to be lexically attached to **un**stressed syllables: "[In Swedish and Limburg Dutch;LW] lexical tone and stress accent are not independent factors: a syllable can only be marked with one of the lexical tones if it has a stress accent. (...) no language has been demonstrated to feature stress accent and lexical tone as independent factors in its word-prosodic system."

Remijsen's argumentation in favor of his analysis of the Ma'ya word-prosodic system takes two routes. One is to argue that the analysis previously proposed by van der Leeden, which is based on a non-contrastive root-final stress accent and four contrastive tones (Low, High, Fall, Rise) leads to a more complex analysis than the alternative proposed by the author, who establishes the existence of a lexical stress contrast within a two-syllable window at the right edge of content words, as well as three tonemes, two of which are lexical (High and Rise) and one of which is default (Fall). I will return to Remijsen's analysis in a moment. The other explores the by now established fact according to which the prominence of the accented syllable in stress-accent languages is definable in terms of a fairly constant set of acoustic parameters.

It was claimed by Bolinger (1958) and Hyman (1977) that, everything else being equal, languages tend to obey a hierarchy as regards the acoustic parameters chosen to implement word stress: the most important factor is *Fundamental Frequency*, or pitch, followed by *duration* and *intensity*, in that order. Later work by Berinstein (1979) showed that the relative importance of specific prosodic parameters for the realization/identification of word-prominence is not a fixed linguistic universal, but instead depends on the phonological structure of the system. Berinstein established what she called the *Functional Load Hypothesis* by studying the relevance of length as a perceptual cue in languages with and without a vocalic length contrast and found that duration was the least important cue for word prominence in languages with contrastive vowel length. For languages with a length contrast on vowels, Berinstein's findings showed that pitch remains the most important perceptual cue for the identification of stress, followed by intensity and duration, a deviation from the hierarchy established by Bolinger[7]. When we combine Bolinger and Berinstein's findings, the following typology emerges[8]:

(4)
Contrastive vowel length   Stress: pitch > intensity > duration
Contrastive tone   Stress: duration > intensity > pitch
None   Stress: pitch > duration > intensity
(Contrastive vowel length
plus contrastive tone   Stress: ?)

Now, if in Ma'ya, which has no contrastive vowel length, tone and stress were different systems, we would expect that in this language, the prominent syllable bears acoustic properties other than pitch, in particular that duration is an important cue in the discrimination between stressed and unstressed syllables. This, then, would distinguish Ma'ya from languages such as Japanese and some dialects of Basque, which mark the prominent syllable exclusively with a pitch contrast[9]. In a very careful experimental analysis of the Ma'ya prosodic features, Remijsen shows that duration, vowel quality and spectral balance values vary significantly as a function of the presence of stress-accent, whereas pitch does not, as is summarized in the tables VII to X in his paper.

Let us briefly return to Remijsen's phonological analysis of Ma'ya stress and tone. The crucial difference between his analysis and van der Leeden's hinges upon the interpretation of word pairs like *mana* 'light of weight' and *mana* 'grease'. According to van der Leeden these words bear witness to a tonal contrast between the Fall (21) and the Low (1) tonemes on their first (unstressed) syllable: $ma^{21}ná^3$ 'light of weight' and $ma^1ná^3$ 'grease'. For Remijsen, on the other hand, the crucial difference between these words resides in the location of stress: $má^{21}na^3$ 'light of weight', with stress on the first syllable, and $maná^3$ 'grease', with stress on the final syllable. Remijsen's reanalysis leads to the elimination of the low toneme from the Ma'ya system of tonemes: low tones exclusively occur in unstressed syllables, where they never contrast with other tones, and which therefore may be considered phonologically toneless. Furthermore, besides entering in a paradigmatic opposition with the High (3) and Rise (12) tonemes on the final syllable of content words, the Fall (21) toneme surfaces on root-final stressed syllables, irrespective of their underlying tone, as a consequence of a number of lexical, morphological, or syntactic operations that neutralize the tone opposition. For this reason Remijsen suggests that the Fall toneme represents the default tone for stressed vowels. This, in turn, together with the fact that prefinal stress always surfaces with the default tone, allows him to establish the lexical contrast of the word pairs under discussion as $mána^3$ 'light of weight' versus $maná^3$ 'grease'. Moreover, when under focus, the prefinal syllable of $má^{21}na^3$ 'light of weight' shows all of the phonetic parameters typical of Ma'ya stressed vowels, as predicted. The author concludes that stress and tone are independent parameters in this language: in polysyllabic content words, stress is unpredictably either final or prefinal, and there is a three-way surface tone contrast on the only or final syllable of content words, of which High and Rise are lexically specified, and of which Fall is assigned by default.

Remijsen's reanalysis of the Ma'ya facts is certainly convincing. It is not entirely clear, however, whether stress and tone are really independent in this language. A comparison with the tonal dialects of Limburg Dutch could be illuminating[10]. Limburg Dutch has both a stress-accent, including phonological rules that refer to the stressed/unstressed distinction, and a (binary) surface tone contrast. Stress is contrastive, as in standard Dutch (e.g. *kanón* 'cannon' versus *cánon* 'canon'). The tonal contrast is limited to stressed syllables, wherever these occur, that contain two sonorant moras. One way to distinguish the contrasting syllables phonologically is to use a privative lexical High tone ~ Ø opposition, as is done in Gussenhoven (1999). Let us compare this state of affairs with the facts of Ma'ya. Instead of a single lexical high tone, Ma'ya has two lexical tones. Seemingly, these tones are lexically assigned to the final syllable of content words, whether stressed or unstressed. As it turns out, however, in words with **pre**-final stress there is no tonal opposition on the last syllable: only the high toneme may occur after a pre-final (default) Fall. Since the final tone is always predictable after a **pre**final stress, the lexical representation of a word like *mána*³ 'light of weight' (versus *maná*³ 'grease') can be further simplified as *mána*, without any tone specification whatsoever. Now, if unstressed final syllables have no lexical tone, the only syllables that do carry a lexical tone specification are stressed syllables. It would thus seem, from the point of view of lexical representation, that the dialects of Limburg Dutch use a single lexical tone that may be attached to any stressed syllable of the required type, whereas in Ma'ya there are two tonemes, but which are restricted to final stressed syllables of content words at the level of lexical representation. All other differences appear to be predictable by rule. From a more abstract point of view, the word-prosodic system of Ma'ya seems to represent a variant of the type 2 in the typology (3) given above.

José Ignacio Hualde, Gorka Elordieta, Iñaki Gaminde and Rajka Smiljanić; (henceforth abbreviated as HEGS) show that some Basque dialects spoken along the Bizkaian coast possess a prosodic system that shares some important characteristics with the one that is known from Tokyo Japanese:

- A lexical accented/unaccented distinction
- A non-accentual phrase-initial rise %LH maintained up to the accented syllable
- Invariable realization of accents as H*L (a pitch fall after the accented syllable)
- No durational correlates of prominence

As a matter of fact, part of the above characteristics defines the relevant variants of Basque as representing a non-stress accent system in terms of Beckman's typology in Table 1. The authors very carefully investigate the dialectal distribution of two of the given parameters: the accented/unaccented distinction and the presence of the initial rise. The results of their experiments are summarized Table 2 below (I have added the Tokyo Japanese and Spanish systems for comparison):

Table 2:

	Tokyo	Northern Dialects	Southern Dialects	Bergara	Spanish
Lexical acc/unacc dist	Yes	yes (among inflected and uninflected words)	yes (only among words uninflected for number)	no (no lexically unaccented content words)	no (no lexically unaccented content words)
%LH	yes	yes	No	No	no
Duration	No	no	yes (?)	yes (?)	yes

One group of the Basque dialects, which belong to the Northern Bizkaian Basque area, seems to share all of the characteristics of the Tokyo pitch accent system. The Southern dialects are different and represent the intermediate case between Northern Bizkaian and Western Bizkaian (Bergara), the latter having a Castilian Spanish type stress-accent system. The interrogation marks in Table 2 indicate that the relevant parameters were not studied for these dialects. Therefore, the values I have filled in must be considered speculative. They are solely motivated by the (not very explicit) observation made by HEGS, that, except for the absence of lexically unaccented words in Bergara, "the accentual systems of Bergara and SB are rather similar". Moreover, the authors mention a study by Etxebarria (1991), who found a consistent difference in the duration of accented and unaccented vowels for the Southern Bizkaian dialect of Zeberio.

I found this paper very interesting for various reasons. First, as HEGS observe in an earlier version of the paper, since Basque has no length opposition, the Northern Bizkaian dialects provide proof that tone can function as the unique phonetic correlate of word-prominence. Moreover, as the authors also note, the very fact that the Northern Bizkaian Basque dialects bear all of the defining characteristics of the Tokyo-Japanese system, without the availability of an areal or genetic explanation, does indeed suggest that the Tokyo 'prototype' presents a relatively unmarked prosodic system. It seems to make sense that a word-prosody that is marked by a pitch fall immediately after the accented syllable, combines with a tonal rise as an initial phrase boundary marker. It seems equally relevant to add to these resemblances the fact that, just as in Tokyo Japanese, in Northern Bizkaian the pitch of the accented syllable (the mora in Japanese) is often higher than any high pitch in the preceding syllables. (For this observation in Japanese, see Poser, 1984; Pierrehumbert & Beckman, 1988; Ramsey, 1999:180.)

As for the way in which some of the Basque dialects have lost the above described word-prosodic features, one should not exclude a priori the possibility of an original variation among the Basque dialects. This would not be unusual, as it also exists among the Limburg dialects as well as among the dialects of Japan. See, in particular, Uwano (1999:157) who discusses the Japanese dialect of Shizukuishi, in which the pitch *rise* is the distinctive word-prosodic feature.

One final comment regards a fact that was not made explicit by the authors, but which strikes me as very relevant for the discussion regarding the overall typology of word-prosodic systems, especially with regard to the discussion whether or not it makes sense to distinguish between tone languages and accentual languages, and, within the latter group, between stress-accent and non stress-accent languages.[11] It was observed earlier that there is some proof for the fact that the Southern Bizkaian dialects show significant variation in duration between stressed and unstressed syllables. We have also seen that these dialects, as a general feature, have preserved the accented/unaccented distinction in content words. Although the prosodic systems of this group of dialects appear not to be sufficiently studied, the facts that are known suggest that further research might confirm the existence of one or more dialects in this group that combines the accented/unaccented distinction with a genuine stress-accent (and maybe with all the further characteristics of a genuine stress-accent language, such as the presence of phonological rules sensitive to the stressed/unstressed distinction[12]). Now, given that there are languages which lack lexically unaccented words, but which mark a single syllable per word exclusively with pitch, such as the Japanese dialects of Northern Honshuu and Kyushu, or the Tanzanian Bantu languages Kinga, Safwa and Hibena[13], and also given the existence of languages like Tokyo Japanese and Northern Bizkaian Basque where some words are marked with pitch and others are unaccented, we would actually expect the existence of word-prosodic systems that combine the accented/unaccented dichotomy with a genuine stress accent. If my speculations turn out to be correct, such a dialect of Southern Bizkaian Basque would fill an empirical gap in the predicted typology of stress-accent systems.

Notes

1 For a far more detailed survey, see Smeets & Adelaar (ms).
2 These, by the way, do not always identify those entities that are considered syllables by phonologists.
3 They do this without actually extracting the corresponding sequences from the word. For example, in my home town dialect, children quickly discover that *l*[ɛː]*pel* 'spoon' is pronounced *l*[iə]*pel* by their friends living on the other side of the railroad.
4 Such as, for example, the willingness to teach the variant considered the norm, as was the purpose of the *Appendix Probi* (e.g. *vetulus* non *veclus*), whose author was happy enough to dispose of an alphabetic writing system.
5 Thanks to Toni Rietveld for useful discussion of the different indexes to be discussed below.
6 This does not necessarily mean that only one of the parameters is enough to account for rhythmic differences among languages. See for this Frota & Vigário (2001), who apply Ramus' method to the European and Brazilian variants of Portuguese.

7   It appears to be the case that the Functional Load Hypothesis has a very old predecessor. Trubetzkoy first addressed the question of the relation between stress and vowel quantity in a paper that deals with the disintegration of the common Russian linguistic unity, which he published in 1925. There Trubetzkoy explains the disappearance of the Old-Slavic ('Urslavisch') pitch accent as a consequence of the loss of quantitative vowel oppositions. According to Trubetzkoy, this supposed causal relation follows from a universal implicational law, that may be formulated as in (i)

   (i) Universal implicational relations between vowel quantity and stress (Trubetzkoy 1925)
      a. If L has contrastive pitch accent, then L has a vocalic length contrast.
      b. If L has a vocalic length contrast, then L cannot also have a contrastive dynamic (stress) accent, which implies:
      c. If L has a contrastive dynamic (stress) accent, then L cannot have also contrastive vowel length.

   In a later paper Trubetzkoy returns to these laws in some more detail and points out that the implications given as (b, c) had already been proposed by Jakobson in 1923, in a study on Czech metrics. The implicational laws in (i) embody the suggestion of a functional division of labor between pitch on the one hand and duration/intensity on the other: languages that use pitch as an across-the-board contrast cannot also use it for purposes of word stress, and, inversely, languages that use duration as a general vocalic opposition cannot use it for the purposes of prominence. Clearly, already in Trubetzkoy's mind the phonetic parameters used to express word prominence are related to the structure of the phonological system (for a detailed discussion of Trubetzkoy's view on the relation between phonological quantity and stress accent, see Wetzels, forthcoming).

8   I have added the fourth logical possibility between parentheses. Languages that have both contrastive tone and contrastive vowel length do exist. I do not know if one could also argue for the relevance of stress in these languages. One would expect that such languages would not exist, or be very rare. Notice further that the parameter expressed as 'intensity' in (4), since it is currently considered both as irrelevant and unreliable as a correlate for stress-accent, should perhaps be replaced by 'spectral balance'. For a recent comprehensive discussion on the phonetics of word prosody, see van Heuven & Sluijter (1996).

9   For an explicit statement regarding the uniqueness of tone as a correlate for prominence in Japanese non-stress accent systems, see Hayata (1999:221), for Basque, see Hualde et al., this volume and below. One should keep in mind, however, that in Japanese length is a contrastive feature of both consonants and vowels.

10 For the facts of Limburg Dutch, see Hermans (1994); Gussenhoven (1999).

11 See, for example, Kaji's (1999) discussion of Odden.

12 For extensive discussion of prototypical tonal and prototypical stress properties, see Odden (1999) and Hyman (forthcoming).
13 See Hayata (1999:221) for Japanese, Odden (1999:198) for Bantu and some other languages.

References

Berinstein, A.
    1979   *A Cross-Linguistic Study on the Perception and Production of Stress.* MA-thesis, UCLA. WPP47.

Bolinger, D. L.
    1958   A theory of pitch accent. *Word*, **14**, 109–149.

Clements, G. N. & Hertz, S. H.
    1996   An integrated model of phonetic representation in grammar. *Working Papers of the Cornell Phonetics Laboratory*, **11**, 34–116.

Comrie, B.
    1989   *Language Universals and Linguistic Typology.* Chicago: University of Chicago Press.

Frota, S. & Vigário, M.
    2001   On the correlates of rhythmic distinctions: the European/Brazilian Portuguese case. *Probus*, **12**, 247–275

Gussenhoven, C.
    1999   Tone systems in Dutch Limburgian dialects. In Kaji (ed.), 127–143.

Hale, Ken
    1998   On endangered languages and the importance of linguistic diversity. In L. A. Grenoble & L. J. Whaley (eds.), *Endangered Languages*, (pp. 192–216). Cambridge: Cambridge University Press.

Hayata, T.
    1999   Accent and tone: towards a general theory of prosody. In Kaji (ed.), 221–234.

Hermans, B.
    1944   *The Composite Nature of Accent. With Case Studies of the Limburgian and Serbo-Croatian Pitch Accents.* Tilburg, Katholieke Universiteit Brabant.

Heuven, V. J. van & Sluijter, A.
    1996   Notes on the phonetics of word prosody. In R. Goedemans, H. van der Hulst & E. Visch (eds.), *Stress Patterns of the World. Part I: Background.* HIL Publications Vol **II**, (pp. 233–269). Den Haag: Holland Academic Graphics

Hyman, L.
    1977   On the nature of linguistic stress. In L. Hyman (ed.), *Studies in Stress and Accent.* Southern California Occasional Papers in Linguistics, **4**, 37–82.

Hyman, L.
  forthcoming Tone systems. In M. Haspelmath, E. König, W. Oesterreicher & W. Raible (eds.), *Language Typology and Language Universals: An International Handbook*. 2 vols. Berlin & New York: Walter de Gruyter.
Jakobson, R.
  1968 *Child Language Aphasia and Phonological Universals*. Mouton: The Hague.
Kaji, S. (ed.)
  1999 *Proceedings of the Symposium Cross-Linguistic Studies of Tonal Phenomena, Tonogenesis, Typology, and Related Topics*. ILCAA, Tokyo University of Foreign Studies.
  1999 Comments on David Odden's paper. In Kaji (ed.), 217–219.
Lambert, W. E.
  1992 *Language, psychology and culture*. Stanford: Stanford University Press.
Odden, D.
  1999 Typological issues in tone and stress in Bantu. In Kaji (ed.), 187–215.
Pierrehumbert, J. & Beckman, M. E.
  1988 *Japanese Tone Structure*. Cambridge, MA: MIT Press.
Poser, W.
  1984 *The Phonetics and Phonology of Tone and Intonation in Japanese*. PhD dissertation, MIT.
Ramsey, R.
  1999 Comments on Professor Uwano Zendo's "Classification of Japanese accent systems". In Kaji (ed.), 179–182.
Ramus, F.
  1999 *Rythme des Langues et Acquisition du Langage*. PhD dissertation. Paris, École des Hautes Études em Sciences Sociales.
Sapir, E.
  1921 *Language*. New York: Harcourt Brace.
Smeets, I. & Adelaar, W.
  ms *Bedreigde Talen*. Department of Descriptive and Comparative Linguistics, Leiden University. 1993.
Trubetzkoy, N.
  1929 Zur allgemeinen Theorie der phonologischen Vokalsysteme. *Travaux du Cercle Linguistique de Prague*, **I**, 39–67.
Wetzels, W. L.
  forthcoming On the relation between quantity-sensitive stress and distinctive vowel length: The history of a principle and its relevance for Romance. In C. Wiltshire & J. Camps (eds.), *Selected Papers of the XXXth Linguistic Symposium on Romance Languages*. Amsterdam: Benjamins.
Zendo, U.
  1999 Classification of Japanese accent systems. In Kaji (ed.), 151–178.

Underspecified recognition

Aditi Lahiri and Henning Reetz

Abstract

The FUL (Featurally Underspecified Lexicon) model assumes phonological representations of morphemes with hierarchically structured features, not all of which are specified. Such underspecified representations are assumed for the mental lexicon as well as for the computerised lexicon employed for automatic speech recognition. In FUL, a segment is lexically represented by sufficient features to separate it from any other segments in the phonology of a particular language. In speech production, adjacent features 'fill in' underspecified slots, thereby accounting for assimilations. In speech perception, incoming speech sounds are compared online to these sets of features with a ternary logic of match, mismatch, and no-mismatch. Features that are present in the acoustic signal do not mismatch with the underspecified (i.e. 'empty') slots in the lexicon. In such an approach, speech perception can deal with different kinds of within- and across-speaker variation found in normal speech, without listing every variant in the lexicon. Along with diachronic data and the results of psycholinguistic experiments, the computational performance of our automatic speech recognition system successfully demonstrates the adequacy of this model.

1. Introduction

The speech signal of the same phonetic segment varies across dialects and speakers, within speakers between segmental and prosodic contexts, and even for the same speaker and context with repetition, speaking rate, emotional state, microphone and line condition, etc.[*] Ambiguities in the signal, whether they come from random noise or whether they are linguistic in nature, like cliticisations of words, or assimilations, partial or otherwise, are the norm rather than the exception in natural language. Human listeners, however, appear not to be too concerned by adverse acoustic conditions and indeed, handle "variations" in the signal with aplomb. Any theory of lexical phonological representation and recognition must be able to account for productive phonological processes such as assimilations, particularly across word boundaries. Explicitly or implicitly, all such theories assume that at the level of the lexical entry there is a single abstract representation, so that not every phonological surface variant form is listed.[1] This leaves unanswered, however, the question of precisely how the system does recognise the different phonetic variants of a word when the relationship between these realisations and the lexical entry is not straightforward.

We will consider here the linguistic, psychological, and computational adequacy of our approach to this question. The approach we advocate assumes a featurally underspecified lexicon, extraction of features from the acoustic signal, and a ternary matching condition which matches the output features to the lexically specified features. The predictions of our model — FUL (Featurally Underspecified Lexicon) — are evaluated on the basis of language comprehension experiments, evidence from language change, and its computational performance in an automatic speech recognition system. The crucial assumptions of FUL are given below.

(1)   Underspecified recognition: the FUL model

   a. The phonological representation is abstract and underspecified. The feature representation for each segment is constrained by universal properties and language specific requirements.
   b. Each morpheme has a unique representation. No phonological variants, morphophonological or postlexical, are stored.
   c. The perception system analyses the signal for rough acoustic features which are transformed into phonological features. There is no conversion into segments or syllables and there is no further intermediate representation.
   d. The phonological features are mapped directly on to the lexical representation. A three-way matching condition (*match, mismatch, no-mismatch*) determines the choice of candidates activated. Along with the phonological information, morphological, syntactic and semantic information is made available.

Each point is discussed briefly in turn. (1a) A segment is represented with a root node and its relevant features, similar to that presented in Lahiri & Evers (1991), Lahiri (2000) and Ghini (2001). The most salient aspects of this representation are that (i) features are privative or monovalent, (ii) vowels and consonants share the same place features, and (iii) the place features split into two nodes: the articulator node consisting of the places of articulation, and the height features under the tongue height or aperture node. Hence [HIGH] and [LOW] (height features) are independent of the places of articulation [LABIAL], [CORONAL] and [DORSAL].

Not all features are represented in the lexicon. The specification of features depends both on universal and language specific grounds. For instance, the FUL system has the feature [ABRUPT] in its inventory, but it is not specified in the lexical representation for German morphemes. Neither is the feature [CORONAL] specified. The assumption is that features like [ABRUPT] and [CORONAL] are left unspecified unless the phonological system of the language requires it. In our model, underspecification is context-free.

Underspecification and underspecified representations have been the source of considerable dissension.[2] A recent critique, re-examining the pros and cons of the issues and providing further evidence in favour of underspecification, is given in Ghini (2001). Ghini shows that a complex pattern of vowel alternation in the dialect of Miogliola supports not only the underspecification of vowel features, but also that two superficially similar dental nasals are underlyingly different – one specified for [CORONAL] which always surfaces as [n], and the other unspecified for place which surfaces as [ŋ], [ɲ] and [n] under prosodically defined conditions. These facts are discussed in more detail with reference to language change in §3.

The next assertion (1b), that no phonological variant is stored, is also linked to the notion of an underspecified representation. No postlexical variants are stored and if morpheme alternants are phonologically related the assumption is that only a single underlying representation is available. From the signal to the phonological representation, the perceptual system extracts rough acoustic characteristics which are converted into phonological features (1c). All features are extracted independent of whether they are specified or unspecified in lexical representations. The features extracted from the speech signal are then compared to those stored in the lexicon. There is no conversion from features into segments; in fact there is no intermediate representation of segments, syllables or any other phonological unit. The mapping from the features to the representation entails a ternary system of matching (1d): *match, no-mismatch* and *mismatch*. The *match* condition can only occur if both signal and lexicon have the same features. This condition is used for the scoring of word candidates and includes a correction formula to account for different sized feature sets. The *mismatch* occurs if signal and lexicon have contradicting features. A mismatch excludes a word from the list of possible word candidates. The mismatching relationship can be bidirectional. For instance, [HIGH] and [LOW] mismatch, independent of which is extracted from the signal and which is stored in the lexicon. A mismatch can occur also in one direction due to underspecification. For example, any one of the place features [LABIAL], [DORSAL], or [CORONAL] can be extracted from the signal but only [LABIAL] and [DORSAL] are stored in the lexicon. If the feature [CORONAL] is extracted from the signal then it mismatches with the features [LABIAL] and [DORSAL]. The other way round, the signal feature [LABIAL] *does not* mismatch with an underspecified coronal sound.

A *no-mismatch* occurs (i) if no feature is extracted from the signal that is stored in the lexicon, or (ii) if a feature is extracted from the signal that is not stored in the lexicon, and (iii) by definition (e.g. [CORONAL] does not mismatch with [HIGH]). Case (i), where no feature is extracted from the signal but features are available in the lexicon, does not lead to a rejection of candidates. The signal simply does not contradict a candidate; only the candidate does not increase its matching score (see below). Case (ii) is exactly the case for the lexical feature [CORONAL]: coronality is not stored in the lexicon. If a place feature like [LABIAL] or [DORSAL] is extracted from the signal, it does not mismatch with a coronal sound in the lexicon.

(2) Examples of *match, mismatch* and *no-mismatch*
     Signal   Matching   Lexicon
     [HIGH]   *mismatch*   [LOW]
     [CORONAL]   *mismatch*   [DORSAL]
     [DORSAL]   *no-mismatch* [UNSPECIFIED PLACE]
     [DORSAL]   *match*   [DORSAL]

All word candidates that agree (match or do not mismatch) with the initial feature set are activated, together with their phonological, morphological, syntactic, and other information. Matching features increase the activation level for potential word candidates, non-mismatching features do not exclude candidates and only mismatching features lead to the rejection of word candidates. The level of activation is measured on the basis of the number of matching features with respect to those specified in the lexicon and the number of features extracted from the signal (Reetz 1998). Each candidate receives a score on the basis of the formula given in (3):

(3) Scoring formula

$$\text{SCORE} = \frac{(\text{NR. OF MATCHING FEATURES})^2}{(\text{NR. OF FEATURES FROM SIGNAL}) \times (\text{NR. OF FEATURES IN THE LEXICON})}$$

To illustrate the scoring method, the features extracted from the signal for the first vowel in the intended German word *müde* [myːdə] 'tired' would optimally be [HIGH, CORONAL, LABIAL]. The features in the lexicon are [HIGH, LABIAL]. Given these features, the scores of other front vowels would be as follows:

(4) Scores for [y]

	Lexical features	Input features of [y]	Score
[y]	[HIGH, LABIAL]	[HIGH, CORONAL, LABIAL]	$2^2/(3 \times 2) = 0.66$
[i]	[HIGH]		$1^2/(3 \times 1) = 0.33$
[Y]	[HIGH, LABIAL, RTR]		$2^2/(3 \times 3) = 0.44$
[ɪ]	[HIGH, RTR]		$1^2/(3 \times 2) = 0.16$

According to these scores, a word like *Mücke* [mYkə] 'mosquito' would be a higher scoring candidate than *Miete* [miːtə] 'rent' for the initial sequence [myː] of *müde*. If for some reason the feature [LABIAL] was not present in the signal, or could not be extracted by the listener, the FUL system predicts that [i] would have the highest score but [y] would still be available. None of the low vowels, however, would be considered if [HIGH] was extracted since it would mismatch with lexically specified [LOW]. We will discuss this in more detail in §4.

In the next three sections we briefly go through some data in support of the FUL model from language comprehension experiments, language change, and finally from the speech recognition system that we are developing.

2. Underspecification in language comprehension

In this section, we focus on the adequacy of the assumptions in FUL for language comprehension. To this end we will summarise some experiments incorporating the concept of underspecification for lexical access.

As we mentioned above, assimilation can lead to surface variants. Assimilation of a coronal sound (e.g. /n/) to a following labial place of articulation (like /b/ in "Where could Mr. Bean be?") often results in the production of a labial (i.e. *Bea[m] be*). The reverse is not usually true, that is, a labial sound does *not* assimilate to a coronal place of articulation (i.e., *la[m]e duck* does *not* become *la[n]e duck*).[3] Simple articulatory mechanics cannot account for such behaviour because an articulatory assimilation would operate in both directions. An explanation can be given by assuming that coronal sounds are underspecified for place, whereas labials and dorsals are not: the labial place of articulation spreads to the preceding coronal sound (if the language has regressive assimilation) because that sound is not specified for place. On the other hand, the specification of a labial place prevents the place features of an adjacent sound from overriding this information. Consequently, coronal sounds can become labial (or dorsal), but labial (or dorsal) sounds do not change their place of articulation.

This explanation is straightforward for speech production, but not so in speech perception. How can a realisation of *gree[m]* in a labial context (like *bag*) or *gree[ŋ]* in a dorsal context (like *grass*) lead to the access of the word *green* in the lexicon? The utterances *gree[m]* and *gree[ŋ]* are nonwords in English. And, at the same time, how should a mechanism be constructed to disallow the activation of the word *bean* if the acoustic input is *bea[m]*, even if *bean* is a word of the language? Human listeners handle these asymmetries (and many other assimilatory effects) within and across words without noticing it, as experimental evidence indicates (Lahiri & Marslen-Wilson, 1991; Gaskell & Marslen-Wilson, 1996; Gow, 2001; Lahiri & van Coillie, to appear). The solution to these seemingly contradictory requirements can be obtained in the FUL system by assuming an underspecified representation in the lexicon, where certain features (like the place feature [CORONAL]) are *not* stored in the lexicon (in speech production, segments with unspecified place are generated with the feature [CORONAL] by default) and by postulating the ternary matching logic in the signal-to-lexicon mapping.

Assuming that phonological lexical representations of words consist of underspecified featural representations, Lahiri & Marslen-Wilson (1991, 1992) argue that the mapping process from the signal to the lexicon crucially depends on the absence and presence of features in the representations of words in the mental lexicon. They contrasted vowel nasality in Bengali and English, where Bengali has underlying nasal vowels as well as contextual nasalisation ([bʰãr] 'clay bowl', /bʰan/ > [bʰãn] 'pretence'). On the other hand, any nasality on a vowel in English comes from a neighbouring nasal consonant. They argued that only underlying contrastive nasal vowels in Bengali are specified for nasality; for other vowels, no nasality is specified. Results show that indeed, the listener always interprets nasality on a vowel as being contrastively nasal even if the stimulus segment contained a vowel which was contextually nasalised. More strikingly, oral vowels in oral contexts, for both English and Bengali (English *bad*, Bengali [bʰɑr] 'weight'), are interpreted by listeners as having either a nasal or an oral context, depending on the distribution of the words in the language. That is, the vowel [æ] in *bad* was equally likely to be a interpreted as being part of *bad* or *ban*, showing that in both languages the oral vowels were represented as unspecified for nasality in spite of the fact that there may be surface phonetic nasalisation present in production of CVN words.

Thus, along with underspecification, the three-way matching – match, no-mismatch and mismatch – gives the asymmetry between coronals on the one hand and labials and dorsals on the other. If [CORONAL] is extracted from the signal, then it mismatches with [LABIAL] (i.e. [n] mismatches with underlying /m/). It does not find a perfect match since /n/ is not specified for [CORONAL], but it does not mismatch either – hence a no-mismatch situation occurs. If [LABIAL] is retrieved from the signal, it matches perfectly with underlying /m/, but it also does not mismatch with /n/. This is not the best match, but it is a no-mismatch. Examples of the three way distinction are given in (5).

(5)   Matching from signal to lexicon

Signal	Matching	Lexicon
[HIGH]	*match*	[HIGH]
[STRIDENT]	*mismatch*	[NASAL]
[LATERAL]	*mismatch*	[NASAL]
[CORONAL]	*mismatch*	[LABIAL]
[CORONAL]	*no-mismatch*	[UNSPECIFIED PLACE]
[LABIAL]	*no-mismatch*	[UNSPECIFIED PLACE]

The system can handle within and across word assimilations and can deal with a certain number of dialectal variants. The asymmetry in assimilation is explained by the fact that since the place feature [CORONAL] is unspecified, the feature [LABIAL] detected in the signal for *gree[m] book* does not mismatch with the lexical representation *green*. However, the feature [DORSAL] detected in the signal for *ho[ŋ]* does mismatch with the feature [LABIAL] in the lexical representation of *home,* and so *home* is rejected. Coronals get a lower score than the labials (or dorsals), which obtain a match, but coronals are not excluded. They remain active as assimilatory variants.

Lahiri & van Coillie (to appear) provide further evidence for the underspecification of [CORONAL], and the efficacy of the three-way matching. We will briefly discuss two experiments. In both experiments, a crossmodal lexical decision task with semantic priming was used. The listeners were auditorily presented with a real word like *Bahn* 'railway' or *Lärm* 'noise' in isolation. At the offset of the acoustic stimulus, the subjects saw a semantically related word like *Zug* 'train' or *Krach* 'bang, racket' and they had to decide whether it was a word or not. Since it is well established in the psycholinguistic literature that semantically related words prime, the expectation was that the subjects would be faster in reacting to *Zug* after they heard *Bahn* as compared to an unrelated word *Maus* 'mouse'. Similarly, *Krach* should be recognised faster after *Lärm* rather than after *Blatt* 'leaf'. The question of course is whether nonword variants of the real word primes would have any effect. That is, would related acoustic variants **Bahm* or **Lärn* prime *Zug* and *Krach* respectively? The first experiment presented here examined word final nasals. The experimental design and predictions are illustrated below.

(6)   Recognition of word final nasals: predictions

Acoustic Test Primes	Target	Lexical Representation	Predicted Reaction Times
	ZUG	Bah /NASAL/	
		|	
		UNSPECIFIED	
{ Bah [n] *Bah [m] }		no-mismatch no-mismatch	FAST FAST
Acoustic Control Prime			
Maus		unrelated	SLOW

Acoustic Test Primes	Target	Lexical Representation	Predicted Reaction Times
	KRACH	Lär /NASAL/	
		|	
		[LABIAL]	
{ Lär [m] *Lär [n] }		match mismatch	FAST SLOW
Acoustic Control Prime			
Blatt		unrelated	SLOW

The claim is that although the acoustic prime *Bahm* is a nonword it does not mismatch with the lexical representation of *Bahn* and therefore successfully activates *Zug*. The signal has the feature [LABIAL] but the lexical representation has no place specified in the lexicon and hence it is not rejected. This is not the case with an underlying labial. When the feature [CORONAL] is extracted from the nonword *Lärn*, it mismatches with the lexically represented [LABIAL] of the real word *Lärm* and hence its semantic associate is not activated. Apart from the nasal, we used additional consonantal variations as primes which deviate from the lexical representation with respect to other features as well. The matching expectations are given in (7).

(7) Other consonantal variants of word final nasals

a. Variants of final /-n/

Acoustic variant	Acoustic features	Lexical Representation of /n/	Matching
Bah[l]	[LATERAL] [CORONAL]	[NASAL] [UNSPECIFIED PLACE]	mismatch no-mismatch
Bah[p]	[ABRUPT] [LABIAL]	[NASAL] [UNSPECIFIED PLACE]	mismatch no-mismatch
Bah[s]	[STRIDENT] [CORONAL]	[NASAL] [UNSPECIFIED PLACE]	mismatch no-mismatch

b. Variants of final /-m/

Acoustic variant	Acoustic features	Lexical Representation of /m/	Matching
Lär[w]	[CONTINUANT] [LABIAL]	[NASAL] [LABIAL]	mismatch match
Lär[p]	[ABRUPT] [LABIAL]	[NASAL] [LABIAL]	mismatch match
Lär[s]	[STRIDENT] [CORONAL]	[NASAL] [LABIAL]	mismatch mismatch

Note that features like [ABRUPT] and [CORONAL] are not specified in the German lexicon. It does not mean that this is always so.

Depending on the grammar of a particular language, [CORONAL] for instance can be specified for nasals and not for stops, as laid out in the next section.

As indicated in (6) and (7), for each word, 4 nonword primes were created by changing the final consonant.[4] Thus for the word *Bahn*, the nonwords were *Bah[m], Bah[l], Bah[s], Bah[p]*. In addition, there was a control prime for each target, where the control was unrelated to the real word prime (e.g. *Maus-Zug*). Thus, in all, for one target there were six different primes. However, each subject was faced with the target only once. Reaction time measurement started at the offset of the auditory prime when the visual target was presented. The results of the experiment are given in Figures 1 and 2. In Figure 1, we see the reaction times when the prime was a variant of an underlying /-n/ unspecified for place. In comparison to the control, there is a significant priming effect for the real word *Bahn* as well as the variant **Bahm* where the final consonant did not mismatch.[5] In all other instances there was no priming effect. Recall that under our assumptions, there is no difference in matching between the surface *Bah[n]* and *Bah[m]* when compared to the real word *Bahn* (see 6). Since the nasal is unspecified for place, both variants with [n] and [m] are no-mismatches. Hence we did not expect any difference between the two conditions and our results bear this out — they do not differ significantly.

In Figure 2, we see the results of the variants of the words with final /-m/. Here, the only word which has a significant priming effect is the real word *Lärm*. In contrast to the word final [n] as in *Bahn*, where its labial variant **Bahm* also caused priming of *Zug*, the variant **Lärn* did not prime the semantically related word *Krach* of the real word *Lärm*. Moreover, there was a significant difference between *Lärm* and **Lär[n]*. The clear difference in the results supports our expectations regarding underspecified features and the match/no-mismatch asymmetry.

The next experiment examined word medial nasals. In the case of word final nasals there is a possibility of assimilation, but word medial nasals, particularly intervocalic nasals, remain untouched. Hence, one could argue that even if underspecification was a reasonable choice for word final nasals, such an option would be

Word final /-n/

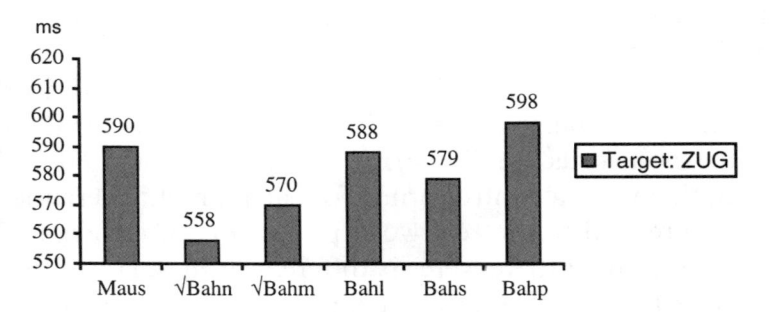

Figure 1: Mean reactions times to a semantically related target for a word ending in /-n/ and its variants (each class consists of 24 words represented here with one example). Significant priming effects with respect to the control are indicated by √.

Word final /-m/

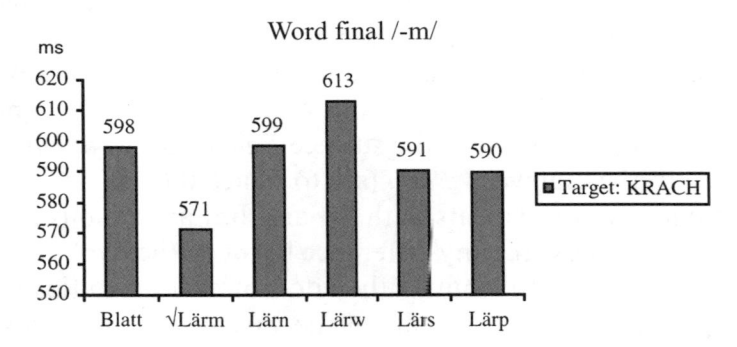

Figure 2: Mean reaction times to a semantically related target for a word ending in /-m/ and its variants (each class consists of 12 words represented here with one example). Significant priming effects with respect to the control are indicated by √.

unnecessary in medial position since there is no possibility of alternation due to assimilation. Under the FUL model, underspecification is not determined by the position in a word. Coronal consonants are unspecified for place no matter what position in a word they occur in. Our prediction is therefore, that the same asymmetry would hold for word medial nasals just as like the word final ones.

In the second experiment, assuming that medial coronal consonants in German are all unspecified for place, both obstruents as well as nasals were examined. For the sake of comparison, only the nasal data are discussed. The task was the same, and the real word primes with medial nasals were converted into two different types of nonwords: a nasal with a different place of articulation and a non-nasal consonant (*Düne* 'dune', **Dü[m]e*, **Dü[l]e*; *Schramme* 'a scratch', **Schra[n]e*, **Schra[v]e*). The targets, as before, were semantically related, and were presented visually at the offset of the prime.[6]

The results of the second experiment confirms our earlier findings. *Düne* 'dune' primes its semantically related word *Sand* 'sand' just as well as nonwords made up with a non-mismatching [LABIAL] nasal (like **Dü[m]e*). In contrast, although *Schramme* 'a scratch' primes its semantically related word *Kratzer*, (also 'a scratch'), the nonword with a coronal (**Schra[n]e*) does not. The asymmetry again shows that when the feature [LABIAL] is extracted from the signal, it does not mismatch with the underlying unspecified [CORONAL], but an extracted [CORONAL] does mismatch with a [LABIAL]. There was no priming in the other nonword conditions. In the next two figures we compare the results for the word medial and word final nasals in the same graph.

The pattern of results of the medial and final coronal nasals are very similar, as shown in Figure 3. Both the real words and their acoustic variants with [m] show significant priming effects with respect to the control. However, there is no priming with the other nonword primes as compared to the control words. This is not the same for the labials, as we can see in Figure 4.

Here, the real words with [m] are significantly faster than the control, but neither the nasal variants nor the non-nasal variants are significantly faster. The nonwords with coronal nasals mismatched and hence were no different from the unrelated controls, and they were also significantly slower than the real words with [m].

Thus, language comprehension experiments suggest that the predictions made by the FUL model combining underspecification with a three-way matching – perfect match, no-mismatch and mismatch – are borne out. The experimental results support the predicted asymmetry between coronals on the one hand, and labials and dorsals on the other.[7]

	Control	√ Word [n]	√Variant [m]	Non-nasal variants
—●—/-n/	590	558	570	588
—□—/-n-/	642	568	587	598

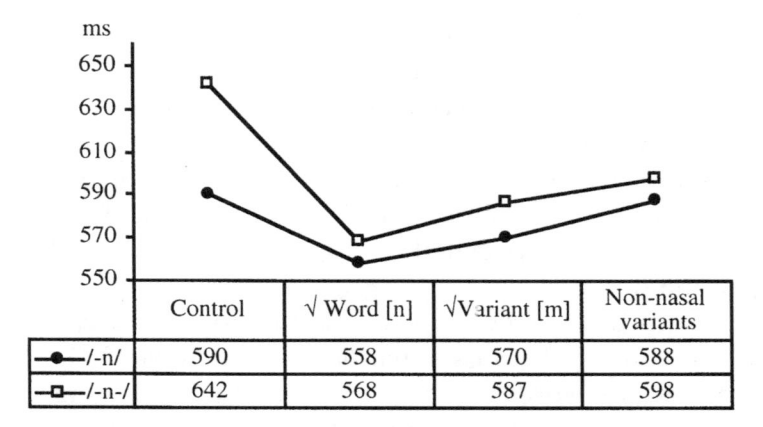

Figure 3: Comparing word final /-n/ and word medial /-n-/. Mean reaction times to the real word primes with the coronal nasal, the primes with the non-mismatching nasal variant [m], and the primes with mismatching non-nasal variants. Significant priming is indicated by √.

	Control	√ Word [m]	Variant [n]	Non-nasal variants
—●—/-m/	598	571	599	613
—□—/-m-/	602	553	601	573

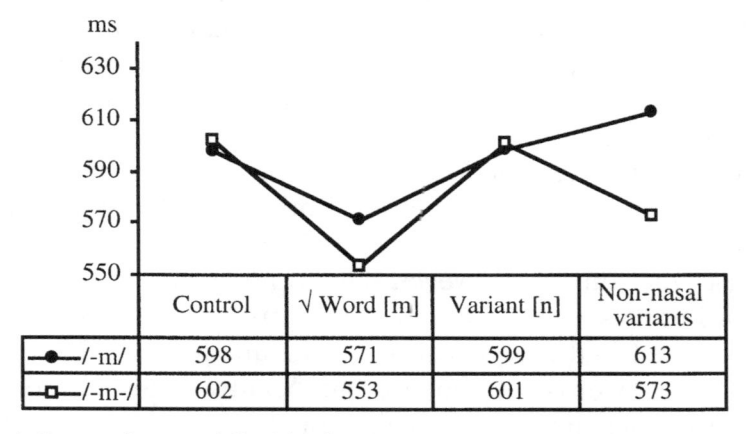

Figure 4: Comparing word final /-m/ and word medial /-m-/. Mean reaction times to the real word primes with the labial nasal, the primes with the mismatching nasal variant [n], and the primes with mismatching non-nasal variants. Significant priming is indicated by √.

3. Underspecification in language change

In general, the proponents and opponents of underspecification have leant on synchronic alternations to support their point. As we mentioned earlier, Ghini (2001) shows that underspecification of vowel and consonantal features is crucial for the understanding of the complex interaction of prosodic and segmental phenomena in Miogliola, an Italian dialect of Liguria. In particular, two superficially similar dental nasals are different in their underlying representation in terms of place specification. One of them is specified for the feature [CORONAL] and always surfaces as [n], while the other is unspecified for place and surfaces as a palatal, dental or velar, depending on context. If underspecification is part of the mental lexicon, as we claim, then it should play a role in language change since part of change is in fact building representations by a new generation. In Ghini (to appear), we find additional support for this representation from language change. The crucial facts are summarised below.

Many Italian dialects like Miogliola have lost the quantity distinction in both obstruents and nasals. Thus all Latin geminates are single consonants in these dialects. For obstruents, however, a further process of spirantisation along with voicing has helped to maintain the distinction between original Latin single consonants and geminates in Miogliola. If we compare Latin, Standard Italian and Miogliola, we find that Latin [p] remained in Italian, but became [v] in Miogliola. In general, Latin single voiceless stops and fricatives became voiced fricatives in Miogliola ([p, f] > [v]; Latin *lupus* 'wolf', Miogliola [lūv]). Geminate obstruents, however, simply degeminated in Miogliola and the stop has not undergone spirantisation. That is, Latin labial stops and fricatives [p:, f:] became simple [p, f] (Latin *cippus* 'pillar', Miogliola [tsæp]). This is shown in (8a). Thus, the original geminate/single consonant contrast of Latin is now maintained as a stop/voiced fricative contrast in Miogliola.[8]

In sonorants, there was no possibility of voicing or spirantisation, and hence, after degemination, there was a general neutralisation of the length contrast: Latin [m:, m] > Miogliola [m]. As we see in the examples in (8b), there is a single labial nasal in Miogliola now and the original geminate/nongeminate [m:]/[m] contrast of Latin has been neutralised. In standard Italian, the original length contrast is still maintained. The spirantisation and voicing processes could play no role in the case of the labial nasal.

(8)   Loss of geminate/nongeminate contrast from Latin to Miogliola

Classical Latin   Italian   Miogliola

a. Latin length distinction changed to segmental distinction for obstruents.

| cippus | 'pillar' | tʃeppo | tsæp | tsæp + ɪ (PL) |
| lupus | 'wolf' | lūpo | lūv | lūv + ɪ (PL) |

b. Sonorants did not lenite – distinction lost with labial nasals

| summus | 'utmost' | sommo | sum | sum + ɪ (PL) |
| fūmus | 'smoke' | fūmo | fym | fym + ɪ (PL) |

However, given the assumption of underspecification, the coronal nasal had the possibility of a dual pattern of change. And this is what happened: the original quantity distinction was transformed to a place distinction. The following examples illustrate this.

(9)   QUANTITY distinction to place distinction for coronal nasals

Classical Latin   Italian   Miogliola

pannus	'cloth'	panno	pān		pān + ɪ		(PL)
canis	'dog'	kāne	kaŋ		kaɲ + ɪ		(PL)
alumnus	'alumni'	alunno	alýn	MASC	alýna	FEM	(SG)
			alýnɪ	MASC	alýnɛ	FEM	(PL)
ūnus	'one'	uno	ø̃ŋ	MASC	œ̃na	FEM	(SG)
			ýɲɪ	MASC	œ̃nɛ	FEM	(PL)

LATIN   MIOGLIOLA
geminate [nː]   >   [n]
single [n]   >   [ɲ] in onset followed by [ɪ], [ŋ] in coda, [n] elsewhere

Both the single /n/ as well as the geminate /nː/ in Latin were unspecified for place. In Miogliola, the original Latin single coronal nasal /n/ remained unspecified for place – that is, there was no change. The geminate /nː/ degeminated, but became specified for place. As a result, the synchronic grammar of Miogliola shows surface neutralisations from two underlyingly different specifications. Latin *pan-*

nus became Miogliola [pān] SG., [pān + ɪ] PLURAL, where Miogliola has lost the geminate/nongeminate contrast. But the [n] in Latin *ūnus* has several surface variants in Miogliola: [øŋ], [ǽna], [ýɲɪ] and [ǽnɛ]. The quality of the nasal depends on whether it is in the coda and on the quality of the following vocalic suffix. Compare now the original Latin *alumnus,* where the /-mn-/ sequence became a geminate at a later point. Here, all four gender and number contrasts are also present as in 'one', but the consonant is always a dental [n]. Note the differences in the masculine plural: [ýɲɪ] (from unspecified /N/) and [alýnɪ] (from specified /n/). The quality of the vowel has no effect on the original geminate /nː/. The change in the representation from Latin geminate coronals to Miogliola is illustrated in (10).

(10) Change of coronal nasals from Latin to Miogliola due to underspecification

Classical Latin
distinction by QUANTITY, not PLACE

			μ
PLACELESS	N	PLACELESS	N
	|		|
	PLACE		PLACE
	unspecified		*unspecified*
SURFACE	[n]		[nː]

Miogliola
distinction by PLACE, not QUANTITY

PLACELESS	N	PLACE SPECIFIC	n
	|		|
	PLACE		PLACE
	unspecified		|
			CORONAL
SURFACE	[n, ɲ, ŋ]		[n]

As can be seen, the placeless /N/ can take place features according to segmental and prosodic contexts and surface as [n, ɲ, ŋ], while the coronal nasal specified for place, surfaces always as a dental [n].

Thus, synchronically, Miogliola has two coronal nasals, only one of which is specified for place. Like many other languages, underspecification is used contrastively. The history of these nasals show that the source of the place-unspecified nasal is the original nongeminate coronal, which maintained its underspecification and has several surface variants depending on prosodic contexts. It is the original geminate coronal nasal which became a single consonant and acquired place specification. This consonant has no surface variants. What is interesting is that it was possible for the language learner to take advantage of the underspecified place representation to maintain the original geminate/nongeminate contrast. This was not possible for the labial nasals which were already specified for place.

Thus, under our view, underspecified phonological representations, being a part of the mental representation, play a role for both processing and change. Some of the notable parallel aspects are summarised in the following table.

(11)   Processing and Change with respect to underspecified phonological representations

PROCESSING	CHANGE
a) Segments can vary according to context, leading to loss of contrast; however, there is asymmetry in the variants.	a) Sound change can lead to loss of contrasts and restructuring; however, there is occasional asymmetry in restructuring.
b) Asymmetry in representation leads to asymmetry in recognition.	b) Asymmetry in representation is reflected in phonological change.
c) Underspecified representations lend themselves to a three-way matching with features from the signal, allowing for the recognition of neutralised segments.	c) Underspecified representations can be exploited by language learners to maintain contrasts which would have otherwise been neutralised.

4. The FUL model of speech recognition

In an attempt to model a system with an underspecified lexicon and a three-way matching described above, we have developed an automatic speech recognition system which runs on these lines (Reetz, 1998, 1999; Lahiri, 1999). The central goal behind this enterprise is to test the actual viability of a feature based extraction system in combination with an underspecified lexicon and a ternary matching condition. Experimental results in language comprehension allowed us to believe that the human system does not use a fully specified phonological representation and that there is an asymmetry in the matching from the signal to the lexicon. Evidence from language change also suggests that the asymmetry in place representation can lead to an asymmetry in the restructuring of forms and to the establishment of an altered pattern of contrasts. Both pieces of evidence are real but do not provide us with a handy means of testing the predictions. We therefore took on the task of building a model based on our premises, with the addition of an acoustic front-end which could handle the online extraction of features.

Given the variation in the speech signal, it is not surprising that automatic speech recognition using simple spectral template matching has problems. Any variation of the signal leads to variation of the spectra that are compared to the stored templates. Klatt (1989) provides a comprehensive review of models which endeavour to solve the variation problem by storing all spectral information in the lexicon. The more popular approach to resolving such variation is a statistical one. Statistical approaches like Hidden Markov Models based on large training sets have led to acceptable results, but are still speaker and transmission-line dependent. Moreover, the success of the HMMs depend more on probabilities of longer strings of data (including word sequence probabilities) rather than on a front-end phonetic analysis. The system presented here operates on completely different principles, both with respect to the front-end as well as the lexicon. No spectral templates are computed from the speech signal to access the lexicon. Neither is the signal analysed in great detail for acoustic evidence of individual segments and their boundaries. The principal aspects of the FUL model are the following:

(12) Characteristics of the FUL speech recognition system
    a. The system is based on the phonological representation of words in the lexicon.
    b. Each word has a unique representation in spite of the large variation. The phonological representation is feature-based and assumes underspecification.
    c. The speech signal is converted into distinctive phonological features. The conversion operates speaker-independently and without prior training.
    d. Once the features are extracted the system never re-evaluates the acoustic signal, i.e. there is no close phonetic investigation of the signal to verify or falsify word hypotheses.
    e. Features extracted from the signal are matched with those stored in the lexicon using a ternary system of matching, non-mismatching, and mismatching features. All word candidates that match with the initial feature set are activated, together with their phonological, morphological, syntactic, and other information.
    f. The word candidates are expanded to include word hypotheses, even without complete acoustic evidence, which are then available for the phonological and syntactic parsing that uses additional prosodic and other information and operates in parallel with the acoustic front-end.

The lexical representations are similar to what we have seen before. Each morpheme is represented with root nodes linked to minimal feature specifications. For the sake of space, in the examples in (13) the features are listed in a linear string for each segment. In all, FUL requires twelve phonological features.[9] Quantity is represented in terms of moras and not by features.

(13) Lexical feature specifications for German

BAHN	/baːn/	
railway	/b/	[CONS] [LAB] [VOICE]
	/aː/	[LOW] [DORSAL]
	/n/	[NASAL]

SPECK	/ʃpɛk/	
bacon	/ʃ/	[STRIDENT]
	/p/	[CONS] [LAB]
	/ɛ/	[RTR]
	/k/	[CONS] [DORSAL]

The conversion of the speech signal to phonological features is performed in two steps. The task of the acoustic front-end described here is (a) to remove linguistically irrelevant information, (b) to use speaker independent acoustic characteristics to compute the features, and (c) not to exclude potential word candidates due to computational faults or poor signal quality. The general design principle of the system is to use simple and only rough measures that cooperate to form a stable system.

First the signal undergoes a spectral analysis that delivers LPC formants and some rough spectral shape parameters computed from the speech signal using a 20 ms window with 1 ms step rate. The output is an 'online' stream of spectral data as shown in the second panel of Figure 5 (only the speech signal and formant tracks are shown in panels 1 and 2).

The spectral parameters are converted by simple logical decisions into phonological features. The intention is to derive a representation of the speech signal that is relatively independent of the speaker and acoustic line properties. Only very broad acoustic characteristics define the 12 phonological features we use (CONSONANTAL, HIGH, LOW, RTR, VOICE, etc.). For example, the feature [HIGH] is defined by the condition that F1 has to be below 450 Hz. It can be the case that parts of the speech signal incidentally meet or miss the criteria for a particular feature. That is, a non-[LOW] sound that is *not* classified as [HIGH] in its lexical representation might have an F1 below 450 Hz, and another sound segment that should be classified as [HIGH] might have an F1 above 450 Hz. But most important, a sound segment that is [LOW] should *not* have an F1 below 450 Hz. In other words, there is a limit to define a member of a feature undoubtfully, but there is a certain range that does not exclude possible members. In general, however, the acoustic characteristics are chosen so that all members of a particular feature are captured and other sounds might be included as well, but members are hardly missed. And, more important, sounds belonging to a mismatching feature are not captured. The matching conditions and the lexicon eliminate unlikely candidates later. The rationale behind this very relaxed procedure is that in running speech a speaker can deviate from any 'norm' of acoustic characteristics of a sound due to assimilation, coarticulation, dialect, vocal tract parameters, and others. The FUL system does not have such a 'norm'. The system only expects that the feature [HIGH] is acoustically characterised by a low first formant.

The conversion from the spectral characteristics of the speech signal into phonological features delivers a stream of features. Features can change every millisecond as a consequence of the window step rate. Features are defined independently from each other and, hence, they can change independently from other features. For this reason, the features are filtered and time aligned within roughly 20 ms to define feature bundles. These bundles of distinctive features extracted from the speech signal are now compared to those sets stored in the lexicon. This comparison is executed only when the computed feature set changes (and not every millisecond), and the matching logic generates *match*, *no-mismatch* and *mismatch* conditions. The ternary logic works in the same way we have discussed before.

The computation of the matching features relative to the number of features computed from the signal and the number of features stored in the lexicon using the formula given in (3) adds a score for each feature bundle computed from the signal for each entry in the lexicon. The scoring of the consecutive feature bundles gives the word score and its ranking in the list of possible candidates. Feature sets at the beginning of a word gain a higher weight than non-initial features sets; the weight is computed by an exponential decaying function. The set of all word candidates is the lexical cohort that is used to generate word hypotheses.

To recapitulate, all word candidates that match with the initial feature set are activated, together with their phonological, morphological, syntactic, and other information. No segmentation or grouping into syllable units is performed. Matching features increase the scoring for potential word candidates, non-mismatch-

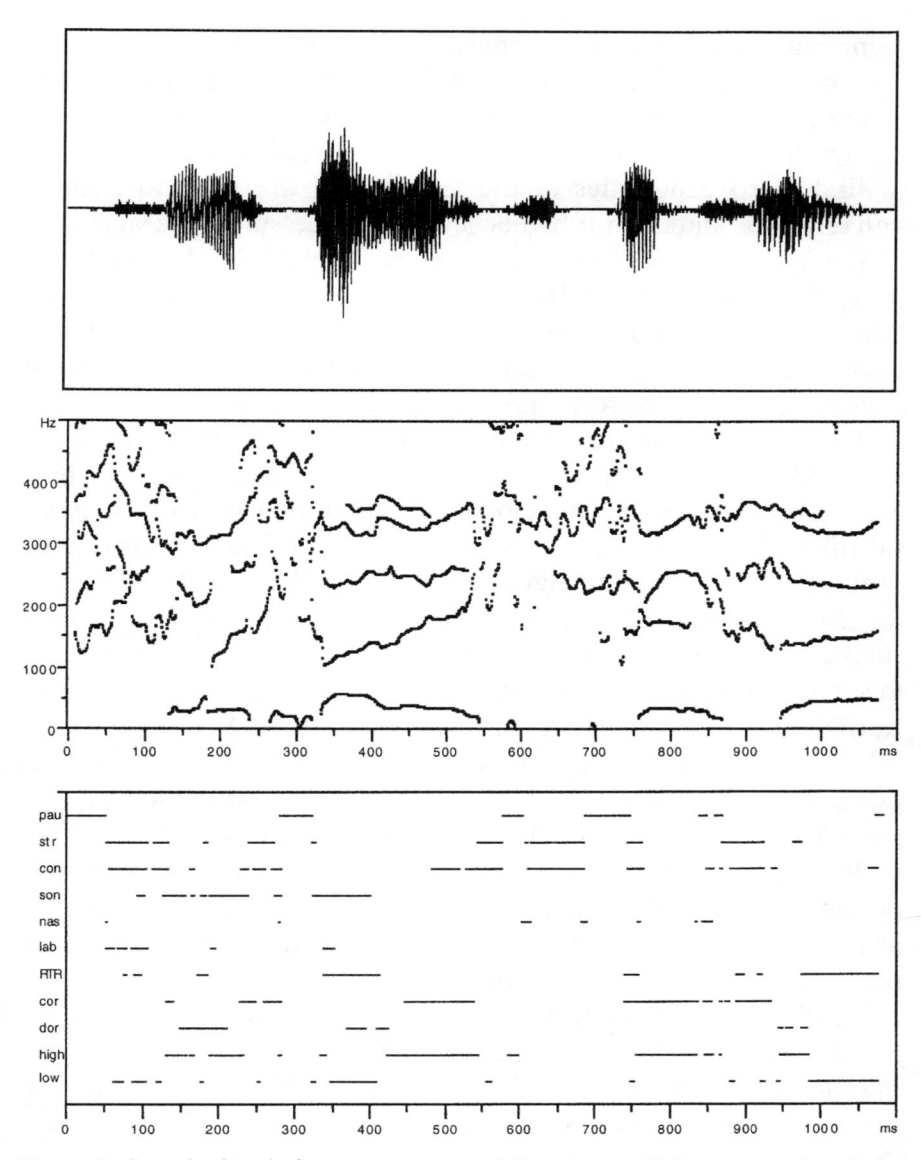

Figure 5: Speech signal, formant tracts and (uncorrected) feature tracks of the sentence "Fußball ist Spitze" (*football is fantastic*), spoken by a male German speaker.

ing features do not exclude candidates, and only mismatching features lead to the rejection of word candidates. The lexicon contains segmental, morphological, semantic, and other information for each word, but for the comparison with the information computed from the acoustic front-end only their representation by phonological features is used. These other information sources are not used to find word candidates in the lexicon but are used to exclude unlikely candidates on a higher level of processing. Characteristic of the system is the operation of these 'higher' level modules in parallel to the acoustic front-end and the lexical access. These 'higher' levels of processing are not described in this paper, which restricts itself to the description of the speech analysis, matching condition and the word hypotheses formation.

For example, the initial feature set [CONSONANTAL][LABIAL][NASAL] activates not only all words beginning with an [m], but also words beginning with other labials that do not mismatch with a nasal (like [b])[10] and also [n] because it is unspecified for place; the ranking of [m] would be higher than [n] [p] [pf] > [b] [f] > [t] [v] > [d]. But if the signal gives [CONSONANTAL][CORONAL][NASAL], a much smaller set is encountered since all dorsal and labial consonants mismatch. The consecutively incoming feature sets deactivate word candidates from the cohort that have mismatching feature sets. In other words, the system overgenerates possible word candidates but does not include impossible word candidates. If the signal gives [HIGH][SONORANT], all high and mid vowels would be activated but *no* low vowels. The rationale behind this mechanism is to include possible variants of sounds (e.g. the vowel /a/ could be pronounced as an [ɔ] or even as [e]) but to exclude variants that will not occur (e.g. the vowel /a/ is never produced as an [i]).

Further, at each point, whenever a word candidate is identified, another new word candidate can begin. Thus, the assumption being that although the signal does not dependably have information of word beginnings or word endings, the lexicon initiates candidates as it goes on.

The main aim of the system is to investigate whether an underspecified representation is suitable to model the linguistic behaviour of humans and their representation of speech. An appropriate evaluation would be therefore a comparison of the system to humans' behaviour. This is beyond our capabilities today with respect to the state of the implementation of the system and to detailed comparable data we have about humans' perception. On the other hand, Hidden Markov Models (HMMs), the standard in automatic speech recognition, operate on different principles and make a direct comparison difficult. HMM systems gain from longer strings of data (states, segments, words, or whatever), because they do not make a definite decision at the smallest unit but delay decisions as long as possible (eventually up to the end of the recognition of a phrase). This is one of the reasons why implausible words might show up in an HMM analysis in the output: the overall probability is maximised even if a part of the string has a very low probability, but there is no 'impossible' label that a part of the string might have. The FUL system makes decisions at the first step, where it rejects candidates about which it is 'sure' that they do not meet a criterion.[11] Thus, this is the first step to compare the FUL system with a HMM system. To make the comparison of single units more compatible, we restrict ourselves to vowels: vowels are more gradient and are more likely to reduce or alter in running speech across speakers and thus allow a more fair comparison.

The Kiel Corpus of Spontaneous Speech (IPDS 1995) served as the database for the comparison. This corpus contains high-quality recordings of spontaneous dialogues of two speakers at a time who were asked to arrange appointments with each other. A total of 54 minutes of speech was recorded for 26 speakers (16 male and 10 female, mostly students from north Germany). The speech data was labelled and transcribed by trained phoneticians. The analysis is based on what the transcribers heard rather than what the speakers intended to say. The Kiel corpus transcription uses 17 vowels in German (all monophthongs, including long-short and tense-lax vowels: [iː, ɪ, yː, ʏ, eː, øː, ɛː, ɛ, œ, aː, a, ɔ, oː, uː, ʊ, ə, ɐ]). For the comparison these were mapped to the 13 vowels the FUL system uses for German since the FUL system does not distinguish long and short vowels on the level of features, but only by moraic representations. Moreover, there is no featural difference in the representation of [a] and [ɐ], and [e] and [ə] which are also only moraically distinguished. Even if we disregard the moraic representation, these simplifications do not lead to a noticeable increase of existing homophones in the lexicon. The complete set of vowels used by both systems is [i, ɪ, y, ʏ, e, ø, ɛ, œ, a, ɔ, o, u, ʊ].

The hidden Markov model had three states and eight mixtures to model every phone;[12] i.e. the system was trained to model the phone and the left and right transitions of that phone (these are the three states) and allowed 8 'variations' of a phone to exist, that are realised by mixtures of Gaussian probability density functions (these are the 8 mixtures of the three states).[13] The phones were modelled left-to-right and no states were skipped. The transformation from the speech waveform to the states was done with 12 MFCC (mel-frequency cepstral coefficients) plus the energy parameters and the corresponding delta-values, giving a total of 26 parameters (cf. e.g. Jelinek, 1997; De Mori, 1998; or Becchetti & Ricotti, 1999 for details about the parameters of stochastic ASR systems). The training of the system was done with a jack-knife procedure, where a subset of the recordings served as training set (i.e. were used to define the pattern sequences for the phones) and another subset (other speakers and other sentences) were used as test set (i.e., had to be 'recognised'). About 80% of the data served as training set and the remaining 20% were used as test set. This procedure was repeated 5 times with different subsets of speakers and sentences selected from the database (i.e. each data set was exactly once in the test set) and the recognition results are averaged over these experiments.

For FUL, we have used only 20 ms of the centre part of the vowels for this comparison. The vowels are classified by combinations of 7 features ([SONORANT], [LABIAL], [CORONAL], [DORSAL], [LOW], [HIGH], [RTR]) and the ternary logic described earlier. Recall, that the FUL system does *not* require any training and therefore there is no separation between training and test sets. Our results are based on a single run.

For both systems, only the top-scoring vowels were counted as 'correct' recognition, i.e., only the vowel(s) with the highest rank were compared to the transcribed phone and counted as correct if they were identical. Note that lower scoring vowels are still contributing to the recognition, both in the HMM and in the FUL system. The results are presented in the Figure 6.

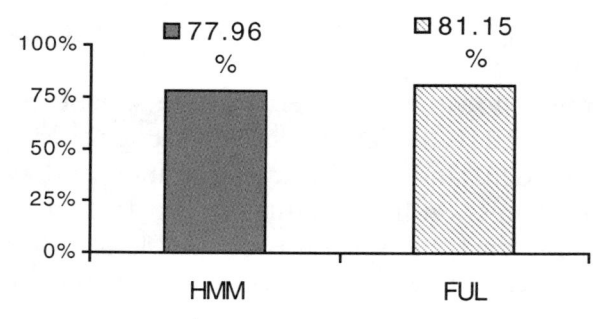

Figure 6: Vowel recognition: HMM and FUL

For the HMM the top-scoring vowels reach 77.96% correct recognition. For the same data set the FUL system achieved 81.15% correct recognition. From these results it seems that the FUL system is able to hold its own in an evaluation format prescribed by stochastic models.

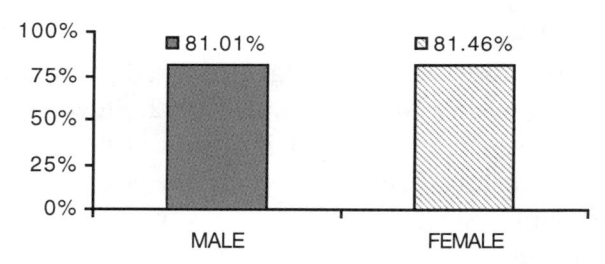

Figure 7: FUL: Vowel recognition by gender

Formants are relatively invariant to spectral tilt, random noise, and overall signal level, which are altered by microphone and transmission-line conditions, hence, these factors do not influence the performance. But formant values do depend on vocal tract size which differs between male and female speakers. For the speakers examined here, the average F1 was 483 Hz for the male speakers and 576 Hz for the female speakers across all vowels, indicating a shorter lip−glottis distance for the female speakers. We therefore examined the differences between the 26 male and 10 female speakers, and found that the vowels were equally well identified across gender. The results are graphically presented in Figure 7. Although there is a very slight bias in favour of the female speakers, the difference is not significant.

In sum, the following characteristics are salient in our implementation of the FUL model in a speech recognition system. It is speaker independent and to a large extent independent of microphone and transmission-line conditions. No training is required, and last but not least, the system is adaptable to other languages because the lexical representation is based on the phonological systems of individual languages.

4.2 Comparable existing models

We now turn to a comparison of our system with existing models which also take recourse to features or related linguistic units, the closest of which are the ACOUSTIC LANDMARK model (Stevens, Perkell & Shattuck-Hufnagel, 1997) and TIME MAP PHONOLOGY (Carson-Berndsen, 1998).

In spirit, the closest model is that proposed by Stevens and his colleagues (1997; earlier LAFF, Stevens, 1992; Stevens et al., 1992), which is also discussed at length in Klatt (1989).[14] The system resembles a more advanced version of the original analysis-by-synthesis principle (Stevens, 1960): A spectrogram is analysed for acoustic characteristics and phonetic segments that relate to these characteristics are proposed as possible candidates. The features associated with these segments are looked up from a table and possible assimilations from neighbouring segments are predicted.[15] The spectrogram is inspected again for acoustic characteristics of these hypothesised features and segment candidates are verified or falsified on basis of this detailed acoustic information. The most prominent acoustic characteristics are hypothesised at segment boundaries (e.g. dropping or missing F1 at VCV boundaries or down-glides of F1 in V-glide-V sequences). The crux of the approach is to examine the speech signal for detailed acoustic characteristics and essentially look for characteristics that might relate to the proposed features. The biggest difference between ACOUSTIC LANDMARK and FUL is that in the former, there is a conversion of the acoustic characteristics into a segment and then features are looked up and searched for. The whole process is not lexicon-driven as the FUL system and is motivated by the acoustical effects at segment boundaries (hence, ACOUSTIC LANDMARKS). The idea behind the system is the handling of allophonic variation after the recognising of the segmental context, whereas the FUL system does neither look for segment boundaries (rather tries to ignore their effects) and handles variations by the matching logic.

Since the system is not implemented by an automatic procedure, it is difficult to compare its performance with FUL or an HMM model.

Another system that converts speech signals into acoustic events and uses them to access the lexicon is most completely described by Carson-Berndsen (1998). The system incorporates two components, the HEAP 'acoustic event' classifier and the SILPA 'phoneme event' recognition module. These two components are described now in more detail.[16]

The HEAP system (Hübener & Carson-Berndsen, 1994) is essentially a statistical categoriser which classifies the speech signal into 24 (later 27, cf. Carson-Berndsen, 1998: 80) 'acoustic events' (like, 'fricative, noisy, nasal, a-like vowel, mid vowel', etc.).[17] This classification is computed from 30 ms frames with a step-rate of 20 ms that are parameterised with 5 cepstrally smoothed PLP coefficients (perceptual linear predictive coefficients, Hermansky, 1990), log energy, and regression coefficients (total 13 coefficients per frame). This recogniser was trained on automatically labelled data on 180 utterances of a single speaker to classify the signal into the acoustic events. To test the performance of HEAP, 20 additional utterances were classified between 77% and 98% correctly for a particular acoustic event.

Because the acoustic events are not synchronously changing with the edges of phonemes, a finite-state parser built up a sequence of 'phonological events' that are in turn used for phoneme recognition. That is, the output of the HEAP classifier (i.e. the acoustic events) are converted by a finite state automaton into 'phonological events'. These are 7 independent 'phonological attributes', each one having several values. For instance, the phonological attribute MANNER includes 'plosive, fricative, nasal, lateral, affricate, vowel-like, diphthong'. The phonological attribute

PLACE includes 'labial, apical, palato-alveolar, velar, palatal, uvular, glottal'.[18] In all there are 31 phonological values. Additionally, all possible onset and coda clusters in German syllables were used to restrict the number of possible phoneme sequences derived from the acoustic events. This parser/automaton includes an "underspecified representation of the syllable", but underspecification is understood here as a method to cluster several phonological segments into one 'phonological event'. In this way, 'underspecification' is understood as a state (or memory) saving task rather than as it is understood in phonology (and in this paper otherwise) as a structure that explains certain processes.

Furthermore, the mapping of the acoustic events computed from the signal onto the constraints of the parser are done in a rather different way than in the FUL system. The SILPA parser operates in the following way: if there are more acoustic events in the signal than a particular node of the finite state network needs, the additional events are ignored and the constraint that this node represents is met. If there are less acoustic events than specified in a node, the network could be parameterised so that more important events for a constraint are weighted higher.

The best empirical evaluation scoring rate given is 66.97% for phonemes in a scheduling task scenario with many speakers and 82 utterances (Carson-Berndsen, 1998: 203).

In sum, the system converts the speech signal into 28 'phonetic events' by statistical means that are in turn converted into 31 different 'phonological events' by a finite state machine. The increase in representational units from the signal to the lexical level itself is contradictary to an 'underspecified' representation and rather it is a generation of a detailed phonetic description. Essentially, the use of terminology here is quite different from the description of the FUL system and the two systems are only superficially similar.

5. Conclusion

Our aim has been to present a model of lexical representation which has significant consequences for various aspects of human behaviour, and which can be computationally implemented for the purposes of machine recognition of speech and the testing of models. A lexicon which is phonologically underspecified is the pivot of the FUL model. Phonological variants of morphemes are not listed, the assumption being that the abstract underspecified representation will subsume any phonetic or phonological variation produced by the speaker. The perceptual system extracts phonological features from the signal and directly maps them on to the lexicon. No other linguistic unit is compiled or extracted at this level. There is no intermediate representation like phoneme or syllable. Incoming phonological features activate word candidates constrained by a ternary matching condition, which in turn are fed directly into the phonological and syntactic parser.

Although morphemes are phonologically underspecified, they have sufficient information to distinguish them from each other - unless of course, they are really homophones. This assumption is directly in contrast to a system which assumes that all variants would be listed. The underspecified representation in the FUL system anticipates that there will be variation, but that the variation is itself constrained even at the level of postlexical phonology.

To illustrate, we can take as an example high coronal vowels which can phonologically reduce/lax/unround in running speech. In words like *Füller* [fʏlər] 'pen', *Fühler* [fylər] 'antenna', *Filler* [fɪlər] 'material for smoothing surfaces' and *vieler* [filər] 'much, many-GEN' the first vowel can be indistinguishable. Depending on phrasal structure, rate of speech, focus, and other factors, all the variants can represent one possible pronunciation of each of the words. That is, underlying /y/ could become [ʏ], [i] or [ɪ]; similarly, /ʏ/ could be realised [ɪ], [y] or [i] and so on. All speakers may not have all of the possible pronunciations for all four words, but across speakers it is possible to obtain all variants. Storing the variants makes it impossible to distinguish one from the other; all variants will have equal status unless there is a weighting for each possibility. If this weighting depends on the statistical distribution, the weights depend on the particular data set and it is possible that two of the three variants would have similar weights. FUL predicts a different hierarchy for each variant. If *Filler* was the mispronounced variant of either *Füller*, *vieler*, or *Fühler*, neither word would be a mismatch, but the scores are different as we can see below.

(14)   Scores for [ɪ] of *Filler*

Lexical features		Input features of [ɪ]	Score
[y] *Fühler*	[HIGH, LAB]	[HIGH, COR, RTR]	$1^2/(3 \times 2) = 0.16$
[i] *vieler*	[HIGH]		$1^2/(3 \times 1) = 0.33$
[Y] *Füller*	[HIGH, LAB, RTR]		$2^2/(3 \times 3) = 0.44$
[ɪ] *Filler*	[HIGH, RTR]		$2^2/(3 \times 2) = 0.66$

Clearly, when [ɪ] is the surface variant, *Filler* has the highest score. Next in line is *Füller* followed by *vieler* and then finally the last choice would be *Fühler*. The FUL system predicts that for the listener, when [ɪ] is heard, [Y] is a better match than [i]. That is, maintaining the laxing (i.e. [RTR]) is preferred. It is entirely possible that storing all the variants with weights would give the same results, but this would have to be done for each lexical item individually. This is not the case for FUL. The predictions would hold for the entire lexicon and would be borne out as a consequence of the underspecified representation and the scoring which incorporates the features extracted from the signal, the features in the lexicon and the matching features.

Since the claim is that FUL models human perception, evidence from both language comprehension experiments and language change were put forward. Language comprehension experiments have shown that listeners extract certain acoustic characteristics reliably, but do not match acoustic details with the lexicon. Rather, the experimental results are best explained with the assumption that lexical access involves mapping of the acoustic signal to an underspecified featural representation such that non-mismatching variants are treated differently from mismatching variants. If an underspecified representation is indeed part of the adult mental lexicon, then one assumes that the language learner is able to construct such a representation. If so, then language change ought to provide evidence that an underspecified representation at a certain point of time lends itself to a different pattern of change than a more fully specified representation. Our example came from the change of geminates to nongeminates from Latin to the northern Italian dialect of Miogliola. Although degemination occurred everywhere, the original length contrast in Latin obstruents could be maintained by spirantising the original nongeminate stops. This was not possible for sonorants where in general the contrast was lost, the exception being the coronal nasals. For these consonants, the original underspecified representations were exploited, such that the Latin nongeminate /n/ remained underspecified in Miogliola, but the geminate /n:/ degeminated but acquired a place feature.

The computational adequacy of these assumptions was verified in implementing an automatic speech recognition system. Again, assuming that speech is variable but that the variation is constrained, the FUL ASR system focuses on solving the problem of recognition not by capturing all possible details from the signal but by extracting acoustic characteristics which can be easily interpreted as distinctive features which are relevant for distinguishing lexical representations. The information retrieved from the signal is not responsible for building lexical representations. The lexical representations in their idealised forms already exist and the information from the signal (i.e. the extracted features) is mapped onto existing representations. Resolving variation is achieved by the fact that given underspecification and the ternary matching logic, a one-to-many matching is possible. Since particular underspecified representations are geared towards accepting only phonologically viable phonetic variants, the one-to-many matching is not random.

We should add at this point, that our main objective is not to construct the most marketable speech recognition system. Product-oriented systems have specific constraints and individual requirements. In principle, the FUL system is adaptable for specific products, but this has not been our main concern. A system to reconfirm flights, for instance, does not require a complex model like FUL. A limited vocabulary combined with an intelligent dialogue is a far better solution. Our aim has been to construct a computational system which operates on the principles we believe are important for human perception. We would like to make it entirely speaker independent and not use any stochastic procedures, thereby no doubt sacrificing possible gains. However, as it stands, FUL can provide a means of testing speech perception theories, particularly details of feature interaction, properties of features, lexical representations, coarticulation and such. It could also be an excellent tool to study dialect variations and possible directions of change. Since FUL takes the speech data as speech and not as any random acoustic signal, and assumes that this speech is produced by speakers who have a real language in their heads, it is intended primarily as a linguistic tool, using linguistic primitives and exploiting linguistic knowledge.

The FUL system is highly constrained – in the allowable lexical representations, in what is extracted from the signal, and in the information used to make the matching decisions. The message has been "Less is More" in a positive sense.

Acknowledgements

We are especially grateful to John Kingston and an anonymous reviewer's very detailed comments. We are much indebted to Jacques Koreman for the HMM classifications. This paper also owes a large debt to Jennifer Fitzpatrick, Sibrand van Coillie and Michael Wagner. The research was partially supported by the SFB 471, the Max-Planck-Forschungspreis and the Leibniz Prize.

Notes

* We would like to dedicate this paper to Mirco Ghini †, without whose abounding enthusiasm and intellectual commitment, a large part of this research would have never been possible.
1 There are other proposals outside phonological approaches, like 'full listing models' that abandon generalisations altogether, or 'exemplar models' (e.g. Medin & Schaffer, 1978; Nosofsky, 1986) that use individual items as representatives for a category, or 'prototype models' (e.g. Klatt, 1979) that compute an average representative for a category. There appear to be misconceptions regarding the terminology. For instance, Bybee (2000: 253) refers to her model of the lexicon as an 'exemplar model', while assuming that "Each experience of a word is stored in memory with other examples of use of the same word". Such an assumption fits with a 'full listing model'. To cover all these models and their variants would go far beyond the scope of this article.

2   For support for underspecification see, for instance, Keating (1988), Kiparsky (1993), and Rice (1996); psycholinguistic evidence is provided in Lahiri, Jongman & Sereno (1990), Lahiri (1991), Lahiri & Marslen-Wilson (1991, 1992), and Fitzpatrick & Wheeldon (2001). Opposing views have been presented, for example, in McCarthy & Taub (1992), Mohanan (1993) and Steriade (1995), and references therein.
3   Mohanan (1993) gives a hierarchy of assimilation possibilities where the most frequent type is coronal assimilation. In languages where labials do assimilate to other places of articulation, a dental/alveolar sound is always subject to assimilation. This persuades Mohanan to assume that there is no underspecification but rather a hierarchy of 'attraction'. In our model, for the labials the assimilation must be a result of delinking-cum-spreading and would be treated differently from coronal assimilation.
4   Full statistical and methodological details are not repeated here since this is an overview and the original paper is being published in an experimental journal. A total of 24 monosyllabic words with final /-n/ and 12 monosyllabic words with final /-m/ were used as primes, each with a semantically related target (e.g. *Bahn-Zug*). The differences in the number of items was due to the fact that there were less words in the language ending with /-m/ where the final consonant could be changed to make nonwords. A total of 144 German native speakers were tested.
5   Significance was tested at a 5% level.
6   There were 20 words each with medial /n/ and /m/. A total of 90 subjects participated in this experiment.
7   For a recent review of the different predictions and experimental evidence for lexical access based on underspecification or full specification, see Fitzpatrick & Wheeldon (2001).
8   Coronal stops also became affricates, but this is not important for the discussion here.
9   The total number of features needed may be language dependent.
10 The signal feature [ABRUPT] mismatches with the lexical feature [NASAL], cf. (7a). If [NASAL] is found in the signal it cannot mismatch with [ABRUPT] because [ABRUPT] is not stored in the lexicon.
11 Note, however, that this is a much more relaxed decision than in many early phonetics-based systems, that tried to determine the set of possible segments.
12 The HMM experiments were run at the University of Saarbrücken by William Barry, Jacques Koreman and their colleagues.
13 To use the left and right context in modelling phones to allow different contexts in ASR was already proposed by Klatt (1979).
14 At a workshop at Schloss Freudental (Konstanz) July 1998 entitled *Speech Recognition: Man and Machine*, Ken Stevens and his colleagues presented the system in detail.
15 The original texts do not make a clear distinction between acoustic characteristics and the phonological features as it is presented here. Both are understood by Stevens and his colleagues as different expressions of the same thing.

16 The 'acoustic events' are very different from phonological features and neither are they acoustic characteristics, as in Stevens' model.
17 The classifier for the acoustic events was originally planned as a deterministic module that uses auditory spectra as input (Hübener, 1991).
18 Overall, the system maps the acoustic events to phonetic descriptions rather than phonological features.

References

Becchetti, C. & Ricotti, L. P.
    1999   *Speech Recognition - Theory and C++ Implementation*. Chichester: John Wiley & Sons.

Bybee, J.
    2000   Lexicalization of sound change and alternating environments. M. B. Broe & J. B. Pierrehumbert (eds.), *Papers in Laboratory Phonology V: Acquisition and the Lexicon*, (pp. 250–268). Cambridge: Cambridge University Press.

Carson-Berndsen, J.
    1998   *Time Map Phonology*. Dordrecht: Kluwer.

De Mori, R.
    1998   *Spoken Dialogues with Computers*. London: Academic Press.

Fitzpatrick, J. & Wheeldon, L.
    2001   Phonology and phonetics in psycholinguistic models of speech perception. In N. Burton-Roberts, P. Carr, & G. J. Docherty (eds.), *Phonological Knowledge – Conceptual and Empirical Issues*, (pp. 131–160). New York: Oxford University Press.

Gaskell, G. & Marslen-Wilson, W. D.
    1996   Phonological variation and inference in lexical access, *Journal of Experimental Psychology: Human Perception and Performance*, **22**, 144–158.

Ghini, M.
    2001   *Asymmetries in the Phonology of Miogliola*. Berlin: Mouton.

Ghini, M.
    to appear   The role of underspecification in the development of metrical systems. In P. Fikkert & H. Jacobs (eds.), *Change in Prosodic Systems*. Berlin: Mouton.

Gow, D.
    2001   Assimilation and anticipation in continuous spoken word recognition. *Journal of Memory and Language*, **44**, 1–27.

Hermansky, H.
    1990   Perceptual linear predictive (PLP) analysis of speech. *Journal of the Acoustical Society of America*, **87**, 1738–1752.

Hübener, K.
1991　　Eine Architektur zur integrierten Analyse von Sprachsignalen. Verbundprojekt ASL, Document Nr. ASL-TR-3-91/UHH, Vers. 2. University of Hamburg.

Hübener, K. & Carson-Berndsen, J.
1994　　Phoneme recognition using acoustic events, *Proceedings of the 3rd International Conference on Spoken Language Processing (ICSLP 94)*, Yokohama, **4**, 1919–1922.

IPDS
1995　　*The Kiel Corpus of Spontaneous Speech, Vol. 1.* CD-ROM. Kiel: Institut für Phonetik und digitale Sprachverarbeitung.

Jelinek, F.
1997　　*Statistical Methods for Speech Recognition.* Cambridge: MIT Press.

Keating, P. A.
1988　　Underspecification in phonetics. *Phonology*, **5**, 275–292.

Kiparsky, P.
1993　　Blocking in nonderived environments. In S. Hargus & E. M. Kaisse (eds.), *Phonetics and Phonology*, (pp. 277–314). New York: Academic Press.

Klatt, D. H.
1979　　Speech perception: a model of acoustic-phonetic analysis and lexical access. *Journal of Phonetics*, **7**, 279–312.

Klatt, D. H.
1989　　Review of selected models of speech perception. In W. Marslen-Wilson (ed.), *Lexical Representation and Process*, 169–226. Cambridge: MIT Press.

Lahiri, A.
1991　　Anteriority in sibilants. *Proceedings of the XIIth International Congress of Phonetic Sciences*, Aix-en-Provence, **1**, 384–388.

Lahiri, A.
1999　　Speech recognition with phonological features. *Proceedings of The XIVth International Congress of Phonetic Sciences*, San Francisco, **1**, 715–718.

Lahiri, A.
2000　　Phonology: structure, representation and process. In Linda Wheeldon (ed.), *Aspects of Language Production*, (pp. 165–225). Hove: Psychology Press.

Lahiri, A. & Coillie, S. van
to appear　　Non-mismatching features in language comprehension.

Lahiri, A. & Evers, V.
1991　　Palatalization and coronality. In Paradis, C. & Prunet, J.-F. (eds.), *The Special Status of Coronals*, (pp. 79–100). San Diego: Academic Press.

Lahiri, A., Jongman, A. & Sereno, J. A.
  1990   The pronominal clitic [dər] in Dutch: a theoretical and experimental approach. *Yearbook of Morphology,* 3, 115–127.
Lahiri, A. & Marslen-Wilson, W. D.
  1991   The mental representation of lexical form: a phonological approach to the recognition lexicon. *Cognition.* 38, 245–294.
Lahiri, A. & Marslen-Wilson, W. D.
  1992   Lexical processing and phonological representation. In G. J. Docherty & D. R. Ladd (eds.) *Papers in Laboratory Phonology II: Gesture, Segment, Prosody,* (pp. 229–254). Cambridge: Cambridge University Press.
McCarthy, J. & Taub, A.
  1992   Review of Paradis and Prunet 1991. *Phonology,* 9, 363–370.
Medin, D. L. & Schaffer, M. M.
  1978   Context theory of classification learning. *Psychological Review,* 85, 207–238.
Mohanan, K. P.
  1993   Fields of attraction in phonology. In John Goldsmith (ed.) *The last Phonological Rule: Reflections on Constraints and Derivations,* (pp. 61–116). Chicago: University of Chicago Press.
Nosofsky, R. M.
  1986   Attention, similarity, and the identification-categorization relationship. *Journal of Experimental Psychology: General,* 115, 39–57.
Reetz, H.
  1998   *Automatic Speech Recognition with Features.* Habilitationsschrift. Universität des Saarlandes.
Reetz, H.
  1999   Converting speech signals to phonological features. *Proceedings of The XIVth International Congress of Phonetic Sciences,* San Francisco, 3, 1733–1736.
Rice, K.
  1996   Default variability: the coronal-velar relationship. *Natural Language and Linguistic Theory,* 14, 493–543.
Steriade, D.
  1995   Underspecification and markedness. In J. Goldsmith (ed.) *The Handbook of Phonological Theory,* (pp. 114–174). Cambridge: Blackwell.
Stevens, K. N.
  1960   Towards a model for speech perception. *Journal of the Acoustical Society of America,* 32, 47–55.
Stevens, K. N.
  1992   Lexical access from features. *Speech Communication Group Working Papers, Research Laboratory of Electronics, MIT,* 8, 119–144.

Stevens, K. N., Manuel, S. V., Shattuck-Hufnagel, S. & Liu, S.
   1992   Implementation of a model for lexical access based on features. *Proceedings of the 2nd International Conference on Spoken Language Processing (ICSLP 92)*, Banff, **1**, 499−502.

Stevens, K. N., Perkell, J. S. & Shattuck-Hufnagel, S.
   1997   Speech Communication. *MIT-Research Laboratory for Electronics Progress Report*, **140**, 353−367.

Comments on Lahiri & Reetz

Dafydd Gibbon

Lahiri and Reetz (LR) take up one of the classical issues of linguistic theory which has always been of special interest to phonologists, the issue of underspecification. The topic has appeared in several guises over the years, involving such notions as privative features, natural classes, redundancy rules, distinctions between general and radical underspecification, the masking of articulatory configurations, and more recently, under the influence of Computational Linguistics and Artificial Intelligence, type inheritance hierarchies and default logics. In a refreshing departure from classical linguistic methodology, the authors touch on so-called internal evidence (evidence from synchronic language structure) only briefly, and examine three types of independent external evidence from neighbouring disciplines in an argumentation strategy somewhat reminiscent of the early work of Morris Halle on external evidence from dialects, secret languages and phonological change (1962), building on the tradition founded by Jakobson's seminal psycholinguistic study (1944); see also the recent contributions in Dziubalska (2001).

The authors' main interest is *underspecification in language comprehension*, and they report two online experiments on this. They flank their primary topic with a discussion of *underspecification in language change*, with reference to the Italian dialect of Miogliola, and *underspecification in speech recognition*, for which they outline an implementation based on a model with the whimsical name of "FUL". I will start by concentrating on what I take to be the central theoretical idea, which has far-reaching consequences for work in theoretical and laboratory phonology: *underspecification processing*. Then I will return to LR's empirical evidence.

What distinguishes LR's approach from previous linguistic and psycholinguistic work on underspecification, which is based on essentially declarative formal rules, is the implication that underspecification has consequences for *processing*. For discussion purposes I will define a process as *an operation on a state of a system at time t_i which yields a state of the system at a later time t_{i+k}*, thereby creating a link between LR's three types of external evidence: human processing, historical processes, and computational processing. To provide a basis for further argumentation I will define *underspecification processing* in what I understand to be the sense intended (though not formalised) by LR, as *an operation on an underspecified state of a system at time t_i which yields a (more) fully specified state of the system at time t_{i+k}*.

But what does this mean in detail? In order to understand underspecfication processing it is necessary to understand the input-to-lexicon matching function which is at the heart of the FUL model, and I think it is worth teasing this out in a little formal detail to provide a handle for precise claims, counter-claims and extensions. I will represent this three-valued function as follows (I being an input feature set and L a lexical feature set for some lexical entry):

$$\text{MATCH}_{LR}: I \times L \rightarrow \{match, mismatch, no\text{-}mismatch\} \times \text{SCORE}$$

In other words, underspecified input feature sets I are matched with underspecified lexicon feature sets L, yielding one of three match values weighted by a score. The feature matching conditions can be precisely characterised using LR's unary feature notation:

(1) $\text{MATCH}_{LR}(i \in I, l \in L) = match$ iff $i,l \in I \cap L$ & $i = l$
(2) $\text{MATCH}_{LR}(i \in I, l \in L) = no\text{-}mismatch$ iff $i,j \notin I \cap L$
(3) $\text{MATCH}_{LR}(i \in I, l \in L) = mismatch$ iff $i,j \in I \cup L$ & $i \neq l$ & contradict (i, l)

Note that an additional contradiction constraint is needed, stating which feature pairs are contradictory and which features contradict their own absence (i.e. are privative as opposed to optional), or else every feature would contradict every other feature. For instance, it needs to be stipulated that [NASAL] and [STRIDENT] mismatch. But this additional constraint defines exactly the equivalence relation which partitions feature sets into multivalent attributes, contradicting LR's claim that they deal in monovalent features. This is a point which Ladefoged has repeatedly made in connection with phonetic features. However, this contradiction does not harm LR's FUL model, as the monovalency assumption is not part of their four fundamental modelling conventions. In the form given above, the LR matching function is indistinguishable from a non-recursive variety of the *unification* operation over feature structures or graphs, in the Unification Grammar paradigm (LFG, HPSG and several other approaches; cf. Jurafsky & Martin, 2000).

The *match* value is weighted by a score, which LR call an activation level, defined in terms of the magnitudes of the feature sets. In present terminology, the score is 0 IFF *contradict* (i, l) for any $i \in I$, $l \in L$, otherwise $|I \cap L|^2 / (|I| * |L|)$. Note that the score is also zero when the intersection of I and L happens to be empty, and the formula is invalid if either I or L or both are empty. So there must be at least one matching feature in this model, unlike some older concepts of radical underspecification.

Now phonologists are of course pretty familiar with thinking in terms of scores, albeit of rather different kinds, like symbol-counting evaluation measures or Optimality Theory constraint violations, both of which are essentially declarative rather than process oriented in the sense defined above. But the novelty of LR's score is that it means *process evaluation*, not symbol or rule/constraint counting. This is the sense in which activation levels determine results in a neural network, or in which a word hypothesis graph at the "speech-language interface" in ASR describes a process and receives a Bayesian probability estimate based on a combination of bottom-up (so-called *a posteriori*) factors and top-down (so-called *a priori*) factors. A standard assumption in ASR, borne out by basic research over a number of decades, is that the speech signal is itself highly underspecified and only provides suboptimal clues for decoder, which is thus highly non-deterministic (in the technical sense of the theory of formal languages) — though not arbitrarily, as LR seem to claim at one point.

High recognition scores in the standard tests (Gibbon et al., 1997) are only reached when top-down syntactic and semantic "language models" are used for hypothesis disambiguation. In the formula for LR's matching function, I is analogous to the *a posteriori* or observational component and L is analogous to the *a priori* component. This similarity between the FUL model and standard ASR models suggests a multidisciplinary line of development for LR's approach, in the direction of integrating the FUL model with existing procedures of top-down hypothesis disambiguation.

A particularly convincing demonstration of the value of underspecified phonological representations in speech recognition was provided in the Time Map model of Carson-Berndsen (CB), which takes Church's classic study (Church, 1988) as a starting point, but uses the Autosegmental-Articulatory Phonology paradigm rather than classical phonotactics (Carson-Berndsen, 1998). CB developed a formalisation in terms of a multi-level event logic in which utterances are described at the phonetic level as parallel acoustic feature trajectories (underspecified because of noise-masking, co-articulation etc.), and at the lexical level as parallel lexical feature trajectories (underspecified on the basis of phonotactic constraints). The logic of underspecified events is mapped to a finite state automaton model with underspecified feature labels on the transitions, and implemented as such. This component interfaces at the bottom-end with an acoustic event detector and at the top-end with event based morphological analyser, lexicon, syntax and translation components.

The word-level architecture, a design study for the VerbMobil speech-to-speech translation project, is shown in Figure 1, a screen snapshot of CB's working Time Map ASR system. There are some striking structural similarities to LR's "feature tracks". The Time Map system is incremental (indicated by the partial structures), providing anytime output as the signal comes in, an important feature for modelling the functionality of human online behaviour. It must be said that this work is not quite accurately represented by LR, who apparently overlook the formal complementarity, from a feature logic and set-theoretic point of view, of feature underspecification (whether general, as with CB, or radical, as with LR) and the definition of phonological natural classes. And in

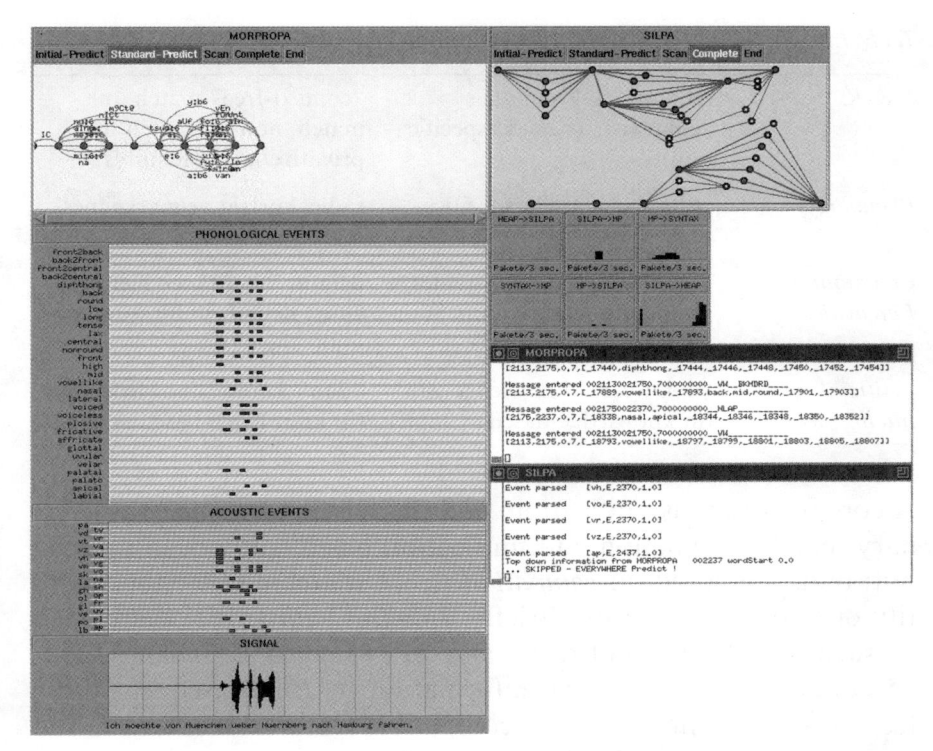

Figure 1: Underspecified event tracks and automata in the Time Map ASR model

fact both define the same compaction operation on memory data structures – compactness reflects generalisation here, as in other areas of phonology. In fact the Time Map model includes several of LR's basic assumptions and provides more evidence for them as well as a number of pointers for further development.

Another point where LR provide a useful link to computational research lies in the underspecified lexicon component. There is a long line of computational work on underspecification in the lexicon (cf. van Eynde & Gibbon, 2000), with regard both to representation by underspecified feature structures, and to processing by unification and inheritance. In this work, distinctions between two main underspecification types are made (in addition to the special case of underspecification of the speech signal), which are summarised in Table 1.

Table 1: Two underspecification types in different disciplines

L & R:	(absent; FUL only has "context-free" underspecification)	"context-free" match, mismatch, non-mismatch for privative/unary features
Phonology:	redundancy underspecification	radical/privative/markedness underspecification
Computational Linguistics:	type inheritance hierarchies, graph and feature unification, attribute value logics	default inheritance hierarchies, default unification, default logics
Artificial Intelligence:	"don't care" knowledge gap (in knowledge-based systems)	"don't know" knowledge gap (in knowledge-based systems)

A core operation is unification, and the relation between LR's ternary matching function and unification has already been pointed out: both are based on *compatibility*, i.e. matching by either identity or underspecification. Briefly, *I unifies with L* IFF there is an *M* such that both *I* and *L* subsume *M* (where *L* subsumes *M* IFF *M* contains at least all the information in *L*); consequently the feature set *M* contains all the compatible features of *L* and *I*. The subsumption relation is transitive, and induces a *subsumption hierarchy* (also known as a *type hierarchy*), which corresponds to implication and set inclusion in other formalisms. It is useful to know this when developing details of a processing model such as FUL, as the subsumption relation is the basis for defining the type of semantic network known as an *inheritance hierarchy*, which is one of the standard computational mechanisms for dealing with underspecification in the lexicon (see various contributions to van Eynde & Gibbon, 2000). A type inheritance hierarchy is defined directly by subsumption, while a default inheritance hierarchy is defined by an additional override relation.

The points made by LR are very timely, and they are in an optimal position to plunder the treasure store of computational linguistics in this area. In fact, on the phonological side, LR could have gone even further, as the default inheritance relation is relevant to the three types of external evidence which they examine, as I will show.

Matching and scoring in the FUL speech recognition program. LR do not examine the performance of their speech recognition program with respect to underspecification, though this would make for an interesting series of experiments, but stipulate it as a property. Nevertheless, the consequences of taking underspecification as a principle for storage and processing do need to be spelled out, and LR provide a suitable example. The relation between [y], [i], [Y] and [I] (in LR's discussion of scores) is reproduced in Table 2. The dependencies are expressed in the tree diagram as a simple default inheritance hierarchy of underspecified nodes, in which specifications at lower nodes override unspecified values at higher nodes. So, for any given input feature, any subtree dominated by a node labelled with this feature contains possible candidate matches. Thus, if only [HIGH] were recognised, the hypothesis space includes all items, so all items inherit [HIGH]. If [LABIAL] is also specified, only [Y] inherits this from [y], so the space of competing hypotheses contains only [y] and [Y]. The use of a default inheritance hierarchy thus permits a much higher degree of underspecification than a tabular representation. The additional structure also provides a configurational account of the radical underspecification facts, and the lexical feature count needed for scoring is simply the sum of the explicitly marked feature counts at the relevant node and its parent nodes (see Table 2). This more formal model underlines the potential of lexical underspecification in this approach.

Table 2: Configurational representation of underspecification dependencies

SEGMENT	HIGH	LABIAL	RETRACTED	
Y	HIGH	LABIAL		i [HIGH]
I	HIGH			I [RTR] y [LABIAL]
Y	HIGH	LABIAL	RETRACTED	
I	HIGH		RETRACTED	Y [RTR]

Language comprehension. To explain the results of the *Bahn-Lärm* experiment, a default inheritance hierarchy can be defined for [n] and [m]: [m] is specified for [LABIAL] (i.e. [PLACE]), and inherits

[NASAL] from [n]. The activation of [n], and thus *Bahn*, by [m], in the input *Bahm*, can be explained elegantly in terms of the need to inherit [NASAL] from [n]; top-down information promotes the overriding [PLACE] information from the [m] node to the [n] node. The inputs with other consonants, which have longer reaction times, do not have this relation. The other way round, with *Lärm* as target and *Lärn* as input, does not involve the inheritance relation, and correctly predicts that [n] will fare about the same as the other consonants. I will not discuss details of the *Schramme* experiment, which can be accounted for in the same way. The dimension which this default inheritance model adds to the LR account is a component of an underlying explanatory processing model in the form of a hierarchical storage data structure; it also provides a configurational explication of the notion of "non-mismatch". Of course I am not claiming that a structure like this is in itself "psychologically real", simply that it is a suitable part of a functionally plausible processing model with the required properties.

Language change. For the fascinating case of Miogliola noncontinuant degemination, the interesting point is that the position of the Latin coronal nasal long/short contrast in the system of oppositions is preserved. So if [n] is only specified for [NASAL], and [nn] for [LENGTH], with [PLACE] specified (e.g. for [m]) one step lower down in a default inheritance hierarchy, it can be argued that consonant degemination did not result in complete neutralisation, and that the [PLACE] feature was promoted upwards one place, innovating an [n] which is robustly specified for [PLACE], and leaving the unmarked and contextually unstable [N]. Without a mechanism such as the one proposed here, LR have no means of predicting which features could have taken the place of [LENGTH] since [n] is also unmarked for other features than [PLACE]. The configurational default inheritance model enhances the value of the underspecification account.

In these comments I have deliberately focussed on computational implications of the idea of *underspecification processing*, and on process oriented underspecification representations, because I see LR's work as a further indication that the same degree of precision is required for representation and processing models in laboratory phonology as for the experimentation itself. It seems to me that LR's approach to searching for new types of independent external evidence in phonological explanation suggests a stimulating set of questions for this kind of multidisciplinary work. Many points still need to be clarified, but LR have made a novel contribution to the interface between classical linguistic methodology on the one hand, and the formal and operational methodologies of psycholinguistics and computational linguistics on the other, on which laboratory phonology thrives. I look forward to further multidisciplinary studies along similar lines.

References

Carson-Berndsen, J.
    1998   *Time Map Phonology: Finite State Models and Event Logics in Speech Recognition.* Dordrecht, NL: Kluwer Academic Publishers.

Church, K.
    1988   *Phonological Parsing in Speech Recognition.* Dordrecht, NL: Kluwer Academic Publishers.

Dziubalska-Kołaczyk, K. (ed.)
    2001   *Constraints and Preferences.* Berlin: Mouton de Gruyter.

Gibbon, D., Moore, R. & Winski, R. (eds.)
    1997   *Handbook of Standards and Resources for Spoken Language Engineering.* Berlin: Mouton de Gruyter.

Halle, M.
    1962   Phonology in Generative Grammar. *Word,* **118,** 54–72.

Jakobson, R.
    1941   *Kindersprache, Aphasie und allgemeine Lautgesetze.* Uppsala Universitets Arsskrift 9 (1942) & Uppsala: Almqvist & Wiksell.

Jurafsky, D. & Martin, J. H.
    2000   *Speech and Language Processing. An Introduction to Natural Language Processing, Computational Linguistics and Speech Recognition.* Upper Saddle River, NJ: Prentice Hall.

Van Eynde, F. & Gibbon, D. (eds.)
    2000   *Lexicon Development for Speech and Language Processing.* Dordrecht, NL: Kluwer Academic Publishers.

Subject Index

accent: correlates of accent 547 ff, 627 ff, *see also* auditory f_0 cues, stress cues
acoustics 112, 193 ff, 268, 299 ff, 338, 341, 351 ff, 419, 423, 455 ff, 515 ff, 585 ff, 655 ff
acquisition, *see* language acquisition
aerodynamics 299 ff, 351 ff, 455 ff, 619
airstream mechanism 299 ff
airstream mechanism: egressive velaric 302, xvi
allophony 101, 103, 105, 111, 118, 120, 122, 123, 125, 129, 130, 132, 134, 330, 334, 352, 498, 665
articulation 299 ff, 341, 351 ff, 419 ff
articulatory timing 419 ff, 444
artificial intelligence 677
aspiration 54, 105, 133, 316, 330, 382, 383 fn 2, 443
assimilation 351 ff, 397, 658, 671, *see also* voice assimilation
audition (auditory system) 171, 351, 455 ff
auditory f_0 cues 61 ff
automatic speech recognition 637 f, 655 ff, 680 ff
autosegmental phonology 354, 388, 411

background noise 276, 280
bilingualism 241, 245, 246, 247, 259, 262 ff
chest pulse 516
clear speech 106, 124, 131, 241 ff, 280 ff
clicks 311, 342 fn 1, 437, 457, 464, 492 ff

cleft questions 82
coarticulation 122, 224, 241, 243, 279, 286 ff, 351 ff, 494, 502, 658, 670
cognition 455 ff, 495 ff, 503
communicative purposes 241 ff, 420
compensatory lengthening 174
computational linguistics 637 ff, 677 ff
consonant deletion 8 ff
continuous activation 284

degemination 651, 669
destressing 213, 215, 216
diachrony 6, 27 f, 175, 352, 420, 443, 549, 579 fn 2, 579 fn 3
dialectal variation 235 fn 7, 352 f, 630, 658, 670
dispersion 268, 459, 477 ff, 502
double articulation 437
downstep 553 ff, 560 ff
duration 3 ff, 330, *see also* vowel duration
durational variability 515 ff

ease of articulation 241
ejectives 341 fn 1, 443, 465 ff, 504 fn 1
emergent phonology 458 ff, 503
endangered languages 615 f
energy, spectral 601 ff
epenthesis 353
exemplar theory 29, 101, 103, 112 ff, 670 fn 1
explosive stops 299 ff

f_0 baseline slope 64 ff
feature matching 638 ff
features, *see* phonological features

fieldwork 455 ff, 503, 547, 551, 555, 615 ff
flapping 106
focus 389 ff
frequency, *see* fundamental frequency, lemma frequency, lexical frequency, phoneme frequency, word frequency
function words 4 ff, 209 ff, 214 ff, 550, 592 ff
functional load 133, 627, 633 fn 7
fundamental frequency 585 ff, 627, *see also* auditory f₀ cues, f₀ baseline slope, pitch

gating experiments 64 ff, 288
gestural overlap 419 ff, 482, 487, 491
gestural phonology 354
glottalization 105, 123, 130, 131, 133, 299 ff, 342 fn 7, *see also* ejectives, laryngealization, preglottalized stops
glottal stops 323

harmonic clusters 427, 442 ff, 444
hearing impairment 182
Hidden Markov Models 655 ff, 671 fn 12
homophones 3, 91, 662, 667
hyper-articulation 241 ff
hypo-articulation 118, 241 ff

implicit priming 89
implosive stops 299 ff, 496
inheritance hierarchy 681
initial rise 572 ff
interrogative intonation 61 ff, 95 f
intonation 61 ff, 91, 101, 105, 387 ff, 411 ff, 580 fn 10
isochrony 173, 515 ff, 539 fn 2
isochrony: objective *vs.* subjective isochrony 518

language acquisition 35 f, 205 ff, 211 f, 215, 222, 231, 232, 265, 283, 459, 461
language change 118, 120, 503, 555, 638 f, 650 ff, 677, 684 ff, *see also* diachrony
language change: analogical sound change 118
language change: Neogrammarian sound change 105, 118, 120
language comprehension 3, 28, 642 ff, 683 f
language production 28, 29
language-specificity 118, 121, 288 f, 492, 671 fn 9
laryngealization 299, 313, 325 f, 340
lemma 3 ff
lemma frequency 3 ff, 92
lenition 8 ff, 103, 107 ff
level of variability 519 ff
lexical access 6, 7, 28, 123, 144, 160 ff, 165, 242, 278 f, 422, 642, 660, 668
lexical category 11 ff
lexical exceptions 228, 235 fn 11
lexical frequency 7
Lexical Phonology [ANNELIES p. 2 of Introduction]
lexical representation 3, 87, 104, *see also* phonological representation
lexicalization 28
lexicon 3 ff, 28, 102, 110, 121, 210, 276, 637
listener-orientation 241 ff
loanwords 228, 550

McGurk effect 171, 180, 191
metrics 633 fn 7
mora 172, 173 ff, 181, 198 fn 4
morphology 87, 101, 106, 110 f, 130, 131, 132, 175, 427, 638, 639

morphosyntax 123
muscular tension 330

nasalization 243
neutralization (temporal ~) 171 ff, 281, 651
nonexplosive stops 299 ff
nuclear falls 387 ff

Optimality Theory 36, 457, 679
orthography 49, 87, 89, 500, 619 f, 632 fn 4
overlap (segmental ~) 38 ff, 46, 51, 53 f
overlap, in articulation, see gestural overlap

pairwise variability 515 ff, 621 ff
palatography 464
paradigm effects 101, 131
perception and production 35 ff, 104, 113 f, 120, 121, 135, 269 f, 279 ff, 463
perception: ~ of stress 203 ff, 275, 518
perception: ~ of vowels 275
perceptual confusion 241
perceptual units 278 f
phoneme frequency 141 ff, 198 fn 4, 285, 315
phoneme inventories 288
phonetic encoding 3 ff, 91, 112
phonetic implementation 101, 133
phonetics and phonology, relation between 101, 172, 300, 456 f, 492, 618
phonological awareness 496 ff, 619 ff
phonological encoding 35 ff, 87 ff, 102 ff, 121, 134, 207, see also phonetic encoding
phonological features 159, 300, 337 f, 340 f, 354, 618 f, 639
phonological features: [obstruent] 299 ff

phonological features: feature geometry 159
phonological features: privative features 677
phonological processing 121 ff, 134, 164 f, 275 ff, 503
phonological representation 29, 101 ff, 159, 203, 211, 341, 491, 637 ff, 643
phonological theory 455 ff, 501, 615 ff
phonotactics 121
phrase boundaries 357, 525
pitch 96, 107, 220, 492
pitch accent 24, 26, 30, 63 ff, 96, 174, 208, 337, 388 ff, 547
pitch-accent languages 547 ff
place of articulation 194, 419 ff, 639 ff, 648 ff
possible word 153, 289 f, 640, 660
predictability 3 ff
preglottalized stops 300, 313, 322, 340
processing, see phonological processing
prosodic hierarchy 388, 520
prosody 13, 92, 101, 121, 124, 360, 539 fn 5
prosody: incremental prosodification
psycholinguistics xiv f, 30 f, 53, 103, 111, 174, 275 ff, 291, 460, 500, 503, 644, 677, 685

quantal theory 308
question intonation, see interrogative intonation

recoverability, perceptual ~ 419 ff
reduction 3 ff, 92, see also vowel reduction
register 62, 283
release burst 299 ff

release, of consonants 300 ff, 465 ff, 487
rhythmic classification 174, 515 ff, 621 ff
rhythmic classification: mora-timed languages 174, 175, 196, 515 ff, 624
rhythmic classification: rhythmically mixed languages 515 ff, 621 ff
rhythmic classification: stress-timed languages 43 ff, 515 ff, 621 ff
rhythmic classification: syllable-timed languages 43 ff, 94 f, 175, 515 ff, 621 ff
rhythmic readjustment 234, 397

secret languages 179, 677, *see also* word games
sentence melody 65
sentence type 388 ff, *see also* interrogative intonation
sign language 182
sociolinguistics 101, 265, 281, 575
sonorants 336 f
sonority 337, 419, 439 ff
sonority sequencing 421, 439 ff
speaker normalization 127, 133, 282
speaker orientation 241 ff
speaking rate 4, 9, 12, 125, 525, 539 fn 5, 637
spectral balance 601 ff
speech errors 88, 131, 174
speech perception 88, 108, 171 ff, 203, 242, 461, 670
speech production 87 ff, 102, 108, 134, 462, 637 ff, *see also* language production, perception and production
speech recognition, *see* automatic speech recognition
speech rhythm, *see* rhythm
speech segmentation 174

stops, *see* explosive stops, implosive stops, nonexplosive stops
stops: lenis stops 329 f
stress 13, 105, 114, 123 f, 203 ff, 283, 387, 518
stress: contrastive *vs.* predictable 203 ff, 585 ff
stress: cues 206 ff, 217, 224 ff, *see also* auditory f_0 cues
stress accent 585 ff, 625
stress 'deafness' 203 ff
stress languages 547 ff
stress-pulse 516
style (speech ~) 106, 123, 130, 174, 254, 283, *see also* clear speech
syllabic consonants 337, 482, 491
syllabification 41, 43, 90, 94, 427, 619
syllable heaviness 215
syllable length 105, 517
syllable priming 35 ff, 94 f
syllable structure 35 ff, 50, 90, 91, 174, 178, 210, 337, 355 ff, 419, 420, 438 f, 482, 487, 518, 526 f, 529 f, 623
syllable structure: vowelless syllables 482 ff, 504 fn 4
syntactic structure 281, 397

talker-control 241 ff
target alignment 387 ff
terminal f_0 rise 65 ff
tonal association 387 ff
tone: boundary tone 62 ff
tone: depression 326 f, 335 f, 343 fn 17
tone: lexical tone 208, 585 ff, 625
tone languages 547 ff
tongue root advancement 305 ff
trills 351 ff
trills: bilabial trills 473 ff, 502
truncation 178
type inheritance hierarchies 677 ff
typology 205 ff, 621, 625

unaccented words 547 ff
underspecification 388, 637 ff, 677 ff
unification 679, 681

variation 3 ff, 637
visual perception 171 ff
vocal tract 305 ff, 332, 455 ff, 658, 663
voice assimilation 443
vowel coalescence 174, 175, 176 ff
vowel devoicing 351, 525
vowel duration/length 171, 247 f, 281, 586, 600
vowel formants 247, 524
vowel harmony 498, 499, 623
vowel inventory 142, 241, 280, 460, 502
vowel mutability 158 f, 165
vowel reduction 118, 233, 518, 527, 530 f
vowel shortening 171 ff

vowel space 107, 114, 244, 257 ff, 460, 478, *see also* dispersion
vowel variability 244, 252
vowels and consonants 54, 141, 145 ff, 157 ff, 279, 283 ff, 500, 521, 639
vowels: devoiced vowels 527

WEAVER model of phonological encoding 92, 94 f, 104
word boundaries 121, 131, 217, 280, 638
word frequency 50, 91, 106, 109, 111, 112 f, 117, 120, 125, 132 ff, 142, 144, 228
word games 495 ff, 503, 619 f
word production 103, 275
word recognition 121 f, 141, 162, 276 ff, 290
word reconstruction 141 ff
word stress, *see* stress
word-prosodic systems 587 ff, 625 ff

Author Index

Abercrombie, D. 43, 515 f, 517, 523, 528
Abry, C.: *see* Schwartz, Abry & Boë
Adelaar, W.: *see* Smeets & Adelaar
Agresti, A. 10
Ahrens, K. V. 28
Al Ani, S.: *see* Port, Al Ani & Maeda
Alcover, A. M. & Moll, F. 354
Alegria, J.: *see* Morais, Cary, Alegria & Bertelson
Alfonso, A. 172, 176
Allopenna, P.: *see* Shi, Morgan & Allopenna
Amiel-Tison, C.: *see* Mehler, Jusczyk, Lambertz, Halsted, Bertoncini & Amiel-Tison
Anderson, S. R. 458
Andruski, J.: *see* Kuhl, Andruski, Chistovich, Chistovich, Kozhevnikova, Ryskina, Stolyarova, Sundberg & Lacerda
Anyawu, R.-J. 333
Aronoff, M.: *see* O'Grady, Dobrovolsky & Aronoff
Arvaniti, A., Ladd, D. R. & Mennen, I. 388, 394, 395, 406
Arvaniti, A.: *see also* Grice, Ladd & Arvaniti
Asher, R. E. 523, 531, 534
Aslin, R. N., Woodward, J., LaMendola, N. & Bever, T. 207, 235 fn 9
Aslin, R. N.: *see also* Saffran, Aslin & Newport
Aston, C. H.: *see* Nakatani, O'Connor & Aston
Auer Jr., E. T.: *see* Luce, Goldinger, Auer Jr. & Vitevitch

Avesani, C.: *see* Hirschberg & Avesani
Azkue, R. M. de 570

Baars, B. J., Motley, M. T. & MacKay, D. 89
Baayen, R. H. & Schreuder, R. 130
Baayen, R. H.: *see also* Schreuder & Baayen
Barry, W. J. 382 fn 1
Bartels, C. & Kingston, J. 81
Bartels, C.: *see also* Kingston, MacMillan, Dickey, Thorburn & Bartels
Basterrechea, J. 570
Bateman, J. 585 f
Bates, E. A.: *see* Elman, Bates, Johnson, Karmiloff-Smith, Parisi & Plunkett
Baumann, M. 94
Beach, D. M. 301
Becchetti, C. & Ricotti, L. P. 662
Beckman, M. E. 174, 286, 516, 517, 518, 577, 585 f, 598, 607, 610, 625, 630
Beckman, M. E. & Edwards, J. 520
Beckman, M. E. & Pierrehumbert, J. B. 388, 409, 413, 548
Beckman, M. E.: *see also* de Jong, Beckman & Edwards; Pierrehumbert & Beckman; Pierrehumbert, Beckman & Ladd; Pierrehumbert, Ladd & Beckman
Beddor, P. S. & Krakow, R. A. 243, 268, 270
Beddor, P. M., Krakow, R. A. & Goldstein, L. M. 480
Bell, A. 482

Bell, A., Jurafsky, D., Fosler-Lussier, E., Girand, C. & Gildea, D. 4, 8, 12, 13
Bell, A.: see also Jurafsky, Bell & Girand; Jurafsky, Bell, Gregory & Raymond
Bell-Berti, F. 305
Bender, E. A. 463
Benedict, H. 209, 210
Benzmüller, R. & Grice, M. 387, 391, 395, 405
Berinstein, A. E. 281, 627
Berkenfield, C. 4, 7, 17, 23
Bernacki, R. H.: see Lively, Pisoni, Van Summers & Bernacki; Van Summers, Pisoni, Bernacki, Pedlow & Stokes
Bertelson, P.: see Morais, Cary, Alegria & Bertelson
Bertoncini, J. & Mehler, J. 501
Bertoncini, J.: see also Christophe, Dupoux, Bertoncini & Mehler; Mehler, Bertoncini, Dupoux & Pallier; Mehler, Jusczyk, Lambertz, Halsted, Bertoncini & Amiel-Tison; Nazzi, Bertoncini & Mehler
Bessel, N.: see Maddieson, Bessel & Smith
Best, C., McRoberts, G. & Sithole, N. 206
Bever, T.: see Aslin, Woodward, LaMendola & Bever
Bezooijen, R. van: see Haan, van Heuven, Pacilly & van Bezooijen
Bhaskararao, P.: see Spajic, Ladefoged & Bhaskararao
Bilbao, X.: see Hualde & Bilbao
Bladon, R. A. W. & Nolan, F. 356
Blasko, D. G.: see Connine, Blasko & Wang; Connine, Titone, Deelman & Blasko
Blecua, B. 352, 374

Blevins, J. 35
Bloch, B. 516, 523
Bluhme, S. & R. Burr 204
Boë, L. J.: see Schwartz, Abry & Boë
Boelhouwer, B. 39, 51
Boersma, P. 242, 457
Boersma, P. & Weenink, D. 66, 600
Bole-Richard, R. 333, 334, 336
Bolinger, D. L. 516, 627
Bolinger, D. L.: see also Dasher & Bolinger
Bond, Z. S.: see Marks, Moates, Bond & Stockmal; Marks, Moates, Bond & Vazquez; Moates, Bond & Stockmal
Bonin, P. 49
Booij, G. E. & Rubach, J. 234 fn 6
Booij, G. E.: see also Rubach & Booij
Bosch, L.: see Pallier, Bosch & Sebastián-Gallés
Bourgeois, T. 234 fn 1
Boysson-Bardies, B. de: see Hallé & de Boysson-Bardies
Bradley, D. C., Sánchez-Casas, R. M. & García-Albea, J. E. 49
Bradlow, A. R. 261, 262, 275
Bradshaw, M. 335
Braida, L. D.: see Krause & Braida; Payton, Uchanski & Braida; Picheny, Durlach & Braida; Uchanski, Choi, Braida, Reed & Durlach
Brakel, A. 539 fn 1
Broe, M. B. & Pierrehumbert, J. B. 268
Browman, C. P. & Goldstein, L. M. 351, 354, 356, 357, 420, 438, 464, 491
Bruce, G. 392, 578, 588
Bruce, G.: see also Gussenhoven & Bruce

Bunnell, H. T.: *see* Martin & Bunnell
Burani, C.: *see* Tabossi, Burani & Scott
Burgess, C.: *see* Simpson & Burgess
Burr, R.: *see* Bluhme & Burr
Bush, N. 14
Bushe, M. M.: *see* Rosenbaum, Engelbrecht, Bushe & Loukopoulos
Butterfield, S.: *see* Cutler & Butterfield; Norris, McQueen, Cutler & Butterfield; Norris, Cutler, McQueen, Butterfield & Kearns
Bybee, J. L. 16, 109, 118, 133, 670 fn 1
Byrd, D. 356, 420, 421, 422, 424, 438
Byrd, D. & Saltzman, E. L. 420
Byrd, D.: *see also* Chitoran, Goldstein & Byrd; Saltzman & Byrd

Campbell, L. 312
Caramazza, A., Laudanna, A. & Romani, C. 130
Carney, A. E., Widen, B. & Viemeister, N. 535
Carson-Berndsen, J. 664, 665, 680 ff
Carson-Berndsen, J.: *see also* Hübener & Carson-Berndsen
Carter, B.: *see* Liberman, Shankweiler, Fischer & Carter
Cary, L.: *see* Morais, Cary, Alegria & Bertelson
Caspers, J. 393
Catford, J. C. 301 f, 305, 312, 332, 342 fn 3, 342 fn 7, 370, 382 fn 1, 454 fn 3, 465, 504 fn 3, 523
Chafcouloff, M.: *see* Faure, Hirst & Chafcouloff
Chafe, W. 81

Chen, A.: *see* Gussenhoven & Chen
Chistovich, I.: *see* Kuhl, Andruski, Chistovich, Chistovich, Kozhevnikova, Ryskina, Stolyarova, Sundberg & Lacerda
Chistovich, L. A. & Lublinskaya, V. V. 248
Chistovich, L. A.: *see* Kuhl, Andruski, Chistovich, Chistovich, Kozhevnikova, Ryskina, Stolyarova, Sundberg & Lacerda
Chitoran, I. 423, 425, 427, 443, 450 ff, 453 fn 1
Chitoran, I., Goldstein, L.M. & Byrd, D. 449
Cho, T. 243
Cho, T.: *see also* Keating, Cho, Fougeron & Hsu
Choi, S.: *see* Uchanski, Choi, Braida, Reed & Durlach
Chomsky, N. 457
Chomsky, N. & Halle, M. 309, 342 fn 5, 449
Christol, A. 482
Christophe, A., Dupoux, E., Bertoncini, J. & Mehler, J. 207
Christophe, A.: *see also* Pallier, Sebastián-Gallés, Felguera, Christophe & Mehler
Church, K. 206, 680
Clark, H. H.: *see* Fox Tree & Clark
Classe, A. 523
Clements, G. N. 338, 344 fn 27, 449
Clements, G. N. & Hertz, S. R. 618
Clements, G. N. & Osu, S. 315, 449, 618
Clements, G. N.: *see also* Halle & Clements
Cluff, M. S. & Luce, P. A. 277
Cohen, A.: *see* 't Hart, Collier & Cohen
Cohen, M.: *see* Perkell, Cohen, Svirsky, Matthies, Garabieta & Jackson

Coillie, S. van: *see* Lahiri & van Coillie
Cole, J. S.: *see* Hualde, Smiljanić & Cole; Sevald, Dell & Cole
Collier, R.: *see* 't Hart, Collier & Cohen; Rump & Collier
Colomé, A. 44
Colomé, A.: *see also* Schiller, Costa & Colomé
Comrie, B. 216, 617
Connine, C. M., Blasko, D. G. & Wang, J. 277
Connine, C. M., Titone, D., Deelman, T. & Blasko, D. G. 160
Content, A., Dumay, N. & Frauenfelder, U. H. 122
Cooper, F. S.: *see* Liberman, Cooper, Shankweiler & Studdert-Kennedy
Cooper, R.: *see* Moon, Cooper & Fifer
Cooper, W. E.: *see* Eady, Cooper, Klouda, Müller & Lotts
Corder, S. P. 523, 531, 534
Costa, A. 44
Costa, A. & Sebastián-Gallés, N. 53
Costa, A.: *see also* Schiller & Costa; Schiller, Costa & Colomé
Couper-Kuhlen, E. 518
Crazzolara, J. P. 477, 480
Creissels, D. 301, 336
Crompton, A. 90
Cummins, F. & Port, R. F. 539 fn 2
Cutler, A. 36, 43, 172, 174, 233, 278, 280
Cutler, A. & Butterfield, S. 242, 280
Cutler, A. & van Donselaar, W. 233
Cutler, A. & Norris, D. G. 36, 122, 290
Cutler, A. & Otake, T. 174, 284, 287

Cutler, A., Demuth, K. & McQueen, J. M. 289
Cutler, A., Mehler, J., Norris, D. G. & Segui, J. 172, 174, 282
Cutler, A., van Ooijen, B., Norris, D. G. & Sánchez-Casas, R. 284
Cutler, A., Sebastián-Gallés, N., Soler Vilageliu, O. & van Ooijen, B. 142, 158, 160, 284, 287
Cutler, A.: *see also* Jusczyk, Cutler & Redanz; McQueen, Norris & Cutler; McQueen, Otake & Cutler; Norris, McQueen & Cutler; Norris, McQueen, Cutler & Butterfield; Norris, Cutler, McQueen, Butterfield & Kearns; Otake, Hatano, Cutler & Mehler; Scott & Cutler; Soto-Faraco, Sebastián-Gallés & Cutler

Dahan, D., Magnuson, J. S., Tanenhaus, M. K. & Hogan, E. M. 122
Dalby, J.: *see* Port, Dalby & O'Dell
Damian, M. F. 93
Damian, M. F., Vigliocco, G. & Levelt, W. J. M. 93
Dasher, R. & Bolinger, D. W. 518 f
Dauer, R. M. 516 f, 518, 519, 522, 523
Davis, B. L.: *see* MacNeilage & Davis
De Boeck, P. L. B. 333
Deelman, T.: *see* Connine, Titone, Deelman & Blasko
Delattre, P. 516
Delgado Martins, M. R. & Lacerda, F. 389
Dell, F. 213
Dell, G. S. 43
Dell, G. S. & Newman, J. E. 282

Author Index

Dell, G. S.: *see also* Sevald, Dell & Cole
Dembowski, J. & Westbury, J. R. 357
Demolin, D. 304, 312, 327 f, 333, 460, 473, 475, 615
Demolin, D. & Soquet, A. 461, 463
De Mori, R. 662
Demuth, K.: *see* Cutler, Demuth & McQueen
Denning, K. 460, 477 f
Derbyshire, A. J.: *see* Ellis, Derbyshire & Joseph
Deterding, D. H. 521, 539 fn 5
Dickey, L. W.: *see* Kingston, MacMillan, Dickey, Thorburn & Bartels
Diehl, R. L. 460
Diehl, R. L.: *see also* Kingston & Diehl; Redford & Diehl
Dilley, L., Shattuck-Hufnagel, S. & Ostendorf, M. 105
Dimmendaal, G. J. 313, 337, 342 fn 8, 456, 460, 482
D'Imperio, M. 387, 388, 393 f, 395, 399
D'Imperio, M. & House, D. 388, 393
Dixon, R. 214
Dobrovolsky, M.: *see* O'Grady, Dobrovolsky & Aronoff
Donald, M. 500
Donohue, M. 586, 587
Donselaar, W. van: *see* Cutler & van Donselaar
Dommergues, U.: *see* Mehler, Dommergues, Frauenfelder & Segui
Druss, B.: *see* Hirsh-Pasek, Kemler-Nelson, Jusczyk, Wright Cassidy, Druss & Kennedy
Duez, D. 243

Dumay, N.: *see* Content, Dumay & Frauenfelder
Dupoux, E. & Peperkamp, S. 205, 206, 210, 213
Dupoux, E., Peperkamp, S. & Sebastián-Gallés, N. 204, 205, 218 ff, 226
Dupoux, E., Pallier, C., Sebastián-Gallés, N. & Mehler, J. 204, 206, 211, 219, 283
Dupoux, E., Kakehi, K., Hirose, Y., Pallier, C. & Mehler, J. 206
Dupoux, E.: *see also* Christophe, Dupoux, Bertoncini & Mehler; Mehler, Bertoncini, Dupoux & Pallier; Mehler, Dupoux & Segui; Pallier, Dupoux & Jeannin; Sebastián-Gallés, Dupoux, Segui & Mehler
Durlach, N. I.: *see* Picheny, Durlach & Braida; Uchanski, Choi, Braida, Reed & Durlach
Dziubalska-Kołaczyk, K. 677

Eady, S. J., Cooper, W. E., Klouda, G. V., Müller, P. R. & Lotts, D. W. 81
Edwards, J.: *see* Beckman & Edwards; de Jong, Beckman & Edwards
Ellis, D.: *see* Greenberg, Ellis & Hollenback
Ellis, L., Derbyshire, A. J. & Joseph, M. E. 288
Elman, J. L. & McClelland, J.L. 161, 164
Elman, J. L., Bates, E. A., Johnson, M. H., Karmiloff-Smith, A., Parisi, D. & Plunkett, K. 459, 462
Elman, J. L.: *see also* McClelland & Elman
Elordieta, A.: *see* Hualde, Elordieta & Elordieta

Elordieta, G. 547
Elordieta, G.: *see also* Hualde, Elordieta & Elordieta; Hualde, Elordieta, Iñaki & Smiljanić; Jun & Elordieta
Elugbe, B.: *see* Ladefoged, Williamson, Elugbe & Uwulaka
Engelbrecht, S. E.: *see* Rosenbaum, Engelbrecht, Bushe & Loukopoulos
Engstrand, O. 243
Engstrand, O.: *see also* Lindblom & Engstrand
Eriksson, A. 516
Etxebarria Ayesta, J. M. 577, 631
Evers, V.: *see* Lahiri & Evers
Evinck, S. 39, 51
Ewan, W. G. & Krones, R. 305, 343 fn 17
Ewan, W. G.: *see also* Hombert, Ohala & Ewan

Face, T. 575
Falé, I. 389
Fant, G. 248, 464, 601, 612 fn 10
Fant, G.: *see also* Jakobson, Fant & Halle
Farnetani, E. 286
Faulkner, D.: *see* Ladd, Faulkner, Faulkner & Schepman
Faulkner, H.: *see* Ladd, Faulkner, Faulkner & Schepman
Faure, G., Hirst, D. J. & Chafcouloff, M. 516
Felguera, T.: *see* Pallier, Sebastián-Gallés, Felguera, Christophe & Mehler
Ferguson, C. A. 6
Ferrand, L. & Grainger, J. 38
Ferrand, L. & Segui, J. 53
Ferrand, L., Segui, J. & Grainger, J. 36 ff, 39, 56, 44, 49, 50 f, 52
Ferrand, L., Segui, J. & Humphreys, G. W. 36 ff, 39, 40, 44, 52

Fidelholz, J. 16
Fifer, W. *see* Moon, Cooper & Fifer
Fischer, F. W.: *see* Liberman, Shankweiler, Fischer & Carter
Fischer-Jørgensen, E. & Hutters, B. 524
Fitzpatrick, J. & Wheeldon, L. 671 fn 2, 671 fn 7
Flege, J. E. 264
Flemming, E. 242, 457
Flemming, E.: *see also* Johnson, Flemming & Wright
Fontdevila, J., Pallarès, M. D. & Recasens, D. 360
Fontdevila, J.: *see also* Recasens, Pallarès & Fontdevila
Fosler-Lussier, E. & Morgan, N. 12
Fosler-Lussier, E.: *see also* Bell, Jurafsky, Fosler-Lussier, Girand & Gildea
Foss, D. J. 464
Fougeron, C.: *see* Keating, Cho, Fougeron & Hsu
Fowler, C. A. 243, 268
Fowler, C. A.: *see* Sancier & Fowler
Fox Tree, J. E. & Clark, H. H. 12
Francis, W. N. & Kučera, H. 23, 146, 157
Frauenfelder, U. H. & Schreuder, R. 130
Frauenfelder, U. H.: *see also* Content, Dumay & Frauenfelder; Grosjean & Frauenfelder; Mehler, Dommergues, Frauenfelder & Segui; Segui & Frauenfelder
Frazier, L. 206
Fre Woldu, K. 473
Fridjhon, P.: *see* Traill, Khumalo & Fridjhon
Friederici, A.: *see* Jusczyk, Friederici, Wessels, Svenkerud & Jusczyk

Frisch, S.: *see* Pierrehumbert & Frisch
Frota, S. 395, 403, 406, 409, 449
Frota, S. & Vigário, M. 632 fn 6
Fujimura, O.: *see* Sproat & Fujimura

Gaitenby, J. 419
Galindo, B.: *see* Teston & Galindo
Gaminde, I. 547
Gaminde, I.: *see also* Hualde, Elordieta, Gaminde & Smiljanić
Gamkrelidze, T. V. & Ivanov, V. 443
Gandour, J. 204
Gandour, J.: *see* Potisuk, Gandour & Harper
Garabieta, I: *see* Perkell, Cohen, Svirsky, Matthies, Garabieta & Jackson
García-Albea, J. E.: *see* Bradley, Sánchez-Casas & García-Albea
Garrett, M. F. 88
Garrido, J. M., Llisterri, J., de la Mota, C. & Ríos, A. 575
Gaskell, G. & Marslen-Wilson, W. D. 643
Gay, T. 539 fn 6
Gelder, B. de: *see* Vroomen & de Gelder
Gerken, L. A. 35
Gerken, L. A., Jusczyk, P. & Mandel, D. 209
Ghini, M. 639, 650
Gibbon, D., Moore, R. & Winski, R. 680
Gibbon, D.: *see also* Van Eynde & Gibbon
Gildea, D.: *see* Bell, Jurafsky, Fosler-Lussier, Girand & Gildea
Girand, C.: *see* Bell, Jurafsky, Fosler-Lussier, Girand & Gildea; Jurafsky, Bell & Girand
Gjerlow, K.: *see* Obler & Gjerlow

Godfrey, J., Holliman, E. & McDaniel, J. 8, 9
Goldinger, S. D. 108 f, 113, 117, 206, 279
Goldinger, S. D., Luce, P. A., Pisoni, D. B. & Marcario, J.K. 160
Goldinger, S. D.: *see also* Luce, Goldinger, Auer Jr. & Vitevitch
Goldsmith, J. 458
Goldstein, L. M.: *see* Beddor, Krakow & Goldstein; Browman & Goldstein; Chitoran, Goldstein & Byrd; Surprenant & Goldstein
Gordon, P. C.: *see* Gow & Gordon
Gósy, M. & Terken, J. 64
Goto, H. 203, 206
Gow, D. W. 643
Gow, D. W. & Gordon, P. C. 277
Goyvaerts, D. 313
Grabe, E. 388
Grabe, E. & Low, E. L. 615
Grabe, E., Post, B. & Watson, I. 520, 525
Grabe, E.: *see also* Low & Grabe; Low, Grabe & Nolan
Gracco, V. L. & Nye, P. W. 428
Grainger, J.: *see* Ferrand & Grainger; Ferrand, Segui & Grainger
Grammont, M. 205, 234 fn 4
Grassias, A. 333
Greenbaum, S.: *see* Quirk, Greenbaum, Leech & Svartvik
Greenberg, J. H. 300, 312, 477
Greenberg, S., Ellis, D. & Hollenback, J. 4, 9
Gregory, M.: *see* Jurafsky, Bell, Gregory & Raymond
Grice, M. 388, 393 f, 395, 413
Grice, M., Ladd, D. R. & Arvaniti, A. 388, 393, 395, 405, 406, 409

Grice, M.: *see also* Benzmüller & Grice
Griffith, N. C.: *see* Lieberman, Harris, Hoffman & Griffith
Grønnum, N. & Viana, M. C. 387, 389, 392, 403, 404
Grosjean, F. 66
Grosjean, F. & Frauenfelder, U. H. 276
Guion, S.G. 352
Gussenhoven, C. 387, 409, 629, 633 fn 10
Gussenhoven, C. & Bruce, G. 588
Gussenhoven, C. & Chen, A. 62, 84
Gussenhoven, C. & van der Vliet, P. 88, 578
Gussenhoven, C., Repp, B. H., Rietveld, A., Rump, H. H. & Terken, J. 72

Haan, J. 82
Haan, J., van Heuven, V. J., Pacilly, J. J. A. & van Bezooijen, R. 62
Haan, J.: *see also* van Heuven & Haan
Hale, K. 617
Hale, M. & Reiss, C. 458
Halle, M. 309, 341, 458, 677
Halle, M. & Clements, G. N. 309
Halle, M.: *see also* Chomsky & Halle; Jakobson, Fant & Halle
Hallé, P. & de Boysson-Bardies, B. 209
Halsted, H.: *see* Mehler, Jusczyk, Lambertz, Halsted, Bertoncini & Amiel-Tison
Hamburger, M.: *see* Slowiaczek & Hamburger
Han, M. S. 174, 516, 517, 523
Hanson, B. F.: *see* Mines, Hanson & Shoup
Haraguchi, S. 174
Hardcastle, W. J. 357, 421, 422
Hardcastle, W. J. & Hewlett, N. 286
Hardcastle, W. J. & Roach, P. 424
Hardcastle, W. J.: *see also* Hoole, Nguyen & Hardcastle
Harnad, S. 535
Harper, M. P.: *see* Potisuk, Gandour & Harper
Harrington, J., Palethorpe, S. & Watson, C. I. 112
Harris, J. G. 323
Harris, K. S.: *see* Lieberman, Harris, Hoffman & Griffith
Hart, J. 't, Collier, R. & Cohen, A. 71
Haruna, A.: *see* Lindsey, Hayward & Haruna
Hatano, G.: *see* Otake, Hatano, Cutler & Mehler
Haudricourt, A. G. 300, 313
Hay, J. B. 110 f, 117, 130
Hay, J. B., Jannedy, S. & Mendoza-Denton, N. 111
Hayata, T. 633 fn 9, 634 fn 13
Hayes, B. P. 208, 214, 216, 217, 233, 388
Hayes, B. & Lahiri, A. 388, 391, 393, 395
Hayward, K. & Hayward, R. J. 504 fn 1
Hayward, K.: *see also* Lindsey, Hayward & Haruna
Hayward, R. J.: *see* Hayward & Hayward
Henderson, J. B. & Repp, B. H. 452
Hermann, E. 62
Hermans, B. 633 fn 10
Hermansky, H. 665
Hertz, S. R.: *see* Clements & Hertz
Heuven, V. J. van & Sluijter, A. 633
Heuven, V. J. van & Haan, J. 64, 87
Heuven, V. J. van: *see also* Haan, van Heuven, Pacilly & van Bezooijen; Sluijter & van Heuven

Hewlett, N.: *see* Hardcastle & Hewlett
Hirose, H.: *see* Sawashima & Hirose
Hirose, Y.: *see* Dupoux, Kakehi, Hirose, Pallier & Mehler
Hirschberg, J. & Avesani, C. 388, 393
Hirschberg, J.: *see also* Prieto, van Santen & Hirschberg
Hirsh-Pasek, K., Kemler-Nelson, D., Jusczyk, P., Wright Cassidy, K., Druss, B. & Kennedy, L. 208, 209
Hirst, D. J.: *see* Faure, Hirst & Chafcouloff
Hockett, C. F. 482, 523
Hoequist, C. J. 517
Hoffman, H. S.: *see* Lieberman, Harris, Hoffman & Griffith
Hogaboam, T. W. & Perfetti, C. A. 7
Hogan, E. M.: *see* Dahan, Magnuson, Tanenhaus & Hogan
Hollenback, J.: *see* Greenberg, Ellis & Hollenback
Holliman, E.: *see* Godfrey, Holliman & McDaniel
Holst, T. & Nolan, F. J. 357, 365
Hombert, J.-M., Ohala, J. J. & Ewan, W. G. 327, 343 fn 17, 344 fn 20
Honda, K. 192
Hoole, P., Nguyen, N. & Hardcastle, W. J. 356
Hooper, J. B. 16
House, A. S.: *see* Stevens & House
House, D.: *see* D'Imperio & House
House, J.: *see* Wichmann, House & Rietveld
Hsu, C.: *see* Keating, Cho, Fougeron & Hsu
Hualde, J. I. 547, 548, 549, 550, 551, 555, 561, 565, 570, 579 fn 2, 579 fn 3, 580 fn 10

Hualde, J. I. & Bilbao, X. 547
Hualde, J. I., Elordieta, G. & Elordieta, A. 547
Hualde, J. I., Smiljanić, R. & Cole, J. S. 548, 553, 577
Hualde, J. I., Elordieta, G., Gaminde, I. & Smiljanić, R. 615, 633 fn 9
Hualde, J. I.: *see also* Smiljanić & Hualde
Hübener, K. 672 fn 17
Hübener, K. & J. Carson-Berndsen 665
Hulst, H. G. van der & Smith, N. S. 547, 587
Hume, E., Johnson, K., Seo, M. & Tserdanelis, G. 351
Humphreys, G. W.: *see* Ferrand, Segui & Humphreys
Hutters, B.: *see* Fischer-Jørgensen & Hutters
Hyman, L. M. 456, 579 fn 1, 627, 634 fn 12
Hyman, L. M. & Magaji, D. J. 335

Indefrey, P.: *see* Price, Indefrey & van Turennout
IPDS 661
Itô, J. 177, 178
Itô, J., Kitagawa, Y. & Mester, R. A. 179
Ivanov, V.: *see* Gamkrelidze & Ivanov

Jackson, M.: *see* Perkell, Cohen, Svirsky, Matthies, Garabieta & Jackson
Jakobson, R. 449, 617, 633 fn 7, 677
Jakobson, R. & Waugh, L. 482
Jakobson, R., Fant, G. & Halle, M. 354
Jannedy, S.: *see* Hay, Jannedy & Mendoza-Denton

Jansen, W. 580 fn 10
Jeannin, X.: *see* Pallier, Dupoux & Jeannin
Jelinek, F. 662
Jescheniak, J. D. & Levelt, W. J. M. 7, 16, 28
Jespersen, O. 4, 15, 17
Jessen, M. 313, 330
Jessen, M. & Roux, J. C. 326
Johnson, K. 113, 117, 127, 282, 460
Johnson, K., Flemming, E. & Wright, R. 242, 459
Johnson, K.: *see also* Hume, Johnson, Seo & Tserdanelis
Johnson, M. H.: *see* Elman, Bates, Johnson, Karmiloff-Smith, Parisi & Plunkett
Johnson, W.: *see* Roca & Johnson
Jones, D. 4
Jong, K. J. de 105
Jong, K. J. de & Obeng, S. G. 460
Jong, K. J. de, Beckman, M. E. & Edwards, J. 105
Jongman, A.: *see* Lahiri, Jongman & Sereno; Warner, Jongman, Sereno & Kemps
Joseph, M. E.: *see also* Ellis, Derbyshire & Joseph
Jun, J.: *see* Silverman & Jun
Jun, S.-A. 388
Jun, S.-A. & Elordieta, G. 547, 549
Jurafsky, D. & Martin, J. H. 679
Jurafsky, D., Bell, A. & Girand, C. 87, 106, 107
Jurafsky, D., Bell, A., Gregory, M. & Raymond, W. D. 8, 13, 14, 15, 16, 29
Jurafsky, D., Bell, A., Fosler-Lussier, E., Girand, C. & Raymond, W. D. 4, 8, 12, 15, 31 fn 1
Jurafsky, D: *see also* Bell, Jurafsky, Fosler-Lussier, Girand & Gildea

Jusczyk, A.: *see* Jusczyk, Friederici, Wessels, Svenkerud & Jusczyk
Jusczyk, P. 231
Jusczyk, P., Cutler, A. & Redanz, N. 204
Jusczyk, P., Friederici, A., Wessels, J., Svenkerud, V. & Jusczyk, A. 204
Jusczyk, P.: *see also* Gerken, Jusczyk & Mandel; Hirsh-Pasek, Kemler-Nelson, Jusczyk, Wright Cassidy, Druss & Kennedy; Mehler, Jusczyk, Lambertz, Halsted, Bertoncini & Amiel-Tison

Kagaya, R. 325
Kaiki. N. & Sagisaka, Y. 194
Kaji, S. 633 fn 11
Kakehi, K.: *see* Dupoux, Kakehi, Hirose, Pallier & Mehler
Karan, M.: *see* Labov, Karan & Miller
Karlsson, F. 214
Karmiloff-Smith, A.: *see* Elman, Bates, Johnson, Karmiloff-Smith, Parisi & Plunkett
Kato, H. 179
Kato, H.: *see also* Takano, Tsuzaki & Kato; Tanaka, Tsuzaki & Kato
Kawasaki, H.: *see* Ohala & Kawasaki
Kaye, J. D. 336
Kearns, R.: *see* Norris, Cutler, McQueen, Butterfield & Kearns
Keating, P. A. 87, 671 fn 2
Keating, P. A., Cho, T., Fougeron, C. & Hsu, C. 105
Kello, C. T., Plaut, D. C. & MacWhinney, B. 92 ff
Kelso, J. A. S., Saltzman, E. L. & Tuller, B. 420

Kemler-Nelson, D.: see Hirsh-Pasek, Kemler-Nelson, Jusczyk, Wright Cassidy, Druss & Kennedy
Kemp, W.: see Yaeger-Dror & Kemp
Kemps, R.: see Warner, Jongman, Sereno & Kemps
Kennedy, L.: see Hirsh-Pasek, Kemler-Nelson, Jusczyk, Wright Cassidy, Druss & Kennedy
Kenstowicz, M. 35, 54, 458
Kent, R. D.: see Shriberg & Kent
Khumalo, J. S. M.: see Traill, Khumalo & Fridjhon
Kingston, J. C. 464, 465, 470, 473, 502
Kingston, J. C. & Diehl, R.L. 462
Kingston, J. C. & MacMillan, N. A. 462
Kingston, J., MacMillan, N. A., Dickey, L. W., Thorburn, R. & Bartels, C. 462
Kingston, J. C.: see also Bartels & Kingston
Kiparsky, P. 671 fn 2
Kirchner, R. 113, 116
Kiriloff, C. 204
Kitagawa, Y.: see Itô, Kitagawa & Mester
Klatt, D. H. 206, 419, 655, 664, 670 fn 1, 671 fn 13
Klouda, G. V.: see Eady, Cooper, Klouda, Müller & Lotts
Knoll, R. L.: see Sternberg, Monsell, Knoll & Wright; Sternberg, Wright, Knoll & Monsell
Kohler, K. J. 457, 523
Kolinsky, R.: see Morais & Kolinsky
Kouwenberg, S. & Murray, E. 588
Kozhevnikova, E.: see Kuhl, Andruski, Chistovich, Chistovich,
Kozhevnikova, Ryskina, Stolyarova, Sundberg & Lacerda
Krakow, R. A. 356
Krakow, R. A.: see also Beddor & Krakow; Beddor, Krakow & Goldstein
Krause, J. C. & Braida, L. D. 242
Krejnovic, E. A. 482
Krikhaar, E.: see Wijnen, Krikhaar & den Os
Kroll, J. & Stewart, E. 93
Krones, R.: see Ewan & Krones
Krull, D. 243
Kubozono, H. 172, 173, 174, 175, 176, 178, 179, 275
Kubozono, H.: see also Ujihira & Kubozono
Kučera, H.: see Francis & Kučera
Kuhl, P., Williams, K., Lacerda, F., Stevens, K. & Lindblom, B. 209
Kuhl, P., Andruski, J., Chistovich, I., Chistovich, L. A., Kozhevnikova, E., Ryskina, V., Stolyarova, E., Sundberg, U. & Lacerda, F. 280
Kühnert, B. & Nolan, F. J. 286
Kutsch Lojenga, C. K. 312, 327 f, 335, 343 fn 18, 482, 483, 486, 490

Labov, W. 6
Labov, W., Karan, M. & Miller, C. 133
Lacerda, F.: see Delgado Martins & Lacerda; Kuhl, Andruski, Chistovich, Chistovich, Kozhevnikova, Ryskina, Stolyarova, Sundberg & Lacerda; Kuhl, Williams, Lacerda, Stevens & Lindblom
Ladd, D. R. 387, 388, 393, 395, 413
Ladd, D. R., Faulkner, D., Faulkner, H. & Schepman, A. 413

Ladd, D. R.: see also Arvaniti, Ladd & Mennen; Grice, Ladd & Arvaniti; Pierrehumbert, Beckman & Ladd; Pierrehumbert, Ladd & Beckman
Ladefoged, P. 300, 303, 304, 307, 333, 338, 342 fn 5, 464, 516, 517, 523
Ladefoged, P. & Maddieson, I. 303, 304, 305, 313, 316, 340, 352, 382 fn 1, 465, 474
Ladefoged, P. & Traill, A. 457 f, 492
Ladefoged, P. & Wu, Z. 482
Ladefoged, P., Williamson, K., Elugbe, B. & Uwulaka, A. 304, 312
Ladefoged, P.: see also Spajic, Ladefoged & Bhaskararao
Lahiri, A. 639, 655, 671 fn 2
Lahiri, A. & van Coillie, S. 643, 644
Lahiri, A. & Evers, V. 639
Lahiri, A. & Marslen-Wilson, W. D. 288, 643, 671 fn 2
Lahiri, A. & Reetz, H. 677
Lahiri, A., Jongman, A. & Sereno, J.A. 671 fn 2
Lahiri, A.: see also Hayes & Lahiri
Lambert, J. 616
Lambertz, G.: see Mehler, Jusczyk, Lambertz, Halsted, Bertoncini & Amiel-Tison
LaMendola, N.: see Aslin, Woodward, LaMendola & Bever
Landauer, T. K. & Streeter, L. A. 142
Laudanna, A.: see Caramazza, Laudanna & Romani
Laver, J. 482, 491, 504 fn 4, 516, 518
Lee, L. & Nusbaum, H. 204
Leech, G.: see Quirk, Greenbaum, Leech & Svartvik

Leeden, A. C. van der 589 ff, 607 f, 610, 611 fn 2, 611 fn 3, 612 fn 3, 612 fn 5, 626, 628
Lehiste, I. 208, 518
Lehiste, I.: see also Peterson & Lehiste
Levelt, C. C., Schiller, N. O. & Levelt, W. J. M. 36
Levelt, W. J. M. 3, 87, 88, 89, 90, 96, 104, 275, 279, 281, 291
Levelt, W. J. M. & Wheeldon, L. 41, 53, 90
Levelt, W. J. M., Roelofs, A. & Meyer, A. S. 7, 41, 43, 90 ff, 275
Levelt, W. J. M.: see also Damian, Vigliocco & Levelt; Jescheniak & Levelt; Levelt, Schiller & Levelt; Schriefers, Meyer & Levelt
Lex, G. 304, 312
Li, P. & Yip, M. C. 28
Liberman, A. M., Cooper, F. S., Shankweiler, D. P. & Studdert-Kennedy, M. 286, 437
Liberman, I.Y., Shankweiler, D. P., Fischer, F. W. & Carter, B. 35
Lieberman, A. M., Harris, K. S., Hoffman, H. S. & Griffith, N. C. 464
Lieberman, P. 341
Liljencrants, J. & Lindblom, B. 268, 459
Lindau, M. 312, 313, 317, 465
Lindblom, B. 118, 131, 241, 268, 381, 455, 457, 458, 459, 478, 618
Lindblom, B. & Engstrand, O. 459
Lindblom, B., MacNeilage, P. F. & Studdert-Kennedy, M. 461, 463
Lindblom, B.: see also Kuhl, Williams, Lacerda, Stevens & Lindblom; Liljencrants & Lindblom; Moon & Lindblom
Lindsey, G. A. 62

Lindsey, G. A., Hayward, K. & Haruna, A. 313
Liu, S.: *see* Stevens, Manuel, Shattuck-Hufnagel & Liu
Lively, S. E., Pisoni, D. B., Van Summers, W. & Bernacki, R. H. 242
Llisterri J., Marín, R., de la Mota, C. & Ríos, A. 575
Llisterri, J.: *see also* Garrido, Llisterri, de la Mota & Ríos
Löfqvist, A. 428
Loftus, E. F.: *see* Loftus & Loftus
Loftus, G. R. & Loftus, E. F. 601
Lotts, D. W.: *see* Eady, Cooper, Klouda, Müller & Lotts
Loukopoulos, L. D.: *see* Rosenbaum, Engelbrecht, Bushe & Loukopoulos
Low, E. L. 520
Low, E. L. & Grabe, E. 520, 525
Low, E. L., Grabe, E. & Nolan, F. J. 519, 520, 521 f, 525, 526, 531
Low, E. L.: *see also* Grabe & Low
Luangthongkum, T. 523, 531, 534
Lublinskaya, V. V.: *see* Chistovich & Lublinskaya
Luce, P. A., Goldinger, S. D., Auer Jr., E. T. & Vitevitch, M. S. 161, 164
Luce, P. A.: *see also* Cluff & Luce; Goldinger, Luce, Pisoni & Marcario; Vitevitch & Luce
Lupker, S. J. 89
Lynch, M.: *see* Slowiaczek, McQueen, Soltano & Lynch

MacClean, M. 357
MacKay, D. G.: *see* Baars, Motley & MacKay; Santiago, MacKay, Palma & Rho
Macken, M. A. 36
MacMillan, N. A.: *see* Kingston & MacMillan; Kingston, MacMillan, Dickey, Thorburn & Bartels
MacNeilage, P. F. 54, 460
MacNeilage, P. F. & Davis, B. L. 459, 460
MacNeilage, P. F.: *see also* Lindblom, MacNeilage & Studdert-Kennedy
MacWhinney, D.: *see* Kello, Plaut & MacWhinney
Maddieson, I. 277, 299, 331, 335, 342 fn 7, 343 fn 14, 455
Maddieson, I., Bessel, N. & Smith, C. 473
Maddieson, I.: *see also* Ladefoged & Maddieson
Maeda, S.: *see* Port, Al-Ani & Maeda
Maekawa, K.: *see* Sukegawa, Maekawa & Uehara
Magaji, D. J.: *see* Hyman & Magaji
Magnuson, J. S.: *see* Dahan, Magnuson, Tanenhaus & Hogan
Makarova, V. 64
Malou, J. 480
Mandel, D.: *see* Gerken, Jusczyk & Mandel
Mann, V. A. 268
Manning, C. D. & Schütze, H. 15
Manrique, A. M. B. & Signorini, A. 516
Manuel, S. V. 243, 267
Manuel, S. V.: *see also* Stevens, Manuel, Shattuck-Hufnagel & Liu
Marcario, J. K.: *see* Goldinger, Luce, Pisoni & Marcario
Marín, R.: *see* Llisterri, Marín, de la Mota & Ríos
Marks, E., Moates, D. R., Bond, Z. S. & Stockmal, V. 159

Marks, E., Moates, D. R., Bond, Z. S. & Vazquez, L. 142, 158
Marslen-Wilson, W. D. 160, 161, 277, 422
Marslen-Wilson, W. D. & Warren, P. 206, 278, 279, 288
Marslen-Wilson, W. D. & Welsh, A. 161
Marslen-Wilson, W. D. & Zwitserlood, P. 160
Marslen-Wilson, W. D.: *see also* Gaskell & Marslen-Wilson; Lahiri & Marslen-Wilson
Martin, J. G. & Bunnell, H. T. 288
Martin, J. H.: *see* Jurafsky & Martin
Martinet, A. 15
Martins, F. 389
Matsumura, A. 175
Matthies, M.: *see* Perkell, Cohen, Svirsky, Matthies, Garabieta & Jackson
Mattingly, I. G. 437, 439 f
Mayer, K.: *see* Meringer & Mayer
McCarthy, J. J. & Taub, A. 671 fn 2
McCawley, J. D. 174, 587
McClelland, J. L. & Elman, J. L. 161, 164, 277, 288
McClelland, J. L.: *see also* Elman & McClelland
McCoy, P. 427
McDaniel, J.: *see* Godfrey, Holliman & McDaniel
McDonald, J.: *see* McGurk & McDonald
McGowan, R. S. 382 fn 1
McGowan, R. S. & Saltzman, E. L. 352
McGurk, H. & McDonald, J. 171
McLaughlin, F. 312, 335
McQueen, J. M. 122
McQueen, J. M., Norris, D. G. & Cutler, A. 160, 278, 288

McQueen, J. M., Otake, T. & Cutler, A. 290
McQueen, J. M.: *see also* Cutler, Demuth & McQueen; Norris, McQueen & Cutler; Norris, McQueen, Cutler & Butterfield; Norris, Cutler, McQueen, Butterfield & Kearns; Pitt, M. A. & J. M. McQueen; Slowiaczek, McQueen, Soltano & Lynch
McRoberts, G.: *see* Best, McRoberts & Sithole
Medin, D. L. & Schaffer, M. M. 670 fn 1
Mehler, J., Dupoux, E. &. Segui, J. 206
Mehler, J., Bertoncini, J., Dupoux, E. & Pallier, C. 209
Mehler, J., Dommergues, J. Y., Frauenfelder, U. H. & Segui, J. 36, 48
Mehler, J., Jusczyk, P., Lambertz, G., Halsted, H., Bertoncini, J. & Amiel-Tison, C. 208 f
Mehler, J.: *see also* Bertoncini & Mehler; Christophe, Dupoux, Bertoncini & Mehler; Cutler, Mehler, Norris & Segui; Dupoux, Kakehi, Hirose, Pallier & Mehler; Dupoux, Pallier, Sebastián-Gallés & Mehler; Nazzi, Bertoncini & Mehler; Otake, Hatano, Cutler & Mehler; Pallier, Sebastián-Gallés, Felguera, Christophe & Mehler; Ramus, Nespor & Mehler; Sebastián-Gallés, Dupoux, Segui & Mehler
Mendes de Luz, M. A.: *see* Vázquez & Mendes
Mendoza-Denton, N. 111
Mendoza-Denton, N.: *see also* Hay, Jannedy & Mendoza-Denton

Mennen, I.: *see* Arvaniti, Ladd & Mennen
Meringer, R. & Mayer, K. 88
Mertens, F. 482, 486
Mester, R. A.: *see* Itô, Kitagawa & Mester
Meyer, A. S. 89
Meyer A. S. & Schriefers, H. 89
Meyer, A. S.: *see also* Levelt, Roelofs & Meyer; Roelofs & Meyer; Schriefers, Meyer & Levelt
Miller, C.: *see* Labov, Karan & Miller
Miller, G. & Nicely, P. 223
Mines, M. A., Hanson, B. F. & Shoup, J. E. 143
Moates, D. R. & Russell, S. 142, 158
Moates, D. R., Bond, Z. S. & Stockmal, V. B. 275
Moates, D. R.: *see also* Marks, Moates, Bond & Stockmal; Marks, Moates, Bond & Vazquez
Mohanan, K. P. 671 fn 2, 671 fn 3
Moll, F.: *see* Alcover & Moll
Moñino, Y. 335
Monsell, S.: *see* Sternberg, Monsell, Knoll & Wright; Sternberg, Wright, Knoll & Monsell
Moon, C., Cooper, R. & Fifer, W. 209
Moon, S.-J. & Lindblom, B. 242
Moore, R.: *see* Gibbon, Moore & Winski
Morais, J. 503
Morais, J. & Kolinsky, R. 503
Morais, J. & Mousty, P. 498
Morais, J., Cary, L., Alegria, J. & Bertelson, P. 503
Morais, J.: *see also* Radeau, Morais & Segui

Morgan, J.: *see* Shi, Morgan & Allopenna
Morgan, N.: *see* Fosler-Lussier & Morgan
Mota, C. de la 575
Mota, C. de la: *see also* Garrido, Llisterri, de la Mota & Ríos; Llisterri, Marín, de la Mota & Ríos
Motley, M. T.: *see* Baars, Motley & MacKay
Moulines, E. & Verhelst, W. 64
Mousty, P.: *see* Morais & Mousty
Müller, P. R.: *see* Eady, Cooper, Klouda, Müller & Lotts
Murray, E.: *see* Kouwenberg & Murray

Nakatani, L. H., O'Connor, J. D. & Aston, C. H. 516
Navarro Tomás, T. 207, 353, 575
Nazzi, T., Bertoncini, J. & Mehler, J. 209
Nespor, M. 519, 523, 530, 535
Nespor, M. & Vogel, I. 209, 388
Nespor, M.: *see also* Ramus, Nespor & Mehler
Newman, J. E.: *see* Dell & Newman
Newman, P. 337, 482
Newman, P. & Ratliff, M. 456
Newport, E. L.: *see* Saffran, Aslin & Newport
Ngonga, H. 496, 498, 500
Nguyen, N.: *see* Hoole, Nguyen & Hardcastle
Nibert, H. 575
Nicely, P.: *see* Miller & Nicely
Nigro, G. N.: *see* Streeter & Nigro
Nolan, F. J.: *see* Bladon & Nolan; Holst & Nolan; Kühnert & Nolan; Low, Grabe & Nolan
Nord, L. 243
Norris, D. G. 121, 161, 164, 277

Norris, D. G., McQueen, J. M. & Cutler, A. 121, 122, 164, 287
Norris, D. G., McQueen, J. M., Cutler, A. & Butterfield, S. 289, 290
Norris, D. G., Cutler, A., McQueen, J. M., Butterfield, S. & Kearns, R. 289
Norris, D. G.: see also Cutler, Mehler, Norris & Segui; Cutler & Norris; Cutler, van Ooijen, Norris & Sánchez-Casas; McQueen, Norris & Cutler
Norman, J. 504 fn 4
Nosofsky, R. M. 670 fn 1
NTT Communication Science Laboratories 198 fn 4
Nusbaum, H.: see Lee & Nusbaum
Nye, P. W.: see Gracco & Nye
Nygaard, L. C. & Pisoni, D. B. 286

O'Connor, J. D.: see Nakatani, O'Connor & Aston
O'Dell, M.: see Port, Dalby & O'Dell
O'Grady, W., Dobrovolsky, M. & Aronoff, M. 155
Obeng, S. G.: see de Jong & Obeng
Obler, L. K. 264
Obler, L. K. & Gjerlow, K. 264
Odden, D. 633 fn 11, 634 fn 12, 634 fn 13
Ohala, J. J. 54, 83, 343 fn 17, 351, 369, 439, 441, 456, 457, 464, 465
Ohala, J. J. & Kawasaki, H. 356, 441
Ohala, J. J. & Ohala, M. 335
Ohala, J. J. & Riordan, C. J. 305
Ohala, J. J., Solé, M. J. & Ying, G. 370
Ohala, J. J.: see also Hombert, Ohala & Ewan; Solé, Ohala & Ying

Ohala, M.: see Ohala & Ohala
Oldfield, R. C. & Wingfield, A. 15 f
Ooijen, B. van 141 f, 155, 157 f, 159, 284
Ooijen, B. van: see also: Cutler, van Ooijen, Norris & Sánchez-Casas; Cutler, Sebastián-Gallés, Soler Vilageliu & van Ooijen
Os, E. den: see Wijnen, Krikhaar & den Os
Ostendorf, M. 24, 30
Ostendorf, M.: see also Dilley, Shattuck-Hufnagel & Ostendorf
Osu, S. 342 fn 9
Osu, S.: see also Clements & Osu
Otake, T., Hatano, G., Cutler, A. & Mehler, J. 36, 290
Otake, T.: see also Cutler & Otake; McQueen, Otake & Cutler
Oyakawa, T. 517

Pacilly, J. J. A.: see Haan, van Heuven, Pacilly & van Bezooijen
Palethorpe, S.: see Harrington, Palethorpe & Watson
Pallarès, M. D.: see Fontdevila, Pallarès & Recasens; Recasens & Pallarès; Recasens, Pallarès & Fontdevila
Pallier, C., Bosch, L. & Sebastián-Gallés, N. 206
Pallier, C., Dupoux, E. & Jeannin, X. 45
Pallier, C., Sebastián-Gallés, N., Felguera, T., Christophe, A. & Mehler, J. 282
Pallier, C.: see also Dupoux, Kakehi, Hirose, Pallier & Mehler; Dupoux, Pallier, Sebastián-Gallés & Mehler; Mehler, Bertoncini, Dupoux & Pallier
Palma, A.: see Santiago, MacKay, Palma & Rho

Paradis, C. 335, 337
Parisi, D.: see Elman, Bates, Johnson, Karmiloff-Smith, Parisi & Plunkett
Payton, K. L., Uchanski, R. M. & Braida, L. D. 242
Pedlow, R. I.: see Van Summers, Pisoni, Bernacki, Pedlow & Stokes
Peereman, R. 49
Peng, S.-H. 424
Peperkamp, S. 210, 228
Peperkamp, S. & Dupoux, E. 275
Peperkamp, S.: see also Dupoux & Peperkamp; Dupoux, Peperkamp & Sebastián-Gallés
Perfetti, C. A.: see Hogaboam & Perfetti
Perkell, J. S.
Perkell, J. S., Cohen, M., Svirsky, M., Matthies, M., Garabieta, I. & Jackson, M. 428
Perkell, J. S.: see also Stevens, Perkell & Shattuck-Hufnagel
Peterson, G. E. & Lehiste, I. 400, 524
Peterson, G. G.: see Shen & Peterson
Phillips, B. S. 16, 109
Picheny, M. A., Durlach, N. I. & Braida, L. D. 242, 248, 280
Pickett, J. M. 141
Pierrehumbert, J. B. 29, 103, 105, 110, 113 ff, 118, 119, 121, 275 ff, 387, 388, 392, 413
Pierrehumbert, J. B. & Beckman, M. E. 107, 133, 388, 392, 394, 395, 399, 548, 552, 631
Pierrehumbert, J. B. & Frisch, S. 105
Pierrehumbert, J. B. & Steele, S. A. 393, 395
Pierrehumbert, J. B. & Talkin, D. 105, 133

Pierrehumbert, J. B., Beckman, M.E. & Ladd, D. R. 103
Pierrehumbert, J., Ladd, D. R. & Beckman, M. E. 503
Pierrehumbert, J. B.: see also Beckman & Pierrehumbert; Broe & Pierrehumbert; Silverman & Pierrehumbert
Pike, E. 580 fn 12
Pike, K. L. 43, 312, 342 fn 3, 515, 523, 528
Pinkerton, S. 312, 465
Pisoni, D. B.: see Goldinger, Luce, Pisoni & Marcario; Lively, Pisoni, Van Summers & Bernacki; Nygaard & Pisoni; Van Summers, Pisoni, Bernacki, Pedlow & Stokes
Pitt, M. A. & McQueen, J. M. 164, 282
Pitt, M. A. & Samuel, A. G. 282
Platt, J. T. & Weber, H. 523, 531
Plaut, D. C.: see Kello, Plaut & MacWhinney
Plunkett, K.: see Elman, Bates, Johnson, Karmiloff-Smith, Parisi & Plunkett
Pointon, G. E. 516
Polivanov, E. 203
Polka, L. & Werker, J. 204, 209
Pols, L. C. W.: see van Son & Pols
Port, R. F., Al-Ani, S. & Maeda, S. 517
Port, R. F., Dalby, J. & O'Dell, M. 174, 517
Port, R. F.: see also Cummins & Port
Poser, W. J. 174, 552, 631
Post, B. 539 fn 5
Post, B.: see also Grabe, Post & Watson
Potisuk, S., Gandour, J. & Harper, M.P. 611

Price, C., Indefrey, P. & van Turennout, M. 280
Prieto, P., van Santen, J. & Hirschberg, J. 388, 403, 575

Quilis, A. 550
Quirk, R., Greenbaum, S., Leech, G. & Svartvik, J. 82

Radeau, M., Morais, J. & Segui, J. 160
Ramsey, R. 631
Ramus, F. 623 ff, 632 fn 6
Ramus, F., Nespor, M. & Mehler, J. 174, 209, 521 f, 533, 536
Ratliff, M.: see Newman & Ratliff
Raymond, W. D.: see Jurafsky, Bell, Gregory & Raymond
Recasens, D. 251, 353, 356, 357, 381
Recasens, D. & Pallarès, M. D. 355, 356, 357
Recasens, D., Pallarès, M. D. & Fontdevila, J. 351, 356, 357, 365
Recasens, D.: see also Fontdevila, Pallarès & Recasens
Redanz, N.: see Jusczyk, Cutler & Redanz
Redford, M. A. & Diehl, R. L. 356, 422
Reed, C. M.: see Uchanski, Choi, Braida, Reed & Durlach
Reetz, H. 641, 655
Reetz, H.: see also Lahiri & Reetz
Reiss, C.: see Hale & Reiss
Remijsen, B. 589, 615
Repp, J. B.: see Gussenhoven, Repp, Rietveld, Rump & Terken; Henderson & Repp
Ressler, W. H.: see Samuel & Ressler
Rho, C.: see Santiago, MacKay, Palma & Rho

Rhodes, R. A. 16
Rialland, A. 132
Rice, K. D. 339, 671 fn 2
Ricotti, L. P.: see Becchetti & Ricotti
Rietveld, A. 204
Rietveld, A.: see also Gussenhoven, Repp, Rietveld, Rump & Terken; Wichmann, House & Rietveld
Riordan, C. J.: see Ohala & Riordan
Ríos, A.: see Garrido, Llisterri, de la Mota & Ríos; Llisterri, Marín, de la Mota & Ríos
Roach, P. 4, 6, 516 f
Roach, P.: see also Hardcastle & Roach
Robins, R. H. & Waterson, N. 453 fn 1
Roca, I. M. & Johnson, W. 159
Roelofs, A. 90, 92, 94 f, 104
Roelofs, A. & Meyer, A. S. 53
Roelofs, A.: see also Levelt, Roelofs & Meyer
Romani, C.: see Caramazza, Laudanna & Romani
Römer, R. 588
Romero, J. 382
Rosenbaum, D. A., Bushe, S. E., Engelbrecht, M. M. & Loukopoulos, L. D. 114
Rotaetxe, K. 570
Roux, J. C. 312, 313
Roux, J. C.: see also Jessen & Roux
Rubach, J. & Booij, G. E. 216
Rubach, J.: see also Booij & Rubach
Rump, H. H. & Collier, R. 81
Rump, H. H.: see also Gussenhoven, Repp, Rietveld, Rump & Terken
Russell, S.: see Moates & Russell

Ryskina, V.: *see* Kuhl, Andruski, Chistovich, Chistovich, Kozhevnikova, Ryskina, Stolyarova, Sundberg & Lacerda

Sadock, J. & Zwicky, A. 62
Saffran, J. R., Aslin, R. N. & Newport, E. L. 14
Sagisaka, Y.: *see* Kaiki & Sagisaka
Salmons, J. 579
Saltzman, E. L. & Byrd, D. 420
Saltzman, E. L.: *see also* Byrd & Saltzman; Kelso, Saltzman & Tuller; McGowan & Saltzman
Samuel, A. G. 464, 535
Samuel, A. G. & Ressler, W. H. 282
Samuel, A. G.: *see also* Pitt & Samuel
Sánchez-Casas, R.: *see* Bradley, Sánchez-Casas & García-Albea; Cutler, van Ooijen, Norris & Sánchez-Casas
Sancier, M. L. & Fowler, C. A. 264
Sands, B. 494
Santen, J. van: *see* Prieto, van Santen & Hirschberg
Santiago, J., MacKay, D. G., Palma, A. & Rho, C. 95
Sapir, E. 203, 620
Sawashima, M.& Hirose, H. 323
Schaffer, M. M.: *see* Medin & Schaffer
Schane, S. A. 213
Schepman, A.: *see* Ladd, Faulkner, Faulkner & Schepman
Schiller, N. O. 36, 38f, 41, 43, 46f, 49, 53, 90
Schiller, N. O. & Costa, A. 40, 42
Schiller, N. O., Costa, A. & Colomé, A. 87
Schiller, N. O.: *see also* Levelt, Schiller & Levelt
Schreuder, R. & Baayen, R. H. 130
Schreuder, R.: *see also* Baayen & Schreuder
Schriefers, H., Meyer, A. S. & Levelt, W. J. M. 89
Schriefers, H.: *see also* Meyer & Schriefers
Schuchardt, H. 15
Schütz, A. 214
Schütze, H.: *see* Manning & Schütze
Schwartz, J. L., Abry, C. & Boë, L.-J. 461
Scott, D. R. & Cutler, A. 281, 491
Scott, D. R.: *see also* Tabossi, Burani & Scott
Scott, N. C. 491
Sebastián-Gallés, N., Dupoux, E., Segui, J. & Mehler, J. 48
Sebastián-Gallés, N.: *see also* Costa & Sebastián-Gallés; Cutler, Sebastián-Gallés, Soler Vilageliu & van Ooijen; Dupoux, Pallier, Sebastián-Gallés & Mehler; Dupoux, Peperkamp & Sebastián-Gallés; Pallier, Bosch & Sebastián-Gallés; Pallier, Sebastián-Gallés, Felguera, Christophe & Mehler; Soto-Faraco, Sebastián-Gallés & Cutler
Segui, J. & Frauenfelder, U. H. 464
Segui, J.: *see also* Cutler, Mehler, Norris & Segui; Ferrand & Segui; Ferrand, Segui & Grainger; Ferrand, Segui & Humphreys; Mehler, Dommergues, Frauenfelder & Segui; Mehler, Dupoux & Segui; Radeau, Morais & Segui; Sebastián-Gallés, Dupoux, Segui & Mehler
Sekiyama, K. 191
Sekiyama, K. & Tohkura, Y. 172
Selkirk, E. O. 388
Seo, M.: *see* Hume, Johnson, Seo & Tserdanelis

Sereno, J. A.: see Lahiri, Jongman & Sereno, Wang, Spence & Sereno; Warner, Jongman, Sereno & Kemps
Sevald, C. A., Dell, G. S. & Cole, J. S. 53, 95
Shady, M. 209
Shankweiler, D. P.: see Liberman, Cooper, Shankweiler & Studdert-Kennedy; Liberman, Shankweiler, Fischer & Carter
Shattuck-Hufnagel, S. 24, 30, 88, 103, 105
Shattuck-Hufnagel, S.: see also Dilley, Shattuck-Hufnagel & Ostendorf; Stevens, Perkell & Shattuck-Hufnagel; Stevens, Manuel, Shattuck-Hufnagel & Liu
Shen, Y. & Peterson, G. G. 516
Shi, R., Morgan, J. & Allopenna, P. 210
Shigeno, S. 172
Shillcock, R.C. 277
Shoup, J. E.: see Mines, Hanson & Shoup
Shriberg, E. 12
Shriberg, L. D. & Kent, R. D. 143
Shryock, A.: see Wright & Shryock
Sibata, T. 172
Signorini, A.: see Manrique & Signorini
Silverman, D. 421, 437
Silverman, D. & Jun, J. 421
Silverman, K. & Pierrehumbert, J. B. 403
Simpson, G. B. 7
Simpson, G. B. & C. Burgess 7
Sithole, N.: see Best, McRoberts & Sithole
Slowiaczek, L. M. & Hamburger, M. 160
Slowiaczek, L. M., McQueen, J. M., Soltano, E. G. & Lynch, M. 160

Sluijter, A. M. C. 598, 601, 607, 610
Sluijter, A. M. C. & van Heuven, V. J. 598, 601, 607, 610, 612 fn 10
Sluijter, A. M. C.: see also van Heuven & Sluijter
Smeets, I. & Adelaar, W. 632 fn 1
Smiljanić, R. & Hualde, J. I. 579
Smiljanić, R.: see also Hualde, Elordieta, Iñaki & Smiljanić; Hualde, Smiljanić & Cole
Smith A. 523
Smith, C.: see Maddieson, Bessel & Smith
Smith, N. S.: see van der Hulst & Smith
Solé, M.-J. 369, 370, 371, 449
Solé, M.-J., Ohala, J. J. & Ying, G. 369, 374
Solé, M.-J.: see also Ohala, Solé & Ying
Soler Vilageliu, O.: see Cutler, Sebastián-Gallés, Soler Vilageliu & van Ooijen
Soltano, E. G.: see Slowiaczek, McQueen, Soltano & Lynch
Son. R. J. J. H. van & Pols, L. C. W. 268
Soquet, A.: see Demolin & Soquet
Sosa, J. M. 388, 575
Soto-Faraco, S., Sebastián-Gallés, N. & Cutler, A. 277, 284
Spajic, S., Ladefoged, P. & Bhaskararao, P. 352, 382 fn 1
Spence, M.: see Wang, Spence & Sereno
Sproat, R. & Fujimura, O. 356
Srebot-Rejec, T. 579
Steele, S. A.: see Pierrehumbert & Steele
Steriade, D. 132, 671 fn 2
Sternberg, S., Monsell, S., Knoll, R. L. & Wright, C. E. 104, 105

Sternberg, S., Wright, C. E., Knoll, R. L. & Monsell, S. 104, 105
Stevens, K. N. 266, 305 f, 308, 309 f, 316, 321, 341, 342 fn 4, 343 fn 17, 370, 379, 383 fn 5, 480, 664, 671 fn 14, 671 fn 15, 671 fn 16
Stevens, K. N. & House, A. S. 251
Stevens, K. N., Perkell, J. S. & Shattuck-Hufnagel, S. 664
Stevens, K. N., Manuel, S. V., Shattuck-Hufnagel, S. & Liu, S. 664
Stevens, K. N.: *see also* Kuhl, Williams, Lacerda, Stevens & Lindblom
Stewart, E.: *see* Kroll & Stewart
Stewart, J. M. 301, 314, 331, 337, 338 f, 344 fn 26
Stockmal, V.: *see* Marks, Moates, Bond & Stockmal; Moates, Bond & Stockmal
Stokes, M. A.: *see* Van Summers, Pisoni, Bernacki, Pedlow & Stokes
Stolyarova, E.: *see* Kuhl, Andruski, Chistovich, Chistovich, Kozhevnikova, Ryskina, Stolyarova, Sundberg & Lacerda
Streeter, L. A. & Nigro, G. N. 278
Streeter, L. A.: *see also* Landauer & Streeter
Studdert-Kennedy, M. 460
Studdert-Kennedy, M.: *see also* Liberman, Cooper, Shankweiler & Studdert-Kennedy; Lindblom, MacNeilage & Studdert-Kennedy
Sugito, M. 174
Sukegawa, Y., Maekawa, K. & Uehara, S. 179 f
Sundberg, U.: *see* Kuhl, Andruski, Chistovich, Chistovich, Kozhevnikova, Ryskina, Stolyarova, Sundberg & Lacerda

Suomi, K. 266
Surprenant, A. M. & Goldstein, L. M. 424
Svenkerud, V.: *see* Jusczyk, Friederici, Wessels, Svenkerud & Jusczyk
Svartvik, J.: *see* Quirk, Greenbaum, Leech & Svartvik
Svirsky, M.: *see* Perkell, Cohen, Svirsky, Matthies, Garabieta & Jackson

Tabossi, P., Burani, C. & Scott, D. R. 160, 277
Takano, S., Tsuzaki, M. & Kato, H. 171
Talkin, D.: *see* Pierrehumbert & Talkin
Tanaka, M., Tsuzaki, M. & Kato, H. 179
Tanenhaus, M. K.: *see* Dahan, Magnuson, Tanenhaus & Hogan
Taub, A.: *see* McCarthy & Taub
Tees, R.: *see* Werker & Tees
Terken, J.: *see* Gósy & Terken; Gussenhoven, Repp, Rietveld, Rump & Terken
Teston, B. & Galindo, B. 466
Thorburn, R.: *see* Kingston, MacMillan, Dickey, Thorburn & Bartels
Thorsen, N. 63
Titone, D.: *see* Connine, Titone, Deelman & Blasko
Titze, I. 477
Tohkura, Y.: *see* Sekiyama & Tohkura
Tongue, R. K. 523, 531
Traill, A. 464, 492
Traill, A. & Vossen, R. 492, 494 f
Traill, A., Khumalo, J. S. M. & Fridjhon, P. 343 fn 17
Traill, A.: *see also* Ladefoged &

Traill
Trubetzkoy, N. S. 308 f, 449, 617, 633 fn 7
Tserdanelis, G.: *see* Hume, Johnson, Seo & Tserdanelis
Tsuzaki, M.: *see* Takano, Tsuzaki & Kato; Tanaka, Tsuzaki & Kato
Tucker, A. 477 f, 482
Tuller, B.: *see* Kelso, Saltzman & Tuller
Turennout, M. van: *see* Price, Indefrey & van Turennout

Uchanski, R. M, Choi, S., Braida, L. D., Reed, C. M. & Durlach, N. I. 242, 248
Uchanski, R. M.: *see also* Payton, Uchanski & Braida
Uehara, S.: *see* Sukegawa, Maekawa & Uehara
Ujihira, A. & Kubozono, H. 188, 196
Uwulaka, A.: *see* Ladefoged, Williamson, Elugbe & Uwulaka
Uwano, Z. 631

Vago, R. M. 215
Vázquez Cuesta, P. & Mendes de Luz, M. A. 353
Vallée, N. 460
Van Eynde, F. & Gibbon, D. 681, 682
Van Summers, W., Pisoni, D. B., Bernacki, R. H., Pedlow, R. I. & Stokes, M. A. 280
Van Summers, W.: *see also* Lively, Pisoni, Van Summers & Bernacki
Vazquez, L.: *see* Marks, Moates, Bond & Vazquez
Verhelst, W.: *see* Moulines & Verhelst
Verhoeven, J. 393

Viana, M. C. 389, 392
Viana, M. C.: *see also* Grønnum & Viana
Viemeister, N.: *see* Carney, Widen & Viemeister
Vigário, M. 389, 390, 395, 403
Vigário, M.: *see also* Frota & Vigário
Vigliocco, G.: *see* Damian, Vigliocco & Levelt
Vitevitch, M. S. & Luce, P. A. 121, 277
Vitevitch, M. S.: *see also* Luce, Goldinger, Auer Jr. & Vitevitch
Vliet, P. van der: *see* Gussenhoven & van der Vliet
Vogel, I. 216
Vogel, I.: *see also* Nespor & Vogel
Vossen, R.: *see* Traill & Vossen
Vroomen, J. & de Gelder, B.

Wang, J.: *see* Connine, Blasko & Wang
Wang, Q. E.: *see* Xu & Wang
Wang, Y., Spence, M. & Sereno, J. A. 204
Warner, N. 465
Warner, N., Jongman, A., Sereno, J. A. & Kemps, R. 281
Warren, P.: *see* Marslen-Wilson & Warren
Warren, R. M. 464
Waterson, N.: *see* Robins & Waterson
Watson, C. I.: *see* Harrington, Palethorpe & Watson
Watson, I.: *see* Grabe, Post & Watson
Waugh, L.: *see* Jakobson & Waugh
Weber: *see* Platt & Weber
Weenink, D.: *see* Boersma & Weenink
Weijer, J. C. van de 207
Welsh, A.: *see* Marslen-Wilson & Welsh

Wenk, B. & Wioland, F. 516, 538 fn 1
Werker, J. & Tees, R. 203, 204, 209
Werker, J.: *see also* Polka & Werker
Wessels, J.: *see* Jusczyk, Friederici, Wessels, Svenkerud & Jusczyk
Westbury, J. R. 305, 306 f
Westbury, J. R.: *see also* Dembowski & Westbury
Wetzels, W. L. 633 fn 7
Whalen, D. H. 244, 278, 288
Wheeldon, L.: *see* Fitzpatrick & Wheeldon; Levelt & Wheeldon
Wichmann, A., House, J. & Rietveld, T. 403
Widen, B.: *see* Carney, Widen & Viemeister
Wijnen, F., Krikhaar, E. & den Os, E. 35
Williams, K.: *see* Kuhl, Williams, Lacerda, Stevens & Lindblom
Williamson, K. 342 fn 9
Williamson, K.: *see also* Ladefoged, Williamson, Elugbe & Uwulaka
Wingfield, A.: *see* Oldfield & Wingfield
Winski, R.: *see* Gibbon, Moore & Winski
Wioland, F.: *see* Wenk & Wioland
Wolff, E. 336

Woodward, J.: *see* Aslin, Woodward, LaMendola & Bever
Wright, C. E.: *see* Sternberg, Monsell, Knoll & Wright; Sternberg, Wright, Knoll & Monsell
Wright, R. 107, 117, 421, 422, 425
Wright, R. & Shryock, A. 327
Wright, R.: *see also* Johnson, Flemming & Wright
Wright Cassidy, K.: *see* Hirsh-Pasek, Kemler-Nelson, Jusczyk, Wright Cassidy, Druss & Kennedy
Wu, Z.: *see* Ladefoged & Wu
Wurm, L.H. 130
Xu, Y. & Wang, Q. E. 588, 607

Yaeger-Dror, M. 110, 117
Yaeger-Dror, M. & Kemp, W. 110, 117
Yeow, K. L. 531
Yigezu, M. 477, 479
Ying, G.: *see* Ohala, Solé & Ying; Solé, Ohala & Ying
Yip, M. C.: *see* Li & Yip

Zhgenti, S. 421
Zipf, G. K. 15, 106
Zsiga, E. C. 424
Zwicky, A.: *see* Sadock & Zwicky
Zwitserlood, P. 160, 277
Zwitserlood, P.: *see also* Marslen-Wilson & Zwitserlood

Language Index

African languages 300, 312
African languages: West-African languages 303, 335, 344 fn 25
Amharic 465 ff, 501, 504 fn 1
Athapaskan languages 339, 580 fn 12
Austronesian languages 214, 585, 588 f, 611 fn 2, 625

Bantu languages 496, 632, 634 fn 13
Basque 547 ff, 625, 629 ff, 633 fn 9
Basque: Northern Bizkaian Basque 547 ff, 629 ff
Basque: Southern Bizkaian Basque 547 ff, 629 ff
Bella Coola 482
Bengali 388, 391, 393, 643

Carrier, Central 580 fn 12
Catalan 251, 351 ff, 522 ff, 623
Catalan: Central Catalan 382, 383 fn 3
Catalan: Roussillon Catalan 382
Catalan: Valencian Catalan 383 fn 3
Chadic languages 336
Chinese 84 fn 3, 191, 588, 607
Chinese: Mandarin 189, 504 fn 4, 523 ff
Chinese: Pekinese 482
Chinese: Szechuanese 491
Czech 633 fn 7

Damin 454 fn 3
Danish 63
Degema 334
Dinka 478, 480

Dutch 35 ff, 61 ff, 90, 91, 94, 141 ff, 219, 233, 284, 287, 393, 515 ff, 578, 598, 601, 607, 623, 625, 629
Dutch: Limburg dialects 588, 626, 629, 631, 633 fn 10
Dutch: Limburg: Roermond 409

Ebrié 333, 334, 336
Ega 336
English 3 ff, 35 ff, 91, 94, 105, 109, 114, 122, 123, 141 ff, 189, 191, 203, 233, 234 fn 7, 241 ff, 284, 287, 289, 290, 306, 310, 322, 357, 387, 388, 392, 393, 408, 424, 432, 452, 460, 515 ff, 551, 586, 598, 607, 623, 625, 643
English: African-American Vernacular English 111 f
English: American English 105, 143, 145, 147, 203, 235 fn 9, 246 f, 452
English: British English 105, 112, 520 ff
English: California Latina 111
English: New York English 6
English: Philadelphia English 6
English: Singapore English 520 ff
Estonian 523 ff

Fijian 214 f, 234 fn 7
Finnish 203 ff
French 35 ff, 94, 110, 203 ff, 306, 454 fn 3, 515 ff, 623
French: Quebec French 110, 117, 120
French: Southern varieties 234 fn 4
Fula 304, 312, 335, 337

Ganda 344 fn 25
Gascon 548

Gbaya 335
Georgian 419 ff, 450 ff
German 35, 94, 387, 388, 391, 405, 515 ff, 578, 639, 641, 646, 648, 656, 661, 666, 671 fn 4
Germanic 106
Germanic languages 35, 36, 38, 43
Greek 227, 393, 394, 517 ff
Greek: Ancient Greek 547
Greek: Cypriot Greek 405
Gwari 335

Hausa 312, 337
Hawaiian 455
Hebrew 264
Hendo 496 ff, 503, 619 ff
Hibena 632
Hindi 203
Hungarian 64, 84 fn 3, 203 ff, 623

Iau 585 f
Igbo 304, 312, 333, 344 fn 25, 625
Ijo 334
Ikwere 299 ff
Indo-European 106
Indo-European languages 300, 482
Indonesian 589, 599
Italian 352 f, 382, 393, 517, 546, 651 ff
Italian: Miogliola Italian 639 ff, 677
Italian: Neapolitan Italian 387, 388, 393, 394
Italian: Palermo Italian 394

Japanese 36, 171 ff, 203, 284, 287, 290, 392, 515 ff, 547, 552, 570, 587, 625, 628, 633 fn 9, 634 fn 13
Japanese: Kyushuu Japanese 632
Japanese: northern Honshuu Japanese 631
Japanese: Shizukuishi Japanese 631
Japanese: Tokyo Japanese 171, 196, 547, 548 ff, 629 ff

Kartvelian languages 420
Kartvelian languages: Proto-Kartvelian 443
Khoe 495
Khoisan languages 492, 495
Kinga 632
Korean 189
Korjak 482
!Kung 455

Latin 110, 227, 383 fn 3, 651 ff, 669, 684
Lendu 312, 327 f, 337, 342 fn 8, 482 ff, 502, 504 fn 4
Luxembourg 523 ff

Ma'ya 585 ff, 625 ff
Malay 523 ff
Mangbetu 333, 473 ff, 501
Marathi 189
Masa 336
Mayan languages 312
Mbatto (Ngula) 333

Nama 302, 457
Ngiti 312, 327 f, 335, 490
Niger-Congo languages 299 ff, 342 fn 9
Nilo-Saharan languages 460, 482
Nilotic languages 477 f
Nuer 477 ff, 502
Nuer: Ethiopian variety 477 f

Papiamentu 587, 626
Polish 203 ff, 623
Portuguese 352 f
Portuguese: Brazilian Portuguese 632 fn 6
Portuguese: European Portuguese 387 ff, 632 fn 6
Portuguese: European Portuguese (Lisbon) 398

Romance languages 35, 36, 43, 548
Rumanian/Romanian 189, 523 ff
Russian 64, 633 fn 7

Language Index

Safwa 632
Seereeer-Siin 312, 335
Serbo-Croatian 547, 578 f
Sesotho 289
Shilluk 478
Sino-Tibetan languages 482
Siswati 327
Slavic languages: Old-Slavic 633 fn 7
Slovenian 579
Spanish 35 ff, 94, 141 ff, 203 ff, 241 ff, 284, 287, 352 f, 382, 383 fn 2, 515 ff, 548, 550, 551, 571, 575 ff, 578, 579 fn 5, 623, 630
Spanish: Iberian Spanish 353
Spanish: Mexican Spanish 246
Sudanic: Central Sudanic languages 465, 473, 475, 482

Swedish 392, 393, 547, 578, 588, 626
Swedish: Swedish dialects 579

Taiwanese 424
Tamil 523 ff
Thai 189, 243, 517 ff, 611 fn 1
Tigrinya 470, 473
Tlingit 473
Toda 352
Tsou 422 f, 425
Turkish 235 fn 9, 623
Twi 460

Una 586, 587

Welsh 523 ff

Xhosa 313, 326
!xóõ 492 ff, 503

Yoruba 625